THE ICONOGRAPHY OF LATE MINOAN AND MYCENAEAN SEALSTONES AND FINGER RINGS

J.G. YOUNGER

(DUKE UNIVERSITY)

Published by Bristol Classical Press
General Editor: John H. Betts

Printed in Great Britain by
Antony Rowe Ltd, Chippenham, Wiltshire
First published in 1988 by:-

BRISTOL CLASSICAL PRESS
226 North Street
Bedminster
Bristol BS3 1JD
© J.G. Younger, 1988

British Library Cataloguing in Publication Data

Younger, J.G.
    The iconography of late Minoan and
    Mycenaean sealstones and finger rings.
    1. Seals (Numismatics)—Greece
    2. Numismatics, Mycenaean 3. Seals—
    (Numismatics)—Greece—Crete
    4. Numismatics, Minoan
    I. Title
    737'. 609388   CD5369

ISBN 0-906515-70-X

TABLE OF CONTENTS

Introduction x
Abbreviations xxii
List of Illustrations xxvi

Part I. PRIMARY MOTIFS
    Graphic Summary of Animal Pose Types 1

    Chapter 1. **Animal Pose Types** (PT's 1-54) 4

    Chapter 2. **People**
        A. Parts of the Human Body 119
        B. Men 121
                Scenes Possibly Secular & Non-Military;
                Military; Religious
        C. Women 131
        D. Men and Women 138
        E. People at Shrines 141

    Chapter 3. **Men and Animals**
        A. Men with Animals 149
        B. Master of Animals 156
        C. Man Hunts Animals 159
        D. Men in Chariots 163
        E. Animal Games 166
                Bull-Catching; Bull-Riding; Bull-Wrestling; Bull-
                Leaping; Man in front of the Bull; Man in back of
                the Bull; Uncertain Poses for bull-leaping; Man
                Rides Other Animals
        F. Animal Sacrifice 176

    Chapter 4. **Women and Animals**
        A. Women with Animals 178
        B. Potnia Theron 182
        C. Woman "Crossed" by a Caprid 183
        D. Miscellaneous Compositions 186

    Chapter 5. **Miscellaneous Animals**
        A. Miscellaneous Quadrupeds 187
        B. Animal Faces 187
        C. Animal Heads 192
        D. Protomes 193
        E. Birds and Waterbirds 195
        F. Alerions 201
        G. Insects 203

CONTENTS

ACKNOWLEDGEMENTS

My debt of gratitude extends to many people for having fostered my interest in seals and for having helped me gain some knowledge of them. The symposia on seals in Marburg arranged by Dr. I. Pini (1974, 1978, and 1985 published as CMS Beihefts 0, 1, and 3 [see Abbreviations below]) and in Paris (1980) arranged by Professors H. and M. van Effenterre have all provided intimate settings for the quick exchange of ideas, and the distinguished scholars who attended have been generous with their thoughts and advice. More recently Drs. Michael Vickers and Ann Brown of the Ashmolean Museum have both been exceedingly kind in opening the cases of its rich collection; John Sakellarakis and Stylianos Alexiou, when they were the Directors of the Prehistoric Collection in the National Museum in Athens and of the Herakleion Museum, respectively, allowed me to examine many of the seals in their care; other museum and excavation directors have been similarly kind: Jean-Claude Poursat, Photios Petsas, Lila Marangou, Mrs Karagiorga-Stamatopoulou, Mrs Deilaki, Mssrs Mervyn Popham and Hugh Sackett, and Professors William McDonald, John Tzedakis, A. Colin Renfrew, Gerald Cadogan, and William and Jane Biers; and private collectors have graciously allowed me to examine the seals under their care. Dr Ingo Pini opened the archives of the CMS to me and without them or his unfailing help I would never have been able to gain a synoptic view of this material; John H. Betts has generously allowed me to make use of his notes and drawings of the material in the Herakleion Museum, and in many other ways has been continuously supportive; A. Colin Renfrew has awakened my interst in technique and the economic and bureaucratic use of seals; and Dr. Margaret A.V. Gill has kept me acutely aware of the personalities, the idiosyncracies, and the genius of the artists who carved these endlessly fascinating gems and rings.

The illustrations are line drawings based on published photographs or figures; they are not to scale. Their intention is to illustrate the iconography, not the style of engraving.

The directing spirits of this study, however, are the late Professor John L. Caskey, who first put seals into my hand, and Mrs. Rae Kappelman, who taught me how to outline my thoughts; for both of them an elemental typology has been the necessary basis for research.

This book has been made possible through the assistance of research grants from the Duke University Research Council and from the National Endowment for the Humanities.

This classification of iconography is based on my PhD dissertation, "Towards the Chronology of Aegean Glyptic in the Late Bronze Age" (University of Cincinnati 1973, University Microfilms 73-24, 867) chapter III, pp. 214-404. Several people have helped in the preparation of the present version: in its initial stages, Cathy Eaglen typed much of the manuscript, Julia Manning arranged some of the catalogue, and Jeffryn Stephens began the concordance; in its final stages, Thomas McCreight, and Christopher Parslow helped proofread and Catherine Rine compiled some of the bibliography. I am especially grateful to Ms Kimberly Flint for her tireless assistance. I am responsible, however, for whatever errors that remain.

The catalogue of motifs was generated by the data-base computer program, Dbase II, and generated as text through the word-processing programs EasyWriter 2.1, PC-Write, and WordPerfect and as graphics through the program Energraphics, all on an IBM PC and XT. The printing was done on a Toshiba P351.

This book is dedicated to Sonny Snead, who has displayed an amazing tolerance of my devotion to "those little rocks" and to the "green screen".

INTRODUCTION

General Remarks

At first glance it may seem to the scholar of Late Bronze Age Greece that the sealstone engraver had at his disposal the whole range of human activity and all of nature from which he could draw the inspiraton for his scenes. Such an impression is intensified as well by the way seals have been used to illustrate numerous aspects of Minoan-Mycenaean life, including sports, architecture, costume, ships, the palaeo-environment, and of course religion.

It is true that of all the artistic media of the Late Bronze Age seals constitute the one with the most examples extant today: over 4500 sealstones, rings, and the impressions they made in clay provide a wealth of iconographic material. It is also true, however, that seal engraving was a major art form, and, like frescoes, they cannot be expected to document much in the way of common behavior, attitudes, or even every-day utilitarian artifacts.

Only 15% of the sealtypes (about a third of these are rings) portray the human figure, and a few others, like those with netted bulls or collared dogs and lions, imply it. The variety of scenes, however, is surprisingly small. The major categories include a man's head, standing solitary figures, men in combat, people saluting either another human figure or a shrine, people participating in rites (tree-pulling, omphalos-embracing), masters and mistresses of animals, and bull-leaping. In short, the scenes are monumental in scope and most may be construed as religious. These seals certainly convey little, if any, information about the concepts that informed these activities, i.e., the where, when, or why they took place (granted, of course, that they all did); little information can be culled even about military garb and gear or about religious costume and furniture. Even such a fundamental distinction as that between divinity and devotee is obscure in almost all scenes, except possibly those depicting epiphanies. Most women identified commonly as goddesses on the seals may not be: the ladies on the Isopata ring could just as well be devotees saluting, the seated women in presentation scenes may be priestesses, the masters and mistresses of animals are simply more conventional versions of the people who restrain lions, dogs, and griffins with leashes.

Depictions of monsters account for about 7% of the catalogued total. The Minotaur is the most common, and of those fourteen seals with known findspots, all but one come from Crete, most from the Knossos area, as one might expect. The griffin, sphinx, genius, and Babylonian Dragon have all received special attention, but there are many other types that have been relatively unstudied: the bull-woman, calf-man, lion-man, winged agrimi, agrimi-man and -woman, lion- and lady-eagle, and a large fish? that attacks animals and chariots. Of these minor monsters, the last may pay honor to the shark, but the former ones may hypothetically represent people dressed up in the garb of totemic animals.

A few seals (5% of the catalogue) depict only plants or geometric motifs. The plant forms are simple branches and provide no insight into the palaeo-environment; even those seals that include better rendered plants of a more specific nature are misleading -- the so-called papyrus on seals bolsters no argument as to whether that plant is native in the Aegean in the Bronze Age, nor does the stylized palm. A few seals carry many compass-drawn circles, up to 25, placed randomly on a face; these seals could have been used as counters, though, if such were necessary, Linear A and B numerals engraved on seals would have been easier to read and more versatile.

The greatest number of seals (62% of the catalogue) carry animals. Some were hunted and killed or captured -- a few depict men fighting lions and trussing them up; lions, agrimia, and bulls are wounded by short lances or long darts (here called picas); lions and dogs are restrained on leashes attached to collars. But most animal scenes consist of a single animal, a pair, or one animal attacking another.

These seals with animals make up the bulk of the iconography; they convey almost no information about Minoan-Mycenaean society and only a little insight into the artists' view of the natural world, limited as it seems to have been to a few animals (most commonly, the lion, the bull, and the agrimi) in 54 (most commonly, 36) conventional poses. Nor can we even trust his vision: the agrimi was certainly indigenous to Crete, the stag to the Mainland, and the bull was common to both, but the argument still runs as to whether the lion, as depicted, was native to the Aegean or a symbol imported from the Near East -- perhaps it is more probable that the lion came to certain palaces as a gift and there paraded about as a palace showpiece (few lion bones have been found in Bronze Age contexts to support the hypothesis that lions were extant there then: from Ayia Irini in Keos comes a lion tooth, and lion bones have been found in early LH levels at Tiryns [AR 1978-9, p. 16 & 1980-81, p. 16]).

With most of his iconography focusing on animals we must not expect the seal engraver to convey much about everyday life. Aside from some articles of costume and some procedures of ritual that are difficult to interpret, the artist seems to have had little interest in recording what he saw around him. What then was he interested in, what were his intentions? His pretext of course was the high demand for sealstones as an item of jewelry and as a sphragistic bureaucratic tool. His preference for animals, however, limited mainly to a few specific animals placed in a select number of standardized poses, implies that his real interest lay in style, not subject.

This iconographic catalogue may help some scholars in their analyses of a few motifs, but its main goal is to facilitate the iconographic interpretation of seals newly found or to encourage a stylistic and iconographic comparison between seals bearing the same motif and between seals and the other artistic media.

Accordingly the present study attempts to organize as many Late Bronze Age sealtypes (motifs) as is possible by their iconography, amounting finally to over 2600. All the legible seals in the Corpus der minoischen und mykenischen Siegel (CMS I, I Supplement, II 1-3, IV, V, VII-X, XII, and XIII), the Ashmolean Museum (CS), the German collections (AGDS), the LM Ib sealings, most of the Knossos sealings (KSPI), and almost all the published seals in the Herakleion Museum (HM) are included, as well as others in other collections or recently excavated.

While the focus of this iconographic catalogue is on the Late Bronze Age, some seals from contexts dating to this period have been excluded and some seals engraved probably in the Middle Minoan period have been included.

Absent are most of the foreign seals, such as Mitannian cylinders (Pini 1983) and most Cypriote seals (except those cylinders which could be considered influenced predominantly by Minoan-Mycenaean styles and iconography [Pini 1979 and 1980]).

Excluded for the most part, however, are Hieroglyphic, Architectonic (cf. Schiering 1984; architectonic motifs as filler, however, are included in this study), and Talismanic seals, since all these date mainly to the Middle Minoan period and are conventional enough to deserve their own study. Such seals are often considered not to have been intended as sphragistic seals, though all three classes were used to seal documents. For example, sealings impressed by Talismanic sealstones do exist: HMs 1022, 1023, 2021 from Chania (Papapostolou 1977: nos. 23 and 24), one from Gournia, and at least one from Ayia Triada (HMs 554; AT 4), Kato Zakro (HMs 58; KZ 91), and Knossos (HMs 1013; Betts 55). For this class we turn to its full study by Artemis Onassoglou (CMS Beiheft 2). Earlier treatments of Talismanic seals include Kenna 1969 and Betts's review (1974).

On the other hand, the male portraits and a few select animal studies from Middle Bronze Age contexts are included since each may serve as a fitting introduction to the way their motif was rendered later; for example, CMS II 1.419 is included because it seems to be the earliest example (MM I-II?) of Animal Pose Type 44.

Such a catalogue of the whole repertory of LBA Aegean sealtypes is mammoth, perhaps, but virtually all iconographic elements, from the filling motifs to the complete scene, are here catalogued. Such a taxonomic endeavor is not intended to limit, but rather to provide a basis for further analysis.

Thus, any two or more seals exhibiting similar compositions form a subgroup of their general category, and each category is organized according to its own idiosyncracies (e.g., Ch. 3 -- the Men with Animals section is organized differently from Ch. 4 -- the Women with Animals). In this way it is hoped that such an organization will clarify what iconographic patterns can be detected.

To present a catalogue of the whole repertory of sealtypes as objectively as possible, the text has been sparing of interpretation; human activity is described in compositional terms, animals have been grouped by poses, and most filling objects and decoration are merely listed. The nomenclature and identifications proposed here occasionally differ from those of other scholars, and these, along with other conventional names, are capitalized. Divergent opinions, the occurences of a motif in other media, or previous discussions will be found, but sparingly, in Part IV, the Iconographic Bibliography with Commentary.

The focus of this study is on the seals themselves; they are usually eloquent: they provide specific instructions, through stringhole alignment or groundlines, on how to orient a seal so that animal poses can be correctly viewed; they provide a remarkably consistent scale of proportions in complex scenes so that one object may be differentiated from another though there are confusing exceptions (e.g., one form when small may be called the Sacred Knot and when large the Sacred Robe); and through the repetition of a motif with subtle variations seals can instruct us

how to sacrifice or vault a bull, hunt a lion, or how the small
outdoor shrine looks from all sides. Seals present their own
"petit univers", as Chapouthier noted years ago (1932: 201), one
whose scenes and even styles seem more to have influenced other
media -- from the Thera Ship fresco to murals in the Pylos Throne
Room, from the Elgin bull plaques to the Lion Gate at Mycenae, or
from the Temple Repositories' faience nanny and kid to the ivory
Delos plaque of a lion attacking a griffin -- than did the other
media influence seals.

General Layout of the Book

   This book is divided into two major iconographic sections: Part
I lists primary motifs of animals and people, and Part II
catalogues the various subsidiary filling motifs. Part III lists
major references for the rarely occurring animals cat, horse, and
ape. Part IV gives a select bibliography and commentary for the
major iconographic motifs. Part V gives a concordance by
publication and/or museum inventory number of the seals included
in this study and their primary iconographic citation. And Part
VI lists the general bibliography. Each section presents its own
problems.

Terminology

   The scenes with human figures present the most difficulties in
organization. The Aegean artist and his clientele were all too
familiar with their own religious, sporting, and social activities
to fill out the trivial or highlight the significant for us. It
has therefore been thought best to group people by their predomi-
nant activity rather than by our surmise of the artist's intention. For example, men in a ship may indeed be marines of a sort,
but men and women together in ships are simply People in Ships,
for their goal could be simple pleasure and their destination
could be a neighboring municipality as well as a shrine.

   The most obvious departure from common usage occurs in the
cataloguing of the religious scenes; only the scenes that depict
people at shrines and the objects found there are termed
religious. The omphalos is occasionally found near a shrine (and
at Phylakopi has actually been excavated at one) and therefore it
is termed a religious object, though the seal that depicts people
embracing it with no shrine in sight is accordingly listed among
the scenes with People, not amongst the scenes with People at
Shrines.

Similarly, certain objects depicted in scenes that are most probably religious have received names that are now conventional. Some now seem romantic and even incomprehensible (e.g., Horns of Consecration, Snake Frame); others are more objective (e.g., Figure-8 Shield and Shrine), though they still may be problematic (Omphaloi or Squills?). Other objects, however, have received no such consensus either of terminology or of identification, and many have never really been named; these are here given descriptive names like Sacred Heart, Heaven Line, Shield-in-Profile, etc. All such conventional names are capitalized and underlined. Most of these objects will be found catalogued separately as filling motifs in Part II and discussed in Part IV.

Most people do seem engaged in religious acts, unless the men among them display their bravery in battle or in the hunt, both of which exude an aura of importance. In fact, the apparently complete lack of purely domestic scenes that one occasionally finds in Classical gem-engraving should mean that the Bronze Age Aegean glyptic artist thought it appropriate to depict only the grander moments in his medium; it could thus be argued that all scenes with people possess a significance that is more or less religious in nature, if it were not for the fact that the term "religious" is already badly overworked. Certain technical features suggest too that people are mostly depicted in religious acts: lentoids carrying animals usually have stringholes vertical to the motif, but those that carry people generally have horizontal stringholes, which are often an indication of a scene's special nature (Younger 1977: 153-7).

A similar monumentality surrounds most of the animals. Not only do their overwhelming numbers command respect, but they also appear in such a limited number of poses that several scholars, Kenna especially, refer to them as "animal studies". Studies they must have been, the artist consciously mimicking a pleasing and aesthetically satisfying composition created by a past or contemporary master, probably selecting it from some sort of pattern-book or collection of representative seals, and recasting the composition in his own distinctive style.

It is probable, too, that some motifs could have served as badges of office. The bulls in PT (Pose Type) 24 could qualify for such an insigne; they are usually engraved on large lentoids of a beautiful red-brown agate and often come from aristocratic burials. HMs 415 from the Royal Tomb at Knossos may have been impressed with a royal seal; its bull is in a unique pose (though here forced to conform, for convenience, to PT 11) and the dado it lies on, Dado 9a, seems reserved for similarly special seals. For

Mesopotamian seals that functioned as badges of office, see Gibson
& Biggs 1977: 61-66.

Thus the vocabulary used here to describe the iconography has
tried to accommodate this pervading monumentality by adopting
terms from heraldry, in spite of the fact, however, that seals do
not seem to have functioned as family badges (pace: Persson 1942:
148): animals may be assis (sitting), couchant (recumbent,
kneeling, or running in a contracted pose), salient (leaping),
rampant (standing on the hindlegs), regardant (looking back over
the shoulder), and with head contorted (stretched back over the
back and upside down); displayed birds or griffins have both
wings spread open to either side of the body, and, when
viewed frontally, displayed birds are called alerions; animal
limbs as filling motifs are "erased"; protomes are the heads
and shoulders, including occasionally the chest, of an animal.

Antithetic means two animals face each other or are belly
to belly; addorsed means rump to rump or back to back. Two
figures may be parallel in axial symmetry or rotating in radial
symmetry.

An object may be "in front" or "in back" of an animal, but if
it is on the near or far side of an animal (vis a vis the viewer),
it is "before" or "behind" respectively.

Animals are also listed in order of their popularity: lions
first, then bulls, agrimia, goats and other caprids, and monsters.

All motifs are described from the impression, not from the
seal. This convention is the one almost always used, following a
long and dogmatic tradition that insists that the engraver
intended his motifs to have meaning only when the seal was used
sphragistically. Such may not be the case, as Biesantz (1954: 5-
10) has argued: presumably right-handed warriors stab their
enemies with the proper hand on the Shaft Grave gold and stone
seals themselves; the bulls on CMS XII 251 and XIII 26, among
others, have their faces shallowly engraved so that the viewer,
looking at the seal, sees the heads realistically nearer to him;
the gold jewel CMS I 293 has small areas of the gold surface pried
up to make sharp flanges that make it very difficult to produce a
clear impression in clay; and Linear B *125 faces its graphic
direction only on the seal AM 1938.1075 (CS 342). But other
people on seals, such as the hunters on CMS I 290 and V 656 or the
cult figures on I 101 and 279, use their right hand in impression.
There cannot, therefore, have been any hard and fast rule that
every motif was only to be read either from the seal or from its

impression; it may instead have depended on the type of seal, its use, or its motif. That one direction was preferred for certain scenes is inescapable. In impression, most agrimia face left, seated women with animals in front are on the right, scratching dogs in PT 12 face right, etc. But which direction, that on the seal or in the impression, was the more significant or the more aethetically pleasing is debatable.

Reading the scene from the impression, however, does have a distinct advantage, for the motif there is always more legible than on the seal itself: the veins in agates and the luminosity of cornelians and limestones, for instance, obscure the motif, as no doubt they were meant to do. In any case, the convex figures in the relief of the impressions correspond more to nature than to the concave intaglio ones on the seals themselves; if such a naturalism was a concern, and if the artist had wanted the motif to be read from the seal, he might have created cameos.

Previous publications have often had difficulty in identifying poses that, in this study, have become standardized and given special rubrics, always capitalized. For example, Animal Pose Type (PT) 14, usually identified as an animal in various degrees of contortion, is here seen as a variant of PT 13, animal with its head under the belly. Thus, all occurences of PT 14, including the Minotaurs, are grouped together with the head under, not over the body, with the result that the filling motifs are then described in relation to that orientation (except: CMS V 246, a composite of two separate scenes). A lion curved around a bull has often been published as: An analysis of stringhole orientation (Younger 1977: 156 n. 74) has led, however, to the conclusion that the lion receives the accent. And so this motif is classed not as a variety of PT 39C, but separately as PT 44.

For the archaeologist, major problems exist in separating the glyptic sheep from the goats, and occasionally the lions from the hounds; bulls, too, can present some problems in identification. It is quite likely that the palace-based Minoans and Mycenaeans had similar difficulties. This study follows a rather simplistic approach. Bulls, dogs, and lions have long tails; lions often have a dot at the tip of the tail to indicate the spur and tuft that occur in nature; dogs occasionally share this trait mistakenly (e.g., CMCG 113b), but they usually also have large

pointed ears, deeper chests, and thinner waists than the lions
do (thereby superceding previously identified lions on several
seals, e.g., CMS I 81 and VII 96, and AM 1938.1065 [CS 350]). In
addition, most dogs wear collars while only a few lions do.

It is more difficult to discriminate among the
goats, sheep, and deer. Perhaps to some extent the author
has been arbitrary in deciding that goats and sheep have
horns that curl back from the top of the head and under the
cheek (e.g., CMS V 732 [goat]   and   I 113 [sheep]):

goat   sheep

Agrimia have long horns that sweep
straight back from the head and
begin to curve only near the tip
(e.g., CMS 119 & 123), thus:

agrimi

Young agrimia, however, are hornless; they may look like dogs,
except they are larger and have long ears and short tails (e.g.,
CMS VII 131; for an actual kid, see Bowman 1978: 22 bottom).
Stags have antlers which make them fairly easy to identify (e.g.,
CMS I 272b). There has, however, been no further attempt to
distinguish other caprids. This is not to say that the glyptic
artist may not have intended here an oryx, there an ibex, as
perhaps did fresco painters, but a seal seems to have had too
small a space to include those minor though important
characteristics that identify the various members of this family.

Bulls have horns that form a S-curve (e.g.,
CMS I 125 & 137) or a pair that form a semi-
circle in profile (e.g., CMS I 142). Calves
also have long tails, but short, pointed horns
as on CMS I 58, 215, & 287b. Certain other
bovines have short, thick, and striated horns

bull

(e.g., CMS I 111 & 124); their long tails, too, give them away.
Depicted alone, a bovine is called a bull for the sake of
convenience only, for it cannot be determined whether a hornless,
solitary bovine was actually intended to be cow, a heifer, or a
bullock. The only certain representations of a cow are the ones
that show her suckling her calf, though one must keep in mind that
sealstone artists were also capable of engraving an obvious father
lion guarding (CMS I 62), licking (I 508), and even suckling (XII

286) his cub.

   If there are difficulties in identifying one animal from
another, there are even more in identifying plants. The author
does not admit to being a naturalist and has here too been rather
arbitrary, classing most plants as small (Weeds), medium (Branches
and Fronds), or large (Trees, usually with bases). Branches and
Trees are here subdivided and given numbers to designate subtypes.
The formal profiles of Lily, Palm, and Cypress were exaggerated;
on seals none of the plants called Papyrus, however, looks indeed
like the real papyrus growing in the author's study (pace Warren
1977) -- the name is retained here only as a convenient carry-
over from Furumark (1977: Analysis FM 11).

The Catalogue Entries

   In Part I all seals are catalogued according to their primary
motif or composition; in Part II, filling motifs have their examples listed by the primary motif or composition of which
they are a part and the specific seals that carry them. A
few technical facts are included, such as the occasional engraving
of a seal's reverse, the orientation of the stringhole (SH), or a
seal's unfinished state. The alloys of the rings and the types
of stones and their colors are not mentioned, even though they
certainly played a part both in the style of the engraving (e.g.,
the Cut Style is perfect for a rock crystal lentoid like Melos
Mus. 568) or in the position of a motif (cf. the placement of the
owl on AM 1938.973 [CS 220]; Gill 1981: 88).

   In the primary catalogue, Part I, therefore, a seal is listed
something like this:

       Category
       Direction
          seal (shape) provenience (context; bibliography)
             primary motif/composition
                secondary/filling motifs

       PT 6 (runs, regardant)
       RIGHT
          HM 1867 (L) Sellopoulo T. 1 (LM III A2-B; AR 1957,
                24-5)
             goat
                Branch 1 ab[ove]

The seals are given by their museum inventory number (with
their pertinent publication given then in the bibliography) or by
their CMS publication (Roman numerals followed by Arabic; e.g., I
144 = CMS volume I no. 144). For convenience, seals in the
Ashmolean Museum, Giamalakis collection, etc. are referred to by
their museum inventory numbers for easier cross-referencing when
these are eventually included in the CMS.

Question marks preceeding the entry denote that there is some
doubt as to whether the motif on this seal actually belongs to the
iconographic category.

The shape of a seal is referred to by its abbreviation (see:
Abbreviations); the shape-abbreviation followed by a "s" means the
sealtype is on a sealing impressed by the shape abbreviated (e.g.,
Ls = impressed by a lentoid).

Provenience is indicated by the name of the site the seal
comes from; most sites are well known and there is therefore no
mention of whether the site is in Crete or on the Mainland. Sites
in quotation marks (e.g., "Knossos") signify that the seal is
reported to have come from there.   It must also be noted that
seals coming from Makry Teichos, Metochi Bougada, and Hellenika
were probably found at Knossos (see PM II map opposite p. 547);
Knossos is also a favorite findspot for dealers and not all seals
said to come from there may actually have; similarly, Boeotia was
a favorite findspot for forgeries. Several collections, the
Hutchinson, Dawkins, Seager, etc., are also mentioned since their
collectors concentrated their archaeological activity in Crete and
many seals in their collections may well have come from there.

Context is that of the pottery context of a seal found in
excavation; only contexts with a rather narrow range are included,
e.g., LH I-II rather than LH I-III. It must be stressed that
these pottery context dates do not date a seal but only give it a
terminus post quem non for the seal's manufacture date. Context
dates are usually found in the seal's publication or in Furumark
1972: Chronology.

The bibliography is that of the seal's primary publication, of
an important republication, or of the most useful illustration.

Under the first line of information and indented from it,
there is then given the description of the primary motif or
composition and, below it and indented further, there are then
given the secondary (filling) motifs (the capitalized and
underlined names of motifs are conventional; some are of long

standing, others are recent or introduced here for the first time
[e.g., <u>Tree 1</u>, a conventional shape, as opposed to "tree", a
tree-like plant form]; these conventional motifs are listed
separately in Part II); finally, important technical details are
cited if they may influence the interpretation of the motif.

When a motif is questionable the question mark is placed
immediately after it.

When at least two seals share the same composition, these are
grouped together under that composition's heading. Thus, PT 19B
(two animals in one direction, the far one regardant) is first
divided into two major subgroups: animals that face left and
animals that face right. Each subgroup is then further
subdivided by the types of animals depicted; under "Left" there
are two seals with goats and one (under "Miscellaneous") with
bulls; under "Right" there are two seals with calves, two with
agrimia, two with goats, and one ("Miscellaneous") with
waterbirds.

ABBREVIATIONS

Bibliographical

Most bibliographical abbreviations are standard and may be
found in <u>AJA</u> (<u>American Journal of Archaeology</u>) 90, 1986, 381-394.
The following may be less obvious:

AGDS	Antike Gemmen in deutschen Sammlungen (Munich 1968 ff.)
AR	Archaeological Reports
AT	D. Levi, "Le cretule di Hagia Triada," ASAtene 8-9 (1925-6) 71-156
Betts	J.H. Betts, "Some Unpublished Knossos Sealings and Sealstones," BSA 62 (1967) 27-45
CMCG	A. X.-Sakellariou, Les Cacehts minoen de la Collection Giamalakis (EtCretoises X; Paris, 1958)
CMS	Corpus der minoischen und mykenischen Siegel (Berlin, 1964 ff.), to be understood before a seal-citation of a Roman numeral followed by an Arabic numeral; e.g., "I 144" = CMS I 144 Gemmae Dubitandae are included in the CMS volumes by the arabic number followed by a "*" in vol. X and by a "D" in the other volumes
CS	V.E.G. Kenna, Cretan Seals (Oxford UP, 1960) a number followed by "P" = Peripheral, a classification Kenna devised for those seals in whch he saw foreign characteristics a number followed by "S" = sealing
GGFR	J. Boardman, Greek Gems and Finger Rings (London, 1970)
KSPI	M.A.V. Gill, "The Knossos Sealings: Provenience and Identification," BSA 60 (1965) 58-98, with references to illustrations
KZ	D.G. Hogarth, "The Zakros Sealings," JHS 22 (1901) 76-93; and D. Levi, "Le cretule di Zakro," ASAtene 8-9 (1925-6) 157-201
PM	A. Evans, The Palace of Minos
Sk	S. Marinatos, "To Minoikon Megaron Sklavokampou," ArchEph 1939-1941, 69-96

Musuems

AM	Ashmolean Museum, Oxford
HM	Herakleion Museum, Herakleion

         HM = stone seals
         HMm = metal (rings and metal seals)
         HMp = pottery
         HMs = clay sealings
         HM G = the Giamalakis Collection, most
               published in CMCG (see above)
         HM M = the Metaxas Collection, most published
           in CMS IV

NMA	National Museum, Athens

Seal Forms

N.B.: sealings have a small "s" as a suffix (e.g., Ls = sealing
     impressed by a lentoid)

   Abbreviated shapes

A	Amygdaloid
APr	Amygdaloidal Prism
C	Cushion or Flattened Cylinder
Cyl	Cylinder
D	Disk (Disc)
L	Lentoid
Pr	Prism
R	Ring
RPl	Rectangular Plate
RPr	Rectangular Prism
Sc	Scarab or Scaraboid

   Unique or rare shapes
      Almond-shaped prism: IX 162 (in PT 3, L; Ch. 5B: Insects
         [butterflies]; and Ch. 5E: Birds & Waterbirds
         [waterbirds, trio])
      Amygdaloid/Lentoid: X 241 in PT 40, L
      Figure-8 Shield: II 4.189 in Ch. 9Q: Misc. Lines (cf. the
         unengraved VII 132)
      Flattened Cylinder: CMS I 389 in PT 11, R
      Scarab: V 424 in PT 40, L

   Miscellaneous technical abbreviation
    SH   Stringhole

Provenience

N.B.: places in quotation marks, e.g., "Knossos", signifies that
      the seal is only said to have been found there)

    ChT   Chamber Tomb
    ShGr   Shaft Grave
    T.   Tomb

Iconographical

    With reference to the sealface
        obv   obverse
        rev   reverse
        SH horizontal   with the stringhole running
                             horizontally
        SH vertical   with the stringhole running
                             vertically
    Miscellaneous
        head   the head viewed in profile
        face   the head viewed en face

Some Conventional or Special Motifs

        Branch 1, Branch 2, etc.   see Part II, Ch. 14A
        Dado 1, Dado 2, etc.   see Part II, Ch. 15C
        Fronds   see Part II, Ch. 14B
        HC (Horns of Consecration)   see Part II, Ch. 12I
        ImpTr Impaled Triangles   see Part II, Ch. 13B
        Mount-Guides   see Part II, Ch. 16B
    Omphaloi/Squills   see Part II, Ch. 12I
        Picas   see Part II, Ch. 12D
        Sacred Hearts   see Part II, Ch. 12I
        Pithoi/Shields-in-Profile   see Part II, Ch. 12I
        Short Columns   see Part II, Ch. 12H
        Small Man or Woman   see Part II, Ch. 10A
        Snake Frames   see Part II, Ch. 12I
        Tree 1, Tree 2, etc.   see Part II, Ch. 14C
        Weed   see Part II, Ch. 14B

Placement of Motifs in the Field

N.B.: with reference to the primary motif (all filling motifs are
        described in this order: **beh**, **bef**; and then clockwise,
        beginning with **infr**, then **ab**, **inb**, and **bel**)

ab	above the primary motif
bef	before (on the near side of) it; engraved over the primary motif
beh	behind (on the far side of) it; the primary motif engraved over the secondary motif
bel	below the primary motif
betw	between two motifs
cl	clockwise
ccl	counterclockwise
inb	in back of the primary motif
infr	in front of the primary motif
L	left
R	right

Compositionally

clockwise	two motifs in a circular composition facing in the direction the clock goes
counterclockwise	two motifs in a circular composition facing in the opposite direction of the way the clock goes
in axial symmetry	one subject in one half of the field is repeated in the other half but reversed
in radial symmetry	one subject in one half of the field is repeated in the other half in mirror image
addorsed	rump to rump, or back to back
antithetic	head to head, or belly to belly
vs	one animal attacks another

LIST OF ILLUSTRATIONS

FIG.	PT	Reference	Subject
1	1A	XII 305	bull in PT 1A, L
2	1B	V 157	bull/calf in PT 1B, L
3	2	I 76	bull in PT 2, R
4	3	V 580	bull in PT 3, L
5	4	XIII 35	bull in PT 4, R
6	5A	Once Evans	bull in PT 5A, R
7	5B	IX 119	bull in PT 5B, R
8	5C	V 252	bull in PT 5C, R
9	6	VII 261	bull in PT 6, R
10	7	XIII 13	bull in PT 7, L
11	8	V 498	lion in PT 8, L
12	8	V 677a	dog in PT 8, R, scratching
13	9	VIII 52	bull in PT 9, L
14	10A	XII 248	bull in PT 10A, R
15	10B	VII 105	calf in PT 10B, L
16	11	I 65	bull in PT 11, R
17	12	VIII 148	bull in PT 12, R
18	13A	XII 268	bull in PT 13A, R
19	13B	VII 99	bull in PT 13B, R
20	14A	XIII 43	bull in PT 14A, R
21	14B	II 4.161	bull in PT 14B, R
22	14C	XIII 21	bull in PT 14C, R
23	15	I 393	agrimi in PT 15, R
24	16A	AM 1938.1019	nanny & kid in PT 16A, R
25	16B	I 168	goat & kid in PT 16B, R
26	17A	I 13	doe & fawn in PT 17A, R
27	17B	VII 233	nanny & kid in PT 17B, R
28	17C	II 3.54	nanny & 2 kids in PT 17C, R
29	18B	VII 236	cow & calf in PT 18B, R
30	19A	I 45	2 agrimia in PT 19A, R
31	19B	V 597	2 bulls in PT 19B, R with bull-leaper
32	19C	IV 256	2 bulls in PT 19C, R
33	19D	XIII 68	2 bulls in PT 19D, R
34	20	HMs 321 etc.	2 lions in PT 20, R
35	21	XIII 3D	2 calves in PT 21, R
36	22	I 71	2 lions in PT 22, R
37	23A	I 276	2 boars in PT 23A, L
38	24	V 433	2 bulls in PT 24, R
39	25A	V 297	2 bulls in PT 25A, L
40	25B	VII 100	2 bulls in PT 25B, R with man infr
41	25C	XIII 59	2 bulls run in PT 25C, R
42	26	I 215	3 calves in PT 26, L

PART I

PRIMARY MOTIFS

CHAPTER 1
Animal Pose Types

Graphic Summary of Animal Pose Types

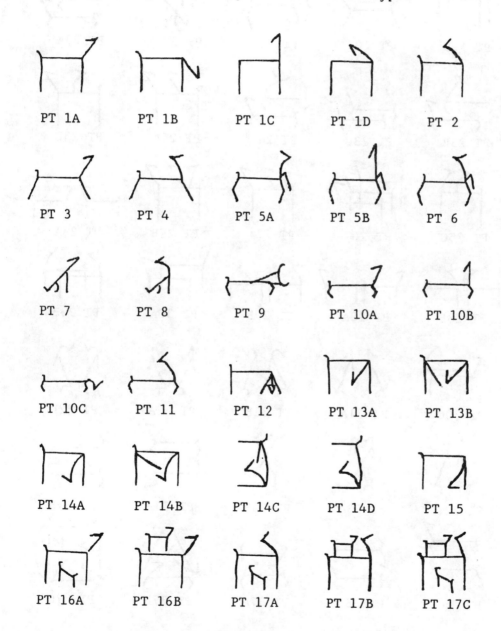

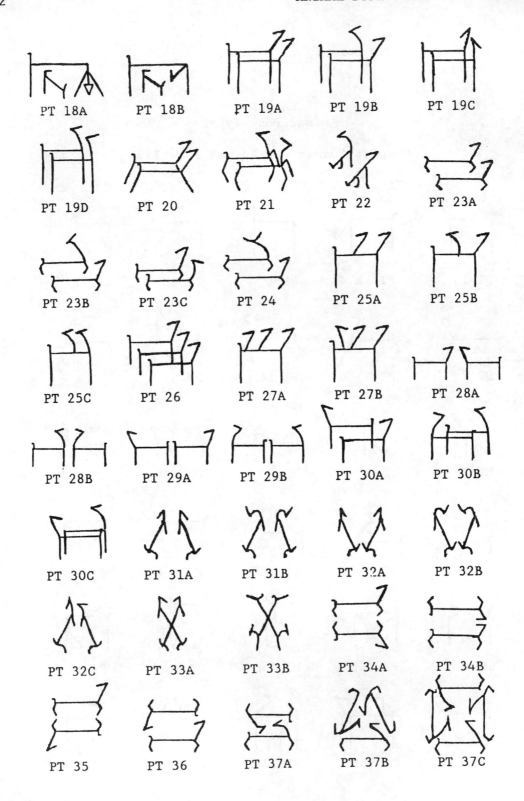

PT 18A   PT 18B   PT 19A   PT 19B   PT 19C

PT 19D   PT 20   PT 21   PT 22   PT 23A

PT 23B   PT 23C   PT 24   PT 25A   PT 25B

PT 25C   PT 26   PT 27A   PT 27B   PT 28A

PT 28B   PT 29A   PT 29B   PT 30A   PT 30B

PT 30C   PT 31A   PT 31B   PT 32A   PT 32B

PT 32C   PT 33A   PT 33B   PT 34A   PT 34B

PT 35   PT 36   PT 37A   PT 37B   PT 37C

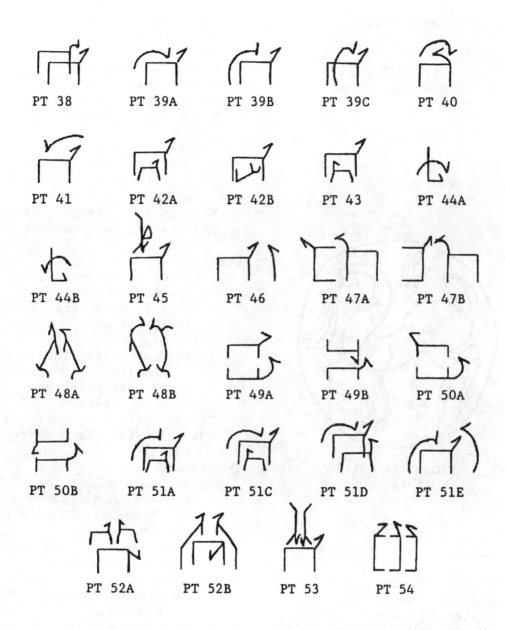

PT 38   PT 39A   PT 39B   PT 39C   PT 40

PT 41   PT 42A   PT 42B   PT 43   PT 44A

PT 44B   PT 45   PT 46   PT 47A   PT 47B

PT 48A   PT 48B   PT 49A   PT 49B   PT 50A

PT 50B   PT 51A   PT 51C   PT 51D   PT 51E

PT 52A   PT 52B   PT 53   PT 54

PART I

PRIMARY MOTIFS

CHAPTER 1
Animal Pose Types

PT 1, L

AM 1941.1242 (L) (CS 335)
   quadruped
      tree beh

FIG. 1 -- XII 305:
bull in PT 1A, R

PT 1A
Animal Standing or Walking

LEFT (see: Ch. 3A: Man &
   Animals, passim; Ch. 3B:
   Master of Animals [lions] --
   AM 1938.1054; Ch. 3D: Animal
   Games [rides other animals]
   -- X 166; & Ch. 4A: Women
   & Animals, passim)

Plain (no filling motifs)
Lion
   V 651 (L) Crete
   ?IX 175 (L)
Agrimi
   I 178 (L) Mycenae
      line encircles
   IV 309 (L) Aphrati
   V 394 (L) Medeon T. 99
      (LH III A)
   X 162 (L) (fat body =
      forgery?; cf. Ch. 3D:
      Animal Games [rides other
      animals] -- X 166)
   XII 196 (L) Seager Coll.
   ?HM G 3258 (L) Knossos
      (CMCG 252)
Goat
   Nafplion no. unknown (L)
      Apollo Maleatas (AR
      1977-8, p. 28 fig. 49
      left)
Griffin
   I 269 (C) Rutsi Tholos 2
         (LH IIA)
      griffiness, wing up
   I 475 (L) Crete
   VII 201 (L)
   HMs 185 (Ls) Kato Zakro
      (KZ 185)
Quadrupeds
   HM no. unknown (L)
      Knossos, MUM (Popham et
      al. 1984: pl. 190a, Misc.
      13)
   HMs no. unknown (Ls) Ayia
      Triada (AT 152)
Miscellaneous
   I 154 (A) Mycenae ChT 518
      (LH I-II)
      bull
   I 192 (L) Midea, ChT 10
         (LH II-III A)
      boar (originally: lion
      vs bull in PT 40A, R
      with "cloud" ab;
      unfinished)

I 353 (Ls) Pylos Palace
    (LH III B2-C1)
  caprid
VII 64 (L)
  dog
    dark V-shaped vein ab
      in place of a
      branch

Filling Motifs
BEFORE
  II 4.46 (L) "Apostoli"
  lion
    tree bef
BEHIND
 HMs 11 (Ls) Kato Zakro
    (KZ 198)
  bull
    Palm 4
ABOVE
  II 3.259 (L) Mochlos
  agrimi
    Pica ab
    2 Mount-Guides flank
  II 4.12 (L) Knossos
  agrimi
    Pica ab
  X 116 (Cyl)
    SH horizontal: agrimi
    Pica ab
    SH vertical: 2 fish in
      PT 35A, ccl
BELOW
  II 4.21 (L) Episcopi T.
  agrimi
    Branch 1 bel
 HM no. unknown (L)
    Knossos, MUM (Popham
    et al. 1984: pl. 189c,
    Misc. 11)
  quadruped
    Pica bel
    SH horizontal

IN FRONT & BEFORE
  II 4.485 (L)
  agrimi

    Branch 1 Tree infr &
      bef
IN FRONT & ABOVE
 Lion
  II 4.207 (L) Mochlos
    object infr & ab
  II 4.75 (L)
    erased hindleg?
    infr Frond ab
 Bull
  IX 174 (L) Knossos?
    Frond infr & bel
    dots ab
  HM G 3518 (L) (CMCG 248)
    Branch 1 infr
    Pica ab
 Agrimi
  V 186 (L)
    Column & Branch 3 infr
  VIII 129 (L) Hutch-
      inson Coll.
    Branch 1 Tree infr
    Frond (bird?) ab
  ?HM no. unknown (L)
    (Younger & Betts
    1979: no. 3)
    branch infr
    objects ab
 Miscellaneous
  V 670 (L) Thebes
    (LH III B)
    quadruped
    Branch 1 infr
    Frond ab
  VII 191 (L) Crete
  goat
    2 Figure-8 Shields
      infr
    bull face ab
  XIII 6 (L)
  stag
    Tree 1 infr
    spear ab
  Munich A.1216b (L)
    Melos (AGDS I
    Munich 70b)

griffin
    object infr (in
        mouth?)
    ImpTr ab

IN FRONT & IN BACK
    V 264   (L)   Armenoi T.
        39 (LM III A2-B1)
    lion
        object infr
        dots inb

IN FRONT & BELOW
Agrimi
    V 248   (L)   Armenoi T. 18
        Branch 1 Tree infr
            & bel (schematic
            bull face? cf. V
            247)
    V 342   (L)   Medeon T.
        29 (LH III A-C)
        Branch 2 infr
        3 strokes bel
    VII 167   (L)
        Branch 1 Tree infr
        branch/arrow ab
        3 Branch 1 & Dado 2c
        bel
    IX 103   (A)
        Branch 1 infr & bel
    X 124   (L)
        zig-zag? infr
        stroke bel
Miscellaneous
    II 4.43   (L)   Knossos
        quadruped
            2 Branch 1 infr,
                ab, & bel
            star bel
    X 176   (L)
        bull
            strokes infr
            Branch 1 bel

ABOVE & BELOW
Agrimi
    II 3.278   (C)   Palai-

kastro House D11
    (LM IIIA?)
    Pica ab
    2 Branch 1 bel
IV 245   (L)   Messara
    Pica ab
    Frond & Dado 2a
        bel
    SH horizontal
V 344   (L)   Medeon T.
    29 (LH III A-C)
    frond ab & bel
X 234   (L)
    strokes ab
    6 strokes bel
Florence 85490   (L)
    Crete? (Laviosa
    1969: no. 9)
    Pica ab
    Branch 1 bel
Miscellaneous
I 38   (RPl)   Mycenae
    quadruped
        1 Branch 2 ab &
            2 bel
        SH vertical
I Supp. 154   (L)
    quadruped
        Branch 2 ab & bel
HMs 320   (Ls) Knossos
    Palace (KSPI R79)
    lion
        branches ab & bel
HM G 3075a   (C) Mallia
    (CMCG 122)
    sheep
        rocks ab
        Dado 2a bel

IN FRONT, ABOVE, & IN BACK
    V 324   (L)   Krissa ChT 1
        (LH III B)
    quadruped
        line infr, ab, & inb
    X 113b   (A)
    agrimi
        Branch 1 infr & inb

        Pica in shoulder,
          arcs, net/reti-
          culation - all
          ab

IN FRONT, ABOVE, & BELOW
  Lion
    I Supp. 97 (L) Crete
      quadruped leg infr
      quadruped belly &
        hindquarter ab
      quadruped leg
        upside down bel
    II 3.104 (L) Kalyvia
      T. 4
      arrow infr
      goat head R ab
      sheep head L bel
  Agrimi
    I Supp. 70 (L) Hydra?
      Branch 2 infr
      Frond ab
      2 groundlines bel
      SH horizontal
    II 3.341 (A)
      Branch 1 infr
      branch ab & bel
      groundline bel
    IV 225 (A) Messara
      a pair of Mount-
        Guides, zig-zags, &
        arcs - all infr
      Bundles ab & bel
      a pair of Mount-
        Guides inb
    IX 101 (L)
      stroke infr
      Branch 1 ab & bel
      groundline bel
      SH horizontal but
        not finished
    X 115 (L)
      3 branches infr
      Pica in neck ab
      Branch 1 bel
      SH horizontal
    XII 308 (L) Seager

      Coll.
      Branch 3 infr
      Pica ab
      Branch 4 bel
    XIII 144 (L)
      Branch 1 infr
      Pica ab
      line (= kid suckling,
        PT 16A, L?) bel
      SH horizontal
    AM 1941.124 (L) (CS
      263)
      Branch 1 ab, infr
        & bel
      SH horizontal?
    HMs 509 (Ls) Ayia
      Triada (AT 73)
      Branch 1 infr & bel
      Pica ab in shoulder
  Miscellaneous
    II 4.214 (L)
      "Palaikastro"
      bull
        Tree 1 infr
        Figure-8 Shield
          ab & bel
    AM AE 1796 (L) (CS 42P)
      quadruped
        Branch 2 infr,
          ab, & bel

IN FRONT, IN BACK, & BELOW
  Agrimi
    XII 252 (L) Seager
      Coll.
      Branch 1 infr,
        inb, & bel
      groundline bel
    HMs 660 (As) Ayia
      Triada (AT 70)
      Branch 1 infr,
        inb, & bel
  Miscellaneous
    V 746 (L) Metaphio
      Tholos (LH III A2)
      bull
        strokes infr,

            inb, & bel

ABOVE, IN BACK, & BELOW
    VII 170 (L)
        agrimi
            Pica ab
            Branch 1 inb & bel
            SH horizontal

IN FRONT, ABOVE, IN BACK, &
    BELOW

    Agrimi
        II 3.153 (APr)
            "Phaistos"
            Branch 1 infr,
                inb, & bel
            Pica ab
            groundline bel
        IV 41D (L) Melambes
            Branch 1 infr, ab,
                inb, & bel
            Pica ab
            groundline bel
        VII 247 (L)
            Branch 1 infr, inb,
                & bel
            Pica & 2 Branch 1
                ab
        IX 102 (C)
            strokes infr & inb
            Pica ab
            Branch 1 bel
        XII 195 (C) Seager
            Coll.
            zig-zags infr & inb
            Branch 3/Pica ab
            Branch 1 bel
        XII 232 (L) Seager
            Coll.
            zig-zags infr
            Pica ab in shoulder
            lines inb & bel
            groundline bel
            SH horizontal
        XIII 44 (A)
            Branch 1 infr, inb,

            & bel
            Pica ab
            Dado 4d bel
        HM G 3045 (L) Mallia
            (CMCG 171)
            zig-zags infr & inb
            Branch 1 ab & bel
        Munich A.1198 (A)
            (AGDS I Munich
            65)
            Branch 1 infr, inb,
                & bel
            Pica ab
            3 groundlines bel
    Miscellaneous
        V 581 (APr) Kasarma
            Tholos (**FIG. 151**;
            LH I-II)
            Babylonian Dragon
            Branch 1 infr, bel
                & inb
            5 arcs & 1 circle
                ab
            groundline bel
        HM 2617? (L) Knossos
            (LM IA; Catling et
            al. 1979: 66 no. 2,
            pl. 14 c & d)
            lion
            branch infr, ab,
                inb, & bel
        Munich acc. 22846
            (L) (AGDS I
            Munich 76)
            bull
            branch infr,
                inb, & bel
            Pica & strokes ab
            SH horizontal

RIGHT (see: Ch. 2A: Body Parts
[man's head] -- HM G 3211;
Ch. 3A: Man & Animals [lion]
-- II 3.24 & HMs 508 [AT
134] & [bull] HM 2076; Ch.
4A: Women & Animals [anti-
thetic] -- VIII 95; [woman

seated at right] -- Chania
1503/1513, & HMs 584 [AT
128], HMs 157 [KN KSPI R91];
[animal inb] -- HMs 191 [KZ
191]; & [woman rides] -- HMs
73 [AT 13])

Plain (no filling motifs)
Lion
    I 332 (Ls) Pylos
      Palace (LH III B2-C1)
    IV 279 (L) Mallia
    AM 1953.121 (L) "Gaza"
      (CS 36P)
Bull
    I 345 (Ls) Pylos Palace
      (LH III B2-C1)
      calf?
    II 3.69 (C) Sellopoulo T.
      1 (LM III A2-B)
    HM 2236 (L) Mochlos
      (Hughes & Warren 1963:
      pl.IH)
      SH horizontal
Agrimi
    II 4.88 (L)
    XII 196 (L) Seager Coll.
    HM G 3306a (Pr) Mallia
      (CMCG 186a)
    Melos 578a (RP1) Phylakopi,
      East Sanctuary (LH III C;
      Renfrew 1985: 282, 289)
Miscellaneous
    I 400 (L) Athens
      quadruped
    I 473 (L) Crete
      griffin
    I Supp. 158 (L)
      quadruped
    V 325 (L) Krissa
      quadruped
    XII 262c (stone Matrix for
    making glass lentoids)
    "Poros"
    AM 1938.953 (C) (CS 200)
    sheep walks
    ?HMs 575 (As) Ayia Triada

    (AT 37)
  dog

Filling Motifs
BEHIND
    I Supp. 174 (Ls) Pylos
      Palace (LH III B2-C1)
    bull
      <u>Tree 5</u> beh
    V 598 (L/D) Mycenae, House
      of the Idols (LH III
      B2)
    goat
      <u>Tree 1</u> beh
    AM 1938.1041 (L) Crete? (CS
      306)
    bull held by a genius R
      beh with a leash
    HM G 3452 (L) Messara
      (CMCG 259)
    agrimi kid
      net/reticulation
        encircles (= beh?)

IN FRONT
Lion
    X 164 (L)
      erased lion/bull
      foreleg infr
    HMp no. unknown (clay
      conoid stamp seal)
      Knossos? (Pini
      1984: 79 pl. 16.3)
      branch infr
Agrimi
    V 250 (L) Armenoi T. 19
      (LM III B1)
    <u>Branch 1 Tree</u> infr
    V 341 (L) Medeon T.
      29 (LH III A-C)
    <u>Branch 2</u> infr
    IX 176 (L)
    <u>Branch 2</u> infr
    Munich inv. no. unknown
      (L) (AGDS I Munich
      78)
    <u>Branch 3</u> infr

Griffin
   I 472 (L) Crete
      <u>Branch 1 Tree</u> infr
   IV 58D (R) Tourtourli
      <u>Altar</u>? infr
   IX 18D (L)
      <u>Branch 1</u> infr
      probably not a forgery
         since it was bought
         in 1898
   HMs 97 (Ls) Kato
      Zakro (KZ 178)
      <u>Tree 1</u> (= <u>Palm 4</u>?)
         infr
Miscellaneous
   II 3.68 (C) Sellopoulo
      T. 1 (LM III A2-B)
      bull
         tree infr
   HMs 298 (Ls) Knossos
      Palace (KSPI K9)
      quadruped (bull?
         agrimi?)
      <u>Figure-8 Shield</u> &
         branch infr
   HMs 387ii/AM 1938.1439aa
      (Cs) Knossos
      Palace (KSPI L25;
      CS 7Sa)
     goat
        object ab
ABOVE
  Bull
     V 258 (L) Armenoi T.
        32 (LM III A2-B1)
      en face
        <u>Sun</u> ab
        SH horizontal
    ?HM no. unknown (L)
        Knossos, MUM
        (predominantly LM
        IIIB; Popham et al.
        1984: pl. 185c, D8)
      branch ab
  Agrimi
    V 29 (L) Argos
      <u>Branch 2</u> ab

V 625 (L) Marathia
   Tholos 2 (LH III
   B-C)
   2 lines ab form a
     profile line for
     back & tail
Goat
   V 357 (L) Medeon T. 29
     (LH III A-C)
   <u>Branch 1</u> ab
  Hannover 1935.119 (L)
     (AGDS IV Hannover
     6)
     <u>Pica</u> ab
     SH horizontal
Miscellaneous
   II 4.67 (L) Mirabello
     caprid?
       lines infr
       branch ab
   V 734 (L) Mega Monas-
     tiri T. Delta (LH
     III A2-B1)
     quadruped
       strokes ab
   X 122* (L)
     sheep
       stroke ab = <u>Pica</u>?
       unfinished?
   HM G 3333 (L) (CMCG
     282)
     quadruped, dappled
       tree ab
  Chania 2065 (Ls) Chania,
     Kastelli (Papapo-
     stolou 1977: no. 7)
     quadruped
       frond ab

IN BACK
  II 3.73 (C) Knossos
     (Geometric)
   waterbird, 1 wing up
     <u>Branch 1 Tree</u> inb
  IV 54D (L) Sokarras
   agrimi
     net inb

BELOW
    I Supp. 185 (Ls) Pylos
          Palace (LH III B2-C1)
        quadruped
          branch bel
    VII 263 (L)
        agrimi
          branch bel
    HMs 88 (Ls) Kato Zakro
          (KZ 42)
        griffin
          rocks? bel
    HMs 154 (Ls) Kato
          Zakro (KZ 154)
        collared lion?
          Dado 8 bel

IN FRONT & BEHIND
    Lion
        Column beh & Quadruped
        Hind-quarters infr

            II 4.18 (L) Ayia
              Irini Tholos E?
            II 4.74 (L)
        Miscellaneous
            IX 149 (L)
              Tree 1 infr & beh
            HMs 315 (Ls) Knossos
                Palace (KSPI
                R41)
              object infr
              Column beh
    Bull
        II 4.195 (L) Kastelli
            Pediada
          Tree 1 infr & beh
        AM 1938.1040 (L)
            "Taygetos" (CS 307)
          Palm 4 variant (bird?
            Fish Monster?) infr
          genius R beh
    Caprids
        I 487 (L) Crete
          kid
              tree infr
              Column beh

    II 3.40 (L) Zafer
        Papoura T. 36 (CS
        7P [once AM
        1941.246],
        "Gortyn"; see
        Younger 1985:
        section A6)
      goat
          Frond inf
          Column beh to which
            the goat is
            leashed loosely

IN FRONT & ABOVE
Lion
    II 4.17 (L) Kalyvia
        T.? (LM III A?)
      lioness
          Figure-8 Shield
            infr & ab
    II 4.45 (L)
        "Tsingounia"
      quadruped neck & head
        infr (= PT 1B, R)
      Column? ab/beh
    II 4.118 (L) Isopata T.
        2 (LM III A1)
      genius R
          infr a horizontal
            row of densely
            packed vertical
            dashes ab (=
            Column?)
    VIII 124 (L) Hutchinson
        Coll.
      erased quadruped
        hindquarters infr
      Column capital? ab
    HM G 3211 (L) (CMCG
        338)
      horse protome (PT 1B?)
        R infr
      man's head in profile
        R ab
    HM G 3526 (L) (CMCG
        266)
      erased quadruped

                    hindleg infr
                object ab
Bull
    I 373 (Ls) Pylos
            Palace (LH III
            B2-C1)
        Tree 5 crown ab (=
            Tree 5 beh?)
        branch infr
    V 159 (L) Kephallenia,
            Kokkolata (LH III
            B[-C])
        Branch 1 ab
        Branch 3 infr
    V 751 (L) Pefkakia
        Cypress Branch infr
        Figure-8 Shield ab
    X 263 (L)
        line infr
        Branch 2 ab
        incised line around
            edge of stone
            (probably for a
            ring setting or
            gilding)
    HMs 330+OD (Ls) Knossos
            Palace (KSPI R48)
        Branch 1 infr & ab
    Melos 569 (L)
            Phylakopi, East
            Sanctuary (LH III
            C; Renfrew 1985:
            282, 290)
        Branch 2 infr & ab
Agrimi
    II 4.123 (L) Mavro-
            spelio T. IV
        Frond infr
        object ab
    I 210 (L) Prosymna
            ChT VI (LH III
            B1)
        Branch 2 infr & ab
    V 338 (L) Medeon T.
            29
        Branch 1 ab
        Branch 3 infr

    V 401 (L) Medeon T.
            239 (LH III C)
        Branch 2 ab & infr
    Melos 570 (L) Phylakopi
            (LH III C; Renfrew
            1985: 282, 290)
        line infr & ab
Goat
    I Supp. 49 (L) Eleusis
            T. Lamda-pi 1 (LH
            III B)
        branches ab & infr
    II 3.111 (L) Kalyvia T.
            9 (LM III A1)
        Branch 1 infr
        Figure-8 Shield ab
    HMp 4813 (Ls, on a
            loomweight)
            Palaikastro
            (Hutchinson
            1939-40: 48, no. 34
            figs. 33 & 34)
        Branch 1 infr
        Figure-8 Shield ab
    HMs 296 (Ls) Knossos
            (KSPI K10)
        Palm 4 infr
        tree ab (ImpTr
            variant?)
Miscellaneous
    V 30 (L) Argos
        quadruped
            branches ab & infr
    Melos 574 (L) Phyla-
            kopi, East
            Sanctuary (LH
            III C; Renfrew
            1985: 283, 290)
        horse?
            branch infr &
            ?ab

IN FRONT & IN BACK
    V 340 (L) Medeon T. 29
            (LH III A-C)
        agrimi
            Branch 2 infr & inb

IN FRONT & BELOW
   Agrimi
      VII 239 (L)
        Frond infr
        branch bel
      AM 1941.134 (L) (CS
          20P)
        Branch 1 infr & bel
   Griffin
      XII 300 (L) Seager
          Coll.
        Branch 1 Tree infr
        branch bel
      XII 301 (L) Seager
          Coll.
        leashed to Column
          infr
        Sun bel
      AM 1941.128 (L) (CS
          23P)
        Column infr
        Figure-8 Shield bel
   Miscellaneous
      I Supp. 157 (L)
        bull
            Branch 2 infr &
            bel

ABOVE & BEHIND
   HMs 208 (Ls) Knossos
      Palace (KSPI R7)
     sheep
       Figure-8 Shield ab
         at left
       Column beh

ABOVE & BELOW
   Bull
      V 630 (L) Chalandritsa?
         (LH III C)
      sword ab
        Dado 4d bel
      VIII 145 (L)
        ImpTr? ab the
         hindquarters
        Figure-8 Shield bel

Agrimi
   I 399 (L) Athens
     branches ab & bel
   V 170 (L) Metaxata T.
       B (LH III [B-]C)
     dot ab & bel
Miscellaneous
   I 39 (L) Mycenae
     quadruped
       lines ab
       Figure-8 Shield
        ab & bel
   I 135 (L) Mycenae ChT
     103
     boar
       Branch 3 ab
       2 groundlines
        bel
   I Supp. 156 (L)
     quadruped
      branch ab & bel
   II 4.216 (L)
     lion
       objects ab & bel
   IV 311 (L) Siteia
     cat? en face
       Figure-8 Shield &
        dots ab
       2 strokes bel
   V 425 (L) Lefkandi
     quadruped
       Branch 1 ab
       Branch 3 bel
   V 615 (L) Olympia,
      Bachoureika T. A
      (LH III [A-]
      B-C)
     quadruped
       Branch 2 ab & bel
   V 740 (L) Mega Monastiri
      T. E (LH III A2-B2)
     quadruped
       strokes ab & bel
   HMs 335 (Cs) Knossos
      Palace (KSPI L26)
     goat
       swastika ab

quadruped/<u>Table</u> bel

IN FRONT, ABOVE, & IN BACK
   IX 201   (L)
   bull
      <u>Branch 1</u> ab, infr,
        & inb

IN FRONT, ABOVE, & BELOW
   Bull
     V 3   (L) Aigina,
       Athena Temple
     <u>Branch 1</u> infr
     4 strokes ab & 3
      bel
     V 683   (L) Tanagra,
       Dendron T. 13
       (LH III A-B)
     <u>Branch 1</u> infr &
      upside down ab
     2 <u>Figure-8 Shields</u>
      ab
     <u>Figure-8 Shield</u> &
      dot bel
   VII 177   (L) Ialysos?
     genius infr appears
        to hold bull
        by the nose
        (not a jug)
      bird ab
      octopus with 6
        arms bel
   X 186   (L)
     bull with short
       tail
      <u>Branch 1</u> infr &
       bel
     star ab
   XII 305   (L) Seager
      Coll. (**FIG. 1**)
     branch infr, ab, &
      bel
   HMs 129/AM 1938.1016
      (Ls) Knossos,
      Palace (KSPI J1;
      CS 45S)
     <u>Palm 4</u> infr

   <u>Figure-8 Shield</u> ab
    & bel
Melos 573   (L)
   Phylakopi East
   Sanctuary (LH
   III C; Renfrew
   1985: 282, 290)
   <u>Branch 2</u> infr, ab,
    & bel
Agrimi
   I Supp. 144   (L)
     <u>Branch 1 Tree</u> infr
     <u>Branch 1</u> ab & bel
   V 158   (L) Kephal-
      lenia, Kokkola-
      ta (LH III B[-
      C])
     <u>Branch 1</u> infr &
      bel
     3 strokes ab
   V 169   (L) Kephal-
      lenia, Metaxata
      T. B (LH III
      [B-] C)
     <u>Branch 3</u> infr & ab
     <u>Branch 1</u> bel
   V 339   (L) Medeon T.
      29 (LH III A-C)
     <u>Branch 2</u> infr
     2 triangles ab & 3
      bel
   X 165   (L)
     strokes/branch infr
     branch? ab
     stroke bel
   HMs 36   (Ls) Kato
      Zakro (KZ 125)
     <u>Branch 3</u> infr
     object ab & bel
Caprid
   I 188   (L) Midea
      Tholos (LH III
      A1)
     goat
       <u>Palm 4</u> variant
        infr
       <u>Tree 2</u> branch

                                    ab
                              rocks bel
                    V 272 (L) Armenoi,
                         T. 54
                         kid
                              Branch 1 Tree
                              infr
                              Branch 1 ab
                              dots bel
                    Nafplion 8839 (L)
                         Midea/Dendra T.
                         6 (LH I; Pini
                         1981: no. 65)
                         goat
                              Figure-8 Shield
                              infr, ab,
                                   & bel
               Miscellaneous
               I 32 (L) Mycenae
                         quadruped
                              strokes/gouges
                                   infr, ab, &
                                   bel
                    Once Evans Coll. (L)
                         (GGFR pl. 115)
                         dog
                              waterbird infr
                              ImpTr ab
                              Dado 5 bel

IN FRONT, IN BACK, & BELOW
     AM 1938.1096 (L) Ayia
          Pelagia Tholos (CS
               19P)
               agrimi
                    Branch 3 infr
                    Frond inb & bel
     HM G 3296 (RP1) (CMCG
          170)
          goat
               tree infr
               vertical stroke inb
               bucranium bel

IN FRONT, ABOVE, IN BACK, &
BELOW

     Bull
          V 227 (L) Oxylithos
               Tholos (LH III A-B)
               Branch 2 infr, ab, &
               inb
               4 Branch 2 bel
          V 254 (L) Armenoi T.
               27 (LM III A1-2)
               Branch 3 infr, inb, &
               bel
               Figure-8 Shield ab
     Agrimi
          IX 202 (L)
               Branch 2 infr, ab, &
               inb
               dot bel
          X 114* (A)
               Branch 1 infr & inb
               6 strokes ab
               Branch 1 bel
          Hamburg 1964.287 (A)
               (AGDS IV Hamburg 5)
               Pica ab
               Branch 1 infr, bel, &
               inb
          HM 2163 (L) Kamilari
               Tholos (MM III-LM
               I; Levi 1961-2: no.
               18 fig. 125)
               vertical stroke infr &
               inb
               Branch 1 ab & bel
     Miscellaneous
          V 510 (L) Zygouries T.
               T. XXXIII (LH III
               B)
               quadruped
                    lines in the field

FIG. 2 -- V 157:
bull/calf in PT 1B, L

PT 1B

Animal Standing or Walking,
Head Down

LEFT (see: Ch. 3A: Men &
    Animals; & Ch. 4A: Women &
    Animals, both passim)

Bull/Calf
    II 4.126 (L) Mavrospelio
        T. XVIIA
        Tree 3 bef
    II 4.150 (L) Phaistos
        2 lines ab
    II 4.221 (L)
        Tree 3 beh
    V 157 (L) Kephallenia,
        Kokkolata (FIG. 2; LH
        III B[-C])
        2 Palm 4 beh
    VII 251 (L)
        Tailed Sun? ab (see
            Ch. 14B: Tailed
            Suns)
    HMs 515 (As) Ayia Triada
        (AT 63)

Boar/Sow
    I 343 (Ls) Pylos Palace,
        (LH III B2-C1)
        3 Palm 4 beh
    V 314 (L) Delos, Artemis
        Sanctuary
        zig-zags ab
        2 groundlines bel
        SH oblique: upper left to
            lower right
    AM 1938.1086 (L) Archanes
        (CS 332; Sakellarakis
        1970: 217 no. B1,
        figs. 8.1 & 9.1)
        on sacrificial Table with
            3 bucranium legs
    HM G 3528 (L) (CMCG 278)
        Branch 3? ab
    Brummer Coll. (L)
        sow
            2 Weeds ab
            groundline bel

Dog
    II 4.92 (L))
    ?HM G 3369 (L) Phaistos
        (CMCG 280)

Miscellaneous
    V 365 (L) Medeon T. 29
        horse?
            Branch 3 ab
    IX 178 (L)
        griffin
            stroke ab
    XII 136 (D) Lasithi
        sheep
            architectonic
                exergue ab
            2 groundlines bel
            SH oblique: lower
                right to upper left
    HMs 561 (As) Ayia Triada
        (AT 40)
        lion
    HM no. unknown (L) Mallia
        (BCH 90, 1966, 584 no.

17, fig. 30.3)
quadruped

RIGHT (see: Ch. 3A: Man &
Animals; & 4A: Woman &
Animals both passim)

Lion/Lioness
I 246   (A/Cyl) Vapheio
Tholos cist (LH IIA)1
lioness
XIII 82 (A) Knossos
rocks bel
HMs no. unknown (Ls) Ayia
Triada (AT 39)
lion/dog
Dado 2a bel
HM G 3331 (D) (CMCG 121)
zig-zag ab
tree beh
2 groundlines bel
reverse: architectonic
HM no. unknown (L) (Younger
& Betts 1979: no. 2)
objects in field
Berlin FG 19 (L) Olympia?
(AGDS II Berlin 41)
agrimi head R bel
SH horizontal

Bull
I 88   (L) Mycenae, ChT 55
2 Palm 4 beh
2 groundlines bel
I 264 (L) Tragana Tholos 2
(LH III A)
Table with 3 legs
upside down ab
II 4.83 (L)
branches ab
V 497 (L) Ayia Irini, the
Temple (LH IIIA-B)
Picas in shoulder
VII 163 (L)
Frond & 2 groundlines bel
IX 157 (L)
Tree 1 beh

SH horizontal
IX 17D (L)
Tree 3/Cypress Tree beh
X 139 (L)
Tree 3 crown ab
X 222 (L)
tall Frond beh
XII 303 (L) Seager Coll.
(published upside down)
branch infr, ab, & bel
HMs 330a/XiEta (Ls)
Knossos Palace (KSPI
R52)
2 Branch 1 bef
HMs 311 (Ls) Knossos
Palace (KSPI R84)
2 Frond ab
Palm 4/Pica bel
HMs 41 (As) Kato Zakro (KZ
99)
HMs 73 (As) Kato Zakro
(KZ 100)
HM no. unknown (L) Kamila-
ri Tholos (MM III-LM
I; Levi 1961-2: no.
16)
net/reticulation beh
HMs no. unknown (Ls) Ayia
Triada (AT 60)
en face, caught in a net
at right
Oxford (MS) Mus. J22 (A)
(Robinson 1949: 309
pl. 39 no. 4-4a)
NMA no. unknown (L)
Prosymna T. 8 (LH
III A2-B; Blegen
Prosymna fig. 587)
Branch 2 ab
branch bel

Agrimi
V 160 (L) Kephallenia
Kokkolata (LH III [B-
B[-C])
Branch 3 ab
Branch 1 bel

V 687 (L) Tanagra,
    Dendron T. 34 (LH III
    A-B)
  line ab
  groundline bel
AM 1938.954 (C) Archanes
    (CS 227)
  stands on rock ledge
    dog bel L
    rocks bel dog
    SH vertical

Boar
  II 4.184 (L) "Knossos,
    Temple T. area"
  object ab
  II 4.40 (L) "Knossos"
  Frond & Pica? ab
  VIII 119 (A) Hutchinson
    Coll.
  2 groundlines bel
  IX 177 (L)
  strokes ab
  XII 240 (L) Seager Coll.
  man bel prone R, head
    regardant

Goat?
  II 4.228 (L)
  XIII 134 (L)
  branches ab

Miscellaneous
  I 350 (Ls) Pylos Palace
    (LH III B2-C1)
  quadruped
    objects ab
  HM G 3102 (L) Knossos
    (CMCG 279)
  donkey?
    object ab
  Oxford, MS J21 (L)
    (Robinson 1949: 309f
    pl. 39 no. 5-5a)
    SH horizontal: sheep
    enface? unfinished
    SH vertical: the original

design might have been
intended to consist of
2 quadrupeds in PT 36
cl
Eretria no. unknown (L)
  Lefkandi T. 12B (Sub-
  Myc; Popham & Sackett
  1980: 225, T. 12B3)
  quadruped

PT 1C

Animal Standing or Walking,
Head Up

LEFT
Bull
  I 479 (L) Crete
  branches? ab
  I Supp. 24 (L) Argive
    Heraeum
  Branch 2 infr & inb
  II 3.217 (L) "Mallia"
  VII 65a (L) Crete
  Pica ab in neck
  2 groundlines
  VII 200 (L)
  Branch 1 infr & ab
  dot bel
  IX 147 (L)
  Branch 1 Tree infr
  Figure-8 Shield ab
  X 167 (L)
  2 lines ab (later re-
  engraved?)

Miscellaneous
  I 495 (L) Crete
  kid
    Branch 1 Tree infr &
    beh
  IX 178 (L)
  griffin

RIGHT (see: Ch. 3A: Man &
    Animals [bull] -- Chania
    1529 & 1530)

Bull
    I 25   (L)   Mycenae
        Branch 2 infr
        Branch 3 ab
    I 147   (L)   Mycenae, ChT
        518 (LH I-II)
        Pica ab
    I Supp. 23   (L)   Argive
        Heraeum
        Branch 2 infr
        Branch 1 ab
    IV 317   (L)
        Branch 1 ab
    AM 1938.969 (L)   Knossos
        area (CS 301)
        calf/bull, arrow in
            chest
        groundline bel

Agrimi
    X 178   (L)
        Branch 2 infr
        Branch 3 ab
    Berlin FG 61   (L)   "Athens"
        (AGDS II Berlin 60)

Miscellaneous
    I Supp. 4   (L)   Mycenae,
        ChT
        quadruped
            Branch 2 encircles
    II 3.160   (L)   "Platanos"
        collared dog
        branch ab

                PT 1D

Animal Standing or Walking,
        Head Back

RIGHT
Bull
    ?I 169   (L)   Mycenae
        branches bel
    IX 108 (L)
        Branch 3 ab & infr
        Frond bel
Miscellaneous
    V 402   (L)   Medeon T. 239
        (LH III C)
        agrimi
            stroke infr
            Branch 2 inb

        PT 1 or PT 2, R

I 138   (L)   Mycenae, ChT 505
    (LH III A2)
    bull
        Branch 2 ab
I 300   (L)   Pylos (LH III
    B2-C1)
    quadruped
AM 1938.1136a   (L)   (CS 398a)
    bull?
AM 1938.1441   (Ls) Knossos?
    (CS 43S)
    lion
        Pica in the back

        PT 1 or PT 5A, L

HM no. unknown   (L)   (Younger &
    Betts 1979: no. 4)
    agrimi
        Branch 1 ab

FIG. 3 -- I 76:
bull in PT 2, R

PT 2

**Animal Standing or Walking,
Regardant**

LEFT (see: Ch. 3A: Man &
Animals [lion] -- HMs 383I
[KSPI L46], [griffin] -- I
223, & [misc.] -- AM 1938.
1062; Ch. 3C: Man Hunts
Animals [lions] -- IX 114 &
HMs 65a [KZ 193]; & Ch. 4A:
Women & Animals [antithe-
tic] -- AM 1938.1097)

Plain (no filling motifs).
Lion
   V 671   (C)   Thebes
     stretching
      SH vertical
   AM 1971.1144   (L)   de
     Jong coll. (Boardman
     1973: no. 9)
   Cyprus no. unknown   (R)
     Enkomi T. 18 (LCyp II;
     SCE I pls. 88.2 & 145,
     21-23
   HM no. unknown   (A)   Zafer

Papoura T. 99 (Evans
   1906: no. 99a3)
HMs 477 (Ls) Ayia Triada
   (AT 38)
   lioness
HMs 470 (Ls) Ayia Triada
   (AT 45)
HM G 3313   (L)   Knossos
   (CMCG 274)

Bull
   I Supp. 117   (L)
   II 4.220   (L)
   VII 97   (C)
   AM AE 697   (L)   (CS 17P)
   HMs 541   (Ls)   Ayia Triada
     (AT 66)
   Munich A.1169   (L) Crete
     (AGDS I Munich 53)

Griffin
   I 475   (L)   Crete
   HMs 60 gamma   (Ls)   Kato
Zakro (KZ 79)

Miscellaneous
   HMs 162 (Ls) Kato
     Zakro (KZ 162)
   collared bitch

Filling Motifs
IN FRONT
   Bull
     IV 284   (L)   Lastros
     tree infr
     V 322   (L)   Krissa ChT 3
      (LH III C?)
     <u>Branch 3</u> infr
   Miscellaneous
     I Supp. 119   (A)
     waterbird
     <u>Branch 1</u> infr

ABOVE
   Lion
     II 3. 152   (L) Mallia,
     Gem-Engraver's

Workshop
Pica ab
II 4.1 (L) Tylissos
Pica ab
AM 1941.155ba (L)
(CS 30Pa)
branch ab
Miscellaneous
I Supp. 15 (L)
Mycenae
quadruped
Branch 1 ab
II 4.220 (L)
bull
Pica ab in the back
V 610 (L) Olympia, New
Mus. T. SigmaTau
(LH III B)
quadruped
2 strokes ab

BELOW
Bull
Berlin FG 33 (L)
"Athens" (AGDS II
Berlin 43)
head unfinished?
groundline bel
HMs 77 (Ls) Ayia Triada
(AT 77)
2 groundlines bel
Miscellaneous
II 4.163 (L) Mallia,
Quartier DeltaA
lion
object bel
AM AE 1795 (L) (CS 29P)
quadruped
2 groundlines bel
IN FRONT & ABOVE
Lion
AM 1873.129 (A) "found"
in Egypt" (CS 330)
lioness
Frond infr
Pica ab
HMs 531 (Ls) Ayia

Triada (AT 36)
rocks infr & ab
Bull
I 59 (R) Mycenae ChT 25
tree infr
Branch 1 & 3 ab
V 282 (L) Armenoi T. 64
(LM III A2[-B1])
Branch 1 Tree infr
Pica? ab
Miscellaneous
X 179 (L)
agrimi?
Branch 2 infr
Branch 1 ab

IN FRONT & IN BACK
Copenhagen 1364 (L) (Betts
1981a: 11 fig. 15)
lioness
2 pairs of Mount
-Guides flank

IN FRONT & BELOW
Bull
I Supp. 48 (L) Eleusis
T. ThetaPi 4 (LH
III A)
Branch 3 infr
Branch 2 bel
V 281 (L) Armenoi T. 64
(LM III A2[-B1])
Branch 2 infr
branch bel
Mallia no. unknown (Ls)
Mallia (LM III
A2?-B; BCH 102,
1978, 836)
Branch 1 infr
Frond bel

ABOVE & BELOW
Lioness
I Supp. 168 (L)
Thebes?
Weeds ab, & inb, & bel
bird? flies R bel

V 304   (L) Volimidia,
        Angelopoulou T. 8
        (LH I-II)
    waterbird L
        regardant ab
    bull face bel
Miscellaneous
    HMs 72 (Ls) Kato Zakro
        (KZ 124)
    caprid
        Pica ab
        Frond bel
    XIII 32 (L)
    bull
        2 Sacred Knots ab
        Figure-8 Shield bel

IN BACK & BELOW
    XIII 57 (L)
    lion
        vertical line inb
    Branch 1 bel
    Dado 4b bel

IN FRONT, ABOVE, & BELOW
    Bull
        IX 123 (L)
        calf head infr
        circle ab rump & bel
        XIII 131 (L)
        branch infr
        Pica ab
        2 dots bel

IN FRONT, ABOVE, IN BACK,
& BELOW
    Lion
        HM G 3285 (A) Apesokari
            (CMCG 260)
        rocks infr, inb, & ab
        waterbird bel in PT
            11, L
        groundline bel
    Munich A.1199 (A) "Melos"
            (AGDS I Munich 66)
        2 Mount-Guides infr
        branch ab

        1 Mount-Guide inb
        arrow in belly bel
Miscellaneous
    V 323 (L) Krissa ChT 2
        (LH III C)
    quadruped
        strokes encircle

RIGHT (see: Ch. 3A: Man & Ani-
    mals [bull] -- HMs 85 [KZ
    102])

Plain (no filling motifs)
Lion
    I Supp. 115 (L)
        unfinished
    II 3.18 (C) Knossos, House
        of the Frescoes (LM
IB?)
    II 4.24 (L) Mallia
        en face
    II 4.7 (L) Knossos
        (Geometric)
        lion/bull
    ?V 652 (L) Crete

Bull
    I 336 (Cs) Pylos Palace
        (LH III B2-C1)
    ?II 4.8 (L) Knossos,
        Demeter Sanctuary
    HMs 563 (Ls) Ayia Triada
        (AT 69)

Deer
    I 181 (L) Midea Tholos (LH
        III A:1)
    IV 269 (L) Messara
    VII 67 (C)

Miscellaneous
    I 365 (Ls) Pylos Palace
        (LH III B2-C1)
        quadruped
    ?I Supp. 190 (Ls) Pylos
        Palace (LH III B2-C1)
        quadruped

V 261   (L)   Armenoi T. 34
    (LM III A2-B1)
  quadruped
V 309   (L)   Pylos
  agrimi
V 443   (L)   Nichoria (LH
    III)
  quadruped
V 583   (Cyl)   Kasarma Tholos
    (LH I-II)
  griffin
V 631   (L)
  quadruped
HMs 2a   (Ls)   Kato Zakro
    (KZ 127)
  quadruped = monster?
Melos 575   (L)   Phylakopi,
    East Sanctuary (LH III
    C; Renfrew 1985: 282,
    290)
  quadruped (lion/bull)

Filling Motifs
BEHIND
  I 76   (L)   Mycenae ChT 42
    (FIG. 3)
    bull
      Tree 2 beh
  VII 155   (L)   Melos
    quadruped
      Branch 2/Column beh
          (cf. Ch. 6B: Genii
          -- VIII 65)

IN FRONT
  Bull
    II 4.141   (L)   Knossos
        (cf. HMs 1014,
        below)
      tree infr
    V 442   (L)   Nichoria (LH
        III)
      Branch 2 infr
    ?V 729   (L)   Mega
        Monastiri T. Gamma
        (LH III A1-B1)
      branch infr

VII 205   (L)
  branch infr
X 314   (L)   Dawkins Coll.
  large Branch 3 infr
HMs 1014   (Ls)   Knossos
  Palace (Betts 46; cf.
  II 4.141, above)
Miscellaneous
  V 42   (L)   Lerna
    quadruped
      Branch 2 infr
  V 378   (L)   Medeon T.
      29 (LH III A-C)
    agrimi
      strokes infr
  X 172   (L)
    lion?
      Branch 1 infr
  Sparta no. unknown (L)
      Ayios Stephanos
    quadruped
      Branch 2 infr

ABOVE
Agrimi/Caprid
  V 343   (L)   Medeon T. 29
      (LH III A-C)
    branch ab
  HMs 22   (Ls)   Kato Zakro
      (KZ 121)
    2 Picas ab
Miscellaneous
  II 4.206   (L)   Mochlos
    lion
      Figure-8 Shield? ab
  V 4   (L)   Aigina, Aphaia
    quadruped
      Branch 3 ab
  V 310   (L)   Pylos ChT E9
      (LH III B?)
    quadruped
      dots ab & bel
  Chania no. unknown (Ls)
      Chania, Kastelli
      (Papapostolou 1977:
      no. 18)
    waterbird

fish (upside down?)
L ab
HM G 3212 (L) (CMCG
241)
bull
branch ab

BELOW
Lion
II 3.302 (L)
"Hierapetra"
lioness
zig-zags bel
Dog
AM 1938.1061 (L) central
Crete (CS 240)
collared bitch, hind-
leg up to scatch
groundline bel
Chania 2053 (Ls)
Chania, Kastelli
(Papapostolou 1977:
no. 6)
collar
groundline bel
HMs 214+287/AM 1938.1014
(Ls) Knossos (KSPI
F2/K4/K7/K12/Q21/R53/
CS 40S; inscribed)
collared bitch
groundline bel
Miscellaneous
I Supp. 147 (L)
sheep (unfinished)
groundline bel
V 275 (L) Armenoi T. 56
bull
Figure-8 Shield bel
VII 190 (A)
agrimi
Figure-8 Shield bel
SH vertical
HMs 24 (Ls) Kato
Zakro (KZ 108)
stag
groundline bel
HMs 503 (Ls) Ayia

Triada (AT 57)
bull (impressed
twice?)
groundline bel

BEHIND & BELOW
HMs 49 (Ls) Kato
Zakro (KZ 103)
bull
tree beh
2 groundlines bel

IN FRONT & ABOVE
Lion
II 4.209 (L)
Palaikastro
line infr
Pica ab
X 303 (L)
lioness
line infr
stroke ab
SH horizontal
HMs no. unknown (Ls)
Ayia Triada (AT 83)
line infr
helmet? & object ab
Bull
V 379 (L) Medeon T.
29a (LH III A-C)
Branch 2 infr & ab
Figure-8 Shield ab
V 417 (L) Medeon T.
264 (LH III C)
Branch 4 infr
Branch 2 ab
IX 204 (L)
Pica/branch infr & ab
X 180 (L)
Branch 2 infr
Branch 1 ab (cf. X 171
for the pose & the
forward lean of the
horns)
XIII 10 (L)
branch infr curls
bef the bull's

shoulder
Palm ab
Miscellaneous
  V 187 (L)
    quadruped
      Branch 2 infr & ab
  V 606 (L) Naxos, Kamini
    T. 3 (LH III C)
    quadruped
      Branch 2 infr & ab
  Munich no. unknown (L)
    (AGDS I Munich 77)
    quadruped
      Branch 3 infr & ab?
  NMA no. unknown (L)
    Athens, Acropolis,
    Mycenaean fountain
    (LH III C1; Broneer
    1939: 414 fig. 99a)
    quadruped
      Branch 1 infr
      2 Figure-8 Shield
        ab

IN FRONT & BELOW
Bull
  II 3.212 (L) "Gouves"
    Branch 1 Tree infr
    Figure-8 Shield bel
    groundline bel
  II 3.336 (L)
    calf
      Branch 1 Tree infr
      Frond bel
  II 4.200 (L) "Mallia"
    line infr
    stroke bel
  V 172 (L) Kephallenia,
    Pronnoi
    Branch 2 infr & bel?
  V 219 (L) Brauron,
    Lapoutsi ChT 19
    (LH III B?)
    3 strokes infr & bel
  V 247 (L) Armenoi T. 18
   en face
      Branch 1 Tree infr

rake/schematic
bull face bel
VII 113 (L) Ialysos
  Palm 4 infr
  Figure-8 Shield bel
VII 162 (L)
  licking its back
  Palm branch
    attached to a
    stand? infr
  Figure-8 Shield
    bel
X 244 (L)
  Branch 2 infr
  dots/Figure-8
  Shield bel
Berlin FG 32 (L) Greek
  islands (AGDS II
  Berlin 52)
  lion en face
  Branch 1 infr
  Figure-8 Shield bel

ABOVE & BELOW
Bull
  V 626 (L) Skoura,
    Kivouria cist grave
    lines ab & bel
  HMs 19 (Ls) Kato
    Zakro (KZ 120)
    rocks ab & bel
  HMs 308I & OH (Ls)
    Knossos Palace
    (KSPI R74/97?)
  Frond ab & bel
Agrimi
  I Supp. 155 (L)
    kid
      branch ab & bel
      reverse: engraved
        lines for a
        quadruped L?
  V 9 (L) Aigina,
    Aphaia Temple?
  branch ab
  Branch 2 bel

IN FRONT, ABOVE, & IN BACK
   IX 151 (C)
      lion
         Pica ab in shoulder
      2 Mount-Guides flank
IN FRONT, ABOVE, & BELOW
   Bull
      I Supp. 142 (L)
         Branch 2 infr
         Figure-8 Shield ab
         Branch 1 bel
      II 4.4 (L) Zafer
         Papoura T. 94
       a column of dots infr
       branch? ab
       Figure-8 Shield bel
      V 315 (L) Delos
         Branch 3 infr
         Branch 2 ab & bel
      V 377 (L) Medeon T. 29a
         (LH III A-C)
         Branch 3 infr
         Pica ab
         Branch 2 bel
      V 512 (L) Korakou
         Branch 3 infr & ab
         2 Branch 3 bel
      VII 161 (L) Sparta
         lance infr
         spear/sword ab
         Frond bel
      VII 204 (L) Kalymnos,
         found in vase BM
         A1015 (LH III C1;
         Walters 1912: s.n.;
         Furumark 1972,
         Analysis: FS 176.1
         & FM 21.28)
       with short tail
         Branch 2 infr & ab
         line bel
     ?VIII 99 (L) Dawkins
         Coll.
        Branch 3 infr
        2 Branch 2 ab
        Branch 2 bel
      X 142* (L)

erased bull hindleg
   infr
Sacred Knot? with
   bull's ear ab
lion protome upside
   down & regardant
   bel
   X 175 (L)
      strokes infr & bel
      Branch 1 ab
      SH diagonal (lower
         left to upper
         right)
   AM 1893.234 (L) bought
      at Rethymnon (CS
      18P)
      branches infr
      tree horizontal ab
      stroke bel
   HM 2301 (L) Archanes
      Tholos B (LM III
      A1; Sakellarakis
      1967a: fig. 7b)
      rocks (Frond?) infr
      3 complete (5,
         including twice-
         drilled) rings ab
      conch bel
Caprid
   I Supp. 14 (L) Mycenae
      lines infr, ab, & bel
   VIII 98 (L) Dawkins
      Coll.
      goat
         Branch 3 infr & ab
         branch bel
Miscellaneous
   ?I Supp. 143 (L)
      quadruped
         Branch 3 infr
         line ab
         Figure-8 Shield
            bel?

IN FRONT, IN BACK, & BELOW
  Bull
      IX 203   (L)
        Branch 2 infr & inb
        dot bel
      Munich A.1308   (L)
          Athens, Olympieion
          (AGDS I Munich 89)
        Branch 3 infr
        3 strokes bel
        6-7 strokes inb

ABOVE, IN BACK, & BELOW
  V 8 (L) Aigina
    bull
        Branch 2 infr, ab,
          inb, & bel

ABOVE, BELOW, & ENCIRCLING
  V 321   (L)   Krissa ChT
      3 (LH III C)
    quadruped
      dot ab & bel
      strokes encircle
      SH horizontal
  X 181   (L)
    goat
        Branch 1 & dot ab
        dot bel
        Branch 2 encircles

IN FRONT, ABOVE, IN BACK, &
  BELOW

  II 3.122   (L)   Porti Tholos
    lioness
        a pair of Mount-Guides
          infr & inb
        lion face ab
        small Tree 1 with 2
          groundlines bel
        SH horizontal

Miscellaneous
  V 161   (L)   Kephallenia,
      Kokkolata cist grave
      (LH III B[-C])

    quadruped
        Branch 3? encircles
  V 345   (L)   Medeon T. 29
      (LH III A-C)
    quadruped
      strokes in the field

PT 2 or Possibly Another PT

2/6
HMs 182   (Ls)   Kato Zakro (KZ
    182)
  bull L
HMs no. unknown   (Ls?)   Mallia
    (AR 1976-7, 63-4)
  agrimi
  foliage
Nafplion no. unknown   (Ls)
    Tiryns (AA 1979, 383-4
    fig. 4)
  bull
    Palm 4 beh

2/8, R
I 516   (Ls)   Knossos?
  quadruped
    Palm 4 beh?

FIG. 4 -- V 580:
bull in PT 3, L

PT 3
Animal Runs in Flying Gallop

(see: PT 43; PT 49B, R -- VII
96; PT 51A, L -- HM 155; & PT
51A, R -- AM 1938.861 [KSPI
G15/CS 50S]; & Ch. 3E: Animal
Games [bull-leaping] passim)

LEFT (see: PT 14B, R/PT 18B,
     R -- IX 156 [calf])

Agrimi
    Munich A.1200 (R) Crete
         (AGDS I Munich 35)
         Branch 1 infr, inb/ab, &
         2 Branch 1 bel
    HMs 153 (Ls) Kato Zakro
         (KZ 153)
         branches bel

Griffin
    IX 162 (Almond-shaped
         prism) Cyprus
         displayed
    HMs 179 (Rs) Kato Zakro
         (KZ 179)
         object infr

Miscellaneous
    I 201 (R) Asine T. 1 (LH
         III A2)
         bull (-leaping?)
              tree? infr
              rocks bel
    V 580 (L) Kasarma (FIG. 4;
         LH I-II)
         bull, head down
              3 Branch 3 beh

RIGHT (see: Ch. 3D: Men In
    Chariots -- HMs 347 [KSPI
    L?/Na?])

Bull
    HM no. unknown (R)

    Kalyvia T. 9 (LM III
         A1; Savignoni 1904:
         520 fig. 11)
         Branch 1 infr & ab
         Dado 1? bel
    HMs 37 (As) Kato Zakro (KZ
         98)
         bull-leaping?

Lion
    I Supp. 146 (L)
         branches encircle
    ?HMs 321 (Rs) Knossos
         Palace (KSPI R37)
         Palm 1 beh

Miscellaneous
    I 394 (L) Perati ChT 1 (LH
         III B2-C1)
         quadruped
              branches ab
              groundline bel
    IV 42D (L) Messara
         Babylonian Dragon
         Sun ab & bel
         branch bel
    VIII 47a (R bezel once on
         vertical swivel pin?)
         Dawkins Coll.
         goat
              4 Weeds bel
    HMs 638-648 (Cs)
         Sklavokambos
         (Sk 12)
         griffin
              object bel

         PT 3, R or PT 4, R

(see: Ch. 3A: Man & Animals
[misc.] -- HMs 167 [KSPI K8])

FIG. 5 -- XIII 35:
bull in PT 4, R; man prone R
bel

PT 4
Animal Runs in Flying Gallop,
Regardant

(see: PT 42A, L --HMs 132 [KSPI
P73]; PT 45 -- Berlin FG 43
[AGDS II 36]; PT47B -- V 642;
PT 51C -- Hannover 1973.2 [AGDS
IV 7])

LEFT
HMs no. unknown (R/As) Ayia
   Triada (AT 46)
      stag

RIGHT
XIII 35 (C) **(FIG. 5)**
   bull
      man prone R bel (a fallen
        bull-leaper?), his
        right leg beh & his
        left leg bef the
        bull's hindlegs
Munich acc. 18211 (C) (AGDS I
   Munich 23)

FIG. 6 -- Once Evans coll.:
bull in PT 5A, R

PT 5A
Animal Runs

LEFT
Plain (no filling motifs)
  Bull.
    I Supp. 145 (L)
    II 4.37 (L) "Knossos"
    II 4.56 (L) "Pediada"
    II 4.82 (L)
    II 4.223 (L)
    VIII 126 (L) Hutchinson
      Coll.
    HMs no. unknown (As)
      Ayia Triada (AT 64)
    HMs 546 (Ls) Ayia
      Triada (AT 72)
  Agrimi
    I 489 (L) Crete
    I Supp. 83 (L) Crete
    II 3.166 (L)
      "Tylissos"
    II 4.31 (L) "Poros"
      agrimi kid
    II 4.106 (L) Tylissos
    II 4.181 (L)

II 4.201 (L)
II 4.152 (L)
IV 261 (L) Knossos
IV 270 (L) Sklavi
IV 292 (L) Messara
IV 297 (L) Sokarras
IV 303 (L) Messara
V 741 (L) Gritsa,
   Lemoni Tholos
VIII 76 (L) Dawkins
   Coll.
VIII 81 (L) Dawkins
   Coll.
IX 173 (L)
X 319 (L)
XIII 127 (L)
XIII 128 (L)
AM 1941.99 (L) (CS
   386)
AM 1971.1149 (L) de
   Jong Coll. (Boardman
   1973: no. 14)
HMs 71 (Ls) Ayia Triada
   (AT 71)
HMs 559 (Ls) Ayia
   Triada (AT 65)
HM G 3086 (L) (CMCG
   242)
HM G 3324b (A) (CMCG
   185b)
HM G 3450 (L) Mallia
   (CMCG 244)
Munich 21767 (L) (AGDS
   I Munich 93)
Goat
   II 4.86 (L)
   IV 308 (L) Messara
   HM G 3500 (L) (CMCG
      239)
   Munich no. unknown (L)
      (AGDS I Munich 52)
Stag
   I 499 (L) Crete
   I 500 (L) Crete
   II 4.174 (L) Gazi
   IX 171 (L)
   XII 104a (Reel) Seager

Coll.
   AM 1925.54 (C) (CS 27P)
Deer
   HM G 3557 (L) (CMCG
      256)
Griffin
   I Supp. 149a (L)
   HMs 66a (Ls) Kato Zakro
      (KZ 40)
Miscellaneous
   I 339 (Ls) Pylos Palace
      (LH III B2-C1)
      quadruped
   II 4.77 (L)
      lion

Filling Motifs
BEHIND
   Bull
      ?HMs 248 (Ls) Knossos
         tree beh

ABOVE
   Lion
      I 504 (L) Crete
         Branch 1 ab
      I 505 (L) Crete
         Branch 1 ab
      II 3.290 (A)
         "Tzermiado"
         Branch 1 ab
      II 4.127 (elliptical L)
         Mavrospelio T. 17B
         arrow?
      V 362 (A) Medeon T. 29
         Branch 1 ab
      VII 94 (Cyl)
         2 registers upside
         down to each other:
         in one, a mule &
         griffin; in the
         other, a lion
         (Branch 1/Pica ab)
         & agrimi
         Frond infr of both
         animals
      dolphin betw

Florence 82690 (A)
    bought in Crete
    (Laviosa 1969: no.
    7)
    Branch 1 & arrow? ab
Bull
  I 494 (L) Crete
    Pica ab
  II 3.174 (L)
    Branch 1
  IV 300 (L) Choumeri
    Pica? ab
  VII 145 (L)
    Branch 1 ab
  IX 19D (L)
    branch ab
  XII 304 (L) Seager
      Coll.
    Pica ab
  HM G 3123 (APr) Messara
      (CMCG 226)
    Pica ab in shoulder
  HM no. unknown (L)
      (Xanthoudides
      1907: pl. 8.148)
    Picas ab
Kid/Calf
  I Supp. 25 (L) Argive
      Heraeum
    lion face upside down,
      goat head R, &
      Baton? ab
    unfinished?
  I Supp. 118 (L)
    Branch 1 ab
  VII 252 (L)
    ImpTr ab
Agrimi
  Pica ab
    I 212 (L) Prosymna
      ChT XIII.3 (LH
      IIB/III A2-B)
    I 481 (L) Crete
    I 482 (L) Crete
    I Supp. 38a (L)
      Amyklaion
    II 3.126 (L)

Tylissos
  II 3.176 (L)
  "Knossos"
  II 3.342 (L)
  II 4.113 (L)
  Knossos, House of
  of the Frescoes
  IV 296 (L)
  Tsoutsouros
  X 251 (A)
    Pica in neck ab
SH vertical
  XIII 76 (L)
  AM AE 700 (L) Dik-
    taian cave (CS 364)
  AM AE 1786 (L) (CS
    371)
    Pica? ab
  AM AE 1793 (L)
    (CS 13P)
  HM G 3146 (L)
    (CMCG 253)
    Pica? ab
  HM G 3502 (L)
    (CMCG 257)
Dot ab
  IV 288 (L) Messara
  2 dots ab
  XII 274 (L)
    Seager Coll.
  XII 275 (L)
    Seager Coll.
Plant ab
  I Supp. 101 (L)
    Crete
    Branch 1 ab
  II 3.200 (C)
    "Astritsi
    Pediada"
    frond ab
  II 4.52 (L)
    branch? ab
  XII 296 (L)
    Seager Coll.
    Tree 5 ab
  Melos 568 (L)
    Phylakopi,

West Sanctuary
(LH III A;
Renfrew 1985:
281, 283)
Frond ab
Stag
    I 501   (L)   Crete
        Pica ab
    II 4.50   (L)
        bird? ab
    VII 152   (L)   Ialysos?
        Pica in the neck ab
Miscellaneous
    II 4.6   (L)   Zafer
        Papoura T.?
        quadruped
    II 4.93
        quadruped
        branches ab
    IV 313   (L)   Tylissos
        griffin
        object ab
    V 228   (L)   Chalkis,
        Trypa T. 8
        quadruped
        Branch 2 ab
    V 400   (L)   Medeon T.
        239 (LH III C)
        winged agrimi
        Branch 1 infr
    HMp 4793-5   (clay Matrix
        for a glass
        lentoid)
        Palaikastro (LM II;
        Hutchinson 1939-40:
        48 no. 32 fig. 32;
        the matrix, with
        design in relief?,
        is identified as an
        impressed
        loomweight)
        horse?
        Branch 1 ab
    HM G 3224   (L)   Knossos
        (CMCG 247)
        deer
        Frond ab

IN BACK
    IV 287   (L)   Messara
        griffin
        branch inb/bel at
            right
    Melos 572   (L)   Phylakopi,
        East Sanctuary (LH III
        C; Refrew 1985: 281,
        288)
        goat
        tree inb
BELOW
    Agrimi
    I Supp. 82   (A)   Crete
        rocks bel
    II 3.343   (L)
        groundline bel
    II 4.180   (L)   "Knossos"
        groundline bel
    Miscellaneous
    I 492   (L)   Crete
        bull
            stroke ab & bel
    V 690   (L)   Thera,
        Acrotiri (LM IA)
        plumed griffiness
            dolphin upside down
                & groundline bel
            SH horizontal
BEHIND & BELOW
    II 3.238   (C)   Gournia, House
        T. (MM II)
        bull
            architectonic beh
            object (unfinished
                calf?) bel
IN FRONT & IN BACK
    X 233   (L)
        winged agrimi
        Frond infr
        branch inb
ABOVE & BELOW
    Agrimi
        VII 42 . (D)
            Pica & Tailed Sun
                (see Ch. 14B:
                Tailed Suns) ab

dog? bel to attack
   R in PT 44
groundline bel
unfinished
VII 15 (L)
<u>Pica</u> ab
3 groundlines bel
VIII 101 (L)
branch ab
1 or 2 groundlines bel
IX 139 (L)
<u>Pica</u> ab
2 groundlines bel
IX 140 (L)
<u>Frond</u> ab
groundline bel
XII 261 (L) Seager
   Coll.
<u>Pica</u> ab
groundline bel
XII 267 (L) Seager
   Coll.
<u>Pica</u> ab
groundline bel
Berlin FG 21 (L) Achaia
   (AGDS II Berlin 56)
<u>Pica</u> ab
2 groundlines bel
Miscellaneous
II 4.140 (C) Knossos
   stag
     <u>Pica</u> ab in? the
      shoulder
     groundline bel
IV 264 (L) Sokarras
   goat
     <u>Frond</u> ab
     groundline bel
HMs 637 (As)
     Skalvokambos (Sk
      11)
     <u>Babylonian Dragon</u>
     3 <u>Fronds</u> ab rocks? bel

IN FRONT, ABOVE, & BELOW
  Agrimi
    II 3.258 (A) Mochlos

<u>Branch 1</u> infr
<u>Pica</u> & branches ab
3 <u>Branch 1</u> bel
groundline bel
hatching bel
XII 308 (L) Seager Coll.
<u>Branch 3</u> infr
<u>Pica</u> ab
<u>Branch 4</u> bel
Miscellaneous
  V 732 (L) Mega
    Monastiri T. Gamma
    (LH III A-B)
  goat
    <u>Branch 1 Tree</u> infr
    <u>Branch 1</u> ab & bel
    2 groundlines bel

RIGHT (see: Ch. 3C: Man Hunts
Animals [boars] -- I 227)

Plain (no filling motifs)
Lion
  I 245 (A) Vapheio Tholos
    (LH II A)
  II 3.330a (L)
    illegible objects in the
    field
Bull
  II 3.20 (L) Knossos, House
    of the Frescoes (LM IB)
  II 4.199 (L)
    "Chersonessos"
  II 4.222 (L)
  IV 322 (L) Messara
  XII 307 (L) Seager Coll.
  HMs 157 (Cs) Kato Zakro (KZ
    157)
  HMs 648 (Cs) Sklavokambos
    (Sk 19)
  HM G 3132 (L) Mallia (CMCG
    229)
Agrimi
  II 3.120 (A) Platanos
  IV 273 (L) Avdou
  VII 242 (L)
  VIII 94 (L) Dawkins Coll.

X 123   (L)
X 168   (L)   Munich A.1165
   (L)   Lappa (AGDS I Munich
   85)
Stag
   X 300   (L)
   AM 1893.235   (L) bought at
      Palaikastro/Polyrrhenia
      (CS 26 P)
   Munich A.1170   (L)   Crete
      (AGDS I Munich 86)
Caprid
   AM AE 1227   (L)   Crete (CS
      384)
   HM G 3305   (L)   Knossos (CMCG
      254)
Miscellaneous
   AM 1953.117   (L)   "Gaza" (CS
      32P)
      griffin

Filling Motifs
ABOVE
   I 122   (L)   Mycenae ChT 86
      calf
         Tree 6 crown ab

BEFORE
   IV 321   (L)   Kastelli
      agrimi
         tree bef

BEHIND
   I Supp. 191   (Ls)   Pylos
      Palace (LH III B2-C1)
      calf
         Tree 1 beh

IN FRONT
   I 54   (L)   Mycenae ChT 11
      lion en face
         Sacred Knot/Robe infr
ABOVE
   Lion
      VIII 75   (L)   Dawkins
         Coll.
      branch ab

VIII 78   (L)   Dawkins
   Coll.
   branch? ab
Bull
   II 3.141   (L)   Vathypetro
      (LM IA)
   branch ab
   HM no. unknown   (L)
      Knossos, MUM
      (Popham et al.
      1984: Misc. 8)
   lion face ab
Once Evans Coll   (L)
      (**FIG.** 6; GGFR pl.
      135)
   Figure-8 Shield ab
Agrimi
   VII 139   (L) Knossos
      Pica ab
   X 185   (L)
      large Branch 1 ab
      SH horizontal
   Munich A.1163a   (L)
      (AGDS I Munich 84a)
      branch ("signs") ab
Miscellaneous
   I Supp. 40   (L) Perachora
      quadruped
         lines ab
         SH horizontal
   HMs 148   (Ls)   Knossos
      Palace (KSPI R2)
      stag
         2 Sacred Knots ab

IN BACK
   I 148   (L)   Mycenae ChT 518
      (LH I-II)
   caprid
      branch? inb
      SH horizontal

BELOW
   Agrimi
      I Supp. 164b   (L)
         the dotted centers of
            164a were drilled

through to the face
of 164b & the
resulting hole bel
the agrimi was made
into a star
II 3.222 (L) "Pediada"
2 groundlines bel
IV 166a (D) Pombia
hind leg up (cf. V
33, below)
branch/spear bel
X 221 (L)
stroke bel
IN FRONT & ABOVE
Bull
I 23 (L) Mycenae
tree infr
Tree 1 ab
V 150 (L) Kephallenia,
Kokkolata Tholos A
(LH III B[-C])
Branch 2 infr
Branch 1 ab
Miscellaneous
I Supp. 39 (L)
Perachora
goat
dots infr
Branch 1 ab
XII 273 (L) Seager Coll.
lion
frond infr
Column ab

ABOVE & BELOW
Bull
II 3.226 (C) Diktaian
Cave
head averted
Pica ab
rocks bel
XII 151a (A) Seager
Coll.
Pica? ab
groundline bel

Agrimi
V 255 (L) Armenoi T. 27
(LM III A1-2)
Figure-8 Shield ab &
bel
5 (6) strokes ab
5 strokes bel
IX 141 (L) Crete
large arrow in the
back ab
2 groundlines bel
X 215 (L)
Pica in back ab
groundline bel
Miscellaneous
V 33 (L) Argos, Deiras
T. 24 (LH III A2)
quadruped, hindleg up
(cf. IV 166a,
above)
Branch 2 ab & bel
V 676 (L) Thebes,
Kolonaki T. 3
calf?
Branch 1 ab
groundline bel
AM 1938.1150 (L) (CS
22P)
Babylonian Dragon
Branch 1 ab
Dado 6a bel
HM 2784 (L) Knossos, MUM
(prob. LM II;
Popham et al. 1984:
pl. 185b, H50)
quadruped
branch

IN BACK & BELOW
Agrimi
I 490 (L) Crete
rocks inb & bel
VIII 93 (L) Dawkins
Coll.
branch inb
arc bel
SH horizontal?

IN FRONT, IN BACK, & BELOW
   II 4.62 (L) Mochlos
      quadruped
        <u>Branch 3</u> infr & inb
      stroke bel

FIG. 7 -- IX 119:
bull in PT 5B, R

PT 5B

Animal Runs, Head Up

LEFT (see Ch. 4D: Women &
Animals [misc.] -- HMs no.
unknown [AT 111])

Plain (no filling motifs)
Bull
   I 8 (L) Mycenae ShGr (LH
     II)
   I 139 (C) Mycenae ChT 513
     (LH III B1)
   I 234 (L) Vapheio Tholos
      (LH IIA)
     SH horizontal
   I 483 (L) Crete
   II 3.89 (L) Knossos
   II 4.105 (L) Tylissos
   II 4.130 (L) Knossos,
     Royal Tomb (LM II; BSA

     Cast 123)
II 4.132 (L) Knossos
     (Geometric)
   rim chipped back (for a
     ring setting?)
IV 281 (L) Aphrati
VII 166 (L)
VII 193 (L) Crete
VIII 77 (L) Dawkins Coll.
IX 121 (L)
X 169 (L)
XII 209 (L) Seager Coll.
XII 211 (A) Seager Coll.
   sinks to knees
XII 298 (L) Seager Coll.
XIII 129 (L)
XIII 130 (L)
   SH horizontal
AM 1925.49 (L) (CS 385)
AM 1971.1143 (L) de Jong
   Coll. (Boardman 1973: no.
   12)
HM 2093 (L) Knossos,
   Royal Road (Hughes &
   Warren 1963: 355)
HM G 3007 (L) Messara
   (CMCG 230)
HM G 3134 (L) (CMCG 245)
HM G 3216 (L) (CMCG 231)
HM G 3219 (L) (CMCG 246)
HM G 3101 (L) (CMCG 232)
HM G 3220 (L) (CMCG 233)
HM G 3214 (L) (CMCG 234)
Younger Coll. (C)
Stag
   I 497 (L) Crete
   I 498 (L) Crete
   IX 170 (L)
   AM 1925.47 (L) (CS 25P)
Miscellaneous
   II 4.61 (L) Gournia
     griffin, 1 wing up
   V 499 (L) Ayia Irini, the
     Temple (LH III)
     kid
       SH horizontal

HM G 3032 (L) (CMCG 236)
goat

Filling Motifs
ABOVE
Bull
Pica ab
IV 278 (L)
Kapetaniana
IX 110a (L)
XII 278 (L) Seager
Coll.
branch/Pica ab
AM 1971.1140 (L) de
Jong Coll.
(Boardman 1973:
no. 11)
HMs 159 (Ls) Kato
Zakro (KZ 159)
Pica in shoulder
Miscellaneous ab
X 297 (L)
stroke ab
Miscellaneous
I 322 (Ls) Pylos Palace
(LH III B2-C1)
caprid
branch ab
I Supp. 81 (A) Crete
lion en face
lance in shoulder
II 4.226 (L)
stag
HMs no. unknown (Ls)
Ayia Triada (AT
155)
calf?
spear & Figure-
8 Shield ab
HM G 3303b (Pr) Mallia
(CMCG 186b)
agrimi
rocks ab

BELOW
X 220* (L)
griffiness

Branch 1/arrow bel

ABOVE & BELOW
Bull/Bovine
AM 1941.137 (L) (CS
11P)
Pica ab
groundline bel
?VIII 47b (R bezel once
on vertical swivel
pin?) Dawkins Coll.
Pica ab
groundline bel
Berlin FG 20 (L)
Peloponnese (AGDS
II Berlin 46)
Pica ab
groundline bel
Chania 1002 (Ls)
Chania, Kastelli
(Papapostolou
1977: no. 3)
calf, hindleg up to
scratch out the
arrow in its
shoulder
groundline? bel

IN BACK & BELOW
HMs 574 (Ls) Ayia
Triada (AT 53)
bull
Pica ab in back
groundline bel

RIGHT (see: Ch. 3E: Animal
Games [bull-leaping, Diving] --
HM G 3209; & Ch. 4C: Women
'Crossed' by a Caprid -- I
221)

Plain (no filling motifs)
Bull
I Supp. 5 (A) Mycenae ChT
78-92
II 4.153 (A) Ayia "T. of
the Painted

Sarcophagus"
calf, 1 hind leg up to
    scratch (at an arrow
    undepicted?
V 399   (L)   Medeon T. 239
    (LH III C)
VII 110   (L)   Melos
    en face
VII 243   (L)
VIII 82   (L)   Dawkins Coll.
IX 14D   (A)
X 296   (L) en face
Caprids
    II 4.11   (L)   Knossos
    stag
    V 644   (C)   Gouvalari Tholos
    1 (LH IIA/IIIB?)
    IX 172   (L)
    kid
    HM G 3217   (L)   Knossos
    (CMCG 243)
    agrimi

Filling Motifs
ABOVE
    II 2.60   (D)   Profitis
        Elias T. VII
    bull sinks to its
        knees
        <u>Pica</u> ab in the
            shoulder
        groundline bel
        SH oblique (lower
            left to upper
            right)
BELOW
    II 3.74   (L)   Knossos,
    Geometric Tb
    stag
        arrow bel in
            chest
    V 645   (A)   Gouvalari
        Tholos 1 (LH
        IIA/III B?)
    bull
        arrow in chest

BEHIND & BELOW
    I 242   (L)   Vapheio Tholos,
    cist (LH IIA)
    agrimi
        <u>Tree 5</u> beh
        arrow in chest & <u>Rocks</u>
        bel

IN FRONT & BELOW
    XII 237   (L)   Seager Coll.
    bull
        <u>ImpTr</u> infr
        2 lines (= spears?)
        bel belly
        groundline bel

ABOVE & BELOW
    Bull
        V 646   (A)   Gouvalari
        Tholos 2 (LH I-
        III B)
        <u>Pica</u>/<u>Spear</u> in back
        2 wavy groundlines bel
        IX 119   (L)   (FIG. 7)
        <u>Pica</u> ab
        <u>Dado 6c</u> bel
        SH horizontal

FIG. 8 -- V 252:
bull in PT 5C, R

PT 5C
Animal Runs, Head Back

LEFT
Bull
    Plain (no filling motifs)
    I 233b (Pr) Vapheio
            Tholos
        II 4.225 (L)
        HMs no. unknown (As)
            Ayia Triada (AT 67)

    Filling Motifs
        I 367 (Ls) Pylos
            Palace (LH III
            B2-C1)
        branch infr & bel
        V 279 (L) Armenoi T.
            60 (LM III B2)
        Pica ab
        V 356 (L) Medeon T. 29
            (LH III A-C)
        calf
            thick line ab

Bull/Bovine
    V 252 (L) Armenoi T. 24
        (FIG. 8; LM III
        A2-B1)
    bull face ab
    IX 191 (L)
    AM 1938.1031 (L)
        Polyrrhenia (CS
        317)
    Figure-8 Shield bel
Chania 1542/1544 (As)
        Chania, Kastelli
        (Papapostolou 1977:
        no. 2)
    calf, hindleg up to
        scratch out the
        Arrow in its
        flank
    rocks bel
Miscellaneous
    I 26 (A) Mycenae
    calf?/kid?

PT 5D
Animal Runs, Head Down

LEFT
II 3.175 (L) "Knossos"
    bull

RIGHT
Bull
    I Supp. 124 (A, published
        upside down)
        Branch 1 infr & inb?
    IV 280 (L) Lastros
        branch ab

PT 5 or PT 6

LEFT
I 338 (Ls) Pylos Palace
        (LH III B2-C1)
    quadruped
I Supp. 204 (Ls) Pylos Palace
        (LH III B2-C1)
    quadruped

RIGHT
II 3.65 (Cyl) Ayios Ioannes
        T. III (LM IIB)
    SH horizontal: 2 lions run R
        (1 regardant)
    SH vertical:
        betw lions are an agrimi
        in PT 5A & waterbird in
        PT 2, to form PT 36 cl
    branches in the field
HMs 160 (Ls) Kato Zakro (KZ
        160)
    bull, head averted
        Pica ab

FIG. 9 -- VII 261:
bull in PT 6, R

PT 6
Animal Runs, Regardant
LEFT (see: Ch. 3A: Man &
Animals [caprid] -- I 199)

Plain (no filling motifs)
Lion
    I 141 (L) Mycenae ChT 515
      (LH IIB)
      hindleg up as if to
        scratch away an
        unengraved arrow
    II 3.19 (L) Knossos, House
      of the Frescoes (LM IB)
    II 4.49 (L) "Chersonessos"
    II 4.188 (L) "Skalani"
    II 4.227 (L)
    IV 277 (L) Atsipades
    HMs 472 (Ls) Ayia Triada
      (AT 44)
    HM G 3085 (L) Phaistos
      (CMCG 271)

Bull
    I 121 (L) Mycenae ChT 86
    I 334 (Ls) Pylos Palace (LH
      III B2-C1)
    I Supp. 100 (L) Crete

head averted
    II 3.225 (L) Diktaian Cave
      en face
    IV 299 (L) Knossos
    XII 262b (stone Matrix for
      glass lentoids) "Poros"
    ?AM 1925.52 (L) (CS 387)
    HM 2780 (L) Knossos, MUM
      (LM II; Popham et al.
      1984: pl. 184b, H104)
    HMs 74 (Ls) Kato Zakro
      (KZ 156)
    HM G 3422 (L) Knossos
      (CMCG 249)
      en face

Agrimi
    I 37 (D) Mycenae
      head tucked down
    I Supp. 58 (A) Perati ChT
      118? (LH III C1)

Stag
    XII 236 (L) Seager Coll.
    AM 1941.1228 (L) (CS
      24P)
    HMs 540 (Ls) Ayia
      Triada (AT 68)
      head contorted

Calf
    V 418 (L) Medeon T. 264
      (LH III C)
    IX 192 (L)

Kid
    V 659 (L) Rhodes, Ialysos?
    ?XII 223 (L) Seager Coll.

Miscellaneous
    I 357 (Ls) Pylos Palace
      (LH III B2-C1)
      quadruped
    IV 318 (L) Phaistos
      griffin
    XII 293 (A) Seager
      Coll.

Babylonian Dragon
AM 1938.1095 (L) (CS
     239)
collared bitch
Melos 576 (L) Phylakopi,
     East Sanctuary (LH
     III C; Renfrew
     1985: 281, 287ff)
bull/stag

Filling Motifs
IN FRONT
  Bull
    VIII 107 (L)
      ImpTr ab/infr
    X 173 (L)
      Branch 2 infr
  Miscellaneous
    VII 262 (L)
      stag
        tree ab/infr resem-
          bling a large
          tulip
    V 162 (L) Kephallenia,
      Kokkolata (LH III
      B[-C])
      quadruped
        branch infr
    HM 2170 (L) Kamilari
      Tholos (MM III-LM
        I; Pini 1981: no.
        70)
      griffin, 1 wing up
        zig-zags infr

ABOVE
  Lion
    II 4.38 (L) "Knossos"
      Pica ab
      2 dots connected by a
        wavy line ab (see:
        PT 6, L; Filler: IX
        169, below)
    II 4.51 (L) "Mallia"
      branch ab
    II 4.76 (L)
      Sun ab

II 4.117 (L) Knossos,
     South House?
  Branch 1 ab
V 604 (L) Naxos (LH
     III C)
  Frond ab
AM 1941.146 (L) (CS
     369)
  Pica ab
AM 1941.147 (L) (CS
     28P)
  branches ab
HM G 3227 (L) (CMCG
     272)
  plant/waterbird? ab
Bull
  I Supp. 22 (A) Midea ChT
     3 (LH III B1)
  branch/Pica ab
  a horizontal line is
     engraved across the
     length of the face,
     as if this were the
     reverse of such an
     amygdaloid as I
     Supp. 58 & X 241
  I Supp. 77 (A) Crete
  head averted
    Pica ab in head
  V 664 (L) Thebes, Me-
     galo Kastelli ChT 4
  branch ab (cf. Ch.
     12J: Tailed Suns)
  V 689 (L) Orchomenos
  head up
    Branch 1 ab
Calf
  II 3.125 (L) Tylissos
    Branch 1 ab
  II 3.134 (L) Nirou
     Chani (LM III B)
    branch ab
Kid
  V 528 (L) Midea (LH
     III B)
    dot ab
  X 136 (L)

Sword/Pica ab in neck
Caprid
  VII 184   (A)
    agrimi
      Branch 1 Tree ab
  Naples 1404 (A?) (GGFR
    pl. 139)
    branch ab
      SH vertical
Griffin
  IV 266 (L)   Lastros
    Frond ab
  HMs 564 (Ls) Ayia
  Triada (AT 99)
    Frond ab

IN BACK
  HM G 3316 (L) Phaistos
    (CMCG 379)
    Minotaur en face
      small Sun inb

BELOW
  Lion
    I 10   (C) Mycenae ShGr
      III (LH I)
    arrow in shoulder
    rocks bel
    II 4.138 (L) Knossos
    dots (= rocks?) bel
    V 242 (L) Armenoi T. 13
      (LM III A2)
    Dado 6a bel
    X 151 (L)
    originally zig-zag?
      bel (cf. X 152,
      below)
  Miscellaneous
    I 484 (A) Crete
    kid
      ImpTr bel
    X 298 (L)
    calf
      stroke/arrow bel

IN FRONT & BELOW
  II 3.337 (L)
    line infr
    Figure-8 Shield bel
  IX 124 (L)
    bull
      Figure-8 Shield &
      circle infr
    groundline bel

ABOVE & BELOW
  Agrimi
    IV 53D (L) Knossos
      Frond ab
      3 strokes bel
    VII 196 (L)
    dot ab
    object bel
      SH horizontal
  Miscellaneous
    VII 249 (A/L)
    dog/lion cub
      bird? ab (turned
      90 degrees)
      dog? head &
      object bel
    SH vertical:
      originally 2 calves
      run in PT 25C, L?
    IX 169 (L)
    bull en face
      Branch 3 = Pica?
      ab
      2 dots connected by
      wavy line bel
      (see: PT 6, L;
      Filler: lion,
      above)
    X 152 (L)
    lion
      rocks/Weed ab (cf.
      IX 7D)
      Dado 6a = zigzag
      bel

HM G 3138 (A) Knossos
    (CMCG 283)
    <u>Babylonian Dragon</u>
    <u>Sun</u> ab & bel
    arc ab

IN BACK & BELOW
  VII 192 (L)
    calf/bull
      tree inb
      2 groundlines bel
      SH horizontal

IN FRONT, IN BACK, & BELOW
  AM 1938.946 (C; spacer
    bead) Rethymnon (CS
    201; Younger 1981:
    fig. on p. 34)
    agrimi
      horizontal stroke/
      <u>Pica</u>? infr
      <u>Tree 3</u> inb
      rocks bel

RIGHT
Plain (no filling motifs)
  Lion
    II 4.190 (C) "Vagonia"
      en face
    XII 262a (stone Matrix
      for making glass
      lentoids) "Poros",
      Knossos
    HMs 520 (Ls) Ayia
      Triada (AT 43)
  Bull
    II 4.154 (L) Episcopi
      Pediada T. Gamma
    V 243 (L) Armenoi T. 13
      (LM III A2)
    ?V 358 (L) Medeon T. 29
    ?V 381/382 (L) Medeon
      T. 29a (LH IIIA-C)
    VII 106 (L)
      en face
    IX 168 (L)
    IX 190 (L)

AM 1925.50 (L) (CS
  388)
?HMs 583 (Ls) Ayia
  Triada (AT 62)
HMs no. unknown (Ls)
  Knossos, MUM (LM II?;
  Popham et al. 1984:
  pl. 190d, Misc. 16)
HM G 3496 (L) (CMCG
  238)
HM G 3517 (L) (CMCG
  235)
Agrimi
  ?II 4.131 (L) Knossos,
    Temple T.
  VIII 127 (L) Hutchinson
    Coll.
  X 121 (D; later re-
    shaping?)
  X 183 (L)
  HM G 3222 (L) (CMCG
    240)
Calf
  II 3.135 (L) Nirou
    Chani (LM III B)
  VIII 66 (L) Dawkins
    Coll.
  VIII 130 (Ls)
    Hutchinson Coll.
Goat
  II 3.131 (L) Karteros
  AM 1941.1233 (L) (CS
    287)
Stag
  V 336 (R) Medeon T. 29
  V 686 (L) Tanagra,
    Dendron T. 31 (LH III
    A-B)
Griffin
  II 4.47 (L) "Lyttos?
  II 4.116 (L) Knossos,
    South House?
Miscellaneous
  I 120 (L) Mycenae ChT
    95
    quadruped

I 164   (Ls)   Mycenae,
    House of Sphinxes
    (LH III B1)
  dog
I 337   (Ls) Pylos Palace
    (LH III B2-C1)
  quadruped
IV 286   (L)   Rotassi
  calf/dog

Filling Motifs
IN FRONT
  I 391   (R)   Perati ChT 1
    (LH III B2 C1)
  quadruped
    branches? infr
  VIII 156   (L)
  bull
    row of dots infr
  XIII 56   (L)
  griffin
    Frond infr

ABOVE
  Lion
    ?II 4.39   (L)   "Knossos"
    branch ab
    II 4.175   (L)
    Branch 1 ab
    IV 319   (L)   Amariano
    Sun ab
  Bull
    I 315   (Ls)   Pylos Palace
      (LH III B2-C1)
    branch ab?
    II 3.197   (L)   "Kato
      Vathia"
    Branch 3 ab
    X 171*   (L)
    Column capital? ab
    AM 1925.53   (L) (CS 389)
    line ab
    AM 1971.1141   (L) Crete?
      (Boardman 1973: no.
      3)
    Pica? ab
  HMs KE   (Ls)   Knossos

    & Ayia Triada (AT
    151/153)
  Branch 1 ab
Agrimi
  I 355   (Ls)   Pylos Palace
  branch ab
  II 4.44   (L)   "Lycastos"
  branch ab
  II 4.87   (L)
  lines ab
  VII 250   (L)
  Frond ab
Calf
  I 287b   (P)   Pylos T.
    Gamma (LH IIA/
    Palace Style)
  Branch 1 ab
  line encircling the
    face encroaches at
    places upon the
    field
  V 316 (L)   Delos
  Frond ab
  V 360/383   (L) Medeon Ts.
    29 (360) & 29a
    (383)
  branch ab
  unfinished
  V 393   (L)   Medeon T.
    99 (LH III A)
  Figure-8 Shield ab
  ?Florence 82820   (L)
    bought at Hera-
    kleion (Laviosa
    1969 = no. 8)
  Frond ab
Goat
  I 24 (L)   Mycenae
  branch ab
  II 4.122   (L) Sello-
    poulo T. 1 (LM
    III A2-B;AR 1957,
    24-5)
  Branch 1 ab
  II 4.144   (L) Knossos
  object ab

Rumania Academy 434 (L)
    (Gramatopol 1974:
    no. 4)
    Frond ab
Miscellaneous
  I 366 (Ls) Pylos Palace
    (LH III B2-C1)
    quadruped
      branch ab
  X 310 (L)
    quadruped
      dot ab

BELOW
  Bull
    II 3.202 (L)
      "Evangelismos"
      2 groundlines bel
    II 4.179 (L) "Knossos"
      Dado 3 bel
    IV 275 (L) Atsipades
      indication of
        ground? bel
    BSA Cast 182 (L)
      2 groundlines bel
  Miscellaneous
    I 328 (Ls) Pylos Palace
      (LH III B2-C1)
      quadruped
      Weed bel
    X 134 (L)
      griffin
        lines bel

IN FRONT & ABOVE
  I 29 (L) Mycenae
    quadruped
      strokes infr & ab
  I 31 (L) Mycenae
    quadruped
      Branch 3 infr
      Branch 4 ab
  II 4.171 (L) "Tylissos"
    griffin
      2 strokes infr
      line (= Pica?) ab

IN FRONT & BELOW
  X 258 (L)
    bull
      row of dots infr
      Figure-8 Shield bel
  AM 1920.116 (L)
    "Greece" (CS 8P)
    agrimi
      Palm infr
      Branch 1 bel

ABOVE & BELOW
  Bull
    V 575 (L) Tiryns,
      Prophitis Elias T.
      19 (LH I-III A)
      8 dots ab (3 Omphaloi/
      Squills, 1 Figure-8
      Shield, 3 dots?)
      Branch 3 bel
    IX 120 (L)
      Frond ab
      2 strokes at right
      angles bel
    AM 1938.1052 (Ls)
      Knossos (BSA 57,
      1962, 53-54; in-
      scribed KN Ws 8153)
      Figure-8 Shield ab &
        bel?
    HM G 3299 (L) Phaistos
      (CMCG 228)
      2 Branch 1 ab & bel
    HM G 3497 (L) (CMCG
      237)
      branch ab
      arrow? bel
  Miscellaneous
    I 83 (L) Mycenae ChT
      48
    calf
      2 curved lines ab
        tail
      rocks? bel
        (unfinished?)

V 667   (L)   Thebes,
        Mikro Kastelli ChT
    caprid
        fish L ab & bel

IN FRONT, ABOVE, & IN BACK
    X 311   (L)
        bull
            Branch 3 infr & inb
        dot ab

IN FRONT, ABOVE, & BELOW
    II 3.90   (L) Knossos
        goat?
            branch ab & infr
            Branch 3 bel
    VII 261   (L)   (FIG. 9)
        bull
            Frond infr & ab
            2 groundlines bel
IN FRONT, IN BACK, & BELOW
    V 403   (L)   Medeon T. 239
        (LH III C)
        quadruped
            8 dots infr
            6 (7?) strokes inb
            4 dots bel

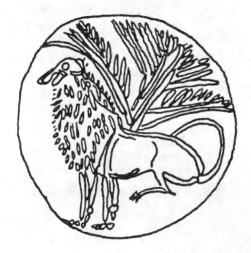

FIG. 10 -- XIII 13:
lion in PT 7, L

PT 7
Animal Assis

LEFT
Lion (cf. Ch. 3A: Man &
    Animals [lion] -- I 512)

    I 512   (L)   Crete
        man beh restrains the
            lion by a collar
        Branch 1 Tree infr
        groundline? bel
    II 4.60   (L)   Gournia
        branch at left
    II 4.78   (L)
    V 192   (L)   Thebes?
        frond ab
        2 groundlines bel
    XIII 13   (L)   (FIG. 10)
        Palm fronds ab
Griffin
    I Supp. 38b   (L)   Amyklaion
        Branch 1 Tree infr
    AM 1941.142 (L)   Milatos
        (CS 368)
        displayed
    AM AE 1200b   (L)   "Ayia
            Pelagia" (CS 15P)
        head up, displayed
            zig-zags ab
    Munich A. 1164   (L)   Crete?
        (AGDS I Munich 55)
    collared

RIGHT (see: Ch. 3A: Man &
    Animals [monster] -- I 285
    & I 309; Ch. 4A: Women &
    Animals [antithetic] -- HM
    G 3054)

I 133   (L)   Mycenae ChT 103
        (FIG. 111)
    lion
        man's torso ab R, his
            left arm stretched R
            ab the lion's head

I 206   (Cyl) Prosymna ChT 2
    (LH II-III A)
    2 rows, upside down to each
       other: griffins, lions

FIG. 11 -- V 498:
lion in PT 8, L

FIG. 12 -- V 677a: dog
in PT 8, R scratching

PT 8
Animal Assis, Regardant

LEFT
Lion
    I 149   (L)   Mycenae ChT 518

        (LH I-II)
       2 groundlines
I Supp. 32   (L)   Epidauros,
      Apollo Maleatas
    Pica ab
    2 groundlines bel
II 3.345   (L)
    arrow ab in the shoulder
    groundline bel
V 498 (L) Ayia Irini, the
       Temple (FIG. 11; LH
       III B-C)
    Frond ab
    2 groundlines bel
VII 235   (A)   Hellenika
      (Knossos?)
    Pica ab
VIII 104   (D)
    line encircles (for a
      ring setting or
      gilding?)
    SH horizontal
IX 15D   (A)
    Frond ab
    2 Mount-Guides flank
X 133*   (L)
    Branch 1 ab (= Pica?)
    Dado 6c bel
    SH horizontal
AM 1941.155bb   (L)   (CS
      30Pb)
    Frond ab
Florence 82528   (L)   bought
      in Greece (Laviosa
      1969: no. 6)
    Pica in back
Hamburg 1964.288   (L)
      (AGDS IV Hamburg 7)
    collared
    branch ab
HM G 3142   (L)   (CMCG 273)
    plant ab
Griffin
    V 215   (L)   Brauron
       2 groundlines bel

V 437   (L)   Nichoria Tholos
        (LH III A2-B1)
    Branch 1 Tree infr
    zig-zags ab
VII 135   (L)
    displayed
IX 138   (L)
    plumed?
Berlin FG 14   (L)   Crete
    (AGDS II Berlin 31)
Dog
    I 256   (L)   Vapheio Tholos
        (LH IIA?)
        scratching
        Dado 5 bel
        SH horizontal
    XII 135a   (D) Seager Coll.
        dog (calf? lion?)
            Frond with circle ab
            (Sceptre?)
            3 groundlines bel
            SH horizontal

RIGHT
Lion
    I 243   (L)   Vapheio Tholos
        2 groundlines bel
        SH horizontal
    II 3.64b   (Pr) Ayios
        Ioannes T. III (LM
        IIB)
        3 Pica infr in chest
        Pica ab in shoulder
    VII 168   (C)   Enkomi T. 1
        Branch 1 ab
    VII 171   (L)
        Pica in shoulder
        2 groundlines bel
    BSA cast 183   (L)
        Branch 1 ab
        groundline bel
    Munich A.1195   (L)   (AGDS I
        Munich 64)
        Branch 1 infr
        branch ab
        groundline bel

Dog, scratching
    I 255   (L)   Vapheio Tholos
        (LH IIA?)
        Dado 8 bel
        SH horizontal
    IV 185   (L)   Kastelliana
    V 677a   (Pr)   Thebes, Kolo-
        naki T. 17 (FIG. 12;
        12; LH III A1)
        collared
        2 groundlines bel
        SH horizontal
    AM 1971.1150   (L)   Crete?
        (Boardman 1973: no.
        3)
        collared
        groundline bel
    HMs 47   (Ls)   Ayia
        Triada (AT 47)
    HMs 106   (Ls)   Kato Zakro
        (KZ 106)
    HMs 571   (Ls)   Ayia Triada
        (AT 82)
        collared
Griffin
    I 85   (A)   Mycenae ChT 52
        displayed
    IV 283a   (L)   Fortetsa

FIG. 13 -- VIII 52:
bull in PT 9, L

PT 9

Bull Half-Couchant,
Head Averted

LEFT
Net/Reticulation in the field
    (= beh?)

    I Supp. 53 (L) Sounion
    VIII 52   (L) Dawkins
        Coll. (FIG. 13)
    AM 1938.1018 (L) (CS
        236)
    HMs 581 (Ls) (AT 61)

Miscellaneous
    HMs 504 (As) Ayia Triada
        (AT 55)
        2 oblique lines infr
        2 horizontal lines ab

RIGHT
HMs 482 (Ls) Ayia Triada (AT
    78)
    Pica in head

FIG. 14 -- XII 248:
bull in PT 10A, R

PT 10A
Animal Couchant

LEFT
Lion
    I 329 (large Ls?) Pylos
        Palace (LH III B2-C1;
        inscribed PY Wr 1331,
        1332, 1334)
        lions & griffins in a
            frieze (griffin,
            lion, griffin)
        Dado 9b of double
            nautili bel
    I 387 (A) Menidi Tholos
        (LH IIIB)
        Branch 1 bel
    I 405 (A) Koukaki
        Branch 1 ab
        2 Mount-Guides flank
    I Supp. 64 (A) Thessaly
        Branch 1 ab
        groundline bel
    II 3.257 (A) Mochlos
        a pair of Mount-Guides
            infr
        zig-zags ab
        groundline bel
    II 3.346 (A)
        Frond ab
        groundline bel
    II 4.19 (L) Ayia Irini T.
        E?
        Frond ab
    II 4.139 (L) Knossos
        Frond ab
    IV 228 (A) Messara
        Frond ab
    V 241 (L) Armenoi, T. 13
        (LM III A2)
        groundline bel
    V 745 (A) Metaphio Tholos
        (LH III A2)
        Frond ab
    VII 178 (A)
        Branch 1 ab
    ?AM 1971.1151 (L) Crete?
        (Boardman 1973: no.
        10)
        Frond ab

HM 2506 (A) Knossos, MUM
     (probably LM II;
     Popham et al. 1984:
     pl. 185a, P 136)
   Frond ab
HM G 3143 (A) Knossos
     (CMCG 261)
   Frond ab
HM G 3324c (APr) (CMCG
     185c)
   Frond ab
Bull
   I 209 (A) Prosymna ChT 3
   I 281 (L) Rutsi Tholos 2
     (LH II-IIIA)
   circle infr
   Branch 1 ab
   2 groundlines bel
   I Supp. 34 (A) Kakovatos
     Tholos 2 (LH IIA)
   Tree 5 beh
   Dado 3 bel
   II 3.64a (Pr) Ayios
     Ioannes T. III (LM
     IIB)
   Tree 2 inb
   SH horizontal
   II 3.293 (L) "Limnes
     Mirambello"
   Tree 6 ab
   groundline bel
   XII 249 (L)
   leashed to a Tree 2 inb
   Dado 3 bel
   XII 272 (L) Seager Coll.
   Frond ab
   XII 289 (L)
   Tree 6 Branch ab
   2 groundlines bel
   AM 1941.125 (L)
     Argyropolis
     (CS 299)
   Branch 1 ab
   2 groundlines bel
Chania 1527 (As) Chania,
     Kastelli (Papapo-
     stolou 1977: no. 9)

3? groundlines bel
HMs no. unknown (As) Ayia
   Triada (AT 50)
HMs 212/1000/1005 (Ls)
     Knossos Palace (KSPI
     R6; Betts nos. 51 &
     52)
   head down
Agrimi
   I 486 (L) Crete
   object ab
   Dado 2a-b/3/4/ bel
   II 3.50 (D) Gypsades T. 18
     (MM III A)
   rocks bel
   SH oblique: lower left to
     upper right
   II 4.183 (L) "Knossos"
   groundline bel
   V 730 (L) Mega Monastiri
     T. Gamma (LH III
     A1-B1)
   agrimi
     Frond ab
     groundline bel
   XII 135b (D) Seager Coll.
   4 groundlines ab
   SH horizontal
   XIII 19 (D)
   2 groundlines bel
   AM 1941.136 (L) Ligortyno
     (CS 190)
   Dado 2d bel
   HM 2507 (L) Knossos, MUM
     (LM II; Popham et al.
     1984: pl. 184d, no.
     J/K3)
   frond infr
   double Pica ab
   groundline bel
   HMs 144 (Ds) Knossos
     Palace (KSPI Pd)
   Munich A.1194 (L) Melos
     (AGDS I Munich 63)
   3 strokes ab
   zig-zags on back =
     hair

        2 groundlines bel
Griffin
    II 3.349 (L)
    1 wing up
    3 small dots at plume &
    2 small dots ab wing
    II 4.71 (L)
    plant? infr
    II 4.72 (L)
    IV 39D (C; gold cover)
    VII 93 (A) Crete
    displayed
    IX 179 (L)
    AM 1953.119 (L) "Gaza"
        (CS 34P)
    groundline bel
    Chania 2067 & 2068 (Ls)
        Chania, Kastelli
        (Papapostolou 1977:
        no. 15)
    Branch 3 ab
    groundline bel
    HM G 3223 (L) (CMCG 337)
    displayed
    HM G 3324a (APr) (CMCG
        185a)
    1 wing up
    zig-zags ab
  Boar
    I Supp. 76 (L) Crete
    4 Branch 1 ab
    groundline bel
    HM 2096 (L) Knossos,
        Ivory Cutter's
        Workshop (LM IB; AR
        1959-60, 23 fig. 27)
    2 Frond ab
    groundline bel
Miscellaneous
    II 4.9 (L) Knossos
    stag?
    XII 137 (D) Seager Coll.
      calf
        Dado 3 bel
    HM G 3325 (L) (CMCG 281)
      dog?
        Pica in back

HM G 3415 (C) Knossos
    (CMCG 169)
  sheep
    Dado 2a bel

RIGHT (see: Ch. 3A: Man &
  Animals [bulls] --HMs 143
  [KSPI Q20]; Ch. 3F: Animal
  Sacrifice [bulls] -- HMs 142
  [Sakellarakis 1970: 217 no.
  B3] & HMs 211 [KN KSPI
  R13])

Lion
    II 3.192 (A) "Herakleion,
        Nea Halikarnassos"
    Branch 1 ab
    IV 229 (A) Siteia
    branch ab
    V 182 (L)
    Frond ab
    2 groundlines bel
    VIII 92 (A) Dawkins Coll.
        2 groundlines bel
    X 132 (A)
    Branch 1 ab
    2 pairs of Mount-Guides
        flank
    groundline bel
    X 277a (APr) Crete
    2 strokes infr
    Pica/stroke in back
    Mount-Guide at right
    groundline bel
    XII 208 (A) Seager Coll.
    1 pair of Mount-Guides
        at right
    Branch 1 ab
    XIII 55 (L)
    XIII 138 (A)
    zig-zag/lion (unfinished,
        though SH was finished
        completely)
    HM 2123 (L) Knossos, Royal
        Road (LM IB; AR 1961-2
        fig. 39)
    Branch 1 ab

52

ANIMAL POSE TYPES -- PT 10A, R

HM 2772 (L) Knossos, MUM
    (apparently LM IA;
    Popham, et al. 1984:
    pl. 186c,no. NP18)
HMs 87 (A/Rs) Kato Zakro
    (KZ 143)
    8 pendent arrowheads?
    ab
HM G 3089 (A) (CMCG 262)
    Frond ab
HM G 3104 (L) (CMCG 275)
HM G 3351 (L) Knossos
    (CMCG 267)
    Sun ab
Bull
  I 236 (A) Vapheio Tholos
    (LH IIA)
    head down
      groundline bel
  I 346 (Ls?) Pylos Palace
    (LH III B2-C1)
    bull face ab
  IV 306 (L) Siteia
    bull?
      frond ab
  V 198 (R) Thebes?
    infr of & leashed to
      Shrine
    rocks ab, bel, at left &
      right
    Tree 2 inb
  XII 248 (L) (FIG. 14)
    Branch 1 Tree inb
    2 groundlines bel
  Berlin FG 22 (L) Mycenae
    (AGDS II Berlin 44)
    on sacrificial Table
      with 4 bucranium legs
      & 2 struts (see: Ch.
      3F: Animal Sacrifice)
    sword in neck
    Palm 4 ab bends R
    groundline bel
  HMs 345B/399 (D/Ls)
    Knossos Palace
    (KSPI L27)
    head averted

    groundline bel
HMs 631 (As?) Sklavokambos
    (Sk 7)
    bull?
Agrimi
  I 143 (L) Mycenae ChT 515
    (LH IIB)
    Pica ab
    SH horizontal & canted
  I 158 (L) Mycenae ChT 529
    (LH IIA)
  I 404 (A) Athens,
    Erechtheion
    Branch 1 & rocks ab
    3 groundlines bel
  II 3.340 (D)
    Dado 3 bel
    SH oblique: upper left to
      lower right
  IV 263 (L)
  X 281 (D)
    Dado 2a bel with arcs & a
      circle
    Branch 1 Tree inb
  BSA Cast 168 (L)
    2? groundline(s) bel
Griffin
  I 316 (Ls) Pylos Palace
    (LH III B2-C1)
  I 383 (R; archaic?) Spata
    ChT
    griffin?
    lines infr
  IV 248 (A) Skalani
    displayed
  VII 140 (L)
  X 170 (L)
    sword/Pica near
      shoulder
    stroke ab (continuation
      of sword/Pica?)
    Branch 1 ab at left
  AM 1893.238 (A) Crete (CS
    327)
    wavy line ab
  AM AE 693 (L) Diktaian
    cave (CS 16P)

Dado 2d bel
HM G 3495 (C) (CMCG 336)
    1 wing up
    vertical stroke? infr
    groundline bel
HM no. unknown (R) Kaly-
        via T. 9 (LM III A1;
        Savignoni 1904: fig.
        12)
    1 wing displayed
        branch infr
Sphinx
    I 129 (R) Mycenae ChT 91
            (LH II)
        displayed, with a lily
            plume on her cap
        rocks infr
        Dado 1 bel
    II 3.39 (R) Zafer Papoura
            T. 7 (LM III A1)
        displayed
        Frond bel at right
    II 3.118 (L) Ayia Triada
        ChT (LM III A)
        1 wing up
        Sun infr (not as a
            pendant on a
            'collar' which is
            really a deep
            scratch in the
            stone)
        groundline bel
Miscellaneous
    V 665 (L) Thebes, Megalo
        Kastelli T. 3
        stag (intended to have
            been 2 bulls in PT
            24, R)
        branch of Tree 5 ab
        2 groundlines bel
    AM 1938.1017 (L) (CS
        237)
        collared dog
        groundline bel

FIG. 15 -- VII 105:
calf in PT 10B, L

PT 10B
Animal Couchant, Head Up

LEFT
Bull
    I 35 (L) Mycenae
        spear ab
        groundline bel
    I 55 (L) Mycenae, ChT 12
        Pica ab
        groundline bel
    IV 305 (L) Knossos
        Frond ab
    V 191b (Pr) Thebes?
        Frond ab
        Dado 4a bel
    ?V 586 (L) Kasarma Tholos
        (LH I-II)
Griffin
    I 474 (L) Crete
    V 208 (A)
        displayed
        hatching bel at
            left
    V 590 (A) Nafplion,
        Evangelistria cemetery
        zig-zags ab
        groundline bel

VII 240   (L)   Hellenika
    (Knossos?)
XIII 54   (L)
HMs 222   (Ls) Knossos
        Palace (KSPI R15)
    displayed
        zig-zags ab
Munich A.1196   (L)   bought
        in Istanbul (AGDS I
        Munich 47)
    zig-zags ab
    groundline bel
Miscellaneous
    V 191c   (Pr)   Thebes?
        agrimi
            Frond ab
            Dado 4a bel
    VII 105   (L)   Mycenae (FIG.
        15)
        calf,
            sword in the back
            2 groundlines bel
    X 150   (L)
        lion
            Palm 1? crown ab

RIGHT
Bull
    I Supp. 79   (L)   Crete
        dot infr
        groundline bel
    HM 2116   (L)   Knossos,
        Royal Road (Pini 1981:
        no. 69)
    Munich A.1197   (L)   Crete
        (AGDS I Munich 48)
        Branch 1 flanked by 2
            dots (= tree ?) ab
        groundline bel
Griffin
    II 3.219   (L)   "Avdou
        Pediados"
        griffiness, 1 wing up
            (logo for Heraklei-
            on's Demarcheion)
    IX 22D   (A)
        displayed

PT 10C
Animal Couchant, Head Down

RIGHT
I Supp. 80   (A)   Crete
    lion, en face
        Pica ab in back
        2 groundlines bel

PT 10 or PT 11

LEFT
I Supp. 186   (Ls)   Pylos
        Palace (LH III B2-C1)
    bull
VIII 88   (L)   Dawkins Coll.
    griffin
        2 groundlines bel

FIG. 16 -- I 65:
bull in PT 11, R

PT 11
Animal Couchant, Regardant

LEFT
Plain (no filling motifs)
    Lion
        II 3.61   (A)   Ayios

Ioannes T. 4 (LM IB-
IIA)
IV 274 (L) Phaistos
VIII 125 (L) Hutchinson
Coll.
HMs 155 (Ls) Kato Zakro
(KZ 155)
HM G 3081 (L) Phaistos
(CMCG 269)
HM G 3083 (L) (CMCG
264)
Griffin
II 3.79 (L) Knossos
plumed
II 4.166 (L) Mallia,
Maison E
IX 104 (L)
XII 253 (L) Seager Coll.
XII 266 (L) Seager Coll.
AM 1953.120 (L) "Gaza" (CS
35P)
HMs 51 (Ls) Kato Zakro (KZ
41)
Chora no. unknown (C)
Tragana Tholos 1 (AR
1981-2, 25 fig. 46
drawn from the seal)
plumed head up,
displayed
Miscellaneous
HMs no. unknown (A?s)
Ayia Triada (AT 75)
bull?

Filling Motifs
ABOVE
Lion
IV 282 (L) Knossos
head up
branch ab
X engraved later
over lion
IV 310 (L) Knossos
Pica ab
VII 121 (A)
sword? ab
AM 1941.98 (L) (CS 373)

Branch 1 ab
Chania 2094 (As)
Chania, Kastelli
(Papapostolou
1977: no. 14)
Branch 1 ab
HMs 580a (Ls) Ayia
Triada (AT 42)
2 Picas/spears in
back
HM G 3177 (L) (CMCG
270)
branch ab
HM G 3434 (L) Lassithi
(CMCG 263)
Frond ab
Hannover 1972.33 (L)
(AGDS IV Hannover
8)
Pica ab

BELOW
Agrimi
HM G 3136 (L) Mallia
(CMCG 172)
rocks bel
I Supp. 92 (L) Crete
4 courses of Dado 3
bel
circle engraved
(later?) at center
Miscellaneous
I 244 (A) Vapheio
Tholos (LH IIA)
lion
2 groundlines bel
I Supp. 152 (L)
griffin
groundline bel
Chania 1557 (Ls)
Chania, Kastelli
(Papapostolou 1977:
no. 8)
bull
groundline bel
HMs 344 (Ds) Knossos
Palace (KSPI La)

deer/cow
   2 groundlines bel

ABOVE & BELOW
  Lion
    I 272a (Pr) Rutsi
       Tholos 2 (LH IIA)
      Branch 1 ab
      3 groundlines bel
      SH horizontal
    I 272b (Pr) Rutsi
       Tholos 2 (LH IIA)
      Branch 1 ab
      2 groundlines bel
      SH horizontal
    I 506 (L) Crete
      Pica ab
      2 groundlines bel
    II 3.277 (D)
       Palaikastro (LM III
       A?)
      Branch 1 ab
      7 strokes bel
      line encircles (for a
       ring setting or
       gilding?)
      SH oblique: lower left
       to upper right
    V 191a (Pr) Thebes?
      Frond/Pica ab
      Dado 4a bel
    VII 151 (L) Ialysos
      Branch 1 ab
      Dado 6c bel
    IX 161 (L)
      Branch 1 ab
      groundline bel
    X 1 (A)
      Branch 1 ab
      groundline bel
    XII 229 (L) Seager
       Coll.
      arrow ab in back
      3 groundlines bel
    HMs 79 (Ls) Kato Zakro
      (KZ 109)
      Pica ab

      2 groundlines bel
  Miscellaneous
    V 684 (L) Tanagra,
      Dendron T. 16 (LH
      III A-B)
    griffin
      zig-zags ab
      2 groundlines bel
    HMs 126/AM 1938.982
      (Ls) Knossos
      Palace (KSPI Pa;
      CS 5S)
    deer
      river, rocks,
       plants, all ab
      groundline bel

IN FRONT, ABOVE, & IN BACK
  HMm 1035 (R) Sellopoulo
    T. 4 (LM III A1;
    Popham 1974: no. J7)
  griffin
    branches

IN FRONT, ABOVE, & BELOW
  V 438 (L) Nichoria Tholos
    (LH III A2-B1)
  griffin
    zig-zags infr & ab
    groundline bel

RIGHT
Plain (no filling motifs)
  Griffin
    1 wing up
      I Supp. 94b (L)
       Crete
      VII 120 (A)
    Both wings up/displayed
      V 672 (A/Cyl) Thebes
       Kadmeion (LH III
       B)
      X 267 (A) bought in
       Tripoli
      HMs no. unknown (Cs)
       Ayia Triada (AT
       94)

HMs 316/317 (Ls)
Knossos Palace
(KSPI R49)
Miscellaneous
VIII 137 (A)
lion

Filling Motifs
IN FRONT
VII 258 (A)
griffin
<u>Frond</u> infr

ABOVE
Lion
I Supp. 116 (A)
<u>Branch 1</u> ab
IV 258 (L) Kousse
<u>Frond</u> ab
V 655 (A) Ialysos T.
20? (LH III C1?)
<u>Pica</u> in the back ab
XIII 23 (A)
2 <u>Fronds</u> ab
XIII 20D (L)
<u>Sun</u> ab
Miscellaneous
I Supp. 138 (L)
griffin displayed
2 baby griffins? ab
antithetic
V 283 (L) Armenoi T. 64
(LM III A2 [-B1])
agrimi?
<u>Branch 4</u> ab
XIII 13D (L)
kid?
2 <u>Picas</u>? in rump
SH oblique: lower
left to upper
right

BELOW
Bull
I 65 (L) Mycenae ChT 26
(LH III A?; **FIG.**

16)
2 groundlines bel
IV 268 (L) Siteia
groundline bel
HMs 415/AM 1938.1082
(Ls) Isopata, the
Royal Tb (LM IIB;
Evans 1906: 141 &
154-5 fig. 138; CS
44S; GGFR pl. 98)
head against flank
<u>Dado 9a</u> bel
Griffin
I 293 (C) Pylos Tholos
IV (MH/LH I-III)
displayed
<u>Dado 8</u> bel
reverse: reticula-
ted & filled
with blue glass
I 389 (Flattened
Cylinder) Menidi
Tholos (LH III B)
displayed
groundline bel
XII 233 (L) Seager
Coll.
groundline bel
HM G 3015 (A) Lasithi
(CMCG 335)
displayed
groundline bel
Miscellaneous
HM 2505? (L) Knossos,
MUM (Popham et al.
1984: pl. 184c no.
M 35)
lion
groundline bel

IN FRONT & ABOVE
II 3.339 (D)
agrimi nanny
kid protome ab
2 thick groundlines
bel
AM 1938.1048 (A) (CS 10P)

lion
    <u>Branch 1</u> ab & infr

ABOVE & IN BACK
  I 56 (A) Mycenae, ChT 12
    lion
        branches ab

ABOVE & BELOW
  IX 105 (A) Crete
    griffin displayed, head
        up
    zig-zags ab
    2 groundlines bel
  XII 235 (L) Seager Coll.
    bull, head averted
        <u>Pica</u>/lance in back ab
        groundline bel
  XIII 9 (A)
    lion
        arrow in shoulder ab
        2 groundlines bel

IN FRONT, ABOVE & BELOW
  Lion
      II 3.292 (D) "Latsida
      Mirabello"
      2 strokes infr
      1 stroke ab
      groundline bel (are
        these lines part of
        an encircling line
        for a ring setting/
        gilding?)
      SH oblique: lower left
        to upper right
    XIII 22 (A)
      pair of <u>Mount-Guides</u>
        infr
      arrow pointed at
        shoulder ab
      2 groundlines bel
  Miscellaneous
    XII 247 (L)
      griffin
        zig-zags infr & ab
        2 groundlines bel

FIG. 17 -- VIII 148:
  bull in PT 12, R

PT 12
Animal Stands, Head En Face
& Down Between the Forelegs

LEFT
Lion
  I 287a (Pr) Pylos T. Gamma
      (LH IIA/Palace Style)
    <u>Cleaver</u> bel
    line encircling the face
      encroaching at places
      in the field
  II 3.227 (L) Karphi (LM
      III C-Sub Minoan)
    SH horizontal
  XII 244 (L)
    a row of dots ab half-
      encircle
    <u>Sun</u> bel
  XIII 19D (L)
    <u>Dado 4d</u> bel?
  AM 1941.1241 (L) (CS
      346)
    en face
      2 agrimia in PT 34B
      run down bel (at
      left in PT 3; at
      right in PT 13A,

head contorted)
all form lion vs
agrimia in PT 41,
L variant
HM G 3181 (L) (CMCG 268)
groundline bel
Berlin FG 16 (L) Gythion
(AGDS II Berlin 40)
hindleg up to scratch
head
Branch 1 infr
Oxford, MS J25 (L)
2 groundlines bel

Bull
I 63 (L) Mycenae, Ch T. 26
(LH IIIA?)
I 66 (L) Mycenae T. 26
head in profile
2 goat heads
antithetic ab
horizontal line ab
erased quadruped hind-
leg & 2 groundlines
bel
2 lines flank
I 237 (A) Vapheio Tholos
(LH IIA)
II 3.101 (L) Kalyvia T. 1
(LM III A1)
en face, hindleg up
circle bef the back
2 circles bel (ab
raised hindleg)
X 143* (L)
Palm 1 beh
AM AE 690b (L) Diktaian
cave (CS 334b)
lion face bef
bull's back

RIGHT (see: Ch. 3A: Men &
Animals [lions] -- Munich
A.1171)

Lion
I 248 (L) Vapheio Tholos
leg up to scratch 2?

arrows in flank
rocks bel
II 4.156 (L) Episcopu
Pediada T. Delta
Weed upside down bel
V 363/364/385 (L) Medeon
T. 29 [363/4], T.
29a [385], & Lefkandi
T. 12B.4? (Popham &
Sackett 1980: 225)
line ab
unengraved object bel
VII 137 (L)
?IX 181 (L)
HMs 587 (As) Ayia Triada
(AT 41)
groundline bel
HMs no. unknown (Ls)
Ayia Triada (AT 48)
hindleg up
arrow in chest
Chania no. unknown (Ls)
Chania, Kastelli
(Papapostolou 1977:
pl. 46a)
object bel
Chania Sigma 92 (L)
Armenoi T. 108 (LM III
A2-B; Pini 1981: no. 74)

Bull
I 265 (L) Tragana Tholos
2 (LH III A)
Switch? ab
Column/Mace bel
I 283 (A) Rutsi Tholos 2
(LH II-IIIA)
head averted
Pica ab
rocks bel
reverse: arcades
filled with blue
glass
VIII 148 (L) (FIG. 17)
groundline bel

X 187* (L)
  horns splayed
    2 centered circles
      ab
HMs 588 (Ls) Ayia Triada
    (AT 88)
  en face
  agrimi head bel
HMs no. unknown (As) Ayia
    Triada (AT 154)
  object? bel

LEFT
Lion
  Head in profile
    I 43 (L) Mycenae
      groundline bel
    II 3.112a (Pr) Kalyvia
      T. 9 (LM III Al)
    II 4.198 (L) "Aropolis"
      quadruped? pendant bel
        (see: PT 13A, R:
        lion -- II 4.48
        both in composition
        & style)
    V 2 (L) Aigina, Aphaia
      Temple
      bull/lion face bel
    Chania 1021 (Ls)
      Chania, Kastelli
        (Papapostolou
        1977: no. 5)
      groundline bel
  Head en face
    V 680 (L) Thebes,
      Taxiarch Church
      Frond ab
      sword in belly
      groundline bel
    HMs 225 (Ls) Knossos
      Palace (KSPI 06)
    HMs 302 (Ls) Knossos
      Palace (KSPI R33)
      Branch 4? ab
Bull
  I 268 (L) Tragana Tholos
    2 (LH III A)
    Pica? ab
  II 3.224 (L) Diktaian
    Cave
    groundline ab
  V 7 (L) Aigina, Athena
    Temple?
    2 Tree 1 ab
  Patras 2440/2442 (L)
    Kallithea, Rambantania
    ChT Theta (LH III; Pini
    1981: nos. 86/87)
  Rumania Academy 433 (L)

PT 13

HMs 286 (Ls) (Gill 1966: 16
    no. 20)
  bull R
  ImpTr ab

FIG. 18 -- XII 268:
bull in PT 13A, R

PT 13A
Animal Stands, Head Under Belly

(Gramatopol 1974: 40
no. 3)
branches ab, beh, & bel
Minotaur
I 216 (L) Prosymnia ChT
41 (LH III A2)
hornless (=calfman)
Figure-8 Shield in
the center
XIII 34 (L)
AM 1938.1071 (L) Diktaian
Cave
Figure-8 Shield & ImpTr
bel
Miscellaneous
J. P. Getty Mus. no.
unknown (L)
(Boardman 1975: p.
83 no. 4)
dog
2 groundlines bel

RIGHT (see: PT 12, L -- AM
1941.1241; & Ch. 3A: Man &
Animals [bulls] -- HMs 267
[KN KSPI R61])

Lion
Head in profile
I 44 (L) Mycenae, ChT 7
unfinished
I 217 (L) Prosymna, ChT
44 (LH IIA)
SH horizontal; with SH
vertical: Lin B
-a-[-na-?] in
center
I 508 (L) Crete
II 4.48 (L) "Evangel-
ismos (Mouchtaro)"
quadruped (small
agrimi?) pendant
bel (see: PT 13A,
L: Lion -- II 4.198
for both composi-
tion & style)
HMs 119 (Ls) Knossos

Palace (KSPI Vc;
inscribed)
Head en face
I 84 (L) Mycenae, ChT
48
I 247 (L) Vapheio
Tholos
VII 114 (L)
IX 150 (L)
Dado 6c bel
X 154 (L)
row of dots infr
branch ab
Lioness
AM 1938.1037 (L) (CS
314)
?HMs 319 (Ls) Knossos
Palace (KSPI R77)
Bull
Head in profile
Plain (no filling
motifs)
II 4.172 (L)
"Trypiti"
V 312a + b (Pr)
Delos, Artemisium
deposit
VII 156 (L)
unfinished
IX 11D (L)
Berlin FG 8 (L) Syra
(AGDS II Berlin
22)
man prone ab
(stands R at
left when SH
is horizontal)
HMs 78 (Ls) Kato
Zakro (KZ 101)
impressed twice?
Filling Motifs
I 493 (L) Crete
groundline bel
II 3.335 (L)
Branch 3? ab
object (plant?)
bel

V 32   (L)   Argos,
     Deiras T. XI
     (LH III A2)
spear? ab
arrow bel
V 153   (L)
     Kephallenia,
     Kokkolata
     Tholos B (LH
     III B[-C])
Branch 3 ab
V 500   (L)   Ayia
     Irini, Temple
     (LH III A-B)
Weed bel
VII 157   (L)
     1 foreleg raised
     short striated
          Column ab
IX 193   (L)
     Dado 6d with 6
     circles ab
     2 groundlines bel
XII 225   (L)   Seager
     Coll.
     line = groundline
     bel
XII 268   (L)   Seager
     Coll. (FIG. 18)
     line/arrow ab
     Sacred Knot bel
     3 horizontal
          strokes bel
          left
     4 vertical strokes
          bel right
XII 297   (L)   Seager
     Coll.
     Pica? ab
HMs 111   (Ls)   Knossos
     Palace (KSPI N6;
     Papapostolou
     1977: pl. 46.6)
     Palm 4? beh
     groundline bel
HMs 147 & 313   (Ls)
     Knossos Palace

          (Gill 1966: no.
          7)
     ImpTr bel
     Munich A.1307   (L)
          Greece (AGDS I
          Munich 88)
     Branch 2 ab
Head en face
     I 64   (L)   Mycenae ChT 26
          (LH III A?)
     II 4.84
     IV 267   (L)   Assimi
          Column? beh
     V 280   (L)   Armenoi T. 60
          (LM III B2)
          2 Branch 2 ab
          triangle bel
     VIII 141   (L)
          en face with lion's
               body
          2 groundlines ab &
               bel
          2 small circles bel
          1 small circle on
               shoulder
     IX 23D   (L)
          bovine
          2 groundlines ab
     Munich A.1188   (L)   (AGDS
          I Munich 61)
          groundline bel
Calf
     ?VII 136   (L)
          3 groundlines ab
          dots bel
          unfinished?
     Melos 571   (L)   Phylakopi,
          East Sanctuary (LH III
          C; Renfrew 1985: 281,
          283ff.)
          Frond ab
          reverse: double ax & 1-
               handled cup [Linear B
               -ki-?])
Agrimi
     I 202   (L)   Nafplion, ChT 2
          kid

I 298 (L) Pylos Palace
        (LH III B2-C1)
    kid
II 4.217 (L)
    agrimi?
Miscellaneous
    XII 238 (L) Seager Coll.
        hornless <u>Minotaur</u> (=
            calf-man?; the
            collar may imply a
            dog-man instead)
        <u>Figure-8 Shield</u> bel
    AM 1938.1100 (L) (CS 367)
        griffin displayed
            bull face infr
            arrow ab
            short <u>Column</u> bel
    HMs 517 (Ls) Ayia Triada
        (AT 81)
        dog

LEFT
Bull
    I 235 (L) Vapheio Tholos
        (LH IIA)
        groundline bel
    IX 109 (A) central Crete
    XIII 31 (L)
        2 groundlines bel
    Chania 1017 (Ls) Chania,
        Kastelli
        (Papapostolou
        1977: no. 4)
        groundline bel
Miscellaneous
    VIII 53 (L) Dawkins Coll.
        boar
    HM G 3221 (L) Phaistos
        (CMCG 265)
        lion en face

RIGHT
Bull
    VII 99 (L) (FIG. 19)
        2 groundlines bel
    XIII 83 (L) Central Crete
        groundline bel
    HM G 3208 (L) (CMCG 224)
        groundline bel
Miscellaneous
    II 3.41 (L) Zafer Papoura
        T. 36
        lion en face
            sword in chest bel
            groundline bel

FIG. 19 -- VII 99:
bull in PT 13B, R

PT 13B
Animal Stands, Head Under
Belly; Hindleg Raised to be
Licked

PT 13C
Animal Stands, Head Under Belly
Hindleg Up to Scratch the Head

RIGHT
Lion
    I 277 (L) Rutsi Tholos 2
        (LH II-III A)
        arrow in flank

SH horizontal
IX 107 (A)
  en face
      stroke/<u>Mount-Guide</u>
          infr
      <u>Frond</u> inb
      arrow/spear in head
          from bel
      groundline bel
Bull
  I 49 (L) Mycenae ChT 9
  I 160 (Rs) Mycenae, House
      of the Oil Merchant
      (LH III B1)
    frontal horn =? crack in
        the ring
    2 groundlines bel
  ?I Supp. 2 (L) Mycenae
      ChT 28
  II 3.216 (L) "Mallia"
  V 200 (L, gold cover)
      Thebes?
    groups of 2 or 3 strokes
        encircle
    spear in the belly bel
  VII 248 (L)
    en face
        2 goat heads bel
  HMs 270 (Ls) Knossos
      Palace (KSPI R34)
Stag
  I 41 (L) Mycenae
    lion
        foreleg & <u>Figure-8</u>
            <u>Shield</u> bel
  IX 122 (L)
    head
        contorted up

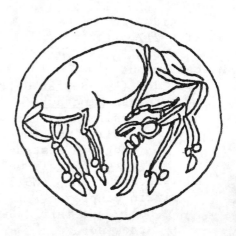

FIG. 20 -- XIII 43:
bull in PT 14A, R

PT 14A
Animal Stands, Head Under
Belly, Upside Down & Facing
Forwards

LEFT (see: Ch. 5D: Protomes --
  HM 2383)

Lion
  V 246 (L) Armenoi T. 17
      (LM III B)
    SH vertical: lion
    SH horizontal: at left,
        man R & kid R (see:
        Ch. 3A: Man & Animals
        [caprids])
  X 302 (L)
    <u>Pica</u>? ab
Bull
  V 320 (L) Krisa
    <u>Figure-8 Shield</u> & <u>Pica</u>?
        bel
  VII 148 (L)
  IX 125 (L)
    <u>Tree 2</u> frond ab & bel

Agrimi
     VII 124   (L)
         SH horizontal?
     X 137   (L)
         2 groundlines ab & bel
         2 circles & Figure-8
             Shield bel

RIGHT (see: Ch. 6B: Genii --
   Berlin FG 12)

Lion
     I 51   (L) Mycenae, ChT 10
         human leg bel
     I 358   (Ls) Pylos Palace
             (LH III B2-C1)
         Palm 4 beh
     VII 115c (Pr)
         groundline bel
     AM 1938.1058 (L) Knossos
         (LM II 'mature'; CS
         315)
     HMs 253 (Ls) Knossos
             Palace (KSPI N1)
         Sun bef, on shoulder
         Branch 4 ab
     HMs 265 (Ls) Knossos
             Palace (KSPI R18)
         small vertical &
             horizontal strokes bel
Bull
     I 496   (RP1) Crete
         dots infr
     V 23   (L)   Sklavi,
             Pharmakokephalo T. 2
             (LM III B)
         Branch 2 ab
     V 319   (L)   Krissa ChT 1
             (LH III B)
     V 588   (L)   Nafplion, Evan-
         gelistria cemetery
     IX 118   (L)
         Branch 3 ab
         branch (approximating
             Linear B -sa-?) bel
     XIII 43   (L) (FIG. 20)
     HM G 3091 (L) Chersonisos

     (CMCG 227)
         Branch 1 ab
Agrimi
     HMs 165 (Ls) Knossos
         Palace (KSPI G12)
     V 587   (L) Nafplion,
             Evangelistria
             cemetery
         2 Palm 4/asphodel bel
Goat
     II 3.303   (L)   "Hierapetra"
     Dr. Hamerton Coll.   (L)
         (Boardman 1973: no. 1)

                 PT 14B

         Animal Stands in PT 14A
         Foreleg Up to Scratch

LEFT
Bull
     X 269   (L) Dawkins Coll.
         goat head L ab
     AM 1938.1085 (L) (CS 345)

         en face, head upside down
             beaked Fish-Monster ab
             L
         waterbird supine R bel
     HM 2384 (L) Sellopoulo T.
         4 (LM III A1; Popham
         1974: fig. 14c)
     Munich A.1189 (L) Piraieus
         (AGDS I Munich 62)
         2 short groundlines bel
         SH oblique: lower left to
             upper right)
Miscellaneous
     I Supp. 71 (L) Melos?
         cow (udder depicted?)
         Figure-8 Shield ab
         Tree 3 bel
     X 321   (L)
         agrimi

Branch 3 bel

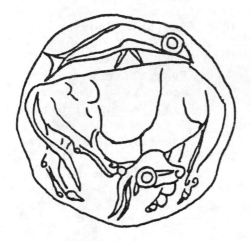

agrimi
Branch 3 ab

FIG. 21 -- II 4.161:
bull in PT 14B, R

FIG. 22 -- XIII 21:
lion in PT 14C, R

RIGHT
Bull
   I 380 (Ls) Pylos Palace
      (LH III B2-C1)
    en face
    Pica ab in neck
   II 4.161 (L) Gournes T. 2
      (FIG. 21; LM III B1)
      5.5)
    Fish-Monster ab R bites
      shoulder
   XIII 33 (L)
    Sacred Knot bel
    Figure-8 Shield in
      center bef the raised
      hind hoof
   HMs 121 (Ls) Knossos
    Palace (KSPI N10;
    inscribed)
   HM G 3372c (Pr) Vasilike
    Anogeia (CMCG 190c)
Miscellaneous
   IX 156 (L) near Antioch
    cow in PT 14B & calf in
      PT 3 forming PT 18B,
      R
   AM 1925.45 (L) (CS 348)

PT 14C
Animal Stands in PT 14A or B,
Turned 90 degrees ccl

LEFT
II 3.67 (L) Sellopoulo T. 1
    (LM III A2-B)
   Minotaur
    ImpTr ab

RIGHT (see: Ch. 2B: Men [pair]
    -- I Supp. 169a)

IX 126 (L) Crete
   bull
    Fish-Monster R ab
XIII 21 (L) (FIG. 22)
   lion, hindleg up to scratch
    head (unfinished?)

PT 14D

Monsters in PT 14C
& Turned 90 degrees ccl

LEFT
Agrimi-Man
    IX 128 (L) Crete
        Sun ab
        Figure-8 Shield bel
    AM 1941.123 (L) (CS 326)
        Branch 1 infr
Minotaur
    X 145 (L)
        man's face bel
    XIII 61 (L)
        SH horizontal?
    AM 1938.1070 (L) Knossos
            area (CS 325)
        groundline ab
        Sun bel

RIGHT
Agrimi-Man
    II 3.331 (L)
    VII 138 (L)
        ImpTr ab

Minotaur
    IX 127 (L) central Crete
        Frond infr
    IX 144 (L) Knossos
        Pica? bel

PT 14 or PT 13

LEFT
Lion
    ?V 599 (L) Mycenae, House
        with the Idols (LH
        III B2; photograph
        upside down
        unfinished?
    V 733 (L) Mega Monastiri

T. Delta (LH III
    A2-B1)
erased animal leg bel
groundline bel

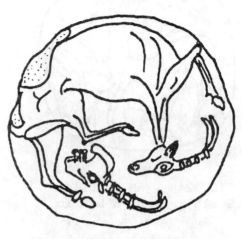

FIG. 23 -- I 393:
agrimi in PT 15, R

PT 15

Animal Stands, Head Under
Belly, Upside Down & Facing
Backwards

LEFT
HM G 3521 (L) (CMCG 225)
    bull

RIGHT
I 393 (L) Perati ChT 1
        (FIG. 23; LH III
        B2-C1)
    agrimi, hindleg up to
        scratch
    agrimi head upside down
        bel
    2 groundlines bel

FIG. 24 -- AM 1938.1019
(CS 316): nanny & kid in PT
16A, R

PT 16A

Mother Animal Stands in PT 1
Offspring Below & Facing to
Suckle

RIGHT (see: PT 1A, L; Filler:
    Agrimi -- XIII 144; PT 39A:
    dog L vs agrimi/kid-man --
    XII 242)

Nanny & Kid
    AM 1938.1019 (L) (FIG. 24;
        CS 316)
        lion beh L forming PT 33A
        with the nanny
    Chania 1018 (Ls) Chania,
        Kastelli (Papapostolou
        1977: no. 12)
        Tree 2 beh
    HMs 122 (Ls) Knossos
        Palace (KSPI N7)
        Tree 2 infr
        rocks bel at left

FIG. 25 -- I 168:
goat & kid in PT 16B, R

PT 16B

Mother Animal Stands in PT 1
Offspring Above

LEFT
?HM G 3011 (L) Mallia (CMCG
    276)
    lion & cub?/quadruped

RIGHT
I 168 (L) Mycenae,
    Clytemnestra Tholos
    (FIG. 25; LH III A)
    kid
        Branch 1 bel
        groundline bel

    PT 16, L or PT 17, L

VIII 91 (L) Dawkins Coll.
    cow & calf

FIG. 26 -- I 13:
doe & fawn in PT 17A, R

PT 17A
Mother Animal Stands, Regardant
Offspring Below

LEFT
Cow & calf
 I 291 (A) Pylos Tholos 4
   calf L, betw cow's
     forelegs
 XIII 30 (L)
   SH horizontal?
 BSA Cast 172 (L)
   double zig-zag ab & infr
 HMs 77 (Ls) Kato Zakro
   (KZ 126)
 HM G 3027 (L) (CMCG 304)
   cow's forelegs raised to
     a horizontal position
Nanny & Kid
 AM 1938.1021 (A) (CS 242)
   collared nanny runs
     man inb holds the
       nanny by a leash
 HMs 163 (Ls) Kato Zakro
   (KZ 163)
   plant? inb

Miscellaneous mother &
 offspring

 I 13 (L) Mycenae ShGr III
   (FIG. 26; LH I)
  doe & fawn
    Branch 4 infr
 XII 286 (L) Seager Coll.
   lioness & cub
     Frond ab

RIGHT
I 364 (Ls) Pylos Palace (LH
  III B2-C1)
 cow & calf?

FIG. 27 -- VII 233:
nanny & kid in PT 17B, R

PT 17B
Mother Animal Stands,
Regardant
Offspring Above

LEFT (see: PT 28B: griffins --
 I 171)

Cow & Calf
 XII 306 (L) Seager Coll.
  cow en face
    branch ab

XIII 133 (L)
HMs 295/329 (R/As)
        Knossos Palace
        (KSPI K6/R46)
    cow couchant in PT 11, L

RIGHT (see: PT 11, R; Filler:
    nanny & kid)

I 62 (L) Mycenae, ChT 26 (LH
        III A?)
    male lion assis & cub
VII 233 (L) (**FIG. 27**)
    nanny & kid

FIG. 28 -- II 3.54:
nanny & 2 kids in PT 17C, R

PT 17C

Mother Animal Stands, Regardant
    Offspring Above & Below

LEFT
VII 66 (L)
    collared bitch & 2 puppies

RIGHT
II 3.54 (L) Isopata T. 3 "The
        Mace Bearer's Tomb" (**FIG.
        28**; LM III A1)
    nanny & 2 kids (bottom kid

unfinished)
    SH oblique: lower left to
    upper right

PT 18A

Mother Animal in PT 12
Offspring Below Facing to
    Suckle

RIGHT
I 106 (L) Mycenae ChT 68
    lioness en face & cub
    ImpTr bel
AM 1938.1087 (stone Matrix for
        a gold or gilded
        lentoid)? Knossos
        Palace (Younger 1979)
    cow & calf
        groundline bel

FIG. 29 -- VII 236:
cow & calf in PT 18B, R

PT 18B

Mother Animal in PT 13A
Offspring Below Facing to
    Suckle

LEFT (see: PT 28A: Misc. -- I
  20)

Cow & Calf
  I 104 (L) Mycenae ChT 68
    calf in PT 11, L
  I 140 (L) Mycenae ChT 515
    (LH IIB)
  I Supp. 178 (Ls) Pylos
    Palace (LH III B2-C1)
  II 3.88 (L) Knossos
    2 waterbirds flank a
        man's face, all ab
  V 663 (L) Thebes, Megalo
    Kastelli, ChT 1
    object (rocks, Pithos/
      Figure-8 Shield in
      profile?) bel calf
  XIII 28 (C) Crete,
    Chersonisos?
  XIII 29 (L)
    Tree 6 infr/ab
  Munich no. unknown (L)
    (AGDS I Munich 74)
Miscellaneous
  Chania 2052 (Ls) Chania,
    Kastelli (Papapo-
      stolou 1977: no. 11)
    nanny & kid

RIGHT
Lioness & Cub
  II 3.344 (L)
    goat head upside down bel
      lioness's neck
      Figure-8 Shield ab
  AM 1938.1060 (L) Gortyna
    (CS 298)
    Figure-8 Shield ab
    agrimi head upside down
        bel betw lion's
        head & forelegs
Cow & Calf
  I 67 (L) Mycenae ChT 27
    6 circles ab
  I 125 (R) Mycenae ChT 90
  I 376 (Ls) Pylos Palace

  (LH III B2-C1)
I 509 (L) Crete
  calf betw cow's hindlegs
    2 groundlines ab
I Supp. 28 (L) Prosymna,
  ChT 33 (LH III A1)
I Supp. 110 (L)
II 3.288 (L) "Kaminaki
  Lasithiou"
?II 4.142 (L) Knossos
  a row of dots ab
II 4.159 (L) Gournes T. 2
  (LM III B1)
  calf standing in PT 2, L
II 4.160 (L) Gournes T. 2
  (LM III B1)
  remains of a calf? bel
IV 272 (L) Knossos
  Frond bel
V 298 (C) Maleme Tholos
  (LM III B)
V 317 (L) Krisa ChT 3 (LH
  III C)
  2 Fronds & circle ab
V 404 (L) Medeon T. 239
  (LH III C)
  reverse: 6 drilled holes
VII 236 (L) (FIG. 29)
IX 155 (L)
IX 156 (L) near Antioch
  cow in PT 14B, R & calf
    in PT 3, L
?IX 194 (L)
  Figure-8 Shield infr
    lion R ab to form PT
    40, R
    calf may be a bitch
      to form, with the
      lion, PT 51C
IX 24D (L)
  cow en face
  fish ab
X 138 (L)
X 216 (L)
  calf couchant between
    cow's hindlegs
    groundline bel

X 217 (L)
X 255 (L)
    cow's head inverted
        X 255 Flower ab
        (cf. Ch. 5E: Birds
        & Waterbirds
        [birds, pair] --
        KN HMs 377 [KSPI
        Va])
    SH horizontal
XII 14D (A)
    Frond? ab
    SH vertical
AM 1938.1032b (L) (CS
    243b)
    calf betw cow's hindlegs
HM 2250 (L) Archanes
        Tholos B (LM III A1;
        Sakellarakis 1967a)
    Branch 1 ab
HMs 221 (Ls) Knossos
        Palace (KSPI R10)
HM G 3309 (L) Knossos
        (CMCG 303)
    calf regardant
        small Weed bel
Berlin FG 24 (L) Greece
        (AGDS II Berlin 47)
    unfinished
    Palm 3/sign (ImpTr
        variant?) ab

Miscellaneous
    Chania 2058 (As) Chania,
        Kastelli (Papapostolou
        1977: no. 10)
    nanny & kid

PT 18C

Mother Animal in PT 14A
Offspring Below Suckling

RIGHT
I 78 (L) Mycenae ChT 42
    lioness & cub

PT 19

LEFT
HMs 284 (Ls) Knossos Palace
        (KSPI G13)
    2 bulls
        objects infr

FIG. 30 -- I 45:
2 agrimia in PT 19A, R

PT 19A

Two Animals Stand in PT 1,
    one beh the other

LEFT (see: Ch. 3A: Man &
    Animals [caprid] -- HMs 93
    [KZ 15])

Caprids
    I 262 (L) Kampos Tholos
        2 goats

VII 179 (L) Ialysos
   2 kids
      kid protome infr as
        if in PT 1B
HMs 525 (Ls) Ayia Triada
   (AT 74)
   2 agrimia
Sparta no. unknown (L)
   the Menelaion
   2 goats stand
      goat protome R at
        right ab (do the
        hind legs at
        extreme right
        belong? cf. PT 26)
      bull face/bucranium
        infr with Branch 1
        betw the horns
Waterbirds
   X 224* (A) Crete
   stand
      waterbird at left
        with 1 wing up
      Branch 1 in center
      groundline bel ending
        in flanking Fronds
   XII 203 (L) Seager Coll.
   swim/copulate
      branch inb
      groundline bel
      SH oblique: lower
        right to upper
        left
   HM G 3210 (L) (CMCG 312)
   wavy groundline bel
Miscellaneous
   HMs 364 (Ls) Knossos
      Palace (KSPI R16)
      2 griffins?

RIGHT (see: PT 26, R: 4
   agrimia -- VII 89; & Ch.
   3A: Men & Animals [caprid]
   -- AM 1938.1024)

2 Bulls/Calves
   V 673 (L) Thebes Kadmeion

      (LH III B)
   calves run
HMs 216 (Ls) Knossos
   Palace (KSPI R86;
   Papapostolou 1977: pl.
   46d)
   bulls, each in PT 1B
      Branch 4 (= Dado 2a)
      bel
2 Agrimia
   I 45 (L) Mycenae ChT 8
   (FIG. 30)
      the far (beh) agrimi is
        infr of the near
        (bef) agrimi
      Branch 1 Tree infr
      groundline bel
   V 641 (L) Gouvalari Tholos
   1 (LH IIA/IIIB?)
   run
2 Goats
   I 93 (L) Mycenae ChT 58
      the far (beh) goat is
        infr of the near (bef)
        goat
   II 4.197 (L)
   Tree 1 infr
   Frond ab
2 Waterbirds (see Ch. 5E: Birds
   & Waterbirds [waterbirds,
   pair])
   I 258 (A) Vapheio Tholos
   (FIG. 136; LH IIA)
      the far (beh) waterbird
      is infr of the near
      (bef) waterbird, which
      has both wings up
   I 471 (L) Crete
      the near (bef) waterbird
      is infr of the far
      (beh) waterbird, which
      has 1 wing raised
   II 3.352 (A)
      one at left with 1 wing
        up
   Weed ab
   IV 246 (A) Mochos

in tandem, left one with
    wing up
2 <u>Fronds</u> with stems
    conjoined to form a
    groundline bel, flank
    & one betw
IV 265 (L) Sklavi
in tandem, both with 1
    wing up
groundline bel
AM 1941.101 (L) Kato
    Choria (CS 290)
swim? branch ab
    groundline bel
Chania 2100 (Ls) Chania,
    Kastelli (Papapostolou
    1977: no. 17)
swim
Miscellaneous
    HMs 1098 (Ls) Myrtos
        Pyrgos, Shrine (Hagg
        & Marinatos 1981: 171
        fig. 3)
    2 boars

FIG. 31 -- V 597:
2 bulls in PT 19B, R
with bull-leaper

PT 19B

Two Animals Stand,
One in PT 2, the other in PT 1

LEFT
2 Bovines
    I 130 (L) Mycenae T. 91
        (LH II-III)
    bull bef & cow? beh
        <u>Branch 1</u> infr & bel
        groundline bel
    I 515/KN HMs 109 (Ls)
        Knossos Palace (KSPI
        J2; Gill 1974: 32-34,
        fig. 1)
        2 bulls
        <u>Palm 4</u> ab
        2 bucrania & a <u>Column</u>
            bel
        groundline bel
2 Goats
    I 74 (L) Mycenae ChT 42
        <u>Palm 4</u> infr
        <u>Palm 1</u>? inb
    II 4.57 (L) Milatos T. 1
        (LM III B1)
    X 299 (L)
        stroke infr
    J. P. Getty no. unknown (L)
        Boardman 1975: 84 no.
        5)
        goat protome infr, head
            down as if in PT 1B

RIGHT (see: Ch. 3E: Animal
    Games [bull-leaping, Diving]
    -- V 597 [**FIG. 31**])

2 Calves Run
    V 673 (L) Thebes Kadmeion
        (LH III B)
    VII 103 (L)
        groundline bel
2 Agrimia
    V 221 (L) Epidauros,
        Apollo Maleatas

XII 241   (L)   Seager Coll.
   run
2 Goats
   VII 98   (C with humped back)
     <u>Tree 1</u> infr
     <u>Frond</u> ab
     SH vertical
   XIII 7   (L)
     <u>Tree 1</u> beh
Miscellaneous
   I 349   (Ls)   Pylos Palace
       (LH III B2-C1)
     2 quadrupeds
   HM G 3025   (Scarab) Knossos
       (CMCG 177)
     2 waterbirds
     2 lines flank =
       marshgrass

FIG. 32 -- IV 256:
2 bulls in PT 19C, R

PT 19C

Two Animals Stand
the Far one in PT 1, the Near
one in PT 2

RIGHT
IV 256   (L)   Elounda (FIG. 32)
   2 bulls
     SH horizontal?

VII 186   (L)   Crete
   2 caprids
     branch infr

PT 19D
Two Animals Stand in PT 2,
One beh the other

LEFT
II 3.106   (L)   Kalyvia T. 8
     (LM III A2)
   2 bulls
IX 189   (L)
   2 agrimi
     zig-zags/branch infr
HM G 3511   (L) (CMCG 328)
   2 waterbirds
     fish ab upside down

FIG. 33 -- XIII 68:
2 bulls in PT 19D, R

RIGHT
XIII 68   (L)   (FIG. 33)
   2 bulls
     2 groundlines bel

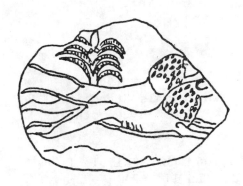

FIG. 34 -- HMs 321 etc.:
2 lions in PT 20, R

PT 20

Two Animals Run in Flying
Gallop (PT 3), One Beh the
Other

LEFT
I 390 (R) Perati ChT 1 (LH
    III B2-C1)
    2 horses?
    branch ab
    Branch 1 divided into
        2 branches
        resembling 2
        Branch 3 bel
    rocks inb & bel

RIGHT
Lions
    HMs 321 &40, Pigorini no.
        unknown (Rs)
        Knossos, Ayia Triada,
        Kato Zakro (FIG. 34;
        KN KSPI R37, AT 146,
        KZ 105)
        Palm 1 beh
        rocks bel
    AM 1938.981 (Ls) Knossos

Palace (KSPI K1; CS
    6S)
lion ab & lioness bel
Miscellaneous
    HMs 456 (Rs) Ayia Triada
        (AT 79)
        2 agrimia?, far one
            regardant
        rocks bel

FIG. 35 -- XIII 3D:
2 calves in PT 21, R

PT 21

Two Animals Run, One Beh
the Other & Regardant

LEFT
Bulls/Calves
    I 69 (L) Mycenae ChT 27
        object ab (cf. I 50,
        below)
    Munich A.1187 (A) (AGDS I
        Munich 82)
        rear bull with hindleg up
            to scratch head
        arrow in the chest of
            the near bull
        branch inb

HMs 232 (Ls) Knossos
        Palace (KSPI R17)
     2 calves run?

RIGHT
Bulls
    I 50 (L) Mycenae ChT 10
       lion or bull face ab
       SH horizontal
    XII 287 (L)
        rear bull en face, near
              bull's horns
              (fore?)shortened
           Frond ab
           groundline bel
Calves
    I 72 (L) ChT 33
    IX 111 (L)
       Frond infr
    XII 263 (C)
    XIII 3D (A) (FIG. 35)
    Berlin FG 44 (A) Athens?
       (AGDS II Berlin 49)
       rear calf's hindleg up to
              scratch head
           Tree 1 inb
    Brussels Mus. Cinq. A1343
       (L) Argos, Deiras &
       Jersualem, Rockefeller
       34.329 (L) Tell Abu
       Hawam (Pini 1981: nos. 71
       & 72)
Miscellaneous
    I 386 (L) Menidi Tholos
        (LH III B)
       2 goats run
    IX 12D (L)
       2 stags

                 PT 21 Variant

VII 159 (L)
    2 ibex/bulls
       lioness in PT 12, R ab

tall Frond beh
2 wavy groundlines
   bel

FIG. 36 -- I 71:
2 lions in PT 22, R

PT 22

Two Animals Assis,
One Beh the Other & Regardant

RIGHT
I 71 (L)
    Mycenae ChT 29 (FIG. 36)
    2 lions
       1 Palm 1 infr & 2 ab

            PT 23A
       2 Animals Couchant,
       1 Beh/Ab the Other

LEFT
2 Boars
    I 276 (L) Rutsi Tholos 2
        (FIG. 37; LH II-IIIA)
       Branch 1 ab
       2 groundlines bel
    HM G 3192 (A) (CMCG 302)

3 <u>Weeds</u> ab
2 pairs <u>Mount-Guides</u>
    flank

FIG. 37 -- I 276:
2 boars in PT 23A, L

RIGHT
2 Boars
    II 3.21 (L) Knossos, House
          of Frescoes (LM I)
    <u>Dado 3</u> bel
    V 666 (L) Thebes, Megalo
          Kastelli T. 3
    groundline bel
    a 3rd boar ab originally
        intended?
    HMs 545 (Ls) Ayia Triada
        (AT 80)
    wavy rocks bel
    Berlin FG 49b (Pr)
        Peloponnese (AGDS II
        Berlin 45b)
    2 <u>Branch 1</u> ab
    groundline with <u>Dado 2c</u>
        bel
    SH horizontal
Miscellaneous
    I 193a (Pr) Midea ChT 10
        (LH II-III A)
        2 agrimia
          2 groundlines bel

I 282 (L) Rutsi Tholos 2
    (LH II-III A)
    2 griffins: 1 beh, far
      infr
    unfinished griffin?
      beh/ab
    <u>Dado 7c</u> bel
    SH horizontal

PT 23B

2 Animals Couchant,
1 Beh & Regardant

I Supp. 112 (L)
    2 bulls L

PT 23B or PT 24

I 91 (R) Mycenae ChT 58
    2 bulls couchant R
    2 <u>Tree 1</u> flank
    <u>Dado 4c</u> bel

PT 23C

Two Animals Couchant,
Miscellaneous

LEFT
II 3.191 (L) "Katsambas"
    2 goats, near goat's head
      averted, far goat
      regardant
IX 136 (L) the Islands
    3 boars
    <u>Dado 6d</u> bel

RIGHT
XIII 24   (A)
   2 lions couchant regardant
      vertical line (single
      <u>Mount-Guide</u>) infr
   half-<u>Frond</u> ab

FIG. 38 -- V 433:
2 bulls in PT 24, R

PT 24

Two Bulls Couchant,
Far One's Head Averted

LEFT
Plain (no filling motifs)
   I Supp. 20   (L)   Midea, ChT
   2 LH III B1 or A2
   [Catling in Popham 1974:
   254])
   X 316   (L)   Crete

Single Groundline bel
   I Supp. 78   (L)   Crete
     unfinished?
   V 195   (L)   Thebes?
   HM G 3218   (L)   (CMCG 292)

Pair of Groundlines bel
   I 142   (L)   Mycenae ChT 515
     (LH IIB)

I 240   (L)   Vapheio Tholos
I 241   (L)   Vapheio Tholos
V 432   (L)   Nichoria Tholos
   (LH III A2-B1)
VII 127   (L)
XIII 78   (L)   Mycenae
AM 1938.1029   (L)   (CS 311)

Miscellaneous Filling Motifs
   I 318   (Ls)   Pylos Palace
     (LH III B2-C1;
     inscribed PY Wr 1328)
     <u>Branch 1</u> ab
   II 3.62   (L)   Ayios Ioannes
     T. III (LM IIB)
     <u>Tree 2</u> infr & inb
     2 groundlines bel
   AM 1938.1030   (L)   Herak-
     leion area (CS 312)
     <u>Pica</u> ab
     groundline bel
   Munich A.1193   (L)   Crete
     (AGDS I Munich 38)
     <u>Frond</u> ab
     groundline bel

RIGHT
Plain (no filling motifs)
   I Supp. 26   (L)   Argive
     Heraeum
   X 254   (L)
   HMs 501   (A?s)   Ayia Triada
     (AT 59)

Single Groundline bel
   II 3.119   (L)   Ayia Triada
     near bull regardant
   XIII 8   (A)
   HM 2393   (L)   Sellopoulo T.
     4 (LM III A1; Popham
     1974: fig. 14a)

Pair of Groundlines bel
   I 109   (L)   Mycenae ChT 78
   V 433   (L)   Nichoria Tholos
     (FIG. 38; LH III A2-B1)

Pair of Groundlines bel, <u>Branch</u>
  <u>1</u> ab

    I 275 (L) Rutsi Tholos 2
      (LH II-III A)
    Berlin FG 49a (Pr)
          Peloponnese (AGDS
          II Berlin 45a)
          SH horizontal

FIG. 39 -- V 297:
2 stags in PT 25A, L

                PT 25A
Animal with Another's Protome
            Above

LEFT
Lions
  2 Lions
    XIII 40 (L)
          2 (3?) bulls couchant
          around periphery cl
          (the bulls were
          engraved after the
          lions, perhaps as a

study); 1 1/2 bulls
are actually
couchant (1 ab
without legs; at
left only a
protome); bel is a
zigzag that was
probably planned to
be a 3rd bull)
    XIII 124 (L)
Lion & Agrimi
    I Supp. 95 (L) Crete
        lion & agrimi
          Branch 1 infr
          line bel
    II 4.79
    II 4.178 "Knossos"
Miscellaneous
    V 297 (C) Malame Tholos
        (**FIG. 39**; LM III B)
        2 stags run
          <u>Figure-8 Shield</u>/
            <u>Pica</u>/<u>Baton</u> ab
          lines bel
    HMs 287 (Ls) Knossos
        Palace (KSPI
        R69)
        2 goats run
          <u>Pica</u> ab

RIGHT
Goats
    V 348/349/350/392 (L)
        Medeon Ts. 29 (348),
        29a (349 & 350), 99
        (392; LH III A)
      <u>Branch 1 Tree</u> infr &, V
        349/350/392, <u>Branch 1</u>
        ab, modelled slightly
        differently
    X 2 (L)
      <u>Branch 3</u> infr
      strokes ab
      <u>Figure-8 Shield</u> bel

Miscellaneous
    I 488 (L) Crete

          2 agrimia run
    I Supp. 141   (L)
          lion couchant & bull

    FIG. 40 -- VII 100:
    2 bulls in PT 25B, R
      with man infr

        PT 25B
    Animal with Another's
Protome Above, Regardant

LEFT
2 Lions couchant
    V 193   (A)   Thebes?
        groundline bel
    V 236   (As)   Chania,
        Kastelli
        Mount-Guides?
    IX 13D   (L)
        2 Weeds ab
        2 groundlines bel
    X 304   (L)
    HM 2345   (L)   Poros ChT (MM
        III-LM I; Lembessi
        1967: pl. 190a & b)
        2 groundlines bel
    HM G 3065   (L)   Knossos
        (CMCG 287)

2 Bulls
    Couchant
        V 196   (L)   Thebes?
            protome of bull ab R
                2 groundlines bel
        V 434   (L)   Nichoria
            Tholos (LH III
            A2-B1)
    Run
        II 4.5   (L)   Zafer
            Papoura T.?
            Figure-8 Shield ab
        II 4.151   (L)   Phaistos
        Berlin FG 26   (L)
            Corinth (AGDS II
            Berlin 48)
            run
                Column ab center
2 Calves Run
    I 348   (glass Ls?)   Pylos
        Palace (LH III B2-C1)
    I 411   (L)   Amorgos
        kids?
    V 359   (L)   Medeon T. 29
        (LH III A-C)
        Branch 4 infr
    HM no. unknown   (L)
        Knossos, MUM (Popham et
        al. 1984: Misc. 12)
Miscellaneous
    Bull
        PT 5
            V 511   (L)   Korakou
                (LH II?)
            & lion protome
            AM 1941.138   (L)   (CS
                12P)
                PT 5B & goat
                    protome
                    Figure-8 Shield
                        bel
        PT 10A, R
            I 183   (L)   Midea Tho-
                los (LH III A1)
                & lion protome
                    groundline bel
            II 4.191   (L)

& sheep protome
Miscellaneous
    V 311 (L) Papoulia
      2 quadrupeds walk
        Frond ab & infr
    X 308 (L)
      2 quadrupeds
        branch infr
        stroke? bel
    XIII 126 (L)
      2 kids run

RIGHT (see: PT 46: lion L vs 2
    bulls -- AM 1938.1153h:A
    [**FIG. 40**]; & Ch. 3A: Men &
    Animals [bulls] -- VII 100)

2 Bulls
    I 175 (L) Mycenae
    run
      2 Picas? ab
    VIII 108 (L)
    tree infr
    ImpTr ab
    HMs 548 (Ls) Ayia Triada
      (AT 58)
    couchant
Caprids
    I Supp. 111 (L)
    goats
    Tree 2 infr
    II 3.123 (L) Tylissos T.
      (LM III B-C)
    agrimi kids
      dot infr & inb
    II 4.89 (L)
    agrimia? run
    V 600 (L) Mycenae, House
      with the Idols (LH
      III B2)
    goats
    Frond infr
    AM 1941.144 (L) (CS 363;
      profile is illustra-
      ted s.n. CS 40P)
    sheep
    Frond infr

HM 2770 (L) Knossos, MUM
    (Popham et al. 1984:
    Misc. 9)
    goats
2 Calves Run
    VII 115b (Pr)
    Frond ab
    AM 1941.92 (L) (CS 383)
    Frond inb
Miscellaneous
    I 115 (L) Mycenae ChT 81
    lion assis en face &
      agrimi
      X & Figure-8 Shield
      infr
      2 groundlines bel
    V 589 (L) Nafplion,
      Evangelistria cemetery
    2 lions assis
    Dado 4a bel
    IX 180 (L)
    lion couchant & agrimi
    protome
    X 249 (C)
    2 dogs run
    HMs no. unknown (Ls) Ayia
      Triada (AT 133)
    2 Babylonian Dragons run?
      2 plants (Papyrus?)
      infr

PT 25C
Animal Regardant with
Another's Protome Ab,
Regardant

LEFT
Lion
    Assis
      & Lion Protome
        I 280 (L) Rutsi
        Tholos 2 (LH
        II-III A)
        torsos of 2 men ab,

the near one
stretches out
his right hand
as if to
restrain the
lions
Munich A.1172 (L)
    Crete (AGDS I
    Munich 54)

& Agrimi Protome/Fore-
quarters

    IV 276 (L) Knossos
    IX 16D (L)
        2 groundlines bel
    X 153 (L)
    X 264 (L)
        groundline bel
    HM G 3130 (L)
        Knossos (CMCG 289)
    HM G 3293 (L)
        Knossos (CMCG 288)
& Miscellaneous
    V 222 (L)
        Epidauros,
        Apollo Maleatas
    & stag protome as
        if in PT 3, R
Couchant
    & Agrimi Protome
    V 725 (L) Mega
        Monastiri T.
        Gamma (LH III
        A-B)
        2 groundlines bel
    VII 197 (L) Crete
        agrimi, PT 3, R
    Berlin FG 30 (L)
        Crete (AGDS II
        Berlin 42)
    SH horizontal
& Miscellaneous
    VII 198 (L) Crete
        & griffin
            displayed (=
            PT3/5A, R?)

Brummer Coll. (L)
    & bull
        groundline bel
Miscellaneous
    V 249 (L) Armenoi T.
        19 (LM III B1)
        2 calves run

FIG. 41 -- XIII 59: 2 bulls
run in PT 25C

RIGHT
Lion
    Assis
        V 750 (A) Achilleion
            & agrimi protome
    Couchant
        VIII 80 (L) Dawkins
            Coll.
            & agrimi? protome as
                if in PT 3, L
        HM G 3064 (L) (CMCG 308)
            & bull protome
2 Agrimia stand
    X 260 (L)
        Branch 1 Tree infr
        agrimi protome bef
    II 3.55 (L) Isopata T. 3,
        The Mace Bearer's Tomb
        (LM III A1)
    AM 1925.43 (L) (CS 313)

2 Goats
  Stand
    I Supp. 140a (L)
      branch infr
    II 4.164 (L) Mallia,
        Quartier Da pl.
        XLV)
      tree infr
    X 174 (L)
      Branch 3 infr
    HM G 3006 (L) (CMCG 294)
      2 quadrupeds
    HM G 3139 (L) Knossos
      (CMCG 295)
      2 quadrupeds
  Run
    I 30 (A) Mycenae
      agrimia?
        2 Weeds ab
        line infr
      lines, tree/ground-
        line, & spear
        bel
    II 4.90 (L)
    ?HM G 3356 (L) Knossos
      (CMCG 293)
Miscellaneous
  XIII 59 (L) Mycenae?
    (FIG. 41; Younger
    1976b: 255)
    bulls run

FIG. 42 -- I 215:
3 calves in PT 26, L

LEFT (see: PT 19A, L -- Sparta
  no. unknown; Ch. 3A: Man &
  Animals [bulls] -- AM
  1938.1026])

I 215 (L) Prosymna T. XLI
  (FIG. 42; LH III B1)
  3 calves run (last calf
    regardant & scratching
    head with a hindleg)
X 252 (L)
  3 agrimia stand
    Pica ab in the last
      agrimi's head, which
      sports splayed horns
    2 groundlines bel
    SH horizontal

PT 26
Three Animals Stand
Overlapping

LEFT & RIGHT
HMs 210 (Ls) Knossos Palace
  (KSPI R29)
  2 registers, each with 3
    couchant sheep: top
    R, bottom L
  Papyrus R separates the
    registers

RIGHT
2 Calves
  I 238 (A) Vapheio Tholos
    (LH IIA)
    stand (middle calf reg,
      calf at right in PT
      1B)
  HMs 110 (Ls) Knossos
    Palace (KSPI N2)
    couchant

Dado 2a? bel
Miscellaneous
   VII 89 (A) Crete
      4 agrimia stand (ab, the
         3rd agrimi with
         head averted; infr,
         the 4th agrimi in
         PT 1B)
      2 groundlines bel
   AM 1938.1066 (L) Knossos
      (CS 343)
      3 waterbirds swim (rear
         waterbird
         regardant)
        Papyrus infr & ab
        water bel

Figure-8 Shield bel inb
Tree 1 bel

FIG. 44 -- I 113:
3 sheep in PT 27B, R

PT 27B

Animal Stands
Protomes of Two Others Above,
One Regardant

RIGHT
Sheep
   I 113 (L) Mycenae ChT 79
      (FIG. 44)
   I 176 (L) Mycenae
      groundline bel
Miscellaneous
   I Supp. 56 (L) Perati ChT
      142 (LH III C1)
      3 deer
      line ab
      2 lines bel
   AM 1941.121 (L) Goulas
      (CS 286)
      3 goats stand
      Tree 1 infr
      Frond ab at left
      groundline ab & bel

FIG. 43 -- I 105:
3 goats in PT 27A, R

PT 27A

Animal Stands
Protomes of Two Others Above

I 105 (L) Mycenae ChT 68
    (FIG. 43)
   3 goats R
   Figure-8 Shield, Tree 1,
    & Palm 4 bel
   Palm 4 bel infr

FIG. 45 -- V 337:
2 bulls in PT 28A

PT 28A
Two Animals Stand Antithetic

2 Bulls
I 19 (R/As) Mycenae, Rhyton
        Well (LH III B1)
    couchant
        Column with HC betw
        birds ab
V 337 (L) Medeon T. 29 (**FIG.**
        45)
    centered dot ab & bel each
    Branch 3 ab
    groundline bel
V 607 (L) Naxos, Kamini T. 4
        (LH III C)
    conjoined with 1 face
        bull face upside down ab
IX 137 (L)
    & 2 calves, each in PT 1B,
        en face conjoined
    the 2 bulls, each in PT 1C,
        are upside down to the 2
        calves

2 Agrimia
I 155 (R) Mycenae ChT 520
        (LH III A2)

Tree 2 betw
Tree 2 beh each
I 297 (L) Pylos Palace (LH
        III B2-C1)
    agrimi at left regardant

2 Griffins (see: Ch. 4B:
    Potnia Theron [monsters] --
    HM 1654)

I 218 (R) Prosymna ChT XLIV
        (LH III B1)
    assis
        Column betw
        rocks ab
        Dado 1 bel
VII 187 (L)
    protomes
        Column betw

Miscellaneous
I 20 (R) Mycenae, Ramp House
    2 pairs of a cow & calf,
        each in PT 18B
        groundline bel
I 87 (R) Mycenae ChT 55
    2 sphinxes assis, each
        crowned by a
        lily plume
        Tree 1 betw
I 189 (R) Midea Tholos (LH
        III A1)
    2 sheep protomes (frontal
        protomes with profile
        heads) each ab a
        triple Snake Frame
    Dado 1 bel
    in an exergue bel: 2
        calves couchant in PT
        28B
I 347 (Ls?) Pylos Palace (LH
        III B2-C1)
    2 quadrupeds
V 747 (L) Ayii Theodoroi,
        Metaphio Tholos (LH III
        A2)
    2 kids

Branch 1 ab each
HMs 23b (Ls) Kato Zakro (KZ
     58)
   bel: 2 waterbirds in PT 28A
   ab: lion face with 2 human
        arms? rising from the top
          & curving out
   object betw
HMs 391 (R?s) Knossos Palace
     (KSPI L38)
   2 pairs owls upside down to
        each other
        rosette in center

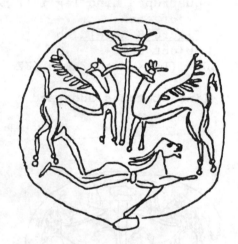

FIG. 46 -- I 171:
2 griffins in PT 28B
with Minotaur prone R bel

PT 28B
Two Animals Stand
Antithetic & Regardant

(see: Ch. 5D: Protomes -- I 189
& Ch. 5E: Owls -- HMs 391)

2 Lions
I 172 (L) Mycenae
   assis flank a genius R
      short lines ab & bel
      line encircles
HMs 42 (Ls) Kato Zakro (KZ
     128)

waisted Altar topped with
     Column betw the 2 lions
   groundline bel
HMs 256a (Ls) Knossos Palace
     (KSPI R88?)
   couchant
      Pica ab in lion's
         shoulder
      2? quadruped(s) bel

2 Bulls
II 4.203 (L) Diktaian Cave
   flank central Column
XIII 27 (R) Mycenae (hoop
     modern?: Kenna 1964: 12)
   couchant flank Tree 1
      Frond ab each bull
      2 groundlines bel
HMs 139 (Ls) Knossos Palace
     (KSPI C51)
   2 pairs upside down to each
        other, all couchant
        bucranium betw each pair
HMs 156 (R/As) Knossos
     Palace (KSPI O7;
     inscribed)
   couchant

2 Calves (see PT 28A -- I 189,
   above)

I 58 (R) Mycenae ChT 25
   leashed, couchant
      Tree 1 betw
      Dado 1 bel
VIII 90 (L) Dawkins Coll.
   2 pairs couchant upside
        down to each other
        Column capital betw each
          pair

2 Griffins
I 171 (L) Mycenae, Perseia
     area (FIG. 46; LH III B)
   leashed to Column with HC
     ab
   horned Minotaur prone R

(originally intended to
be a bull?)
I 304   (Rs) Pylos Palace (LH
III B2-Cl)
griffinesses each with her
baby fledgling in PT 17B
I 398   (L) Athens
2 quadrupeds
branches
V 5   (L) Aigina, Athena Temple
(Archaic)
2 quadrupeds
Branch 2 ab each
IX 113   (L)
2 birds/storks
strokes ab & bel
SH horizontal

I 40   (L) Mycenae
2 goat forequarters
I 375   (Rs?) Pylos Palace
(FIG. 47; LH III B2-Cl)
2 calves couchant
3 Palm 4 betw
I 4.65   (L) Palaikastro
bull protome at left &
lion?
protome regardant at right
II 4.218   (L)
2 lion protomes
quadruped hind leg infr
of each
Figure-8 Shield ab
object bel
HMs 60a   (Ls) Kato Zakro (KZ
111)
2 lion protomes addorsed

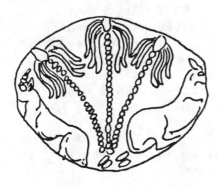

FIG. 47 -- I 375:
2 calves couchant in PT 29A

PT 29A
Two Animals Stand Addorsed

(see: Ch. 3C: Man Hunts Animals
[lions] -- I 307 & I Supp. 173;
Ch. 4B: Potnia Theron [water-
birds] -- IX 154; & [lions] --
X 242, & Kassel no. unknown
[AGDS III 6]; & Ch. 6A: Animal-
People [bull-people] -- BSA
cast 186)

FIG. 48 -- AM 1938.1126
(CS 340): 2 lions in PT 29B

PT 29B
Two Animals Stand Addorsed
& Regardant

(see: Ch. 5D: Protomes -- X
309)

Griffins

I 102   (R)   Mycenae ChT 68
  2 <u>Cypress</u> branches flank
  <u>Dado 1</u> bel
HMs 259   (Ls)   Knossos Palace
      (KSPI C15)
  1 wing up
      baby griffin? betw

Miscellaneous

V 151   (L)   Kephallenia,
      Kokkolata Tholos A (LH
      III B[-C])
  2 bulls
      <u>Branch 2</u> ab
VII 126   (L)   Cyprus
  2 collared dog protomes
            flank
      genius running L
VIII 84   (L)   Dawkins Coll.
  2 kids? conjoined
      2 branches flank
      branch bel
AM 1938.1094   (L)   (CS 336)
  2 calf protomes en face
      <u>ImpTr</u> & <u>Figure-8 Shield</u>
      ab
      bull's face bel
      vertical line at left
AM 1938.1126   (R)   "Mycenae"
      (**FIG. 48**; CS 340)
  2 lions leashed to central
          <u>Column</u>
      <u>Sacred Knot</u> ab each lion

PT 30A

Two Animals in Opposite
Directions Overlapping

2 Bulls

I 372   (Ls)   Pylos Palace (LH
      III B2-C1)

both in PT 4 branch bel
    (line of the seal's gold
    cap bel?)
I Supp. 91   (L)   Crete
  <u>Branch 1</u> & <u>Figure-8 Shield</u>
      ab
  groundline dotted like a
      <u>Baton</u> with 2 <u>Branch 1</u>
      <u>Trees</u> at each end
XIII 11   (L)   (**FIG. 49**)
  2 circles ab

FIG. 49 -- XIII 11:
2 bulls in PT 30A

2 Goats

I 48   (L)   Mycenae ChT 9
  circle on far goat's neck &
      near goat's neck & hip
?I 97   (L)   Mycenae ChT 58
Patras 2443   (L)   Kallithea,
  Rambantania ChT Theta
      (Pini 1981: no. 88)

Miscellaneous

I 124   (L)   Mycenae ChT 88
  2 stags
      a vertical dog/lion in
          PT 5A/3 bef each stag
I 187   (L)   Midea Tholos (LH
      III A1)

2 sheep
  <u>HC</u> at left
  <u>Dado 2a</u> bel
I 352 (Ls) Pylos Palace (LH
  III B2-C1)
  2 quadrupeds
?I 362 (Ls) Pylos Palace (LH
  III B2-C1)
  2 quadrupeds
I 381 (Ls) Pylos Palace (LH
  III B2-C1)
  lion & sheep en face
IV 240 (L) Knossos
  2 boars couchant
    groundline bel
IV 294 (L) Fortetsa
  2 lions?
    tree beh?

FIG. 50 -- I 197:
2 bulls in PT 30B

PT 30B
Two Animals in Opposite
Directions, Overlapping
& Regardant

(see: PT 46: lion L vs 2 bulls
-- AM 1938.1153h:A)

I 197 (L) Asine ChT 1 (**FIG.
  50**; LH III A2)

2 bulls couchant
  3 circles ab
  <u>Dado 7a</u> & 5 circles bel

PT 30C

Two Animals in Opposite
Directions Overlapping,
One Regardant

IX 112 (A)
  lions couchant, far one
    regardant
  <u>Frond</u> ab
HM 2271 (L) Archanes (LM III
  A1; Sakellarakis 1966:
  fig. 7)
  agrimia stand, near one
    regardant
  <u>Figure-8 Shield</u> ab at
    left
  <u>Frond</u> ab at right

FIG. 51 -- IV 40D:
2 lions in PT 31A

PT 31A
Two Animals Salient &
Antithetic

(see: PT 54: 2 lions vs man
[Master of Animals?] -- IV
293; Ch. 2E: People at a
Shrine [person at right] -- HMs
141 [KN KSPI M1-5]; Ch. 3B:
Master of Animals [lions] --
HMs ?218 [KN KSPI R44], 219
[KSPI 43], 382 [KSPI R44, R43,
& Ca], & Nafplion no. unknown
from Asine, [caprids] -- I 163
& V 594; Ch. 3C: Man Hunts
Animals [lions] -- I 228; Ch.
3D: Men In Chariots -- I 230;
Ch. 4B: Potnia Theron [lions]
-- BSA Cast 135, & [caprids] -
- I 379)

2 Lions
I 46 (L) Mycenae ChT 8
  conjoined with 1 face,
    stand on waisted Altar
I 319 (Ls) Pylos Palace (LH
    III B2-C1; inscribed: PY
    Wr 1325)
Column betw
?I Supp. 63 (Scarab) Dimini
Tholos
IV 304 (L) Knossos
central Column/Palm 4?
IV 40D (L) Elounda (FIG. 51)
  waisted Altar & Tree 1 betw
HMs 285 (Ls) Knossos Palace
    (KSPI G14)
  2 dogs/lions en face
    dot ab each?
HMs 577 (Ls) Ayia Triada (AT
    49)
  on waisted Altar

2 Agrimia
?I 90 (R) Mycenae ChT 58
  branches everywhere
I 266 (L) Tragana Tholos 2

(LH III A)
Tree 2 betw
HMs 288 (Ls) Knossos Palace
    (KSPI R85)
kid? upside down betw

2 Griffins
I 73 (L) Mycenae ChT 42
  conjoined with 1 face, stand
    on waisted Altar
    ImpTr at right
HMs no. unknown (As) Ayia
    Triada (AT 96)
Papyrus betw
groundline bel
SH vertical

Miscellaneous
?I Supp. 205 (R?/Ls) Pylos
    Palace (LH III B2-C1)
  2? quadrupeds
HM G 3078 (L) Knossos (CMCG
    378)
  2 genii?

PT 31B
Two Animals Salient,
Antithetic, & Regardant

2 Lions
II 3.306 (L) "Chandras"
  collared
    bull's face flanked by &
      joined to 2 dots betw
    Figure-8 Shield inb of
      each
    groundline bel
Berlin FG 34 (L) Crete (FIG.
    52; AGDS II Berlin 39)
  the lions stand on a
      waisted Altar or
      small Table with one
      leg shaped like a
      bucranium

Sun ab
Lamia inv. no. unknown & BE
     956 (L) Kalapodi, Plakia
     T. 1 & Stavros, Kaltsis
     T. 5 (both LH III; Pini
     1981: 48-81 nos. 81 & 82,
     respectively)
  BE 956 adds a Frond ab &
  models the lion at right
  differently

2 Waterbirds
I 213 (C) Prosymna ChT XIII
     (LH IIB/III A2-B 2)
Branch 1 betw
HMs 4b (Ls) Kato Zakro (KZ
     52)
  geese? protomes?
     flower ab center betw
HMs 495 (Cs) Ayia Triada (AT
     27)
  stroke inb of each
  Branch 1 betw
  groundline bel

2 Griffins
I 98 (L) Mycenae ChT 58
  on waisted Altar
  Column supporting epistyle
     betw
I 196 (L) Midea
  leashed together
  Branch 1 (& wavy rocks?)
     bel
HMs 163 (Ls) Knossos Palace
     (KSPI R92)
  squat

Miscellaneous
I 99 (L) Mycenae ChT 61
  2 agrimia (no waisted Altar
     bel = unfinished?)
V 353/354 (L) Medeon T. 29
  2 calves?
     a thick line bel (354:
        engraved with a row
        of short lines =

striated?)
HMs 233 (Ls) Knossos Palace
     (KSPI R88)
  2 collared dogs on waisted
     Altar
     Sun ab in center
     5 dots ab each dog
HM G 3311 (L) Phaistos (**FIG.
     132**; CMCG 355)
  2 monkeys
     kantharos betw

FIG. 52 -- Berlin FG 34
     (AGDS II Berlin 39):
     2 lions in PT 31 B

PT 32A

Two Animals Salient & Addorsed

(see: Ch. 3B: Master of
Animals [lions] -- HM G 3117
[CMCG 358]; & Ch. 4B: Potnia
Theron [lions] -- HMs 158/662
[KN KSPI R32])

HMs 68 (Ls) Kato Zakro (**FIG.
     53**; KZ 177)
  griffin at left & agrimi at
     right
     kantharos betw

FIG. 53 -- HMs 68 (KZ 177):
griffin & agrimi in PT 32A

FIG. 54 -- I 123:
2 agrimia in PT 32B

PT 32B
Two Animals Salient,
Addorsed, & Regardant

2 Bulls
I 198 (C) Asine ChT 1 (LH III
      A2)
   conjoined with 1 face
      branch betw
HMs 118 (Ls) Knossos Palace

(KSPI 05; inscribed)

2 Agrimia
I 123 (L) Mycenae ChT 88
      (FIG. 54)
   2 tiered building bel each
   Palm 2 betw
II 3.107 (L) Kalyvia T. 8
   Figure-8 Shield betw
II 3.133 (L) Nirou Chani T.
      (LM III B)
   kid rampant R betw

2 Caprids
II 3.5 (L) "Axos"
   2 bull faces betw:
      top one is schematic
         Snake Frame bel the
            horns
      goat head upside down &
         bel the caprid at
         right

Miscellaneous
I 161 (Ls) Mycenae, House of
      the Oil Merchant (LH III
      B1)
   2 dogs flank a genius

PT 32C

Two Animals Salient &
Addorsed, One Regardant

HMs 68 (Ls) Kato Zakro (KZ
      181)
   lion regardant at left &
      plumed griffin at right
      Dado 6a bel lion

PT 33A
Two Animals Crossed, Heads Up

2 Lions
I 117 (L) Mycenae ChT 83
     (**FIG. 55**)
   caprid bel in PT 10, L
I 385 (L) Menidi Tholos (LH
     III B)
   assis

Miscellaneous
V 355 (L) Medeon T. 29 (LH
     III A-C)
   2 goats
     SH horizontal
AM 1938.1019 (L) (CS 316)
   lion L & nanny R
     kid bel nanny to form PT
       16A, R
HM G 3372a (Pr) Vasilike
     Anogeia (CMCG 190a)
   2 caprids (agrimia?)
     central vertical stroke

2 bulls regardant

FIG. 56 -- IX 133:
2 bulls in PT 33B

FIG. 55 -- I 117:
2 lions in PT 33A

PT 33B
Two Animals Crossed, Heads Down

IX 133 (L) (**FIG. 56**)

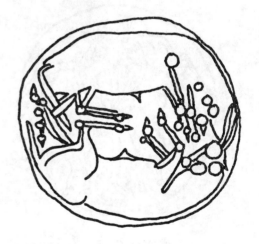

FIG. 57 -- X 256:
2 bulls in PT 34A

PT 34A
Two Animals in One Direction,
Bodies Parallel & Antithetic

(see: Ch. 4B: <u>Potnia Theron</u>
[dolphins] -- II 3.327)

2 Bulls
X 256 (L) (FIG. 57)
HMs 292+Zeta (Ls) Knossos
    Palace (KSPI R19/30)
  object betw
    2 groundlines flank (a
      groundline ab each bull)

Miscellaneous
II 3.108 (L) Kalyvia T. 8
  2 goats, each in PT 10A
HMs 367 (Ls) Knossos Palace
  (KSPI R38)
  2 lions flank bull face
    SH vertical = on axis

FIG. 58 -- I 92:
2 bulls in PT 34B

PT 34B

Two Animals in One Direction,
Bodies Parallel & Addorsed

(see: PT 12, L: lion -- AM
1941.1241; Ch. 2B: Men [pair]
-- I 131; Ch. 4B: Potnia Theron
[lions] -- HM 2568)

2 Bulls
Separate
  I 92 (L) Mycenae ChT 58

(FIG. 58)
  each in PT 13A
    branch bel one bull
    branch betw

Conjoined with One Head En Face
II 4.158 (L) Gournes T. 1
  (LM III B1)
  Figure-8 Shield ab
Sparta no. unknown (Ls) the
  Menelaion (Dawkins
    1909-1910: fig. 5; LH III
    B1)
  arrows betw

Miscellaneous
I 60 (L) Mycenae ChT 25
  2 lions, each in PT 14A
    Branch 1 betw
I 157 (L) Mycenae ChT 523 (LH
  III A2)
  2 quadrupeds
    branch betw

FIG. 59 -- IX 131:
2 bulls in PT 35

PT 35

Two Animals in Radial Symmetry,
Antithetic

CLOCKWISE (see: Ch. 5I:
 Dolphins [pair] -- I 259
 [**FIG. 141**])

Bulls in PT 1B
Head In Profile
 II 3.102 (L) Kalyvia T. 1

En Face
 IX 131 (L) Crete (**FIG. 59**)
 HMs 240/1023 (Ls) Knossos
  Palace (KSPI G3/Betts 17;
  KSPI fig. 2)

Miscellaneous
II 3.109 (L) Kalyvia T. 8
 2 calves?
II 3.110 (L) Kalyvia T. ?
 2 goats
HM no. unknown (L) (Younger &
  Betts 1979: no. 1)
 2 lion forequarters
   conjoined
  erased quadruped
   hindquarters infr
   of each

COUNTERCLOCKWISE (see: Ch.
3B: Master of Animals [lions]
-- I Supp. 27; Ch. 4B: Potnia
Theron [dolphins] -- Nafplion
no. unknown from Aidonia T.
8; Ch. 5H: Fish [pair] -- HM
no. unknown from Kato Souli;
Ch. 5I Dolphins [pair] -- I
Supp. 121)

I 239 (L) Vapheio Tholos
 2 bulls couchant
I 396 (Cypriot conoid)
  Perati ChT 24
 2 agrimia protomes
  conjoined
HMs 512 (Ls) Ayia Triada (AT
  86)
 lion ab & collared lioness
  bel

 2 groundlines bel
HM G 3372b (Pr) Vasilike
  Anogeia (CMCG 190b)
 2 bull protomes conjoined
  man protome above each,
  one arm up as if to
  restrain them (= Master
  of bulls?)

                PT 35 or PT 36

CLOCKWISE
I 103 (L) Mycenae ChT 68
 2 pairs: lion vs an upside
  down sheep, each in PT
  39A

FIG. 60 -- II 3.115:
2 goats in PT 36, cl

PT 36
Two Animals in Radial Symmetry,
Addorsed

(see: PT 1B, R [misc.] --
Oxford [MS] J21)

CLOCKWISE
2 Bulls
I 53   (L)   Mycenae ChT 10
  2 <u>Tree 1</u> betw
I 317   (Ls)   Pylos Palace   (LH
    III B2-C1; inscribed: PY Wr
    1329)
XII 250   (L)
  couchant & en face
    <u>Double Ax</u> betw the horns
      of each
    betw: sign (Linear B -a-
      ?)
    groundline bel each
HM G 3525   (L)   (CMCG 305)
  run

2 Goats
II 3.115   (L)   Kalyvia T. 8
  (FIG. 60)
  man's face betw in the
    center
  SH horizontal to the man's
    face (= on axis)
HMp 4819 (?s on a coarse LM
    III pot handle) Palai-
    kastro, House Pi38
    (Hutchinson 1939-40: 47,
    no. 31 fig. 31)
  line encircles?
HMs 331/332   (Ls)   Knossos
    Palace (KSPI R76)
  2 goat protomes run

2 Griffins
HMs 180   (Ls)   Kato Zakro   (KZ
    180)
  griffin & quadruped

Miscellaneous
I 184   (L)   Midea Tholos (LH
    III A1)
  2 boars
    groundline bel each
I Supp. 29   (L)   Prosymna ChT
    33
  2 calves

II 4.16   (L)   Kalyvia T. 8
    (LM III A1)
  2 quadrupeds en face or
    with heads up
    regardant
V 351/352   (L)   Medeon T. 29
  2 calves, each in PT 5B

COUNTERCLOCKWISE (see: Ch. 3B:
  Master of Animals [monsters]
  -- V 669; & Ch. 5H: Fish
  [pair] --HMs 480 [AT 33])

2 Lions
I 249   (L)   Vapheio Tholos
  each in PT 13A
HM G 3432   (A)   Knossos
    (CMCG 296)
  run
    centered circle infr
      of each
BSA cast 184   (L)   (Betts
    1981a: 7 fig. 10)
  run
    2 <u>Branch 1</u> bel one lion
    zig-zags bel other
      lion & betw both

2 Bulls
II 3.310   (L)   Siteia   (GGFR
    pl. 125)
  run en face
    sign (Linear A #52/B
      -a-?) betw
II 4.36   (L)   "Knossos"
  each in PT 13A, R
?IV 291   (L)   Messara

Miscellaneous
I 360   (Ls)   Pylos Palace
    (LH III B2-C1)
  2 quadrupeds
I 371   (Ls)   Pylos Palace
    (LH III B2-C1)
  2 quadrupeds

98

FIG. 61 -- V 318:
2 bulls in PT 37A ccl

PT 37A
Two Animals in Radial
Symmetry Addorsed Regardant

CLOCKWISE
2 Lions
I 250 (L) Vapheio Tholos
I Supp. 93 (L) Crete
V 493 (L) Ayia Irini, Keos
    (LM Ib/LH II)
  dot & groundline bel each
    lion?
VII 90 (L)
IX 143 (L)
AM 1941.95 (L) central Crete
    (CS 244)
AM 1941.94 (L) Knossos (CS
    245)
Hamburg 1964.289 (L) (AGDS
    IV Hamburg 8)
HM 3133 (L) Knossos (CMCG
    300)
HM G 3503 (L) (CMCG 297)
HM G 3505 (D) (CMCG 298)
HM G 3514 (L) Knossos
    (CMCG 299)

2 Calves
I Supp. 188 (Ls) Pylos
    Palace (LH III B2-C1)
II 4.143 (L) Knossos

Miscellaneous
AM 1938.1069 (L) (FIG.
    145; CS 321)
  lion-man with head up &
    Minotaur

COUNTERCLOCKWISE
2 Lions
I Supp. 94a (L) Crete
II 3.348 (L)
II 4.66 (L) "Diktaian
    Cave"
HM 888 (L) (Betts 1981a: 7
    fig. 9)
HM G 3066 (L) Mallia
    (CMCG 277)
HM G 3080 (L) (CMCG 301)
KN Strat. Museum (Ls) Knossos
    (Younger & Betts 1979:
    no. 9; Betts 1981a: 5,
    fig. 3)
  each in PT 3
Victoria & Albert 8793-1863
    (L) (Betts 1981a: 7,
    fig. 8)

2 Bulls
V 318 (L) Krisa ChT 2
    (FIG. 61; LH III B-C)
  SH horizontal = on axis
Miscellaneous
II 3.10 (L/R stone?) Knossos
    Palace
  lion-man vs stag-man
Chania 1014/1016 (Ls) Chania,
    Kastelli (Papapostolou
    1977: no. 19)
  waterbird regardant &
    argonaut
HMs 289 (Ls) Knossos (KSPI
    R3)
  2 calves

branch betw
HMs 452 (Ls) Ayia Triada
    (AT 95)
griffin & griffiness
        displayed
        groundline bel one
HMs LamdaDelta/AM 1938.1047
    (Ls) Knossos (CS 49S;
    KSPI Q15/17)
goats
    infr of one: <u>ImpTr</u>
    infr of the other:
        <u>Figure-8 Shield</u>

FIG. 62 -- X 250:
3 lions in PT 37B, cl

PT 37B

Three Animals in Radial
Symmetry, Addorsed & Regardant

CLOCKWISE
X 250 (L) (FIG. 62)
    3 lions, each in PT 3 with
        head contorted up
HMs 136 (Ls) Knossos (KSPI
        G8)
    3? quadrupeds
        man's beardless face in
            center

COUNTERCLOCKWISE
I 47 (L) Mycenae ChT 8
    3 quadrupeds (bulls?)
        <u>Branch 3</u> betw each
I 194 (L) Midea
    3 lions en face

FIG. 63 -- XIII 12:
4 bulls in PT 37C, ccl

PT 37C

Four Animals in Radial
Symmetry Addorsed & Regardant

COUNTERCLOCKWISE
I 323 (Ls) Pylos Palace (LH
        III B2-C1)
    cross quarters the field, a
        caprid in PT 6 in each
        quadrant
    an arc has been engraved
        over the center of the
        seal
XIII 12 (L) Boiotia (FIG.
        63)
    4 bulls, each in PT 5B
        cross quarters the
        field, a bull in each
        quadrant

PT 38

Attacker Before the Victim
Both in One Direction

AM 1938.1036 (L) "Athens"
    (CS 318)
  lion bef & vs bull, both
        stand L
    tree beh
    3 circles infr

FIG. 64 -- VIII 149:
lion L vs bull in PT 39A, L

PT 39A
Attacker Above the Victim
Both in One Direction

LEFT & RIGHT
I 324 (Rs) Pylos Palace (LH
    III B2-C1)
  2 pairs of griffins vs
      stags, forming PT 29A,
      flank 2 Masters (top
      Master R, bottom Master
      L; each wearing a
      Bull-Tail)

LEFT
Lion vs
  Bull
    I 100   (L) Mycenae ChT
        65
    V 678   (L) Thebes,
        Kolonaki T. 17 (LH
        III A1)
      bull in PT 13A, L
    VIII 149 (L) (FIG. 64)
    AM 1938.1064 (L) (CS
        5P)
    Berlin FG 42 (A)
        Eleusis (AGDS II
        Berlin 37)
      bull in PT 13
      couchant?
    HMs 209 (Ls) Knossos
        (KSPI G10)
      lion en face
    HM G 3033 (L) (CMCG
        311)
      small lion vs bull in
        PT 5B, L
  Agrimi
    IV 262 (L) Axos
      groundline? bel
  Miscellaneous
    X 129 (L)
      stag in PT 5B
        regardant
      Figure-8 Shield ab
        dot inb

Dog vs (see: the Sclumberger &
Morgan cylinders, below)

V 184a (L)
  dog in PT 6 vs stag
    Figure-8 Shield ab
XII 242 (Cyl) Knossos
    harbor
  SH vertical: agrimi/
    kid-man R reg
      goat head L ab at
        left
  SH horizontal (top to

bottom): lion in PT
5A, sphinx in PT 5A,
dog vs stag in PT 40,
fawn? bel -- all R
  stag in PT 11 (stag
    & fawn in PT
    16A, variant?)
filling motifs: 2 dots (=
  Figure-8 Shield?) bel
  lion; 4 dots infr of,
  & X inb of, & sign &
  stroke bel sphinx;
  Pica? bel dog; sche-
  matic Column? bel &
  schematic palm? infr
  of stag; & X or
  crossed tail inb of
  fawn
Mount-Guides top & bottom
AM 1941.119 (L)
  Palaikastro (CS 3P)
  kid in PT 6
  ImpTr ab
  Palm 1 horizontal bel
Berlin FG 18 (A) "Greek
  Islands" (AGDS II
  Berlin 38)
  quadruped (dog?) vs bull?
  en face in PT 1B &
  with a short tail

Griffin vs
Bull
  Cabinet des Medailles,
    Coll. Schlumberger
    43 (Cyl) (Pini
    1980: no. A6)
  SH horizontal: griffin
    vs bull regardant,
    both L
      Sun ab
      2 Figure-8
        Shields at
        right
  SH vertical: man stabs
    bull with a sword;
    griffin vs stag in

PT 49, both R
  dog upsidedown
    ab also vs
    stag
L. Morgan Library 1077
  (Cyl) (Pini 1980:
  no. A5)
  SH horizontal: griffin
    vs bull, both L
  2 calves/dogs in PT
    34A, L bel
  waterbird flies R
    at left
  zig-zag inb
  SH vertical: goat-man
    L with arms up
  ImpTr at left &
    waterbird (zig-
    zag bel) flies
    L, all ab
  Figure-8 Shield &
    Palm 4 infr
  2 Mount-Guides flank
    the field, top &
    bottom
Miscellaneous
  HM G 3561 (A) (CMCG 306)
  stag, head up &
    regardant

Miscellaneous vs miscellaneous
  I 395 (A) Perati ChT 4
    (LH III B-C1)
    quadruped vs quadruped
  Berlin FG 31 (L) (AGDS II
    Berlin 57)
    Fish-Monster (quadruped?)
      vs agrimi
      6 strokes infr

RIGHT (see: PT 5A, R; Filler:
  bull -- HM no. unknown [KN
  MUM Misc. 8]; PT 18B, R:
  cow & calf --IX 194; PT 39A:
  lion R vs bull/Ch. 3D: Men
  In Chariots -- Cyprus Museum
  1953/IX-3/6)

Lion vs
  Bull
    I 70   (L)   Mycenae ChT
          28
      bull en face
      tree ab
    I 185   (L)   Midea Tholos
          (LH III A1)
      lion en face vs bull
          in PT 3
      rocks/waves bel
    II 3.173   (L)   "Knossos"
      lioness en face vs
          bull in PT 6, R,
          head up
            groundline bel
    V 220   (L)   Brauron, ChT
          19 (LH III B?)
      bull in PT 6
        SH horizontal
    V 235   (Ls)   Chania,
          Kastelli
      lion in PT 14
    V 361   (L)   Medeon T.
          29 (LH III A-C)
      Branch 3 encircles
      SH horizontal
    V 602   (L)   Mycenae (LH
          III B)
      bull in PT 5B en face
    VIII 97   (L)   Dawkins
          Coll.
      bull in PT 6, R
    VIII 121   (L)   Hutchinson
          Coll.
      bull in PT 5B, R
    X 127   (L)
      lion en face vs bull
          in PT 14
    ?X 218   (L)
      Branch 1 & groundline
          bel
      SH horizontal
    X 257   (L)
      bull in PT 5B
        2 objects ab
    AM 1938.1035   (A) central

      Crete (CS 331)
      lion en face vs bull
          in PT 5B en face
    HM G 3260   (L)   (CMCG
          307)
      groundline bel
    Cyprus Museum 1953/IX-3/6
          (Cyls) Analiondas,
          surface (Pini 1980:
          no. B2)
      bull in PT 3
        2 men run R
        man in chariot
            drawn by a lion
            R
  Miscellaneous
    II 3.210   (L)   "Lyttos"
      stag in PT 11

Griffin vs
  X 125   (L)
    kid in PT 5B
  X 126   (A)
    stag in PT 6
  HMs 521   (As)   Ayia Triada (AT
        97)
    lion in PT 4, R

Miscellaneous vs miscellaneous
  I 407   (R)   Dimini Tholos
        (is this ring
        Archaic?)
    quadruped vs quadruped
  I 511   (L)   Crete
    dog vs agrimi
      Branch 2 infr
      branch ab
  X 184   (L)
    quadruped vs quadruped
      SH horizontal = on
        axis
  AM 1938.1084   (L)   Archanes
        (CS 344)
    cat vs waterbird
      displayed
      waterbird R ab regar-
        dant bel

HMs 26 (Ls) Ayia Triada
  (AT 87)
    quadruped vs quadruped
    regardant

PT 39A or PT 40

RIGHT
AM AE 695 (L) (CS GD pl. 20)
  lion vs bull in PT 5A en
  face

PT 39B

Attacker Salient
in Back of the Victim,
Both in One Direction

LEFT
Lion vs Bull
V 688 (L) Orchomenos
  2 groundlines bel
  SH horizontal
X 301* (A)
  bull in PT 10A
    forgery?
HM 2128 (L) Knossos (LM
    IB; AR 1961-2 fig. 38)
  bull in PT 5B

RIGHT
VII 68 (R)
  2 agrimia copulating
    rocks bel

FIG. 65 -- I 204:
lion L vs bull in PT 39C, L

PT 39C

Victim Both Salient Behind
Attacker in One Direction

LEFT
Lion vs Bull
I 204 (L) Argos ChT 7
    (FIG. 65; LH III A)
  bull in PT 2
VIII 89 (L) Dawkins Coll.
  bull in PT 5B
    groundline bel

RIGHT
I 252 (L) Vapheio Tholos (LH
    IIA)
  lion vs bull
    rocks bel
AM AE 1787 (L) (CS 372)
  (lion vs ?) goat in PT 1B

PT 40
Attacker Above a Regardant
Victim, Both in One Direction

LEFT
Lion vs
  Bull
    I 214 (L) Prosymna ChT
        XLI (LH III B1)
      lion in PT 14A vs
            bull in PT 10
        Picas? ab
    II 4.80 (L)
    V 424 (Scarab) Lefkandi
        (LH III C early)
    V 435 (L) Nichoria
          Tholos (LH III
          A2-B1)
      bull couchant
    VII 237 (L)
    HMs 293 (Ls) Knossos
        (KSPI R4)
      bull in PT 5D, L
  Miscellaneous
    X 271 (L) Crete
      calf in PT 5C
    XII 285 (L) Seager
          Coll.
        agrimi, head
          contorted

Dog vs
X 158 (L)
  kid in PT 5C
    SH oblique: lower left to
      upper right
Munich A.1192 (A) bought in
      Istanbul (AGDS I Munich
      37)
  male dog vs agrimi in PT 4
  groundline bel

FIG. 66 -- V 660:
lion R vs bull in PT 40, R

RIGHT (see: PT 18B, R: cow &
calf -- IX 156)

Lion vs
  Bull
    I 310 (Ls) Pylos Palace
      (LH III B2-C1)
    II 3.129 (L) Katsamba
      T. B (LM III A1)
    II 3.333 (L)
    IV 259 (L) Tsoutsouros
      bull in PT 5C
    V 660 (L) Salamis,
        Gymnasium ChT Theta
        (**FIG. 66**; LH III
        A1-C)
      lion in PT 12 en face
        SH horizontal
    VII 260 (L)
      lion en face
    IX 142 (L)
      bull with stag horn
    X 241 (A/L; unique
        shape)
      bull in PT 5C
        inverted V infr
        Fence betw (see:
        Ch. 13A: Fence)

XIII 21D (L)
   SH horizontal
HM 2243 (L) Olous T.
      24 (EtCretoises 8,
      10-11, 41, title p.
      ill., pls. 37 & 47)
   bull in PT 5B
HMs 310 (Ls) Knossos
      (KSPI R42)
Miscellaneous caprids
   I 193b (Pr) Midea ChT
      10 (LH II-III A)
   agrimi
   II 3.100 (L) Kalyvia T.
      1 (LM III A1)
   caprid in PT 6, R
   II 4.219 (L)
   agrimi kid in PT 6, R
AM 1941.89 (L) (CS 4P)
   stag
Munich acc. 21768 (L)
      (AGDS I Munich
   44)
   caprid (unfinished)

FIG. 67 -- IX 195:
dog R vs agrimi in PT 41

PT 41
Attacker Above the Victim,
Both in Opposite Directions

ATTACKER LEFT (see: PT 12, L:
   lion -- AM 1941.1241)

Lion vs
   ?I 333 (Ls) Pylos Palace
      (LH III B2-C1)
   quadruped
   II 3.334 (L)
      griffin in PT 14A, L, one
      wing up, vs bull in
      PT 5B, R
   HMs 205 (clay Conoid Stamp
      Seal) Knossos Palace
      (KSPI O1; Pini 1984:
      78-9 pl. XV)
      lion in PT 13A, L vs
      calf in PT 5A, R

ATTACKER RIGHT
Lion vs
   Bull
      HMs 106 (Ls) Knossos
         (KSPI O3)
         lion in PT 12, R
      ?NMA no. unknown (L)
         Tiryns (AJA 30,
         1926, 442)
   Miscellaneous
      V 265 (L) Armenoi T.
         40 (LM III B1[-2])
      caprid
      Berlin FG 15 (L)
         "Athens" (AGDS II
         Berlin 34)
         lion in PT 12 en face
         vs stag

Dog vs
VII 160 (L) Calabria
   cow & calf in PT 18B
IX 195 (L) (**FIG. 67**)
   agrimi
      2 groundlines ab
      SH horizontal = on axis

Miscellaneous vs miscellaneous
Berlin FG 51 (C) Syme (AGDS

II Berlin 33)
griffin displayed vs
kneeling kid

FIG. 68 -- Cylinder from
Koukounara:
dog vs agrimi in PT 42A, R

PT 42A
Attacker Bel the Victim,
Both in One Direction

LEFT
Dog vs
I 363   (A/Ls?)   Pylos Palace
(LH III B2-C1; inscribed:
PY Wr 1358-1360)
stag
Tree 1 infr
spear? ab
HMs 132   (As)   Knossos (KSPI
P73)
deer in PT 4
tree inb

RIGHT
Lion vs
II 3.44   (L)   Zafer Papoura T.
99 (LM III B1)
lion en face vs bull
VII 125   (L)   Crete
agrimi

Sacred Knot bel
HMs 328/1008   (Ls)   Knossos
(Betts 66)
lion en face vs quadruped

Dog vs Agrimi
I 308   (A/Rs)   Pylos Palace (LH
III B2-C1; inscribed PY Wr
1457+01 "apudosi")
XIII 71   (L)
kid in PT 2
Pylos no. unknown (Cyl)   Koukounara, Phyties Tholos 2
(FIG. 68; LH IIA; Korres
1974: 151 pl. IIIa3-b)
both in PT 3

PT 42B
Attacker Regardant Bel the
Victim, Both in One Direction

LEFT
I 190   (L)   Midea ChT 8 (LH
IIA/Palace Style)
lion vs bull in PT 5C

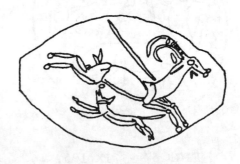

FIG. 69 -- XII 15D:
dog L vs agrimi in PT 43, L

PT 43
Attacker Bel the Victim
Both in Opposite Directions

ATTACKER LEFT (see: Ch. 3E:
Animal Games [bull-leaping,
Diving] -- AM 1938.1074 [CS
209])

Dog vs agrimi in PT 3
V 726   (L)   Mega Monastiri T.
Gamma (LH III A-B)
strokes ab
XII 15D   (A)   (**FIG. 69**)
Pica ab in shoulder

Miscellaneous vs miscellaneous
AM 1938.1059   (L)   Crete (CS
319)
lion en face vs agrimi
goat head L ab

ATTACKER RIGHT
HMs no. unknown 85   (As)   Ayia
Triada (AT 85)
2 dogs/lionesses

PT 44A
Attacker Bef a Pendant
Victim, Both in One Direction

ATTACKER LEFT
Lion en face vs bull
I 116   (L)   ChT 83
II 3.60   (L)   Ayios Ioannes T.
2 (LM IB-II)
V 194   (L)   Thebes?
bull's head cut off by the
sealstone's rim
V 436   (L)   Nichoria Tholos
(LH III A2-B1)
2 groundlines bel bull
AM AE 1230   (L)   Ayia Pelagia

Tholos   (CS 14P)
HMp 4798-4802   (As on a loom-
weight) Palaikastro
(Hutchinson 1939-40: 49 no.
38 fig. 23)

Miscellaneous
AM 696   (L)   Diktaian cave
(CS 324)
Minotaur vs caprid?

FIG. 70 -- I 278:
lion R vs bull PT 44A

ATTACKER RIGHT
Lion en face vs bull
I 36   (L)   Mycenae
I 278   (L)   Rutsi Tholos 2
(**FIG. 70**; LH II-III A)
I 384   (L)   Menidi Tholos
(LH III B)
II 1.419   (clay L? attached
to a clay stamp) Mallia,
Chrysolakkos (MM I-II?)
II 3.283   (L)   Palaikastro area
groundline bel at left
X 131   (A)
2? pairs of Mount-Guides
flank?
XII 213   (A)   Seager Coll.
lion in PT 14A vs kid/calf
2 pairs of Mount-Guides

flank
XIII 58 (L) Munich A.1186
    (L) (AGDS I Munich 40)

Miscellaneous
NMA no. unknown (L) Asine
    ChT 1 (LH III C1;
    Frodin & Persson, 1938:
    374 fig 242.2)
    lion vs calf (neck & head
    only)

                PT 44B
          Attacker & a Pendent
        Victim, Both in Opposite
              Directions

ATTACKER LEFT
I 77 (L) Mycenae ChT 42
    lion-man L vs kid? protome
    bel upsidedown

ATTACKER RIGHT
I 251 (L) Vapheio Tholos (LH
    IIA)
    lion R vs bull bef

                PT 45

      Attacker Pendent Above Victim

VICTIM LEFT
Griffin displayed vs
Lion
    AM 1971.1137 (L) (Boardman
        1973: no. 8)
        cub? infr of the lion
    II 4.73 (L)
Bull
    XII 228 (L) Seager
    Coll. (**FIG. 71**)

AM 1941.130 (L) Sybrita
    (CS 366)
    bull in PT 14A, L

FIG. 71 -- XII 228:
Griffin vs bull L in PT 45

VICTIM RIGHT
Griffin vs (see: PT 41:
    griffin vs bull -- II 3.334)

II 3.25b (L) Knossos, South
    House? (LM IB)
    griffin displayed & boar
    form PT 36 cl
Berlin FG 43 (A) "Athens"
    (AGDS II Berlin 36)
    griffin displayed & en face
    vs lion in PT 4, R

                PT 46

      Attacker Salient in Front of
        Victim, Both in Opposite
              Directions

ATTACKER LEFT (cf. Ch. 3C: Man
    Hunts Animals [lion] --
    I 9)

Lion vs
VII 115a (Pr) (FIG. 72)
    bull in PT 1D, R
        Frond ab groundline ab
IX 148 (L)
    griffin in PT 1A, R
        Sun ab
AM 1938.1153h:A (Ls) Knossos
    Palace (Pini 1982; the
    sealing was also
    impressed twice by a
    rectangular bar seal
    carrying hieroglyphs)
    2 bulls in PT 25B or, if the
        lion was engraved bef,
        PT 30A
        Dado 2e bel

Miscellaneous vs miscellaneous
HMs 90 (Ls) Kato Zakro (KZ
    164)
    genius L at right vs
        bird displayed

FIG. 72 -- VII 115a:
lion L vs bull in PT 46

ATTACKER RIGHT
Lion vs bull
I 253 (R) Vapheio Tholos
    (LH IIA)
    rocks bel
        Palm 1 beh bull & at right
I 388 (AP1) Menidi Tholos
    (LH III B)
    bull in PT 5C, R

Miscellaneous vs miscellaneous
IX 20D (L)
    griffin R vs stag in PT 6,
        L, head contorted
        V (= seagull-like bird?)
            ab
        Table bel

PT 47A
Attacker in Front of Salient
    Victim Antithetic

ATTACKER LEFT
XII 271 (L) Seager Coll.
    lion vs kid?

ATTACKER RIGHT
XII 265 (L) Seager Coll.
    dog vs bull (cf. Ch. 6B:
        Genii with Animals)
    with SH horizontal =
        bull in PT 14A, L
    with SH vertical =
        Figure-8 Shield at
        top left, dot at
        bottom left;
        groundline bel
AM 1941.129 (L) (CS 347)
    griffin vs lion upside
        down?
        SH horizontal?

FIG. 73 -- VIII 154:
lion L vs agrimi kid in PT 47B

PT 47B
Attacker in Back of Salient
Victim Both in One
Direction

ATTACKER LEFT
Griffin vs
V 642 (C) Gouvalari Tholos 1
    (LH IIA/III B?)
   stag in PT 4
   <u>Mount-Guide</u> inb
XII 291 (L) Seager Coll.
   <u>Babylonian Dragon</u>
      2 groundlines ab & bel
         (= <u>Mount-Guides</u> flank-
         ing the monster)
      <u>Weed</u> at left
      SH horizontal
HMs 51 (Ls) Kato Zakro (KZ
    183)
   griffin in PT 3, L vs
      agrimi at left infr

Lion vs
VIII 154 (L) (FIG. 73)
   agrimi kid
AM 1938.1083 (A) Mirabello
   (CS 328)

lion en face vs displayed
     bird
   <u>Frond</u> & <u>Branch 1</u> ab
HMs no. unknown (R?s) Ayia
   Triada (AT 98)
   lion? vs agrimi at left
    kid R
    rocks bel

ATTACKER RIGHT
?HM G 3278 (L) Knossos (CMCG
   380)
   genius R holds stag upside
    down in PT 6
Edith Eccles Coll. (L) (Betts
   1979: 277-8; 1981a: 10
   fig. 14)
   en face vs kid
    zig-zags ab

FIG. 74 -- VII 180:
lion vs agrimi in PT 48A

PT 48A

Attacker & Victim Salient &
Antithetic

Lion vs
VII 180 (L) (FIG. 74)
   lion at right vs agrimi at
    left regardant

at left man's head L
dots betw
<u>Figure-8 Shield</u> bel
SH horizontal
Munich A.1181 (L) (AGDS I
Munich 46)
lion at right vs stag at
left regardant
upside down <u>Dado 4?</u> bel

PT 48B

Attacker Regardant & Victim,
Both Salient & Addorsed

**Lion at right vs bull at left,
regardant**

Berlin FG 17 (L) (AGDS II
Berlin 35)
bull en face

FIG. 75 -- XIII 26:
lioness vs bull in PT 49A, R

PT 49A
Attacker Upside Down Bel
Victim, Both Antithetic & in
One Direction

LEFT
I 330 (Ls) Pylos Palace (LH
III B2-C1)
lion vs bull

RIGHT
Lion vs
I 286 (L) Rutsi Tholos 2
(LH II-IIIA)
lion vs bull in PT 6
<u>Pica</u> ab bull in the back
groundline bel
XIII 26 (L) (**FIG. 75**)
lioness in PT 13A en face vs
bull
XIII 4D (L)
in PT 13A en face vs bull
HMs no. unknown (As) Ayia
Triada (AT 89)
caprid
rocks bel
HMs no. unknown (As) Ayia
Triada (AT 90)
lion? vs bull?

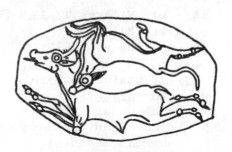

FIG. 76 -- VII 96:
dog vs bull in PT 49B, R

PT 49B
Attacker Bel Upside Down
Victim, Both Addorsed & in One
Direction

LEFT
Lion vs kid
I 182   (L)   Midea Tholos (LH
    III A1)
Figure-8 Shield bel
II 4.182   (L)   "Knossos"
    small quadruped vs stag
    (dog?)
V 428   (L)   Veve Tholos
AM 1971.1136   (C)   (Boardman
    1973: no. 7)

Miscellaneous
I 267   (L)   Tragana Tholos 2
    (LH III A)
    bull vs bull
V 649   (L)   Crete
    dog vs goat
        Figure-8 Shield betw
HM G 3112   (L)   Knossos
    (CMCG 309)
    lion vs caprid
HM G 3527   (L)   (CMCG 310)
    quadruped vs quadruped

RIGHT
Lion vs
II 4.58   (L)   Milatos T. 1
    (LM III B1)
    lion? en face vs bull? in PT
    5B
        Tree 1 upside down infr
        (the Tree 1 reveals
        the actual composi-
        tion: lion upside down
        ab bull, both L)
II 4.167   (L)   Mallia, Maison E
    small lion en face vs stag
        in PT 5B regardant
IV 285   (L)   Knossos
    agrimi kid
    lion en face

XII 243   (L)   Seager Coll.
    small lion vs bull
AM 1941.148   (L)   (CS 370)
    bull

Dog vs
VII 96   (A)   (FIG. 76)
    R vs bull in PT 3, L
        photo of reverse is that
        of VII 87)

Miscellaneous
I 335   (Ls)   Pylos Palace
    (LH III B2-C1)
    2 quadrupeds
V 209   (L)   Crete, Arkades
    genius carries agrimi
    kid R

PT 50A

Attacker & Victim
in Radial Symmetry, Antithetic

COUNTERCLOCKWISE
I 303   (Ls)   Pylos Palace (LH
    III B2-C1)
    lion R vs goat

PT 50B

Attacker & Victim in Radial
Symmetry, Addorsed

ATTACKER LEFT/CLOCKWISE
Lion vs
    Bull
        I 254   (L)   Vapheio
            Tholos (LH IIA)
            lion en face vs bull?
            R

II 4.25 (L) "Tylissos"
   lion vs bull?
HM no. unknown (L)
     Knossos, MUM
     (Popham et al.
     1984: pl. 187b,
     Misc. 2)
   cl, lion regardant vs
     bull in PT 5B
Caprid
   X 128 (L) (FIG. 77)
     lion in PT 2, L vs
       stag
     <u>Figure-8 Shield</u>
       bel
   X 279 (L)
     lioness regardant vs
       2 deer (1 deer
       ab & 1 deer
       protome)
     SH horizontal

FIG. 77 -- X 128:
lion L vs stag in PT 50B

Miscellaneous vs miscellaneous
I 510 (L) Crete
   quadruped R vs quadruped in
     PT 6, L
VIII 150 (L)
   dog L vs stag in PT 6, L
HMs 636/647 (Ls) Sklavokambos
     (Sk 10)
   quadruped (bull?)
HM G 3259 (L) Knossos (CMCG
     290)
   couchant vs quadruped

FIG. 78 -- II 4.202:
lioness & cub vs agrimi
in PT 51A, R

PT 51A
Victim in PT 1A;
One Attacker Ab in PT 39A,
Another Bel in PT 42A

ATTACKER RIGHT/COUNTERCLOCKWISE
II 3.25a (L) Knossos, South
     House? (LM IB)
   griffin R vs stag in PT 13,
     both forming PT 34B
IV 302 (L) Spilia
   lion in PT 8, R vs
     quadruped
HM G 3100 (L) (CMCG 291)
   small lion
     couchant vs bull

LEFT
II 4.202 (L) Diktaian Cave
     (Xanthoudides 1907
     pl. 8.116)

2 lions en face vs bull in
    PT 3
    <u>Weed</u> infr
    plant ab
    <u>ImpTr</u> bel

RIGHT
II 3.99 (L) Kalyvia T. 1
    (**FIG. 78**; LM III A1)
    lioness & cub vs agrimi
        salient R regardant
        rocks bel agrimi
AM 1938.861 (Ls) Knossos
    Palace (KSPI G15; CS 50S;
    KN Ws δ152, countermarked
    with LANA & inscribed
    with ne-ki-ri-de =
    "shroud"? [BSA 57, 1962,
    53-4])
    2 lions en face vs bull

FIG. 79 -- AM 1925.128:
lion & dog vs agrimi
    in PT 51B, L

PT 51B
Victim in PT 2
One Attacker Ab in PT 40,
    Another Bel in PT 42A

LEFT
AM 1925.128 (L) (**FIG. 79**; CS
    6P)
    lion ab & dog bel vs agrimi
        in PT 6, L
    <u>Figure-8 Shield</u> bel dog

FIG. 80 -- I 412:
2 dogs vs stag R in PT 51C

PT 51C
Victim in PT 1A
One Attacker Ab in PT 39A,
    Another Bel in PT 43

VICTIM LEFT
2 Dogs vs agrimi
AM 1938.1063 (L) east Crete
    (CS 349)
    kid in PT 6
        puppy bel turned 90
            degrees
        object bel
        SH horizontal
Hannover 1973.2 (L) Argolid
    (AGDS IV Hannover 7)
    agrimi in PT 2 (the dog ab
        is in PT 4, R)
    rocks bel
BSA Cast 170 (L)
    kid in PT 3, L

Miscellaneous vs miscellaneous
  VII 175   (L)
      bird ab & dog
        bel vs agrimi in
        PT 6, L

VICTIM RIGHT (see: PT 18B, R:
cow & calf -- IX 194)

2 Dogs vs
I 412 (L) Syros (**FIG. 80**)
  stag?
    <u>Figure-8 Shield</u> in the
        center
      dog ab upside down
I Supp. 96 (L) Crete
    2 dogs? in PT 37A, cl vs
    boar in PT 5A, R
X 130 (L)
    kid
        tree infr

FIG. 81 -- XII 251:
2 lions vs bull in PT 51D, R

                PT 51D
          Victim in PT 1A
    One Attacker Ab in PT 39B,
    Another Bel in PT 42C

RIGHT
2 Lions vs bull
    XII 251 (L) (**FIG. 81**)
      bull in PT 5C
        bottom lion upside
            down
    HMs 1097 (As) Myrtos
        Pyrgos, Shrine (Hagg &
        Marinatos 1981: 171
        fig. 2)
      bull in PT 5D, R

FIG. 82 -- I 186:
2 lions vs bull R in PT 51E

                PT 51E
          Victim Regardant
    One Attacker Infr, & Another
        Inb, Both Salient

VICTIM LEFT
HMs 113 (Ls) Knossos Palace
        (KSPI G11)
    2 lions vs bull in PT 6, R

VICTIM RIGHT
I 186 (L) Midea Tholos (**FIG.**

82; LH III A1)
2 lions vs bull in PT 2, R

FIG. 83 -- V 313:
2 lion cubs vs bull L in PT 51F

PT 51F
Victim Regardant
Two Attackers Antithetic
Leap Ab

VICTIM LEFT
V 313 (L) Delos (**FIG. 83**)
    2 lionesses or cubs vs bull
      in PT 6, L

VICTIM RIGHT
HMs 255 +? (Rs) Knossos
      (Pini 1973)
    2 griffins vs stag in
      PT 6, R
      <u>Sun</u> flanked by 2 baby
      griffins? ab

PT 52A
Two Attackers Stand Antithetic
Ab Victim

VICTIM LEFT
VII 176 (L)
    dog & cat ab vs calf in PT
    1B, L

VICTIM RIGHT
V 216 (L) Brauron
    2 griffins stand on the
      stomach of a bull up-
      side down in PT 5C, R
      <u>Frond</u>/<u>Pica</u> in bull's back
AM 1938.1075 (L) Crete (CS
      342)
    2 griffins, each in PT 1B vs
      bull en face in PT
      13B, L
      the griffins flank Lin. B
      *125 (CYPERUS)

FIG. 84 -- I 81:
2 dogs vs stag in PT 52B, L

PT 52B
Two Attackers Stand Salient
& Antithetic Over Victim

I 81 (L) Mycenae ChT 47
    (**FIG. 83**)
    2 dogs vs stag in PT 11, L
V 596 (Ls) Mycenae, House of
    the Idols (LH III B2)

2 griffins vs quadruped
(bull?) in PT 1A, L/5A, L

FIG. 85 -- IX 145:
2 dogs vs kid L in PT 53

FIG. 86 -- XIII 20:
2 lions vs stag in PT 54

PT 54

Two Attackers Salient &
Antithetic Flank a
Salient Victim

PT 53
Two Attackers Pendant Ab
Victim

VICTIM LEFT
IX 145 (L) **(FIG. 84)**
    2 dogs vs kid in PT 10B, L
        regardant
    SH horizontal

VICTIM RIGHT
2 Dogs vs
VII 117 (L)
    dogs in PT 34B vs kid in PT
    5B, L
AM 1938.1065 (L) (CS 350)
    2 addorsed dogs vs agrimi
        kid in PT 6, R
    ImpTr inb
HMs 300/NH (Ls) Knossos
    Palace (KSPI R12/14/27)
    agrimi kid
        ImpTr betw the dogs

2 Lions vs
I 368 (Ls) Pylos Palace (LH
    III B2-C1)
    bull L & regardant
II 4.30 (L) "Poros"
    caprid R
IV 293 (L) Vonni
    vs? man (Master of lions?;
    see Ch. 3B: Master of
    Animals)
VII 181 (L)
    vs bull in PT 6
?IX 135 (L)
    2? lions vs salient calf L
    SH unfinished
XIII 20 (L) Mycenae
    (FIG. 86)
    2 lions vs stag salient R
        with head contorted
        back
    groundline bel

Miscellaneous vs miscellaneous
I Supp. 109 (L)
   2 dogs vs stag in PT 6, R
      with SH horizontal
VII 116 (L) Ialysos
   griffin at left & lion at
      right en face vs a bull
           en face L

CHAPTER 2
People

2A
Parts of the Human Body

FIG. 87 -- V 431
man's face

FIG. 88 -- HMs 179a (KSPI P71):
man's head

Man's Face, Beardless (see:
PT 36 c1 -- II 3.115; Ch.
2B: Men [battles] -- I 16;
Ch. 3B: Master of Animals
[lions] I 89; Ch. 6A:

People-Animals [sphinxes] --
HMs 10a & 50a)

II 3.88 (L) Knossos
cow & calf in PT 18B, L
ab: 2 waterbirds flank
a man's face
V 431 (L) Nichoria Tholos
(**FIG. 87;** LH III A2-B1)
long hair, pleated hem of
tunic at neck
SH horizontal
HMs 10a (Ls) Kato Zakro
(KZ 78)
male sphinx
HMs 50a (Ls) Kato Zakro
(KZ 76)
male sphinx?
corona beh
HMs 653 (Ls) Knossos, Little
Palace? (KSPI U?)
ab & betw the horns of a
bull face flanked? by 2
objects
HMs 654 (Ls) Knossos, Little
Palace (KSPI U106)
flanked by 2 waterbirds
ccl, feet to center
waterbird at right
regardant
Nafplion no. unknown (Heart-
shaped pendant) Tiryns,
Geometric T. 1972.6 (AAA
7, 1974, 24, fig. 22)

Man's Head
Beardless
Frontal
HM 2807a (D) Knossos
Strat. Mus. Extension
(Warren 1980;
Weingarten 1983;
141 & 10: "reel-
shaped")
To Left (see: PT 48A: VII
180)

X 278* (A)
  at right: boy's head,
    L
  center: bearded man's
    head, R
  both wear circular
    earrings
  unfinished object ab
Berlin FG 122 (D)
  "Athens" (AGDS II
  Berlin 13)
To Right
  IX 6Da (Pr)
    boy's?
  XIII 22D (L) Mycenae
    heads cl from man's
      head: horse?,
      boar, bull?, dog,
      goat, agrimi; all
      R
    center faces: bull ab
      central lion
    rocks bel
    SH horizontal?
  HM G 3211 (L) (CMCG
    338)
    lion in PT 1A, R
    horse protome (as if
      in PT 1B) R infr
    man's head ab
  HMs 26b (Ls) Kato Zakro
    (KZ 70)
    palm/feathers inb
      (= Harpy?)
  HMs 179a (Ds) Knossos
    Palace (**FIG. 88**)
    (KSPI P71; GGFR pl.
    14)
  HMs 180a (Ds) Knossos
    Palace (KSPI Pf;
    GGFR pl. 15)
    boy's?
  New York Metropolitan
    26.31.218 (D)
    SH vertical

Bearded (see: Ch. 3: Master of
Animals [lions] -- I 89)

To Right
  I 5 (D) Mycenae ShGr
    Gamma (MH-LH I)
  II 3.13a (D) Knossos,
    Little Palace
    SH horizontal
  VIII 110b (APr)
    with a circular
      earring
    bow (at left) & arrow
      (at right) bel
    SH vertical
  IX 6Db (Pr)
  X 278* (A)
    center: bearded man's
      head, R
    at right: beardless
      boy's head, L
    both wear circular
      earrings
    unfinished object ab
  XIII 22D (L) Mycenae
    man's & animal heads
      (goat, dog, bull,
      boar, agrimi,
      horse)
    center faces: bull
      ab central lion
    rocks bel
    SH horizontal?
  AM 1971.1148 (L) de
    Jong Coll. (Boardman
    1973: no. 2)

To Left
  II 3.196 (L) Anopolis
    Pediada
    man's & 3 animal
      heads (all bulls?)

Woman's Head (see Ch. 2A: Body
Parts [man's face] --
HMs 26b [KZ 70], above)

IX 6Dc (Pr)
person (woman's ?) head R

Face Parts (see: Ch. 2C:
Women [single] -- AM
1919.56)

HM G 3298 (A) Messara (CMCG
426)
eye ab an ear?
2 dot-rosettes flank

FIG. 89 -- HMs 153 (KSPI R102)
braceleted hand holds a <u>Lily</u>

Parts of the Body (see Ch.
3D: [men in chariots] --
II 3.199; Ch. 6A: People-
Animals [animal-people]
woman] -- HMs 55a [KZ 46],
[squatting human legs] --
HMs 10b [KZ 48], 27b [KZ
45])

HMs 54 (Ls) Kato Zakro
(KZ 47)
3 hands, each with bracelet
top & bottom hand to
left, middle to hand
HMs 153 (Ls) Knossos Palace
(**FIG. 89**; KSPI R102)
right hand from the right

holds a <u>Lily</u> & wears
a double strand
bracelet

2B

Men

Scenes possibly secular & non-military

Single (see: Ch. 3A: Man &
Animals [bird] -- AM
1938.1050 & HMs 134)

Carrying an Ax
I 225 (A) Vapheio
Tholos
man L salutes,
carrying lunate
ax
the lunate,
open-work
blade is
presumably
not Aegean,
though such a
lunate ax was
found in the
cist
(Tsountas
1899: pl.
8.1;
Catling
1964:
104)
SH vertical
II 3.147 (A) Mallia
man R in a long robe
groundline bel
SH vertical
II 3.198 (A) Vathy
Pediados
man L, regardant,

holds lunate ax
(see I 225
above)
SH vertical
HMs 133 (As) Knossos
Palace (KSPI 02)
man L
fish upside down
inb
groundline bel
Miscellaneous
I 68 (A/Cyl) Mycenae
ChT 27
man stands R, arms
akimbo, holding
a leash? (for a
leashed animal
[griffin?];
unfinished?)
SH vertical (for
shape of cf.
Ch. 8G: Sacred
Knots/Robes --
I 205)
I 107 (Cyl) Mycenae
ChT 68
man R flanked by 5
Columns
I Supp 169a (Pr)
SH horizontal:
acrobat in PT 14A,
L
SH vertical: papyrus,
at right
XIII 16Db (D)
frontal with legs
spread?
SH vertical?
Chania 1563 (Rs, axis
vertical) Chania,
Kastelli (LM 1B [-
II?]; Hallagar
1985)
4 zones, top to
bottom:
4: man stands left,
his left arm

akimbo, his
right stretched
out holding a
staff or spear
(point down)
infr
wears kilt &
boots, a
necklace,
a bracelet
& arm
bracelet
on his
left arm
infr of the
staff, ob-
ject ab &
human leg?
bel
inb, a bull's
head? R
3: he stands on
the roof of a
central 2-storey
building atop a
gate? built on a
large rock?/
mountaintop?
(zone 2) &
flanked symme-
trically by 2
building units,
each consisting
of (from center
out) a 3-storey,
a 1-storey, & a
2-storey buil-
ding, all with
windows & topped
by rounded mer-
lins (HC?); 2
parts of a (con-
tinuous?) wall
flanks the
rock?/mountain-
top? each part
with a large

(closed?) gate
with half-
rosette frieze
over the lintel
2: central rock?/
mountain-top?
spreading thinly
to either side
for ground with
arcades
projecting down
1: net/reticulation
with loops
filling the
diamonds (=
water?)
HM no. unknown (C)
Archanes,
Anemospilia Temple
(MM IIIb [LM I?];
Sakellarakis 1981:
220, fig. on 221)
man R poles boat R
with animal-head
(regardant) stern
aegis
HMs 91 (R?s) Kato Zakro
(KZ 196)
man stands L holds
staff inb
at right: vertical
stroke?
groundline bel
HMs 171 (Ls) Kato Zakro
(KZ 171)
man (frontal) squats
HMs 1017 (?s) Knossos
Palace (Betts 53)
man (supine L, knees
up, L)
groundline bel?
HMs no. unknown (Ls)
Kato Zakro (KZ 187)
man

2 Men
Acrobats
I 131 (L) Mycenae
ChT 91 (LH II)
2 men, head down
3 Lotos/Papyrus
flowers betw,
2 groundlines
(= Mount-Guides)
bel each man
Boxers
HMs 336 (Rs?) Knossos
Palace (KSPI L50)
L-R: man? fallen,
man stands L with
clenched? fists,
lower part of a
Pylon with Pylon
box
Sailors
I Supp. 167 (A)
"Thebes"
pole L a boat out-
fitted with a cabin
at right & a
branch-headed prow
at left & stern
at right
V 184b (L)
in a boat R
bird flies R
regardant ab
Stand/Walk
Left
AM 1953.122 (L)
"Gaza" (CS 37P)
both men in long
robes
later line cuts
obliquely
across the face
SH horizontal
HMs 611 (Ls) (Skla-
vokambos (Sk 1)
Right
HMs 18a (Ls) Kato
Zakro (KZ 186)

Dado 2b bel
HMs no. unknown (Ls)
    Kato Zakro (KZ 8)
Miscellaneous
    I Supp. 113 (A/Cyl)
        2 men greet
            at left: man in
                long robe
            at right: man
                in kilt

FIG. 90 -- HMs 343 (KSPI L47):
        warrior & dog

3 or More Men
    Sailors
        I Supp. 193 (Rs?)
            Pylos Palace
            3 men (busts) L in a
                boat?
                the legs of a man
                    L ab the
                    gunwale in the
                    center
        HMs 242 (Ls) Knossos
            Palace (KSPI R50)
            2 registers, separa-
            ted by a line: 5
                (top) + 6
                (bottom) men row R

FIG. 91 -- AM 1938.1049
        (CS 294): archer

Military Scenes
Single
    Warrior
        HMs 343 (C?s) Knossos
            Palace (FIG. 90;
            KSPI L47)
            man walks R holding a
                small Tower
                Shield on his
                left arm &? a
                spear (although
                the spear
                appears to be
                beh) & wears a
                conical helmet
                collared dog
                walks R bef
    Archer
        AM 1938.1049 (A)
            Knossos (FIG. 91;
            CS 294)
            man L carries a bow?
                beh, the tip of
                which shows
                above his
                shoulder
            a single Mount-
                Guide at the

the top (bottom?
     now chipped
     away)
SH vertical
HMs 69 (As) Ayia Triada
     (AT 112)
man kneels L & holds
     bow
SH vertical
Miscellaneous
     V 239 (L) Chania,
          Kastelli (LM III
          B?)
     man carries a <u>Figure-
          8 Shield</u>, arms
          outstretched
     2 strokes/lances/
          spears flank
     SH horizontal
XIII 137 (L)
     man frontal, arms
          out, wears
          <u>Figure-8 Shield</u>
     2 vertical strokes/
          spears flank
     SH horizontal
HMs 337 (Rs) Knossos
     Palace (KSPI L49)
man on boat L carries
     a spear, an object
     at right (cabin?
     rigging?)
animal-head prow
     aegis of 2nd boat
     R bel

2 Men
     Wear <u>Figure-8 Shields</u>
     II 3.32 (L) Mavrospelio
          T. VII
     walk L, wearing
          plumed boar's tusk
          helmets
     man at left holds
          spear upright
          infr
XIII 136 (L)

walk L
     SH horizontal
HMs 459 (Cs) Ayia
     Triada (AT 116)
arms up
     2 vertical lines
     flank

FIG. 92 -- V 643: 2 duelists

Duel
     Both Duelists Equal
     V 643 (C) Gouvalari
          Tholos 1 (FIG.
          92) (LH IIA/III
          B?)
     each has a dagger &
          a sword with a
          feathered plume
          (=scabbard?)
     Berlin FG 6 (L)
          Athens (AGDS II
          Berlin 25)
     2 men run center
          each with a
          sword; 1 arm
          touches the
          other's face;
          man at right
          regardant
     a dot bel each,
          betw the legs of

each, & at right

FIG. 93 -- VII 129:
2 duelists

Frond ab L
SH horizontal?

FIG. 94 -- I 11: 2 duelists

Left Duelist Dominant
        (see: Ch. 2B: Men
        [battles] --   IX
        158, & HMs 8a [KZ
        12/13])
?V 180b   (L)
        man at left: holds
            his sword ab
            his head
        man at right:
            Figure-8 Shield
            & sword
        SH horizontal
VII 129   (L)   Crete
        (FIG. 93)
        man at left:
            sword, scabbard
        man at right:
            spear, Tower
            Shield
XII 292   (L)   Seager
        Coll.
        man at left: sword
        man at right:
            helmet, Tower
            Shield, spear

Right Duelist Dominant
        (see: Ch. 2B: Men
        [battles] -- I 16)

I 11   (C) Mycenae
        ShGr III (FIG.
        94; LH I)
        man at left:
            helmet, Figure-8
            Shield, lance
        man at right:
            sword, scabbard
I 12   (A) Mycenae
        ShGr III (LH I)
        man at left:
            Figure-8
            Shield, helmet
        man at right:
            Figure-8 Shield,
            helmet, sword
        branch? at right
        2 groundlines bel
XII D   (L)   Seager
        Coll.
        man at left: helmet
        man at right:
            Figure-8 Shield,

sword
SH horizontal?
HMs 43 (Cs?) Kato
    Zakro (KZ 14)
man at left:
    falling
man at right: stabs
    the other with
    a spear
?HMs 190 (Ls) Kato
    Zakro (KZ 190)
man at left:
        fallen?
        supine R?
    Branch 1 inb
man at right:
    hurls spear L
HMs no. unknown (Ls)
    Ayia Triada (AT
    115)
man at left:
    fallen
man at right:
    holds 1 sword
    in the crook of
    his arm &
    wields another
    with his right
    hand

3 or More Men
  Processions
    HMs 260 (Rs?) Knossos
        Palace (**FIG. 95**;
        KSPI R60 + 63)
      L-R: man R (playing a
        flute-like
        instrument?) & 3
        men, all R, each
        with a Figure-8
        Shield (&
        helmet?); the
        the helmeted
        center man also
        holds a staff infr
    HMs 362 (Rs) Knossos
        Palace B (KSPI K16)
      3 men walk R, each
        with a Figure-8
        Shield
      2 horizontal lines
        beh
      groundline & Dado
        9a bel

FIG. 96 -- I 263: battle

Battles
  I 16 (R) Mycenae ShGr
        IV (LH I)
    in center: duel
        dominant man at

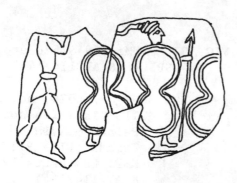

FIG. 95 -- HMs 260 (KSPI R60):
frieze of warriors

right: helmet &
dagger; man at
left: sword
man at left:
helmeted, inb of
Tower Shield, aims
lance at the
dominant duelist
man at right: bearded
& nude, sits L
rocks surround the
scene
?I 263 (L) Tragana
Tholos 1 (FIG. 96;
LH III A1; now
Chora Mus. 2705)
man L at center
touches a flexed
man L at left with
a Pica/Baton
man at right: upside
down, wears a
helmet
SH horizontal
?I 306 (Rs) Pylos
Palace
2-3 men preserved,
all nude, in
various postures
I 340 (Rs?) Pylos
Palace
2 (3?) men, legs
crossed, in
various postures
VII 130 (L) Crete
man at left: flexed L
man in center: with
boar's tusk
helmet?, touches
the back of the
head of the man at
left
man at right: with
sword/Baton,
touches the center
man's helmet
SH horizontal

IX 158 (L)
duel at right:
dominant man
at left wields
sword; helmeted man
at right
man at left: falling
upside down
SH horizontal
HMs 8a (Rs) Kato Zakro
(KZ 12/13)
duel in center:
dominant man at
left spears
man at right armed
with a sword?
fallen warrior? bel

FIG. 97 -- HMs 369 & 526 etc.
(KN KSPI Ec & AT 114/144)

HMs 369, 447, 526, no. No
116 (Rs) Knossos
Palace & Ayia
Triada (FIG. 97;
KSPI Ec [Betts 12]
& AT 114/144)
man at left pursues
man at right, both
R, & restrains him
by the hair

fallen warriors bel
HMs 483 (Rs) Ayia
      Triada (AT 113)
   duel in center, <u>Column</u>
         with volute
         capital?
      betw: dominant man
         at right wears
         helmet
   fallen, nude helmeted
      man R at right

FIG. 98 -- II 3.7: man at <u>Altar</u>

Religious Scenes
Single
   At an <u>Altar</u>
      II 3.7 (L) Idaean
            Cave (**FIG. 98**)
      at left: man R
            wearing a skirt
            blows conch
            <u>Branch 1 Tree</u>
            inb
      at right: waisted
         <u>Altar</u> topped with
         <u>HC</u> with <u>Branch 1</u> &
         flanked by 2 <u>Branch</u>
         <u>1</u>
      <u>Sun</u>/star at right &
         object (bucket?) at
         left (i.e.,

betw man & the
<u>Altar</u>) flank
   the <u>Altar</u>
2 groundlines bel

FIG. 99 -- V 608: man at <u>Altar</u>

V 608 (C) Naxos, Aplo-
      mata T. B (**FIG.
      99**; LH III C)
   at right: man L holds
      a spear, blade up,
      directly infr of
      him in his out-
      stretched right?
      hand (cf. the same
      pose on Ch. 2E:
      People at a <u>Shrine</u>
      [person at right]
      -- HMs 141] & the
      Chieftain's cup)
   bel the arm: jug,
      rhyton, bucket,
      sword (blade up)
      [cf. tablet KN
      K93a, *226 VAS],
      all resting on a
      (curtailed?) two-
      legged <u>Table</u>
   at left: <u>Palm 4</u>
      SH vertical

HMs XZ (Cyls) Knossos
        Palace (KSPI
        R70)
    L-R: agrimi head
        upside down as
        if in PT 14A,
        head bent up;
        man stands R;
        waisted Altar

FIG. 100 -- HMm 1034:
man kneels at an Omphalos

Kneels at an Omphalos
HMm 1034 (R)
        Sellopoulo T. 4
        (FIG. 100; LM
        III A1; Popham
        1974 = 223 no.
        J8)
    L-R: Pithos/Shield-
        in-Profile; bird
        flies R with
        Sacred Heart bel
        (dangling from?
        its mouth; nude man
        kneels R at an
        Omphalos, regar-
        dant & his right
        arm up to salute?
        the bird; Tree 2
        grows from rocks

Cypress Branch ab
Miscellaneous
    II 3.330b (L) Tylissos?
    man R, arm out R
        2 objects (Sacred
            Knots?) flank
        SH horizontal

Two Men
    Salute
        I 195 (L) Midea
            man R at left with
                both hands up
            man L at right with
                left hand up
            branch & dashes in
                the field
        I Supp. 179 (Rs) Pylos
            Palace
        V 11 (C) Aigina,
            Perdika
            with 1 hand
                strokes fill the
                field
        V 189 (L) Salamis
            Kaloumenou ChT (LH
            III B-C)
            2 men? both arms up?
                lines in the field
        AM 1895.3 (L) (CS 40P;
            illustrated
            profile is that
                given for CS
                363)
            both arms up
        HMs 18b (Ls) Kato
            Zakro (KZ 188)
            salute L
        V 244 (L) Armenoi T.
            15
            2 men? flank a tree
        HMs 155 (Ls) Knossos
            Palace (KSPI R89)
            helmeted man at left,
            man R at right with
                arms akimbo
            sacrificial Table? ab

3 or More Men
  Saluting
      I 42 (L) Mycenae
          acropolis
        3 men stand, salute
            with their right
            hand
          Branch 2 encircles
          SH horizontal
      I 369 (Ls) Pylos
          Palace
        3 men salute with
            their right hand
            up
          Figure-8 Shield
            betw each
          Branch 4 ab
            (encircles?)
      I Supp. 177 (Rs) Pylos
          Palace
        3 men L salute with
            both? hands
    HMs no. unknown (Rs)
          Kato Zakro (KZ
          2)
        2 men salute & flank
            a man R in the
            center with staff

Procession, with cult?
  furniture

      I 170 (Rs?) Mycenae
          House of the Wine
          Merchant (LH III B1)
        3 men procession R, arms
            out to carry
            something
          groundline bel
    HMs 441 (Rs) Ayia Triada
          (AT 125)
        2 men walk L (man at
            left carries
            staff)
          vertical lines at
            right = Shrine?
    HMs 485 (Rs) Ayia Triada

          (AT 135)
        at left: man R
        at right: 2 men L
            (man at extreme
            right carries
            staff)
          groundline bel
    HMs no. unknown (Rs)
          Kato Zakro (KZ 6)
        2 men R
          man at left:
            carries Double
            Ax
          man at right:
            carries Sacred
            Robe?
    HMs no. unknown (Ls)
          Kato Zakro (KZ
          7)
        in center: 2 men hold
            hands
          man at right:
            carries staff

                2C
              Women

Single
Stands frontally
  Plain
      II 4.28 (L) "Trypiti"
        arms out
          SH horizontal
      IV 283b (L) Fortetsa
          groundline bel
          SH horizontal
    HM 610? (L) (Xanthou-
          dides 1907 pl. 8.147)
    HM G 3103 (L) (CMCG
          366)
        2 groups of 3 dots
            flank
    HMs 467 (Ls) Ayia
          Triada (AT 105)
        2 vertical strokes

(Mount-Guides?)
flank
HMs no. unknown (Ls)
    Ayia Triada (AT 119)
Arms akimbo
    I 513 (L) Crete
    flanked by 2 Columns
    groundline bel
    II 4.112 (L) Knossos,
        House of the
        Frescoes (LM IB)
    2 sets of 4 lines
        each flank
    SH horizontal
    AM 1941.126 (L) (CS
        41P)
    SH horizontal
Arms up
    II 3.239 (R) Sphoun-
        garas (MM III-LM I)
    circles in the field
    IV 55D (L) Knossos
    2 strokes flank
    SH horizontal
    X 270 (L)
        in a building made
        of 2 concentric
        boxes of Branch 3,
        & flanked by
        Columns (see: Ch.
        2E: People at a
        Shrine [woman in
        Shrine])
    ?HMs 199 (Ls) Kato
        Zakro (KZ 199)
    HMs 669 (Ls) Knossos
        Palace (KSPI C9)
        flanked by 2? Branch 1
Salutes with 1 hand
    VIII 128 (L) Hutchinson
        Coll.
        salutes with her left
        hand
        2 strokes flank
        SH horizontal
    HM 1969/2094 (L)
        Knossos, Royal

Road
    salutes with her right
        hand?
    SH horizontal
Stands Left
    Plain
        II 3.3 (L) Kalyvron
            Mylopotamou
        arms akimbo
            2 Suns flank
            SH horizontal
        II 3.72 (L) Knossos,
            Geometric Tb.
        arms outstretched
            2 pairs of
                Branch 1
                flank
            SH horizontal
    Salutes
        XII 12D (L) Seager
            Coll.
            head L?,salutes a
                Branch 1 Tree
            SH horizontal?
        HM G 3145 (L) (CMCG
            367)
            flower inb
        ?HMs 578 (Ls) Ayia
            Triada (AT 121)
            1 arm out L
            2 branches flank
    Both arms out
        HM G 3349 (L) Knossos
            (CMCG 368)
            2 Branch 1 flank
Stands Right
    Plain
        II 4.165 (L) Mallia,
            Maison E
            2 Branch 1 flank
            SH horizontal
        II 4.55 (L?) "Pediada"
            2 circles flank
            unfinished
        HMs 159 (Ls?) Ayia
            Triada (AT 84)
            object inb

Salutes
   II 3.170 (L) "Knossos"
     head L, left arm up
       SH horizontal
   II 3.304 (L) Ierapetra
     woman with her left
       arm raised
      Sun at right
       SH horizontal
   II 3.124 (L) Tylissos
     her left arm up
      2 objects flank
   II 3.171 (L) "Knossos"
     salutes with her left
       hand
       Sun at right
       branch (rocks?)
        at left
       SH horizontal
   X 262 (L)
     salutes with her left
       hand
       SH horizontal
   HM G 3446 (L) Knossos
      (CMCG 361)
      Sun infr
   HMs 523 (Rs) Ayia
      Triada (AT 138)
     L-R: woman; 2
      Omphaloi/Squills;
      Tree 5 grows from
      rocks
   HMs no. unknown (Rs)
     Ayia Triada (AT 160)

Carries an object
  Left
   II 38 (L) Knossos
     Double Ax & Sacred
       (Knot/) Robe
      Dado 6d inb
      SH horizontal
   II 3.16 (C) Knossos
      (LM IA)
     sword in her right
      hand
     a whip? (lituus:

"lustral
  sprinkler"?)
  in her left hand
   SH vertical
HMs 534 (As) Ayia
    Triada (AT 120)
  object
   SH vertical
HMs 535 (Ls) Ayia
    Triada (AT 123)
  Sacred Robe hanging
    from a Yoke inb
    of the woman

FIG. 101 -- Berlin FG 50a
   (AGDS II 12a):
woman R holds a Papyrus

Right
   I 226 (A) Vapheio
      Tholos
    staff ab
      groundline bel
      SH vertical
   Berlin FG 2 (L) Crete
      (AGDS II Berlin
      20)
    kneels with bow
   Berlin FG 50a (APr)
      Crete (FIG. 101;
      AGDS II Berlin
      12a)

Papyrus?
Papyrus inb
    SH vertical
HM 2807b (D) Knossos,
    Strat. Mus. Ext.
    (Warren 1980;
    Weingarten
    1983: 141 & 10:
    "reel-shaped")
Sacred Robe?
HM G 3158 (L) Knossos
    (CMCG 363)
Sacred Robe

Single, Religious
At an Altar
  I 410 (R) Melos, building
      H2: 14 (LM I; Renfrew
      1985: 295-6)
  woman stands L infr of
      Altar/3(4?)-legged
      Table topped with HC
  the woman may hold the
      stick that is
      crowned with 2
      arcs ending in a
      star-like object ab
      the HC
  2 Branch 3 (Palm
      fronds?) inb of
      the woman
  arcs (decoration?) bel
      the Altar/Table

At an Omphalos/Squill
  AM 1919.56 (R) Mycenae?
      (Sourvinou-Inwood
      1971)
  L-R: woman stands R, her
      left hand touches her
      bosom, her right arm
      inb of her; woman
      kneels R at 2
      Omphaloi/Squills
  ab & betw the women is
      a small man R, with
      his right arm

stretched out inb
of him
ab the kneeling woman
    are an eye & ear
Dado 2a bel
HMs no. unknown (Rs)
    Ayia Triada (AT
    143)
at left, woman kneels
    L & salutes R
2 butterflies
    antithetic &
    Sacred Robe at right
    Heaven Line ab
HMs no. unknown (Rs)
    Kato Zakro, Rm
    XXVIIII (Platon 1971:
    159)
"butterfly inb"

Single, Miscellaneous
Sits/Squats frontally
  HMs 176a (Ls) Kato
      Zakro (KZ 176)
  HMs 642 (Ls)
      Sklavokambos (Sk 13)
  HMs 642 (Ls)
      Sklavokambos (SK 14)

In a boat
  Ayios Nikolaos 4653 (A)
      Makrygialos, E. Crete
      (Davaras 1976: 327,
      fig. 189)
  woman salutes L in the
      prow? of a ship R
  cabin at left
  HMs 434 (Rs) Ayia Triada
      (AT 118)
  woman poles a boat R
      (backward?) with
      an animal-head
      (regardant) stern/
      prow? aegis & a
      Frond prow/stern?
      aegis; waves bel

Miscellaneous
  HMs 392 (As) Knossos,
      Palace (KSPI Cc)
    woman stands L/reclines
      shell pattern beh
      SH vertical?
  HMs 661 (Ls) Knossos
      Palace (KSPI Cb)
    at left, woman seated
      on a footstool R
      holds jug/krater
    at right, Branch 1

Two Women
Plain or unclear
  VII 241 (L)
  HM 1608 (L) Knossos,
    Kephala Tholos (LM I &
    IIIA; Hutchinson 1956:
    80 no. 18, fig. 2.18)
  HMs 642 (Ls) Sklavokambos
    (Sk 15)

Stand Left
  II 3.146 (L) Mallia,
      Quartier Da
    curtailed Dado 7a infr

Salute
  Center
    I Supp. 133 (L)
      dots flank
      SH horizontal
    I Supp. 134 (L)
      dots flank
      SH horizontal
    I Supp. 135 (L)
      dots in field
    II 4.22 (L) Mallia,
      Maison E
      SH horizontal
    II 4.70
      SH horizontal
    IX 164 (L)
      2 Fronds flank
    AM 1889.289 (L) bought
        at Smyrna (CS 375)

frontal
HM 1961 (L) Knossos,
    Royal Road
HMs 200 (Ls) Kato Zakro
    (KZ 200)
  flowers? in field
  rocks? bel

FIG. 102 -- XII 168:
  2 women salute L

Left
  II 3.169 (L)
  XII 168 (L) Seager
      Coll. (FIG. 102)
    in conical hats
    woman at right carries
      staff
    SH horizontal?
  AM 1938.1146 (L)
      Knossos (CS 253)
    SH horizontal
  Florence 84708 (L)
      Korai, Knossos
      (Laviosa 1969: no. 8)
Right
  II 3.17 (C) Knossos,
      House of Frescoes
      (LM I)
    Sun infr
    SH vertical

II 3.236 (L) Gournia,
    "oldest part of
    town"
SH horizontal
AM 1938.1147 (L) (CS
    252)
HMs 486 (Ls) Ayia
    Triada (AT 122)
Flank an object
HMs 576 (Rs) Ayia
        Triada (AT 137)
    Tree 5 grows from
        rocks
        at left, woman has
          her left arm
          out to Tree 5
        at right, woman
          sits? on
          rocks?, arms up

Woman at left salutes woman at
    right (see: Ch. 2C:
    Women [pair] -- HMs
    576 [AT 137])

HMs 522 (Rs) Ayia Triada
        (AT 139)
    top center, small woman
        L
    rocks bel & inb of
        small woman
HMs no. unknown (Ls) Kato
        Zakro (KZ 5)
    woman at right seated L
        on campstool?
HMs no. unknown (Rs) Kato
        Zakro (KZ 9)
    top center, Sacred Heart
Miscellaneous
    I 134 (L) Mycenae ChT 103
        2 women's torsos
        2 groundlines bel
        SH horizontal

Three Women
Stand Left
    Ayios Nikolaos 11384 (R)

Mallia, House Delta-
    A, Space 8 (MM III-
    LM I; Kopake 1984)
all salute L

Stand Right
    I 132 (L) Mycenae ChT 103
        woman at right originally
          intended to be a
          Figure-8 Shield
        Figure-8 Shield inb &
          ab
    I 162 (Rs) Mycenae, House
        of the Oil Merchant
        both hands up
    BM no. unknown (stone matrix
        for a ring) Enkomi
        (Sakellarakis 1981:
        168, fig. 4)
    all salute R

2 Women Flank a Central Woman
    Flanking Women Smaller,
    All Face R (see: Ch. 2E:
    People at a Shrine -- HMs
    unknown [AT 140])

    I 159 (L) Mycenae,
        Philadelpheus' T. 4
        (LH III B1)
        SH horizontal
    II 3.218 (L) Mochos Pediado
        groundline bel
        SH horizontal
        tool marks on the reverse
        (J. Betts)
Miscellaneous
    I 321 (Ls) Pylos Palace,
        flanking women salute
    AM 1938.1013 (L) Chania
        (CS 295)
        central woman seated on
          a Column?
        SH horizontal
    Chania 1528 a & b (Rs?)
        Chania, Kastelli
        (Papapostolou 1977:

no. 29)
    central woman seated R
      (on rocks?)

Four or More Women (cf.: where-
  abouts unknown: a lentoid
  from Nerokourou, Crete, with
  5 women; Kapaka 1984: 12 no.
  36)

Stand Left
  HM 1559 (stone matrix for
      a ring) (Sakellara-
      akis 1981: 168, figs.
      2 & 3)
      6 women stand, flanked
      by 2 branches

Stand Right
  HMs 668 (Cs) Knossos
      Palace (KSPI C10)
      4? salute with their
      left arm

3 Women Face Seated Woman
  Face Left
    I 313 (Rs) Pylos
      Palace, (CMS I
      p. 349 accurately
      describes the ring
      type)
      3 salute L

  Face Right
    I 17 (R) Mycenae
      Treasure (**FIG.
      103**)
      L-R: 2 large women
        & small woman,
        all R; woman
        seated on rocks
        L; Tree 6;
        small woman L
        pulls at the
        Tree 6
      woman at left holds
        Lilies in both

hands
small woman at left
    holds some
    plants in both?
    hands
    rocks bel
seated woman holds, in
    her right hand,
    poppies at which
    the second large
    woman gestures
    with her left
    hand
at left: a vertical
    row of 6 lion
    faces
ab, at left: small
    man? R wears a
    Figure-8 Shield &
    holds a spear
ab, center: crescent
    Moon & Sun ab a
    wavy Heaven Line

FIG. 103 -- I 17:
3 women face R
a woman seated at right

I 361 (Rs) Pylos
    Palace, (inscribed:
    PY Wr 1361)
    3 women R offer

objects to woman
seated L at right

Miscellaneous
    II 3.51 (R) Isopata T. 1
        (FIG. 104; LM
        IB-II)
        L-R: woman R en face with
        both arms up, woman en
        face ab center with
        her right arm up, a
        pair of women L with
        both arms up
    wavy Heaven Line ab
        ab: Cypress Branch at
            left & small woman
            at right
        bel: Sacred Heart &
            eye at left
        4 plants (asphodels?) in
            the field

FIG. 104 -- II 3.51:
3 women salute & small woman

2D
Men & Women

Pair
Man at left, Woman at right
    Salute

AM 1938.1009 (CS 284)
    L-R: man & woman
        salute L
    SH horizontal
HMs 114 (Rs) Knossos
    Palace (KSPI
    K2/11)
    L-R: man R salutes
        woman frontal
        with both arms
        up
    groundline? bel
Chania 1024   (Rs)
    Chania, Kastelli
    (Papapostolou
    1977: no. 31)
    L-R: man R & woman L
        flank & salute
        Column/Pylon betw
    at left: double
        Omphalos/Squill
        with frond
            object ab
    2 groundlines bel

Greet
    X 261* (L)
        at left: man R;
        at right: seated
            woman L; they
            reach out with 1
            hand each to
            touch boar? head &
            Cypress Branch ab
        rocks bel
        incised line around
            edge of stone
            probably for a
            ring setting or
            gilding
Woman Seated
    I 101 (R) Mycenae ChT
        66
        L-R: man R with a
            staff in his
            in his right
            hand & woman

seated L on a
stool/bench
the man points with
his left hand,
the woman with
her right hand,
both to center,
as if the two
were conversing
rocks at right
groundline bel
HMs 421 (Ls?) Knossos,
Little Palace (KSPl
U2)
L-R: man R offers
object to woman
seated L on a
campstool
HMs no. unknown (Ls)
Ayia Triada (AT
142)
L-R: man R presents
object? to a
woman seated L
rocks bel

Flank a central object
HMs 655 (Ls) Knossos,
Little Palace (KSPl
U?)
L-R: man & woman
flank? & hold a
tree growing from
a tripod cauldron
II 3.145 (L) Mallia
man at left, woman in
pantaloons at right,
flank a Sacred Robe/
Knot

Woman Kneels at an Omphalos
I 219 (R) Vapheio
Tholos
L-R: Pithos/Shield-in-
Profile from which
a Tree 6 grows &
bends R; a nude

man stands on
rocks L & pulls
the Tree 6; woman
R with both arms
out & hands up;
Figure-8 Shield in
profile topped
with Sacred Knot
in profile
ab right: Sacred
Heart,Cypress
Branch, & Double
Ax with festoons

Woman at Left, Man at Right
II 3.305 (R) Avgo
L-R: woman R salutes
Tree 5, man L
rocks bel
HMs 195 (L?s) Kato Zakro
(KZ 195)
salute R at right:
Column topped with
helmet
Figure-8 Shield in
profile inb
HMs 592 (Rs?) Ayia Triada
(AT 124)
both carry L a Double Ax
HMs no. unknown (Rs) Kato
Zakro (KZ 10)
HMs no. unknown (?s) Ayia
Triada (AT 141)
at right: another man
groundline bel

Man and Women
Two Women Flank a Man
HMs 149 (As?) Knossos
Palace (KSPl S4)
2 saluting woman flank a
man L, raised ab
(only legs
preserved; cf. Ch.
2B: Men [3 or
more] -- I Supp.
193)

SH vertical

FIG. 105 -- V 173:
man leads 2 women L

Man & Two Women (see: Ch.
2D: Men & Women [misc.]
-- AM 1938.1130, the
Ring of Nestor, below])

V 173 (R) Athens, Agora
T. VIII (**FIG. 105**;
LH III A1)
L-R: man leads 2 women,
all left
man holds a long <u>Frond</u>
or staff (cf. XIII
39) & leads the
women on a double
leash
<u>Frond</u> ab
short <u>Column</u> inb (at
right)
groundline bel

Miscellaneous
Men & Women & Boat
I 180 (R) Tiryns Treasure
L-R: masted ship with 2
rowers R below a
canopy, steersman
L, & man R on prow;

woman R & man L
salute each other;
building, inside
which a man & woman
greet each other
at right: an object
3 buildings (town) ab
with rocks
dolphin(s?) bel ship
AM 1938.1129 (R) "Harbor
Town of Knossos" =
Poros (PM II 250 fig.
147b; IV 953 fig. 923;
Alexiou 1958b)
L-R: <u>Pithos/Shield-in-
Profile</u>; woman
frontal, her right
arm akimbo & her
left hand at? her
bosom; man R, one
arm stretched out
R; a boat with 5
rowers, a
steersman at left,
& a man sitting?
near the prow at
right
boat's hull is
decorated with
zig-zags
ab boat: a small man
salutes L &
objects (<u>Omphaloi</u>/
<u>Squills</u>?)
bel boat: 3 dolphins R

Miscellaneous
AM 1938.1130 (R)
"Kakovatos" (the Ring
of Nestor; CS pl. 20;
PM III 145ff.)
a tree quarters the
bezel
in the quadrants
clockwise from
upper left:
at left: a man &

woman sit
antithetic; at
right: a man &
woman stand
antithetic; 2
butterflies
antithetic & 2
Sacred Hearts
ab

lion in PT 11, L
on 3-legged
Table, ivy
infr

2 small women bel;
2 women, each
with 1 arm up,
flank 2 griffin-
women saluting
a griffin in PT
7, L on a small
Table

man leads 2 women
R, man inb (cf
Ch. 2D: Men &
Women [man &
women] -- V 173
above)

Babylonian Dragon runs
R on ground bel
tree

2E
People at a Shrine

Shrine (see: Ch. 4B: Potnia
Theron [lions] -- BSA Cast
135)

At the Shrine
HMs no. unknown (Rs) Ayia
Triada (AT 140)
at left: 2 small women flank
a large woman
at right: Tree 5 grows from

Shrine
Frond (Palm 1?) betw women &
Shrine
Dado 1 bel

Saluting the Shrine
Person at left, Shrine at right
Person
HMs 418 (Rs?) Knossos,
Little Palace (KSPI
E1)
at left: person R
salutes (with left
arm) a Shrine
topped with HC,
Columns inside
Shrine
betw person & shrine:
a shorter Shrine?
topped with HC
Man
I 292 (R) Pylos, Tholos
4, stone cist
L-R: man salutes R;
pile of rocks
(mountain?) topped
with Shrine;
agrimi in PT 1A,
L, its front legs
on the rocks betw
the saluting man &
the Shrine
ab: a slightly
smaller man? L
with both arms up
bel: plant growing
from rocks

Woman
Plain
II 3.15 (R) Knossos,
Hogarth's House
A (LM IB)
L-R: Pithos/
Shield-in-
Profile; woman
R; object(s);

at right,
<u>Shrine</u>
(peribolos?)
wall & topped
with 2 <u>HC</u>; from
the <u>Shrine</u> a
<u>Tree 2</u> grows
hanging L over
the wall

IX 163 (L)
Ligortyno
at left: woman
salutes R a
<u>Shrine</u> at right
topped with <u>HC</u>?
& a <u>Tree 3</u>
    arc (= neck-
      lace?) bel
    <u>Shrine</u>

AM 1938.1127 (R)
Knossos (CS 250;
  PM I fig. 115)
L-R: rocks & plant;
woman R salutes
small man ab
center standing
L, holding a
staff? infr of
him in an out-
stretched hand;
<u>Pylon</u>?; <u>Shrine</u>
with small
<u>Column</u> inside
porch & <u>Tree 2</u>
growing from it;
rocks at left
with plant or
<u>Squills</u>

HMs 487 (Ls) Ayia
    Triada (AT 136)
at left: woman R
salutes <u>Shrine</u>
at right topped
with 2 <u>HC</u>
necklace?/festoon?/
  swag? hangs
  inside <u>Shrine</u>

Averts her head (see: Ch.
2E: People at a
<u>Shrine</u> [person at
left] -- I 191,
below)

Chania 2055 (L/R?s)
Chania, Kastelli
(Papapostolou
1977: no. 28)
at left (in
center?): woman
stands facing L,
touching her
downturned face
with her right
hand, her left
hand stretched
inb toward a
2-tiered <u>Shrine</u>
at right: a 2-
tiered <u>Shrine</u>
topped with 2 <u>HC</u>
& a <u>Tree 5</u>
growing from it

FIG. 106 -- The Mochlos Ring:
woman visits a <u>Shrine</u> by boat

Sits in a boat
  II 3.252 (R)
        Mochlos, over T.
        IX (**FIG. 106**;
        the Mochlos
        Ring; LM IB;
        Sourvinou-Inwood
        1973; an
        electrotype copy
        is now on
        display in the
        HM)
      at left: part of a
        <u>Shrine</u> (peri-
        bolos?) wall
        2 small
        <u>Omphaloi/</u>
        <u>Squills</u> ab infr
        rocks form the
        ground bel infr
      at right: boat R
        with a
        <u>Babylonian</u>
        <u>Dragon's</u> head
        prow aegis & a
        stern looking
        like bunched
        sheaves (of
        <u>Papyrus</u>?)
      in the boat, L-R:
        woman sits L,
        her right arm
        bent to salute;
        2-tiered
        <u>Shrine</u>/cabin
        from which a
        <u>Tree 6</u> grows
      ab: <u>Sacred Heart</u>
        at left,
        <u>Short Column</u> at
        right
      bel: <u>Dado 4a</u> at
        left
Two women
  I 191 (R) Midea ChT 10
      (LH II-III A)
      2 women R (woman at

right with her
head averted L,
salute a <u>Shrine</u> at
right
  the <u>Shrine</u> consists of
  a 2-tiered
  structure covered
  by a porch
  supported by a
  short <u>Column</u> from
  the top tier & by a
  tall <u>Column</u> infr of
  the structure; <u>HC</u>
  crowns the porch; 2
  birds within the
  porch; rocks form
  the floor of the
  porch
  small tree at left
  V 728 (R) Mega
      Monastiri T. Gamma
      (LH III A-B)
      L-R: half-<u>Shrine</u>
        topped with <u>HC</u>; 2
        women R salute a
        <u>Shrine</u> topped with
        2 <u>HC</u> object (<u>Stand</u>?
        <u>Altar</u>?) betw women
        & <u>Shrine</u>

Three Women
  I 86 (R) Mycenae ChT 55
      3 women R salute with
        their left hand a
        <u>Shrine</u> at right
        with a <u>Column</u>
        inside & topped
        with <u>HC</u>; the
        women's hands,
        especially their
        lowered right
        hands, seem to
        hold objects like
        flowers or grain
        sheaves
      at left, <u>Frond</u>
      <u>Dado 1</u> bel

I 108 (R) Mycenae ChT
71
3 women R, middle
woman saluting,
face a Shrine
topped with HC

Person at right, Shrine at left
Man
HMs no. unknown (Rs)
Kato Zakro (KZ 1)
at right: man salutes
L a Shrine at left
topped with 2 HC
object (Shrine?
tree?) inb of man
ab center: small
woman? R leans
back

Woman
I 279 (L) Rutsi Tholos
2, last burial (LH
II-IIIA)
at right: woman L
holds 2 Lilies in
her right hand
ab a Shrine at left
topped with HC with
2 branches
SH horizontal
XII 264 (L) Seager
Coll.
in center: nude woman
L pulls at Tree 3
growing from
Shrine at left;
Tree 3 bends R
rocks bel Shrine
SH horizontal?

Two women
V 422b (R matrix, for a
relief ring?)
Eleusis T. Eta-pi 3
2 women L infr of
Shrine? at left

woman at right
holds Fronds
woman at left
(infr of
Shrine) raises
both arms ab
Shrine
Shrine seems to
consist of 3 thick
Pylons, each
topped with 1 or 2
Double Axes
Fronds flank &
separate the women

Man & Woman
HMs 141 (Rs) Knossos
Palace (KSPI M1-5)
L-R: 2-tiered Shrine
with the upper tier
containing Columns
& topped with HC; a
woman R, holding a
staff infr of her
(for the pose: Ch.
Ch. 2B: Men [reli-
gious] -- V 608; &
the Chieftain's
Cup), stands on a
mountain of rocks
flanked by 2
collared? lions
rampant on the
mountain in PT 31A;
man salutes L

Two women antithetic
Shrine betw
I 127 (R) Mycenae ChT
91 (FIG. 107; LH
II)
2 women flank & salute
a Shrine on a
"mountain?"
(the mountain
could be a
built

structure in
3 tiers with
door bel)
2 <u>Cypress
Branches</u> on
the middle
tier flank
3 or 4 small
<u>Omphaloi/
Squills</u> top the
<u>Shrines</u>
at left: rocks &
plants
at right: <u>Cypress
Tree</u>
<u>Dado 4c</u> bel

FIG. 107 -- I 127:
2 women flank
& salute a <u>Shrine</u>

Chania 2071 & 2112   (Rs)
Chania, Kastelli
(Papapostolou
1977: no. 27)
center: 2 women face
each other & hold
hands
betw: <u>Branch 1 Tree</u>
(growing from
<u>Shrine</u>?)
2 <u>Shrines</u> flank, each

topped with <u>HC</u>?
Two <u>Shrines</u> flank (see:
Ch. 2E: People at a
<u>Shrine</u> [2 women
antithetic] -- Chania
2071/2112, immediately
above)

II 3.56 (R) Isopata T.
6 (LM III A1)
in center: 2 women
face & hold hands
2 <u>Shrines</u>? flank at
right

Woman in a <u>Shrine</u>
X 270 (L)
woman frontal with arms
up in a building?
flanked by <u>Columns</u>?
(see: Ch. 2C: Woman
[single])
building made of 2
concentric boxes of
<u>Branch 3</u> & topped
with <u>HC</u>? & branches?
Woman Sits on <u>Shrine</u> (see:
Ch. 4B: <u>Potnia Theron</u>
[lions] -- BSA Cast 135)

Man salutes the woman
V 199 (R) Thebes?
L-R: man R salutes a
woman sitting L on a
2-tiered <u>Shrine</u> topped
with <u>HC</u> with a branch
the lower tier &
the back wall
are both
supported by a
<u>Column</u>; the back
wall? is convex
L
ab: <u>Heaven Line</u> with <u>Sun</u>
ab
<u>Dado 1</u> bel

Woman salutes the woman
    Berlin Antike Abteilung (R)
        (Bielefeld 1968: no.
        263 pl. CIIa;
        forgery?)
        at left: woman R sits on
        2-tiered Shrine topped
        with 2 HC & with HC
        with Column inside,
        her right hand raised
        towards the standing
        woman at left, her
        left hand on her knee
        at right: woman stands L,
        her right hand raised
        toward the seated
        woman
            Papyrus inb (at
                extreme right)
    Chania 2097 (Ls) Chania,
        Kastelli (Papapostolou
        1977: no. 30)
        at left: small skirted
        person R holds Sceptre
        at right: woman seated L
        on 3-tiered Shrine,
        holds her right hand
        to her bosom

2 Women face seated woman
    HMs 277-283 (Rs) Knossos
        Palace & Kato Zakro
        (LM IB; KSPI Q22/R1/
        R51/R54;KZ 3; Pini
        1984: 79-80)
        L-R: woman L offers
        goblet to woman
        seated L on a 2-
        tiered Shrine, feet
        on a footstool
        groundline bel

Tree-pulling without Omphalos-
    kneeling

Man
    ?I 119 (R) Mycenae ChT 84

(FIG. 108)
    L-R: agrimi in PT 1A, R,
    with the crown of a
    Tree 3 ab; man R
    touches a Tree 3
    growing from a Shrine
    rocks bel the
        Shrine
    groundline bel

FIG. 108 -- I 119:
man touches a tree
growing from a Shrine

Man pulls, woman accompanies
    I 126 (R) Mycenae ChT 91
        (FIG. 109; LH II)
        L-R: Shrine or Table,
        inside or bel which
        are a Sacred Heart?,
        2 necklaces, & a
        vertical stroke; a
        woman L bends over
        the Shrine/Table &
        laying her folded arms
        on it, rests her head
        on her arms; woman
        stands R, arms akimbo;
        man R, head averted L,
        pulls at a Tree 2
        growing from a Shrine,
        inside which is a

pillar or Column
ab left (ab woman at
   Shrine/Table: 3 Branch
   2
ab right (betw the
   standing woman & the
   Tree 2): 2 Heaven
   Lines?
Dado 1 bel

FIG. 109 -- I 126:
man & woman in a sanctuary

Man & Woman pull, Woman
   accompanies
Once in the Evans coll. (R)
   "Knossos, above the
   Temple Tomb" (The
   Ring of Minos; PM IV
   947 ff.)
on the top of a
   mountain, decorated
   with an arcade
   pattern are 3 large
   Omphaloi from which
   rises a Shrine from
   which grow 2 Tree 5
at left: a nude man R
   pulls at the left
   Tree 5 with his left
   hand & holds a jug
   (Sacred Heart?) with

his right hand
2 2-tiered masonry
   platforms (Shrines?
   Altars?) flank the
   mountain
   at left: the
      platform is
      topped with a
      HC; a woman
      sits R on the
      top tier, her
      left hand
      touches her
      shoulder; 3
      Omphaloi bel
   at right: a nude?
      woman pulls at
      a Tree 5
      growing from
      the top tier; 2
      Omphaloi bel
   ab: at left (betw the
      left seated woman
      & the left Tree 5
      top center), a
      small woman L
   bel: a woman poles a
      boat L with a
      Babylonian
      Drangon's head
      prow aegis and
      frond stern
      in the boat are
         2 Shrines,
         each topped
         with HC

Man kneeling at an Omphalos
   II 3.114 (R) Kalyvia
      T. 11 (LM III A2)
   L-R: Pithos/Shield-in-
      Profile bird flies R,
      nude man R kneels at
      Omphalos, woman R
      pulls at Tree 6
      growing from Shrine &
      bending L

        wavy line of dots   <u>Heart</u>
           (necklace?) ab   <u>Dado 3</u> bel
           bird
        rocks? bel shrine
     groundline bel

FIG. 110 -- HMm 989:
man & woman in a sanctuary

HMm 989 (R) Archanes
     Tholos A (**FIG. 110**; LM
     III A1; Sakellarakis
     1967a: fig. 13)
  L-R: <u>Shrine</u> with <u>Tree 4</u>
     growing from it &
     bending R; man L pulls
     at the <u>Tree 4</u>; woman
     R, her face averted L,
     her left arm up; man
     kneels R, his head
     averted L, at <u>Omphalos</u>
  ab & betw woman &
     kneeling man: (top
     to bottom) eye, <u>Small</u>
     <u>Column</u>, butterfly,
     "dragonfly"
  ab kneeling man: <u>Sacred</u>

CHAPTER 3
Men and Animals

3A
Man with Animals

FIG. 111 -- I 133:
man & lion in PT 7, R

Men in Chariots see Ch. 3D

Man & Lion
Single Man
  Lion stands
    Man beh
      I 133 (L) Mycenae T
        103
        lion in PT 7, R,
        man's torso ab
          R, his left arm
          stretched R ab
          the lion's head
      I 512 (L) Crete
        lion in PT 8, L
        man L beh lion, his
          left arm akimbo
          & his right
          restraining the
          lion by a Leash
          around its neck
        Branch 1 Tree infr
        groundline bel

II 3.24 (L) Knossos,
    Houses So. of
    palace (LM IB)
  lion in PT 1A, R
  man R beh lion, his
    right arm
    akimbo & his
    left down
    bef the
    lion's chest
  2 groundlines
    bel
II 3.27 (A) Mavro-
    spelio T.
    III.13
  lion in PT 2, R
  man R beh with
    right arm up &
    left arm down
    framing the
    lion's head
  2 pairs of Mount
    -Guides flank
  groundline bel
II 3.52 (C) Isopata
    T. 1 (LM II
    [IIB?])
  lion in PT 1A, L
    wearing a
    beaded Collar
  man L beh lion,
    his left arm
    akimbo
  man inb, his left
    arm akimbo
  2 circles infr
    circle ab
II 3.329 (A)
  lion in PT 2, R
  man R beh lion,
    both arms down
  2 Mount-Guides infr
  1 Mount-Guide inb
VII 169 (A)
  lion in PT 1A, L
    man L beh
    Shrine? infr

X 135*   (L)
  collared lion in
    PT 2, R
  man R, his right
    arm akimbo; his
    left arm
    restrains the
    lion by a leash
  Dado 6c bel
HMs 194   (Ls) Kato
    Zakro (KZ 194)
  lion in PT 1A,
    left
  man L beh, his
    right arm held
    to his chest &
    his left arm
    down
Man bef (see: Ch. 3C:
    Man Hunts Animals
    [lion] -- IX 114)

XII 207   (A) Seager
    Coll.
  lion in PT 2, R
  man R bef, his
    right arm akimbo
    & his left hand
    unseen beh the
    lion's shoulders
  2 pairs of Mount-
    Guides flank
  groundline bel
HMs 508   (As) Ayia
    Triada (AT 134)
  lion in PT 1A/2, R
  man R bef, his
    right arm thrown
    inb holds a
    leash?
  groundline bel
  SH vertical
HMs 383I   (Ls) Knossos
    Palace (KSPI
    L46; CS 8S)
  lion in PT 2, L
  man, wearing a cap,

L bef, his right
    arm outstretched
    & holding a
    staff infr of
    him
  2 groundlines bel
Man infr
  I 359 (Ls) Pylos
    Palace, (LH III
    B2-C1)
  lion at right in PT
    12, L vs man at
    left running L
    regardant?
  II 3.9 (L) Knossos
  lion vs bull in PT
    39A, R?
  man L infr at the
    bull's horns
Man inb
  X 161*   (L)
  at left: a lion in
    PT 1A, L
  at right: a man
    inb restrains
    the lion by a
    leash
  wavy line (bow?)
    inb
Miscellaneous
  II 3.221 (L)
    Pediada
  2 lion protomes
    conjoined to
    one body in
    axial symmetry
    cl
  man L at right
    (cf. Ch. 3A:
    Man & Animals
    [bulls] -- HM G
    3372b, below)

2 Men flank a lion
  I 374   (Rs?) Pylos Palace
    (LH III B2-C1)
  2 men salute with their

inner arms & flank
a lion salient R
<u>Dado 7b</u> bel
Munich A.1171 (L) Crete
(AGDS I Munich 87)
2 men flank lion upside
down in PT 13? en
face

Man & Bovines
Man beh
VII 102 (L) Crete
bull in PT 1A, L
man beh L holds the bull
by a leash attached
to its horns
groundline bel
X 259 (L)
bull in PT 1B, L
man L beh, his left arm
akimbo?; his right
arm stretches out
over the bull's neck
Chania 1529 & 1530 (Ls)
Chania, Kastelli
(Papapostolou 1977:
no. 25)
collared calf in PT 1C, R
man beh R restrains the
animal by a leash
groundline bel
Man bef
IX 146 (L)
bull in PT 1B, R
man R bef, hands
up-raised (engraved
later?)
2 dots/balls ab
SH horizontal
Man infr
VII 100 (A) Crete (**FIG.
40**)
2 bulls in PT 25B, R
man infr kneels? R, his
right arm inb to touch
the head of the
forward bull

<u>ImpTr</u> & <u>Figure-8 Shield</u>
ab
<u>Branch 3</u> & X bel
HMs 85 (Ls) Kato Zakro (KZ
102)
bull in PT 2, R
<u>Tree 5</u> beh
man L infr, right hand up
holding a cup? & left
arm bent down
a vertical line bel his
hands (genius? holding
a vessel; a <u>Column</u>
bel his hands?)
HMs 143 (Ls) Knossos
Palace (KSPI Q20)
bull in PT 10A, R?
man L infr, his right arm
up near his face &
his left hand holding
a double leash? close
to his chest (in the
PM fig. the man is
restored as a
barricade)
?object bel man
Piraieus no. unknown Varkiza
T. I (LH III A2-B; AAA
7, 1974, 423-433)
L-R: bull in PT 1A, R;
<u>Tree 1</u>; helmeted? man
runs L (clutching the
tree?, struggling
with a leash?)
<u>Tree 1</u> beh ab bull
rocks bel man
object (<u>Pithos/
Shield-in-
Profile</u>?) inb
<u>Dado 1</u> bel
Man inb
AM 1938.1021 (A) (CS 242)
collared cow runs & calf
in PT 17A, L
man L inb leans forward
to restrain cow by a
leash

AM 1938.1026 (L) (CS 300)
  3 bulls stand in PT 26,
    L; last bull
    regardant
  man L inb leans over the
    last bull & touches
    its muzzle
  2 groundlines bel
AM 1938.1076 (L)
    Peloponnese (CS 247)
  bull in PT 6, R
    bull in PT 1A, R
    bel
  man R inb stretches his
    left arm out over the
    top bull's back
  3? Weeds at right
HMs 267 (As) Knossos
    Palace (KSPI R61)
  cow? in PT 1A/2/13A, R
  man R inb, arms down
    (milking?)
Man bel
  XIII 35 (C)
    bull in PT 4, R, chin
      tucked under
    man prone R bel, his
      right leg up & beh
      the bull's
      hindquarters
  HMs 251 (Rs) Knossos
    Palace (KSPI R9)
    bull in PT 3, R
    man prone R bel
Man carries a bovine simulacrum
  HMs 585 (As) Ayia Triada
    (AT 127)
    man walks R, carrying a
      calf simulacrum
    groundline bel
    SH vertical
  HMs 1010 (As) Knossos
    Palace (Betts 54)
    man walks L carrying a
      bull simulacrum?
    SH vertical

Man & conjoined bulls
  HM G 3372b (Pr) Vasilike
    Anogeia (CMCG 190b)
  2 bull protomes conjoined
    in radial symmetry
    ccl
  man protome ab each
    (as if beh each),
    one arm up as if to
    restrain them (cf.
    Ch. 3A: Man &
    Animals [lion] --
    II 3.52, above)

Man & bull aligned with
  different SH orientations

  Berlin FG 8 (L) Syra (AGDS
    II Berlin 22)
  SH horizontal:
    below: dappled bull in
      PT 13A, R
  SH vertical:
    at right: man L (cf.
      Ch. 3A: Man &
      Animals [man & bull
      with different
      SH alignment -- HM
      33, below)
  BM 97.4.64 (Cyl) Enkomi OT
    2 (Pini 1980: no. C3)
  SH horizontal:
    at left: man sits R on
      a campstool, arms
      out
    at right: another man
      sits (without a
      campstool); 2 dogs?
      antithetic; bull in
      PT 1A, L ab
  SH vertical:
    ab: eagle-woman, head
      R
    bel: a pair of wings
      ab a bull in PT
      5A, L

Man & Caprids (see: Ch. 2B:
Men [single] -- HMs
XZ/N-Theta [KSPI R70]; &
Ch. 6A: People-Animals
[winged man] -- XIII 60)

Man beh
  AM 1938.1024 (L) (CS
      309)
    2 sheep in PT 19A, R
    2 groundlines beh
Man infr
  HMs 93 (A?s) Kato Zakro
      (KZ 15)
    2 caprids in PT 19A, L
      man infr: man R at
        left, arms out to
        touch the caprids
  V 246 (L) Armenoi T. 17
      (LM III B)
    SH horizontal:
      at left: man R
        regardant inb of
        of kid in PT 5B, R
        at right
    SH vertical: lion in PT
      14A, L
  HMs 131 (Ls) Knossos
      Palace (KSPI Pe)
    sheep in PT 1A, R
      spear horizontal R ab
      man squats R bel (cf.
        HM 2214)
      net/reticulation beh
Man & salient agrimi
  I 199 (C) Asine ChT 1
      (LH III A2)
    at right: man L holds
      the head of an agrimi
      at left salient L,
      head contorted back
    SH vertical
  II 3.33 (Cyl) Mavrospelio
      T. VIIA (LM IA)
    L-R: man R, arms
      stretched out ab an
      agrimi infr salient R

  & regardant quadruped
  salient R; regardant
  quadruped in PT 7, R;
  man's face & object ab
  lines ab
HMs 583a (Ls) Ayia Triada
    (AT 126)
  man walks L, carrying a
    staff? over his
    shoulder
  agrimi? salient L infr
  groundline bel
2 Men & Stag
  II 3.66 (L) Sellopoulo T.
      1 (LM III A2-B)
    SH vertical: stag in PT
      6, R
    SH horizontal: 2 men,
      both R, flank the stag
      now vertical, head
      upside down the men's
      inner arms stretch
      across the stag's back

Man & Birds (see: Ch. 2A: Body
Parts [man's face]/5E: Birds
& Waterbirds [waterbirds,
pair] -- HM 206)

AM 1938.1050 (A) Knossos (CS
    293)
  man R holds bird
  groundline bel
  SH vertical
HMs 134 (Ls) Knossos Palace
    (KSPI Q14)
  man R holds staff infr
  2 plants (Asphodels?
    Lilies?) flank
  2 birds fly antithetic bel
    ab a knob-shaped object
    (Omphalos?)
HMs 569-570 (Rs?) Ayia Triada
    (AT 93)
  at left: person L
  at right: 2 waterbirds in PT
    34B

Man & Miscellaneous Quadrupeds
    (see: Ch. 2B: Men [single]
    -- HMs 343 [KSPI L47]; &
    Ch. 4D: Women with Animals
    [Misc.] -- Nafplion no.
    unknown, side b from Asine)

Single
    I 377 (Ls) Pylos Palace,
        LH III B2-C1)
        at left a man R
            an ape? infr, L with
                arms raised up
    I Supp. 175 (Ls) Pylos
        Palace, (LH III
        B2-C1)
        quadruped in PT 1A, L
            man ab?
    XII 240 (L) Seager Coll.
        boar in PT 1B, R
        man prone R bel, head
            regardant
    AM 1938.1062 (L) central
        Crete (CS 238)
        collared dog in PT 2, L
        man L beh, leans
            backward, &
            stretches out his
            right arm to hold
            the dog by its
            collar
    HMs 167 (L?s) Knossos
        Palace (KSPI K8)
        2 registers
        top: quadruped in
            PT 3/4/5, R
        bottom: man R with
            both arms out
                hatching beh
    HMs 1039 (Ls) Knossos
        Palace (Betts 6)
        man R carries quadruped
        R (cf. HMs 275B)
    HMs no. unknown (Ls) Kato
        Zakro (KZ 145)
        man & animal

Two or more
    HMs 160 (Ls) Knossos
        Palace (KSPI Q19)
        in the center: man R
            with "pony-tail"
        at right: ape seated L
            on a campstool, its
            left arm up to salute
        bel: calf? in PT 10A, R
            bef the man's feet?
        Weeds fill the field
    HMs 650 (Ls) Knossos,
        Little Palace (KSPI
        U?)
        man stands R carrying a
            Yoke over his
            shoulders from which
            hang a boar at left &
            a kid? at right, the
            two forming PT 34B
            upside down
    HMs 656 (Ls) Knossos,
        Little Palace (KSPI
        U115)
        filling the field: a man
            sitting R, animal
            heads (bull, agrimi,
            dog?) all R, & a
            centered circle

Man & Monsters
Griffins
    Stand
        I 223 (L) Vapheio
            Tholos (LH II)
            man L in long robe
                stands bef & holds
                a griffin in PT 2,
                L by a leash
                the leash is
                    attached to a
                    collar tied
                    with a small
                    Sacred Knot
            3 groundlines bel
    Frieze with Seated Griffins
        I 285 (Cyl) Rutsi

Tholos 2, last
burial (LH II-III
A)
  at left: griffin in PT
    7, R
  at right: helmeted?
    man R infr, his
    left arm akimbo,
    his right arm
    stretches out infr
I 309 (Cyl?s) Pylos
Palace (LH III
B2-C1)
  frieze: griffin? in
    PT 7, R; 2 men
    flank a smaller
    griffin in PT 7,
    R

Miscellaneous
II 3.328 (Cyl)
  2 panels separated by
    a pair of
    vertical lines
  in one panel: man
    walks L
  in the other
    panel: griffin
    salient L
      rocks bel

Miscellaneous
I Supp. 3 (Cyl) Mycenae,
ChT 47 (Pini 1980,
no. C6)
  L-R: helmeted man?
    salutes; man? with
    quadruped head
    (calf?); lion-headed
    person (with quadru-
    ped head [calf's?]
    conjoined to right,
    or perhaps this is
    another Figure-8
    Shield [see below]);
    agrimi-person -- all
    L

filler
  bel: dog? in PT 8, R
    infr of the quad-
    ruped-headed
    person; bull-face
    infr of the
    lion-headed person;
    object (lion face?)
    infr of the agrimi-
    headed person;
    Fish-Monster infr
    of the man
  ab: Figure-8 Shield
    inb of the
    quadruped-headed
    person

FIG. 112 -- VII 95:
2 men flank a genius

VII 95 (A) Hydra (FIG.
112)
  2 men flank genius
    standing L, arms posed
    as if to hold the jug
    that is typically
    present but missing
    here
      each man holds his
        outside arm
        across the waist
        & his inside arm

out toward the
genius
SH vertical
AM 1938.1091 (Cyl) Crete
(CS 358; Pini 1980:
no. B1)
frieze, L-R: 2 agrimia
salient R, 2 men R
wearing caps, genius R
holding a jug
supported by a <u>Column</u>
(waterbird R ab), man
R with bull horns on
his head
filler: <u>Short Column</u>
separates the agrimia
from the man, a sword?
betw the 2 men, a
<u>Column</u>?/<u>Stand</u>? + 2
dots separate the men
from the genius, &
a vertical line topped
with a rayed dot
betw the horned man &
the agrimia; dotted
arcs ab the 2 men;
<u>Mount-Guide</u> top &
bottom
HMs 291 (Ls) Knossos
Palace (KSPI R35)
collared sphinx in PT
1A, L
man L infr

3B
Master of Animals

FIG. 113 -- AM 1938.1054
(CS 9P): Master of lions

FIG. 114 -- V 201:
Master of griffin
& winged goat

Lions (see: PT 54: 2 lions vs
man -- IV 293)

PT 31A
?HMs 218 (Ls) Knossos
Palace (KSPI R44)
Master L in a kilt
flanked? by 2? lions

salient in PT 31A,
over which he flexes?
his arms
HMs 219 (Ls) Knossos (KSPI
    R43)
    Master L flanked by 2
    lions up in PT 31A,
    over which he
    stretches out his
    arms

PT 32A
HM G 3117 (L) Knossos
        (CMCG 358)
    Master L flanked by 2
    lions in PT 32A

PT 34A
AM 1938.1054 (L) (FIG. 113;
    CS 9P)
    Master R, arms stretched
    out over 2 upright
    lions in PT 34A,
    each in PT 1A
        SH horizontal?

PT 35
I 89 (R, stone) Mycenae
    ChT 58
    bearded Master R, arms
    out to hold 2 lions in
    PT 35, ccl
        lion at left in PT
        6
I Supp. 27 (L) Prosymna,
    ChT 33 (LH III A1)
    Master R flanked by 2
    lions in PT 35, ccl
    (lion at left
    regardant); he holds
    both arms stretched
    out over the lions

Miscellaneous
V 675 (Cyl) Thebes
    Kadmeion, (LH III B)
    SH vertical: Master L

regardant, arms out-
stretched, bel which
& flanking him are 2
lions upside down
(both in PT 11, L
with SH horizontal)
    SH horizontal: griffin
    vs stag in PT 39A, L
HMs 382 (L?s) Knossos
    Palace (KSPI Ca)
    Master R flanked by 2
    lions/dogs apparently
    assis, which he holds
    by leashes drawn
    tightly into his
    chest; the master
    wears a plumed? cap
        at left: a
        vertical row of
        objects
Vienna 1357 (L) (GGFR pl.
    189)
    Master L flanked by 2
    upside down lion
    protomes en face
    (hanging from an
    undepicted yoke?)

Caprids
Agrimia
I 163 (Ls) Mycenae, House
    of the Sphinxes (LH
    III B1; inscribed: MY
    Wt 501-506)
    Master flanked by 2
    agrimia salient in PT
    31A
IV 38D (L) Vrondissi
    Master L flanked by 2
    agrimia in PT 31B,
    which he holds by the
    neck

Stags?
V 594 (Ls) Mycenae, South
    House (LH III B1;
    inscribed: MY Wt 700)

Master L, arms
    up-raised, flanked by
    stags? in PT 31A

Monsters
Griffins
    I 324   (Rs)   Pylos Palace
        (LH III B2-C1;
        inscribed: PY Wr 1327)
    2 pairs of griffins vs
        stags, each pair in
        PT 39A, form PT 29A
        flanking 2 Masters
    top Master (at the level
        of the griffins) runs
        R to restrain? the
        griffin at the right
        by its wing
    bottom Master (at the
        level of the stags)
        runs L to restrain?
        the stag at the left
        by its haunch?
    each Master wears a Bull-
        Tail (for the curved,
        plume-like object at
        his head, cf. Ch. 6C:
        Griffins -- I 171)
    II 3.167   (L)   "Knossos"
    Master L flanked by a
        griffin at left & a
        lion at right, both
        salient
            line inb of lion
    V 669   (Ls)   Thebes,
        Kadmeion (LH III B2)
    Master R regardant, arms
        stretched out over 2
        griffins in PT 36, ccl

Genii
    V 201   (L)   Crete, Pyrgos
        Psilonero (**FIG. 114**)
    Master stands L, arms
        akimbo, on a HC,
        flanked by a winged
        agrimi at left salient

R & a genius at right
    standing L with jug
Berlin FG 10   (L)   Phigaleia
    (AGDS II Berlin 27)
    Master R flanked by 2
        genii, each with one
        arm up towards a dot
        where the Master's
        chest should be; the
        Master holds the
        genii by their jaws
Villa Giulia no. unknown
    (L)   (Battaglia 1982:
    no. 1; PM IV, fig.
    389)
    Master R flanked by 2
        genii, each holding a
        jug; the Master holds
        his arms out over the
        genii's head

Miscellaneous   (see: Ch. 3C:
Man Hunts Animals
[fisherman] --   V 181)

    I 356   (Rs?)   Pylos Palace,
        (LH III B2-C1)
    Master R, arms akimbo,
        flanked by 2 quadrupeds
        Pica? ab quadruped
            at right
        Dado 1 bel
    II 3.193   (L)   "Poros"
    Master R, arms akimbo,
        flanked by 2 dogs in PT
        31A

FIG. 115 -- IX 7D:
2 men R at left vs lion

3C
Man Hunts Animals

(see: Ch. 3D: Men in Chariots
-- I 15)

Lions
One Man
    Man at left, Lion salient
    at right

        I 228   (L)   Vapheio
        Tholos
            man at left carries R
            a Figure-8 Shield
            (seen in profile)
            & aims a sword at
            the head of a lion
            at right salient L
            SH horizontal?
        I 290   (A) Pylos Tholos
        4
            man R at left stabs
            with a sword the
            mouth of a lioness
            at right salient L
        II 3.14   (L) Knossos,
        Little Palace

lion in PT 12/14, L
    spear? in lion's
    chest
IV 233   (A) Siteia
    man at left holds a
    sword in his right
    hand & aims for the
    head of the lion at
    right salient L, en
    face
IX 7D   (C)   (FIG. 115)
    2 men R left vs lion
    at right salient L
    man at extreme
        left carries
        a Figure-8
        Shield & aims
        a spear at
        the lion
    2nd man aims a
        bow & arrow
        at the lion
    rocks/weeds bel

Man at right, Lion salient
at left

    I 9   (C) Mycenae ShGr
    III (LH I)
        at right: man with a
        sword L vs lion R
        at left (cf. PT
        46)
    I 165   (Ls) Mycenae,
    House of the
    Shields (LH III
    B1)
        man at right runs L
        towards a lion at
        left salient R;
        the man (his hair
        streaming to
        either side)
        touches the lion's
        nose with his
        right arm & holds
        a dagger/short

sword with his
left hand
    dog runs L bel
    the man
I 302 (Rs) Pylos
Palace (LH III
B2-C1)
  at left: a man L at
  right vs a lion?
  at left salient?
  R; the man holds
  his right arm up
  at right: a chariot?
  L drawn by one
  horse in PT 2, L
IX 152 (L)
  man at right L with
  plumed helmet
  spears lion at
  left salient R;
  the man's chest is
  incised with short
  horizontal strokes
  (=textured
  corselet/blouse?)
    2 groundlines
    ab
  SH horizontal
Munich Antike Sammlung
  SL681 (Cyl)
  Kakovatos Tholos
  (LH IIA; Gill
  1964: no. 50)
  man at right stabs
  the mouth of a lion
  at left salient
  with a sword; a
  scabbard?
  horizontal at the
  man's waist
    genius (with-
    out jug) inb
    of the man,
    holds its
    paws (as if
    to hold the
    jug that

typically
accompanies)
around the
tip of the
scabbard?
SH horizontal

2 Pairs of Man vs salient
Lion, in bilateral
symmetry

I 307 (Rs) Pylos Palace
  (LH III B2-C1)
  Preserved: 2 addorsed
  pairs of a man vs a
  lion, the men
  addorsed in the
  center, the lions
  salient, en face, &
  biting? each man's
  outside arm; the
  man at left holds
  his left arm up as
  if wielding a sword
  (may not be im-
  pressed by the same
  ring that im-
  pressed I Supp.
  173?; see I Supp.
  p. 16 & Sakellari-
  ou, 1966: 61; im-
  pressed by a ring
  from the same mould
  that, later, with
  changes & addi-
  tions, produced the
  Danicourt ring?;
  see below)
I Supp. 173 (Rs) Pylos
  Palace (LH III
  B2-C1)
  Preserved: 2 addorsed
  pairs of a man vs
  a lion, the men
  addorsed in the
  center, the lions
  salient, en face,

& biting? each
man's outside arm;
the man on the
left holds his
left arm up as if
wielding a sword
(may not be im-
pressed by the
same ring that im-
pressed I 307?:
see I Supp. p. 16 &
Sakellariou, 1966:
61; impressed by a
ring from the same
mould that, later,
with changes &
additions, produced
the Danicourt
ring?; see below)
Peronne no. unknown (R)
   Thessalonike tomb
   (The Danicourt
   Ring; Boardman
   1970: 3-8)
   2 pairs, addorsed, of
   a man vs salient
   lion biting his
   inside arm; the
   man at right
   raises his sword
   ab his head with
   his right hand;
   the man at left
   stabs his lion in
   its chest with his
   left hand; each
   man wears a
   <u>Bull-Tail</u>
      <u>Tree 1</u> bel each
      lion
      <u>Dado 9a</u> bel
Miscellaneous
  I 112 (A) Mycenae ChT
  79
    man at left R spears
    through the shoulder &
    chest of a lion at

right in PT 8, R
  IX 114 (A)
    lion in PT 2, L
    man left bef, his left
      hand holds a sword
      above the lion's
      head & his right
      holds a leash
      attached to the
      lion's beaded
      collar
      SH vertical

Two Men flank Lion
  Attacking
    I 331 (Rs) Pylos Palace
    (LH III B2-C1)
    2 men flank a lion
    salient L; the man
    at right runs L to
    stab the lion in
    the neck with a
    dagger/short sword;
    the man at left
    stands, holding
    both arms up-raised
  Berlin FG 7 (L) Syme
    (AGDS II Berlin 24)
    2 men flank & attack a
    lion salient L en
    face; each man
    holds the top of
    the lion's head &
    stabs his chest/
    shoulders with a
    sword
      dog bel lion
      attacks in PT
      6, R
Tying the lion up
  I 224 (L) Vapheio
    Tholos (LH IIA)
    2 men flank &, using
    rope, tie up a lion
    upside down R in PT
    1C, en face
      SH horizontal

HMs 65a (Cs) Kato Zakro
      (KZ 193)
   2 men flank & rope
      together the legs
      of a lion in PT 2
      upside down

FIG. 116 -- V 656:
man hunts an agrimi

Agrimia/Kids
Agrimi/kid salient
   V 656 (L) Rhodes, Ialysos
      T. 21 (FIG. 116; LH
      III C1)
      at left, man runs R to
      stab an agrimi at
      right salient in PT
      6, R with a dagger/
      short sword; the man
      stretches his left
      arm out to hold a
      Barbell ab the
      agrimi's neck; he
      wears a Bull-Tail
         a dog in PT 7, R
            attacks the
            agrimi from bel
   VII 131 (L)
      at left, man runs R to
         spear the neck of a
         kid salient L at

right in PT 13A; man
also wears a sword
just above his waist
& a Bull-Tail
AM 1938.962 (C) (CS 226)
   agrimi obliquely salient
      R; man beh runs R; his
      left arm touches the
      agrimi's neck; his
      right hand holds
      either a sword or one
      of the agrimi's horns
         dog at right leaps
            up bel the
            agrimi to form,
            with the SH
            horizontal, PT
            42A, R
   AM 1938.1022 (L) Mirabello
      (CS 320; GGFR pl. 122)
      SH horizontal: at right,
         man running L stabs
         the neck of an agrimi
         at left salient R with
         a sword
            bull face upside
               down betw the
               man's legs
Miscellaneous
   AM 1938.1023 (A) Ayia
      Pelagia (CS 285)
      agrimi supine R, head
         brought forward; man
         beh steps R with his
         left foot onto the
         agrimi's belly, holds
         one of the agrimi's
         horns with his right
         hand, & may stab the
         agrimi in the neck

Boars (see Ch3A: Man & Animals
[misc.] -- XII 240)

I 227 (L) Vapheio Tholos (LH
      IIA)
   at right, man L spears the

head of a male boar
at left charging in PT
5A, R
      rocks? ab
I 294 (L) Pylos Grave Circle
    (LH II-III)
 a circular composition, the
    the feet of the figures
    set on the periphery:
 at right: a helmeted man
    L spears the head of a
    boar at left in PT 5A, R
    bel the man, a dog
         runs L
    SH probably parallel
       to the spear
Berlin FG 40 (A) Peloponnese
    (AGDS II Berlin 23)
 at left: man R leans in to
    spear the head of a boar
    protome at right
    charging L
       stylized rocks bel

Miscellaneous quadrupeds
Chania 1536 (Ls) Chania,
    Kastelli (Papapostolou
    1977: no. 26)
 at left: man R holds onto
    the collar of a
    quadruped (dog?) with
    his right hand & wields
    a spear, apparently at
    the animal, with his
    left

Fishermen (see: Ch. 2B: Men
    [single, with an ax] --
    HMs 133/KN 02; & Ch. 4D:
    Women in Misc. Compositions
    [fisherwoman] AM 1938.1093
    [CS 282])

V 181 (L)
 man R, arms out-stretched
    to hold 2 fish upside
    down by the tail

2 Branch 1 flank & 2
    Branch 1 betw fish
    & man
VII 88 (A)
 man L holds infr of him a
    large (tunny?) fish by
    a fishing line
    SH vertical
AM 1938.956 (C) NW of
    Knossos (CS 205)
 man stands L, his right
    hand holds an octopus
    infr on a fishing line &
    his left grips a skaros-
    fish inb
    SH vertical
HMs 164 (Ls) Knossos Palace
    (KSPI K3)
 man R?
    dolphin upside down inb
    arcs in field

3D
Men in Chariots

Lion-drawn chariot
V 585 (Cyl) Kasarma Tholos
    (LH I-II)
 man in chariot R drawn by
    2 lions in PT 21, R; the
    man leans forward,
    holding the reins in
    his left hand; with his
    right arm, he wields a
    whip ab the lions
    an object, perhaps
       scabbard & its
       thong, flies out
       inb of the driver
    upright pole infr/inb
       (goal?/turning
       post?)
Nicosia 1953/IX-3/6 (Cyl)
    Analiondas, impression

on a pithos (Pini 1980:
   no. B2)
L-R: man in chariot R drawn
   by a lion; lion vs bull
   in PT 39A
         2? (impressed twice?)
         men run R

Agrimi-drawn chariot
AM 1938.1051 (R, stone)
   Spiliardia, Avdou rock
   tomb (CS 308; GGFR
   color pl. 9 & black/white
   pl. 110; Vermeule &
   Karageorghis 1982: 183
   fig. 3)
2 men drive chariot L drawn
   by 2 agrimia; the
   charioteer (at right)
   holds the reins in his
   left hand & a whip
   apparently in his right
   hand unseen beh his
   passenger
Once Arndt Coll.   (L) (GGFR
   pl. 186)
man in chariot L drawn by 2
   agrimia
         groundline bel

Horse-drawn chariot
One Man   (see: Ch. 3D: Men In
   Chariots -- II 3.199,
   below)

   Left
      VII 87   (A) Knossos
         man in 2-horse
            chariot L; he
            holds the reins
            with his left hand
            &, ab the team, a
            whip with his
            right hand
                  2 pairs of
                     Mount-Guides
                  flank

photo of
reverse
appears on
VII p. 134
Right
   I 230   (A) Vapheio
      Tholos (LH IIA)
   man? in a 2-horse
      chariot R
   IV 37D   (L) Lastros
   man in/ab 2-horse
      chariot L
            groundline bel
   HMs 516, 632-636 (Rs)
      Ayia Triada,
      Sklavokambos (AT
      117/Sk 8)
   man in chariot R
      drawn by 2 horses;
      man touches the
      back of the horses
      with a whip

Two Men
   Left
      Louvre AO 2188   (Cyl)
         (Pini 1980: no. A8)
      2 men in chariot L
         drawn by one horse
         (bull? goat? with a
         long tail)
            Fish-Monster up-
               side down bel
            2 Figure-8
               Shields bel
      the passenger leans
         forward to aim a
         bow & arrow
            Barbell ab
      in the field:
         ab: dog in PT 3, L
            chases a stag
            in PT 5B, L
            lance ab &
               Sun inb of
                  dog
            hand ab stag

inb & upside down:
lion? vs bull?
in PT 40, R
Right
   I 15 (R) Mycenae ShGr
          IV (LH I)
     2 men in 2-horse
     chariot R; horses
     in PT 20, R; the
     passenger? (since
     no reins are
     depicted, it is
     unclear which
     figure is the
     driver) leans
     forward to aim a
     bow & arrow at a
     stag at right in PT
     6, R ab the horses
        a tree bel
           horizontal R
           forms a
           groundline
           bel
        rocks ab
   I 229 (L) Vapheio
       Tholos
     2 men in 2-horse
     chariot R; the
     passenger carries a
     lance
        2 groundlines
        bel

Griffin-drawn chariot
II 3.199 (Cyl) Astrakoi
     2 registers, each upside
       down to the other &
       separated by a line
          1: man in chariot L
          drawn by a
          griffin, man infr
          & man inb (both
          L), 2 wings
          placed vertically
          & joined by a
          circle, <u>Potnia</u>

flanked by 2 lions
in PT 31A
          2: man in chariot L
          drawn by a horse,
          hand ab, man L inb
          holding a sword/
          vertical line, 2
          lions in PT 33A,
          woman L as <u>Potnia</u>
          to the lions infr &
          an upside down
          agrimi inb, & a man
          wearing <u>Bull-Tails</u>?
          with his right arm
          ab the agrimi & his
          left holding the
          horse L (of the
          horse-drawn
          chariot) by a leash
       a single <u>Mount-Guide</u>
       ab & bel
HMs 347 (Rs) Knossos (KSPI
       L?)
     man leans far forward in
     chariot R drawn by 2
     griffins, wings up, in
     PT 3, R
        groundline bel

                3E
          Animal Games

(see: PT 4 -- XIII 35; Ch. 3A:
Man & Animals [bull] -- HMs
251/KSPI R9)

Bull-Catching (see: PT 9)
I 274 (A) Rusti Tholos 2,
       (**FIG. 117**; LH IIA)
     at left: bull in PT 13C, R
       man R bel holds the
         bull's horns, his
         legs curved inb of him
       net covers the bull's

forequarters   bull L
rocks ab & bel   man upright clutching
<u>Branch 1 Tree</u> at right   the horns
                                    bull face ab

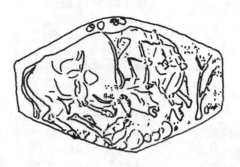

FIG. 117 -- I 274:   FIG. 118 -- I 137:
   bull-catching   bull-wrestling

Bull-Riding   **Bull-Wrestling** (Bull-
HMs 500 (As) Ayia Triada   Grappling; CMCG pp. 85-89,
   (AT 56)   especially 87f. catagory
   bull in PT 3, R, head down   III, to which we refer
man on the horns   below [no. III.7 = CMS I
   rocks ab & bel   199 is catalogued in Ch.
HMs 544 (Rs) Ayia Triada   3A: Men & Animals [caprid])
   (AT 109)
   bull in PT 3, R, head down   Man bef
man upside down on the   Standing
   horns, his back towards   I 95 (L) Mycenae ChT
   the bull's head, his   58 (CMCG no.
   right? leg curved over   III.5)
   the bull's neck   bull in PT 14A, R
HMs no. unknown (Rs) Ayia   man L bef regardant
   Triada (AT 108)   holds the bull by
   bull in PT 3, R, head down   both its head
   & en face   (chin? neck?) & its
man upside down on the   haunch
   horns, his back towards   Kneeling
   the bull's head, his   I 342 (Ls) Pylos
   left leg curved over the   Palace, (LH III
   bull's neck   B2-C1)
HMs no. unknown (?s) Knossos   bull runs in PT 5C,
   Palace (KSPI C42)

R, head averted
man kneels R bef
   regardant, his
   right arm holds
   the bull's head,
   his left arm the
   bull's haunch/
   tail
   I Supp. 35 (L)
      Lykosura? (PM
      III fig. 162:
      Mycenae; CMCG
      no. III.4)
   bull in PT 13A, R,
      head against its
      flank
   man kneels R bef,
      regardant,
      holding onto the
      bull's head with
      both arms
         branch/sign
            ab
   II 3.105b (C) Kalyvia
      T. 7 (LM III A2;
      CMCG no. III.3)
   bull stands in PT
      13A, R, head
      against its
      flank
   man kneels R bef;
      each hand holds
      the tip of a
      horn

Man beh (see: Ch. 4D: Women &
   Animals [misc.] -- HMs no.
   unknown [AT 111])

I 137 (A) Mycenae ChT 504
   (FIG. 117; LH III B; CMCG
   no. III.6)
   bull in PT 1A, L
   man L beh (his legs curve
      infr & bef the bull's
      forelegs) leans back to
      restrain the bull simul-

taneously by both its
   horns & its haunch
   ImpTr ab

Man bel
   AM 1938.1080/HMs 239 (Ls)
      Knossos Palace (KSPI
      G 5/6; CS 52S;
      inscribed: KN Ws
      1703; CMCG no. III.1)
   bull in PT 14A, L
   man semi-prone L bel,
      puts his right arm
      around the bull's
      neck & holds onto the
      bull's left? horn
      with his left hand
   HMs 670 (Ls) Knossos
      Palace (KSPI C43; Bk;
      CMCG p.87 no. III.2)
   bull in PT 1B, R
   man semi-prone R bel,
      reaches up to hold
      onto the bull's neck?

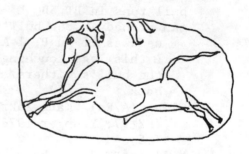

FIG. 119 -- HMs 102/AT 145
bull-leaping: Evans's Schema

FIG. 120 -- HMs 396/KSPI L48:
bull-leaping: Evans's Schema

Bull-Leaping (cf. HMs 161/KZ
    161; see Younger 1976, to
    which we refer below)

Evans's Schema
    I 517 (Ls) Knossos? (Gill
        1974; Younger 1976:
        I.2)
        bull runs in PT 5B, L
        man arched ab the bull's
            neck as if in PT 14A,
            L, his legs touching
            the bull's withers/
            back
    HMs 17a (A/Rs) Kato Zakro
        (KZ 97; Younger 1976:
        I.5)
        bull in PT 3, R, head
            stretched forward
        man curved supine R ab,
            his arms apart at the
            bull's horns, his legs
            apart dangling ab the
            bull's hindquarters,
            his hair flying out to
            either side
                2 groundlines bel
    HMs 102/Pigorini 71974 (Rs)

Ayia Triada, Gournia,
    Sklavokambo (FIG. 119;
    AT 145, Sk 3; Betts
    1967 figs. 6 & 7;
    Younger 1976: I.3)
bull in PT 3, L
man supine curved L ab
    the bull's neck, feet
    apart & dangling ab
    the bull's back
        2 groundlines bel
HMs 189 (Ls) Kato Zakro
    (KZ 189; Younger
    1976: I.7)
bull in PT 1A/5A, R
man curved supine R ab
    the bull's horns, his
    legs dangling ab the
    bull's back
        man inb, his
            right? arm
            stretched out
            infr (= rear
            assistant)
HMs 396 (Ls) Knossos
    Palace (FIG. 120; KSPI
    L48; Papapostolou
    1977: pl. 46g; Younger
    1976: I.1)
bull in PT 3, L
man curved L ab the
    bull's back
        man R inb, his
            right arm
            stretched out
            inb of him
            (alighting
            leaper? rear
            assistant?)
HMs 630 (Rs?)
    Sklavokambos (Sk 6)
bull in PT 1A, R, head
    up
man supine curved R ab
    the bull's horns, his
    arms straddles the
    bull's horns & his

feet (apart?) dangle
down ab the bull's
back
HMs no. unknown (L?s) Kato
Zakro (KZ 123; Younger
1976: I.4)
bull in PT 3, R
man curved supine R ab
the bull's back, both
his legs & arms
dangle ab the bull's
back

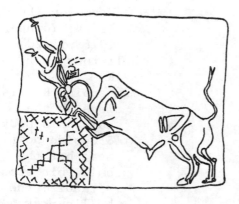

FIG. 121 -- AM 1938.964
(CS 202): bull-leaping:
Diving Leaper Schema

Diving Leaper Schema
Man ab the bull's neck
AM 1938.964 (C) "Priene"
(FIG. 121; CS 202;
GGFR pl.58; Younger
1976: II.6)
bull salient L on
square object
(cistern/box),
forelegs raised on
it with front
hooves & nose
apparently inside
man dives from the

upper left down R
onto the bull's
head
zig-zags outline
& criss-cross
the cistern/
box
HMs 502 (Rs?) Ayia
Triada (AT 51)
bull in PT 3, R
man upside down, head
L, ab the bull's
neck
Man ab the bull's withers
HMs 12, 625 (Rs) Kato
Zakro, Sklavo-
kambos (KZ 96, Sk
5; Betts 1967:
fig. 4; Younger
1976: II.8)
bull in PT 3, R, head
slightly up
man L ab, torso
almost vertical,
his arms apart &
stretching down
just ab the bull's
withers
HMs 516 (Rs) Ayia
Triada (AT 110;
Betts 1967: fig.
11a; Younger 1976:
II.9)
bull in PT 3, R
man upside down? ab
the bull's
withers, his arms
dangle ab the
bull's withers
object? bel
Man ab the bull's back
Bull left
V 267 (R) Armenoi
T. 43 (LH III
B1)
bull runs in PT 3,
L

man? curved ab the
bull's back
Bull right
I 200   (R) Asine T. 1
(LH III A2;
Younger 1976:
II.17)
bull runs in PT 3?,
R
man supine ab, head
L, his feet to
the left of the
bull's haunch,
his arms stretch
out beh the
bull's neck &
back
tree? infr
I 314 (A/Rs) Pylos
Palace, (LH III
B2-C1)
bull runs in PT 4,
R
man bel prone R
man curved ab to
left, head down
just ab the
bull's hind-
quarters, his
arms stretched
back towards the
bull's head
(presumably his
legs would have
curved R over
the bull's head)
V 597   (L) Mycenae,
House with the
Idols (FIG. 30;
LH III B2; 1976:
II.10)
2 bulls in PT 19B,
R
man curved ccl ab,
his legs ab the
far bull's head
& his head ab

its back; one of
the man's hands
touches the far
bull on its
muzzle
Tree 1 infr
groundline
bel
SH oblique
(upper
left to
lower
right)
V 674   (C/A) Thebes/
Kadmeion (LH
III B; Younger
1976: II.20)
bull runs in PT 3,
R
man supine R, his
legs ab the
bull, his body
& upside down
head bef the
bull, his arms
straddle? the
bull's neck
VII 108   (L) Crete
(Younger 1976:
II.16)
bull runs in PT
5A, R en face
man curved ab, his
arms placed
about the
horns, his head
tucked down
above the
bull's back,
his feet L &
straddling
the bull's
hindquarters as
if about to
land

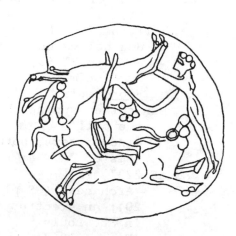

FIG. 122 -- AM 1938.1077
(CS 246): bull-leaping:
Diving Leaper Schema

AM 1938.1077 (L)
    Peloponnese
    (FIG. 122; CS
    246; Younger
    1976: II.19)
    2 bulls in PT 36,
    ccl (top bull
    en face), both
    in PT 3
man L upside down
    ab the en face
    bull, his hands
    straddling
    the bull's back
    & his feet
    thrown forward
    over his head
man stands L infr
    of the other
    bull with both
    arms out-
    stretched
HM G 3209 (L)
    Knossos (CMCG
    357; Younger
    1976: II.13)
    bull in PT 5B, R

man slightly
    curved supine R
    ab, head down,
    his arms apart
    flanking the
    bull's head
HMs 108 (R?s) Knossos
    Palace (KSPI 04;
    Betts 1967: fig.
    11b; Younger
    1976: II.7)
    bull in PT 3, R
man's arms? apart &
    dangle ab the
    bull's back &
    hindquarters
HMs no. unknown (Ls)
    Knossos
    bull in PT 3, R
man's arms or legs
    apart ab the
    bull's withers
HMs 613-24, 626, 627,
    649 (R/As)
    Sklavokambos (Sk
    4; Younger 1976:
    IV.2)
    bull in PT 3, R en
    face
man supine curved R
    ab the bull's
    back, his legs
    apart & dangling
    down ab the
    bull's tail
    Dado 9a bel
HMs 250 (Rs?)
    Knossos Palace
    (KSPI R8; PM I
    fig. 504d, III
    fig. 153;
    Younger 1976:
    II.14)
    bull in PT 3, R
man horizontal
    supine R ab the
    bull's back,

head down &
arms together
stretched R

Man ab the bull's hind-
quarters

I 152   (A) Mycenae ChT
        518 (LH I-II;
        Younger 1976:
        II.21)
    bull in PT 3, L, head
        down
    man horizontal ab,
        head L (torso only
        visible; the gold
        cap covers an
        ancient?
        fracture), hands
        (his left hand is
        visible, the other
        is beh the bull's
        back) stretched
        out over his head
        ab the bull's back
I 370   (Rs) Pylos
        Palace, (LH III
        B2-C1; Younger
        1976: II.22;
        inscribed PY Wr
        1374)
    bull (lion?) runs in
        PT 3, L
    man supine ab, head
        L, his braceleted
        right arm touches
        the withers
            Dado 7b bel
II 4.162 (L) Mallia
        Palace
    bull runs in PT 3, R
    leaper? alighting, 1
        arm stretched out R
        over the bull's
        back
AM 1938.1074 (L)
        Gythion (CS 209;

Younger 1976:
II.18)
    bull in PT 3, L
    dog bel vs bull to
        form PT 43,
        Victim L
    Frond infr
man curved supine ab
    the bull's
    hindquarters, both
    arms up
AM AE 2237 (R)
    "Archanes" (CS pl.
    20); an electrotype
    in St. Louis
    (Hoopes 1947)
    bull in PT 3, R
    man curved L ab, feet
        inb of the bull's
        hindquarters & his
        hands straddling
        the bull's back
            Sacred Knot infr
            Dado 3 bel

Floating Leaper Schema
Bull left
    II 4.81   (L) (CMCG p. 87
        no. II.4)
    bull in PT 5B, L?
    man prone? L ab (see:
        Ch. 3A: Man & Animals
        [man & bull with
        different SH])
    VII 109   (L) (Younger
        1976: III.3)
    bull in PT 1A, L
    man ab L, body
        horizontal, head &
        feet up, his right
        hand holds on to
        either the bull's
        horn or his frontal
        assistant's left
        hand; the leaper's
        left arm reaches
        down to the bull's

withers
  man infr R, his
  right arm
  reaches to the
  bull's chest,
  his arm touches
  the bull's horn
  either to hold
  it or the
  leaper's right
  hand
VII 257 (L) (Younger 1976:
    III.11)
  bull runs in PT 5A, L
    en face
  man ab curved L, head &
    feet up
AM 1938.1078 (L) (CS
    248; Younger 1976:
    III.6)
  bull runs in PT 5B, L
  man horizontal prone ab,
  head & feet up
    frond infr
HM M 1385 (L) (FIG. 123;
    Tamvaki 1973; Younger
    1976: III.9)
  bull in PT 5A, L en face
  man prone L ab, torso &
    left leg up, his
    right? arm stretched
    out towards the bull's
    horns
HMs no. unknown (Ls)
    Knossos, Little Palace
    (KSPI U5; Younger
    1976: III.7)
  bull in PT 5A, L en
    face
  man prone L ab, head &
    foot (feet?) up, his
    right arm up towards
    or ab the bull's left
    horn, his left arm
    down

FIG. 123 -- HM Metaxas 1385:
    bull-leaping:
    Floating Leaper Schema

Bull right
  I 79 (L/A) Mycenae ChT 44
    (Younger 1976: III.13)
    bull in PT 1A, R
    man ab, head R, holds
      onto the top of the
      bull's head
      SH horizontal
  I 378 (Ls) Pylos Palace
    (LH III B2-C1; Younger
    1976: III.17)
    bull runs in PT 5, R
    man horizontal ab,
      leg(s?) up
  I 408 (L) Dimini Tholos
    (Younger 1976: III.5)
    bull in PT 5B, R
    man prone R ab, legs &
      head up, his left
      hand ab the bull's
      nose, his right hand
      down bef the bull's
      shoulder
  II 3.271 (L) Praisos T. D
    (Younger 1976:
    III.12)
    bull in PT 10A, R

Frond infr
man prone R ab, each
  hand clasps a horn
    oblique line ab
      with zig-zags
      ab
  Dado 2c bel
II 4.157 (L) Gournes T. 1
  (LM III B1; Younger
  1976: III.8)
  bull in PT 5A, R en face
  man prone ab, head &
    one leg up, his hands
    grasping? the bull's
    horns
IV 289 (L) Messara
  bull in PT 3, R
  man prone R ab?
V 517 (L)
  bull runs in PT 3, R
  man horizontal ab, legs
    & head up, his right
    hand touches the
    bull's neck & his
    left hand holds the
    bull's upper horn
    Dado 8 bel
X 141 (L) (FIG. 124)
  bull in PT 5A, R en face
  man curved supine R ab,
    head down, his left
    hand touches the
    bull's left horn, his
    right hand dangles
    down, his feet apart
    straddling the bull's
    hindquarters
    SH horizontal
XII 284 (L) Seager Coll.
  bull in PT 1B, R, head
    low
  man R horizontal,
    ab; his left arm
    stretches out to touch
    the bull's neck
AM 1938.1079 (L) (CS 249;
  GGFR pl. 103; Younger

1976: III.16)
  bull runs in PT 3, R
  man ab R, his left leg
    up, his right arm ab
    the bull's horns; his
    left hand touches
    the bull's neck
    prone man bel R

FIG. 124 -- X 141:
bull-leaping:
Floating Leaper Schema

AM 1938.1108 (L) (CS 341;
  GGFR pl. 124; Younger
  1976: III.10)
  bull in PT 5A, R en
    face
  man prone horizontal
    ab, one leg head up,
    his right hand almost
    touches the bull's
    right horn, his left
    arm stretches toward
    the bull's face
    Figure-8 Shield
    infr
Munich A.1180 (L) (AGDS
  I Munich 45; Younger
  1976: III.4)
  bull in PT 5A, R
  man prone horizontal R

ab, his right arm
akimbo, his left
hand holds the tip
of the bull's horn,
& his right leg up
    Tree 1 infr
Columbia, Missouri
    University 57.8 (L)
    "Phigaleia" (Younger
    1984)
    bull in PT 1A, R
    man prone horizontal ab,
    his head & feet up,
    his right hand
    clasping the bull's
    horn, his left arm
    touches the bull's
    neck
        man L infr, his
        arms straddling
        & holding the
        bull's head

Man infr of the bull
I 305 (Rs) Pylos Palace
    (LH III B2-C1; Younger
    1976: II.3)
    bull in PT 3, L
    man R infr, both arms
    stretched out towards
    the bull's head
    Dado 9a bel
?HMs 1001 (Rs) Knossos
    Palace (Younger 1976:
    II.1)
    bull in PT 3, R?
    genius or man steps L
        infr
    Palms beh or Weeds bel
    Weed bel betw the legs
        of the genius or man
    Dado 3 bel

Man inb of the bull
Chania 1547-1556 (R/As)
    Chania, Kastelli (Papapo-
    stolou 1977: no. 1)

bull in PT 3, R, head up
man at left ab, leaning
    forward slightly R, his
    left arm stretched out
    R, feet together
HMs 101, 497, 628, 629
    (R?s) Gournia,
    Sklavokambos, Ayia
    Triada (Sk 2, AT 54;
    Betts 1967: fig. 1a;
    Younger 1976: AL.4)
    bull in PT 3, L
    man at right ab, leaning
    forward slightly L, his
    arm stretched out L,
    feet together
        2 groundlines bel
HMs 1033 (?s) Knossos Palace
    (Betts 10; Younger 1976:
    AL.1)
    bull in PT 1A?, R
    man R inb, his right arm
    down & his left
    arm stretched out R

Uncertain poses
I 82 (L) Mycenae ChT 47
    (Younger 1976: IV.3)
    bull in PT 3, R
    man L at left regardant,
    his right arm bent R
    to touch the bull's
    horn, his left arm
    back R to touch the
    base of the bull's
    neck or its shoulder
    (vaulting?); his
    hair streams to
    either side
        Tree 1 horizontal R
        bel
HMs 37 (As) Kato Zakro (KZ
    98)
    bull in PT 3, R, head
    stretched forward
    man ab, his arms or legs
    straddling the horns

HMs 251   (Rs?)   Knossos Palace
    (KSPI R9)
  bull in PT 3/4, R
  man prone R bel, his right
    arm stretched out infr,
    his left arm back

FIG. 125 -- V 638:
man rides an agrimi

Man rides other animals (see:
  Ch. 3A: Men & Animals
  [caprid] -- HM 1863)

V 638   (L)   Akona Tholos 1
    (FIG. 125; LH III;
    Younger 1976: III.15)
  agrimi in PT 5A, L
    girth? around its waist
  man prone L ab, his left
    leg up, both arms down
    to touch the agrimi's
    shoulder
        2 vertical
           groundlines inb at
           right
        2 Weeds bel
        groundline bel
        SH horizontal
X 166   (L)
    stag in PT 1A, L

man supine horizontal L
    ab
    forgery? (see: PT 1A, L:
    Plain [agrimi] -- X
    162)

3F
Animal-Sacrifice

(see: Sakellarakis 1970, to
which we refer below)

Bull-sacrifice
I 203   (L)   Nafplion ChT 2
    bull in PT 10A, L on a 2-
    legged Table, its legs
    crossed (& presumably
    tied) on either side of
    the Table
        3 circles ab
II 3.338   (L)
    bull in PT 10A, R, head
    down & en face, feet
    brought together
    (crossed & tied?)
    2-legged Table bel
        bull head R bel
    ImpTr ab
Berlin FG 22   (L)   Mycenae
    (AGDS II Berlin 44)
    bull lies in PT 10A, R, head
    down, on a Table with 4
    legs in the shape of
    bull faces & 2 thin
    supports set betw
    a sword stands
        vertically lodged
        in the bull's neck
    Palm 4 horizontal R ab
    groundline bel
HMs 142   (Ls)   Knossos Palace
    (Sakellarakis 1970: 217
    no. B3)
    bull in PT 10A, R, head down

        2-(3-?) legged <u>Table</u> bel
        groundline? bel
HMs 211   (R?s) Knossos Palace
        Staircase (KSPI R13;
        Sakellarakis 1970: fig.
        8.4)
    bull in PT 10A, R, head down
        2 men R stand beh
        2-legged <u>Table</u> bel
        <u>Dado 3</u> bel
HMs 1049 (Ls) Mallia (Long
        1974: fig. 11; Sakellara-
        kis 1970: 169 fig. 8.5)
    bull in PT 10A, R, head
        down, legs crossed &
        tied? on a 2-legged <u>Table</u>
        bel
            ab: sword/spear,
                bucket/basket?, <u>HC</u>
                with another
                bucket/basket? ab
            man R inb, arms
                stretched forward

Boar-sacrifice (see: PT 1B,
    L: boar -- AM 1938.1086; Ch.
    4D: Women & Animals [misc.])

CHAPTER 4
Women & Animals

4A
Women with Animals

Woman stands
Woman & Animal antithetic
  Animal stands
    V 595 (Ls) Mycenae, the
      House of the Idols
      (LH III B2)
      at left: woman R
      at right: bull protome
        in PT 1B, L
          seal was broken
            before the
            sealing
    VIII 95 (L) Dawkins
      Coll.
      at left: griffin in PT
        1A, R
      at right, woman L
        salutes
    X 160 (L)
      at left: woman holds
        the nose of an
        agrimi at right in
        PT 1A, L
          SH horizontal
    AM 1938.1097 (L) (CS 21P)
      at left, woman R
        salutes with her
        left arm
      at right: bull in PT
        2, L
        Palm 1 beh
    AM 1971.1139 (L) de
      Jong Coll. (Board-
      man 1973: no.6)
      at left, agrimi in PT
        1A, R
      at right: woman L
        holds? the agrimi
        by its chin
          2 Fronds ab with

a row of dots
ab
2? groundlines
bel
SH horizontal
HMs 192 (Ls) Kato Zakro
  (KZ 192)
  at left: griffin? R
    (raised foreleg?)
    spear? in the
    chest
  at right: woman leans
    L
HM G 3054 (L) Siteia
  (CMCG 359)
  at left: monkey sits
    R holding an
    object (vessel?)
  at right: woman L
    hatching ab
    branch inb
    Dado 2a bel

Animal rampant
  II 3.168 (L) "Knossos"
    in the center: woman
      sits L
    at right: boar
      rampant L
        SH horizontal
        unfinished?
  VIII 146 (L)
    at left: woman R
    at right: griffin
      rampant L,
      displayed (its
      left wing crosses
      bef the woman's
      neck), regardant
        SH horizontal
  XIII 135 (L)
    at left: quadruped
      rampant R
    at right: woman L
      dots inb
      SH horizontal

Miscellaneous
    II 4.125 (L) Mavro-
        spelio T. VII B
      woman L
        waterbird placed
            antithetic &
            upright
        staff inb (held?)

Animal inb of the Woman
    II 3.309 (A) Siteia
      at left: bull in PT 2, R
        head averted
      at right: woman R
        object ab
        groundline bel
    HMs 191 (Rs) Kato Zakro
        (KZ 191)
      at left: agrimi in PT
        1A, R
      at right: woman R
    HMs no. unknown (Rs)
        Ayia Triada (AT 129)
      at left: woman L, her
        left arm stretched out
        inb of her to the
        agrimi's horns
      at right: agrimi in PT
        1A, L

FIG. 126 -- Berlin FG 3
(AGDS II Berlin 21):
woman holds agrimi

Woman inb of the Animal
    Rampant
    I Supp. 180 (Ls) Pylos,
        outside the SW
        building & Berlin
        FG 3 (L) Elis
        (FIG. 126; AGDS II
        Berlin 21)
      at left: woman R holds
        agrimi at right
        rampant R
          SH horizontal
    IV 307 (L) Roussochoria
      at left: woman R
        salutes
      at right: quadruped
        rampant R
          SH horizontal
    BSA cast 188 (L)
      at left: woman R
        inb: ab, HC with
          vertical line;
          bel, Frond
      at right: goat
        rampant R
        bel: Frond &
          groundline
      betw: 2 X's
      SH horizontal
Running/Flying away
    HMm 1017 (R) Archanes
        Tholos B (LM III
        A1; Sakellarakis
        1967b: pl. 137a)
      at left: woman with
        her left arm
        stretched out over
        the griffin's wing
        holding a leash,
        traces of which
        might be visible
        just below her
        left hand
      at right: griffin in
        PT 3, R

Woman seated L at right (cf.
    Ch. 4A: Women & Animals
    [friezes] -- HMm 44, below)

Lion
    HMs 157 (Ls) Knossos
        Palace (KSPI R91)
        at left: lion in PT 1A,
            R
        rocks bel
        at right: woman L seated
            on rocks

FIG. 127 -- I 128:
griffiness stands infr
of a seated woman

Agrimi
    HMs 584 (Rs) Ayia Triada
        (AT 128)
        at left: agrimi in PT
            1A, R
        at right: woman L seated
            on rocks
    Chania 1503 & 1513 (Rs)
        Chania, Kastelli
        (Papapostolou 1977:
        no. 32)
        at left: agrimi R
        at right: woman seated L
            on a 2-legged Table,
            touching the agrimi's

muzzle (feeding it?)
    head with her right
    hand, her left arm
    bent at the elbow,
    hand up
        groundline bel

Boar's Head
    HMs no. unknown (Rs)
        Ayia Triada (AT 130)
        at left: boar's head R
        at right: woman sits L

Monsters
    I 128 (R) Mycenae ChT 91
        (**FIG. 127**; LH II-III)
        at left: griffiness in
            PT 7, R
        at right: woman seated L
            on a chair holding the
            griffin by a leash
            Dado 1 bel
    I 179 (R) Tiryns Treasure
        (the ring may be a
        forgery; see Gill
        1964: 12-13. The
        representation of a
        campstool was first?
        published in Evans
        1901: 18 fig. 7a)
        L-R: a frieze of 3 genii
            R each carrying a jug
            (cf. Marinatos &
            Hirmer 1960: pl. 95)
            supported by a
            Cypress Branch; the
            genius at right
            carries a jug
            supported by a
            Column; woman L
            seated on a chair,
            holding aloft a
            chalice (Warren 1969:
            type 15)
                inb of the chair:
                    ab, bird L
                        regardant

bel, a half-
     bench?
     decorated
     with a half-
     rosette
 ab: wavy <u>Heaven</u>
     <u>Line</u>, ab which
     are (L-R):
     <u>Cypress Branch</u>,
     crescent <u>Moon</u>,
     <u>Cypress Branch</u>,
     <u>Sun</u>, 2 <u>Cypress</u>
     <u>Branches</u>; dots
     (<u>Stars</u>?) fill
     the area
 <u>Dado 8</u> bel

Woman rides an animal
<u>Babylonian Dragon</u>
  I 167 (L) Mycenae,
       Clytemnestra Tholos
       (LH III A)
   woman rides L <u>Babylonian</u>
   <u>Dragon</u> in PT 1A, L,
   her right hand
   touching the back of
   the monster's head,
   her left hand
   touching its tail
       rocks/waves bel
  HMs 73 (As) Ayia Triada
       (AT 132)
   woman rides <u>Babylonian</u>
   <u>Dragon</u> R in PT 1A, R,
   her right arm bent at
   the elbow with the
   hand up, her left arm
   bent & held close to
   the chest (her head
   turned L?)
       2 short vertical
          strokes flank
          woman
Miscellaneous
  V 584 (Cyl) Kasarma
       Tholos (LH I-II)
   woman rides lion R in

PT 1A, R
     griffin infr in PT
     7, (chip at
     lower rim may
     have prompted
     the artist to
     make the griffin
     sit on it)

Friezes
I Supp. 114 (R)
   L-R: lion rampant R; woman
        seated L, her right hand
        raised up (to salute?);
        <u>Palm 1</u>
II 3.103 (R) Kalyvia T. 2
     (LM III A1)
   L-R: woman salutes R;
        tailed animal (monkey?)
        rampant R; woman kneels
        L; <u>Column</u>
            ab: <u>Cypress Branch</u> &
               objects ab
II 3.282 (Cyl) Palaikastro,
     (LM III)
   L-R: woman, head R; tree?;
        genius R; human figure
        with animal head?, R;
        tree? with groundline
        bel
HMs 272 (Cyls) Knossos
     Palace (KSPI R66; PM
     IV fig. 593)
   L-R: woman R?; kid upside
        down in PT 2, R; lion?
        rampant L, vertical
        stroke crossed by 3
        horizontal strokes

FIG. 128 -- I 144:
<u>Potnia</u> & lions

4B
<u>Potnia Theron</u>

Lions (see: Ch. 2E: People at
a <u>Shrine</u> [person at right]
-- BSA Cast 135, & HMs 141;
& Ch. 3D: Men In Chariots
-- II 3.199)

<u>Potnia</u> holds <u>Snake Frame</u>
Lion protomes in PT 29A
X 242 (L) "the Islands"
<u>Potnia</u> frontal holds
triple <u>Snake Frame</u>
ab her head
2 groundlines
bel each
protome
SH horizontal
Kassel no. unknown (L)
Menidi (LH III B;
AGDS III Kassel 6)
<u>Potnia</u> frontal? with
arms up supports
double/triple
<u>Snake Frame</u> ab her
head

bel her arms &
ab each lion
protome is a
long convex
line
Lions in PT 31A
I 144 (L) Mycenae ChT
515 (FIG. 128; LH
IIB)
<u>Potnia</u> R holds double
<u>Snake Frame</u> with
<u>Double Ax</u> ab her
head
<u>Dado 2b</u> bel
SH horizontal
I 145 (L) Mycenae
ChT 515 (LH IIB)
<u>Potnia</u> R holds double
<u>Snake Frame</u> with
<u>Double Ax</u> ab her
head
<u>Dado 2b</u> bel
SH oblique/
horizontal
Lions in PT 34B, heads up
IV 295 (L) Knossos
<u>Potnia</u> L holds? double
<u>Snake Frame</u> ab her
head

With no <u>Snake Frame</u>
BSA Cast 135 (R)
<u>Potnia</u> sits L, her right
arm raised, on <u>Shrine</u>
or <u>Table</u> flanked by
lions rampant on it
groundline bel
HMs 158 & 662 (Ls) Knossos
Palace Staircase (KSPI
R32)
<u>Potnia</u> R holds the jaws
of the 2 lions
flanking her in PT 32B

Waterbirds
I 233a (Pr) Vapheio Tholos
<u>Potnia</u> R holds 2 addorsed

waterbirds by the neck
VII 134 (L)
  <u>Potnia</u> L, arms bent at
    the elbow & hands out
    to hold 2 addorsed,
    flying waterbirds
     <u>Dado 6b</u> bel
IX 154 (L)
  <u>Potnia</u> R holds 2 addorsed
    waterbirds by the
    neck
     SH horizontal

Dolphins
I 344 (Ls) Pylos Palace
  (LH III B-C)
  <u>Potnia</u> R, arms akimbo,
    flanked by 2 dolphins
    upside down in PT 34A?
II 3.327 (L)
  <u>Potnia</u> R, arms raised,
    flanked by 2 dolphins in
    PT 34A, heads down
    SH horizontal
?AM 1971.1145 (L) (Boardman
  1973: no. 5)
  <u>Potnia</u> R, arms up, flanked
    by 2 dolphins/fish
    upside down

Griffins in PT 28A, 1 wing up
II 3.63 (L) Ayios Ioannes
  T. 3 (LM II)
  <u>Potnia</u> frontal (feet L),
    holds a double <u>Snake</u>
    <u>Frame</u> with <u>Double Ax</u>
     2 groundlines bel
     SH horizontal
II 3.276 (L) Sphakia Tholos
  <u>Potnia</u> frontal holds a
    triple <u>Snake Frame</u>
     griffins rampant on a
      short vertical
      line
     groundline bel each
      griffin
V 654 (L) Rhodes, Ialysos

T. 20 (LH III C1)
  <u>Potnia</u> R hold a double
    <u>Snake Frame</u> with <u>Double</u>
    <u>Ax</u>
     2 groundlines bel
      each griffin
     SH horizontal
AM AE 689 (L) Diktaian cave
  (CS 351)
  <u>Potnia</u> R holds a triple
    <u>Snake Frame</u>
     groundline bel each
      griffin
     broken, no SH

Miscellaneous Animals
I 379 (Ls) Pylos Palace,
  (LH III B2-C1)
  <u>Potnia</u> R, arms up, wears a
    triple <u>Snake Frame</u> with
    <u>Double Ax</u> on her head
     flanked by 2 stags (if
      bulls, this scene
      is unique) in PT
      31A?, salient?
     flanked by 2 genii ab
      each stag & facing
      the <u>Potnia</u> &
      holding a <u>Cypress</u>
      <u>Branch</u>/sword

4C
Woman "Crossed" by a Caprid

Woman with caprid vertical
  infr, its head raised back
  bef the woman (see:
  Sakellarakis 1972b, to whose
  pls. 94 & 95 we refer)

Woman stands; caprid rampant
   infr in the same direction;
   (SH presumed horizontal)

Caprid's head not stretched
   back bef the woman's

   HM G 3034 (L) (CMCG 362)
      woman L

FIG. 129 -- I 221:
woman "crossed" by a sheep

Caprid's head stretched back
   bef the woman's

   Caprid's head unclear
      Woman R
         II 3.213 (L) Cher-
            sonisos (Sakel-
            larakis 1972b: pl.
            94 zeta, drawn
            from the seal)
         II 4.35 (L)
         II 4.196 (L)
         "Gonies"
      Woman L
         II 3.287 (L) (Sak-
            ellarakis 1972b:
            pl. 94 e, drawn
            from the seal)

Frieze
   HM G 3264 (Cyl)
      (CMCG 362)
      L-R: woman L
         saluting? a
         goat; woman L
         with rampant
         goat? inf;
         woman R
         saluting
Caprid in PT 1A
   I 220 (L) Vapheio
      Tholos (LH IIA;
      Sakellarakis
      1972b: pls. 88 eta
      & 95a)
      woman L & goat
         woman L inb,
         salutes
         2 groundlines bel
      reverse carries a
         cartoon of the
         2nd woman
   I 221 (L) Vapheio
      Tholos (FIG. 129;
      IIA; Sakelarakis
      1972b: pl. 95b)
      woman R & sheep
      SH horizontal
   II 3.117 (L) Ayia
      Triada, West area
      (LM IB; Sakellar-
      akis 1972b: pl.
      94b)
      woman L & caprid
      SH horizontal?

Caprid in PT 1B, head bef
   the woman's

   II 4.111 (L) Knossos,
      House of Frescoes
      (LM IB; Sakellar-
      akis 1972b: pl.
      94d)
      woman R & caprid
   VIII 144 (L; Sakel-

larakis 197b: pl.
94i)
woman L & quadruped
SH horizontal
XII 276a (L) Seager
Coll. (Sakellarakis
1972b: pl. 94 iota-
gamma)
woman R & quadruped
SH horizontal
AM 1941.120 (L) (CS
283; Sakellarakis
1972b: pl. 94 ia)
woman R & goat
SH horizontal
Epidauros no. unknown
(L) Apollo
Maleatas Sanctuary
(Ergon 1975, 106
fig. 10.1)
woman L & sheep
SH horizontal

Caprid in PT 2, neck elong-
ated & head bef the
woman's

I 222 (L) Vapheio
Tholos (LH IIA;
Sakellarakis
1972b: pl. 94a)
woman L? & kid?
SH horizontal
II 3.86 (L) Knossos
(Sakellarakis
1972b: pl. 94 eta)
woman R & caprid
II 4.204 (L) Gournia
(Sakellarakis
1972b: pl. 94
gamma)
woman R & caprid
SH horizontal
XII 239 (L) Seager
Coll. (Sakel-
larakis 1972b: pl.
94ib)

woman R & kid?
a vertical row of
3 short hori-
zontal lines
inb
SH horizontal?
XIII 5D (L)
woman L & quadruped
SH horizontal?
HMs no. unknown (Ls)
Kato Zakro (KZ 4;
Sakellarakis
1972b: pl. 95
gamma)
woman R & caprid
vertical stack of
short hori-
zontal strokes
infr (=
Shrine?)

FIG. 130 -- AM 1938.1093
(CS 282): fisherwoman

4D
Miscellaneous Compositions

Fisherwoman
AM 1938.1093 (L) (**FIG. 130**; CS
      282)
   at right: woman L holds fish
      upside down
         SH horizontal

Bull-Wrestling (Bull-
   Grappling)?

HMs no. unknown (R?s) Ayia
      Triada (AT 111)
   animal (bull?) L
   woman L beh, leans forward
      to stretch her right arm
      over the animal's back,
      her left hand holding a
      whip

Boar-Sacrifice/Slaughter (see:
   Ch. 3E: Animal Sacrifice
   [boars])

I 80 (L?) Mycenae ChT 47
         (**FIG. 130**)
   boar lies upside down R
      on a 3-legged <u>Table</u>
   woman stands R bef, arms
      stretched over the boar's
      belly; she holds a knife?
      in her left hand &
      steadies it with her
      right hand

FIG. 131 -- I 80:
woman slaughters a boar

CHAPTER 5
Miscellaneous Animals

5A
Miscellaneous Quadrupeds

Cats (cf. VII 45c)
Cat vs Waterbird
   I Supp. 75 (A) Crete
      at left: cat in PT 3, R
      chases waterbird at
      right in PT 2, R,
      1 wing up
         Weed ab
         2 Weeds bel
   II 3.172 (A) "Knossos"
      at right: cat in PT 3, L
      catches (in PT 39A/B)
      waterbird at left both
      wings up; waterbird
      displayed, flies up R
      ab cat
         5 Weeds bel
         groundline bel

FIG. 132 -- HM Giamalakis 3311
   (CMCG 355): 2 monkeys

Monkeys/Apes (see: PT 31B:
   HM G 3311/CMCG 355 [**FIG.**

132]; Ch. 3A: Men & Animals
[misc. animals] -- I 377 &
HMs 160)

V 233 (Ls?) Chania, Kastelli
3 monkeys

5B
Animal Faces

Lion (see: Ch. 5E: Birds &
Waterbirds [waterbirds,
single] -- IV 257)

Simple
   ?I Supp. 159a (L)
   schematic
      SH horizontal
   HMs 29a (Ls) Kato Zakro
   (KZ 67)
   HMs 39b (Ls) Kato Zakro
   (KZ 68)
   HMs 141 (Ls) Kato Zakro
   (KZ 141)
   Munich A.3161 (L) Kos
      (AGDS I Munich 51)
      schematic
      SH horizontal

With a Snake Frame
   In the mouth
      HMs 38 gamma (Ls) Kato
         Zakro (KZ 60)
         object ab (half a
         Double Ax?/Waisted
         Altar?)
      HMs 39 (Ls) Kato Zakro
         (KZ 167)
         curtailed Snake
         Frame?
            Branch 1 ab
   ABOVE
      HMs 81b (Ls) Kato
         Zakro (KZ 56)

topped by <u>Snake Frame</u>
enclosing 2 bird
heads addorsed
2 human legs flank
lion face

4 or More Lion Faces, noses to
center

HMs 60b (Ls) Kato Zakro
(KZ 93)
4 lion faces
HMs 93 (Ls) Kato Zakro
(KZ 135)
6 lion face "masks"
rosette in center

With Other Faces/Heads
I 110 (L) Mycenae ChT 78
cl: lion face, waterbird
L regardant, goat head
L, lion protome L with
2 groundlines ab,
quadruped in PT 3, L
with groundline bel
XIII 22D (L) Mycenae
lion face in the center
bull face ab
heads, cl from
beardless man's:
horse, boar,
bull?, dog,
goat, agrimi;
all R
rocks bel
SH horizontal?

Bull (see: Ch. 2A: Body
Parts [man's face] -- HMs
653; Ch. 5D: Protomes -- HMs
90; Ch. 8E: Helmets -- HMs
37)

Single
Simple
I 467 (L) Crete
II 3.96c (Pr) Knossos

VIII 116 (L) Hutchinson
Coll.
SH horizontal
XII 162a (Pr) Seager
Coll.
HM no. unknown (L)
Knossos MUM
(Popham et al.
1984: no. Misc.
7)]
SH horizontal
HMs 69a (Ls) Kato
Zakro (KZ 87)
HMs 84a (Ls) Kato
Zakro (KZ 95)
HMs 190a (?s) Knossos
Palace (KSPI P72)
HM G 3307 (L) Knossos
(CMCG 353)
HM G 3520 (L) (CMCG
352)

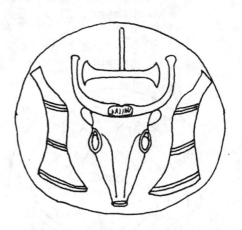

FIG. 133 -- Lentoid
from the Argive Heraeum:
bull-face

Objects ab
<u>Sun</u>
II 3.149 (L) Mallia
X 68 (C)
<u>Double Ax</u>
II 3.11 (C) Knossos

Palace (L)
Argive Heraeum
SH vertical
Once Schliemann (L)
Argive Heraeum
(**FIG. 133**;
Schliemann
1880: fig./no.
541)
flanked by 2
Sacred Knots/
Robes
Double Ax upside
down ab

Fence (see PT 40: lion
R vs bull -- X 241,
Fence = Pica in
bull's back)

V 592 (C) Nafplion,
Evangelistria
cemetery
HMs 665 (L/R?s)
Knossos Palace
(KSPI R101)
branches/lines
encircle

2 Quadruped heads (neck
to neck)

AM 1938.1039 (L)
Psychro (CS 292)
agrimi heads on the
horns
Palm Frond ab
SH horizontal
AM 1938.976 (L) (CS
291)
quadruped heads
flanking
a Palm Frond ab
SH horizontal
Miscellaneous
HMs 152 (As) Knossos
Palace (KSPI S5)

X betw horns
dotted circle ab
SH vertical
HMs 165 (Ls) Kato
Zakro (KZ 165)
rosette ab betw
horns
2 lines (Snake
Frame?) flank
Horns ending in legs
HMs 23 (Ls) Kato Zakro
(KZ 84)
human legs
loop ab, flanked by
2 objects

With Snake Frame in mouth
Simple
HMs 24a (Ls) Kato
Zakro (KZ 81)
flanked by 2 birds
antithetic double
Snake Frame
dot bel
HMs 24 (Ls) Kato
Zakro (KZ 82)
Curtailed
HMs 6b (Ls) Kato
Zakro (KZ 83)
horns ending in kid
heads
wavy line with
3 dots ab
HMs 642 (Ls) Skla-
vokambos (Sk 16)
ABOVE
HMs 15a (Ls) Kato
Zakro (KZ 88)
schematic bull face
flanked by 2
waterbirds
addorsed
double Snake
Frame ab
Wheel ab

As Filler/Part of a larger
composition

    XIII 22D (L) Mycenae
      lion face in center
        bull face ab
          heads, cl from
            beardless
            man's: horse,
            boar, bull?,
            dog, goat,
            agrimi, all R
          rocks bel
          SH horizontal?
    HMs 312 (Ls) Knossos
        (Gill 1966: 15 no. 8)
      in the center, bull face
        ImpTr ab
        flanked: at left,
          goat head; at
          right, quadruped
          leg?
    HMs 367 (Ls) Knossos
        Palace (KSPI R38)
      2 lions in PT 34A
        flank bull face

Two Bull Faces
One above the other
    ?IV 301 (L) Messara
    XII 294 (L) Seager Coll.
      lines in field

Addorsed
    HMs 46 (Ls) Kato Zakro
        (KZ 85)
      each with quadruped
        legs for horns
    HMs 580 (Ls) Ayia Triada
        (AT 7)

Bucrania
Single
  Simple
    V 347 (L) Medeon T. 29
        (LH III A-C)
      3 dots ab

V 513 (L) Korakou
    Branch 3, line, &
      strokes ab
    strokes at left
    SH horizontal
V 748 (L) Ayii
    Theodoroi, Metaphio
    Tholos (LH III A2)
    Branch 3 encircles
VIII 110a (APr)
    bucranium hangs from
      a chain (cf.
      Vermeule & Kara-
      georghis 1982: 54
      no. V.103 & a LM
      larnax in Germany)
    SH vertical
X 236 (L)
    2 Branch 3 ab
    2 sets of 7 strokes
      bel
    SH horizontal
XII 310 (L) Seager
    Coll.
    branches & lines ab
    SH horizontal
Munich acc. 21765 (L)
    (AGDS I Munich 24)
    Branch 3 almost
      completely
      encircles
    SH horizontal
Turkey, museum unknown
    (L) Besiktepe (LH
    III B?)
    Branch 3 bisects the
      face parallel
      to the SH
        bottom:
          bucranium
        top: 2 centered
          circles (each
          with two
          rings) flank
          a wedge
    the whole design
      resembles a

stylized human
face
Branch 3 encircles
As Filler
   V 346 (L) Medeon T. 29
     (LH III A-C)
   at left: caprid in PT
     2, R
   at right: bucranium
     on its side
   Branch 2 encircles &
     ab & bel caprid

Pair, Addorsed, SH parallel
to the central axis

V 31 (L) Argos
  vertical stroke
    separates
V 326 (L) Krissa ChT 3
    (LH III C)
  Branch 1 betw
  strokes encircle
V 327 (L) Krissa ChT 3
    (LH III C)
  Branch 1 betw
V 328 (L) Krissa ChT 3
    (LH III C)
  strokes encircle?
V 398 (L) Medeon T. 162
    (LH III C end)
V 623 (L) Ayios Ilias,
    Seremeti Tholos (LH
    III C)
  2 parallel lines ab each
  2 dots flank with
    strokes
V 661 (L) Salamis,
    Chalioti ChT 2
  lines flank
V 682 (L) Tanagra,
    Ledesa T. 27 (LH III
    B-C)
  lines flank
VII 264 (L)
  lines/branches flank
IX 198 (L)

IX 199 (L)
  lines flank
X 198 (L)
  Branch 2 flanks/
    encircles
X 200 (L)
  line encircles
AM 1938.952 (L) "Greek
    Islands" (CS 104)
  Branch 1 betw
  dots encircle
Bodrum no. unknown (L)
    Kas wreck
  double arcs frame
    each bucranium
Nafplion no. unknown
    (L) Tiryns (LH III C
    early; AA 1979, 405
    fn. 75, fig. 30 lower
    R)

Three Bucrania addorsed
AM 1938.951 (L) central
    Crete (CS 105)
    2 lines flank each

Lion & Bull Faces
I 18 (R) Mycenae, Treasure
  2 registers separated by
    Dado 9b & flanked by 2
    Tree 3
  top: lion, bull, lion
  bottom: bull, lion,
    bull

Stag Faces
HMs 643 & 644 (Ls)
    Sklavokambos (Sk 17)
  rosette betw horns ab

Boar Faces
Simple
    AM 1938.1032a (L) (CS
      243a)
    Palm Frond/Branch 1
      ab
    SH horizontal

With a <u>Snake Frame</u> in the
mouth

    HMs 3b (Ls) Kato Zakro
       (KZ 64)
    HMs 29a (Ls) Kato Zakro
       (KZ 69)
    <u>Palm Frond</u> ab
    HMs 31b (Ls) Kato Zakro
       (KZ 65)
    HMs 53 (Ls) Kato Zakro
       (KZ 62)
    curtailed <u>Snake Frame</u>
    HMs 80a (Ls) Kato Zakro
       (KZ 66)
    double <u>Snake Frame</u> ab
    with half <u>Double Ax</u>/
    <u>Waisted Altar</u> in
    center
    HMs 81a (Ls) Kato Zakro
       (KZ 63)

Part of a large composition
    HMs 21b (Ls) Kato Zakro
       (KZ 71)
    flanked by 2 lion
       legs & topped with
       butterfly wings
       flanking a bird tail

Miscellaneous Faces
    HMs 169 (Ls) Kato Zakro
       (KZ 169)
    bird face?
    HMs 527 (Ls) Ayia Triada
       (AT 8)
    cl: calf/mule face; dog
      head, lion head, bull
      head, all R

         5C
      Animal Heads

Lion
Right (cf. HMs 172B from
   Knossos)

    II 2.48 (D) Profitis
      Elias T. V
    dots encircle
    II 3.87 (L) Profitis
      Elias
    arcs & objects infr
    VIII 115 (D) Hutchinson
      Coll.
    collared lioness
    SH horizontal

Left
    HMs 61 (Ls) Kato Zakro (KZ
      113)
    collared? with foreleg

Bull, R (see: Ch. 2A: Body
   Parts [man's head] -- II
   3.196; Ch. 5C: Animal Heads
   [misc.]-- HMs 656)

I Supp. 151 (L)
II 2.36 (D) Mavrospelio
    T . XVII (MM IIB)
    SH oblique, lower right to
      upper left
II 2.57b (D) Profitis Elias
    T. VII
    SH horizontal
    (published upside down)
II 2.211 (D) Knossos
    horns displayed
    SH horizontal
II 3.13b (D) Knossos, Little
    Palace
II 4.129 (L) Knossos,
    Geometric
IV 168 (L) Knossos
    SH oblique, lower left to
      upper right
AM 1938.970 (L) Mirabello
    (CS 206)
    ab: 2 dots, each

flanked by 2 lines
bel: 1 dot flanked by 2
    lines
HM no. unknown (D) Knossos,
    MUM (LM IA?; Popham et
    al. 1984)
    mouth open

Calf, two addorsed
I Supp. 169c (Pr)
Chania 2066 (L/Prs) Chania,
    Kastelli Papapostolou 1977:
    no. 22)

Sheep
Four left
I 257 (L) Vapheio Tholos (LH
    IIA)
    SH oblique (lower left to
        upper right)

Six Right/Cl
    HMs 386 (Ls) Knossos
        Palace (KSPI L24)
        their horns meet center
        to form a multiple
        spiral

Caprid (see: Ch. 5B: Animal
    Faces [lions] -- XIII 22D)

I 21 (L) Mycenae acropolis
    2 pairs of antithetic
        caprid heads
        <u>Branch 2</u> encircles
I 166 (L) Mycenae, House of
    Lead (LH III B1)
    7 caprid heads? L
    branch ab
HMs 423 (A?s) Knossos,
    Little Palace (KSPI U12)
    2 stag heads R
    SH vertical

Boar (see: Ch. 4A: Women &
    Animals [woman at right] --
    HMs no.unknown [AT 130]; &

Ch. 5B: Animal Faces
[lions] -- XIII 22D)

II 2.213a (D) Knossos
boar head R
    knife/short sword/dagger
    ab

Dog (see: Ch. 5B: Animal Faces
    [lions] -- XIII 22D; & Ch.
    8E: Helmets -- HMs 25)

HMs 394 (Ls?) Knossos Palace
    (KSPI L35)
    3 ccl

Groups of Misc. Heads (see:
    Ch. 5B: Animal Faces
    [lions] -- XIII 22D)

HMs 527 (Ls) Ayia Triada (AT
    8)
    cl: calf/mule face; dog
        head, lion head, bull
        head, all R
HMs 656 (Ls) Knossos, Little
    Palace (KSPI U115)
    heads R: agrimi, bull, dog?
    man seated R (see: Ch. 3A:
        Man & Animals (several
        animals)
    centered circle ab at left

5D
Protomes

Lion, two addorsed (see: Ch.
    4B: <u>Potnia Theron</u> [lions]
    -- X 242 & AGDS IV Kassel 6;
    Ch. 5B: Animal Faces [lions]
    -- I 110; & Ch. 5C: Animal
    Heads [lions] -- HMs 61)

II 4.218   (L)
    a quadruped hindleg infr
        of each
        Figure-8 Shield ab
        object bel

HMs 60a   (Ls)   Kato Zakro (KZ
    111)

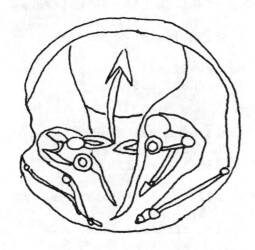

FIG. 134 -- HM 2383
2 bull protomes

Bull   (see: Ch. 3A: Man &
    Animals [bull] -- HM G
    3372b; & Ch. 4A: Woman &
    Animals [antithetic]-- V
    595)

AM 1938.1094   (L)   (CS 336)
    2 bull protomes en face,
        addorsed & conjoined
        ImpTr & Figure-8
            Shield betw the
            heads (ab center)
            bull face bel
HM 2383   (L)   Sellopoulo T. 4
    (FIG. 134; LM III A1;
    Popham 1974 = 224 s. n.
    S2
    2 bull protomes in PT 14A,
        antithetic & conjoined
        arrow betw their

heads & bef their
    common body

Caprid
I 189   (R)   Midea Tholos
    (LH III A)
    Dado 1 separates 2 registers
    top: 2 frontal sheep
        protomes, heads
        turned to center
            triple Snake Frame
            bel each
        bottom: 2 calves
            couchant in PT 28B
I 396   (Cypriote conoid)
    Perati ChT 24 (LH III
    C1)
    2 agrimia protomes addorsed
        & conjoined in radial
        symmetry ccl
I 403   (L)   Crete
    2 goat protomes addorsed &
        conjoined
        a vertical line & dots
            infr of each
        Figure-8 Shield betw the
            heads (ab, center)
    branch? bel
VIII 84   (L)   Dawkins Coll.
    2 caprid protomes, each
        regardant, addorsed &
        conjoined in PT 29B
            Tree 1 infr of each
            branch bel
X 309   (L)
    2 caprid? protomes,
        each in PT 6, addorsed &
        conjoined
HMs 90   (Ls)   (KZ 170)
    sheep frontal

Miscellaneous
I 381   (Ls)   Pylos Palace
    (LH III B2-C1)
    at left: a sheep? protome
        en face?
    at right: a lion protome

in profile, addorsed &
the two protomes
conjoined

II 4.65 (L) Palaikastso
    bull protome at left & lion?
    protome regardant at
    right addorsed in PT 25A

FIG. 135 -- I 150:
bird flies L

5E
Birds & Waterbirds

Bird
Single
    Stands (see: Ch. 5F:
        Alerions)

        Frontal
            HMs 108 (Ls) Ayia
                Triada (AT 91)
                displayed, head L
        Left
            II 3.269 (L) Sykia
                T. (LM III C -
                Geometric)
                regardant
                    2 Weeds? ab
                    hatched arcs
                        (half-
                        bundles)

encircle
X 192b* (L)
    frontal,
        displayed
    lines/scratches
    bel
    groundline bel
HMs 58 (Cs) Kato
    Zakro (KZ 91)
    Talismanic bird?
    net/reticula-
    tion beh
    SH horizontal
Right
    VII 165 (L)
        line infr
        groundline bel
    X 117 (L)
        fish/dolphin R bel
        3 arcs bel & 2
            sets of 3 arcs
            flank bird
        SH oblique (lower
            left to upper
            right)
    XII 214 (L) Seager
        Coll.
        1 wing up
        Tree 1 infr
Flies
Left
    I 150 (L) Mycenae
        ChT 518 (**FIG. 135**;
        LH I-II)
    II 2.43 (D)
        Profitis Elias
        T. V
        alights L on a
        branch at left
        SH unfinished
    II 3.387 (L)
        bird or fish L &
        zig-zags bel
        (unfinished?)
    V 605 (L) Naxos,
        Kamini T. 1 (LH
        II C)

head regardant & up
VII 164   (A)
head regardant & up
HMs 493   (Ls) Ayia
Triada (AT 14)
HMs 586a (Ls) Ayia
Triada (AT 28)
net/reticulation
beh
Right
I Supp. 7 (A)
Mycenae ChT 533
(LH II-III B;
Pini 1981: no.
93)
at left, displayed
glass seal pro-
bably en-
graved,
unfinished?
X 289   (A)
1 wing up
Chania 2045 (As)
Chania, Kastelli
(Papapostolou
1977: no. 16)
object (<u>Sacred
Heart</u>?; chip in the
seal face?) infr
Hamburg 1964.286 (L)
(AGDS IV Hamburg
6)
1 wing up
<u>Frond</u> infr
HMs 435   (Cs) Ayia
Triada (AT 13)
Up
XII 141   (L)   Seager
Coll.
head R
zig-zags ab
SH horizontal

Pair (see: Ch. 5F: Alerions
-- Berlin FG 36)

II 4.194   (L)   "Liliani"

displayed & antithetic
2 branches flank each
HMs 134   (Ls) Knossos
Palace (KSPI Q14)
2 fly antithetic bel man
R holding a staff
infr
knob-shaped object
(<u>Omphalos</u>?) bel

Owls (cf. Talismanic birds
II 3.180 & 354)

AM 1938.973b (A)   near Lappa
(CS 220; Gill 1981: 88
fig. 1b)
at lower right: owl en
face, placed in an area
of clear stone
HMs 391   (R?s) Knossos
Repository (KSPI L38)
2 registers (upside down to
each other, separated by
a rosette), each con-
taining a pair of owls in
PT 28, en face

Miscellaneous Birds
VIII 135   (RP1)
pelican L with fish in bill
arcs bel
XII 174b/AM 1938.9481 AE 1802b
(CS 11Sb)/HMs no.
unknown (Ls) "Poros",
Kato Zakro (KZ 29)
back end of eagle? topped
with a crest
HMs 92b (Ls) Kato Zakro
(KZ 54)
2 bird (hoopoes?) protomes
addorsed
frond bel center

Waterbirds (see: Ch. 5E:
Birds & Waterbirds [water-
birds, single] -- IV 257,
below)

Single
  Frontal
    HMs 11 (Ls) Kato Zakro
        (KZ 129)
        head R
  Swims
    II 3.350 (L)
        swims L, 1 wing up
          2 Branch 1 & branch
            (Papyrus?) ab
          groundline as water
          bel
    HM G 3135 (L) Knossos
        (CMCG 313)
        swims R

FIG. 136 -- I 258:
waterbirds in PT 19A

Stands (see: Ch. 5A: Misc.
  Animals [quadrupeds] -- I
  Supp. 75 & II 3.172)

  Left
    II 3.96b (Pr)
        Knossos
        regardant
    II 4.146 (L) Knossos
        head up
          groundline bel
    HM G 3205 (L) (CMCG
        425)

plants inb
HMs 358 (?s)
    Knossos Palace
    (KSPI L?)
    2 registers? sepa-
      rated by a wavy
      line: portion
      of top register
      preserved with
      1 waterbird
HMs 547 (Ls) Ayia
    Triada (AT 21)
    plant ab
HMs 579 (Ls) Ayia
    Triada (AT 19)
    Weeds from peri-
      phery encircle
Right
  I Supp. 99 (L)
      Crete
      Branch 1 ab
  II 4.13 (L) Knossos
      regardant at right
      dolphin upside
        down at left
  II 4.145 (L) Knossos
      regardant
      branch infr
  VII 44 (C)
      head slightly up
      Weed ab & 3 Weeds
        bel
  XII 210 (Cyl)
      Seager Coll.
      SH vertical:
      waterbird bel
      in PT 2, R
        wing? ab
        centered
          circle ab
      SH horizontal:
      alerion?
      in the field: 5
      centered
      circles & lines
  AM 1938.978 (A)
      Kritsa (CS 223)

zig-zags ab
HM no. unknown   (L)
    (Xanthoudides
    1907: pl.
    8.104)
2 <u>Suns</u> ab & 1 <u>Sun</u>
    bel

FIG. 137 -- IV 257:
    2 waterbirds

Flies
  Right
      IV 257 (L) Mallia
          (FIG. 137)
          cl: waterbird flies
          R; schematic
          lion face; <u>Sun</u>;
          waterbird stands
          R
      X 305* (L)
          takes off R, 1 wing
          up
          rocks? bel
      XII 150a (A) Seager
          Coll.
          <u>Sacred Heart</u>? in
          beak
      AM 1938.979 (APr)
          Herakleion area
          (CS 181)
      2 <u>Weeds</u> ab bird

V 234 (Ls) Chania,
    Kastelli
    takes off R
    <u>Frond</u> ab
    rocks bel

Pair
  One Stands, One Lands
      II 3.250 (A) Gournia/
          Avgo
          at left, waterbird
          stands
          at right, waterbird
          lands, 1 wing up
          <u>Branch 1</u> ab
          groundline as water
          bel
          2 pairs of <u>Mount-</u>
          <u>Guides</u> flank

Stand (see: PT 19A [e.g.,
    I 258 in PT 19A, R; FIG.
    136])

  Left
      I Supp. 33 (A)
          Pylos Palace,
          (LH III B2-C1)
          waterbird at right
          with 1 wing up
          <u>Weeds</u>? ab
          groundline?
          bel
      II 3.78 (L) Knossos
          waterbird at right
          with 1 wing
          up
          <u>Branch 1</u> betw
          2 groundlines
          bel
      II 4.191 (L)
          "Partira"
          <u>Frond</u> ab each
          groundline bel
      ?HM 2124 (L)
          Knossos, Royal
          Road North (LM

II)
Right
　II 3.142　(C)
　　2 Weeds ab
　II 3.179　(C)
　　Knossos
　　2 Weeds flank &
　　　1 Weed betw
　　dots betw & inb
　　zig-zag ab
　II 3.307　(L)
　　2 registers se-
　　parated by a
　　line with 2
　　dots: a pair of
　　waterbirds in
　　each register
　　upside down to
　　each other;
　　waterbird at
　　right in each
　　pair regardant;
　　1 waterbird of
　　each pair has
　　1 wing up
　II 3.351　(A)
　　2 branches ab
　　groundline bel
　II 3.352　(A)
　　waterbird at left
　　　with 1 wing up
　II 3.353　(A)
　AM 1938.1068/HMs377/
　　OTheta (bimetal-
　　lic? Ls) Knossos
　　Palace (KSPI Va/
　　CS 51S; Gill
　　1974: 34-6)
　　2 registers separa-
　　　ted by a ho-
　　　rizontal line
　　top: 2 water-
　　　birds R sepa-
　　　rated by a
　　　Papyrus at
　　　right; water-
　　　bird regar-

dant
bottom: water-
　bird R regar-
　dant flanked
　by 2 Papyri
SH horizontal?
AM 1941.1231　(A)　(CS
　289)
　branch inb
　groundline bel
　　becomes branch
　　at right

Stand in Antithetic Poses
　PT 28B: 2 birds/storks --
　　IX 113
　PT 31B: 2 geese?
　　protomes? -- HMs 4b
　　(KZ 52)

Swim R
　II 3.352　(A)
　HMs no. unknown　(Ls)
　　Ayia Triada (AT
　　22a)
　　plant ab center betw
　　the heads

Fly (see: Ch. 5F:
Alerions [head L] --
Berlin FG 36)

　Left
　V 439　(A)　Nichoria
　　Tholos, (LH III
　　A2-B1)
　　take off L
　　2 Branch 1 & 2
　　　pairs of
　　　Mount-Guides
　　　flank
　　groundline bel
　AM 1938.1020　(L)　N.
　　of Knossos
　　(FIG. 139; CS
　　302)
　　at left: flies L

at right: butter-
fly in profile
(see: Ch. 5G:
Insects [but-
terflies,
trio])
in the center &
bel: argonaut
swims L (see:
Ch. 5K: Shell-
fish
[argonauts])
Miscellaneous
I 151 (L) Mycenae
ChT 518 (LH
I-II)
fly up
I 273 a+b (Pr) Rutsi
Tholos 2, cist
2 (LH IIA)
fly R

Flanking (see: PT 31B;
Ch.2A: Body Parts [man's
face] -- HMs 654)

II 3.88 (L) Knossos
flank a man's face
(see Ch. 2A: Man's
Face [beardless]),
all ab a cow & calf
in PT 18B, L
II 3.279 (Cyl)
Palaikastro (LM II;
Pini 1980: no. C5)
flank a Tree 1
2 dolphins (see: Ch.
5I: Dolphins),
upside down, flank
Woman-Eagle L
HMs 659 (Ls) Knossos,
Little Palace (KSPI
U117)
flank a Waisted Altar
waterbird at left,
regardant
branch ab waterbird

at right
Miscellaneous poses
V 422a (R matrix, for a
relief ring?)
Eleusis T. Eta-pi 3
waterbird L
chick L infr
dot ab the head
of each
Branch 1 ab
dot + branch bel
15 dots encircle
HM G 3210 (L) (CMCG 312)
2 waterbirds L, 1 ab
the other
wavy line bel
HM G 3511 (L) (CMCG 328)
2 waterbirds in PT
19D, L
fish upside down L
ab
HMs 569-570 (Rs?) Ayia
Triada (AT 93)
at left: person? (see:
Ch. 3A: Man &
Animals [bird])
at right: 2 waterbirds
in PT 34B, L
HMs 1096 (As? on a pot
handle) Myrtos
Pyrgos

Trio
Left
IX 162b (Almond-shape
Pr) Cyprus
stand
branch ab
HMs 572 (A/Rs) Ayia
Triada (AT 25)
3 (4?) fly L
HMs no. unknown (Ls)
Ayia Triada (AT
26)
3 (4?) fly L
Right
V 582 (APr) Kasarma

Tholos (LH I-II)
  land/take off
    <u>Branch 1</u> infr of
      each, their
      lower stalks
      create a wavy
      groundline
AM 1938.971 (L)
    Mirabello (CS 297)
  swim: at left, 1
    waterbird with
    wing up; at right,
    1 waterbird regar-
    dant; betw them &
    slightly bel: 1
    waterbird with
    head outstretched
    water bel
AM 1938.1066 (L) (CS
  343)
  3 waterbirds swim in
    PT 26, R (rear
    waterbird regar-
    dant)
      <u>Papyrus</u> infr &
        2 ab
      water bel
HMs 590 (As) Ayia
  Triada (AT 23)
  stand
    branch ab each
Four
  HMs 561 (Ls) Ayia Triada
    (AT 24)
  4 waterbirds, heads to
    center, swim cl

5F
Alerions

(seals are presumed to have a
horizontal SH, unless otherwise
stated)

Head Left
II 3.132 (L) Karteros
II 3.194 (L) "Poros"
II 3.356 (L)
II 4.168 (L)
II 4.176 (L) "Poros"
II 4.32(L) "Ayios Ioannes"
VIII 155 (A)
IX 62 (A)
X 147* (A)
  2 strokes inb of head
X 248 (L)
  SH vertical: alerion at
    top
  SH horizontal: at right
    waterbird L with wing up
  <u>Branch 1</u> ab
  groundline bel
XII 162b (Pr) Seager Coll.
  lines ab
XII 254 (L)
  2 dots flank the head
XII 255 (L) Seager Coll.
  head up
AM 1941.1238 (A) (CS 235)
Berlin FG 36 (L) Syra
    (AGDS II Berlin 58)
  2 birds fly R upside down
    ab
HMs 492 (Ls) Ayia Triada
  (AT 16)
HMs 513 (Ls) Ayia Triada
  (AT 18)
?HMs 1348 (Ls) Ayia Triada
  (AT 15)
HM G 3198 (L) (CMCG 418)
HM G 3507 (L) (CMCG 420)
HM G 3350 (L) Knossos (CMCG
  423)
  alerion/griffin
    2 <u>Suns</u>? flank
HM no. unknown 216- (Heart-
  shaped) Kamilari Tholos
  (MM III-LM I)
Nafplion no. unknown (RP1)
  Apollo Maleatas (AR 1977-8,
  28 fig. 49 R)

Melos 578b (RP1) Phylakopi,
    East Sanctuary (LH III
    C; Renfrew 1985: 282,
    289)
  alerion/eagle
Munich A.1201 (A) Crete
    (AGDS I Munich 49)

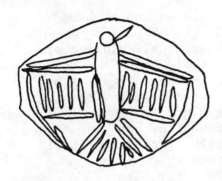

FIG. 138 -- VIII 57:
    alerion, head R

Head Right
I 468 (L) Crete
?I 469 (L) Crete
I Supp. 84 (L) Crete
  branch ab L
I Supp. 132 (L)
I Supp. 169b (Pr)
II 3.94 (L) Knossos
II 3.95 (L) Knossos
  broken groundline bel
II 3.96a (Pr) Knossos
II 3.148 (L) Mallia
II 3.254a (Pr) Mochlos (LM
  IB; Pini 1981: no. 11)
II 3.354 (L)
II 3.355 (A)
IV 260 (L) Krassi
  Frond at left
IV 298 (L) Messara
  Frond at left
V 174 (A) Athens, Agora T.

XL (LH III A1)
VIII 57 (A) Dawkins Coll.
  (FIG. 138)
VIII 83 (L) Dawkins Coll.
VIII 158 (A)
IX 61 (A)
X 277b (APr) Crete
  zig-zags ab
X 318 (A)
  zig-zags ab & bel
  groundline bel the zig-
    zags to either side of
    the body
XII 219 (A) Seager Coll.
?XIII 4 (L)
  SH vertical
XIII 118 (L)
  2 Fronds flank the head
AM 1938.977 (Heart-shaped)
  Knossos (CS 187)
HMs 493 (Ls) Ayia Triada (AT
  17)
HM G 3288 (L) Mallia (CMCG
  419)
HM G 3365 (L) Knossos (CMCG
  421)

With Other Heads
HMs 16 (Ls) Kato Zakro (KZ
    33)
  lion face

Head Direction Unknown or
Irrelevant

I 211 (L) Prosymna, ChT XI
    (LH III A2)
  branches? in the field
I 406 (L) Thebes, Ayia Anna
    T. 2 (LH I-II)
XII 210 (Cyl) Seager Coll.
  SH horizontal: alerion?
  SH vertical: waterbird bel
    in PT 2, R; wing?
    ab; centered circle ab
  in the field: 5 centered
    circles & lines

?XII 279 (L)   Seager Coll.
XII 281 (L)   Seager Coll.
  alerion/eagle-woman
?XII 282 (L)   Seager Coll.
?XII 283 (L)   Seager Coll.

FIG. 139:
AM 1938.1020/CS 302:
butterfly, waterbird, &
argonaut

5G
Insects

Butterflies (see: Popham et
al. 1984: 192; for animals
& monsters with butterfly
wings see KZ 21b in Ch. 5B:
Animal Faces [boar]; & KZ
71, 72, 74, & 75 in Ch. 6A:
People-Monsters [sphinx])

Single, displayed
  II 3.46 (A) Gypsades T. 2
    (LM III A2)
    2 pairs of <u>Mount-Guides</u>
    flank top & bottom
  V 677b (Pr) Thebes,
    Kolonaki T. 17 (LH III
    A1)
  VII 71 (L) Crete
    2 oblique pairs of lines

    form an arch ab with
    a central dot
VIII 152 (L)
X 95 (A)
  originally intended to
    be a butterfly (with
    SH vertical), turned
    into a flying fish
    (with SH horizontal)
    net/reticulation
    fills field
X 102 (A)
  2 <u>Weeds</u> bel
  SH vertical
AM 1938.968 (L) (CS 233)
  SH horizontal
AM 1941.1229 (L) (CS 234)
Chania 1005 (Ls) Chania,
  Kastelli (Papapostolou
  1977: no. 20)
Chania 2018 (Ls) Chania,
  Kastelli (Papapostolou
  1977: no. 21)
HM G 3185 (L) (CMCG 329)
HMs 91b (Ls) Kato Zakro
  (KZ 72)
  quadruped (lion?) face
    ab
HMs no. unkown (Ls) Ayia
  Triada (AT 29)
HMs 552 (Ls) Ayia Triada
  (AT 30)
  2 circles ab

Trio?
  II 3.22 (L) Knossos, South
    House, Palace or
    Little Palace (PM I
    705-6: "sealing from
    the Little Palace"; IV
    490 fig. 421: "sealing
    from the Palace site";
    CS s.n. 302: "from
    Houses So. of
    Knossos")
  1 displayed/en face,
    whose tail forms part

of a whirligig with
the tails of 2 abbre-
viated others of which
only the left wing of
each is engraved
    SH horizontal

As filler (see: Ch. 2C:
Women [single, religious] -
- AT 143; Ch. 2D: Men &
Women [misc.] -- AM
1938.1130 [The Ring of
Nestor; & Ch. 2E: People at
a Shrine [tree-pulling] --
HMm 989)

AM 1938.1020 (L) N. of
    Knossos (FIG. 139; CS
    302)
    at right: butterfly in
    profile
    at left: waterbird
    flies L (see: Ch. 5E:
    Birds & Waterbirds
    [pair])
    in the center & bel
    waterbirds: argonaut
    swims L (see: Ch. 5K:
    Shellfish
    [argonauts])
IX 162a (Almond-shape Pr)
    Cyprus
    SH horizontal: at
    right, butterfly
    displayed
        zig-zags ab
    SH vertical: at top,
    Lion Mask
HMs 530 (A?s) Ayia Triada
    (AT 35)
    2 argonauts in PT 36,
    ccl (see: Ch. 5K:
    Shellfish [argo-
    nauts])
        butterfly bel &
        betw in profile

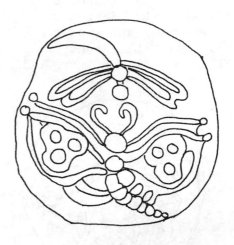

FIG. 140 -- V 677c:
butterfly & "dragonfly"

**Butterfly & "Dragonfly", heads
to center**

I 270 (A) Rutsi Tholos 2 (LH
    IIA)
II 3.237 (L) Gournia
    (LM IB)
V 677c (Pr) Thebes, Kolonaki
    T. 17 (FIG. 140; LH III
    A1)
    SH horizontal
HM no. unknown (L) Knossos,
    MUM (Popham et al. 1984:
    Misc. 1)

Scorpions
Single
    XII 142 (C) Seager Coll.
    lines in the field
    SH vertical

Pair
    ?HM 2344c (APr) Poros ChT
        (MM III-LM I; Lembessi
        1967: pl. 189)
        2 scorpions?
    HMs 149 (Ls) Kato Zakro
        (KZ 149)

2? scorpions (addorsed in
     radial symmetry?)
  necklace? bel
?HMs 393 (Ls) Knossos
    Palace (KSPI L39)
  scorpion cl
     there is room for
        another to make PT
        36

Spiders
?II 3.93 (L) Knossos
V 579 (L) Kasarma Tholos
    (LH I-II)
  Frond betw 2 pairs of legs
  SH horizontal

Miscellaneous Insects
IV 33D (D) Kapetaniana
?grasshopper R
  branch ab/beh
  SH oblique: lower left to
     upper right?
VII 70 (L)
  flying insect displayed
     2 groundlines ab with 3
        Weeds

                5H
               Fish

(see: Ch. 3C: Man Hunts
Animals [fishermen] -- VII 88;
Ch. 8J: Miscellaneous [misc.]
-- X 69)

Single
Flying Fish
  Left
     HMs 476 (Ls) Ayia
        Triada (AT 32)
        dolphin/flying fish L
           plants encircle
     HMs no. unknown (Ls)

        Ayia Triada (AT
        11)
     net/reticulation beh
  Right
     II 3.49 (A) Gypsades T.
        7
     Weed ab upside down
     Weed bel
     AM 1938.972 (A) Arcadia,
        Klitara (CS 232)
  Upright
     II 3.246 (L)
        Sphoungaras
        lines in the field
     HM 2346 (L) Poros ChT
        (MM III-LM I; Lem-
        bessi 1967: pl.
        190)
        flying fish/alerion
        zig-zags bel

Conventional Fish
  Left
     II 3.209 (L) "Viannos"
     II 3.245 a & b (L)
        Sphoungaras (MM
        III-LM I)
     AM 1925.44 (L) (CS 189)
        centered circle ab
        net/reticulation bel
     AM 1938.1052 (crystal R
        bezel) Spiliari-
        dia, Avdou Tb (CS
        224)
     Weeds encircle
     SH vertical
  Right
     Berlin FG 50c (APr)
        Crete (AGDS II
        Berlin 12c)
        branch ab & bel
     HMs 128 (Ls) Knossos
        Palace (KSPI Pb)
     octopus bel
        rocks & seaweed
        encircle

Pair
Stacked
    XII 138 (C) Seager Coll.
        2 fish swim obliquely up
            L
        Weeds ab & bel
HMs 474 (stone R?s) Ayia
        Triada (AT 9)
        2 flying? fish swim L
        2 Weeds at the
            periphery betw top
            left & top right
        zig-zag bel left
Munich A.1321 (A) Crete
        (AGDS I Munich 50)
        2 fish swim L in PT 35
II 3.316 (A) Palaikastro
II 3.317 (A) Palaikastro
X 116 (Cyl)
        SH vertical: 2 fish in
            PT 35, ccl
        SH horizontal: agrimi
            in PT 1A, L
        Pica ab in the back
HMs 480 (Ls) Ayia Triada
        (AT 33)
        net/reticulation betw
        2 lines ab each fish
?HM no. unknown (C) Kato
        Souli

Trio
Top to Bottom: L, R, L
    HMs 348 (Ls) Knossos
        Palace (KSPI L42)

Top Two swim R, bottom swims L
    (see: Ch. 5I: Dolphins
    [trio] -- I Supp. 37)

    IX 74 (L)
    XIII 5 (A)
        in the center: flying
            fish R
        flying fish top & fish
            bottom flank & form
            PT 36, cl

SH vertical

FIG. 141 -- I 259:
2 dolphins in PT 35, cl

5I
Dolphins

(see: Ch. 4B: Potnia Theron
[dolphins] -- AM 1971.1145)

Single
Left
    II 3.34 (A) Mavrospelio T.
        IX
        2 large blobs ab
        2 strokes 1 large blob
            bel
    II 3.375 (L)
        Sun bel
    IV 166b (D) Pombia
        at top
            flaked bel
    HMs 404a (Ls) Knossos
        Palace (KSPI L41)
        net/reticulation beh

Right
    I Supp. 120 (D)
        at top
        flaked bel

rev. flaked (see: Ch.
   9P: Flaked
   Obsidian Disks)
II 4.13 (L) Knossos
  with SH vertical: dolphin
   R
  with SH horizontal: bird
   stands R regardant
II 4.155 (L) Episcopi
   Pediada T.
  hatching bel

Pair, Swim
Stacked
  AM 1938.963 (C, gilded)
    Palaikastro (CS 203)
    swim R
     rocks ab & bel
     incised line circum-
      scribes at the rim
      to secure the gold
      plate
     SH vertical
  AM 1941.91 (D) (CS 191)
    swim L
     groundline/prow of
      ship/rocks bel

In axial symmetry
  PT 34 -- I 409 (barrel-
   shaped Cyl) Skopelos ChT
   (LH IIA)
  PT 34B -- flying fish,
   hatching in the field

In radial symmetry
  PT 35 cl
    I 259 (L) Vapheio
     Tholos (**FIG. 141**)
    II 3.71 (L) Knossos,
     Temple Tomb
     net/reticulation
      betw (in the
      center)
     zig-zags encircle

PT 35 ccl
  I Supp. 121 (L)
  HM G 3046 (L) Mallia
   (CMCG 320)
   net/reticulation betw
    (in the center)
  HM G 3519 (L) (CMCG
   321)
   net/reticulation betw
    (in the center)
As filler
  II 3.279 (Cyl) Palaikastro
   (LM II)
   2 dolphins, upsidedown,
    flank Woman-Eagle L
   2 waterbirds (see: Ch.
    5E: Waterbirds
    [pair]) flank a <u>Tree 1</u>

Trio
All swim right-side up
Left
  ?I Supp. 30 (C)
    Prosymna ChT 36
    SH vertical
  V 176 (A)
    branch bel
    SH vertical
Right
  IX 73 (RP1) Crete
   a horizontal line bel
    each, the bottom
    line slightly
    thicker (perhaps a
    fish? R)
   SH vertical
  HMs no. unknown (L?s)
    Knossos Palace
    (KSPI R105, pl.
    17)
   rocks ab
   object bel

Bottom dolphin upsidedown
  I Supp. 37 (A) Amyklaion
   top pair L; bottom
    dolphin R

horizontal line
    separates the top
    pair from the
    bottom dolphin
V 620 (L) Ayios Ilias,
    Seremeti Tholos (LH
    III C)
  all L

In Axial Symmetry, cl
  HM G 3067 (L) Mallia
      (CMCG 319)
    <u>Sun</u> in center
    short groundline

Four Swim
Left
    XII 158 (C) Seager Coll.
      SH vertical
    XIII 77 (Cyl)
      fish?
        gouges & hatching betw
    AM 1938.1007 (Cyl) east
        Crete (CS 355)
        zig-zags betw
        SH horizontal

in Radial Symmetry
    II 3.75 (L) Knossos
        Geometric T.
        4 form a whirligig cl,
          noses to center
        3 fish? fill the
          available space

More than Four
I 312 (Ls) Pylos Palace
    (inscribed: PY Wr
    1326+1330)
  7 dolphins around central
    octopus (see: Ch. 5J:
    Octopus [naturalistic])

FIG. 142 -- V 496:
simplified octopus

5J
Octopus

Simplified
V 496 (L) Ayia Irini, Keos
    (**FIG. 142**; LH III A1)
  6 arms

Cut-Style
II 3.251 (L) Mochlos T. 1
    (MM III)
    central octopus with 6? arms
        & 5 large circles for
        suckers
    dolphin R ab & bel
    fish? R bel
    dot with short rays (sea
        urchin?) at left
    <u>Branch 3</u> at upper left
        half-encircles
    SH oblique (lower left
        to upper right)

Naturalistic (Furumark, 1972a:
    FM 21.1 [LH IIA]; see:Ch.
    5J: Fish [single] -- HMs
    128)
I 312   (Ls) Pylos   (LH III
       B2-C1; inscribed: PY Wr
       1326+1330)
    in the center: 7 dolphins
       (see: Ch. 5I: Dolphins
       [4 or more]) swim around
       it
IX 10D   (L)
AM 1938.967   (L)   (CS 195)

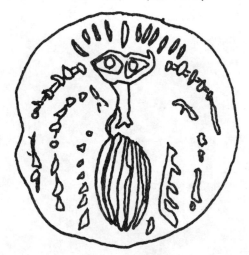

FIG. 143 -- XIII 67:
conventionalized octopus

Conventionalized (Furumark
    1972a: FM 21.9 [LH III B]
    or 14 [LH III A2]), SH
    horizontal

II 3.92   (L)   Knossos
II 4.63   (L)   Sykia
IX 184   (L)   Ligortyno
XII 205   (L)   Seager Coll.
XIII 67   (L)   (FIG. 143)

Abstracted, SH horizontal
V 386   (L)   Medeon T. 29a (LH
    III A-C)
V 749   (L)   Ayii Theodoroi,

Metaphio Tholos   (LH III A2)

5K
Shellfish

Argonauts (see: PT 10A, L:
    lions & griffins -- I 329)

II 3.91   (L) Knossos
    2 argonauts swim L
    Dado 6b bel
AM 1938.1020   (L) N. of
       Knossos (FIG. 139; CS
       302)
    in the center & bel:
       argonaut swims L
    at right: butterfly in
       profile (see: Ch. 5G:
       Insects [butterflies,
       trio])
    at left: waterbird flies L
       (see: Ch. 5E: Birds &
       Waterbirds [waterbirds,
       pair])
HMs 530   (A?s) Ayia Triada
       (AT 35)
    2 argonauts in PT 36, ccl
       butterfly bel & betw in
          profile (see: Ch. 5G:
          Insects [butterflies])

Crab
AM 1938.1440a/HMs 388b   (Ls)
       Knossos Palace (KSPI
       L40; CS 9S)
    horizontal lines beh

Shells
VII 188   (L)
    2 murex shells/hearts/
       peppers
       object (sign?) betw
       line engraved hori-
          zontally across the
          center

AM 1938.975 (L) (CS 379)
    5 murex shells/hearts/
        peppers: 3 across the
        center (the middle one
        upside down to the
        flanking pair), & 2
        others added against the
        periphery
AM 1938.1439a (Ls) Knossos
        Palace (KSPI L13; CS
        75a)
    4 shells arranged as a
        rosette
HMs 340 (Ls) Knossos Palace
        (KSPI L43)
    2 conch/murex shells in
        radial symmetry

CHAPTER 6
Monsters

6A
People-Animals

FIG. 144 -- VII 143:
eagle-woman, head L

Winged Man
XIII 60 (L)
    walks R, as if carrying the
    stag upside down ab in
    PT 14A, R
        branch bel
        hatching inb
HMs 3a (Ls) Kato Zakro (KZ
    36)
    runs L

Eagle-Woman (presumed
    displayed & to have a
    horizontal SH, unless
    otherwise stated)

Head Left
    I 476 (L) Crete
        branches ab
    I Supp. 98 (L) Crete
    II 4.104 (L) Tylissos
    IV 290 (L) Embaros
        head also up

VII 143 (L) (FIG. 144)
XII 277 (L) Seager Coll.
XIII 16Da (D)
HMs 39a (Ls) Kato Zakro
    (KZ 38)
    sits R, regardant, not
    displayed
HMs no. unknown (Ls) Ayia
    Triada (AT 102)
    sits L on a <u>Table</u>?, not
    displayed
HMs no. unknown (Ls) Kato
    Zakro (KZ 20)
HMs no. unknown (Ls) Kato
    Zakro (KZ 23)
HM G 3022 (L) Knossos
    Palace (CMCG 374)
HM G 3157 (L) (CMCG 375)

Head Right (see: Ch. 3A: Men
& Animals [bull] -- BM
97.4.64)

II 3.4 (L) "Axos"
II 3.77 (L) Knossos,
    Field of Terracottas
    (cf. HM 2109)
    squats R
II 4.137 (L) Knossos
    2 large dogs flank
IV 35D (A) Knossos
?V 274 (L) Armenoi T. 55
    (LM III A2-B1)
    branch at right
    SH vertical
IX 165 (L)
XIII 3 (L)
    head also up
HMs 539 (Ls) Ayia Triada
    (AT 104)
HMs 791 (Ls) Ayia Triada
    (AT 103)
HMs no. unknown (Ls)
    Kato Zakro (KZ 27)
HM G 3031 (C) Knossos
    Palace (CMCG 373)
    SH vertical

HM G 3088 (L) Knossos
   (CMCG 376)
  2 <u>Branch 1</u> ab
HM G 3113 (L) Knossos
   (CMCG 422)
HM G 3556 (L) (CMCG 424)
Florence 82822 (L) Crete
   (Laviosa 1969: no. 13)
Munich no. unknown (L)
   (AGDS I Munich 94)

Head Direction Unknown
  HM G 3115 (L) Messara
    (CMCG 365)
  HM G 3437 (L) Knossos
    (CMCG 377)

With Other Heads
  Lion's
    HMs 173 (Ls) Kato Zakro
      (KZ 173)
      en face
  Bull's
    I 477 (L) Crete
      en face
    HMs 5a (Ls) Kato Zakro
      (KZ 43)
      head R, displayed
  Flower
    HMs 10 (Ls) Kato Zakro
      (KZ 44)
      with eyes & nose
    ?HMs no. unknown (Ls)
      Kato Zakro (KZ 28)

With Helmet instead of a
  Head

    XII 174a (Ls) Poros,
      Kato Zakro (KZ 21;
      CS 11Sa)
      helmet on shoulders
    AM AE 1802
    HMs no. unknown (Ls)
      Kato Zakro (KZ 24)
    HMs no. unknown (Ls)
      Kato Zakro (KZ 25)

HMs no. unknown (Ls)
  Kato Zakro (KZ 26)

No Head
  HMs 89 (Ls) Kato Zakro
    (KZ 32)
  HMs no. unknown (Ls) Kato
    Zakro (KZ 22)
    body topped by double
    <u>Snake Frame</u> & object

Lion-Man (see: PT 37A [lion-
  man & <u>Minotaur</u>] -- AM 1938.
  1069 [**FIG. 145**]; Ch. 3A: Men
  & Animals [monsters] -- I
  Supp. 3; Ch. 6A: People-
  Animals [caprid-people] --
  HM 1527, below)

FIG. 145 -- AM 1938.1069
  (CS 321): Lion-man &
  <u>Minotaur</u> in PT 37A

XII 174c/AM AE 1802c (Ls)
  "Poros", Kato Zakro (KZ
  61; CS 11Sc)
  2 human legs up & bent out
    to frame a lion face,
    whose mouth holds a
    truncated <u>Snake Frame</u>
      a vertical row of 6

strokes ab, betw
the legs
HMs 7a (Ls) Kato Zakro (KZ
175)
winged lion-man displayed,
with mask (= face with no
eyes)

Sphinx (see: PT 10A, R: HMm
980; PT 28A: I 87)

Frontal, Displayed
HMs 7b (Ls) Kato Zakro
(KZ 75)
groundline & rocks bel
HMs 23a (Ls) Kato Zakro
(KZ 74)
with butterfly wings,
head R
flanked by 2 objects
(rocks?)

Beardless Male Sphinx
HMs 10a (Ls) Kato Zakro
(KZ 78)
frontal, en face
rocks? flank
groundline bel
HMs 50a (Ls) Kato Zakro
(KZ 76)
sphinx face?, corona beh

Bull-People (see: Ch. 3A: Men
& Animals [monsters] -- I
Supp. 3)

Bull-Men
Minotaurs (see: PT 14C --
II 3.67 [**FIG. 146**]; PT
13A: XII 238 [**FIG. 147**];
PT 37A: AM 1938.1069;
Ch. 6C: Griffins -- I
171)

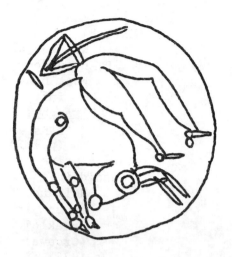

FIG. 146 -- II 3.67:
Minotaur in PT 14C

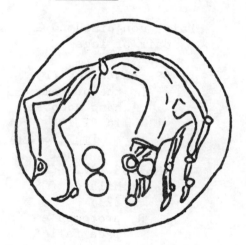

FIG. 147 -- XII 238:
hornless Minotaur
(Calf-man?) in PT 13A, L

Single
Sits L
?HMs 6a (Ls) Kato
Zakro (KZ 18)
groundline bel
Sits R
HMs 2b (Ls) Kato
Zakro (KZ 17)

Runs
    XIII 84 (L)
        Knossos area
    L, head down
        goat head
        infr
        Branch 1
            Tree
            (palm?)
            inb
    Lentoid in
        Holland,
        bought in
        Herakleion
        (Crouwel
        1975)
        R regardant en
        face

Pair, conjoined to 1
    pair of legs

    BSA cast 186 (L)
        L, the protomes
        hang addorsed
        in PT 14A
            ImpTr & Sun
            bel
    AM 1938.1072 (L)
        Milatos (CS
        323)
        R, protomes en
        face fall &
        flank the
        legs
            3 Branch 1
                Tree in
                field
            Figure-8
                Shield at
                right

Bull-Women, protomes
HMs 11a (Ls) Kato Zakro (KZ
    92a)
    L, arms up, stag horn

Squatting Legs topped with a
    Bucranium

HMs 55a (Ls) Kato Zakro (KZ
    46)
    arms over the head instead
        of horns
        groundline bel

FIG. 148 -- HM 2624:
    2-bodied Goat-Man
conjoined to 1 pair of legs

Caprid-People
Agrimi-Man (see: Ch. 3A: Men
    & Animals [monsters] -- I
    Supp. 3)

    Simple
        ?HMs 45b (Ls) Kato
            Zakro (KZ 19)
            R
        HMs 5b (Ls) Kato Zakro
            (KZ 39)
            winged, sits R
    Conjoined, with a Lion-man
    II 3.332 (L)
        the 2 protomes fall
            to either side
            (agrimi L, lion en
            face R); legs R

Agrimi-Woman
  Winged
    XII 276b (L)   Seager
      Coll.
     head R
      dot bel head
      SH horizontal
    HMs 89a (Ls) Kato
      Zakro (KZ 35)
     displayed, head R
  Miscellaneous
    II 4.136 (L) Knossos
     stands L
      2 waterbirds flank
      SH horizontal

Goat-Man
  Single, Winged
    HMs 31 (Ls) Kato Zakro
     (KZ 34)
     displayed, R
    HMs 92a (Ls) Kato
     Zakro (KZ 37)
     sits R, displayed
    HMs 345/141? (Ls) Kato
     Zakro (KZ 55)
     displayed R
    HMs no. unknown (Ls)
     Kato Zakro (KZ 138)
    Present whereabouts un-
     known (L) (Furt-
     wangler 1900: pl.
     VI.6)
     dog infr
     3 ImpTr in field

  Pair conjoined to one pair
    of legs

    ?I 325 (Ls) Pylos
     Palace (LH III B2-C1)
    ?I 326 (Ls) Pylos
     Palace (LH III B2-C1)
    HM 2624 (L) Kato Souli
     (**FIG. 148**; post LM
     IA; AR 1976-7, p.
     64 fig. 113)

    runs R, the 2 protomes
     fall to either side
      goat in PT 1B, R
      ab
     SH horizontal
    HMs 226 (Ls) Knossos
     Palace (KSPI R103)
    runs L, the 2 protomes
     in axial symmetry
     each in PT 14A
    HMs 1007 (Ls) Knossos
     Palace (Betts 47)
    L, the 2 protomes fall
     to either side
     groundline bel

Stag-Man (see: PT 37A: Lion-
  man & Stag-man -- II 3.10)

Stag-Woman
HMs no. unknown (Ls) Kato
  Zakro (KZ 139)
  protome head R, arms up

**Squatting Human Legs topped
with a Bird-Tail**

HMs 10b (Ls) Kato Zakro (KZ
  48)
  wavy line with dots
HMs 27b (Ls) Kato Zakro (KZ
  45)

6B
Genii

Single
Left (see PT 32B: 2 dogs flank
  a genius -- I 161; PT 47A:
  dog vs bull -- XII 265; &
  the last entry in this
  chapter)

FIG. 149 -- V 440:
Genius stands L

Holding jug (see: Ch. 3B:
Master of Animals
[monsters] -- V 201)

   I 232   (A) Vapheio
       Tholos (LH IIA)
     SH vertical
   V 440   (A) Nichoria
       Tholos (LH III
       A2-B1)
     Column bel
     Weed inb
   XII 212   (A) Seager
       Coll.
     2 rows of spirals
       flank
         SH vertical
   Berlin FG 41   (A) (AGDS
       II Berlin 26)
     SH vertical
   HMs 202   (RPl) Knossos
       Palace (KSPI H?)
     flower infr
     Branch 1 inb
Running
   HMs 1042   (Ls) Knossos
       Palace (Betts 4)

Right, with Jug
   ?HMs 360   (Ls) Knossos
       Palace (KSPI Q16)
     object inb
With Animals
   Holds lion protome
     HMs 1347   (As) Ayia
       Triada (AT 107)
       collared lion protome
       with head upside
       down en face
         SH vertical
     Berlin FG 11   (L) Crete
       (AGDS II Berlin
       28)
       genius carries R a
        Yoke from which 2
        lion protomes hang
        en face as if in PT
        12
Carries bull in PT 1B, R
   IX 129   (L)
     R
   AM 1938.1045   (L) Zafer
       Papoura (CS 303)
     R
   Berlin FG 13   (L)
       Thessalonike   (AGDS
       II Berlin 30)
     L
Carries caprids
   II 3.105a   (C) Kalyvia
       T. 7 (LM III A2)
     carries agrimi kid R
       kid vertical, anti-
       thetic,
       regardant
   V 209   (L) Arkades,
       Crete
     carries agrimi kid R
       kid horizontal as
       if in PT 1B, R
   Berlin FG 12   (L) Crete
       (AGDS II Berlin 29)
     genius L carries stag
       in PT 14A, R
         branch infr of

genius
2 <u>Suns</u> bel stag
flank the
genius
Miscellaneous
AM 1938.1046/HMs 257
(Ls) Knossos Palace
(KSPI R81/CS 46S;
AJA 74, 1970, 405)
L-R: genius, lion
salient, human
legs?, all R
AM 1938.1042 (L) Melos
(CS 305)
R bef lion in PT 1A, R
SH horizontal

Two, antithetic
Flanking
<u>Column</u>
II 4.64 (L) Palaikastro
schematic
crude lines flank
XII 302 (L) Seager
Coll.
AM 1938.1044 (L) (CS
338)
Miscellaneous
I 231 (L) Vapheio
Tholos (LH IIA)
<u>Waisted</u>/bucranium
<u>Altar</u> topped with
<u>HC</u> with 3 <u>Branch 1</u>
the genii hold
pitchers aloft
I Supp. 137 (L)
genii flank nothing
at left: another,
smaller genius
R
V 367 (L) Medeon T. 29
2 dots just bel their
muzzles (paws?
jugs?) may be
supported by lines
(= <u>Columns</u>?)
AM 1938.1043 (A)

central Crete (CS
304)
tree
2 <u>Fronds</u> flank the
genii, who hold
jugs
SH vertical

6C
Griffins

(see: PT's passim [PT 5A, L:
FIG. 150]; Ch. 3A: Men & Ani-
mals [monsters] -- II 3.167 &
HMs 291/KSPI R35; Ch. 3B: Mas-
ter of Animals [griffins] -- V
675; Ch. 3D: Men In Chariots
-- HMs 347/KSPI L?; Ch. 4A:
Women & Animals [antithetic]
-- VIII 146, [friezes] -- II
3.282, [woman rides] -- V 584 &
HMs 73 [AT 132]; Ch. 4B: <u>Potnia</u>
<u>Theron</u> [griffins] -- V 654 &
AM AE 689)

FIG. 150 -- V 690:
griffiness in PT 5A, L

Single
I 341 (Cs) Pylos Palace
V 650 (Cyl) Crete
   griffin R (unfinished)
I Supp. 200
   PT 5B, L

Pair
I 171 (L) Mycenae, Perseia
     area (LH III B)
   in PT 28A, leashed to a
      Column betw
      bull-headed man (cf. Ch.
      3B: Master of Animals
      [monsters] -- I 324)
      prone bel

With Other Animals
I Supp. 176 (Ls?) Pylos
     Palace
   PT 10, R displayed ab a
     quadruped (to L?)
II 3.25b (L) Knossos, Houses
     So. of palace
   griffin & dappled stag in PT
     45, victim L
HM 2092 (Cyl) Knossos, Royal
     Road
   top: lion salient R
     regardant, agrimi R,
     waterbird
   bottom: animal salient R,
     griffin couchant L

6D
Miscellaneous Monsters

Babylonian Dragon (see: Ch.
   4A: Women & Animals [woman
   rides animal]; Ch. 12C:
   Boats)

PT 1A, L; Filler -- V 581 [**FIG.**
151]
PT 3, R -- IV 42D
PT 5A, L; Filler -- HMs 637
   (Sk 11)
PT 5A, R; Filler -- AM 1938.
   1150 (CS 22P)
PT 6, L;
   Plain -- XII 293
   Filler -- HM G 3138 (CMCG
     283)

FIG. 151 -- V 581:
Babylonian Dragon in PT 1A

Fish-Monster (see: PT 14B
   [cow & calf]: II 4.161 [**FIG.**
   21; Ch. 3A: Men & Animals
   [monsters] -- I Supp. 3)

Combinations of Monsters (see:
   Ch. 3A: Men & Animals
   [monsters] -- I Supp. 3; Ch.
   3B: Master of Animals
   [monsters] -- V 201)

Miscellaneous Winged Animals
Winged Agrimi
   PT 5A, L; Filler: winged
     agrimi -- V 400
   Ch. 3B: Master of Animals --
     V 201

Winged Lion Protome, head R
   HMs 8 (Ls) Kato Zakro (KZ
      184)
     frontal, displayed
   HMs 598 (Ls) Ayia Triada
      (AT 100)
     frontal, displayed
Miscellaneous
   ?HM 2785 (L, broken)
      Knossos, MUM (Popham
      et al. 1984: no. Misc.
      10)
     2? (winged bird-)people?
     flank a <u>Papyrus</u>
       SH horizontal
   HMs 1a (Ls) Kato Zakro (KZ
      80)
     2 winged forelegs, anti-
      thetic & conjoined
     with bucranium topped
     by a loop
   HMs 1a & AM AE 1801 (Ls)
      Poros & Kato Zakro (CS
      10Sa)
     winged bucranium topped
     by a loop
   HMs 27a (Ls) Kato Zakro
      (KZ 53)
     bird tail topped with 2
     bird-heads addorsed
   HMs 597 (Ls) Ayia Triada
      (AT 101)
     winged monster displayed

Winged Objects
IV 314
IV 320

Miscellaneous
HMs no. unknown (?s) Kato
     Zakro, Shrine (Platon
     1971: 147)
   "lion, monster, libation
     jug" (is the "monster" a
     genius?)

220

PLANTS -- 7A: BRANCHES [Branch 1]

CHAPTER 7
Plants

7A
Branches

branch
I Supp. 62 (C) Thebes, Ayia
  Anna ChT 2 (LH I-II)
V 617 (L) Olympia, Trypes T.
  E (LH III A-C)

Branch 1
One Branch 1
  I Supp. 149b (L)
    SH horizontal
  V 390 (L) Medeon T. 29a
    (LH III A-C)
    SH horizontal
  V 593 (bronze C) Mycenae
    (MH-LH III A2)
    probably a kind of
    scoring prior to
    gilding (cf. V 614
    below; & II 3.98,
    256, & 324)
  V 614 (R) Olympia, New
    Museum T. Theta cist
    (LH III B)
    probably a kind of
    scoring prior to
    gilding (cf. V 593
    above)
  V 742 (L) Gritsa, Lemoni
    Tholos
    SH horizontal
  V 743 (L) Gritsa, Lemoni
    Tholos
    SH horizontal
  X 206 (L) Chania Sigma 58
    (L) Armenoi T. 67 (LM III
    A-B; Pini 1981: no. 73)

Two Branch 1
  I Supp. 61 (C) Thebes,

    Ayia Anna ChT 2 (LH I-II)
  V 156 (L) Kephallenia,
    Kokkolata Tholos B (LH
    III B[-C])
    dots betw
  V 217 (L) Brauron,
    Lapoutsi ChT 13 (LH III
    B?)
  V 229 (L) Chalkis, Trypa
    T. 8?
  V 373 (L) Medeon T. 29
    (LH III A-C)
  V 731 (L) Mega Monastiri
    T. Gamma (LH III A-B)
    flanking 2 depressions
  VII 194 (L) Ialysos

Three Branch 1
  HMs 229 (Ls) Knossos
    Palace (KSPI R36)
  HMs 555 (Ls) Ayia Triada
    (AT 10)

Branch 2
One Branch 2
  V 444 (L) Nichoria (LH
    III A2-B)
    in field
  AM 1889.999 (L) "Athens"
    (CS 397)
    S-shaped

Two Branch 2
  I Supp. 10 (RPr) Mycenae
    flanking 3 centered
    circles
  AM 1941.107 (L) (CS 194)
    2 pairs quarter the
    field; a centered
    circle in each
    quadrant

Branch 3 (see: Ch. 7A:
  Branches [Branch 4] --X
  238, below)

V 163 (L) Kephallenia,

Kokkolata cist grave (LH
III B[-C])
2 <u>Branch 3</u>
X 209 (L)
2 <u>Branch 3</u> encircle central
dot

<u>Branch 4</u>
X 210 (L)
encircles
X 238 (L)
at left with 2 <u>Branch 3</u>
(center <u>Branch 3</u> flanked
by 2 lines)
SH horizontal

7B
Miscellaneous Plants

<u>Palmettes & Branch 4</u>
AM 1938.948 (L?s) Knossos?
(CS 2S)
2 palmettes in radial
symmetry
<u>Branch 4</u> encircles

<u>branch/lines</u>
Florence 82530 (L) bought
in Greece (Laviosa: 1969
no. 15)

<u>Lily</u> (see: Ch. 2A: Body Parts
[body parts] -- HMs 153)

AM 1938.1053 (R, axis
vertical) Knossos area
(CS 251)
ivy bel
dots encircle

<u>Papyrus</u>
X 120 (As) (Brice III.17)
HMs 15 (Ls) Kato Zakro (KZ
132)
3 <u>Papyrus</u> flowers separate 3
boss rosettes (see: Ch.
9R: Misc. Patterns)
HMs 172a (Ls) Kato Zakro (KZ
172)
<u>Papyrus</u> flower tops a volute
spiral (see: Ch. 9E:
Spirals [volute])

<u>Grains</u>
XII 151b (A) Seager Coll.
5 <u>Grains</u>
line ab & bel
strokes in the field

"Dandelion Puff"/<u>Sun</u> (see:
Ch. 5E: Birds & Waterbirds
[waterbirds, single] --IV
257; & the painted "puff" on
the prows of ships in the
Thera ship fresco)

CHAPTER 8
Miscellaneous

8A
Writing

(except Hieroglyphics & signs
on the reverse of seals)

I 156 (L) Mycenae ChT 523 (Lh
    III A2)
  signs
      Branch 2 encircles
      SH horizontal?
II 2.213b (D) Knossos
  Archanes script (cf. Yule
    1981: p. 170)
II 3.23 (A) Knossos, South
    House?
  Linear A: Brice V.12; Linear
    C = CMS II 3 p. 1 s.n. 23
II 3.38 (R) Mavrospelio T. IX
    (MM III)
  Linear A inscription (19
    signs) arranged in a
    spiral
 V 415 (L) Medeon T. 239 (LH
    III C)
  Linear B: e-ku-ja (on seal;
    hapax legomenon?)
  SH horizontal

8B
Buildings

HMs 25a (Ls) Kato Zakro (KZ
    49)
  5 tower-like buildings, the
      center tower with gate
  rocks bel
HMs 45 (Ls) Kato Zakro (KZ
    131)

city buildings
  rocks at left
  2 Figure-8 Shields bel

8C
Ships

(except Talismanic Ships)

AM 1938.957 (C) Knossos area
    (CS 228)
  prow & sails of a ship R
HMs 146 (Ls) Knossos Palace
    (KSPI J3)
  ship L
HMs 384 (Ls) Knossos Palace
    (KSPI L15/22; Betts
    1968)
  3 ship-prows with oarlocks?
    from rocks at left

8D
Vessels

I 114 (L) Mycenae ChT 79
  jug R
    SH horizontal
HM 2343a (Pr) Poros ChT (MM
    III-LM I; Lembessi 1967:
    pl. 188
  kantharos
HM 2344b (APr) Poros ChT (MM
    III-LM I; Lembessi 1967:
    pl. 189)
  kantharos

8E
Helmets

Plumed
Plume sits on top
   IX 166 (L)
      2 sets of 4 straps flank
        SH horizontal
   IX 167 (L)
      2 pairs of horizontal
        straps flank & 2
        straps? hang down from
        the helmet's lower rim
        SH horizontal

To Left
   I 153 (Pr) Mycenae ChT 518
      (LH I-II)
   X 149* (L)
      1 vertical strap hangs
        from the helmet's
        lower rim
        SH horizontal
   X 243 (L)
      cheek piece hangs from
        the helmet's rim
        vertical row of 8-9
        dots at right
        SH horizontal
   AM 1971.1142 (L) de Jong
      Coll. (Boardman 1973: no.
      4)
   HMs 494 (Ls) Ayia Triada
      (AT 6)
   3 pairs of straps hang
        from the helmet's rim
      row of dots ab & at right
   HMs PA (Ls) Knossos Palace
      KSPI L14)
      Branch 4 at right
      object (helmet from
        rear?) at left

To Right
   VII 195 (L)
      2 horizontal straps?

      flank
      SH horizontal?
   HMs 25 (Ls) Kato Zakro (KZ
      130)
      2 dog heads addorsed on
        helmet

2 Plumes
   I 260 (L) Vapheio Tholos
      (LH IIA)
      the 2 plumes curve in to
        center
      straps hang from the
        helmet's rim
      2 straps? flank

Winged
HMs 28 (Ls) Kato Zakro (KZ
      31)
   winged helmet topped with
      an ivy-leaf (cf. HMs 29
      gamma/KZ 30)
HMs 37 (Ls) Kato Zakro
      (KZ 86)
   winged helmet topped with
      bull face

8F
<u>Figure-8 Shields</u>

(see: Ch. 8J: Miscellaneous --
VII 158, below)

Simple
II 3.113 (R) Kalyvia, T. 10
      (LM III A2)
   3
      2 <u>Cypress Branches</u> flank
      dots betw each &
        flanking
      <u>Dado 9a</u> top & bottom?
?V 574 (L) Tiryns, Geometric
      T.

schematic?
    SH horizontal
VII 203 (L)
a wavy line with strokes
    (<u>Branch 3</u>?) encircle
HMm 1002-4 (R's) Archanes
    Tholos A (LM III A1;
    Sakellarakis 1966: fig.
    8)
    3
    <u>Dado 1</u> encircles
HMs 266 (Rs?) Knossos Palace
    (KSPI R22)
    2 registers:
        top: <u>Figure-8 Shields</u> (&
        animal?)
        bottom: conch/murex
        shells obliquely
        arranged, head down

8G
<u>Sacred Knots/Robes</u>

I 205 (A/Cyl) Argos ChT 7
    (LH III A)
    2 <u>Sacred Robes</u>, 1 atop the
        other
        SH vertical (photographs
        upside down; for shape
        cf. Ch. 2B: Men
        [single] -- I 68)
HM 2343b (Pr) Poros ChT (MM
    III-LM I; Lembessi
    1967: pl. 188)
<u>Double Ax</u> crosses just below
    the loop of a <u>Sacred Knot</u>
HMs 150 (A/Ls) Knossos Palace
    (KSPI S6)
    2 <u>Sacred Knots</u> flank <u>Palm 1</u>
    (if made by an
        amygdaloid, the SH is
        vertical)
HMs 168 (Ls) Kato Zakro (KZ

168)
<u>Sacred Knot</u>
    the base of the loop is
    crossed with a <u>Snake</u>
    <u>Frame</u>

8H
Friezes:
<u>Figure-8 Shields</u>
& <u>Sacred Knots/Robes</u>

HMm 990 (R) Archanes Tholos A
    (LM III A1; Sakellarakis
    1966: fig. 8)
    2 registers, each with a
    central <u>Figure-8 Shield</u>
    flanked by 2 <u>Sacred Knots</u>
    & 2 smaller <u>Figure-8</u>
    <u>Shields</u>
        <u>Dado 1</u> separates the
        registers
HMs 664 (Rs) Knossos Palace
    (KSPI C11)
    3 <u>Sacred Robes</u> flanked by 2
    <u>Figure-8 Shields</u>, each
    topped with a loop
    <u>Dado 9b</u> bel

8I
<u>Double Axes</u>

(cf. the <u>Double Ax</u> impressions,
made by a metal? object, on the
two terracotta pieces of cult
furniture from Mallia, tripod
base HMp 5516 from the MM II
Sanctuary & an offering table
HMp 8516 [BCH 90, 1966, 536
figs. 22 & 23, respectively])

HMs 264 (Ls) Knossos Palace
      (KSPI R100)
   4 <u>Double Axes</u> with the
      hafts to center &
      perpendicular to
      each other
          rosette in center

dotted intersections
bel

FIG. 152 -- VII 158:
       trophy?

              8J
         Miscellaneous

VII 158 (L) (**FIG. 152**)
   trophy?: <u>Figure-8 Shield</u>
      topped with a helmet,
      plume to left; arms
      extend from the top of
      the shield out, each
      holding a sword up,
      supported by a human leg
      bel
          SH horizontal?
X 69* (L)
   river with fish?
      3 <u>Fronds</u> ab
      net/reticulation with

CHAPTER 9
Geometric Motifs

9A
Paisleys

(cf. Ch. 7A: Branches [Branch 1] -- V 731)

Single
Large
    V 329 (L) Krissa
        curled, strokes fill &
            encircle

Small
    V 371 (L) Medeon T. 29 (LH
            III A-C)
        strokes fill & encircle
    V 627 (L) Kataraktis?
        strokes fill & encircle
    AM 1938.1099 (L) Archanes
            (CS 394; GGFR pl. 197)
        Branch 3 fills; strokes &
            lines fill the field

Double, antithetic
I Supp. 166 (L) Salamis ChT 2
    strokes fill & Branch 3
        encircles
Nafplion no. unknown (L)
        Tiryns (LH III C; AA
        1979, 405 fn. 75, fig. 30
        middle right)
    strokes encircle

9B
Centered Circles

(cf. EH II: the stamped hearth
rim fragments V 451-455, & the

similar fragment Pigorini
75206/7 from Ayia Triada [LM
IB?; Borda 1946: 63 nos. 2 & 3,
'libation tables']; MM: HM no.
unknown [Stamp] from Kommos,
Hillside room 29: centered
circle & 3 Branch 2 [Shaw 1981:
216 n. 11, pl. 51f], with which
compare CMS II 1.334)

(see: Ch. 9H: Cross -- VII 244
& 245, & V 494)

One
V 225 (L) Medeon?
V 419 (L) Medeon T. 264 (LH
        III C)
    lines

Two
Plain
    I Supp. 16 (RPr) Mycenae
        on each face

On two opposing faces of a
    rectangular prism

    I Supp. 11 (RPr) Mycenae
            acropolis
        sides a & c: in a box
        sides d & e: reticula-
                tion
        ends: X
    I Supp. 60 (RPr) Brauron,
            Lapoutsi ChT 2
        long sides
        short sides: reticula-
                tion (see: Ch. 9M:
                Reticulation)
        SH recessed with large,
                deep socket for
                swivel pin?
    V 448 (RPr) Nichoria (LH
            III A2-B)
        the sides
        the faces: lines (see:
            Ch. 9Q: Misc. Lines)

With Miscellaneous Filler
  I 173 (L) Mycenae
    branches, lines encircle
  I Supp. 50 (L) Glyphada,
      Alyki T. Gamma (LH
      III)
    branch in field
  II 3.127 (L) Tylissos
    2 Branch 3 flank
    S-shaped spiral betw
  II 4.42 (L) Knossos
    a line bisects the face
      top: 2 centered
        circles flank a
        branch
      bottom: lines &
        hatching
  V 13 (L) Aigina
    branch encircles
  V 376 (L) Medeon T. 29
    (LH III A-C)
    line in center
    Branch 3 encircles
  V 429 (L) Akones, Veve
    Tholos
    2 Branch 3
  X 196 (L)
    2 Branch 4
    S-shaped Branch 4 betw
      with 2 wedge-shaped
      gouges flanking

Three
Plain
  II 4.68 "Myrtidia" (RP1)
    sides
  V 154 (L) Kephallenia,
    Kokkolata Tholos B (LH
      III B [-C])
  V 612 (L) Olympia, New
    Museum T. H (LH III B)

On two opposing faces of a
prism

  V 420 (APr) Medeon T. 264
    (LH III C)

sides
faces: reticulation (see:
  Ch. 9M: Reticulation)

With lines
  II 3.84 (L) Knossos,
    Demeter Sanctuary
    a line bisects the face
    in top half: 3 centered
      circles separated by 2
      lines
    in bottom half: a row of
      6-7 oblique lines
  X 190 (L)
  X 195 (L)
  X 288 (L)
    really a bird?
    SH horizontal

With miscellaneous filler
  I Supp. 46 (L) Perachora,
    Hera Limenia
    Sanctuary
    Branch 2 & Branch 4 in
      field
  I Supp. 164a (L)
    a Frond betw each at the
      periphery
  HM 922 (L) Tylissos
    (Khatzidakis 1912:
      pl. 15a)
    3 groundlines bel

Four (see: Ch. 9H: Cross,
below)

Plain
  I 177 (L) Mycenae,
    acropolis
  I 397 (L) Athens,
    acropolis
  II 4.115 (RP1) Knossos,
    House of the Frescoes
      (LM I)
    sides
  V 175 (L) Athens, Agora
    T. VII (LH III [B-]C1)

V 226   (L)   Medeon? T. 29
   (LH III A-C)

With miscellaneous filler
I 34   (L) Mycenae,
       acropolis
    cross
I 402   (L) Athens,
       acropolis
    lines, Branch 2
I Supp. 45   (L) Perachora,
       Hera Limenia
       Sanctuary
    2 Branch 2
I Supp. 165   (L)
    Branch 2
II 4.147   (C) Knossos
    lines in the field
II 4.169   (C) Mallia
    lines in the field
II 4.235   (C)
    a line bisects the face
       lengthwise
    2 centered circles top &
       bottom
V 152   (L) Kephallenia,
    Kokkolata Tholos A (LH
    III B[-C])
    2 Branch 2 in center
    2 Branch 1 flank
V 495   (L) Ayia Arini
    lines
VIII 143   (A)
    a: 4 centered circles
    b: flaked
X 193   (L)
    2 vertical & 1 horizontal
       Branch 2 quarter the
       field, a centered
       circle in each
       quadrant
II 4.135   (L) Knossos,
       Demeter Sanctuary
    lines bisect the face, 2
       circles in each half
    SH horizontal

Six
Plain
    II 4.68   (RPl) "Myrtidia"
    II 4.208   (A) Mochlos

With second SH
    V 330   (L) Krissa, ChT 2
       (LH III B)
    lines encircle
    V 413   (L) Medeon T. 239
       (LH III C)

With miscellaneous filler
    II 3.57   (A) Fortetsa T. P
       (PG-LG)
    separated into 2 rows of
       3 by a line, all
       enclosed in a diamond
    V 387   (L) Medeon T. 29a
       (LH III A-C)
    7 strokes

Seven
II 3.384   (A)
    3 strokes at left & at
       right
II 4.185   (A) "Knossos"
    lines in the field
V 414   (L) Medeon T. 239 (LH
    III C)
    lines encircle
HMs 309a   (As) Knossos Palace
    (KSPI R82)

Eight
Plain
    II 3.323   (L) "Palaikastro"
    HMs 309I   (Ls) Knossos
       Palace (KSPI R83)

On two opposing sides of a
rectangular plate seal

    II 4.115   (RPl) Knossos,
       House of the Frescoes
       (LM I)
    faces: 2 rows of 4

                   separated by a line
                sides: 4
        V 270 (RP1) Armenoi T. 54
                faces: 2 rows of 4
                   separated & flanked
                   by lines
                sides: 4
        X 189 (RP1)
                faces: 2 rows of 4
                   separated & flanked
                   by lines
                sides: 4
Miscellaneous
        II 4.186 (L) "Knossos"
                encircle & connected by
                   rays to a central dot
                   to form a rosette

Miscellaneous
Countable
        I 14 (L) Mycenae, ShGr III
                (LH I)
             10 centered circles
                encircle 1 large
                centered circle;
                these are linked by
                tangents to resemble
                running spirals (cf.
                Ch. 9G: Rosettes
                (early) -- X 105)
        II 3.70 (L) Knossos,
                Temple Tomb
             34 (one uncentered)
                encircle Sun
        II 4.99 (A)
                20? in 4 panels contain-
                   ing 4?, 6?, 6, 4
        II 4.109 (L) Tylissos
                (Khatzidakis 1912: pl.
                15b)
             16 centered circles
        II 4.134 (L) Knossos,
                Geometric T.
             10
        II 4.148 (Cyl) Knossos
                50 in 4 panels contain-
                   ing 13, 15, 13, 9

        II 4.187 (L) "Knossos"
             15
        II 4.236 (L)
             9
        II 4.237 (L)
             10 encircle a Sun?
        X 58 (L)
             9 centered circles
                encircle Sun
        X 188 (RP1)
                faces: 7 & 8 centered
                   circles
                sides: 3 & 4 centered
                   circles
        X 192a* (L)
             17 centered circles
        XII 269 (L) Seager Coll.
             12 centered circles
                encircle central
                centered circle
             7 hand-incised circles
                betw

Within a limited range
        X 191 (L)
             4-7 centered circles
        X 194 (L)
             6-8 centered circles
        AM AE 1790 (L) Diktaian
                cave (CS 392)
             7 (-14 ?) centered
                circles

At least:
        I 401 (L) Athens,
                acropolis
             25 centered circles
        IV 271 (L) Messara
             19 centered circles
        V 259 (L) Armenoi T. 32
                (LM III A2-B1)
             16 centered circles
        XII 79 (Cyl) Seager Coll.
             15 centered circles
                a groove spirals
                   around the face

9C
Arcs

Plain
HM 2343c (Pr) Poros ChT MM
    III - LM I (Lembessi
    1967: pl. 188)
  1 arc (unfinished?)

Hyperbolas
One
  I Supp. 139 (L)
    2 sets of 3 arcs form a
      hyperbola, with a dot
      at each focus
  VII 202 (L)
    2 sets of 3 form a
      hyperbola; 2 dots
      between, on the
      conjugate axis

Two
  V 245 (L) Armenoi T. 15
    4 pairs of arcs quarter
      the field, a dot in
      each quadrant (= 2
      crossed hyperbolas, a
      dot at each focus)
    dot in the center

9D
Dots

I 354 (Ls) Pylos Palace
    3 (-4?) rows of 5? dots each
II 3.85 (C) Knossos, Demeter
    Sanctuary
  a: 2 rows of dots (total:
    10) quarter the field
      upper left quadrant: 3
        dots & a centered
        circle

upper right quadrant:
  a centered circle
  in each lower quad-
    rant: a large dot
    (remains of a
    centered circle?)
  b: 14 dots & 3 centered
    circles preserved
X 197 (L)
  4 dots encircled by 2 hand-
    engraved circles

9E
Spirals

"Running Spirals"
HMs 147 (Ls) Kato Zakro (KZ
    147)
  2 circles with tangential
    line = 2 running
    "spirals"
    Branch 1 ab & bel

Plain
II 2.57a (D) Profitis Elias
    T. VII
  4 tight spirals
V 685 (L) Tanagra, Dendron
    T. 18 (LH III A-B)
  2 opposing spirals
    strokes encircle
Nafplion no. unknown (L)
    Tiryns T. 1972.6 (PG; AAA
    7, 1974, 24, fig. 22
    right)
  2 opposing spirals
    strokes encircle

S-Spirals
?V 738 (L) Mega Monastiri T.
    Delta (LH III A2-B1)
  curved strokes encircle
X 203 (L)

formed from 3 parallel
      lines
   strokes encircle

C-Spirals
HMs 1/AM AE 1801 (Ls) Poros,
    KZ (KZ 134; CS 10Sb)
   cross made by interlocking
      C-spirals
   a diamond in the center
HMs 116 (Ls) Knossos Palace
    (KSPI O11)
   3 addorsed & connected
      C-spirals
      wedge betw each at the
         periphery & in the
         center

V-Spirals
HMs 112 (Ls) Knossos Palace
    (KSPI N11)
   3 V-spirals

Volute-Spirals
X 235 (L)
   outlined by arcs
HMs 172a (Ls) Kato Zakro (KZ
    172)
   volute spiral topped by
      Papyrus flower? (see:
      Ch. 7B: Misc. Plants
      [Papyrus])

9F
Meanders

Squared
HMs 30 (Ls) Kato Zakro (KZ
    133)

Curved
V 332 (L) Krissa

dot in center
strokes encircle

9G
Rosettes

Early
Quatrefoils
   Modeled
      II 3.322 (L) Palai-
         kastro, near MM
         ossuary
      2 parallel chords in
         each quadrant
      II 4.133 (L) Knossos,
         Geometric T.
      frond betw each petal
      X 201 (L)
         Branch 3 betw
      AM 1938.947a, b (Ls)
         Knossos Palace (CS 47S
         & 48S; KSPI R94)
      HMs 57 (Ls) Kato Zakro
         (KZ 94)
         chords
         hatching in the field
      HMs 484 (Ls) Ayia
         Triada (AT 12)
         Branch 3 encircles

   Cut
      ?AM 1971.1138 (L) de
         Jong Coll. (Board-
         man 1973: no. 17)
         Papyrus betw the
         petals

Drilled, terminating in arcs
   7 Arcs
      V 180a (L)
         circle in center,
            lines connecting
            arcs to circle zig-

zags at periphery
XII 157 (L) Seager
    Coll.
    large dot with super-
    imposed circle in
    center
    lines radiate from
    center (cf. X 105
    above, Ch. 9B:
    Circles (count-
    able) -- I 114
10 Arcs (cf. I 14 [Spirals,
    below])
    X 105 (L)
    large centered circle
    in center con-
    nected to arcs by
    lines (cf. Ch. 9B:
    Circles [count-
    able] -- I 14)

Late
Quatrefoils
I Supp. 59 (L) Brauron,
    Lapoutsi ChT 2
    line encircles
V 165 (L) Kephalennia,
    Kokkolata cist grave
    (LH III B[-C])
    line/wedges encircles
V 166 (L) Kephallenia,
    Kokkolata cist grave
    (LH III B[-C])
    3 lines encircle
V 167 (L) Kephallenia,
    Kokkolata cist grave
    (LH III B[-C])
    frond betw
V 369 (L) Medeon T. 29
    (LH III A-C)
    line encircles
V 370 (L) Medeon T. 29
    (LH III A-C)
    parallel curved arcs
    surround each
    "grain/leaf"
V 406 (L) Medeon T. 239

(LH III C)
    lines encircle
V 407 (L) Medeon T. 239
    (LH III C)
    line encircle
    Frond betw each leaf
V 736 (L) Mega Monastiri
    T. Delta (LH III
    A2-B1)
    3 lines encircle
IX 197 (L)
    lines encircle
Hannover 1967.30 (L) Crete
    (AGDS IV Hannover 9)
    line & _Branch 3_ encircles

Miscellaneous
I Supp. 161 (L)
    7 petals
    Branch 2 encircles
II 4.186 (L) "Knossos"
    7 concentric circles
    encircle & are
    connected by rays to
    a central dot
V 395 (L) Medeon T. 99 (LH
    III A)
    5 petals
    lines encircle
V 408 (L) Medeon T. 239
    (LH III C)
    8 petals around a
    centered circle
V 737 (L) Mega Monastiri
    T. Delta (LH III
    A2-B1)
    11 cut petals
Nafplion no. unknown (L)
    Tiryns (LH III C
    early; AA 1979, 405
    fn. 75, fig. 30 top
    right)
    3 petals

9H
Cross

Chevrons in the quadrants (see:
EB II seals [Yule 1981:
motif 29])

I 28 (L/Sc) Mycenae,
acropolis
I Supp. 162 (L)

Hatched
II 3.186   (L) "Knossos"
II 3.187   (L) "Knossos"
II 3.188   (L) "Knossos"
II 3.378   (L)
II 3.379   (L)
II 3.380   (L)
II 3.381   (L)
II 3.382   (L)
II 4.59   (L) Diktaian Cave
II 4.119   (A) Isopata T. 3
II 4.120   (L) Zafer Papoura
T. 81
II 4.215   (L) Palaikastro
IV 222   (L) Tsoutsouros
V 271   (L) Armenoi T. 54
V 277   (L) Armenoi T. 59 (LM
III A2-B1)
V 375   (L) Medeon T. 29   (LH
III A-C)
V 389   (L) Medeon T. 29a (LH
III A-C)
V 412   (L) Medeon T. 239 (LH
III C)
V 653   (L) Crete V 735 (L)
Mega Monastiri T. Delta
(LH III A2-B1)
V 739   (L) Mega Monastiri T.
E (LH III A2-B2)
X 208   (L)
XII 147   (L) Seager Coll.
HM 2067   (L) Galia T. B (LM
III B; Pini 1981: no. 79)
HM 2348   (A) Poros ChT (MM
III A; Pini 1981: no. 80)

HM no. unknown (L) Knossos,
MUM (Popham et al. 1984:
Misc. 6)
HM no. unknown (L) Kommos
(LM III B; Shaw 1982: 166
pl. 40b)

**Centered circle in each
quadrant**

I Supp. 163 (L)
with 2 centered circles in
opposing quadrants,
hatching in the other
two quadrants
II 3.150 (L) Mallia
zig-zags encircle
II 4.14 (A) Knossos
lines in the field
II 4.97 (L)
V 494 (L) Keos
1 central centered circle
VII 244 (L)
VII 245 (L)

Miscellaneous
II 4.211 (C) "Eleounda"
an X quarters the face
top & bottom: 3 centered
circles
left & right: lines
V 190 (Cyl) Thebes?
two squares:
in one: cross whose ends
are capped with arcs;
an arc betw each leg;
a circle in the center
in the other: random
cuts, strokes, arcs, &
circles
VII 38b (D)
flaking
X 118 (L)
quadrant

9I
Stars

II 3.140   (L)   Episkopi
HM no. unknown   (L)   Knossos,
      MUM (Popham et al. 1984:
      Misc. 5)
   6-pointed Star, with the
      points connected by a
      double chord

9J
Quadripartite Designs

I Supp. 47   (L)   Eleusis W.
      Cemetery T. theta-pi 2
      (MH-LH I early)
   V's & hatching

9K
Lines/Strokes/Gouges

   (lines are long, strokes
short, gouges thick & short)

Lines   (see: Ch. 7B: Plants
   [misc.]-- Florence 82430)

AM 1971.1147   (L)   de Jong
      Coll. (Boardman 1973: no.
      18)
AM AE 1798   (L)   (CS 48P)
HM no. unknown   (L)   Knossos,
      MUM (Popham et al. 1984:
      Misc. 14)
   both faces: lines & dashes
Brummer Coll.   (L)
Thera no. unknown   (Stamp)

Thera (Marinatos 1975:
   32 pl. 56d)
central line with 3 lines
   perpendicular

Strokes   (see: Ch. 9E: Spirals
   -- X 203, below])

I 301   (RPr)   Pylos Palace (LH
      III B2-C1)
   a & c: 2 rows of 7? oblique
      dashes each
   b (& d originally?): 7
      columns of short strokes
      in the following pattern:
      3, 4, 4, 3, 4, 4, 3
      (total: 25)
V 224   (L)   Medeon ?
V 409   (L)   Medeon T. 239 (LH
      III C)
V 628   (L)   Kato Goumenitsa
      (LH III A1-2)
X 204   (L)
   line encircles at the
      periphery, possibly for
      a ring setting or for
      gilding?)

Gouges
I Supp. 9   (L)   Mycenae
   with a line or cross
II 4.2   (L)   Tylissos
   with lines
V 331   (L)   Krissa ChT 1 (LH
      III B)
   with strokes
V 410   (L)   Medeon T. 239 (LH
      III C)
V 411 (L) Medeon T. 239 (LH
      III C)

9L
Hatching

(a few broad, intersecting
cuts)

I Supp. 140b (L)
II 2.68 (D) Profitis Elias
II 4.26 (C) "Tylissos"
  both sides
II 4.27 (L) "Tylissos"
IV 221 (A) Mallia
V 278 (L) Armenoi T. 59 (LM
  III A2-B1)
V 374 (L) Medeon T. 29 (LH
  III A-C)
VII 256 (L)

9M
Reticulation

(thicker lines usually form an
  overall "diaper net")
[except: V 420 sides b & d]

(usually on soft stones)
[except: lentoid from Kommos]

Rectangular Prisms
I Supp. 11 (RPr) Mycenae
  sides a & c: 2 concentric
    circles in a box (see:
    Ch. 9B: Concentric
    Circles [2])
  sides d & e: reticulation
  ends: X
I Supp. 60 (RPr) Brauron,
    Lapoutsi ChT 2
  long sides: 2 concentric
      circles (see: Ch. 9B:
      Concentric Circles
      [2])
  short sides: reticulation

SH recessed with large,
  deep socket for
  swivel pin?
V 391 (APr) Medeon T. 29a (LH
  IIIA-C)
V 420 (APr) Medeon T. 264
  (LH III C)
  sides: 3 centered circles
    (see: Ch. 9B: Centered
    Circles [3])
  faces: reticulation

Miscellaneous Shapes
I Supp. 102 (A) Crete
  between 2 pairs lines
II 4.193 (L) "Rousochoria"
  zig-zags encircle
HM no. unknown (L) Kommos
    (LM III?; Shaw 1979: 152
    pl. 53d)
  vertical strokes fill each
    diamond
HMs 146 (Cs) Kato Zakro (KZ
  146)
  horizontal grooves ab &
    bel

9N
Architectonic

("Cut Style": thin lines cross
at right angles, in a "diaper
net", or in combination)

AM 1953.116 (L) "Gaza" (CS
  31P)
Berlin FG 39 (D) "the
  Islands" (AGDS II Berlin
  14)
HMp? no. unknown (A/Ls on a
  Medallion pithos; the seal
  was broken when used)
Knossos Palace (PM I 564,

fig. 410)
HMs 671/AM no No.8   (Cs?)
    Knossos, E. Wing (KSPI Ce)
HMs 666   (Cs) Knossos, NE
    House (KSPI Ve)

90
Chevrons

X 205   (L)
    8 parallel chevrons
        line encircles at the
        periphery, possibly for a
        ring setting or for
        gilding

9P
Flaked Obsidian Disks

(Renfrew, et al. 1985: 296-7)

I Supp. 120   (D)
    a: flaking, one flake
        re-cut? as a dolphin
        (see: Ch. 5I: Dolphins)
    b: flaked
IV 166   (D)
    a: agrimi in PT 5A, R;
        branch/spear bel
    b: flaking, one flake re-cut
        as a dolphin (see: Ch.
        5I: Dolphins)
VII 37a & b   (D)
VII 38 (D)
    a: flaking
    b: flaking & cross
VIII 39a & b   (D)
VIII 40a & b   (D)

9Q
Miscellaneous Lines

Lines Only
II 4.29   (L) "Trypiti"
II 4.54   (L) "Mallia"
    both sides
II 4.238   (L)
V 164   (L) Kephallenia,
    Kokkolata (LH III B[-C])
V 171   (L) Kephallenia,
    Lakkithra T. Gamma (LH III
    C)
V 368   (L) Medeon T. 29 (LH
    III A-C)
V 372   (L) Medeon T. 29 (LH
    III A-C)
V 396 (L) Medeon T. 99 (LH
    III A)
V 427   (C) Akones Tholos
V 446   (A) Nichoria (MH-LH
    I)
V 448   (RPr) Nichoria (LH III
    A2-B)
    faces: lines
    sides: 2 centered circles
        (see: Ch. 9B: Centered
        Circles [2])
V 613   (L) Olympia, New
    Museum T. Theta (LH III
    B)
    parallel lines
X 202   (L)
    encircling center dot
X 207   (L)
    lines oblique to a central
    vertical line
XII 270   (Cyl) Seager Coll.
HM 2347   (A) Poros ChT (MM
    III-LM I; Lembesis 1967:
pl. 191 c + d)

Lines &
I Supp. 12   (L) Mycenae
    circles
II 4.189
Figure-8 Shield

HC with a circle top &
    bottom
lines flank
Branch 1 ab & bel
V 397   (RPr) Medeon T. 131
    (LH III C end)
flanking Branch 2 in box
V 679   (RStamp) Thebes,
    Kolonaki T. 17 (LH III
    A1)
Branch 2
X 199   (L)
dots, line encircles?
X 237   (L)
dots

AM 1938.941   (Ls)   Knossos
    Palace (CS 1S (KSPI L1-
    6?)
knot pattern
HMs 15   (Ls)   Kato Zakro (KZ
    132)
3 bosses
3 Papyrus flowers betw each
    (see: Ch. 7B: Misc.
    Plants)
HMs 63   (Ls)   Ayia Triada (AT
    31)
triangle
    2 vertical strokes flank
HMs no. unknown   (Rs)   Ayia
    Triada (AT 1)
blank ring bezel

9R
Miscellaneous Patterns

Wheels (cf. wheels of ivory
    [Poursat 1977b: no. 262] &
    lead [Schliemann 1880: 74
    fig. 120])

V 34   (bronze Stamp) Argos,
    Deiras T. XXII (LH IIIC1)
V 572   (pithos impressed by a
    stamp/Wheel) Tiryns (LH
    III C)

Miscellaneous
II 4.177   (C)   "Poros"
    a diamond flanked by lines
        & containing lines
II 4.210   (C) Palaikastro
    a: 2 X's with hatching
    b: a ladder-pattern flanked
        by lines
V 744   (L) Gritsa, Tholos
        Lemoni
    diamond, 2 sides of which
            are doubled;
        line cuts across

PART II

FILLING MOTIFS

CHAPTER 10

People

10A
People

Normal Size
Men
  Single
    BEHIND
      PT 7, L; lion -- I 512
    IN FRONT
      Ch. 3D: Bull-Leaping
      (Floating Leaper
      Schema) -- VII 109
      & Columbia, Mis-
      souri University
      57.8
    ABOVE
      PT 13A, L: bull --
      Berlin FG 8
      (AGDS II 22)
      prone R (stands L
      at right when
      SH is horizontal
    IN BACK
      PT 17A, L: nanny & kid
      -- AM 1938.1021
      (CS 242)
      holds the nanny by
      a leash
    BELOW, prone R
      PT 1B, R; boar -- XII
      240
      head regardant
      PT 4, R: bull -- XIII
      35
      a fallen bull-
      athlete?

Ch. 3E: Animal Games
  (bull-leaping,
    (Diving) -- I
    314
    (Floating) -- AM
    1938.1079 (CS
    249)
Ch. 6C: Griffins -- I
  171
  bull-headed
In the Field
  PT 14A, L: lion -- V
    246
    SH horizontal: at
    left, man R &
    kid R
  PT 39A, L: griffin vs
    bull --
    Schlumberger 43
  man stabs a bull
  with a sword
Ch. 2B: Men (battles)
  -- HMs 483 (AT
  113)
  nude, fallen,
    helmeted man at
    right to right
Ch. 2D: Men and Women
  (pair, alone)
  -- HMs no. un-
  known (AT 141)
  at right, another
  man
Ch. 5C: Animal Heads
  (groups) -- HMs
  656 (KSPI U115)
  man seated R
Ch. 5E: Birds &
  Waterbirds
  (waterbirds,
  pair) -- HMs
  569-570 (AT 93)
  at left, person?
Two Men
  PT 39A, L & R: 2 pairs
  of griffins vs
  stags -- I 324

2 Masters in the
center
PT 39A, R: lion vs bull
-- Nicosia
1953/IX-3/6
2 men run R

Small
Men
   Ch. 2C: Women (single,
      religious) -- AM
      1919.56
      ab & betw the women, R
      with his right arm
      stretched out behind
      him
   Ch. 2C: Women (4 or more) --
      I 17
      ab, at left, R wearing a
      Figure-8 Shield &
      holding a spear
   Ch. 2E: People at a Shrine
      (person at left)
      I 292 -- ab, L with both
      arms up
      AM 1938.1127 (CS 250) --
      ab center, L holding a
      staff? infr of him

Women
   Ch. 2C: Women (4 or more)
      -- II 3.51
      at right, ab a wavy
      Heaven Line
   Ch. 2E: People at a Shrine
      (woman sits on Shrine) --
      Chania 2097: at left,
      small skirted person
      R holds Sceptre
      (tree-pulling, no
      Omphalos) -- Once in
      the Evans coll., The
      Ring of Minos: ab: at
      left, a small woman L
      (person at right) --
      HMs no. unknown (KZ
      1): ab center, small

woman leaning L
backwards?
Ch. 3D: Men In Chariots --
II 3.199
second register: flanked
by 2 lions & a man
holding an agrimi

10B
Body Parts

Torsoes/Protomes (see: Ch. 2A:
Parts of the Human Body
[protomes]; & Ch. 2C: Women
[pair, salute] -- I 134)

ABOVE
PT 7, R; lion -- I 133
R, his left arm
stretched R ab the
lion's head
PT 25C, L: 2 lions -- I
280
2 men
PT 35 ccl: 2 bull protomes
-- HM G 3372b (CMCG
190b)
one above each bull
protome

Man's Face
In the Center
PT 36 cl: 2 goats -- II
3.115
PT 37B cl: 3? quadrupeds --
HMs 136 (KSPI G8)
Ch. 5E: Birds & Waterbirds
(waterbirds, pair) --
II 3.88
ABOVE
PT 18B, L: cow & calf -- II
3.88
flanked by two

waterbirds
Ch. 3A: Man & Animals
      (caprids) -- II 3.33
BELOW
   PT 14D, L: <u>Minotaur</u> -- X
   145

Man's Head
PT 1A, R; Filler: lion -- HM G
      3211 (CMCG 338)
   ab, R
PT 48A: lion vs agrimi -- VII
      180
   at left, L
Ch. 5B: Animal Faces (lion,
      with other) -- XIII 22D
   R

Parts of the Human Face
Eye
   Ch. 2C: Women (4 or more)
         -- II 3.51
      bel
   Ch. 2E: People at a <u>Shrine</u>
         (tree-pulling, man at
         <u>Omphalos</u>) -- HMm 989
      in the field

Eye & Ear
   Ch. 2C: Women (single,
         kneels at <u>Omphalos</u>)
         -- AM 1919.56
      ab the kneeling woman

Arms & Hands
PT 28A: 2 waterbirds -- HMs 23b
      (KZ 58)
   ab: lion face with 2 human
      arms? rising from the
      top & curving out
Ch. 3D: Men In Chariots
   II 3.199
   Louvre AO2188
Ch. 8J: Misc. -- VII 158
   arms hold a sword up

Legs (see: Ch. 5B: Animal

Faces [bull] -- HMs 23 gamma
[KZ 165])

Two Flank an Animal Face
   Ch. 5B: Animal Faces
         (lion) -- HMs 81b (KZ 56)
         (bull) -- XII 174c/AM AE
         1802 (CS 11Sc; KZ 61)

Miscellaneous
   PT 14A, L: lion -- I 51
      bel
   Ch. 2B: Men (1) -- Chania
      1563
      leg? infr of the man
   Ch. 8J: Misc. -- VII 158
      arms hold out a sword,
         each supported by a
         human leg bel

CHAPTER 11

Quadrupeds

11A
Quadrupeds

Lions (see: Ch. 3A: Master of
Animals [lions])

BEFORE
PT 1/2, R; genius -- HMs 372

IN FRONT
PT 45: griffin vs lion L --
    AM 1971.1137 (Boardman
    1973: no. 8)
    cub? infr of the lion

ABOVE
PT 18B, R: cow & calf -- ?IX
    194
    lion R ab to form PT 40
PT 21, variant: 2 ibex/bulls
    -- VII 159
    lioness in PT 12, R ab

In the Field
PT 5A, L; Filler: lion --
    VII 94
    Branch 1/Pica ab
PT 5/6, R: lions -- II 3.65
    2 lions run R (1
    regardant)
PT 39A: dog L vs agrimi/kid-
    man -- XII 242
    lion in PT 5
Ch. 2A: Parts of the Human
    Body (man's head,
    beardless) -- HM G
    3211 (CMCG 338)
    lion in PT 1A, R
Ch. 2D: Men & Women [man & 2
    women] -- AM 1938.
    1130, The Ring of

Nestor
in upper right quadrant:
    lion in PT 11, L on a
    Table

Bovines
Bulls
PT 25A, L: 2 lions -- XIII
    40
    3 bulls couchant around
        periphery cl
Ch. 3A: Man & Animals (man
    & bull with different
    SH) -- BM 97.4.64
    bull in PT 5A, L

Cow & Calf in PT 18B, L
Ch. 2A: Parts of the Human
    Body (man's face)/Ch.
    5E: Birds & Waterbirds
    (waterbirds,pair) -- II
    3.88

Calves
Single
Ch. 3A: Man & Animals
    (man, several
            animals) -- HMs
        160 (KSPI Q19)
        bel
Two in PT 28B, couchant
PT 28A: 2 sheep
        protomes/Ch. 5D:
        Protomes (caprid)
        -- I 189
    in an exergue bel

Agrimia
Single
In the Center
PT 5/6, R: lions -- II
    3.65
    SH vertical: in PT
        5A, betw lions in
        PT 36 cl

In the Field
PT 5A, L; Filler: lion
-- VII 94
Ch. 2B: Men (single,
salute) -- HMs XZ
(NTheta/KSPI R70)
in PT 14A, head bent
up
Ch. 2E: People at a
Shrine
(person at left) -- I
292
at right, in PT
1A, L on the
rocks/mountain
(tree-pulling, no
Omphalos) -- ?I 119
in PT 1A, R
Ch. 5H: Fish (pair) -- X
116
SH horizontal: in PT
1A, L

Two
PT 12, L: lion -- AM
1941.1241 (CS 346)
run in PT 34B down bel

Miscellaneous Caprids (see:
PT 1A, L; agrimi -- XIII
144 [kid? suckling])

PT 31: 2 agrimia -- HMs 288
(KSPI R85)
kid? upside down betw
PT 32B: agrimia -- II 3.133
kid rampant R betw
PT 33A:
2 lions -- I 117
caprid bel in PT 10, L
lion vs nanny -- AM
1938.1019 (CS 316)
kid bel nanny
PT 39A:
dog L vs agrimi/kid-man --
XII 242
fawn? bel

dog vs stag in PT 40A in
the field
PT 47B: lion? L vs agrimi --
HMs no. unknown (AT 98)
at left, a kid R
Ch. 5B: Animal Faces (bucrania,
single) -- V 346
at left, caprid in PT 2, R
Ch. 6A: People-Animals [caprid-
people] -- HM 2624
goat in PT 1B, ab

Dogs
Single
Attacking from BELOW with
hunter

Ch. 3C: Man Hunts Animals
(lions)
I 165 -- runs L
Berlin FG 7 (AGDS
II 24) --
attacks in PT
6, R
(agrimia)
V 656 -- attacks
in PT 7, R
AM 1938.962 (CS
226) -- at
right, leaps up
(boars) -- I 294
runs L
Attacks an animal
Agrimi
PT 1B, R; agrimi --
AM 1938.954 (CS
227)
dog bel L
PT 5A, L; Filler:
agrimi -- VII
42
dog? bel to attack
R in PT 44
Stag, dog in PT 39A
dog L vs agrimi/kid-
man -- XII 242
dog vs stag in PT

40A
griffin L vs bull --
Coll. Schlum-
berger 43 (Pini
1980: no. A6)
at left, dog
salient L also
vs stag
Miscellaneous
PT 51C: 2 dogs vs kid
L -- AM 1938.
1063 (CS 349)
puppy bel turned
90 degrees
Ch. 2B: Men
[warriors] --
HMs 343 (KSPI
L47)
collared, walks
bef the man
Ch. 3E: Animal Games
(bull-leaping,
Diving) -- AM
1938.1074 (CS
209)
dog bel vs bull in
PT 43
In the Field
PT 30A: 2 stags -- I 124
a vertical dog/lion in
PT 5A/3 bef each stag
Ch. 3A: Man & Animals
(monsters) filler
-- I Supp. 3
dog? bel
Ch. 6A: People-Animals
[caprid-people] --
Lentoid (Furt-
waengler 1900:
pl. VI.6)
dog infr
Two
PT 39A: griffin L vs bull --
L. Morgan Library
1077 (Pini 1980: no.
A5)

SH horizontal: 2
calves/dogs in PT 34A,
L bel
Ch. 3A: Man & Animals (bull)
-- BM 97.4.64
SH horizontal: 2 dogs?
antithetic

Miscellaneous Quadrupeds
Identifiable
PT 5A, L; Filler: lion --
VII 94
mule & griffin
Ch. 4D: Women in Misc.
Compositions -- I 80
(boar-sacrifice)
boar lies upside down R
on a 3-legged Table

Quadruped
PT 1A, R; Filler: goat --
HMs 335 (KSPI L26)
quadruped/Table bel
PT 28B: lions -- HMs 256a
2? quadruped(s) bel
Ch. 5B: Animal Faces (lion,
with other) -- I 110
quadruped in PT 3, L
Ch. 6: Griffin & lion,
agrimi, waterbird --
HM 1966/2092
quadruped salient R
Ch. 8F: Figure-8 Shields --
HMs 266 (KSPI R22)

Quadruped Parts
Protomes (see: PT's 19 & 25)

Lion (see: Ch. 4B: Potnia
Theron [lions] -- X 242;
& 6B: Genii -- HMs 1347
[AT 107] & Berlin FG 11)

PT 2, R; Filler: bull --
X 142*
bel
Ch. 3B: Master of

Animals (lions) --
Vienna 1357
2 flank Master
Ch. 5B: Animal Faces
    (lions) -- I 110
protome L
Bull
    Ch. 4A: Women & Animals
        (antithetic) -- V
        595
    at right, bull
        protome in PT 1B,
        L
Caprid
    PT 11, R: II 3.339
        kid ab nanny?
    PT 19A, L: Sparta no.
        unknown
        goat ab
Horse
    PT 1A, R; Filler: lion
        -- HM G 3211 (CMCG
        338)
    infr R
    Ch. 2A: Parts of the
        Human Body (man's
        head, beardless)
        -- HM G 3211 (CMCG
        338)
    as if in PT 1B, R
        infr

Animal Faces   (cf. PT 13A, L
-- V 2)

Lion (see: PT 31B [lions]:
II 3.306; Ch. 3A: Man &
Animals [monsters] -- I
Supp. 3]; Ch. 5B [Animal
Faces; lions; lion &
bull])

    PT 2, R; Filler: lioness
        -- II 3.122
        ab
    PT 5A, L; Filler:
        kid/calf -- I Supp. 25

PT 5A, R; Filler: bull --
HM no. unknown
(Popham et al. 1984:
Misc. 8)
PT 12, L: bull -- AM AE
    690b (CS 334b)
bef bull's back
PT 21, R: 2 bulls -- I 50
lion or bull face ab
PT 28A: 2 waterbirds --
HMs 23b (KZ 58)
ab: lion face with 2
    human arms?
Ch. 2C: Women (4 or more)
    -- I 17
at left: a vertical
    row of 6 lion faces
Ch. 5B: Animal Faces
(bulls) -- HMs 91b
    (KZ 72)
    quadruped (lion?)
    face ab
Ch. 5E: Birds &
    Waterbirds
    (waterbirds,
    single) -- IV 257
schematic
Ch. 5F: Alerions (other
    heads) -- HMs 16
    (KZ 33)
en face
Ch. 5G: Insects (butter-
    flies,
single) -- HMs 91b (KZ
    72)
    quadruped (lion?)
    face ab
trio) -- IX 162a
    at left, lion mask

Bull (see: Ch. 5B [bull,
lion & bull, misc.])

In the Center
    PT 32B: misc. -- II
    3.5
    2 in the center

(the one ab
holds a <u>Snake
Frame</u>)
PT 34A: 2 lions --
HMs 367 (KSPI R38)
Ch. 2A: Parts of the
Human Body (man's
face) -- HMs 653
(KSPI U?)
Ch. 5B: Animal Faces
(bulls) -- HMs
367 (KSPI R38)
flanked by 2 lions
in PT 34A
IN FRONT
PT 13A, R: griffin --
AM 1938.1100 (CS
367)
Ch. 3A: Man & Animals
(monsters) -- I
Supp. 3
infr of the lion-
headed person
ABOVE
PT 1A, L; Filler:
goat -- VII 191
PT 5C, R: bull -- V
252
PT 10A, R: bull -- I
346
PT 21, R: 2 bulls --
I 50
lion or bull face
ab
PT 28A: 2 bulls con-
joined -- V 607
upside down
PT 31B: 2 lions -- II
3.306
flanking & joined
to 2 dots
Ch. 3E: Animal Games
(bull-riding) --
HMs no. unknown
(KSPI C42)
Ch. 5B: Animal Faces
(lions) -- XIII 22D

Ch. 8E: Helmets
(winged) -- HMs 37
(KZ 86)
BELOW
PT 2, L; Filler:
lioness -- V 304
PT 2, R; Filler: bull
-- V 247
<u>Rake</u>/schematic
bull face
PT 29B: 2 calf
protomes -- AM
1938.1094 (CS
336)
In the Field
Ch. 3C: Man Hunts
Animals
(agrimia) --
AM 1938.1022 (CS
320)
upside down betw
the man's legs
Ch. 5D: Protomes
(bull) -- AM
1938.1094 (CS
336)
Bucranium/Schematic Bull
Face (cf. branch/<u>Branch 1</u>
as on V 248)

PT 2, R; Filler: bull --
V 247
bel
PT 19A, L: caprid --
Sparta no. unknown
infr with <u>Branch 1</u>
betw the horns
PT 19B, L: bull -- I
515/KN HMs 109
(KSPI J2)
2 bel
PT 28B: 2 pairs of bulls
-- HMs 139 (KSPI
C51)
betw each pair
PT 31B: lions -- Berlin
FG 34 (AGDS II

Berlin 39)
one leg of the
Table/Altar is
shaped like a
bucranium
Ch. 5B: Animal Faces
(bulls) -- HMs 15a
(KZ 88)
flanked by 2
waterbirds
Miscellaneous
PT 31B: lions -- II
3.306
animal/man's face
betw

Heads
Lion (see: Ch. 5B: Animal
Faces [misc.] -- HMs 527)

Bull (see: Ch. 5C: Animal
Heads [groups] -- HMs 527 &
656)

?PT 13A, L: lion -- V2
bel
Ch. 2A: Parts of the Human
Body (man's head,
bearded) -- II 3.196
3 animals heads (one is
a bull's)
Ch. 2B: Men (1) -- Chania
1563
R, inb of man
Ch. 3F: Animal-Sacrifice --
II 3.338
bel
Ch. 3A: Man & Animals
(several animals) -- HMs
656 (KSPI U115)
Ch. 5B: Animal Faces
[lions] -- XIII 22D

Calf
PT 2, L -- IX 123
infr

Agrimi (see: Ch. 5B: Animal
Faces; Ch. 5C: Animal Heads
[groups])

ABOVE
PT 2, R; Filler: agrimi
-- AM 1925.43 (CS
313)
BELOW
PT 1B, R; lion -- Berlin
FG 19 (AGDS II 41)
PT 12, R: bull -- HMs 588
(AT 88)
PT 18B, R: lioness & cub
-- AM 1938.1060 (CS
298)
upside down
In the Field
Ch. 3A: Man & Animals
(several animals) --
HMs 656 (KSPI U115)
Ch. 5B: Animal Faces
[lions] -- XIII 22D

Goat (see: Ch. 5B: Animal Faces
[lion, with other] --I 110)

Single
IN FRONT
PT 18B, R: lioness &
cub -- II 3.344
upside down
Ch. 6A: People-Animals
(bull-people) --
XIII 84
ABOVE
PT 1A, L; Filler: lion
-- II 3.104
PT 5A, L; Filler: kid/
calf -- I Supp. 25
PT 14B, L; Filler:
bull -- X 269
PT 39A, L: dog vs
agrimi/kid-man
-- XII 242
PT 43: lion L vs
agrimi -- AM

1938.1059 (CS
319)
BELOW
    PT 32B -- II 3.5
upside down bel
caprid at right
In the Field
    Ch. 5B: Animal Faces
(bull, filler) --
HMs 312
Two
    PT 12A, L: bull -- I 66
antithetic ab
    PT 13C, R: bull -- VII
248
bel

Sheep
    PT 1A, L; Filler: lion --
II 3.104
bel
    Ch. 5B: Animal Faces
[lions] -- XIII 22D

Caprid
    Ch. 5B: Animal Faces
(lions) -- XIII 22D
stag? head R
(bulls) -- HMs 6b (KZ
83)
horns end in kid
heads

Dog (see: Ch. 3A: Man &
Animals [several animals] &
5C: Animal Heads [groups]
-- HMs 656; & Ch. 5B:
Animal Faces [misc.] -- HMs
527)

    PT 6, L; Filler: dog/lion
cub -- VII 249
dog? head bel
    Ch. 5B: Animal Faces [lion]
-- XIII 22D
    Ch. 8E: Helmets (plumed, R)
-- HMs 25 (KZ 130)

2 dog heads addorsed on
helmet

Boar (see: Ch. 5B: Animal
Faces [lion] -- XIII 22D)

    Ch. 2D: Men & Women (pair,
alone) -- X 261*
    Ch. 4A: Women & Animals
(woman seated L at
right) -- HMs no.
unknown (AT 130)

Horse
    Ch. 5B: Animal Faces
(lions) -- XIII 22D

Quadrupeds (see Ch. 5B: Animal
Faces [bull] -- AM
1938.976])

    PT 1A, R: lion -- II 4.45
infr as if in PT 1B, R
    Ch. 4A: Women & Animals
(friezes) -- II 3.282

Parts of the Animal Head
PT 2, R; Filler: bull -- X 142*
animal ear ab <u>Sacred Knot</u>

Erased Limbs
Single
IN FRONT
    PT 1A, L; Filler: lion --
VIII 124
X 164
HM 27
HM G 3526 (CMCG 266)
    PT 1A, R; Filler: lion --
II 4.74
    PT 2, R; Filler: bull --
X 142*
bull hindleg
    PT 29A: 2 lion protomes
-- II 4.218
infr of each

BELOW
>   PT 12, L: bull -- I 66
>   PT 14 or 13, L: lion -- V
>   733

IN FRONT, ABOVE, & BELOW
>   PT 1A, L; Filler: lion --
>   I Supp. 97

In the Field
>   Ch. 5B: Animal Faces
>   (bulls) -- HMs 312
>   (2 bull faces) -- HMs
>   46 (KZ 85)
>   each with quadruped
>   legs for horns

Two
>   Ch. 5B: Animal Faces (boar)
>   -- HMs 21b (KZ 71)
>   2 lion legs flanking
>   PT 35 c1: 2 lion forequar-
>   ters conjoined -- HM
>   no. unknown (BSA 74,
>   1979, 270-3 no. 1)
>   quadruped hindquarters
>   infr of each lion
>   forequarter

11B
Birds & Waterbirds

Birds
ABOVE
>   PT 1A, L; Filler: agrimi --
>   VIII 129
>   PT 1A, R; Filler: bull --
>   VII 177
>   PT 5A, L; Filler: stag --
>   ?II 4.50
>   PT 6, L; Filler: dog/lion
>   cub -- VII 249
>   turned 90 degrees
>   PT 28A: 2 bulls -- I 19
>   PT 46: griffin R vs stag --

IX 20D
>   V (= seagull-type bird?)
>   ab
>   Ch. 2B: Men (pair, sailors)
>   -- V 184b
>   flies R

IN BACK
>   Ch. 4A: Women & Animals
>   [woman at right] -- I
>   179
>   inb of the seated
>   woman's chair

BELOW
>   PT 2, L; Filler: lioness --
>   I Supp. 168
>   flies R

In the field (see: HMm 1034,
below)

>   Ch. 2B: Men (single,
>   Omphalos) -- HMm
>   1034
>   bird flies R
>   Ch. 2E: People at a Shrine
>   (person at left) -- I
>   191
>   2 birds fly within the
>   Shrine
>   (tree-pulling, man at
>   Omphalos) -- II
>   3.114
>   bird flies R

Miscellaneous
>   Ch. 2B: Men (single,
>   Omphalos) -- HMm
>   1034
>   bird flies R
>   Ch. 5B: Animal Faces (bulls)
>   -- HMs 24a (KZ 81)
>   2 birds antithetic flank
>   Snake Frame
>   Ch. 5E: Birds & Waterbirds
>   (birds, single) --II

3.387
bird or fish L bel
unfinished?
(waterbirds, pair) -- V
422a
chick L infr
Ch. 5F: Alerions (head L) --
Berlin FG 36 (AGDS II
58)
2 birds fly R upside down
ab

Waterbirds (see: Ch. 4B:
Potnia Theron [waterbirds])

IN FRONT
PT 1A, R; Filler: dog --
Once Evans Coll. (GGFR
pl. 115)
Ch. 4A: Woman & Animals
(antithetic)
waterbird upright infr of
a woman

ABOVE
PT 2, L; Filler: lioness --
V 304
regardant
PT 6, L; Filler: lion -- HM
G 3227 (CMCG 272)
plant?
PT 18B, L: cow & calf/Ch.
2A: Parts of the Human
Body (man's face) --
II 3.88
ab: 2 waterbirds flank a
man's face
Ch. 3A: Man & Animals
(several animals) -- AM
1938.1091

BELOW
PT 2, L; Filler: lion -- HM
G 3285 (CMCG 260)
in PT 11, L
PT 14B, L: bull -- AM
1938.1085 (CS 345)

supine R
Ch. 5F: Alerions (head
direction unknown) --
XII 210
SH vertical: in PT 2, R

In the field
PT 5/6, R: lions -- II 3.65
SH vertical: betw lions
is a waterbird in PT
2
PT 34A: 2 dolphins L -- HMs
370
waterbird (1 wing up) L
betw
PT 39A:
griffin L vs bull -- L.
Morgan Library
1077
SH horizontal:
waterbird flies R
at left
SH vertical:
waterbird flies L
cat R vs waterbird -- AM
1938.1084 (CS 344)
waterbird R ab regar-
dant & bel
Ch. 2A: Parts of the Human
Body (man's face) --
HMs 654 (KSPI U 106)
2 waterbirds ccl flank,
feet to center
waterbird at right
regardant
Ch. 5A: Misc. Quadrupeds --
II 3.172
waterbird frontal,
displayed, flies up ab
cat
Ch. 5B: Animal Faces
(lion) -- I 110
L regardant
(bull) -- HMs 15a (KZ
88)
2 flank
Ch. 5E: Birds & Waterbirds

BELOW
    Ch. 5E: Birds &
       Waterbirds
      (birds, single)
       II 3.387
         bird or fish L
         bel
          (unfinished?)
       X 117
         fish/dolphin R
         bel
In the Field
    Ch. 5E: Birds &
       Waterbirds [misc.]
      -- VIII 135
      fish in the bill of a
      pelican
    Ch. 5I: Dolphins (pair)
      -- I 409
      flying fish

Two or more
    PT 1A, L: agrimi -- X 116
      SH vertical: 2 fish in PT
      35A, ccl
    PT 6, R; Filler: caprid -- V
      667
      fish L ab & bel
    Ch. 5I: Dolphins [4 or more]
      -- II 3.75
      3 fill available space

Dolphins (see: Ch. 4B: <u>Potnia</u>
<u>Theron</u> [dolphins])

Single
    Flakes re-cut as dolphins
      Ch. 9D: Flaked Obsidian
      Disks -- I Supp. 120a
      & IV 166b

    Miscellaneous
      PT 5A, L; Filler:
      lion -- VII 94
        plumed griffiness -- V
        690
          upside down bel

Ch. 3C: Men In Chariots
    -- Louvre AO2188
    dolphin/fish monster

Two
    Ch. 5E: Birds & Waterbirds
      (waterbirds, pair) --
      II 3.279
      upside down, flank
      woman-eagle L
    Ch. 5J: Octopus
      (cut-style) -- II 3.251
      ab & bel, both R
      (naturalistic) -- I 312
      7 swim around the
      octopus

Three or more
    Ch. 2D: Men & Women (& a
      boat)
      -- I 180 & AM 1938.1129
      bel the boat

Octopus
BELOW
    PT 1A, R; Filler: bull --
      VII 177
      octopus with 6 arms bel
    Ch. 5H: Fish (single,
      conventional) -- HMs 128
      (KSPI Pb)

Argonauts
Ch. 5E: Birds & Waterbirds
    (waterbirds pair) -- AM
    1938.1020 (CS 302)
    2 in the center & bel

Shells
PT 2, R; Filler: bull -- HM
    2301
    conch bel
Ch. 2B: Men (single, <u>Altar</u>) --
    II 3.7
    man R blows conch
Ch. 5K: Shellfish (shells,
    murex?) -- VII 188

2 murex shells/hearts/
    peppers
AM 1938.975 (CS 379)
    5 murex shells/hearts
Ch. 8F: <u>Figure-8 Shields</u> --
    HMs 266 (KSPI R22)
    bottom register: frieze of
    conch/murex shells
    obliquely arranged, top
    down

Miscellaneous
Ch. 5J: Octopus (cut-style) --
    II 3.251
    sea urchin at left

Omphalos) -- HMs no.
unknown (AT 143)
    Ch. 2D: Men & Women (misc.)
        -- AM 1938.1130, The
        Ring of Nestor
    in the upper left
        quadrant

Miscellaneous
Ch. 2E: People at a <u>Shrine</u>
    (tree-pulling, man at
    <u>Omphalos</u>) -- HMm 989
    "dragonfly"

11E
Monsters

11D
Insects

Butterflies (see: Ch. 5G:
    Butterflies [as filler])

Single
    Ch. 2C: Women (single, at
        <u>Omphalos</u>) -- HMs no.
        unknown (Platon 1971:
        159)
    Ch. 2E: People at a <u>Shrine</u>
        (tree-pulling) -- HMm 989
    Ch. 5B: Animal Faces
        (bulls) -- HMs 91b (KZ
            72)
        (boars) -- HMs 21b (KZ
            71)
    Ch. 5E: Birds & Waterbirds
        (waterbirds, pair)/Ch.
        5K: Shellfish (argonauts)
        -- AM 1938.1020 (CS 302)

Two
    Ch. 2C: Women (single, at

People-Animals
PT 28B: 2 griffins -- I 171
    man with bull horns prone R
    bel
PT 39A: dog L vs agrimi/kid-
    man -- XII 242
    sphinx in PT 5
PT 39A: griffin L vs bull --
    L. Morgan Library 1077
    SH vertical: goat-man L
        with arms up
Ch. 2D: Men & Women (man & 2
    women) -- AM 1938.1130,
    The Ring of Nestor
    in the lower right
        quadrant: 2 griffin-
        women salute a griffin
Ch. 3A: Man & Animals (bull,
    with different SH) -- BM
    97.4.64
    SH vertical: ab, eagle-
        woman, head R
Ch. 4A: Women & Animals
    (friezes) -- II 3.282
    human figure R with animal
        head?

Genii
Single (see: Ch. 3A: Man &
  Animals (bulls) -- HMs 85
  [KZ 102])

  IN FRONT
      PT 1A, R; Filler: lion
          -- HM 907
      PT 1A, R; Filler: bull
          -- VII 177
  IN BACK
      Ch. 3C: Man Hunts
          Animals (lions) --
          Munich Antike
          Sammlung SL 681
      without jug, inb of
          the man, holds
          its paws (as if to
          hold a jug) around
          the tip of the
          man's scabbard?
  BEHIND
      PT 1A, R; Filler: bull --
          AM 1938.1040 (CS 307)/
          1938.1041 (CS 306)
  In the Center
      PT 28B: 2 lions -- I 172
      PT 29B: 2 dog protomes --
          VII 126
      PT 32B: 2 dogs -- I 161
  In the Field
      Ch. 4A: Women & Animals
          (friezes) -- II 3.282
      Ch. 6B: Genii -- I Supp.
          137

Two or more
  Ch. 4A: Women & Animals
      (woman seated L at
      right) -- I 179
  a frieze of 3 genii R
      carrying jugs sup-
      ported by a Cypress
      Branch
  Ch. 4B: Potnia Theron
      (misc.) -- I 379
  2 genii flank & face

the Potnia, standing
  in PT 28A ab each stag

Griffins (see: PT 28A:
  protomes -- VII 187; Ch. 4A:
  Women & Animals [antithetic]
  -- VIII 95 & 156, & HMs
  192/KZ 192, [woman seated L
  at right] -- I 128)

Adult
  Alone
      As Filler
          PT 23A, R: 2 griffins
              -- I 282
          beh
          unfinished?
          Ch. 2D: Men & Women
              (misc.) -- AM
              1938.1130, The
              Ring of Nestor
          on a small Table
              saluted by 2
              griffin-women
          Ch. 4A: Women &
              Animals (woman
              rides) -- V
              584
          infr
          Ch. 6C: Griffins --
              HM 2092
          bel
      Attacking a Stag
          PT 39A: griffin L vs
              bull -- Coll.
              Schlumberger 43
              (Pini 1980: no.
              A6)
          in PT 49
          Ch. 3B: Master of
              Animals (lions)
              -- V 675
          in PT 39A, L

Babies
  Single
      PT 29B: 2 griffins --

HMs 259 (KSPI C15)
betw

Pair
PT 11, R; Filler:
griffin -- I Supp.
138
ab antithetic
PT 28B: griffins -- I
304
each regardant ab its
mother
PT 51F: 2 griffins vs
stag R -- HMs 255
+?
2 baby griffins? ab
flanking a Sun

Babylonian Dragon (see: Ch.
4A: Women & Animals [woman
rides] -- I 167 & HMs
73/AT 132)

Ch. 2D: Men & Women (misc.) --
AM 1938.1130, The Ring
of Nestor
Babylonian Dragon runs R on
ground bel tree

Fish-Monster (see: Ch. 3A: Man
& Animals [monsters])

PT 14B, L: bull -- AM 1938.1085
(CS 345)
ab L
PT 14B, R: bull -- II 4.161
ab R biting the shoulder of
the bull
PT 14C, R: bull -- IX 126
ab R
PT 18B, R: cow & calf -- IX 24D
ab
Ch. 3A: Man & Animals
(monsters) -- I Supp. 3
infr of the man
Ch. 3C: Men In Chariots --
Louvre AO2188

dolphin/Fish-Monster

Winged-Agrimi (see: Ch. 3B:
Master of Animals [genii]
-- V 201)

CHAPTER 12

Man-Made Objects

12A
Apparel

Clothing (see: Chs. 1-2: Men,
Women, Men & Women)

Body Garments (see: Ch. 3C: Man
Hunts Animals [boars] -- XII
240)

Ch. 2A: Parts of the Human
Body (man's face) -- V
431
pleated hem of a tunic at
the neck
Ch. 2B: Men (pair) -- I
Supp. 113
one man in a long robe,
the other in a kilt
Ch. 3A: Men & Animals (man,
griffin) -- I 223
man in long robe

Caps
Plain
Ch. 2C: Women (pair,
salute L) -- XII
169
conical hats
Ch. 3A: Men & Animals
(lions) -- HMs 383I
(KSPI L46)
man wears a cap
(several animals) --
AM 1938.1091 (CS
358)
2 men R wear caps
Plumed
PT 10A, R: sphinx -- I
129?
a Lily plume

PT 28B: Griffins -- I 171
man prone R bel with
bull-head (Mino-
taur?) with 2
plumes/horns
(see I 324, below)
Ch. 3B: Master of Animals
(lions) -- HMs 382
(KSPI Ca)?
(griffins) -- I 324?
plume-like object
at the head of
each Master (see
I 171, above)

"Bull-Tails" (resembling ropes
with tassels suspended
from the waist; cf. the
Egyptian "animal-tail"
as a mark of royalty)

PT 39A: 2 pairs of griffins
vs stags/Ch. 3B: Master
of Animals: Griffins -- I
324
Ch. 3C: Man Hunts Animals
(agrimia) -- V 656 & VII
131
(lions) -- Peronne no.
unknown from
Thessalonike, The
Danicourt Ring

Jewelry
Earrings
Ch. 2A: Parts of the Human
Body (man's head,
beardless)
VIII 110b -- circular
earring
X 278* -- both men,
bearded & beardless,
wear circular
earrings

Bracelets
     Ch. 2A: Parts of the Human
             Body (hands)
        HMs 54 (KZ 47) -- 3
        hands, each with one
        HMs 153 (KSPI R102) --
        double strand bracelet
     Ch. 2B: Men (1) -- Chania
             1563
        bracelet & arm-bracelet
        on man's left arm
     Ch. 3E: Animal Games (bull-
             leaping, Diving) -- I
             370
        leaper wears a bracelet

Necklaces
     In Shrines
        Ch. 2E: People at a
                Shrine
                (person at left)
                IX 163 -- arc (=
                necklace) bel
                the Shrine
           HMs 487 (AT 136)
              -- inside Shrine
           (tree-pulling, no
                Omphalos) --
                I 126
           2 inside or bel
     Miscellaneous
        Ch. 2B: Men (1) -- Chania
                1563
           man wears one
        Ch. 2E: People at a
                Shrine (tree-
                pulling, man at
                Omphalos) -- II
                3.114
           wavy line of dots
           (necklace?) ab
           bird
        Ch. 5G: Insects (scor-
                pions) -- HMs
                149 (KZ 149)
           necklace? bel

12B
Furniture & Vessels

Seats
Chairs
     Ch. 4A: Women & Animals
             (woman seated L at right)
             -- I 128 & I 179

Campstools
     Ch. 2C: Women
             (pair, salutes) -- HMs
                 no. unknown (KZ 5)
             woman at right seated
                 L
             (4 or more)/Ch. 2D:
                 Men & Women (pair,
                 alone) -- HMs 421
                 (KSPI U2)
             woman seated L
     Ch. 3A: Men & Animals
             (bull, with different SH)
             BM 97.4.64
             man sits R on
                 campstool
             (several animals) -- HMs
                 160 (KSPI Q19)
             at right: ape sits
                 L on a campstool
Stools/Benches
     Ch. 2C: Women (single,
             (misc.) -- HMs 661
             (KSPI Cb)
             at left, woman seated on
             a footstool R
     Ch. 2C: Women (4 or
             more)/Ch. 2D: Men &
             Women (pair, alone)
             -- I 101
             woman seated L on a
             stool/bench
     Ch. 2E: People at a Shrine
             (woman sits on Shrine)
             -- HMs 277-283 (KZ 3;
             KSPI Q22/R1/R51/R54)
     Ch. 4A: Women & Animals

(woman seated L at
right) -- I 179
bel, half a bench?
decorated with a
half-rosette

<u>Tables</u> (see: Sakellarakis
1970)

With People
Ch. 2B: Men
(single, salute) -- HMs
155 (KSPI R89)
sacrificial <u>Table</u>? ab
(single, <u>Altar</u>) -- V 608
a (curtailed?)
2-legged <u>Table</u>
?Ch. 2C: Women (single,
religious) -- I 410
?Ch. 2E: People at a <u>Shrine</u>
(tree-pulling) -- I
126
at left
Ch. 4A: Women & Animals
(woman seated L at
right) -- Chania
1503/1513
(Papapostolou
1977: no. 32)
at right, woman seated
L on a 2-legged
<u>Table</u>
Ch. 4B: <u>Potnia Theron</u>
[lions] -- BSA Cast
135
<u>Potnia</u> sits on <u>Shrine</u>
or <u>Table</u>

With Animals
Lion
?PT 31B: lions -- Berlin
FG 34 (AGDS II
Berlin 39)
one leg shaped like a
bucranium
Ch. 2D: Men & Women
(misc.) -- AM 1938.

1130, the Ring of
Nestor
lion in PT 11, L on 3-
legged <u>Table</u>
Bulls
PT 1B, R; bull -- I 264
<u>Table</u> with 3 legs
upside down ab
PT 10A, R: bull --
Berlin FG 22 (AGDS
II 44)
on sacrificial <u>Table</u>
with 4 bucranium
legs & 2 stick legs
Ch. 3E: Animal-Sacrifice
I 203 -- lies on a 2-
legged <u>Table</u>
II 3.338 -- 2-legged
<u>Table</u> bel
Berlin FG 22 (AGDS II
44) -- lies on a
<u>Table</u> with 4 legs
in the shape of
bull-faces & 2
thin supports set
betw
HMs 142 from Knossos
-- 2- (3-?) legged
<u>Table</u> bel
HMs 211 (KSPI R13) --
2-legged <u>Table</u> bel
HMs 1049 from Mallia
-- 2-legged <u>Table</u>
bel
Boars
PT 1B, L; boar -- AM
1938.1086 (CS 332)
on sacrificial <u>Table</u>
with 3 bucranium
legs
Ch. 3E: Animal-Sacrifice
-- AM 1938.1086
(CS 332)
in PT 1B, L on a 3-
legged <u>Table</u>
Ch. 4D: Women in Misc.
Compositions

(boar-sacrifice)
-- I 80
boar lies upside down
R on a 3-legged
Table
Griffins
PT 46: griffin R vs stag
-- IX 20D
Table bel
Ch. 2D: Men & Women
(misc.) -- AM
1938.1130, the
Ring of Nestor
on a small Table
Miscellaneous
PT 1A, R; Filler: goat
-- HMs 335 (KSPI
L26)
goat & quadruped/
Table bel

Vessels
Jugs
Ch. 2B: Men (single, Altar)
-- V 608
bel the arm: jug
Ch. 2C: Women (single,
misc.) -- HMs 661
(KSPI Cb)
at left, woman R holds
jug/krater
Ch. 2E: People at a Shrine
(tree-pulling, no
Omphalos) -- Once in
the Evans coll., the
Ring of Minos (PM IV
947 ff.)
at left, a nude man holds
a jug (Sacred Heart?)
with his right hand
Ch. 3A: Men & Animals
(several animals) --
AM 1938.1091
genius R holding a jug
Ch. 3B: Master of Animals:
Genii
V 201 -- genius L with

jug
Villa Giulia no. unknown
(Battaglia 1980:
no. 1) --
genii hold a jug
Ch. 4A: Women & Animals
(woman seated L at
right) -- I 179
3 genii R carry jugs
Ch. 6B: Genii
I 232
V 440
XII 212
AM 1938.1043 (CS 304)
Berlin FG 41 (AGDS II 26)
HMs 202 (KSPI H?)
HMs 360 (KSPI 16)
Ch. 6C: Misc. Monsters --
HMs no. unknown
(Platon 1971: 147)
"libation jug"

Miscellaneous Drinking Vessels
PT 13A, R calf -- Melos 571
reverse: 1-handled cup
(Linear B -ki-?)
Ch. 2E: People at a Shrine
(woman in a Shrine)
-- HMs 277-283 (KZ 3;
KSPI Q22/R1/R51/R54)
woman R offers goblet to
seated woman
Ch. 3A: Men & Animals
(bulls) -- HMs 85 (KZ
102)
man holds a cup?
Ch. 4A: Women & Animals
(woman seated L at
right) -- I 179
woman L seated on a
chair holds aloft a
chalice
Buckets
Ch. 2B: Men (single, Altar)
?II 3.7 -- at left
V 608 -- bel the arm
Ch. 3E: Animal-Sacrifice --

HMs 1049
bucket/basket? ab

Miscellaneous
    PT 2, R; Filler: VII 162 --
    stand? for a Palm branch
    Ch. 2B: Men (single, Altar)
        -- V 608
    bel the arm: rhyton
    Ch. 2D: Men & Women (pair,
        alone) -- HMs 655
        (KSPI U?)
    a tree grows from a
        tripod cauldron
    Ch. 4A: Women & Animals
        (antithetic) -- HM G
        3045 (CMCG 359)
    at left, monkey sits R
        holding an object
        (vessel?)
    Ch. 6B: Genii -- I 231
    the genii hold pitchers

12C
Conveyances

Chariots (see: Ch. 3D: Men
  In Chariots)

PT 39A: lion R vs bull --
    Nicosia 1953/IX-3/6
chariot drawn by a lion
Ch. 3C: Man Hunts Animals
    (lions) -- I 302
  at right: a chariot? L
    drawn by one horse in PT
    2, L

Chariot Wheels
Ch. 5B: Animal Faces (bull,
    Snake Frame) -- HMs 15a
    (KZ 88)
  ab

Boats (see: Ch. 2B: Men
[pair, sailors]; 2C: Women
[single, in boat]; 2D: Men &
Women [& a boat])

Special Characteristics
  Animal-Head Prow Aegis
    Ch. 2B: Men (single,
      misc.)
      HMs 337 (KSPI L49) an
      object at right
      (cabin? rigging?)
      animal-headed prow
      of 2nd boat bel
    HM no. unknown from
      Archanes,
      Anemospilia
      Temple
    man poles animal-
      headed boat L
    Ch. 2E: People at a
      Shrine
    (person at left) -- II
      3.252: The Mochlos
      Ring
    at left: boat L
      with a prow
      in the shape
      of a Babylo-
      nian Dragon's
      head
    (tree-pulling, no
      Omphalos) --
    Once in the Evans
      Coll., the Ring
      of Minos
    bel: a woman poles
      boat L with a
    prow in the
      shape of a
      Babylonian
      Dragon's head
  Branch Prow & Stern Aegis
    Ch. 2B: Men (pair,
      sailors) -- I Supp.
      167
    branch prow aegis at

left & stern aegis at
right

Branch Prow & Animal-Head
Stern Aegis

Ch. 2C: Women (single,
in boat) -- HMs
434 (AT 118)
woman poles a boat R
with a dog-head
(regardant) stern
& Frond prow aegis

Cabins (see: Ch. 2E: People at
a Shrine [person at
left] -- II 3.252, the
Mochlos Ring])

Ch. 2B: Men (single, misc.)
-- HMs 337 (KSPI L49)
an object at right
(cabin? rigging?)
Ch. 2B: Men (pair, sailors)
-- I Supp. 167
Ch. 2C: Women (single, in
boat) -- Ayios Nikolaos
4653

Miscellaneous
Ch. 2B: Men (pair, sailors)
-- V 184b
Ch. 5I: Dolphins (pair) --
AM 1941.91 (CS 191)
groundline/prow of
ship/rocks bel

12D
Weapons & Hunting Implements

Arrows (see: Bows & Arrows,
below)

Wounding
Lions
PT 2, L; Filler --
Munich A.1199
(AGDS I Munich
66)
in belly
PT 6, L; Filler -- I 10
in shoulder
PT 8, L -- II 3.345
in shoulder
PT 11, L; Filler -- XII
229
ab in back
PT 11, R; Filler -- XIII
9
in shoulder
PT 12, R:
I 248 -- 2 in flank
HMs no. unknown (AT
48) -- in chest
PT 13C, R: I 277
in flank
Bulls
PT 1C, R; calf/bull -- AM
1938.969 (CS 301)
in chest
PT 5B, R; Filler -- V 645
in chest
PT 21, L: -- Munich A.
1187 (AGDS I 82)
in near bull's chest
Calves
PT 5B, L: -- Chania 1002
(Papapostolou 1977:
no. 3)
in shoulder
PT 5C, R: -- Chania
1542/1544 (Papapos-
tolou 1977: no. 2)

in flank
Agrimia
    PT 5A, R; Filler -- IX
        141
        large arrow in the
            back
    PT 5B, R; Filler -- I 242
        in chest
Stags
    PT 5A, R; Filler -- II
        3.74
        bel in chest

In the field
Lion
    PT 1A, L; Filler -- II
        3.104
        infr
    PT 4A, L; Filler --
        Florence 82690
        ab
    PT 6, L; Plain -- I 14
    PT 10A, R -- HMs 87 (KZ
        143)
        8 pendent arrowheads?
        ab
    PT 11, R; Filler -- XIII
        22
        pointed at shoulder
        ab
Bull
    PT 6, R;
        Plain -- VII 106
        "broken dart"
        Filler -- HM G 3497
            (CMCG 237)
            bel
    PT 13A, R
        V 32 -- bel
        XII 258 -- line/arrow
        ab
    PT 34B: 2 bulls
        conjoined --
        Sparta no. unknown
        from the Menelaion
        betw
Ch. 5D: Protomes (bull)

-- HM 2383
        betw & bef
Calf
    PT 6, L; Filler -- X 298
        stroke/arrow bel
Agrimia
    PT 5A, L; Filler --
        II 4.127
        arrow? ab
        II 4.224
        ab
Griffins
    PT 5B, L; Filler;
        griffiness -- X
        220*
        Branch 1/arrow bel
    PT 13A, R -- AM
        1938.1100 (CS 367)
        ab

Bows
Ch. 2B: Men (single, archer)
    AM 1938.1049 (CS 294) --
        man carries a bow? beh
    HMs 69 (AT 112) --man holds
        bow
Ch. 2C: Women (single, carries
    object R) -- Berlin FG 2
    (AGDS II 20)
    kneels R with bow
Ch. 3A: Men & Animals (lions)
    -- X 161*
    wavy line (bow?) inb

Bows & Arrows
Ch. 2A: Parts of the Human
    Body (man's head, bearded)
    -- VIII 110b
Ch. 3C: Man Hunts Animals
    (lions) -- IX 7D
Ch. 3D: Men In Chariots
    I 15 -- the passenger?
    (since no reins are
    depicted, it is unclear
    which figure is the
    driver) leans forward to
    aim a bow and arrow at a

stag at right in PT 6, R
Louvre AO2188 -- the
passenger leans forward
to aim a bow & arrow

Picas (see spears/lances,
below)

With People
Ch. 2B: Men (battles) -- I
263
man touches another with
a Pica

With Animals
IN FRONT
?PT 6, L; Filler: agrimi
-- AM 1938.946 (CS
201)

ABOVE (see: PT 1A, L; 1A, R;
5A, L; 5B, L -- these
have 10 or more
examples, not listed
here)

In the Head
PT 9, R: bull -- HMs
482 (AT 78)
PT 26, L: 3 agrimia
-- X 252
In the Neck
PT 1C, L; bull -- VII
65a
PT 6, L; Filler:
bull -- I Supp. 77
kid -- X 136
PT 14B, R: bull -- I
380
In the Shoulder
PT 1B, R:
bull -- V 497
?boar -- II 4.40
PT 2, R; Filler: lion
II 3.132 & IX 151
PT 5A, L; Filler: stag
-- II 4.140

PT 6, L; Filler: bull
-- VIII 47b
PT 8, R: lion -- VII
171
PT 10A, R: griffin --
X 170
sword/Pica near
the shoulder
stroke ab
(continuation
of sword/Pica?)
PT 28B: lion -- HMs
256a (KSPI R88?)
PT 43: dog L vs
agrimi -- XII 15D
In the Back
PT 1/2, R; lion -- AM
1938.1441 (CS 43S)
PT 2, L; Filler: bull
-- II 4.220
PT 5A, R; Filler:
agrimi -- X 215
PT 5B, R; Filler:
bull -- V 646
Pica/spear
PT 8, L; lion --
Florence 82528
PT 10A, L: dog -- HM
G 3415 (CMCG 169)
?PT 10A, R: lion -- X
277a
PT 10C, R: lion -- I
Supp. 80
PT 11, L; Filler: lion
-- HMs 580a (AT
42)
2 Picas/spears
PT 11, R; Filler
lion -- V 655
bull -- XII 235
Pica/lance
PT 52A: 2 griffins vs
bull R -- V 216
Frond/Pica
Ch. 5H: Fish (pair) --
X 116

In the Rump
   PT 11, R; Filler: kid?
      -- XIII 13D
    2
In the field
   PT 1C, R; bull -- I
   147
   PT 2, L; Filler:
     lion --II 3.152 &
       AM 1873.129 (CS
       330)
     lioness -- HM 923
     bull -- V 282 &
       XIII 131
     caprid -- HMs 72
       (KZ 124)
   PT 2, R; Filler
     lion -- II 4.209
      ab
     bull
      V 377
      IX 204 --
       Pica/branch
       infr & ab
     agrimi/caprid --
       HMs 22 (KZ
       121)
     2
   PT 5A, R; Filler
     bull -- II 3.226 &
       XII 151a
     agrimi -- VII
      139
   PT 5B, R; Filler: bull
     -- IX 119
   PT 5C, L; Filler: bull
     -- V 279
   PT 5/6, R: bull -- HMs
     160 (KZ 160)
   PT 6, L; Filler
   lion
     II 4.38
     AM 1941.146 (CS
      369)
   bull
     I Supp. 22
      branch/Pica

    ab
   IX 169
    Branch 3 =
     Pica? ab
PT 6, R; Filler
  bull
   AM 1971.1141
   (Boardman
   1973: no. 3)
   Munich A.1190
   (AGDS I
   39)
   Frond = Pica
    infr & ab
  griffin -- II
   4.171
   line (= Pica?)
    ab
PT 8, L; lion
  I Supp. 32
  VII 235
  X 133*
   Branch 1 ab =
    Pica?
PT 8, R: lion -- II
  3.64b
PT 10A, L: agrimi --
  HM 2507
   (Knossos, MUM
   no. J/K3)
  double
PT 10A, R: agrimi --
  I 143
PT 10B, L: bull -- I
  55
PT 11, L; Filler;
  lion
  I 506
  IV 310
  V 191a --
   Frond/Pica
  Hannover no.
  unknown
  (AGDS IV 8)
  HMs 79 (KZ 109)
PT 12, R: bull -- I
  283

PT 13A, L: bull -- I
268
PT 13A, R: bull -- XII
297
PT 14A, L: lion -- X
302
PT 24, L; Filler: 2
bulls -- AM
1938.1030 (CS 312)
PT 25A, L
2 goats -- HMs 187
(KSPI R69)
2 stags -- V 297
Figure-8 Shield/
Pica/Baton
PT 25B, R: 2 bulls --
?I 175
2 _Picas_?
PT 40: lion L vs bull
-- I 214
PT 49A, R: lion vs
bull -- I 286
Ch. 3B: Master of
Animals (misc.) --
I 356
BELOW
PT 1A, L; quadruped -- HM
no. unknown (Knossos,
MUM; Misc. 11)
PT 1B, R; bull -- HMs 311
(KSPI R84)
PT 14A, L: bull -- V 320
PT 14D, L: Minotaur -- IX
144
PT 39A: dog L vs agrimi/
kid-man -- XII 242
bel dog

Spears/Lances (see _Picas_,
above)

With People
Men
Ch. 2B: Men (single,
secular) -- Chania
1563
man L holds spear?

(point down) infr
Altar) -- V 608
at right: man L
holds a spear
Ch. 2C: Women (4 or more)
-- I 17
ab, at left: small
man? R holds one
As Warriors
Ch. 2B: Men
(single, warrior)
HMs 343 (KSPI L47)
(single, misc.)
V 239 -- 2
strokes/lances/
spears flank
XIII 137 -- 2
vertical
strokes/spears
flank
HMs 337 (KSPI L49)
-- man on boat
L carries a
spear
(pair, wear Figure-8
Shields)
II 3.32 -- man at
left: spear
(2 men, duel)
VII 129 -- man at
right: spear
I 11 -- man at
left: lance
XII 292 -- man at
right: spear
HMs 43 -- (KZ 14)
man at right:
stabs the other
with spear
HMs 190 (KZ 190)
-- man at
right: hurls
spear L
(battles)
I 16 -- lance
aimed at the
dominant

                              duelist
                              HMs no. unknown
                              (KZ 12) --
                              dominant man
                              at left spears
                              man at right
              As Hunters
                    Ch. 3A: Man & Animals
                              (caprids) -- HMs
                        131 (KSPI Pe)
                    horizontal R ab
                    Ch. 3C: Man Hunts Animals
                        (lions)
                        I 112
                        II 3.14;
                        IX 7D
                        IX 152
                        (agrimia) -- VII 131
                        (boars)
                        I 227
                        I 294
                        Berlin FG 40 (AGDS
                            II 23)
                        (dog?) -- Chania 1563
                            (Papapostolou 1977:
                            no. 26)
                    Ch. 3D: Men In Chariots
                        -- I 229
                    the passenger carries
                    a lance
                    Ch. 4A: Women & Animals
                        (antithetic) --HMs 192
                            (KZ 192)
                        spear? in the chest
                        (animal's raised
                        foreleg?)

        With Animals
              Wounding
                    Lions
                        PT 5B, L; Filler -- I
                            Supp. 81
                        lance in shoulder
                        PT 11, L; Filler --
                            HMs 580a (AT 42)
                        2 Picas/spears in
                            back

        PT 13C, R -- IX 107
            arrow/spear in head
                from bel
        Bulls
            PT 1A, R; Filler -- II
                2.60
            ab in back
            PT 5B, R; Filler --
                V 646
                Pica/spear in
                back
            PT 11, R; Filler --
                XII 235
                Pica/lance in
                back
            PT 13C, R -- V 220
                spear in the belly

    In the Field
        Bulls
            PT 2, R; Filler --
                VII 161
                infr
            PT 5B, R; Filler --
                XII 237
                2 lines (=spears?)
                bel belly
            PT 10B, L -- I 35
                ab
            PT 13A, R -- V 32
                ab
            Ch. 3F: Animal
                Sacrifice
                (bull) -- HMs
                1049
                ab
        Agrimi
            PT 1A, L; Filler --
                XIII 6
                ab
            PT 5A, R; Filler/Ch.
                9P: Flaking --
                IV 166a
            branch/spear bel
        Miscellaneous
            PT 5B, L; Filler:
                calf -- HMs no.

unknown (AT
155)
ab
PT 25C, R: goat -- I
30
bel
PT 49A, L: dog vs
stag -- I 363
ab

Swords
With People
Men
Ch. 2B: Men (single,
Altar) -- V 608
Women
Ch. 2C: Women (single,
carries object L)
-- II 3.16
in her right hand
As Warriors
Ch. 2B: Men
(pair, duel)
I 11 -- man at
right has a
sword
I 12 -- man at
right has a
sword
V 180b -- each has
a sword
V 643 -- each has a
sword
VII 129 -- man at
left has a sword
XII 292 -- man at
left: sword
XII 13D -- man at
right: sword
Berlin FG 6 (AGDS
II 25) -- each
has a sword
HMs no. unknown
(AT 115) -- man
at right has 2
swords

(battles)
I 16 -- man at
left: sword
VII 130 -- man at
right: sword/
Baton
IX 158 -- duel at
right: dominant
man at left
wields sword
HMs no. unknown (KZ
12) -- man at
right armed
with a sword?

As Hunters
PT 39A, L: griffin vs
bull -- Coll.
Schlumberger 43
man stabs bull
PT 46: man vs lion -- I
9
Ch. 3C: Man Hunts
Animals
(lions)
I 9
I 165 -- dagger/
short sword
I 228
I 290
I 331 -- dagger/
short sword
IV 233
IX 114
Berlin FG 7 (AGDS
II 24)
Munich Antike
Sammlung SL681
Peronne no.
unknown from
Thessalonike,
The Danicourt
Ring (Boardman
1970)
(agrimia)
V 656 -- dagger/
short sword
VII 131

AM 1938.1022 (CS
320)
AM 1938.962 (CS
226)
Ch. 3D: Men In Chariots
-- II 3.199
man inb L holding
a sword/vertical
line
Ch. 3E: Animal-Sacrifice
Berlin FG 22 (AGDS II
44) -- a sword
stands vertically
lodged in the
bull's neck
HMs 1049 -- sword/
spear
With Animals
Wounding
Lions
PT 13A, L -- V 680
in belly
PT 13B, R -- II 3.41
in chest
Miscellaneous
PT 6, L; Filler: kid
-- X 136
sword/Pica ab in
neck
PT 10A, R: bull --
Berlin FG 22
(AGDS II 44)
in neck
PT 10B, L: calf -- VII
105
in back
In the Field
PT 1A, R; Filler: bull --
V 630
ab
PT 2, R; Filler: bull --
VII 161
ab
PT 10A, R: griffin -- X
170
sword/Pica near
shoulder

stroke ab
(continuation
of sword/Pica?)
PT 11, L; Filler: lion --
VII 121
ab
PT 39A: griffin L vs bull
-- Coll. Schlumberger
43
Ch. 3A: Man & Animals
(several animals)
-- AM 1938.1091
Ch. 4B: Potnia Theron
(misc.) -- I 379
genii hold a Cypress
Branch/sword
Ch. 5C: Animal Heads
(boar) -- II 2.213a
knife/short sword/
dagger ab

Scabbards
Ch. 2B: Men (pair, duel)
I 11 -- man at right:
scabbard
V 643 -- each has a
feathered plume (=
scabbard?)
VII 129 -- man at left:
scabbard
Ch. 3C: Man Hunts Animals
(lion) -- Munich
Antike Sammlung SL681
Ch. 3D: Men In Chariots --
V 585
an object, perhaps
scabbard & its thong,
flies out inb of the
driver

Whips
Ch. 2C: Women (single, carries
object L) -- II 3.16
a whip? (lituus?) in
her left hand
Ch. 3D: Men In Chariots
V 585 -- man in chariot

wields, with his right
arm, a whip
VII 87 -- man in 2-horse
chariot L holds a whip
with his right hand
above the team
AM 1938.1051 (CS 308) -- the
charioteer holds a whip
apparently in his right
hand unseen beh the
passenger
HMs 516, 632-636 (AT 117/Sk
8) -- man touches the
back of the horses with
a whip
Ch. 4D: Women in Misc.
Compositions (bull-
wrestling) -- HMs no.
unknown (AT 111)
woman holds a whip

Miscellaneous
Cleavers
PT 12, L: lion -- I 287a
bel

Daggers (see Swords: I 165 &
331, & V 656, above)

Ch. 2B: Men (pair, duel)
I 16 -- dominant duelist
has a dagger
V 643 -- each has a
dagger

Knives
Ch. 4D: Women in Misc.
Compositions (boar-
sacrifice) -- I 80
woman holds a knife?
Ch. 5C: Animal Heads (boar)
-- II 2.213a
knife/short sword/dagger
ab

Fishing Lines
Ch. 3C: Man Hunts Animals

(fisherman)
VII 88 & AM 1938.956
(CS 205)

Net (see: Ch. 17E:
Net/Reticulation)
Ch. 3D: Bull-Catching -- I
274
net covers the bull's
forequarters

Rope
Ch. 3C: Man Hunts Animals
(lions)
I 224 -- 2 men flank &
tie a lion with rope
HMs 65a (KZ 193) -- 2 men
flank & tie a lion
with rope

Switch
PT 12, R: bull -- I 265
ab

Yokes
Ch. 2C: Women (single,
carries object L) --
HMs 535 (AT 123)
Sacred Robe hanging from
a Yoke
Ch. 3A: Man & Animals
(several animals) --
HMs 650 (KSPI U?)
man carries Yoke from
which hang a boar & a
kid
?Ch. 3B: Master of Animals
(lion) -- Vienna 1357
2 lion protomes
positioned as if
hanging from an
undepicted Yoke
carried by the man
Ch. 6B: Genii -- Berlin FG
11 (AGDS II 28)
genius carries the
protomes on a Yoke

12E
Collars & Leashes

Collars
Lions
   PT 1A, R; Filler: lion? --
      HMs 154 (KZ 154)
   PT 8, L; lion -- Hamburg
      1964.288 (AGDS Hamburg
      IV 7)
   PT 31B: 2 lions -- II 3.306
   PT 35, ccl: 2 lions -- HMs
      512 (AT 86)
      collared lioness
   Ch. 2E: People at a <u>Shrine</u>
      (person at right) -- HMs
      141 (KSPI M1-5)
   Ch. 3A: Men & Animals
      (lion) -- II 3.52
      beaded collar
   Ch. 5C: Animal Heads (lion)
      VIII 115 -- lioness
      HMs 61 (KZ 113)
   Ch. 6B: Genii -- HMs 1347
      (AT 107)
      lion protome

Bovines
   Ch. 3A: Men & Animals
      (bull)
      AM 1938.1021 (CS 242) --
      cow
      Chania 1529/1530 -- calf

Dogs
   PT 1B, R: misc. -- II 3.160
   PT 2, L; Plain: bitch --
      HMs 162 (KZ 162)
   PT 2, R; Filler:
      dog -- Chania 2053
      bitch -- AM 1938.1061 (CS
         240) & HMs 214/287
         (KSPI F2/K4/K7/K12/
         Q21/R53/CS 40S)
   PT 6, L; Plain: bitch -- AM
      1938.1095 (CS 239)

PT 8, R: dog scratching
   V 677a
   AM 1971.1150 (Boardman
      1973: no. 3)
   HMs 106 (KZ 106)
PT 10A, R: dog -- AM
   1938.1017 (CS 237)
PT 17C, L: bitch & 2 puppies
   -- VII 66
PT 31B: 2 dogs -- Kn HMs 233
   (KSPI R88)
Ch. 2B: Men (single) -- HMs
   343 (KSPI L47)
Ch. 3A: Men & Animals
   (misc.) -- AM 1938.1062
   (CS 238)
Ch. 3C: Man Hunts Animals
   (misc.) -- Chania 1536
   (Papapostolou 1977: no.
   26)

Monsters
Sphinx
   PT 10A, R: sphinx -- II
      3.118
   Ch. 3A: Men & Animals
      (monsters) -- HMs 291
      (KSPI R35)
Miscellaneous
   PT 7, L; griffin --
      Munich A.1164 (AGDS I
      55)
   PT 13A, R: hornless
      Minotaur (= calf-man?)
      -- XII 238

Leashes
With Men (no animal depicted)
   Ch. 2B: Men (single) -- I 68
      man holds a leash?
   Ch. 2D: Men & Women (man &
      women) -- V 173
      man leads the women on a
      double leash

With Men & Animals
   Lions
      Ch. 3A: Men & Animals
        (lions)
          I 512
          X 161*
          HMs 508 (AT 134)
      Ch. 3B: Master of
        Animals (lions) --
        HMs 382 (KSPI Ca)
      2 lions/dogs
   Bulls
      Ch. 3A: Men & Animals
        (bulls)
          VII 102
          HMs 143 (KSPI Q20)
            double leash?
          Piraieus no.
            unknown, ring
            from Varkiza T.
            I

With Women & Griffins
   Ch. 4A: Women with Animals
      (woman seated L at
        right) -- I 128
        at right, woman
        seated L on chair
      (woman inb) -- HMm 1017

With Animals
   Bulls
      PT 10A, L -- XII 249
      PT 10A, R -- V 198
      PT 28B: 2 calves -- I 58
   Griffins
      PT 1A, L; Filler:
        griffin -- XII 301
          leashed to Column
            infr
      PT 28B: 2 griffins/ Ch.
        6C: Griffins -- I 171
          leashed to a
            Column betw
      PT 31B -- I 196
        leashed together

Collars & Leashes
Lions
   Ch. 3A: Men & Animals
      (lion) -- X 135*
   Ch. 3C: Men Hunts Animals
      (lion) -- IX 114
        beaded collar, leash
        attached

Miscellaneous
   PT 1A, R; Filler: caprid --
      AM 1941.246 (CS 7P) = II
      3.40
        caprid with collar?,
        leashed to Column
        beh
   PT 17A, L: nanny & kid -- AM
      1938.1021 (CS 242)
     man restrains a collared
     nanny with a leash
   Ch. 3A: Men & Animals
      (bull) -- Chania
      1529/1530 (Papaposto-
      lou 1977: no. 25)
        man restrains a
          collared calf in
          PT 1C, R by a
          leash
      (griffins) -- I 223
        man restrains the
          griffin by a leash
          attached to a
          collar tied with a
          small Sacred Knot

12F
Hand-Held Sticks

Staves (Cf. Ch. 2B: men [1] --
   Chania 1563)

Men Carry them
   Ch. 2B: Men

(1) -- HMs 91 (KZ 196)
  man holds staff inb
(religious)
  HMs 260 (KSPI R60/63)
    central man holds
      a staff infr
  HMs 441 (AT 125)
    man at left carries
      staff
  HMs 485 (AT 135)
    man at extreme
      right carries
      staff
  HMs no. unknown (KZ
    2)
    central man with
      staff
  HMs no. unknown (KZ
    7)
    man at right:
      carries staff
Ch. 2D: Men & Women
(pair) -- I 101
  man R with a staff in
    his right hand
(man & women) -- V 173
  man holds a long
    Frond or staff
    (cf. XIII 39)
Ch. 2E: People at a Shrine
(person at left) -- AM
    1938.1127 (CS 250)
  small man ab center
    holds a staff?
    infr of him in an
    outstretched hand
    (Pylon?)
Ch. 3A: Men & Animals
(lion) -- HMs 383I (KSPI
  L46)
(caprid) -- HMs 583a (AT
  126)
(bird)/Ch. 5E: Birds &
  Waterbirds (birds) --
  HMs 134 (KSPI Q14)
    man R holds
      staff infr

Women Carry them
  Ch. 2C: Women
    (single) -- I 226
      ab
    (pair, religious) --
      XII 168
        woman at right
          carries staff
  Ch. 2E: People at a Shrine
    (person at right) -- Kn
    HMs 141 (KSPI M1-5)
      woman on mountain
        holds a staff infr
  ?Ch. 4A: Women & Animals --
    II 4.125
      inb of woman

Barbells (see: Ch. 3A: Men &
Animals [bull] -- IX 146)

Ch. 3C: Man Hunts Animals
(agrimia) -- V 656
  ab the agrimi's neck
Ch. 3D: Men In Chariots --
Louvre AO2188
  in the field

Batons
PT 5A, L; Filler: kid/calf -- I
Supp. 25
  ab
PT 25A, L: 2 stags -- V 297
Figure-8 Shield/Pica/Baton
  ab
Ch. 2B: Men (Battles) -- ?I
263
  man at center L touches a
    flexed man at left with
    a Pica/Baton

Miscellaneous
PT 12, R: bull -- I 265
column/mace bel
PT 8, L; dog/calf/lion -- XII
135a
  Frond with circle ab
    (Sceptre?)

Ch. 2C: Women (single)
  II 3.16 -- whip/lituus/
    "lustral sprinkler"
  I 410 -- the woman seems to
    hold a stick crowned
    with 2 arcs ending in
    a star-like object
    (wand?)
Ch. 2E: People at a Shrine
  (woman sits on Shrine) --
  Chania 2097 (Papapostolou
  1977: no. 30)
    at left, small skirted
      person R holds Sceptre

12G
Armor

Helmets (Boar's Tusk, unless
  otherwise stated)

Hunters
  Ch. 3A: Men & Animals
    (bulls) -- Piraieus no.
      unknown, ring from
      Varkiza T. I
    (griffins) -- I 285
  Ch. 3C: Man Hunts Animals
    (lions) -- IX 152
    (boars) -- I 294

Warriors
  Ch. 2B: Men
    (single, warrior) -- HMs
        343 (KSPI L47)
      conical helmet
    (pair wear Figure-8
      Shields) -- II 3.32
        plumed
    (pair, duel)
      I 11 -- man at left
      I 12 -- man at left &
        man at right

XII 292 -- man at
  right
XII 13D --man at left
(battles)
  I 16 -- man at left &
    duellist at right
  I 263 -- upside down
    man at right
  VII 130 -- man in
    center
  IX 158 -- helmeted
    man at right
  HMs 483 (AT 113) --
    duelist at right &
    fallen nude man at
    right
(3 or more, processions)
  -- HMs 260 (KSPI
    R60/63)
  each wears a helmet

Agrimi-Women
  Ch. 6A: Agrimi-Woman, helmet
    head
    XII 174a (KZ 21; CS 11Sa)
    HMs no. unknown (KZ 24)
    HMs no. unknown (KZ 25)
    HMs no. unknown (KZ 26)

Miscellaneous
  PT 2, R; Filler: lion -- HMs
    no. unknown (AT 83)
    ab
  Ch. 3A: Men & Animals
    (monsters) -- I Supp.
    3
    cap-like helmet
  Ch. 2D: Men & Women (pair,
    alone) -- HMs 195 (KZ
    195)
    tops a Column at right
  Ch. 8J: Miscellaneous
    (trophy) -- VII 158
    trophy?: Figure-8 Shield
      topped with a helmet,
      plume L

Tower Shields
Ch. 2B: Men
   (single, warrior) -- HMs 343
      (KSPI L47)
     man holds a small Tower
     Shield
   (2 men, duel)
     I 16 -- man at left
     VII 129 -- man at right
     XII 292 -- man at right

Figure-8 Shields
Carried by Men
  As Warriors
    Ch. 2B: Men
     (single, misc.) -- V
       239 & XIII 137
     (pair wear Figure-8
       Shield)
     II 3.32
     XIII 136
     HMs 459 (AT 116)
     (2 men, duel)
       I 11 -- man at left
       I 12 -- man at left
        & man at right
       V 180b -- man at
        right
       XII 13D -- man at
        right
     (3 or more,
       processions)
     HMs 260 (KSPI
       R60/63)
       3 men, each
        with a
        Figure-8
        Shield
     HMs 362 (KSPI K16)
       3 men walk R,
        each with
        Figure-8
        Shield
    Ch. 2C: Women (4 or
      more) -- I 17
     ab, at left: small
     man? R wears a

Figure-8 Shield
As Hunters
  Ch. 3C: Men Hunts
    Animals (lions)
    I 228 -- man at left
     carries a Figure-8
     Shield (seen in
     profile)
    IX 7D
  Ch. 3D: Men In Chariots
    -- Louvre AO 2188

Filler, with animals
  Single
    In the Center (BETWEEN)
      PT 14B, R: bull --
        XIII 33
      in center bef the
        raised hind
        hoof
      PT 32B: agrimia -- II
        3.107
      PT 51C: 2 dogs vs
        stag? R -- I 412
      PT 49B, R: dog vs
        goat -- V 649
      Ch. 5D: Protomes
        (bull) -- AM
        1938.1094
        (CS 336)
        betw the heads
        (ab in the
        center)
        (caprid) -- I 403
        betw the heads
        (ab in the
        center)
    IN FRONT
      PT 1A, R; Filler:
       quadruped -- HMs
       298 (KSPI K9)
      PT 6, L; Filler: bull
       -- IX 124
      PT 18B, R: cow & calf
       -- IX 194
      PT 25B, R: lion &

agrimi -- I 115
PT 37A, ccl: goats --
HMs LamdaDelta/AM
1938.1047 (CS 49S)
PT 39A: griffin L vs
bull -- L. Morgan
Library 1077 (Pini
1980: no. A5)
Ch. 3E: Animal Games
(bull-leaping,
Floating) -- AM
1938.1108 (CS 341)
ABOVE (cf.PT 6, R -- V
575)
PT 1A, R; Filler:
bull -- V 254 & V
751
goat -- II 3.111 &
HMp 4813
sheep -- HMs 208
(KSPI R7)
at left
cat? -- IV 311
PT 1C, L; bull -- IX
147
PT 2, R; Filler: bull
-- V 379 & I Supp.
142
PT 5A, R: lion -- II
4.206
bull -- Once Evans
Coll. (GGFR pl.
135)
PT 5B, L: calf? -- HMs
no. unknown (AT
155)
PT 6, R; Filler: calf
-- V 393
PT 14B, L: cow -- I
Supp. 71
PT 18B, R: lioness &
cub
II 3.344 & AM
1938.1060 (CS 298)
PT 25A, L: 2 stags --
V 297
Figure-8 Shield/

Pica/Baton ab
PT 29B: 2 calf
protomes -- AM
1938.1094
(CS 336)
PT 30A: bulls -- I
Supp. 91
PT 30C: 2 agrimia --
HM 2271
ab at left
PT 39A:
lion L vs stag --
X 129
dog L vs stag -- V
184a
Ch. 3A: Men & Animals
(bulls) -- VII 100
IN BACK
Ch. 3A: Men & Animals
(monsters) -- I
Supp. 3
inb of the quadru-
ped-headed
person
BELOW
PT 1A, R; Filler:
bull -- V 683 &
VIII 145
griffin -- AM
1941.128 (CS
23P)
PT 2, L; Filler: bull
-- XIII 32
2 bel
PT 2, R; Filler
lion -- Berlin FG
32 (AGDS II 52)
bull
II 3.212
II 4.4
V 275
VII 113
VII 162
X 244 --
dots/Figure-8
Shield bel
agrimi -- VII 190

quadruped -- ?I
Supp. 143
PT 5C, R; Filler: bull
-- AM 1938.1031 (CS
317)
PT 6, L; Filler: bull
-- II 3.337
PT 6, R; Filler: bull
-- X 258
PT 13A, L: Minotaur --
AM 1938.1071
PT 13A, R: hornless
Minotaur (= calf-
man?) -- XII 238
PT 13C, R: stag -- I
41
PT 14A, L:
bull -- V 320
agrimi -- X 137
PT 14D, L: agrimi-
man -- IX 128
PT 18B, R: lion & cub
-- II 3.344
below lion's neck
PT 25A, R: goats -- X
2
PT 25B, L: 2 bulls --
AM 1941.138 (CS
12P)
PT 27A, R: 3 goats --
I 105
bel inb
PT 29A: 2 lion pro-
tomes -- II 4.218
PT 34B: 2 bulls -- II
4.158
PT 39A, L:
dog vs agrimi/kid-
man -- XII 242
dots (=
Figure-8
Shield?)
griffin vs bull --
Coll. Schlumber-
ger 43
PT 47A: dog R vs bull
-- XII 265

bel bull
PT 48A: lion vs
agrimi -- VII 180
PT 49B, L: lion vs
kid -- I 182
PT 50B: lion L vs
stag -- X 128
PT 51B, L: lion & dog
vs agrimi -- AM
1925.128 (CS 6P)
IN FRONT & ABOVE
PT 1A, R; Filler:
lioness -- HM 178
ABOVE & BELOW
PT 1A, L; Filler:
bull -- II 4.214
PT 1A, R; Filler:
bull -- HMs 129
(KSPI J1; CS
45S)
quadruped -- I 39
PT 5A, R; Filler:
agrimi -- V 255
PT 6, R; Filler: bull
-- AM 1938.1052
In the Field
PT 13A, L: I 216 --
calf-man in the
center
PT 39A, L: griffin vs
bull -- L. Morgan
Library 1077
Ch. 6A: Animal People
(bull-people) --
AM 1938.1072 (CS
323)
at right
Two or more
PT 1A, L; Filler: goat
-- VII 191
infr
PT 1A, R; Filler
bull
V 683 -- 2 ab & 1
bel
HMs 129 (KSPI J1)
-- ab & bel

goat -- Nafplion 8839
  infr, ab, bel
PT 2, R; Filler:
  quadruped -- NMA no.
    unknown from
    Athens, Acropolis
    ab
PT 39A: griffin L vs bull
  -- Coll. Schlumberger
    43
  bel

With People in Religious?
  Compositions

  Viewed frontally (see: I
    17, Carried by Warriors,
    above)

    Ch. 2B: Men (3 or more,
        salute) -- I 369
      betw each
    Ch. 2C: Women (trio,
        stand R) -- I 132
      woman at right
          originally
          intended to be a
          Figure-8 Shield
      Figure-8 Shield
        inb & ab
    Ch. 3A: Men & Animals
        (bulls) -- Piraieus
      no. unknown, ring
      from Varkiza T. I
    object (Shield) inb

  Viewed in profile (see: Ch.
    12J: Shields-in-Profile)

    ?PT 18B, L: cow & calf --
      V 663
        bel
    Ch. 2D: Men & Women
      (pair, alone)
        I 219 -- topped
          with Sacred Knot
          in profile

HMs 195 (KZ 195) --
  Figure-8 Shield
  in profile inb

Miscellaneous
  Ch. 8B: Buildings -- HMs 45
    (KZ 131)
    2 Figure-8 Shields bel
  Ch. 8J: Miscellaneous
    (trophy) -- VII 158
    trophy?: Figure-8 Shield
    topped with a helmet

12H
Architecture

Shrines (see: Ch. 2E: People
  at a Shrine)

Special Characteristics
  ?Platforms -- Ch. 2E:
    People at a Shrine (tree
    pulling)
      Once in the Evans's
        Coll., The Ring of
        Minos
        2 flank a
        mountain
  Two-Tiered (see: Shrine/
      Boat Cabin, below)
    Ch. 2E: People at a
      Shrine
      (person at left)
      I 191 -- with
        porch sup-
        ported by 2
        Columns, a
        short one from
        the top tier &
        a tall one infr
        of the Shrine
      Chania 2055 (Papa-
        stolou 1977:

no. 28)
(person at right) --
HMs 141
   topped with HC
     upper tier
     contains
     Column
(woman sits on
   Shrine)
   V 199 -- roof of
   the Shrine
   supported by a
   Column; its
   back wall? is
   convex L
   Berlin Antike
   Abteilung no.
   unknown (Biele-
   feld 1968: 34
   no. 263 pl.
   CIIa)
   HMs 277-283 (KZ 3,
   KSPI Q22, etc)
(tree-pulling, no
   Omphalos) --Once in
   the Evans Coll.,
   The Ring of Minos
Three-tiered
  Ch. 2E: People at a
    Shrine
  (two women antithetic)
   I 127 -- a Shrine
    on a "mountain"?
    that could be a
    built structure
    in 3 tiers with
    a door bel
  (woman sits on Shrine)
   Chania 2097 (Papa-
   postolou 1977: no.
   30)
On a Mountain
  Ch. 2E: People at a
    Shrine
  (man) -- I 292
   pile of rocks
    (mountain?)

(two women antithetic)
  -- I 127
(tree-pulling,
  Omphalos) -- Once
  in the Evans Coll.,
  The Ring of Minos
Containing a Short Column
  Ch. 2E: People at a
    Shrine (person at
    left) -- AM 1938.1127
    (CS 250) & II 3.15
With Animals
  PT 10A, R: bull -- V 198
  Ch. 3A: Man & Animals
    (lions) -- VII 169
    infr

Shrine/Boat Cabin
Ch. 2E: People at a Shrine
  (woman sits in a boat) -- II
  3.252, the Mochlos Ring
  in the boat, 2-tiered
  Shrine/Cabin
(tree-pulling, Omphalos) --
  Once in the Evans Coll.,
  the Ring of Minos
  bel: a woman poles a
  boat L in which
  are 2 Shrines

Half-Shrines
Ch. 2E: People at a Shrine
  (person at left)
  V 728 -- at right
  HMs 418 (KSPI E1) -- betw
    person & Shrine, a
    shorter Shrine?

Possible Shrines
Ch. 2B: Men (3 or more,
  salute) -- HMs 449 (AT 125)
    vertical lines at right
    = Shrine?
Ch. 2E: People at a Shrine
  (person at right) -- V 422b
    Shrine at left
    consists of 3 Double

Axes on thick Pylons
Ch. 4B: Potnia Theron (lions)
-- BSA Cast 135
Potnia flanked by lion
sits on Shrine or
Table
Ch. 4C: Women "Crossed" by a
Caprid -- HMs no. unknown
(KZ 4)
vertical stack of short,
horizontal strokes
infr (= Shrine?)

**Miscellaneous Buildings &
Constructions**

Ch. 2B: Men (1) -- Chania 1563
wall with 2 gates encloses?
2 building units of 3
buildings each (peak
sanctuary?; citadel?)
Ch. 2D: Men & Women (& a boat)
-- I 180
3 buildings (town) ab
Ch. 2E: People at a Shrine
(woman in a Shrine) -- X
270
woman in a building?
made of 2 concentric
boxes of Branch 3
Ch. 3A: Man & Animals (bulls)
-- HMs 143 (KSPI Q20)
PM illustrates the man
at a barricade
Ch. 3D: Animal Games (bull-
leaping, (Diving) -- AM
1939.964 (CS 202)
bull rampant on a box/
cistern decorated
around the edges &
diagonally from corner
to corner with
zig-zags
Columns
With People
Associated with a Shrine/
Building

Ch. 2C: Women (single,
stands frontal)/
Ch. 2E: People at a
Shrine (woman in a
Shrine) -- X 270
in a building flanked
by Columns
Ch. 2E: People at a
Shrine
(person at left)
I 86 -- Column
inside
I 191 -- a Shrine
at right con-
sists of a 2-
tiered structure
covered by a
porch supported
by a short
Column from
the top tier
& by a tall
Column infr
of the structure
HMs 141 (KSPI M1-4)
-- Columns in-
side upper tier
HMs 418 (KSPI E1)
-- Columns
inside
(woman sits on Shrine)
V 199 -- roof of the
Shrine sup-
ported by a
Column
Berlin Antike
Abteilung no.
unknown (Biele-
feld 1968: 34
no. 263 pl.
CIIa) -- Column
inside
(tree-pulling, no
Omphalos)
I 126 -- inside is
a pillar or
Column

Miscellaneous
  Ch. 2B: Men
    (single, misc.) -- I
      107
      flanked by 5
        Columns
    (battles) -- HMs 483
      (AT 113)
      central Column
        with volute
        capital?
  Ch. 2C: Women
    (single, stands
      frontal) -- I 513
        flanked by 2
          Columns
    (3, misc.) -- AM
      1938.1013 (CS 295)
      central woman
        seated on a
        Column?
  Ch. 2D: Men & Women
    (pair, alone)
      Chania 1024 --
        Column/Pylon
      HMs 195 (KZ 195)
        -- at right
  Ch. 3A: Man & Animals
    (several) -- AM
      1938.1091 (CS 358)
    Column?/stand?
  Ch. 4A: Women & Animals
    (woman seated L at
      right) -- I 179
      genius at right
        carrying a jug
        supported by a
        Column
    (friezes) -- II 3.103
      at right

With Animals (see Ch. 6C:
  Genii)

Central
  PT 25B, L: bull -- Berlin FG

26 (AGDS II 48)
PT 28A
  2 bulls -- I 19
    HC & Column betw
  2 griffins --I 218 & VII
    187
PT 28B
  lions -- HMs 42 (KZ 128)
    Waisted Altar topped
      with a Column
  bulls -- HM 156
  calves (2 pairs) -- VIII
    90
    Column capital betw
      each pair
  griffins -- I 171
    leashed to the Column
PT 31A: 2 lions
  I 319
  IV 304 --central Column/
    Palm 4?
PT 31B: 2 griffins -- I 98
  Column supporting an
    epistyle betw
  Ch. 6C: Griffins I 171 --
    leashed to the Column
  XII 302
  AM 1938.1044 (CS 338)
BEHIND
  PT 1A, R; Filler:
    lion -- HMs 315 (KSPI
      R41)
      II 4.18
      II 4.74
      ?II 4.45
    sheep -- HMs 208 (KSPI
      R7)
    goat -- AM 1941.246 (CS
      7P) = II 3.40
      leashed to the Column
    caprid kid -- I 487
  PT 2, R; Filler: quadruped
    -- VII 155
  PT 13A, R: bull -- IV 267
IN FRONT
  PT 1A, L; Filler:
    griffin -- XII 301

leashed to the Column
quadruped -- V 186
PT 1A, R; Filler: griffin
-- AM 1941.128 (CS 23P)
ABOVE
   PT 1A, R; Filler: lion
     HM 907 -- a horizontal
     row of densely
     packed vertical
     dashes ab (= Column?)
     VIII 124
     capital? ab
   PT 5A, R; Filler: lion --
     XII 273
   PT 6, R; Filler: bull -- X
     171*
     capital? ab
BELOW
   PT 12, R: bull -- I 265
   Column/Mace bel
   PT 19B, L: 2 bulls -- I
     515/KN HMs 109 (KSPI J2)
   PT 39A: dog L vs agrimi/
     kid-man -- XII 242
   schematic Column
   Ch. 3A: Man & Animals
     (misc) -- AM 1938.1091
     bel jug held by a
     genius
   Ch. 6C: Genii -- V 440

Short Columns
With People
   Inside a Shrine
     Ch. 2E: People at a
       Shrine (person at
       left) --II 3.15 & AM
       1938.1127 (CS 250)
   In the Field
     Ch. 2D: Men & Women (man
       & 2 women) -- V 173
       at right
     Ch. 2E: People at a
       Shrine
       (person at left) --
       II 3.252, the
       Mochlos Ring

ab right
(tree-pulling, man at
   Omphalos) -- HMm
   989
   ab right
Ch. 3A: Man & Animals
   (several) -- AM
   1938.1091

With Animals
   ABOVE
     PT 13A, R: bull -- VII
       157
       striated
   BELOW
     PT 13A, R: griffin -- AM
       1938.1100 (CS 367)
     PT 39A: dog L vs
       agrimi/kid-man -- XII
       242

Pylons/Poles
Ch. 2B: Men (pair, boxers)
   -- HMs 336 (KSPI L50)
   at right: lower Pylon
   with Pylon box
Ch. 2D: Men & Women (pair)
   -- Chania 1024
   Column/Pylon between a
   man & woman saluting
Ch. 2E: People at a Shrine
   (person at R) -- V 422b
   Shrine at left con-
     sists of 3 Double
     Axes on thick
     Pylons
   (woman, plain) -- AM
     1938.1127 infr of the
     Shrine
Ch. 3D: Men In Chariots -- V
   585 goal?/turning post?

12I
Religious Objects

Horns of Consecration
Topping a Shrine
   Ch. 2E: People at a Shrine
     (person at left)
       I 86
       I 108
       I 191 -- the porch of
          a Shrine
       II 3.15
       V 728
       IX 163
       Chania 2055 --
          (Papapostolou
          1977: no. 28)
       HMs 418 (KSPI E1)
       HMs 487 (AT 136)
     (person at right)
       I 279
       HMs no. unknown (KZ
          1)
     (woman in a Shrine) -- X
     270
     (woman sits on Shrine)
       V 199
       Berlin Antike
          Abteilung no.
          unknown
          (Bielefeld 1968:
          34 no. 263 pl.
          CIIa: forgery?)
     (two women antithetic)
       -- Chania 2071 & 2112
       (Papapostolou 1977:
       no. 27)
     (tree-pulling, no
       Omphalos) -- Once
       in the Evans Coll.,
       "The Ring of Minos"
       (PM IV 947 ff.)
          platform at left
             is topped with
             a HC; in the
             boat are 2

             Shrines, each
             topped with HC
Miscellaneous
   PT 28A: 2 bulls --I 19
     betw
   Ch. 2B: Men
     (1) -- Chania 1563
       HC?/rounded merlins
         top buildings
     (religious) -- II 3.7
       top a Waisted Altar
   Ch. 2C: Women (single, at
       Altar) -- I 41
     top Altar/3 (4?)-legged
       Table
   Ch. 3B: Master of Animals
       (monsters) -- V 201
     Master stands on a HC
   Ch. 3F: Animal-Sacrifice --
       HMs 1049 from Mallia
       (Sakellarakis 1970:
       169 fig. 8.5)
     HC? ab
   Ch. 4A: Women & Animals
     (woman inb) -- BSA cast
       188
       HC & vertical line ab
   Ch. 6B: Genii --I 231
     Waisted/bucranium Altar
       with HC

Altars
PT 1A, R; Filler: griffin -- IV
   58D
   infr
PT 28B: 2 lions -- HMs 42 (KZ
   128)
   betw, topped with a Column
PT 31A (see: Ch. 4B: Potnia
   Theron [misc.] -- I 379)
   2 lions
     I 46 -- (conjoined)
       on Waisted Altar
     IV 40D -- Waisted Altar
       betw
     HMs 577 (AT 49) -- on
       Waisted Altar

2 griffins -- I 73
　　on Waisted Altar
PT 31B (cf. I 99; no
　　Waisted Altar depicted)
2 lions -- Berlin 34
　　(AGDS II 39)
　　　on Waisted Altar/Table
2 dogs -- HMs 233 (KSPI
　　R88)
　　　on Waisted Altar
2 griffins -- I 98
　　　on Waisted Altar
Ch. 2B: Men (single)
　　II 3.7 -- Waisted Altar
　　　at right
　　HMs NTheta (KSPI R70) --
　　　Waisted Altar
Ch. 2C: Women (single, at
　　altar) --
　　I 410
　　　woman stands L infr of
　　　　of Altar/3(4?)-
　　　　legged Table
?Ch. 2E: People at a Shrine
　　(2 women antithetic) --
　　　II 3.56
　　　Altar/Shrine at right
　　(tree-pulling) -- Once Evans
　　　Coll., The Ring of Minos
　　　　2 flank a mountain
Ch. 5B: Animal Faces
　　(lion, Snake Frame) --
　　　HMs 38 gamma (KZ
　　　60)
　　　object ab (half of a
　　　Double Ax or half a
　　　Waisted Altar)
　　(bull, Snake Frame) -- XII
　　　174c & AM AE 1802 (CS
　　　11Sc; KZ 61)
　　　half a Double Ax/
　　　　Waisted Altar ab
　　(boar) -- HMs 80a (KZ 66)
　　　half Double Ax/
　　　　Waisted Altar in
　　　center
Ch. 5E: Birds & Waterbirds

(waterbirds, pair) --
　　HMs 659 (KSPI U117)
　　　flank/on a Waisted
　　　Altar
Ch. 6B: Genii -- I 231
　　Waisted/bucranium Altar

Pithoi/Shields-in-Profile
Ch. 2B: Men (single,
　　Omphalos) -- HMm 1034
　　　at left
Ch. 2D: Men & Women:
　　(pair) -- I 219
　　(& boat) -- AM 1938.1129
　　　at left
Ch. 2E: People at a Shrine
　　(person at left) -- II 3.15
　　　at left
　　(tree-pulling) -- II 3.114
　　　at left
Ch. 3A: Man & Animals
　　(bulls) -- Ring from
　　　Varkiza
　　　at left

Omphaloi (see: Ch. 2B: Men
　　[single, Omphaloi]; 2C:
　　Women [single]; 2E: People
　　at a Shrine [tree-pulling,
　　Omphalos]; 3A:Man & Animals
　　[bird] -- HMs 134 [KSPI
　　R14])

Omphaloi/Squills (cf. PT 6, R
　　-- V 575)

Ch. 2C: Women
　　(single, kneels at Omphalos)
　　　-- AM 1919.56
　　　woman at right kneels
　　　　at 2 Omphaloi/
　　　　Squills
　　(stands R) -- HMs 523 (AT
　　　138)
　　　2 Omphaloi/Squills
Ch. 2D: Men & Women
　　(pair, alone) -- Chania 1024

(Papapostolou 1977: no.
31)
at left, double
Omphalos (/Squill?)
(& boat) -- AM 1938.1129
objects (Omphaloi/
Squills?) ab boat
Ch. 2E: People at a Shrine
(person at left) -- II
3.252, The Mochlos Ring
ab R, 2 small
Omphaloi/Squills
(two women antithetic) -- I
127
2 small Omphaloi/
Squills top the

Sacred Hearts
Ch. 2B: Men (single, Omphalos;
see HMm 989, below) -- HMm
1034
in the bird's beak (see
XII 150a, below)
Ch. 2C: Women (pair, woman
salutes woman) -- HMs no.
unknown (KZ 9)
top center
Ch. 2D: Men & Women
(pair) -- I 219
ab R
(misc.) -- AM 1938.1130,
The Ring of Nestor
2 ab
Ch. 2E: People at a Shrine
(person at left) -- II
3.252, The Mochlos Ring
ab R
(tree-pulling)
I 126 -- inside/bel
Shrine/Table
HMm 989 -- ab kneeling
man (see I 219 & HMm
1034, above)
Once in the Evans coll.,
The Ring of Minos
at left, a nude man
holds a jug/Sacred

Heart? with his
right hand
Ch. 5E: Bird & Waterbirds
(waterbirds, single) --
XII 150a
in the bird's beak (see
HMm 1034, above)

Double Axes
With People
Carried
Ch. 2B: Men (3 or more,
salute) -- HMs no.
unknown (KZ 6)
man at left
Ch. 2C: Women (single,
carries object) -- II
3.8
Ch. 2D: Men & Women
(pair, alone) -- HMs
592 (AT 124)
woman & man both
carry L a
Double Ax

In the Snake Frame held by
a Potnia Theron

Ch. 4B: Potnia Theron
(lions) -- I 144 & I
145
(griffins) -- II 3.63
& V 654
(misc., stags) -- I
379
Associated with a Shrine
Ch. 2E: People at a
Shrine (person at
right) -- V 422b
Shrine at left con-
sists of 3 Double
Axes on thick
Pylons
In the Field
Ch. 2D: Men & Women
[pair] -- I 219
ab R, Sacred Heart

& Double Ax with
festoons

With Animals
    PT 36cl: 2 bulls -- XII 250
      betw the horns of each
    Ch. 3A: Man & Animals
      (bulls) -- VII 100
        bel
    Ch. 5B: Animal Faces
      (lion with a Snake Frame)
        XII 174c/CS 11Sc (KZ
        61) -- betw the
        legs of the lion-
        man (see: Ch. 6A:
        People-Animals
        [lion-man])
      ?HMs 38 gamma (KZ 60)
        -- half a Double Ax
      bel?
    (bull, single)
      II 3.11
      Once Schliemann Coll.
      from the Argive
      Heraeum
        upside down ab
    (boar) -- HMs 80a (KZ 66)
      double Snake Frame
      ab with half Double
      Ax/Waisted Altar in
      center

Miscellaneous
    PT 13A, R calf -- Melos 571
      on the reverse of the
      sealstone
    Ch. 6A: People-Animals
      (lion-man) -- XII 174c/
        CS 11Sc (KZ 61)
      betw the legs of the
      lion-man
    Ch. 8G: Sacred Robes/Knots
      -- HM 2343b
      crossing bel the loop of
      the Sacred Knot

Snake Frames
Held above the Head of a
    Potnia Theron -- Ch. 4B:
    Potnia Theron

    Double
      Lions
        I 144
        I 145
        IV 295
        Kassel no. unknown
          from Menidi
          (AGDS III 6)
          double/triple?
      Griffins
        II 3.63
        V 654
    Triple
      Lions -- X 242
      Misc., stags -- I 379
      Griffins
        II 3.276
        AM AE 689 (CS 351)

In the Mouth of Animals
    Single
      Conventional
        Ch. 5B: Animal Faces
        (lion, Snake
          Frame) -- HMs
          38 gamma (KZ
          60)
        (bull, single,
          simple)
        HMs 24 gamma
          (KZ 82)
        HMs 165 (KZ
          165) -- 2
          lines (Snake
          Frame?)
          flank
        (boar)
        HMs 3b (KZ 64)
        HMs 29b (KZ 69)
        HMs 31b (KZ 65)
        HMs 81a (KZ 63)

Curtailed
  Ch. 5B: Animal Faces
    (lion, Snake Frame)
      -- HMs 39 (KZ
        167)
    (bull, Snake Frame)
      XII 174c & AM AE
        1802 (CS
        11Sc; KZ 61)
      HMs 6b (KZ 83)
      HMs 642 (Sk 16)
    (boar) -- HMs 53
      (KZ 62)
Double
  Ch. 5B: Animal Faces
    (bull, Snake Frame) --
      HMs 24a (KZ 81)
    (boar) -- HMs 80a (KZ
      66)
ABOVE Animals
  PT 32B: misc. -- II 3.5
    bel horns of top bull
    face
  Ch. 5B: Animal Faces
    (lion, Snake Frame) --
      HMs 81b (KZ 56)
    (bull, Snake Frame) --
      HMs 15a (KZ 88)
  Ch. 6A: People-Animals
    (eagle-woman, head misc.)
    -- HMs no. unknown (KZ
    22)
      body topped by a
        double Snake Frame

BELOW Animals
  Ch. 5D: Protomes (caprid) --
    I 189
      bel each protome

Miscellaneous
  Ch. 8G: Sacred Knots/Robes
    (Sacred Knot) -- HMs 168
    (KZ 168)
      the base of the loop
        is crossed with a
        Snake Frame/2 legs?

Sacred Knots/Robes
Single
  PT 2, R; Filler: bull -- X
    142*
    with animal ear ab
  PT 5A, R; Filler: lion -- I
    54
    Sacred Knot infr
  PT 11, L; Plain: griffin --
    Pylos/Chora no.
    unknown
    at the neck
  PT 13A, R: bull -- XII 268
    bel
  PT 14B, R: bull -- XIII 33
    bel
  PT 49A, R: lion vs agrimi
    -- VII 125
    bel
  Ch. 2B: Men
    (single, salute) -- II
      3.145
      2 men flank & hold
        Sacred Robe
    (2 or more, salute) --
      HMs no. unknown
      (KZ 6)
      man at right: carries
        Sacred Robe?
  Ch. 2C: Women (single,
    (carries object L)
      II 3.8 -- Sacred
      Knot/Robe
      HM 2807b -- Sacred
      Robe
      HMs 535 (AT 123) --
        Sacred Robe hangs
        from a Yoke
    (carries object R) -- HM
      G 3158 (CMCG 363)
      Sacred Robe
    (kneels at Omphalos) --
      HMs no. unknown
      (AT 143)
      at right, Sacred Robe
  Ch. 2D: Men & Women [pair]
    -- I 219

at right, Figure-8
Shield in profile
topped with Sacred
Knot in profile
Ch. 3A: Man & Animals
(griffins) -- I 223
collar tied with a small
Sacred Knot
Ch. 3E: Animal Games (bull-
leaping, Diving) -- AM
AE 2237
Sacred Knot infr
Ch. 8G: Sacred Knots/Robes
(Sacred Knot) -- HM
2343b
Double Ax crossing just
below the loop of a
Sacred Knot

Double
PT 2, L; Filler: bull --
XIII 32
2 Sacred Knots ab
PT 5A, R; Filler: stag --
HMs 148 (KSPI R2)
2 Sacred Knot ab
PT 29B: 2 lions -- AM
1938.1126 (CS 340)
a Sacred Knot ab each
lion
Ch. 2B: Men (single, misc.)
-- II 3.330a
2 objects (Sacred Knots?)
flank
Ch. 5B: Animal Faces (bulls)
-- Once Schliemann
Coll. from the Argive
Heraeum
flanked by 2 Sacred
Knots/Robes
Ch. 8G: Sacred Knots/Robes
(Sacred Knot) -- HMs
150 (KSPI S6)
2 Sacred Knots flank Palm
1

Loops Associated with Sacred
Knots/Robes (e.g., Ch. 8G:
Sacred Knots/Robes [Sacred
Knot] -- HMs 168 [KZ 168])

Ch. 5B: Animal Faces (bulls)
-- HMs 23 gamma (KZ 84)
loop ab
Ch. 6C: Misc. Monsters -- HMs
1a (AM AE 1801/CS 10Sa/KZ
80)
bucranium topped by loop
Ch. 8H: Friezes of Figure-8
Shields & Sacred Knots
-- HMs 664 (KSPI C11)
each Shield is topped with
a loop

12J
Miscellaneous Objects

Chain -- Ch. 5B: Animal Faces
(bucrania, single) -- VIII
110a
bucranium hangs on a
chain

Corona -- Ch. 2A: Parts of the
Human Body (man's face)/Ch.
6A: People-Animals (sphinx)
-- HMs 50a (KZ 76)
corona beh

Flute? -- Ch. 2B: Men (3 or
more, processions) -- HMs
260 (KSPI R60/63)
man plays a flute-like
instrument?

Girth -- Ch. 3D: Man Rides
Other Animals -- V 638
girth? around the
agrimi's waist

Masks -- Ch. 5B: Animal Faces
    (lion, 4 or more) -- HMs 93
    (KZ 135)
        6 lion face "masks"

Rake? -- PT 2, R; Filler: bull
    -- V 247
        rake/schematic bull head
            bel

<u>Wheel</u> -- Ch. 5B: Animal Faces
    (bull, <u>Snake Frame</u>) -- HMs
    15a (KZ 88)
        <u>Wheel</u> ab

CHAPTER 13
Signs

13A
Writing

Linear B
PT 13A, R:
   lion -- I 217
     SH vertical: -a- [or
      -na-?] in center
   calf -- Melos 571
     reverse: <u>Double Ax</u> & 1-
     handled cup [Linear B
     -ki-?])
PT 14A, R: bull -- IX 118
   branch (approximating
     Linear B -sa-?) bel
PT 36 cl: 2 bulls -- XII 250
   -a-? betw (tailed -a-:
   Vermeule 1966: 145 & n.5)
PT 36 ccl: 2 bulls -- II 3.310
   -a- betw (Linear A #52?;
   tailed -a-: Vermeule 1966:
   145 & n. 5)
PT 52A: 2 griffins vs bull R
     -- AM 1938.1075 (CS 342)
   the griffins flank Lin. B
     *125 (CYPERUS)

Fence
Between
   PT 40: lion R vs bull -- X

241

Above
   Ch. 5B: Animal Faces (bull,
     single, simple)
   V 592
   HMs 665 (KSPI R101)

Miscellaneous
PT 5A, R; Filler: agrimi --
   Munich A.1163a (AGDS I

84a)
     branch ("signs") ab
PT 39A, L: dog vs agrimi/kid-
man -- XII 242
       sign bel sphinx
Ch. 3D: Bull-Wrestling --
   I Supp. 35
     branch/sign ab

13B
<u>Impaled Triangles</u>

BETWEEN
PT 53, Victim R -- HMs 300
   (KSPI R12/14/27)
   betw the attackers

IN FRONT
PT 5B, R; Filler: bull -- XII
   237
PT 6, L; Filler: bull -- VIII
   107 ab/infr
PT 37A ccl: 2 goats -- HMs
   Lamda-Delta/AM 1938.1047
   (CS 49S; KSPI Q15/17)
     infr of one goat

ABOVE
PT 1A, L; Filler: griffin --
   Munich A.1216b (AGDS I
   70b)
PT 1A, R; Filler
   bull -- VIII 145
   dog -- Once Evans Coll.
     (GGFR pl. 115)
PT 5A, L; Filler:
   kid/calf -- VII 252
PT 6, R; Filler: bull -- HM
   2126
   <u>ImpTr</u>/<u>Palm 4</u> ab
PT 13, R: bull -- HMs 286
   (Gill 1966: 16 no. 20)
PT 14C, L: <u>Minotaur</u> -- II 3.67

PT 14D, L: agrimi-man -- VII
    138
PT 18B, R: cow & calf --
Berlin FG 24 (AGDS II
    47)
        unfinished Palm 3/sign
            (ImpTr variant?) ab

PT 25B, R: 2 bulls -- VIII 108
PT 29B: 2 calf protomes -- AM
  1938.1094 (CS 336)
PT 39A, L: dog vs kid -- AM
    1941.119 (CS 3P)
Ch. 3A: Man & Animals (man,
    bull) -- VII 100
Ch. 3D: Bull-Wrestling -- I
    137
Ch. 3E: Animal-Sacrifice -- II
    3.338
Ch. 5B: Animal Faces (bull,
    filler) -- HMs 312 (Gill
1966: 15 no. 8)

BELOW
PT 6, L: kid -- I 484
PT 13A, L: Minotaur -- AM
    1938.1071 (CS 322)
PT 13A, R: bull -- HMs 147 &
    313 (Gill 1966: no. 7)
PT 18A, R: lioness & cub -- I
    106
PT 51A, L: 2 lions vs bulls in
    PT 3 -- HM 155
Ch. 6A: Minotaurs (2) --
BSA cast 186

In the Field
PT 31A: 2 griffins -- I 73 at
    right
PT 39A, L: griffin vs bull --
    L. Morgan Library 1077
    (Pini 1980: no. A5)
        at left
Ch. 5D: protomes (bull) -- AM
    1938.1094 (CS 336)
        betw the heads
Ch. 6: Winged Goat-Man --

Lentoid (Furtwaengler
1900: pl. VI.6)
    3 in field

CHAPTER 14
Heavenly Bodies

14A
Heaven Lines

Alone
Ch. 2C: Women
    (single) -- HMs no. unknown
        (AT 143)
        ab
    (4 or more) -- II 3.51
        ab: wavy
Ch. 2E: People at a Shrine
    (tree-pulling, no Omphalos)
    -- I 126
        ab R (betw the standing
        woman & the Tree 2): 2
        Heaven Lines

With Heavenly Bodies
Ch. 2C: Women (4 or more, face
    R) -- I 17
        ab, center: crescent Moon
        & Sun ab a wavy Heaven
        Line
Ch. 2E: People at a Shrine
    (woman sits on Shrine) -- V 199
        ab, Sun ab a Heaven Line
Ch. 4A: Women & Animals (woman
    seated L at right) -- I 179
        ab: crescent Moon & Sun
        ab a wavy Heaven Line;
        dots (Stars?) fill the
        area

14B
Suns

(see: Chs. 9I & 16L: Stars; &
Ch. 14A: Heavenly Bodies
[Heaven Lines & Heavenly

Bodies] -- I 17 & 179, & V
199, above)

Simple
With People
Single
    IN FRONT
        Ch. 2B: Men (single,
            Altar) -- II 3.7
        Ch. 2C: Women
            (single, stands R)
            -- HM G 3446 (CMCG
            361)
    IN BACK
        Ch. 2C: Women (2,
            salute R) -- II
            3.17
    Miscellaneous
        Ch. 2C: Women
            (single)
            II 3.171 & II
            3.304
        Ch. 3D: Men In
            Chariots -- Louvre
            AO2188
    Two
        Ch. 2C: Women (single,
            stands L) -- II 3.3
            flank

With Animals
Single
    In the Center
        Ch. 5I: Dolphins (3) --
            HM G 3067 (CMCG 319)
    IN FRONT
        PT 10A, R: sphinx -- II
            3.118
    BEFORE
        PT 14A, R: lion -- HMs
            253 (KSPI N1)
            bef the shoulder
    ABOVE
        Lions
            PT 6. L; Filler: lion
                -- II 4.76
            PT 10A, R: lion -- HM

G 3351 (CMCG 267)
PT 11, R; Filler:
lion -- XIII 20D
PT 31B: 2 lions --
Berlin FG 34 (AGDS
II 39)
Bulls
PT 1A, R; Filler:
bull -- V 258
?PT 6, L; Filler:
bull -- V 664
branch (Tailed
Sun?) ab
Ch. 5B: Animal Faces
(bulls)
II 3.149 & X 68
Miscellaneous
PT 14D, L: agrimi-man
-- IX 128
PT 31B: 2 collared
dogs -- HMs 233
(KSPI R88)
PT 46: lion L vs
griffin -- IX 148
PT 51F: 2 griffins vs
stag R -- HMs 255
+? (Pini 1973:
221-230)
Ch. 5H: Fish (single,
conventional) -- II
3.245a
BELOW
PT 1A, L; Filler: griffin
-- XII 301
PT 12, L: lion -- XII 244
PT 14D, L: Minotaur -- AM
1938.1070 (CS 325)
Ch. 5I: dolphins -- II
3.375
Ch. 6A: People-Animals
(bull-people) -- BSA
cast 186

Miscellaneous
In the Center, Encircled
by Geometric Motifs

Ch. 9B: Centered
Circles (misc.)
II 3.70
II 4.237
X 58
Miscellaneous
PT 6, L; Filler:
Minotaur -- HM G
3316 (CMCG 379)
small Sun inb
Ch. 5E: Birds & Water-
birds [waterbirds,
single] -- IV 257
"dandelion
puff"/Sun

Two
BELOW
Ch. 6B: Genii -- Berlin
FG 12 (AGDS II 29)
flank the genius
ABOVE & BELOW
PT 3, R: Babylonian
Dragon -- IV 42D
ab & bel
PT 6, L; Filler:
Babylonian Dragon --
HM G 3138 (CMCG 283)
Ch. 5E: Birds & Water-
birds (waterbirds,
single) -- HM no.
unknown (AE 1907 pl.
8.104)
2 ab & 1 bel

Tailed Suns (cf. PT 6, L --
V 664)

PT 5A, L; Filler: agrimi --
VII 42
PT 1B, L: bull/calf -- VII 251

CHAPTER 15
Plants

15A
Conventionalized Branches

Branch 1 (see: Ch. 7A:
    Branches; & PT 1A, L, PT
    1A, R, & PT 5A, L -- these
    have 10 or more examples &
    are not listed here)

PT 1B, R:
    agrimia -- V 160
        bel
    bull -- HMs 330a+OGamma?
        (KSPI R52)
        2 bef
PT 1C, L; bull -- VII 200
    infr & ab
PT 1C, R; bull
    ABOVE -- I Supp. 23 & IV 317
PT 1/5A, L: agrimi -- HM no.
    unknown (Younger & Betts
    1979: no. 4)
        ab
PT 2, L; Filler
    IN FRONT
        calf -- Mallia no.
            unknown
        waterbird -- I Supp.
            119
            infr
    ABOVE
        bull -- I 59
        agrimi -- X 179
        quadruped -- I Supp. 15
    BELOW
        lion -- XIII 57
PT 2, R; Filler
    IN FRONT
        lion? -- X 172
        bull
            II 3.212 -- Branch 1
            Tree
            II 3.336 -- Branch 1

Tree
    calf
    quadruped -- NMA no.
        unknown from Athens,
        Acropolis

ABOVE
    bull
        X 180 & X 175
    goat -- X 181
BELOW
    bull -- I Supp. 142
PT 3, L: agrimi -- AGDS I
    Munich 35
    infr, infr/ab, & bel
PT 3, R: bull -- HM no.
    unknown from Kalyvia T. 9
    infr & ab
PT 5A, R; Filler
    ABOVE
        bull -- V 150
        calf? -- V 676
        agrimi -- X 185
            large
        goat -- I Supp. 39
        Babylonian Dragon -- AM
            1938.1150 (CS 22P)
PT 5B, L; Filler: griffiness
    -- X 220*
    Branch 1/arrow bel
PT 5D, R; Filler: bull -- I
    Supp. 124
    infr & inb
PT 6, L; Filler
    ABOVE
        lion -- II 4.117
        bull -- V 689
        calf -- II 3.125
        agrimi -- VII 184
            Branch 1 Tree ab
PT 6, R; Filler
    ABOVE
        lion -- II 4.175
        bull -- HMs KE (AT
151/153)
        calf -- I 287b
        goat -- HM 1867

BELOW
    agrimi -- AM 1920.116
       (CS 8P)
ABOVE & BELOW
    bull -- HM G 3299 (CMCG
      228)
PT 7, L; griffin -- I Supp.
  38b
Branch 1 Tree infr
PT 8, L: lion -- X 133
  ab (= Pica?)
PT 8, R:
IN FRONT
    lion -- Munich A.1195
      (AGDS I 64)
    griffin -- V 437
      Branch 1 Tree infr
ABOVE
    VII 168 & BSA cast 183
PT 10A, L:
ABOVE
    lion
      I 405
      I Supp. 64
      VII 178
    bull
      I 281
      AM 1941.125 (CS 299)
    boar -- I Supp. 76
      4 Branch 1 ab
BELOW
    lion -- I 387
PT 10A, R:
  ABOVE
    lion
      II 3.192
      X 132
      XII 208
      HM 2123
    agrimi
      I 404
    griffin
      X 170 -- Branch 1 ab
        at left
  IN BACK, Branch 1 Tree
    bull -- XII 248
    agrimi -- X 281

PT 11, L; Filler
lion
    I 272a
    II 3.227
    VII 151
    IX 161
    X 1
    AM 1941.98 (CS 373)
    Chania 2094
stag -- I 272b
PT 11, R; Filler
lion
    I Supp. 116 -- ab
    AM 1938.1048 (CS 10P) --
      ab & infr
PT 12, L: lion -- Berlin FG 16
  (AGDS II 40)
    infr
PT 14A, R: bull -- HM G 3091
  (CMCG 227)
    ab
PT 14D, L: agrimi-man -- AM
  1941.123 (CS 326)
    infr
PT 16B, R: goat & kid -- I 168
  bel
PT 18B, R: cow & calf -- HM
  2250
    ab
PT 19A, L:
  2 goats -- Sparta no.
  unknown from the
      Menelaion
    bucranium infr with
      Branch 1 betw the
      horns
  waterbirds -- X 224*
    in center
PT 19A, R: 2 agrimia -- I 45
  Branch 1 Tree infr
PT 19B, L: 2 bovines -- I 130
  infr & bel
PT 20, L: 2 horses? -- I 390
  bel
PT 23A, L: 2 boars -- I 276
  ab
PT 23A, R: 2 boars -- Berlin

FG 49b (AGDS II 45b)
   2 ab
PT 24, L; Filler: 2 bulls -- I
   318
      ab
PT 24, R; Filler -- 2 bulls
   ABOVE
      I 275
      Berlin FG 49a (AGDS II
         45a)
PT 25A, L: lion & agrimi -- I
   Supp. 95
      infr
PT 25A, R: 2 goats - V 348/
   350/392
      infr on V 348
      infr & ab on V 349/350/
         392
PT 25C, R: 2 agrimia -- X 260
<u>Branch 1 Tree</u> infr
PT 28A: 2 kids -- V 747
   ab each
PT 30A: 2 bulls -- I Supp. 91
   ab & groundline dotted like
      a <u>Baton</u> with 2 <u>Branch 1
      Tree</u> at each end
PT 31B:
   2 waterbirds, in the center
      I 213 & HMs 495 (AT 27)
   2 griffins -- I 196
      bel
PT 34B: 2 lions -- I 60
   betw
PT 36 cl: 2 lions -- BSA cast
   184 (Betts 1981a: fig. 10)
      2 bel 1 lion
PT 39A: lion R vs bull -- ?X
   218
      bel
PT 47B: lion L vs bird -- AM
   1938.1083 (CS 328)
      ab
Ch. 2B: Men (duel) -- ?HMs 190
   (KZ 190)
      inb
Ch. 2B: Men (religious) -- II
   3.7

Waisted Altar with <u>Branch 1</u>
   & flanked by 2 <u>Branch 1</u>;
   <u>Branch 1 Tree</u> inb of the
   man
Ch. 2C: Women (single;
   (frontal) -- HMs 669 (KSPI
      C9)
   flanked by 2
   (stands L) --
      II 3.72
      2 pairs flank
      XII 12D
         salutes a <u>Branch 1
         Tree</u>
      HM G 3349 (CMCG 368)
      2 flank
   (stands R) -- II 4.165
      2 <u>Branch 1</u> flank
   (misc.) -- HMs 661 (KSPI Cb)
      at right
Ch. 2E: People at a <u>Shrine</u> (two
   women antithetic) -- Chania
   2071 & 2112 (Papapostolou
   1977: no. 27)
      betw, <u>Branch 1 Tree</u> grows
         from <u>Shrine</u>?
Ch. 3A: Men & Animals (lion)
   -- I 512
      <u>Branch 1 Tree</u> infr
Ch. 3C: Man Hunts Animals
   (fisherman) -- V 181
      2 flank & 2 betw fish &
      man
Ch. 3E: Animal Games (bull-
   catching) -- I 274
      <u>Branch 1 Tree</u> at right
Ch. 5B: Animal Faces
   (lion, Snake Frame) -- HMs
      39 (KZ 167)
      ab
   (bucrania, pair), betw
      V 326
      V 327
      AM 1938.952 (CS 104)
   (boar) -- AM 1938.1032a (CS
   243a)
      ab

Ch. 5E: Waterbirds
   (single, stands R) -- I
     Supp. 99
       ab
   (single, swims) -- II 3.350
    ab
   (pair, 1 stands/1 lands) --
    II 3.250
      ab
   (pair, fly L) -- V 439
    2 flank
   (pair, misc.) -- V 422a
    ab
   (trio) -- V 582
    infr of each
Ch. 5F: Alerions (head L) -- X
248
  ab
Ch. 6A: People-Animals
   (agrimi-women, head R) --
    HM G 3088 (CMCG 376)
      2 ab
   (Minotaur)
     XIII 84 -- Branch 1 Tree
      (from HC or Palm) inb
     AM 1938.1072 (CS 323) --
      3 Branch 1 Tree in
       field
Ch. 6B: Genii -- I 231
   Altar holds 3 Branch 1
Ch. 9B: Centered Circles (4)
  -- V 152
    2 flank
Ch. 9E: Spirals -- HMs 147 (KZ
174)
   ab & bel
Ch. 9Q: Misc. Lines -- II
4.177
   ab & bel

Branch 2
PT 1A, L;
  IN FRONT
   agrimi -- I Supp. 70
   caprid? -- V 342
  ABOVE & BELOW
   quadruped -- I 38 & I

    Supp. 154
IN FRONT, ABOVE, & BELOW
   quadruped -- AM AE 1796
    (CS 42P)
PT 1A, R; Filler
IN FRONT
   agrimi
    V 339
    V 341
    V 342
    IX 176
ABOVE
   bull -- V 29 & X 263
IN FRONT & ABOVE
   bull -- Melos 569
   agrimi -- I 210 & V 401
Miscellaneous
   bull
    I Supp. 157 -- infr &
     bel
    V 227 -- infr, ab,
     inb, & bel
    Melos 573 -- infr, ab,
     & bel
   agrimi
    V 340 -- infr & inb
    X 202 -- infr, ab, &
     inb
   quadruped
    V 615 -- ab & bel
    XII 305 -- infr, ab, &
     bel
PT 1B, R;
  bull -- NMA no. unknown
   from Prosymna T. 8
    ab
  dog -- II 3.160
   bel
PT 1C, L; bull -- I Supp. 24
infr & inb
PT 1C, R;
  IN FRONT
   bull -- I 25 & I Supp.
    23
   agrimi -- X 178
Miscellaneous
   quadruped -- I Supp. 4

encircles
PT 1D, R; agrimi -- V 402
    inb
PT 1/2, R; bull -- I 138
    ab
PT 2, L; Filler
    IN FRONT
        bull -- V 281
        agrimi -- X 179
    Miscellaneous
        bull -- I Supp. 48
            bel
PT 2, R; Filler
    BEHIND
        quadruped -- VII 155
    IN FRONT
        bull
            I Supp. 142
            V 172
            V 442
            X 180
            X 244
        quadruped
            V 42 & Sparta no.
                unknown
    ABOVE
        bull -- V 417
            ab
    BELOW
        bull -- V 377
        agrimi -- V 9
    IN FRONT & ABOVE
        bull -- V 379 & VII 204
        quadruped -- V 187 & V
            606
    ABOVE & BELOW
        bull
            V 315
            VIII 99 -- 2 ab? & 1
                bel
    Miscellaneous
        bull
            V 8 -- infr, ab, inb,
                & bel
            ?V 172 -- infr & bel
            IX 203 -- infr & inb
        goat -- X 181

encircles
PT 5A, L; Filler: quadruped --
    V 228 -- ab
PT 5A, R; Filler
    bull -- V 150
        infr
    quadruped -- V 33
        ab & bel
PT 6, L; Filler: bull -- X 173
    infr
PT 13A, R: bull
    ABOVE
        Munich A.1307 (AGDS I 88)
        V 280 -- ab
PT 14A, R: bull -- V 23
    ab
PT 28B: 2 quadrupeds -- V 5
    ab each
PT 29B: 2 bulls -- V 151
    ab
PT 39A: dog R vs agrimi -- I
    511
        infr
Ch. 2B: Men (3 or more, salute)
    -- I 42
        encirles
Ch. 2E: People at a Shrine
    (tree-pulling, no Omphalos)
    -- I 126
        ab L (ab woman at left):
            3 Branch 2
Ch. 5B: Animal Faces
    (bucrania, single) -- V
    346
            encircles & ab & bel
            caprid
    (bucrania, pair) -- X 198
        flanks/encircles
Ch. 5C: Animal Heads (caprid)
    -- I 21
        encircles
Ch. 8A: Writing -- I 156
    encircles
Ch. 9B: Centered Circles
    (3) -- I Supp. 46
        in field

(4)
    I 402
    I Supp. 45 -- 2
    I Supp. 165
    V 152 -- 2 in center
    X 193 -- 2 vertical & 1
      horizontal
Ch. 9G: Rosettes (late) -- I
  Supp. 161
    encircles
Ch. 9Q: Misc. Lines
  V 397 -- flanking, in box
  V 679 -- in the field

<u>Branch 3</u>
PT 1A, L;
  agrimi
    XII 195 -- <u>Branch 3</u>/
      <u>Pica</u> ab
    XII 308 -- infr
  quadruped -- V 186
    infr
PT 1A, R; Filler
  IN FRONT
    bull
      V 159 & V 254
    agrimi
      V 338
      AM 1938.1096 (CS 19P)
      HMs 36 (KZ 125)
      Munich no. unknown
        (AGDS I 78)
  Miscellaneous
    boar -- I 135
      ab
    quadruped -- V 425
      bel
    agrimi -- V 169
      infr & ab
PT 1B, L;
  ABOVE
    boar -- HM G 3528
    horse? -- V 365
PT 1B, R: agrimi -- V 160
  ab

PT 1C, R: ABOVE
    bull -- I 25
    agrimi -- X 178
PT 1D, R; bull -- IX 108
  ab & infr
PT 2, L; Filler: bull
  I 59 -- ab
  I Supp. 48 -- infr
  V 322 -- infr
PT 2, R; Filler
  IN FRONT -- bull
    I Supp. 143
    V 315
    V 377
    VIII 99
    Munich A.1308 (AGDS I
      89)
  ABOVE: quadruped -- V 4
  IN FRONT & ABOVE
    goat -- VIII 98
    quadruped -- Munich no.
      unknown (AGDS I 77)
  Miscellaneous
    bull -- V 512
      infr, ab, & 2 bel
    quadruped -- V 161
      encircles
PT 3, L: bull -- V 580
3 <u>Branch 3</u> beh
PT 5A, L; Filler: agrimi --
  XII 308 -- infr
PT 6, L; Filler
  bull -- IX 169
    ab = <u>Pica</u>? ab
  calf -- II 3.134
PT 6, R; Filler
  bull
    II 3.197
    V 575 -- bel
    X 311 -- infr & inb
  agrimi -- I 31
    infr
  goat -- II 3.90PT 10A, L:
  griffin -- Chania 2067 &
    2068 (Papapostolou 1977:
    no. 15)
      ab

PT 13A, R: bull
?II 3.335
V 153 -- ab
PT 14A, R: bull -- IX 118
ab
PT 14B, L: agrimi -- X 321
bel
PT 14B, R: agrimi -- AM
1925.45 (CS 348)
    ab
PT 25A, R: 2 goats -- X 2
infr
PT 25C, R: 2 goats -- X 174
infr
PT 28A: 2 bulls -- V 337
ab
PT 37B ccl: 3 quadrupeds
(bulls?) -- I 47
    betw each
PT 39A: lion R vs bull -- V
361
    encircles
Ch. 2C: Women (single;
stands frontal)/Ch. 2E:
    People at a <u>Shrine</u>
    (woman in a <u>Shrine</u>) --
    X 270
        building made of 2
        concentric boxes
        of <u>Branch 3</u>
    at <u>Altar</u>) -- I 410
        2 <u>Branch 3</u> (<u>Palm</u>
        fronds?) inb of the
        woman
Ch. 3A: Man & Animals (bull)
-- VII 100
    bel
Ch. 5B: Animal Faces
(bucrania, single)
    ABOVE
        V 513
        X 236 -- 2 encircles
        V 748
        Munich 21765 (AGDS I
        24)
        Turkey mus. unkn. --
        bisects the face &

encircles
Ch. 5J: Octopus (cut-style) --
II 3.251
    at left, half-encircles
Ch. 7A: <u>Branches</u> (<u>Branch 4</u>) --
X 238 -- 2
Ch. 8F: <u>Figure-8 Shields</u> --
VII 203
    a wavy line with strokes
    (<u>Branch 3?</u>) encircle
Ch. 9A: Paisley
I Supp. 166 -- encircles
AM 1938.1099 (GGFR pl. 197)
    -- fills
Ch. 9B: Centered Circles (2)
II 3.127 -- 2 flank
V 376 -- encircles
V 429 -- 2
Ch. 9G: Rosettes
(early)
    X 208 -- betw
    HMs 484 (AT 12) --
    encircles
(late) -- Hannover no.
unknown (AGDS IV 9)
encircles

<u>Branch 4</u>
PT 1A, L; Filler: agrimi -- XII
308
    bel
PT 2, R; Filler: bull -- V 417
infr
PT 6, R; Filler: agrimi -- I 31
ab
PT 11, R; Filler: agrimi? --
V 283
    ab
PT 13A, L: lion -- HMs 302
(KSPI R33)
    ab
PT 14A, R: lion -- HMs 253
(KSPI N1)
    ab
PT 17A, L: doe & fawn -- I 13
infr
PT 19A, R: 2 bulls -- HMs 216

(KSPI R86)
    bel
PT 25B, L: 2 calves -- V 359
   infr
Ch. 2B: Men (3 or more,
   salute) -- I 369
     ab (encircles?)
Ch. 7B: Misc. Plants -- AM
   1938.948 (CS 2S)
     Branch 4 encircles
Ch. 9B: Centered Circles
   (2) -- X 196
     2 & 1 S-shaped betw
   (3) -- I Supp. 46
     in the field

15B
Conventionalized Plants

Fronds
PT 1A, L; Filler:
   ABOVE
     lion -- HM 27
     agrimi -- I Supp. 70 &
      VIII 129
   BELOW
     agrimi -- IV 245
       bel
   IN FRONT & BELOW
     bull -- IX 174
PT 1A, R; Filler:
   IN FRONT
     agrimi -- VII 239 & II
      4.123
     goat -- II 3.40
PT 1B, R; bull
   VII 163 -- bel
   X 222 -- tall, beh
   HMs 311+KZ (KSPI R84) -- 2
    ab
PT 1D, R; bull -- IX 108
   bel
PT 2, L; Filler:

lioness -- AM 1873.129 (CS
   330)
   infr
caprid -- HMs 72 (KZ 124)
   bel
PT 2, R; Filler:
IN FRONT
     bull -- HM 2301
      rocks (Frond?)
BELOW
     bull -- VII 161
     calf -- II 3.336
ABOVE & BELOW
     bull -- HMs 308I & Rho
      Zeta (KSPI R74/97?)
PT 5A, L; Filler:
IN FRONT
     lion -- VII 94
     winged agrimi -- X 233
ABOVE
     agrimi -- IX 140 & Melos
      568
     goat -- IV 264
     deer -- HM G 3224 (CMCG
      247)
     Babylonian Dragon -- HMs
      637 (Sk 11)
       3
PT 6, L; Filler:
ABOVE
     lion -- V 604
     agrimi -- IV 53D
     griffin -- IV 266 & HMs
      564 (AT 99)
PT 6, R; Filler:
IN FRONT
     griffin -- XIII 56
ABOVE
     calf -- V 316 & Florence
      82820
     agrimi -- VII 250
     goat -- Rumania Academy
      434
IN FRONT & ABOVE: bull
   VII 261
   Munich A.1190 (AGDS I
    39) = Pica

PT 8, L: lion
   ABOVE
      V 498
      IX 15D
      XII 135a -- with circle
      AM 1941.155b (CS 30Pb)
PT 10A, L:
   ABOVE
      lion
         II 3.346
         II 4.19
         II 4.139
         IV 228
         V 745
         AM 1971.1151
           (Boardman 1973:
           no. 10)
         HM 2506
         HM G 3143 (CMCG 261)
         HM G 3324c (CMCG
          185c)
      bull -- XII 272
      agrimi -- V 730
      boar -- HM 2096
         2
PT 10A, R:
   lion
      V 182 -- ab
      HM G 3089 (CMCG 262) --
         ab
   sphinx -- II 3.39
      bel, at right
PT 10B, L:
   ABOVE
      bull
         IV 305
         V 191b
      agrimi
         V 191c
PT 11, L; Filler: lion
   ABOVE
      V 191a
      HM G 3434 (CMCG 263)
PT 11, R; Filler:
   IN FRONT
      griffin -- VII 258
   ABOVE -- lion

      IV 258 -- ab
      XIII 23 -- 2
PT 13A, L: lion -- V 680
   ab
PT 13A, R: calf -- Melos 571
   ab
PT 13C, R: lion -- IX 107
   at left
PT 14D, L: <u>Minotaur</u> -- IX 127
   infr
PT 17A, L: lioness & cub --
   XII 286
      ab
PT 18B, R: cow & calf
   ABOVE
      V 317 -- 2
      XII 14D
   BELOW
      IV 272
PT 19A, L: waterbirds --
   X 224*
      groundline bel ending
         in flanking <u>Fronds</u>
PT 19A, R:
   2 goats -- II 4.197
      ab
   2 waterbirds -- IV 246
      2 flank & one betw
PT 19B, R: 2 goats -- VII 98
   ab
PT 21, R:
   2 bulls -- XII 287
      ab
   2 calves -- IX 111
      infr
PT 21, variant: 2 ibex/bulls
   -- VII 159
      tall beh
PT 23C, R: 2 lions -- XIII 24
   half-<u>Frond</u> ab
PT 24, L: 2 bulls -- Munich
   A.1193 (AGDS I 38)
      ab
PT 25B, L: 2 quadrupeds -- V
   311
      ab & infr

PT 25B, R:
  IN FRONT
    2 goats -- V 600
    2 sheep -- AM 1941.144
      (CS 363)
  Misc.
    2 calves
      VII 115b -- ab
      AM 1941.92 (CS 383)
        -- inb
PT 27B, R: 3 goats -- AM
1941.121 (CS 286)
    ab at left
PT 28B: 2 bulls -- XIII 27
ab each bull
PT 32C:
  2 lions -- IX 112
    ab
  2 agrimia -- HM 2271
    ab at right
PT 31B: 2 lions -- Lamia BE
956
    ab
PT 46: lion L vs bull -- VII
115a
    ab
PT 47B: lion L vs bird -- AM
1938.1083 (CS 328)
    ab
PT 52A: 2 griffins vs bull R --
V 216
    Frond/Pica in bull's back
Ch. 2B: Men (pair, duel) --
XII 292
    ab L
Ch. 2C: Women
(single, in boat) -- HMs 434
    (AT 118)
    a boat has a Frond prow
      aegis
(pair, salute) -- IX 164
    2 flank
Ch. 2D: Men & Women (man & 2
women)
    V 173 -- ab & man holds
      a long Frond or staff
    Chania 1024 -- ab double

Omphalos/Squill
  HMs no. unknown (AT 140)
    betw woman & Shrine
Ch. 2E: People at a Shrine
(person at left) -- I 86
  Frond at left
(person at right) -- V 422b
  flank & separate the
    women
Ch. 3E: Animal Games (bull-
  leaping,
  Diving) -- AM 1938.1074 (CS
  209)
    infr
  Floating) -- II 3.271
    infr
Ch. 4A: Women & Animals
(antithetic) -- AM
  1971.1139 (Boardman
    1973: no.6)
    2 ab with a row of
      dots ab
(woman inb) -- BSA cast 188
  bel
Ch. 5E: Birds & Waterbirds
(birds, single) -- Hamburg
  no. unknown (AGDS IV 6)
    infr
(waterbirds, single)
    V 234 -- ab
    Jantzen Coll. (Zazoff
      1963: no 6)
      infr
(pair) -- II 4.191
    ab each
Ch. 5F: Alerions (head R)
  at left -- IV 260 & IV 298
  2 flank the head -- XIII
  118
Ch. 5G: Insects (misc.) -- V
579
    betw 2 pairs of legs
Ch. 6A: Genii -- AM 1938.1043
(CS 304)
    2 flank
Ch. 8J: Misc. (river with
fish?) -- X 69*

3 ab
Ch. 9B: Centered Circles (3)
-- I Supp. 164a
betw
Ch. 9G: Rosettes -- V 407
betw each leaf

Weeds
PT 1A, R; Filler: bull -- ⋁
HM 79
3 ab
PT 1B, L; sow -- Brummer Coll.
2 ab
PT 2, L; Filler: lioness -- I
Supp. 168
ab & bel
PT 3, R: goat -- VIII 47a
4 bel
PT 6, L; Filler: lion -- X 152
rocks/Weed ab (cf. IX 7D)
PT 6, R; Filler: quadruped -- I
328
bel
PT 12, R: lion -- II 491
upside down bel
PT 13A, R: bull -- V 500
bel
PT 18B, R: cow & calf -- HM G
3309 (CMCG 303)
small Weed bel
PT 19A, R: waterbird -- II
2.52
ab
PT 23A, L: 2 boars -- HM G
3192 (CMCG 302)
3 ab
PT 25B, L: 2 lions -- IX 13D
2 ab
PT 25C, R: 2 goats -- I 30
2 ab
PT 47B: griffin L vs Babylonian
Dragon
XII 291
at left
Ch. 3A: Man & Animals
(several animals) -- HMs 160
(KSPI Q19)

fill the field
(bulls) -- AM 1938.1076 (CS
247)
3? at right
Ch. 3E: Animal Games
(man in front) -- HMs 1001
(Betts 63)
Palms beh or Weeds
bel

Weed bel betw the legs of
the genius or man
(rides other animals) -- V
638
2 bel
Ch. 5A: Misc. Quadrupeds -- I
Supp. 75
ab & 2 bel
Ch. 5E: Birds & Waterbirds
(waterbirds,
single)
VII 44 -- ab & 3 bel
AM 1938.979 (CS 181) --
2 ab bird
HMs 579 (AT 19) -- from
periphery encircle
pair)
I Supp. 33 -- ab
II 3.142 -- 2 ab
II 3.179-- 2 flank & 1
betw
Ch. 5G: Insects
(butterflies) -- X 102
2 bel
(misc.) -- VII 70
2 groundlines ab with 3
Weeds
Ch. 5H: Fish
(single)
AM 1938.1052 (CS 224) --
encircle
II 3.49 -- ab upside
down & bel
(pair)
XII 138-- ab & bel
HMs 474 (AT 9)-- ab, at
left, & 2 at the
periphery bel each

fish
Ch. 6B: Genii -- V 440
   inb
Ch. 9H: Cross -- X 118
   in each quadrant

15C
Conventionalized <u>Trees</u>

<u>Tree 1</u>
PT 1A, L;
   bull -- II 4.214
      infr
   stag -- XIII 6
      infr
PT 1A, R; Filler:
IN FRONT
    griffin -- HMs 97 (KZ
        178)
       variant (= <u>Palm 4</u>?)
BEHIND
    goat -- V 598
IN FRONT & BEHIND
    lion -- IX 149
      small
    bull -- HM 604
PT 1B, R; bull -- IX 157
   beh
PT 2, R: lioness -- II 3.122
  small <u>Tree 1</u> bel
PT 5A, R; Filler:
   bull -- I 23
      ab
   calf -- I Supp. 191
      beh
PT 13A, L: bull -- V 7
   2 ab
PT 19A, R: 2 goats -- II 4.197
   infr
PT 19B, R: 2 goats
   VII 98 -- infr
   XIII 7 -- beh
PT 21, R: 2 calves -- Berlin

FG 44 (AGDS II 49)
   inb
PT 23B/24, R: 2 bulls -- I 91
   2 flank
PT 27A, R: 3 goats -- I 105
   bel
PT 27B, R: 3 goats -- AM
   1941.121 (CS 286)
      infr
PT 28A: 2 sphinxes -- I 87
   betw
PT 28B:
BETWEEN
    2 bulls -- XIII 27
    2 calves -- I 58
PT 31A: 2 lions -- IV 40D
   betw
PT 36 cl: 2 bulls -- I 53
   2 betw
PT 49A, L: dog vs stag -- I
   363
      infr
PT 49B, R: lion vs bull
   infr upside down
Ch. 3A: Man & Animals
(bull)
    Ring from Varkiza T. I
      -- <u>Tree 1 Frond</u> in
      the center beh bull
Ch. 3C: Man Hunts Animals
(lion) -- Peronne no.
   unknown from Thessalo-
   nike, The Danicourt Ring
      bel each lion
Ch. 3E: Animal Games (bull-
   leaping;
IN FRONT
    Diving) -- V 597
    Floating) -- Munich
      A.1180 (AGDS I 45)
BELOW
    uncertain poses) -- I
      82
      horizontal R
Ch. 5D: Protomes (caprid) --
   VIII 84
    infr of each protome

Ch. 5E: Birds & Waterbirds
  (birds, single) -- XII 214
    infr
  (waterbirds, pair) -- II
      3.279
    betw
Ch. 5I: Dolphins (pair) -- II
    3.279
  flanked by 2 waterbirds

Tree 2
PT 1A, R; Filler: goat -- I
  188
    branch ab
PT 2, R; Filler: bull -- I 76
  beh
PT 10A, L: bull
  IN BACK -- II 3. 64a &
    XII 249
PT 10A, R: bull -- V 198
  inb
PT 14A, L: bull -- IX 125
  frond ab & bel
PT 16A, R: nanny & kid
  HMs 122 (KSPI N7)
    infr
  Chania 1018 (Papapostolou
      1977: no. 12)
    beh
PT 24, L; Filler: 2 bulls -- II
    3.62
  infr & inb
PT 25B, R: 2 goat -- I
    Supp. 111
  infr
PT 28A: 2 agrimia -- I 155
  Tree 2 betw & beh each
PT 31: 2 agrimia -- I 266
  betw
Ch. 2B: Men (single, Omphalos)
  -- HMm 1034
    grows from rocks
Ch. 2E: People at a Shrine
  grows from a Shrine
    (person at left)
        II 3.15 & AM 1938.1127
          (CS 250)

(tree-pulling, no
    Omphalos) -- I 126

Tree 3
PT 1B, L; bull
  II 4.126 -- bef
  II 4.221 -- beh
PT 1B, R; bull
  IX 17D -- Tree 3/Cypress
    Tree beh
  X 139 -- Tree 3 crown ab
PT 6, L; Filler: agrimi -- AM
  1938.946 (CS 201)
    inb
PT 14B, L; Filler: bull -- I
  Supp. 71
    bel
Ch. 2E: People at a Shrine
  grows from a Shrine
    (person at left) -- IX
      163
    (person at right) -- XII
      264
    crown ab an agrimi
    (tree-pulling, no
      Omphalos) -- I 119
Ch. 5B: Animal Faces (lion &
  bull) -- I 18
    2 flank

Tree 4
Ch. 2E: People at a Shrine
  (tree-pulling, man at
  Omphalos) -- HMm 989
    grows from a Shrine

Tree 5
PT 1A, R; Filler: bull
  I 373 -- ab
  I Supp. 174 -- beh
PT 5A, L; Filler: agrimi
  I 242 -- beh
  XII 296 -- ab
PT 5B, R; Filler: agrimi -- I
  242
    beh

PT 10A, L: bull -- I Supp. 34
  beh
PT 10A, R: stag -- V 665
  branch ab
Ch. 2C: Women
  (single, stands R) -- HMs
    523 (AT 138)
      grows from rocks
  (pair, flank object) -- HMs
    576 (AT 137)
      grows from rocks
Ch. 2D: Men & Women (pair) --
  II 3.305
    betw
Ch. 2E: People at a Shrine
  grows from a Shrine
    (person at left) --
      Chania 2055 (Papapos-
      tolou 1977: no.28)
    (tree-pulling, no
      Omphalos) -- Once
      in the Evans coll.,
      The Ring of Minos
    (at the Shrine) -- HMs
      no. unknown (AT 140)
Ch. 3A: Man & Animals (bull)
  -- HMs 85 (KZ 102)
    beh

<u>Tree 6</u>
PT 5A, R; Filler: calf -- I
  122
    crown ab
PT 10A, L: bull
  II 3.293 -- ab
  XII 289 -- branch ab
PT 18B, L: cow & calf -- XIII
  29
    infr/ab
Ch. 2C: Women (4 or more) -- I
  17
    inb
Ch. 2D: Men & Women (pair)
  -- I 219
    grows from a Pithos/
      Shield-in-Profile &
      bends R

Ch. 2E: People at a Shrine
  grows from a Shrine
    (person at left) --
      II 3.252, The Mochlos
      Ring
    (tree-pulling, man at
      Omphalos) -- II
      3.114

Identifiable Trees
<u>Cypress</u>
  <u>Tree</u>
    PT 1B, R: bull -- IX 17D
      <u>Tree 3</u>/<u>Cypress</u> beh
    Ch. 2E: People at a
      Shrine (2 women
      antithetic) -- I
      127
        at right
  <u>Branch</u>
    PT 1A, R; Filler:
      bull -- V 751
        infr
    PT 29B: 2 griffins -- I
      102
        2 flank
    Ch. 2B: Men (single,
      Omphalos) -- HMm 1034
        ab
    Ch. 2C: Women (4 or more)
      -- II 3.51
        ab Heaven Line at
          left
    Ch. 2D: Men & Women
      (pair)
        I 219 -- ab
        X 261 -- ab
    Ch. 2E: People at a
      Shrine (2 women
      antithetic) -- I 127
        2 on the middle
          tier flank the
          Shrine

Ch. 4A: Women & Animals
(woman seated L at
  right) -- I 179
    ab wavy <u>Heaven</u>
      <u>Line</u> & sup-
      porting jugs
      carried by
      genii
(friezes) -- II 3.103
  ab
Ch. 4B: <u>Potnia Theron</u>
(misc.) -- I 379
    <u>Cypress Branch</u>/
      sword held by
      each of the 2
      genii flanking
      the <u>Potnia</u>
Ch. 8F: <u>Figure-8 Shields</u>
  -- II 3.113
  2 flank

<u>Palms</u> (see Ch. 2A: Body Parts
[man's face] -- HM 26b [KZ
70])

<u>Palm 1</u>
  PT 3, R: lion -- HMs 321
    (KSPI R37)
  beh
  PT 10B, L: lion -- X 150
  crown ab
  PT 12, L: bull -- X 143*
  beh
  PT 19B, L: 2 goats -- I
    74
  inb
  PT 20, R: 2 lions -- HMs
  321 & 40, Pigorini
  no. (KN KSPI R37, AT
  146, KZ 105)
    beh
  PT 21, R: 2 lions -- I
    71
  infr & 2 ab
  PT 39A: dog L vs kid --
  AM 1941.119 (CS 3P)
    horizontal bel

PT 46: lion R vs bull --
  I 253
    beh bull & at right
Ch. 2E: People at a
<u>Shrine</u> (at the <u>Shrine</u>)
  -- HMs no. unknown (AT
  140)
    <u>Palm 1</u>? betw women
      & <u>Shrine</u>
Ch. 4A: Women with
Animals
  (antithetic) -- AM
    1938.1097 (CS
    21P)
      beh the bull
  (friezes) -- I
    Supp. 114
Ch. 8G: <u>Sacred Knots</u>/
<u>Robes</u> (<u>Sacred Knot</u>)
  -- HMs 150 (KSPI S6)
    flanked by 2 <u>Sacred</u>
    <u>Knots</u>

<u>Palm 2</u>
  PT 32B: 2 agrimia -- I
  123
    betw

<u>Palm 3</u>
  PT 18B, R: cow & calf --
  Berlin FG 24 (AGDS II
  47)
    unfinished <u>Palm</u>
    3/sign (<u>ImpTr</u>
    variant?) ab

<u>Palm 4</u> (see: Ch. 15B: Con-
ventionalized Plants
[<u>Tree 1</u>] -- HMs 97 [KZ
178], above)

PT 1A, L; bull -- HMs 211
  (KZ 198)
PT 1A, R; Filler:
  bull (IN FRONT)
    AM 1938.1040 (CS
    307) -- variant
    HMs 129 (KSPI J1;
    CS 45S)

goat (IN FRONT)
  I 188 -- variant
  HMs 296 (KSPI K10)
PT 1B, L;
  bull -- V 157
    2 beh
  boar -- I 343
    3 beh
PT 1B, R; bull
  I 88 -- 2 beh
  HMs 311/KZ (KSPI R84)
    -- Palm 4/Pica bel
PT 2, R; Filler: bull --
  VII 113
    infr
PT 2/6, R; bull --
  Nafplion no. unknown
  from Tiryns
    beh
PT 2/8, R; quadruped --
  I 516
    beh?
PT 6, R; Filler: bull
  -- HM 2126
    ImpTr/Palm 4 ab
PT 10A, R: bull --
  Berlin FG 22 (AGDS II
  44)
    ab
PT 13A, R: bull -- HMs
  111 (KSPI N6)
    beh
PT 14A, R:
  lion -- I 358
    beh
  agrimi -- V 587
    2 Palm 4/Asphodel
    bel
PT 19B, L:
  2 goats -- I 74
    infr
  2 bulls -- I 515/HMs
    109 (KSPI J2)
      ab
PT 27A, R: 3 goats -- I
  105
    bel, infr

PT 29A: 2 calves -- I
  375
    3 betw
PT 31A: 2 lions -- IV
  304
    central Column/
    Palm 4?
PT 39A: griffin L vs bull
  -- L. Morgan Library
  1077 (Pini 1980: no.
  A5)
    infr
Ch. 2B: Men (single,
  Altar) -- V 608
    at left
Ch. 3E: Animal-Sacrifice
  -- Berlin FG 22 (AGDS
  II 44)
    horizontal R ab

Miscellaneous Palms
  PT 2, R;
    Plain: bull -- XIII 10
    ab
    Filler: bull -- VII
    162
      branch attached
      to a stand?
      infr
  PT 6, R; Filler: agrimi
    -- AM 1020.116 (CS 8P)
    infr
  PT 7, L; lion -- XIII 13
  fronds ab

  PT 39A: dog L vs agrimi/
    kid-man -- XII 242
      schematic, infr of
      stag
  Ch. 2C: Women (single, at
    Altar) -- I 410
      2 Branch 3 (Palm
      fronds?) inb of
      the woman

Ch. 3E: Animal Games (man
    infr) -- HMs 1001
    (Betts 63)
        Palms beh or Weeds
        bel
Ch. 5B: Animal Faces,
    frond ab
        (bulls) -- AM 1
        938.976 (CS 291)
        (boars) -- HMs 29b

15D
Flowers

(see Ch. 3A: Man & Animals
[bird] -- HMs 134 [KSPI Q14])

Lilies
Ch. 2A: Parts of the Human
    Body (hands) -- HMs 153
    (KSPI R102)
        hand from the right
        holds Lily
Ch. 2C: Women (4 or more) -- I
    17
    woman at left holds Lilies
    in both hands
Ch. 2E: People at a Shrine
    (person at right) -- I 279
        at right, woman holds
        2 Lilies in her
        right hand

Miscellaneous Flowers
PT 18B, R: cow & calf -- X
    255
    X 255 Flower ab (cf. Kn HMs
    377 = KSPI Va)
PT 31B: 2 geese? -- HMs 4b
    (KZ 52)
        flower ab center
Ch. 2C: Women

(single, stands L) -- HM G
    3145 (CMCG 367)
        flower inb
(pair, salute center) --
    HMs 200 (KZ 200)
        flowers in field
(4 or more) -- I 17
    seated woman holds
        poppies in her
        right hand
(misc.) -- II 3.51
    bel: 4 plants
        (Asphodels?)
Ch. 5E: Birds & Waterbirds
    (birds, misc.) -- HMs 92b
    (KZ 54)
        flower bel center
Ch. 6A: People-Animals
    (caprid-people, agrimi-
    woman)
        HMs 10 gamma (KZ 44)
        HMs no. unknown (KZ
        28)

15E
Papyrus

PT 8, R: lion -- Munich A.1194
    (AGDS I Munich 64)
PT 26, L & R: 3 sheep -- HMs
    210 (KSPI R29)
        R, separates the
        registers
PT 26, R/Ch. 5E: Birds &
    Waterbirds (waterbirds,
    trio)
        3 waterbirds -- AM
        1938.1066 (CS 343)
        2 ab & 1 infr
PT 31: 2 griffins -- HMs no.
unknown (AT 96)
    betw

Ch. 2B: Men (pair) -- I 131
   3 lotos/<u>Papyrus</u> flowers
      betw
Ch. 2C: Women (single) --
   Berlin FG 50a (AGDS II
   12a)
      inb
Ch. 2E: People at a <u>Shrine</u>
   (woman sits on <u>Shrine</u>) --
   Berlin Antike Abteilung
   no. unknown
      inb (at extreme right)
Ch. 5E: Birds & Waterbirds
   (waterbirds, pair) -- AM
   1938.1068/HMs 377/
   OTheta (KSPI Va/CS
   51S)
      top: waterbirds
         separated by a
         <u>Papyrus</u>
      bottom: waterbird
         flanked by 2 <u>Papyri</u>
Ch. 6D: Misc. Monster (2 winged
   bird-people?) -- ?HM 2785
   from Knossos, MUM (Popham
   et al.1984: Misc. 10)
      flanked
Ch. 7B: Plants (misc.)/Ch. 9R:
   Geometric (misc.) -- HMs 15
   (KZ 132)
      3 <u>Papyrus</u> flowers betw
         each boss
Ch. 7B: Plants (misc.)/Ch. 9E:
   Spirals (volute-spiral) --
   HMs 172a (KZ 172)
      spiral topped by <u>Papyrus</u>
         flower?
Ch. 9G: Rosettes (early) -- AM
   1971.1138 (Boardman 1973:
   no. 17)
      betw rosette petals

15F
Rosettes

(see: Chs. 5K: Shellfish -- HMs
387i [CS 7Sa] & 16C: <u>Dado 8</u>)

PT 28A: 2 pairs of owls/Ch.
   5E: Birds (owls) -- HMs 391
   (KSPI L38)
      in center
Ch. 2A: Parts of the Human
   Body (parts of the face) --
   HM G 3298 (CMCG 426)
      2 dot rosettes flank
Ch. 4A: Women & Animals
   (monsters) -- I 179
      half-rosette decorates
      the bench inb
Ch. 5B: Animal Faces
   (lions, 4 or more) -- HMs
   93 (KZ 135)
      in center
   (bulls, single, simple) --
   HMs 165 (KZ 165)
      ab, betw horns
   (stag) -- HMs 643 & 644
   (Sk 17)
      ab, betw horns
Ch. 5E: Birds & Waterbirds
   (birds, misc.) -- HMs 391
   (KSPI L38)
      2 registers of owls
         separated by a
         rosette
Ch. 7B: Misc. Plants (<u>Papyrus</u>)
   -- HMs 15 (KZ 132)
      3 boss rosettes
Ch. 8I: <u>Double Ax</u> -- HMs 264
   (KSPI R100)
      in center

15G
Miscellaneous Plants

branches (see: PT 1A, R & PT
2, R; these have 10 or more
examples & are not listed
here)

PT 1A, L; Filler
IN FRONT
    agrimi
        X 115
        HM no. unknown
            (Younger & Betts
            1979: no. 3)
    ABOVE
    agrimi -- VII 167
    quadruped -- V 670
    ABOVE & BELOW
        lion -- HMs 320 (KSPI
        R79)
    IN FRONT, ABOVE, & BELOW
        bull
            XII 305
            Munich acc. 22846
                (AGDS I 76)
    IN FRONT, ABOVE, IN BACK,
    & BELOW
        lion -- HM 2617?
PT 1B, L; quadruped -- HM no.
unknown (Eccles photo)
    ab
PT 1B, R; bull
    II 4.83 -- ab
    XII 303 -- ab & bel
    NMA no. unknown from
        Prosymna T. 8 -- bel
PT 1C, L; bull -- I 479
    ab
PT 1C, R: dog -- II 3.160
    ab
?PT 1D, R; bull -- I 169
    bel
PT 2, L; Filler:
lion
    ABOVE

AM 1941.155ba (CS
    30Pa)
Munich A.1199 (AGDS
    I 66)
bull
    V 281 -- bel
    XIII 131 -- infr
PT 2, R; Filler: bull -- II
4.4
    ab
PT 3, L: agrimi -- HMs 153
(KZ 153)
    bel
PT 3, R:
lion -- I Supp. 146
    encircle
quadruped -- I 394
    ab
Babylonian Dragon -- IV 42D
    bel
PT 5A, L; Filler:
ABOVE
    bull -- IX 19D
    agrimi -- VIII 101 & HM
        384
    quadruped -- II 4.93
IN BACK
    griffin -- IV 287
    winged agrimi -- X 233
PT 5A, R; Filler:
ABOVE
    lion -- VIII 75 & VIII
        78
    bull -- II 3.141
    agrimi -- Munich A.1163a
        (AGDS I 84a)
IN BACK
    caprid -- I 148
    agrimi -- VIII 93
Miscellaneous
    agrimi -- IV 166a
        branch/spear bel
    quadruped -- HM no.
        unknown (Knossos, MUM
        no. H50)
            in the field

PT 5B, L; Filler: ABOVE
   bull -- XII 278
     branch/<u>Pica</u>
     caprid -- I 322
PT 5C, L; Filler:
   bull -- I 367
    infr & bel
PT 5D, R: bull -- IV 280
  ab
PT 5/6, R: lions -- II 3.65
  in the field
PT 6, L; Filler:
  IN FRONT: quadruped -- V
  162
  ABOVE
    lion -- II 4.51 & AM
      1941.147 (CS 28P)
    bull
      I Supp. 22 --
        branch/<u>Pica</u> ab
     V 664
    calf -- II 3.134
    caprid -- Naples 1404
PT 6, R; Filler:
  IN FRONT
    goat -- II 3.90
    quadruped -- I 391
    branches? infr
  ABOVE
    lion? -- II 4.39
    bull -- I 315 & HM G 3497
      (CMCG 237)
    calf -- V 360/383
      unfinished
    agrimi -- I 355 & II 4.44
    goat -- I 24
    quadruped -- I 366
PT 7, L: lion -- II 4.60
  ab
PT 8, L: lion -- Hamburg
  1961.288
    ab
PT 8, R: lion -- Nafplion Mus.
  no. unknown from Aidonia T.
  7
    infr
PT 10A, R

lion -- IV 229
  ab
griffin -- HM no. unknown
  from Kalyvia T. 9
    infr
PT 11, L; Filler
lion, ABOVE
    IV 282 & ?HM G 3177
        (CMCG 270)
  griffin -- HMm 1035-
  in the field
PT 11, R: lion -- I 56
  ab
PT 13A, L: bovine -- Rumania
Academy 433
    ab, beh, & bel
PT 13A, R: lion -- X 154
  ab
PT 14A, R: bull -- IX 118
branch (approximating
    Linear B -sa-?) bel
PT 17B, L: cow & calf -- XII
306
    ab
PT 19A, L: waterbirds -- XII
203
    inb
PT 19A, R: waterbirds -- AM
1941.101 (CS 290)
    ab
PT 19C, R: 2 caprids --
VII 186
    infr
PT 19D, L: 2 agrimia -- IX
189
    zig-zags/branch infr
PT 20, L: 2 horses? -- I 390
  ab
PT 21, L: 2 bulls -- Munich
A.1187 (AGDS I 82)
    inb
PT 25B, L: 2 quadrupeds -- X
308
    infr
PT 25C, R: 2 goats -- I Supp.
140a
    infr

PT 28B: 2 quadrupeds -- I 398
   in the field
PT 29A: 2 animals -- HM 1262
   ab
PT 29B: 2 kids? conjoined --
   VIII 84
      2 flank
      branch bel
PT 30A: 2 bulls -- I 372
   bel
PT 31: 2 agrimia -- I 90
   in the field
PT 32B: 2 bulls conjoined -- I
   198
      betw
PT 34B:
   2 bulls -- I 92
      bel 1 bull & betw
   2 quadrupeds -- I 157
      branch betw
PT 37A ccl: 2 calves -- HMs
   289 (KSPI R3)
      betw
PT 39A, R: misc. vs misc.
   -- I 511
Ch. 2B: Men
   (duel) -- I 12
      at left
   (religious) -- I 195
      at right
Ch. 2C: Women (single)
   (stands L) -- HMs 578 (AT
      121)
         2 flank
   (stands R) -- ?II 3.171
      at left
   (4 or more) -- HM 1559
      2 flank
Ch. 2E: People at a Shrine
   Shrine topped with HC &
   branches
         (person at right) -- I
            279
         (woman sits on Shrine) --
            V 199 & X 270
Ch. 3E: Animal Games (bull-
   wrestling) -- I Supp. 35

   branch/sign ab
Ch. 4A: Women & Animals
   (antithetic) -- HM G 3054
      (CMCG 359)
         inb
   (woman rides) -- HM G no.
   unknown
      infr
Ch. 5B: Animal Faces
   (bull, single, simple) --
      HMs 665 (KSPI R101)
   branches/lines encircle
   (bucrania,
      single) -- XII 310
         ab
      pair) -- VII 264
         lines/branches flank
Ch. 5C: Animal Heads (caprid)
   -- I 166
      ab
Ch. 5D: Protomes (caprid)
   BELOW -- I 403 & VIII 84
Ch. 5E: Birds & Waterbirds
   (bird, single,
      stands R) -- II 4.145
         infr
      flies L) -- II 2.43
         alights L on a branch
            at left
   (birds, pair) -- II 4.194
      2 branches flank each
   (waterbirds,
      single) -- II 3.350
         2 ab
      pair)
         II 3.78 -- ab
         II 3.351 -- ab
         V 422a -- bel
         AM 1941.1231 (CS 289)
            -- inb
            groundline bel
               becomes branch
               at right
         HMs 659 (KSPI U 117)
      trio), ABOVE
         IX 162b
         HMs 590 (AT 23)

Ch. 5F: Alerions
    (head R) -- I Supp. 84
        ab L
    (head direction unknown) --
        I 211
Ch. 5G: Insects (misc.) -- IV
    33D
        ab/beh
Ch. 5H: Fish (single,
    conventional)
        II 3.245a -- 2 ab
        Berlin FG 50c (AGDS II
            12c) -- ab & bel
Ch. 5I: Dolphins (3) -- V 176
    bel
Ch. 6A: People-Animals
    (caprid-people) -- XIII 60
        bel
    (agrimi-woman,
        head L) -- I 476
            ab
        head R) -- V 274
            at right
Ch. 6B: Genii -- Berlin FG 12
    (AGDS II 29)
        infr
Ch. 9B: Centered Circles (2)
    Encircle -- I 173 & V 13
    In the field -- I Supp. 50
        & II 4.42

fronds
PT 1A, L; agrimi
    I Supp. 70 -- ab
    IV 245 -- bel
    V 670 -- ab
    V 344 -- ab & bel
PT 1A, R; Filler: quadruped
    -- Chania 2065
        ab
PT 2, R; Filler: bull -- V
    729
        infr
PT 5A, L; Filler: agrimi --
    II 3.200
        ab
PT 5A, R; Filler: lion --

XII 273
    infr
PT 7, L; lion -- V 192
    ab
PT 10A, L: agrimi -- HM 2507
    infr
PT 10A, R: bull? -- IV 306
    ab
Ch. 3E: Animal Games (bull-
    leaping, Floating) --
    AM 1938.1078 (CS 248)
        infr
Ch. 9G: Rosettes (early)
    betw -- V 167 & HM 229

trees
PT 1A, L; Filler:
    lion -- II 4.46
        bef
    bull -- AM 1941.1242 (CS
        335)
            beh
    kid -- I 487
        infr
PT 1A, R; Filler:
    IN FRONT
        bull -- II 3.68
        goat -- HM G 3296 (CMCG
            170)
    ABOVE
        goat -- HMs 296 (KSPI
            K10)
            sign?
        quadruped -- HM G 3333
            (CMCG 282)
PT 1B, L; bull -- VII 251
    ab
PT 1B, R; lion -- HM G 3331
    (CMCG 121)
        beh
PT 2, L; Filler: bull
    IN FRONT -- I 59 & IV 284
PT 2, R; Filler: bull
    AM 1893.234 (CS 18P) --
        horizontal ab
    HM 2043 -- infr
    HMs 49 (KZ 103) -- beh

PT 3, L: bull (-leaping?) -- I
201
    infr
PT 5A, L; Filler: goat --
Melos 572
    inb
PT 5A, R;
  bull -- I 23
    infr
  agrimi -- IV 321
    bef
PT 6, L; Filler:
  calf/bull -- VII 192
    inb
  stag -- VII 262
    ab/infr resembling a
      large tulip
PT 10B, R: bull -- Munich
A.1197 (AGDS I 48)
    ab
PT 25B, R: 2 bulls -- VIII 108
infr
PT 25C, R: 2 goats
I 30 -- tree/groundline bel
HM 1439 -- infr
PT 30A: 2 lions -- IV 294
beh?
PT 38,L: lion vs bull -- AM
1938.1036 (CS 318)
    beh
PT 39A: lion R vs bull -- I 70
ab
PT 49A, L: dog vs deer -- HMs
132 (KSPI P730)
    inb
PT 51C: 2 dogs vs kid -- X 130
infr
Ch. 2B: Men (pair, salute) --
V 244
    flanked by 2 men?
Ch. 2D: Men & Women
(pair, alone) -- HMs 655
  (KSPI U?)
    grows from a tripod
      cauldron & flanked
      by a man & a woman
(misc.) -- AM 1938.1130, The

Ring of Nestor
    quarters the bezel
Ch. 2E: People at a Shrine
(person at left)
  I 191 -- small tree
    at left
  AM 1938.1127 (CS 250) --
    at left
  (2 Shrines flank) -- II 3.56
    at left?
Ch. 3D: Men In Chariots -- I
15
    horizontal bel to right
      forms a groundline
Ch. 3E: Animal Games (bull --
leaping, Diving) -- I 200
    infr
Ch. 4A: Women & Animals
(friezes) -- II 3.282
    2 trees?
Ch. 6B: Genii -- AM 1938.1043
(CS 304)
    flanked
Ch. 8C: Ships -- HMs 384
(KSPI L15/22)
    3 grow from rocks at left?

Miscellaneous Plants
PT 2/6; Filler: agrimi -- HMs
no. unknown from Mallia
    foliage
PT 8A, L; Filler: lion -- HM G
142 (CMCG 273)
    plant ab
PT 10A, L;: griffin -- II 4.71
plant? infr
PT 11, L; Filler: deer -- HMs
126 (KSPI Pa)
    river, rocks, plants
      all ab
PT 13A, R: bull -- II 3.335
plant? bel
PT 17A, L: nanny & kid -- HMs
163 (KZ 163)
    plant inb

PT 19B, R: 2 waterbirds --
    HM G 3025 (CMCG 177)
        2 lines flank =
            marshgrass
PT 25B, R: 2 Babylonian
Dragons -- HMs no. unknown
(AT 133)
        plant infr
PT 51A, L; II 4.202 -- 2 lions
    vs bull
        Weed infr
        plant ab
Ch. 2C: Women (4 or more) -- I
17
        small woman holds some
            plants
Ch. 2E: People at a Shrine
    (person at left) -- I 292
        bel, plant growing from
            rocks
Ch. 3A: Man & Animals (birds)
    -- HMs 134 (KSPI Q14)
        2 plants flank
Ch. 3C: Man Hunts Animals
    (lions) -- IX 7D
        rocks/weeds bel
    (boars) -- XII 240
        plant? part of the man's
            kilt bel
Ch. 5E: Birds & Waterbirds
    (waterbirds, single)
        plant ab
            IV 257 -- "dandelion
                puff"/Sun
            HMs 547 (AT 21)
            HM G 3205 (CMCG
                425)
Ch. 5H: Fish (single, flying
    fish) -- HMs 476 (AT 32)
        plants encircle
Ch. 5K: Shellfish -- VII 188
    murex shells/hearts/peppers
Ch. 6B: Genii -- HMs 202
    (KSPI H?)
        plants infr & inb
Ch. 7B: Misc. Plants (Lily)
    -- AM 1938.1053 (CS 251)

        ivy bel
Ch. 8E: Helmets (winged) --
    HMs 28 (KZ 31)
        topped with an ivy-leaf
Ch. 9G: Rosettes -- V 370
    grain/leaf

CHAPTER 16
Setting

16A
Rocks

(presumed to be bel,
unless otherwise stated)

With Buildings
Ch. 2B: Men (1) -- Chania 1563
as ground/coastline (with
projecting arcades) &
mountain top?
Ch. 2D: Men & Women (& a boat)
-- I 180
rocks bel the 3 buildings
Ch. 2E: People at a Shrine
(person at left)
I 191 -- rocks form the
floor of the porch
I 292 -- pile of rocks
(mountain?)
II 3.252, The Mochlos
Ring -- rocks infr of
the Shrine at right
(person at right)
XII 264 -- rocks bel
Shrine
HMs 141 (KSPI M1-4) --
mountain on which a
woman stands
(tree-pulling, man at
Omphalos) -- II 3.114
rocks? bel Shrine
(tree-pulling, no Omphalos)
-- Once in the Evans
coll., The Ring of Minos
mountain, decorated
with an arcade
pattern, supports a
Shrine
(2 women antithetic) --
I 127
mountain supports a

Shrine
at left: rocks
Ch. 8B: Buildings
HMs 25a (KZ 49)
HMs 45 (KZ 131) -- rocks at
left

With People
Ch. 2B: Men (1, religious) -- I
219
Ch. 2C: Women (1) -- ?II 3.171
Ch. 2D: Men & Women (woman at
left, man at right) -- I
101 & II 3.305
Ch. 2E: People at a Shrine
(person at right) -- HMs
141 (KSPI HM1-5)

With Animals
IN FRONT
PT 10A, R: sphinx -- I 129
ABOVE
PT 1A, L; Filler: agrimi --
HM G 3075 (CMCG 122)
PT 2, R; Filler: bull -- HM
2301
Frond?
PT 5B, L; Filler: agrimi --
HM G 3303b (CMCG 186b)
PT 6, L; Filler: lion -- X
152
rocks/Weed ab (cf. IX
7D)
PT 10A, R: agrimia -- I 404
PT 11, L; Filler: deer --
HMs 126 (KSPI Pa)
Ch. 3C: Man Hunts Animals
(boars) -- I 227
Ch. 3D: Men In Chariots --
I 15
Ch. 5I: Dolphins (3) -- HMs
no. unknown (KSPI R105)
BELOW
General
PT 1A, R; Filler:
goat -- I 188
griffin -- HMs 88 (KZ

42)
PT 1B, R;
   lion -- XIII 82
   agrimi -- AM 1938.954
    (CS 227)
       stands on rock
         ledge
       rocks bel dog
PT 3, L: bull
   (-leaping?) -- I 201
PT 5A, L; Filler:
   agrimi -- I Supp. 82
   Babylonian Dragon --
    HMs 637 (Sk 11)
PT 5A, R; Filler:
   bull -- II 3.226 & HM
    160
PT 5B, R; Filler: agrimi
   -- I 242
PT 5C, R: calf -- Chania
   1542/1544 (Papaposto-
   lou 1977: no. 2)
PT 6, L; Filler:
   lion -- I 10 & ?II
    4.138
   agrimi -- AM 1938.946
    (CS 201)
PT 6, R; Filler:
   bull -- IV 275
   calf -- I 83
PT 10A, L: agrimi -- II
   3.50
PT 11, L; Filler: agrimi
   -- HM G 3136 (CMCG
   172)
PT 12, R:
   lion -- I 248
   bull -- I 283
PT 16A, R: nanny & kid --
   HMs 122 (KSPI N7)
    at left
PT 18, L: cow & calf -- V
   663
   Figure-8 Shield?
PT 20, R:
   2 lions -- HMs 40/321
    etc. (KSPI R37,

AT 146, KZ 105)
   2 agrimia? -- HMs 456
    (AT 79)
PT 23A, R: 2 boars -- HMs
   545 (AT 80)
   wavy
PT 39A: lion R vs bull --
   I 185
    rocks/waves bel
PT 39B, R: 2 agrimia
   copulating -- VII 68
PT 39C: lion R vs bull --
   I 252
PT 47B: lion? L vs agrimi
   -- HMs no. unknown (AT
   98)
PT 49A, R: lion vs caprid
   -- HMs no. unknown (AT
   89)
PT 51C: 2 dogs vs agrimi
   L -- Hannover no.
   unknown (AGDS IV 7)
Ch. 6A: People-Animals
   (sphinxes) -- HMs 7b
   (KZ 75)
Ch. 2A: Parts of the
   Human Body (man's
   head, bearded) --
   XIII 22D
Ch. 2C: Women (pair,
   salute) -- HMs 200
   (KZ 200)
Ch. 2D: Men & Women
   (pair, alone)
    II 3.305
    X 261*
    HMs no. unknown
     (AT 142)
Ch. 2E: People at a
   Shrine (tree-pulling,
   no Omphalos) -- I 119
Ch. 3C: Man Hunts
   Animals
   (lions) -- IX 7D
    rocks/Weeds bel
   (boars) -- Berlin FG
    40 (AGDS II 23)

Ch. 4A: Women & Animals
(rides an animal) --
I 167
    rocks/waves bel
Ch. 5B: Animal Faces
(bull, filler) --
XIII 22D
Ch. 5E: Birds & Water-
birds (waterbirds,
single) -- V 234 & X
305*
Ch. 5I: Dolphins (pair)
-- AM 1941.91 (CS
191)
    groundline/prow of
        ship/rocks bel

Specific areas/figures of a
    composition

PT 51A, R: lioness & cub
vs agrimi -- II 3.99
rocks bel agrimi
Ch. 2B: Men (1, Omphalos)
I 219 -- a nude man
    stands on rocks L
HMm 1034 -- Tree 2
    grows from rocks
Ch. 2C: Women
(1, stands R) -- HMs
    523 (AT 138)
    Tree 5 grows from
        rocks
(pair, flank) -- HMs
    576 (AT 137)
    Tree 5 grows from
        rocks bel woman
        at right
(trio, misc.) --
    Chania 1528a & b
    (Papapostolou 1977:
    no. 29)
        central woman
            seated R on
            rocks?
(4 or more) -- I 17
    woman seated on

rocks L
    rocks bel
Ch. 2D: Men & Women
    (pair, alone)
I 101 -- at right
I 219 -- woman stands
    on rocks
Ch. 2E: People at a
    Shrine
I 191 -- = porch floor
I 292 -- bel agrimi
II 3.114 -- bel Shrine
XII 264 -- bel Shrine
Ch. 3A: Man & Animals
(bulls) -- Piraieus
no. unknown, ring
from Varkiza T. I
    rocks bel man
Ch. 4A: Women & Animals
    (woman seated L at
    right)
HMs 157 (KSPI R91)
    rocks bel
    at right, woman L
        seated on rocks
HMs 584 (AT 128) -- at
    right, woman L
        seated on rocks
Ch. 6A: People-Animals
(Sphinx) -- HMs 7b
(KZ 75)
Ch. 8C: Ships -- HMs 384
(KSPI L15/22)
    3 trees from rocks
        at left?

IN FRONT & ABOVE
    PT 2, L; Filler: lion --
    HMs 531 (AT 36)

IN FRONT & IN BACK
    ?Ch. 6A: People-Animals
        (sphinxes) -- HMs 23a
    (KZ 74)

ABOVE & BELOW
    PT 2, R; Filler: bull --
    HMs 19 (KZ 120)

Ch. 3E: Animal Games
(bull-catching) -- I 274
rocks ab & bel
(bull-riding) -- HMs 500
(AT 56)
rocks ab & bel
Ch. 5I: Dolphins (pair) --
AM 1938.963 (CS 203)

IN BACK & BELOW
PT 5A, R: agrimi -- I 490
PT 20, L: 2 horses? -- I
390
Ch. 2C: Women (pair,
salutes) -- HMs 522 (AT
139)
rocks inb of small
woman & bel

IN FRONT, ABOVE, & IN BACK
PT 2, L; Filler: lion -- HM
G 3285 (CMCG 260)

IN FRONT, ABOVE, IN BACK, &
BELOW
PT 10A, R: bull -- V 198

Encircle
Ch. 2B: Men (pair,
warriors) -- I 16
Ch. 5H: Fish (single) --
HMs 128 (KSPI Pb)

Miscellaneous
PT 11, L; Filler: deer --
HMs 126 (KSPI Pa)
river, rocks, plants
all ab
Ch. 2C: Women (single) --
II 3.171
branch? at left
Ch. 2D: Men & Women (pair)
-- I 101
at right
Ch. 2E: People at a Shrine
-- II 3.252, the Mochlos
Ring

as ground infr of the
Shrine
Ch. 6A: People-Animals
(sphinx) -- HMs 23a (KZ
74)
flank

16B
Water

(for water assumed but not
figured, see: Ch. 2C: Women
[single, in a boat]; Ch. 2D:
Men & Women [men & women &
boat]; Ch. 5E: Birds &
Waterbirds; Ch. 12C: Boats)

ABOVE
PT 11, L; Filler: deer -- HMs
126 (KSPI Pa)
river, rocks, plants all ab
PT 26, R/Ch. 5E; Birds & Waterbirds (waterbirds, 3) -- AM
1938.1066 (CS 343)

BELOW
PT 39A, R: lion vs bull -- I
185
rocks/waves
Ch. 2B: Men (1) -- Chania 1563
net/reticulation = water?
Ch. 2C: Women (single, in boat)
-- HMs 434 (AT 118)
Ch. 4A: Women & Animals (woman
rides) -- I 167
rocks/waves
Ch. 5E: Birds & Waterbirds
(waterbirds, single), -- II
3.350
(pair, 1 stands/1 lands) --
II 3.250
(trio) -- AM 1938.971 (CS
297)

16C
Dadoes

Dado 1   ●●●●●
PT 3, R: bull -- HM no.
unknown from Kalyvia T.
9
PT 10A, R: sphinx -- I 129
PT 28A:
2 sheep protomes -- I
189
2 griffins -- I 218
PT 28B: 2 calves -- I 58
PT 29B: 2 griffins -- I 102
PT 46: lion L vs bull --
I 253
Ch. 2E: People at a Shrine
(person at left) -- I 86
(woman sits on Shrine)
-- V 199
(tree-pulling, no
Omphalos) -- I 126
(at the Shrine) -- HMs
no. unknown (AT 140)
Ch. 3A: Man & Animals
(bull) -- Pireieus no.
unknown, ring from
Varkiza T. I
Ch. 3B: Master of Animals:
(misc.) -- I 356
Ch. 4A: Women with Animals
(woman seated L at
right) -- I 128
Ch. 5D: Protomes (caprid)
-- I 189
separates the registers
Ch. 8F: Figure-8 Shields --
HMm 1002-4
encircles
Ch. 8H: Figure-8 Shields/
Sacred Knots
(friezes) -- HMm 990
separates the registers

Dado 2   ⊓⊓⊓⊓
2a
PT 1A, L; Filler:
agrimi -- IV 245
sheep -- HM G 3075a (CMCG
122a)
PT 1B, R; Filler: lion/dog
-- HMs no. unknown (AT
39)
PT 10A, L: goat -- HM G 3415
(CMCG 169)
PT 10A, R: agrimi -- X 281
with axes & a circle
PT 26, R: 3 calves -- HMs
110 (KSPI N2)
PT 30A: 2 sheep -- I 187
Ch. 2C: Women (single,
kneels at Omphalos) --
AM 1919.56
Ch. 4A: Women & Animals
(antithetic) -- HM G 3054
(CMCG 359)

2b   ⊞⊞⊞⊞
Ch. 2B: Men (pair, walk R)
-- HMs 18a (KZ 186)
Ch. 4B: Potnia Theron
(lions) -- I 144 & I 145

2c   ⧄⧄⧄⧄
PT 1A, L; Filler: agrimi --
VII 167
PT 23A, R: 2 boars -- Berlin
FG 49b (AGDS II 45b)
groundline with Dado
2c (2 groundlines &
oblique strokes)
Ch. 3D: Bull-Leaping
(Floating Leaper Schema)
-- II 3.271

2d   ⋈⋈⋈⋈⋈
PT 10A, L: agrimi -- AM
1941.136 (CS 190)
PT 10A, R: griffin -- AM AE
693 (CS 16P)

2e

    PT 46: lion L vs 2 bulls
    -- AM 1938.1153h:A

Dado 3

PT 6, R; Filler: bull -- II
    4.179
PT 10A, L:
    bull -- I Supp. 34 & XII
       249
    calf -- XII 137
PT 10A, R: agrimi -- II 3.340
PT 11, L; Filler: agrimi -- I
    Supp. 92
    4 courses of Dado 3
PT 23A, R; Filler: 2 boars --
    II 3.21
Ch. 2E: People at a Shrine
    (tree-pulling) -- HMm 989
Ch. 3E: Animal Games
    (bull-leaping, Diving) --
       AM AE 2237
    (man infr) -- HMs 1001
       (Betts 63)
Ch. 3F: Animal-Sacrifice --
    HMs 211 (KSPI R13)

Dado 4

4a

    PT 10B, L:
    bull -- V 191b
    agrimi -- V 191c
    PT 11, L; Filler: lion -- V
    191a
    PT 25B, R: 2 lions -- V 589

4b

    PT 2, L; Filler: lion --
    XIII 57

4c

    PT 23B/24, R: 2 bulls -- I
    91
    Ch. 2E: People at a Shrine
    (2 women antithetic) --
    I 127

4d

    PT 1A, L; Filler: agrimi --
    XIII 44
    PT 1A, R; Filler: bull -- V
    630
    ?PT 12, L: lion -- XIII 19D

Dado 2a-b 3/4/5

PT 10A, L: agrimi -- I 486

Dado 5

PT 1A, R; Filler: dog -- Once
Evans Coll. (GGFR pl. 115)
PT 8, L; dog scratching -- I
256

Dado 6

6a

    PT 5A, R; Filler:
    Babylonian Dragon -- AM
       1938.1150 (CS 22P)
    PT 6, L; Filler: lion
    V 242 & X 152 -- Dado 6a
    = zig-zag bel
    PT 32: lion & griffin --
    HMs 68 (KZ 181)
       bel lion

6b

    PT 6, L; Filler:
    bull/caprid -- HMs 246a
    Ch. 4B: Potnia Theron
    (waterbirds) -- VII 134
    Ch. 5K: Shellfish
    (argonauts) -- II 3.91

6c

    PT 5B, R; Filler: bull --
    IX 119
    PT 8, L; lion -- X 133*
    PT 11, L; Filler: lion --
    VII 151
    PT 13A, R: lion -- IX 150
    Ch. 3A: Men & Animals
    (lions) -- X 135*

6d
PT 13A, R: bull -- IX 193
Dado 6d with 6 circles
ab
PT 23C, L: 3 boars -- IX
136
Ch. 2C: Women (single,
carries object) -- II 3.8
Dado 6d inb

Dado 7
7a
PT 30B: 2 bulls -- I 197
Dado 7a with 5 circles
bel
Ch. 2C: Women (single,
misc.) -- II 3.146
curtailed infr of the
woman

7b
Ch. 3A: Men & Animals
(lions) -- I 374
Ch. 3E: Animal Games (bull-
leaping, Diving) -- I
370

7c
PT 23A, R: 2 griffins -- I
282

Dado 8
PT 1A, R; Filler: lion? -- HMs
154 (KZ 154)
PT 8, R: dog scratching -- I
255
PT 11, R; Filler: griffin -- I
293
Ch. 2B: Men (1): ab lintel of
lower gates -- Chania 1563
Ch. 3E: Animal Games (bull-
leaping, Floating) -- V 517
Ch. 4A: Women & Animals (R)
-- I 179

Dado 9
9a
PT 10A, R; Filler: bull --
HMs 415
Ch. 2B: Men (3 or more,
processions) -- HMs
362 (KSPI K16)
Ch. 3C: Man Hunts Animals
(lions) -- Peronne no.
unknown, the Danicourt
Ring
Ch. 3E: Animal Games
(bull-leaping, Diving)
-- HMs 613-24/626/
627/6499 (Sk 4)
(man infr) -- I 305
Ch. 8F: Figure-8 Shields --
II 3.113
ab & bel?

9b
PT 10A, L: lion & griffins
-- I 329
Dado 9b of double
nautili bel
Ch. 5B: Animal Faces (lion
& bull) -- I 18
separates 2 rows of
animal faces
Ch. 8H: Figure-8 Shields/
Sacred Knots (friezes)
-- HMs 664 (KSPI C11)

16D
Groundlines

Single
ABOVE
PT 13A, L: bull -- II 3.224
PT 14D, L: Minotaur -- AM
1938.1070 (CS 325)
PT 46: lion L vs bull -- VII
115a

BELOW
    PT 1A, L;
        agrimi
            II 3.153
            II 3.341
            IV 41D
            IX 101
            XII 232
            XII 252
        <u>Babylonian Dragon</u> -- I
           Supp. 70 & V 581
    PT 1A, R; Filler: bull -- II
    2.60
    PT 1B, L; sow -- Brummer
    Coll.
    PT 1B, R; agrimi -- V 687
    PT 1C, R; calf/bull -- AM
    1938.969 (CS 301)
    PT 2, L; Filler:
        lion -- HM G 3285 (CMCG
        bull -- Berlin FG 33
           (AGDS II 43)
    PT 2, R; Filler:
        bull -- II 3.212 & HMs
           503 (AT 57)
        stag -- HMs 24 (KZ 108)
        sheep -- I Supp. 147
        dog -- Chania 2053 (Papa-
           postolou 1977: no. 6)
        bitch -- AM 1938.1061 (CS
           240) & HMs 214+287
           (KSPI F2/K4/K7/K12/
           Q21/R53/CS 40S)
    PT 3, R: quadruped -- I 394
    PT 5A, L; Filler:
        bull -- II 4.180
        agrimi
            II 3.343
            II 3.258 -- hatching
               bel
            V 69
            VII 42
            VIII 101
            IX 140
            XII 261
            XII 267
        goat -- IV 264

        stag -- II 4.140
        griffiness -- V 690
    PT 5A, R; Filler:
        bull -- XII 151a
        calf -- V 676
        agrimi -- X 215
    PT 5B, L; Filler:
        bull
            VIII 47b
            AM 1941.137 (CS 11P)
            Berlin FG 20 (AGDS II
               46)
            HMs 574 (AT 53)
        calf -- Chania 1002
    PT 5B, R; Filler: bull
        II 2.60
        IX 119
        ?XII 237
    PT 6, L; Filler: bull -- IX
    124
    PT 7, L: lion -- I 512
    PT 8, L; lion -- II 3.345
    PT 8, R
        lion -- BSA cast 183 &
           Munich A.1195 (AGDS I
           64)
        dog -- AM 1971.1150
    PT 10A, L: (cf. PT 36 --
        XII 250 below)
        lion
            I Supp. 64
            II 3.257
            II 3.346
            V 241
        bull -- II 3.293
        agrimi
            II 4.183
            V 730
            HM 2507
        boar -- I Supp. 76 &
           HM 2096
        griffin -- AM 1953.119
           (CS 34P) & Chania
           2067/2068
    PT 10A, R
        lion -- X 132 & X 277a

bull
    I 236
    Berlin FG 22 (AGDS II
      44)
    HMs 345B/399 (KSPI
      L27)
    dog -- AM 1938.1017
      (CS 237)
    griffin -- HM G 3495
      (CMCG 336)
    sphinx -- II 3.118
PT 10B, L
    bull -- I 35 & I 55
    griffin -- V 590 & Munich
      A.1196 (AGDS I 47)
PT 10B, R: bull-- I Supp. 79
  & Munich A.1197 (AGDS I
  48)
PT 11, L; Filler:
    lion -- X 1 & IX 161
    bull -- Chania 1557
    deer -- HMs 126 (KSPI Pa;
      CS 5S)
    griffin -- I Supp. 152 &
      V 438
PT 11, R; Filler
    lion -- II 3.292 & ?HM
      2505
    bull -- IV 268 & XII 235
    griffin
      I 389
      XII 233
      HM G 3015 (CMCG 335)
PT 12, L: lion -- HM G 3181
  (CMCG 268)
PT 12, R:
    lion -- HMs 587 (AT 41)
    bull -- VIII 148
 PT 13A, L: lion
    I 43
    V 680
    Chania 1021
PT 13A, R: bull
    Plain
      I 493
      HMs 111 (KSPI N6)
      Munich A.1188 (AGDS I

      61)
    Miscellaneous
      XII 225 -- line =
        groundline bel
PT 13B, L: bull -- I 235 &
  Chania 1017
PT 13B, R:
    lion -- II 3.41
    bull -- XIII 83 &
      HM G 3208 (CMCG 224)
PT 13C, R: lion -- IX 107
PT 13/14: lion -- V 733 PT
PT 14A, R: lion -- VII 115c
PT 16B, R: goat & kid -- I
  168
PT 18A, R: cow & calf -- AM
  1938.1087
PT 18B, R: cow & calf -- X
  216
PT 19A, L: waterbirds
    X 224* -- groundline bel
      ending in flanking
      <u>Fronds</u>
    XII 203
    HM G 3210 (CMCG 312)
    wavy
PT 19A, R:
    agrimia -- I 45
    waterbirds -- IV 246 &
      AM 1941.101 (CS 290)
PT 19B, L: 2 bulls -- I 130
  & I 515/KN HMs 109 (KSPI
  J2)
PT 19B, R: 2 calves -- VII
  103
PT 21, R: 2 bulls -- XII
  287
PT 23A, R: 2 boars
    V 666
    Berlin FG 49b (AGDS II
      45b)
    groundline with <u>Dado</u>
      <u>2c</u> (2 groundlines
      & oblique strokes)
PT 24, L: 2 bulls
    I Supp. 78
    V 195

AM 1938.1030 (CS 312)
HM G 3218 (CMCG 292)
Munich A.1193 (AGDS I 38)
PT 24, R; Filler: 2 bulls
II 3.119
XIII 8
HM 2393
PT 25B, L
2 lions -- V 193
2 bulls -- I 183
PT 25C, L
2 lions -- X 264
bull & lion -- Brummer
Coll.
PT 25C, R: 2 goats -- I 30
tree/groundline bel
PT 26, L & R: 3 sheep --
HMs 210 (KSPI R29)
PT 27B, R: 3 sheep -- I 176
PT 28A
2 bulls -- V 337
2 pairs of cow & calf --
I 20
PT 28B: 2 lions -- HMs 42
(KZ 128)
PT 30A
2 bulls -- I Supp. 91
groundline dotted like
a Baton
2 boars -- IV 240
PT 31A: 2 griffins -- HMs
no. unknown (AT 96)
PT 31B:
2 lions -- II 3.306
2 waterbirds
HM G 3210 (CMCG 312)
wavy groundline
HMs 495 (AT 27)
PT 36 cl:
2 bulls -- XII 250
bel each
2 boars -- I 184
bel each
PT 37A cl: 2 lions -- V 493
bel each?
PT 37A ccl: griffin &
griffiness -- HMs 452

(AT 95)
groundline bel 1
PT 39A:
lion L vs agrimi -- IV
262
lion R vs bull
II 3.173
X 218
HM G 3260 (CMCG 307)
PT 39C: lion L vs bull --
VIII 89
PT 40: dog L vs agrimi --
Munich A.1192 (AGDS I
37)
PT 44A: lion R vs bull --
II 3.283
PT 47A: dog R vs bull --
XII 265
PT 48A: lion vs stag --
Munich A.1181 (AGDS I
46)
PT 49A, R: lion vs bull --
I 286
PT 54: 2 lions vs stag R --
XIII 20
Ch. 2B: Men
(single, with ax) -- II
3.147 & HMs 133 (KSPI
O2)
(single, misc.) -- HMs
91 (KZ 196) & HMs
1017 (Betts 53)
(3 or more, processions)
-- HMs 362 (KSPI K16)
(3 or more, salute) --
I 170 & HMs 485 (AT
135)
Ch. 2C: Women
(single, stands frontal)
-- I 513 & IV 283b
(carries object R) --
I 226
(2 flank central woman)
-- II 3.218
groundline bel
tall woman

Ch. 2D: Men & Women
    (pair, alone)
        I 101
        HMs 114 (KSPI K2/11)
        HMs no. unknown (AT
            141)
    (man & 2 women) -- V 173
Ch. 2E: People at a Shrine
    (tree-pulling, man at
        Omphalos) -- II 3.114
    (tree-pulling, no
        Omphalos) -- I 119 &
        HMs 277-283 (KZ 3;
        KSPI Q22/R1/R51/R54)
Ch. 3A: Man & Animals
    (lion)
        I 512
        XII 207
        HMs 508 (AT 134)
    (bulls) -- VII 102 &
        Chania 1529/1530
    (caprids) -- HMs 583a (AT
        126)
    (birds) -- AM 1938.1050
        (CS 293)
    (simulacra) -- HMs 585
        (AT 127)
Ch. 3D: Men In Chariots
    Plain
        IV 37D
        HMs 347 (KSPI L?/Na?)
        Once Arndt Coll. (GGFR
            pl. 186)
    Miscellaneous
        I 15 -- a tree bel
            horizontal to right
            forms a groundline
            bel
Ch. 3E: Animal Games
    (bull-leaping, Diving) --
        V 597
    (rides other animals) --
        V 638
Ch. 3F: Animal-Sacrifice --
    Berlin FG 22 (AGDS II 44)
    & HMs 142 from Knossos
Ch. 4A: Women with Animals

(animal inb) -- II 3.309
    & BSA cast 188
(woman seated L at right)
    -- Chania 1503/1513
Ch. 4B: Potnia Theron
    (lions) -- BSA Cast 135
    (griffins, groundline bel
        each griffin) -- II
        3.276 & AM AE 689 (CS
        351)
Ch. 5B: Animal Faces (lions)
    -- I 110
    bel quadruped
Ch. 5E: Birds & Waterbirds
    (waterbirds, single)
        II 4.146
        VII 165
        X 192b*
    (waterbirds, pair)
        Plain
            I Supp. 33
            II 3.351
            II 4.191
            V 439
        Miscellaneous
            AM 1941.1231 (CS
                289) --
                groundline bel
                becomes branch
                at right
Ch. 5F: Aleirons
    (head L) -- X 248
    (head R)
        II 3.95
            broken groundline
                bel
        X 318
            groundline bel the
                zig-zags to
                either side of
                the body
Ch. 5I: Dolphins
    (2) -- AM 1941.91 (CS
        191)
        groundline/prow of
        ship/rocks bel

(3) -- HM G 3067 (CMCG
      319)
   short
Ch. 6A: People-Animals
   (bull-people)
      HMs 2b (KZ 17)
         groundline bel/
            infr
      HMs 55a (KZ 46)
   (sphinxes) -- HMs 7b
      (KZ 75)
   (caprid-people) -- HMs
      1007 (Betts 47)

1 or 2 Groundlines
BELOW
   PT 5A, L; Filler: agrimi
      -- VIII 101

2 Groundlines
ABOVE
   PT 13A, R: bovine -- IX 23D
   PT 18B, R: cow & calf -- I
      509
   PT 41: dog R vs agrimi --
      IX 195
   Ch. 3C: Man Hunts Animals
      (lions) -- IX 152
   Ch. 5B: Animal Faces
      (lions) -- I 110
         ab lion protome
   Ch. 5G: Insects (misc.) --
      VII 70

IN BACK
   Ch. 3E: Animal Games (rides
      other animals) -- V 638
         vertical, at right
BELOW
   PT 1A, L; Filler:
      boar -- I 135
      agrimi -- I Supp. 70
   PT 1B, L
      boar -- V 314
      sheep -- XII 136
   PT 1B, R
      lion -- HM G 3331 (CMCG

121)
   bull -- I 88 & VII 163
   boar -- VIII 119
PT 1C, L: bull -- VII 65a
PT 2, L; Filler:
   bull -- HMs 77 (AT 77)
   quadruped -- AM AE 1795
      (CS 29P)
PT 2, R; Filler
   lioness -- II 3.122
   bull -- HMs 49 (KZ 103)
PT 5A, L; Filler:
   agrimi
      ?VIII 101
      IX 139
      Berlin FG 21 (AGDS II
         56)
   goat -- V 732
PT 5B, R; Filler:
   bull -- V 646
   agrimi -- II 3.222 & IX
      41
PT 6, L; Filler: calf/bull
   -- VII 192
PT 6, R; Filler: bull -- II
   3.202 & VII 261
PT 7, L: lion -- V 192
PT 8, L
   lion
      I 149
      I Supp. 32
      V 498
   griffin -- V 215
PT 8, R
   lion -- I 243 & VII 171
   dog -- V 677a
PT 10A, L:
   bull
      I 281
      XII 289
      AM 1941.125 (CS 299)
   agrimi -- XIII 19 &
      Munich A.1194 (AGDS I
      63)
PT 10A, R:
   lion -- V 182 & VIII 92
   bull -- XII 248

agrimi -- BSA Cast 168
stag -- V 665
PT 10B, L: calf -- VII 105
PT 10C, R: lion -- I Supp.
80
PT 10/11, L: griffin --
VIII 88
PT 11, L; Filler:
lion
I 244
I 506
HMs 79 (KZ 109)
deer/cow -- HMs 344
(KSPI La)
griffin -- V 684
PT 11, R; Filler:
lion -- XIII 9 & XIII 22
bull -- I 65
nanny agrimi & kid -- II
3.339
griffin -- IX 105 & XII
247
PT 12, L:
lion -- Oxford, MS Mus.
J25
bull -- I 66
PT 13A, L: dog -- Getty no.
unknown
PT 13A, R: bull -- IX 193
PT 13B, L: bull -- XIII 31
PT 13B, R: bull -- VII 99
PT 13C, R: bull -- I 160
PT 14A, L: bull -- BSA Cast
182
PT 14B: bull -- Munich
A.1189 (AGDS I 62)
short
PT 15, R: agrimi -- I 393
PT 19D, R: 2 bulls -- XIII
68
PT 21, variant: 2 ibex/bulls
-- VII 159
wavy
PT 23A, L:
2 boars
I 276
Berlin FG 49b (AGDS II

45b)
with Dado 2c
2 agrimia -- I 193a
PT 24, L; 2 bulls
I 142
I 240
I 241
II 3.62;
V 432
VII 127
XIII 78
AM 1938.1029 (CS 311)
PT 24, R; Filler: 2 bulls
I 109
I 275
V 433
Berlin FG 49a (AGDS II
45a)
PT 25B, L:
2 lions -- IX 13D & HM
2345
2 bulls -- V 196
PT 25B, R: lion & agrimi --
I 115
PT 25C, L:
2 lions -- IX 16D
lion & agrimi protome --
V 725
PT 25C, R: 2 lions -- HM
2085
PT 26, L: 3 agrimia -- X 252
PT 26, R: 4 agrimia -- VII
89
PT 28B: 2 bulls -- XIII 27
PT 35: 2 lions -- HMs 512
(AT 86)
PT 39B, L: lion vs bull --
V 688
PT 41: Attacker Right -- IX
195
dog vs agrimi
PT 44A: lion L vs bull --
V 436
bel bull
Ch. 2B: Men
(pair, acrobats) -- I 131
bel each man

(pair, duel) -- I 12
(religious) -- II 3.7
Ch. 2C: Women (pair, misc.)
-- I 134
Ch. 2D: Men & Women (pair,
alone) -- Chania 1024
Ch. 3A: Man & Animals
(lion) -- II 3.24 & HMs
383I (KSPI L46)
(bull) -- AM 1938.1026
(CS 300)
(caprid) -- AM 1938.1024
(CS 30)
Ch. 3D: Men In Chariots --
I 229
Ch. 3E: Animal Games
(man inb) -- HMs
101/497/628/629 (Sk 2,
AT 54)
(bull-leaping, Evans) --
HMs 17a (KZ 97) & HMs
102/Pigorini 71974
(AT 145, Sk 3)
Ch. 4A: Women & Animals
(antithetic) -- AM
1971.1139
Ch. 4B: Potnia Theron
(lions) -- X 242
2 bel each protome
(griffins)
V 654
2 bel each griffin
HM 1654
Ch. 4C: Women "Crossed" by
a Caprid -- I 220
Ch. 5E: Birds & Waterbirds
(waterbirds, pair) -- II
3.78

ABOVE & BELOW
PT 13A, R: bull with lion's
face -- VIII 141
PT 14A, L: agrimi -- X 137
PT 27B, R: 3 goats -- AM
1941.121 (CS 286)
PT 47B: griffin L vs
Babylonian Dragon -- XII

291
2 Mount-Guides flank
the monster

3 Groundlines
ABOVE
?PT 13A, R: calf -- VII 136

BELOW
PT 1A, L; agrimi -- Munich
A.1198 (AGDS I 65)
PT 5A, L; Filler: agrimi --
VII 153
PT 8, L; dog/calf/lion --
XII 135a
PT 10A, L: bull -- Chania
1527
PT 10A, R: agrimia -- I 404
PT 11, L; Filler: lion -- I
272a & XII 229
Ch. 3A: Man & Animals
(griffins) -- I 223
Ch. 9B: Centered Circles (3)
-- HM 922

4 Groundlines
ABOVE
PT 10A, L: agrimi -- XII
135b

CHAPTER 17
GEOMETRIC MOTIFS

17A
Lines/Strokes/Gouges

(see: the Filler sections of PT
1A, L; PT 1A, R; & PT 2; & Chs.
7 & 9; these all have 10 or
more examples & are not listed
here)

PT 1B, L;
    bull -- II 4.150
        2 ab
PT 1B, R;
    agrimi -- V 687
        line ab
    boar -- IX 177
        strokes ab
    griffin -- IX 178
        stroke ab
PT 1C; bull -- X 167
    2 lines ab (later re-
        engraving?)
PT 1D, R; agrimi -- V 402
    stroke infr
PT 2, L; V 610 -- quadruped
    2 strokes ab
PT 5A, L; Filler: bull -- I 492
    ab & bel
PT 5A, R; Filler:
    agrimi
        V 255 -- 5 (6) strokes ab
            & 5 bel
        X 221 -- stroke bel
    quadruped
        I Supp. 40
            lines ab
        II 4.02
            stroke bel
PT 5B, L; Filler: bull -- X 297
    stroke ab
PT 5B, R; Filler: bull -- XII
    237
    2 lines (= spears?) bel

belly
PT 5C, L; Filler: calf -- V
    356
thick line ab
PT 6, L; Filler
bull -- II 3.337
    line infr
calf -- X 298
    stroke/arrow bel
agrimi
    IV 53D -- 3 strokes bel
    AM 1938.946 (CS 201) --
        stroke/Pica infr
PT 6, R; Filler:
bull
    AM 1925.53 (CS 389) --
        line ab
    HM G 3497 (CMCG 237) --
        3 strokes infr & inb
            (for gilding?)
calf
    I 83 -- 2 curved lines
        ab tail
    I 287b -- line encircles
agrimi -- II 4.87
    lines ab
quadruped
    I 29 -- strokes infr &
        ab
    V 403 -- 6 (7?) strokes
        inb
griffin
    X 134 -- lines bel
    II 4.171 -- 2 lines infr
        line (= Pica?) ab
PT 9, L: bull -- HMs 504 (AT
    44)
    2 oblique lines infr
    2 horizontal lines ab
PT 10A, L: agrimi -- Munich
    A.1194 (AGDS I 63)
    3 strokes ab
PT 10A, R
    lion -- X 277a
    2 strokes infr
    Pica/stroke in back
griffin

X 170 -- ab
  (continuation
  of sword/<u>Pica</u>?)
HM G 3495 (CMCG 336) --
  vertical stroke? infr
PT 11, L; Filler: lion -- II
  3.277
7 strokes bel
line encircles
PT 11, R; Filler: lion -- II
  3.292
2 strokes infr & 1 ab
PT 12, L:
lion -- I 287a
  line encircles
bull -- I 66
  lines infr, ab, & inb
PT 12, R: lion -- V 363/364/385
& Lefkandi T. 12B.4?
  line ab
PT 13A, R: bull
XII 225 -- line = groundline
  bel
XII 268 -- line/arrow ab & 6
  strokes bel
PT 13C, R
lion -- IX 107
  stroke/<u>Mount-Guide</u> at
    right
bull -- V 200
  groups of 2 or 3 strokes
    encircle
PT 14A, R: lion -- HMs 265
  (KSPI R18)
small vertical & horizontal
  stroke bel
PT 19B, L: 2 goats -- X 299
stroke infr
PT 19B, R: 2 waterbirds -- HM G
  3025 (CMCG 177)
2 lines flank = marshgrass
PT 23C, R: 2 lions -- XIII 24
vertical line infr
PT 25A, L
lion & agrimi -- I Supp. 95
  line bel
2 stags -- V 297

lines bel
PT 25A, R: 2 goats -- X 2
strokes ab
PT 25B, L: 2 quadrupeds -- X
  308
stroke? bel
PT 25C, R: 2 goats -- I 30
lines infr & bel
PT 27B, R: 3 deer -- I Supp. 56
line ab & 2 bel
PT 28B: 2 lions -- I 172
short lines ab & bel
  line encircles
2 birds/strokes -- IX 113
PT 29B: 2 calf protomes -- AM
  1938.1094 (CS 336)
vertical line at left
PT 31B
2 calves -- V 353/354
  a thick line bel (354:
    engraved with a row
    of short lines =
    striated?)
2 waterbirds -- HMs 495 (AT
  27)
  stroke infr & inb
PT 36 cl: 2 goats? -- HMp 4819
line encircles?
PT 39A:
dog L vs agrimi/kid-man --
  XII 242
  stroke bel sphinx
<u>Fish-Monster</u>/quadruped L vs
  agrimi -- Berlin FG 31
  (AGDS II 57)
    6 strokes infr
PT 40: lion R vs bull -- XIII
  21D
lightly encised line around
  edge = ring setting?
PT 43: dog L vs agrimi -- V
  726
strokes ab
PT 48A: lion vs stag -- Munich
  A.1181 (AGDS I 46)
3 strokes bel
Ch. 2B: Men

(1, salute)
  I 195 -- dashes
  V 11 -- strokes fill the
    field
  V 189 -- lines in the
    field
(1, misc.)
  V 239 -- 2 strokes/
    lances/spears flank
  AM 1953.122 (CS 37P) --
    later line cuts
    obliquely across the
    face
  HMs 91 (KZ 196) -- at
    right: vertical
    stroke?
  HMs 242 (KSPI R50) -- 2
    registers separated by
    a line
(pair wears Figure-8
  Shield)
  XIII 137 -- 2 vertical
    strokes/spears flank
  HMs 459 (AT 116) -- 2
  vertical lines flank
(3 or more, processions)
  V 239 -- 2 strokes/
    lances/spears flank
  HMs 362 (KSPI K16) -- 2
    horizontal lines beh
(3 or more, salute) -- HMs
    449 (AT 125)
  vertical lines at right
    = Shrine?
Ch. 2C: Women (1, stands
    frontal)
  II 4.112 -- 2 sets of 4
    lines flank
  IV 55D -- 2 strokes flank
  VIII 128 -- 2 strokes flank
  HMs 467 (AT 105) -- 2
    vertical strokes flank
    (Mount-Guides?)
Ch. 2D: Men & Women (pair,
    alone) -- X 261*
  incised line around edge
    of stone (= ring

    setting?)
Ch. 2E: People at a Shrine
  (tree-pulling, no Omphalos)
    -- I 126
  a vertical stroke inside
    Shrine or Table
Ch. 3A: Men & Animals
  (lion) -- X 161
    wavy line (bow?) inb
  (bull) -- HMs 85 (KZ 102)
    a vertical line (Column?)
    bel his hands
  (caprid) -- II 3.33
    lines ab
  (griffin) -- II 3.328
    2 panels separated by a
      pair of vertical lines
  (several) -- AM 1938.1091
    vertical line topped with
    a rayed dot
Ch. 3D: Men In Chariots -- II
    3.199
  man holds a sword/vertical
    line
Ch. 3E: Animal Games (bull-
  leaping, Floating) -- II
  3.271
    oblique line ab
Ch. 4A: Women & Animals
  (woman inb) -- BSA cast 188
    HC with vertical line
  (woman rides) -- HMs 73 (AT
    132)
    2 short vertical strokes
    flank woman
  (friezes) -- HMs 272 (KSPI
    R66)
    vertical stroke crossed
    by 3 horizontal
    strokes
Ch. 4B: Potnia Theron
  (griffins) -- II 3.276
    each griffin rampant
      over a short vertical
      line

(lions) -- Kassel no.
  unknown
  a convex line ab each
  lion protome
Ch. 4C: Women "Crossed" by a
  Caprid
  XII 239 -- a vertical
  row of 3 short
  horizontal lines inb
  HMs no. unknown (KZ 4) --
  vertical stack of short
  horizontal strokes infr
  (= _Shrine_?)
Ch. 5B: Animal Faces (bulls)
  V 31 -- vertical stroke
  separates
  V 326 -- strokes encircle
  V 328 -- strokes encircle?
  V 513 -- line & strokes ab
  & strokes at left
  V 623 -- 2 parallel lines
  ab each
  V 661 -- lines flank
  V 682 -- lines flank
  VII 264 -- lines/branches
  flank
  IX 199 -- lines flank
  X 200 -- line encircles
  X 236 -- 2 sets of 7
  strokes bel
  XII 294 -- lines in field
  XII 310 -- lines ab
  AM 1938.951 (CS 105) -- 2
  lines flank each
  HMs 165 (KZ 165) -- 2 lines
  (_Snake Frame_?) flank
  HMs 665 (KSPI R101) --
  branches/lines encircle
Ch. 5C: Animal Heads (bulls)
  AM 1938.970 (CS 206)
  a pair of lines flank
  dots ab & bel
Ch. 5D: Protomes (caprid) -- I
  403
  a vertical line & dots infr
  of each protome
Ch. 5E: Birds & Waterbirds

(waterbirds, 1)
  VII 165 -- line infr
  X 192b* -- lines/
  scratches bel
  XII 210 -- lines in the
  field
(waterbirds, pair)
  II 3.307 -- line
  separates registers
  HMs 201 -- 2 registers
  separated by a
  horizontal line
Ch. 5F: Alerions (head L)
  X 147 -- 2 strokes inb of
  head
  XII 162b -- lines ab
  XII 210 -- lines in the
  field
Ch. 5G: Insects (scorpions)
  VII 71 -- 2 oblique lines
  form an arch ab
  XII 142 -- lines in the
  field
Ch. 5H: Fish
  (1) -- II 3.245b
  lines in the field
  (pair) -- HMs 480 (AT 33)
  2 lines ab each fish
Ch. 5I: Dolphins
  (1) -- II 3.34
  2 bel dolphin
  (3)
  IX 73 -- a horizontal
  line bel each, the
  bottom line slightly
  thicker perhaps a
  fish? R)
  I Supp. 37 -- horizontal
  line separates the top
  2 from the bottom
  dolphin
  (4) -- XIII 77
  gouges betw
Ch. 5K: Shellfish
  (crab) -- AM 1938.1440a/HMs
  388b (KSPI L40; CS 9S)
  horizontal lines beh

(shells, murex?) -- VII 188
line engraved horizon-
tally across the
center
Ch. 6B: Genii
II 4.64 -- crude lines
flank the genii
Ch. 7A: Branches -- X 238
center Branch 3 flanked by
2 lines
Ch. 7B: Misc. Plants
II 3.144
XII 151b -- line ab & bel,
strokes in the field
Ch. 8F: Friezes -- VII 203
wavy line with strokes (=
Branch 3?) encircles

17B
Mount-Guides

(see Part IV: Iconographic
Bibliography, p. 353, for a
definition)

Single
IN FRONT
PT 10A, L: lion
II 3.257 & X 277a
PT 13C, R: lion -- IX 107
PT 23C, R: 2 lions -- XIII
24

IN BACK
PT 47B: griffin L vs stag
-- V 642

IN FRONT & IN BACK (Flank)
PT 1A; Filler: agrimi -- II
3.259
PT 2, R; Filler:
lion -- IX 151
lioness -- II 3.122
PT 8, L: lion -- IX 150

PT 10A, L: lion -- I 405
?Ch. 2C: Women (1) -- HMs
467 (AT 105)

ABOVE & BELOW
PT 39A:
dog L vs agrimi/kid-man
-- XII 242
griffin L vs bull -- L.
Morgan Library 1077
Ch. 2B: Men (pair, misc.)
-- I Supp. 113
Ch. 3A: Man & Animal [misc]
-- AM 1938.1091

Double (cf. Ch. 2B: Men [pair]
-- I 131)

IN FRONT
PT 10A, R: lion -- XII 208
PT 11, R; Filler: lion --
XIII 22

IN FRONT & IN BACK (Flank)
PT 1A, L; Filler: agrimi --
IV 225
PT 2, L; Filler: lioness --
Copenhagen 1364
PT 10A, L: lion -- I 405
PT 10A, R: lion -- X 132
PT 23A, L: 2 boars -- HM G
3192 (CMCG 302)
PT 25B, L: 2 lions -- V 236?
PT 44A:
lion R vs bull -- X
131
lion R vs kid/calf --
XII 213
PT 47B: griffin vs Babylon-
ian Dragon -- XII 291
flank the monster (= 2
groundlines top &
bottom)
Ch. 2B: Men (pair) -- I 131
2 groundlines bel each
acrobat

Ch. 3A: Men & Animals (lion)
-- II 3.27 & XII 207
Ch. 3D: Men In Chariots --
VII 87
Ch. 5E: Birds & Waterbirds
(waterbirds, pair)
II 3.250 & V 439

ABOVE & BELOW
Ch. 2B: Men (warriors) -- AM
1938.1049 (CS 294)
ab & bel?
Ch. 5F: Alerions -- II 3.46
Ch. 5G: Insects (butter-
flies, 1) -- II 3.46

Double IN FRONT & Single IN
BACK

PT 2, L; Filler: lion --
Munich A.1199 (AGDS I
66)
Ch. 3A: Men & Animals
(lion) -- II 3.329

17C
Wavy Lines

(cf. Ch. 16D: Groundlines)

PT 6, L; Filler:
lion -- II 4.38
2 dots connected by wavy
line
bull -- IX 169
2 dots connected by wavy
line bel
PT 10A, R: griffin -- AM
1893.238 (CS 327)
ab
Ch. 3A: Man & Animals (lion)
-- X 161*
bow? inb

Ch. 5B: Animal Faces (bulls)
-- HMs 6b (KZ 83)
Ch. 5E: Birds & Waterbirds
(waterbirds, 1) -- HMs
358 (KSPI L?)
separates the 2
registers
(waterbirds, pair) -- HM G
3210 (CMCG 312)
bel
Ch. 6D: Misc. Monsters -- HMs
10b (KZ 48)
with dots
Ch. 8F: Figure-8 Shields --
VII 203
a wavy line with strokes
(Branch 3?) encircles

17D
Zig-Zags

(see: Ch. 16C: Dadoes [Dado
6a])

PT 1A, L; Filler: agrimi
IV 225 -- infr
X 124 -- infr
XII 195 -- infr & inb
XII 232 -- infr
HM G 3045 (CMCG 171) -- infr
& inb
PT 1B, L; boar -- V 314
ab
PT 1B, R; lion -- HM G 3331
(CMCG 121)
ab
PT 2, R: lioness -- II 3.302
2 bel
PT 6, L; Filler:
lion -- X 151?
originally a zig-zag bel?
(cf. PT 6, L; Filler:
X 152)

griffin -- HM 2170

PT 7, L; griffin -- AM AE 1200b
    (CS 15P)
        ab
PT 8, L; griffin -- V 437
    ab
PT 10A, L:
    lion -- II 3.257
    agrimi -- Munich A.1194
        (AGDS I 63)
        on back = hair
    griffin -- HM G 3324a (CMCG
        185a)
        ab
PT 10A, R: lion -- XIII 138
    lion sketched as a zig-zag
PT 10B, L: griffin, ABOVE
    V 590
    HMs 222 (KSPI R15)
    Munich A.1196 (AGDS I 47)
PT 11, L; Filler: griffin
    V 438 -- infr & ab
    V 684 -- ab
PT 11, R; Filler: griffin
    IX 105 -- ab
    XII 247 -- ab & infr
PT 17A, L: cow & calf -- BSA
    Cast 172
        double zig-zag ab & infr
PT 19D, L: 2 agrimia -- IX 189
    zig-zags/branch infr
PT 36 cl: 2 lions -- BSA cast
        184
    double zig-zags bel one
        lion & betw
PT 39A: griffin L vs bull --
    L. Morgan Library 1077
        inb
PT 47B: lion R vs kid -- Edith
    Eccles Coll.
        double zig-zags ab
Ch. 2D: Men & Women (& a boat)
        -- AM 1938.1129
    decorate the boat's hull
Ch. 3E: Animal Games (bull-
        leaping,

Diving) -- AM 1938.964 (CS
    202)
    bull salient on cistern/
        box decorated with
        zig-zags
Floating) -- II 3.271
    oblique line ab with
        zig-zags ab
Ch. 5E: Birds & Waterbirds
    (birds, 1), ABOVE --
XII 141 & AM 1938.978
    (CS 223)
Ch. 5F: Alerions (head R)
    X 277b -- ab
    X 318 -- ab & bel
Ch. 5G: Insects (butterflies,
    trio) -- IX 162a
        ab
Ch. 5H: Fish, BELOW
    (1) -- HM 2346
    (pair) -- HMs 474 (AT 9)
Ch. 5I: Dolphins
    (pair) -- II 3.71
        encircle
    (4) -- AM 1938.1007 (CS
        355)
        betw
Ch. 9G: Rosettes -- V 180a
    around periphery
Ch. 9H: Cross -- II 3.150
    encircle = around periphery
Ch. 9M: Reticulation -- II
    4.193

                17E
            Net/Reticulation

(see: Ch. 12D -- Weapons
[Nets])

PT 1A, L; Filler: agrimi -- X
    113b
        ab

PT 1A, R; Filler:
  agrimi -- IV 54D
    inb
  agrimi kid -- HM G 3452
      (CMCG 259)
    encircles (= beh?)
PT 1B, R: bull
  HM no. unknown from Kamilari
    beh
  HMs no. unknown (AT 60)
    at right
PT 9, L: bull, BEHIND
  I Supp. 53
  VIII 52
  AM 1938.1018 (CS 236)
  HMs 581 (AT 61)
PT 11, R: griffin -- I 293
  reverse: reticulated &
    filled with blue glass
Ch. 2B: men (1) -- Chania 1563
  bel (= water), each diamond
    filled with a loop
Ch. 3A: Man & Animals (caprids)
  -- HMs 131 (KSPI Pe)
    beh
Ch. 5E: Birds & Waterbirds
  (birds, 1), BEHIND -- HMs
  58 (KZ 91) & HMs 586a (AT
  28)
Ch. 5H: Fish
  (1)
    AM 1925.44 (CS 189)
      bel
    HMs no. unknown (AT 11)
      beh
  (pair) -- HMs 480 (AT 33)
    betw
Ch. 5I: Dolphins
  (1) -- HMs 404a (KSPI
      L41)
    beh
  (pair, net/reticulation
    betw/in the center) --
      II 3.71
      HM G 3046 (CMCG 320)
      HM G 3519 (CMCG 321)
Ch. 8J: Misc. Patterns -- X

69*
  bel
Ch. 9B: Centered Circles
  (2)
    I Supp. 11 -- on sides
      d & e
    I Supp. 60 -- on the
      short sides
  (3) -- V 420
    on the faces

17F
Architectonic

PT 1B, L; sheep -- XII 136
  exergue ab
PT 1B, R; lion -- HM G 3331
  (CMCG 121)
    reverse
PT 5A, L; Filler: bull --
  II 3.238
    beh

17G
Hatching

PT 5A, L; Filler: agrimi -- II
  3.258
  bel groundline
PT 10B, L: griffin -- V 208
  bel at left
Ch. 3A: Man & Animals (misc.)
  -- HMs 167 (KSPI K8)
    beh
Ch. 4A: Women & Animals
  (antithetic) -- HM G
  3054 (CMCG 359)
    ab

Ch. 5I: Dolphins
  (1) -- II 4.155
      bel
  (pair) -- I 409
      in the field
  (4) -- XIII 77
      betw
Ch. 6A: People-Animals (winged
  man) -- XIII 60
      inb
Ch. 9B: Centered Circles (2) --
  II 4.42
Ch. 9G: Rosettes -- HMs 57 (KZ
  94)
  in the field
Ch. 9H: Cross -- I Supp. 163
  in 2 quadrants
Ch. 9J: Quadripartite -- I
  Supp. 47
Ch. 9R: Misc. Patterns -- II
  4.210

17H
Dots/Blobs

PT 1A, L; Filler:
  lion -- V 264
      beh
  bull -- IX 174
      ab
PT 1A, R; Filler:
  bull -- V 683
      bel
  agrimi
      V 170 -- ab & bel
      V 272 (kid) -- bel
      IX 202 -- bel
  cat -- IV 311
      ab
PT 1C, L; bull -- VII 200
  bel
PT 2, L; Filler: bull -- XIII
  131

2 bel
PT 2, R; Filler:
  bull
      II 4.4 -- arrow of dots
          infr
      IX 203 -- bel
      X 244 -- dots/<u>Figure-8
          Shield</u> bel
  goat -- X 181
      bel
  quadruped
      V 310 -- ab & bel
      V 321 -- ab & bel
PT 5A, L; Filler: agrimi
  ABOVE
      IV 288 -- 2 ab
      XII 274
      XII 275
PT 5A, R; Filler: goat -- I
  Supp. 39
      infr
PT 6, L; Filler
  lion
      II 4.38 -- 2 dots con-
          nected by wavy line ab
      II 4.138 -- dots (=
          rocks?) bel
  bull -- IX 169 -- 2 dots
      connected by wavy line
      bel
  agrimi
      V 528 (kid) -- dot ab
      VII 196 -- dot ab
PT 6, R; Filler:
  bull
      V 575 -- 8 ab
      VIII 156 -- row of dots
          infr
      X 258 -- row of dots
          infr
  quadruped
      V 403 -- 8 infr & 4 bel
      X 310 -- ab
PT 10A, L: griffin -- II 3.349
  3 dots form part of the
      plume
  2 dots ab wing

PT 10B, R: bull -- I Supp. 79
infr
PT 12, L: lion -- XII 244
a row of dots ab half-
    encircle
PT 13A, R
lion -- X 154
    row of dots infr
calf -- VII 136?
    dots bel
PT 14A, R: bull -- I 496
infr
PT 18B, L: cow & calf -- ?II
4.142
PT 25B, R: 2 agrimi kids -- II
    3.123
infr & inb
PT 28A: 2 bulls -- V 337
centered dot ab & bel each
PT 31A: 2 dogs/lions -- HMs 285
    (KSPI G14)
ab
PT 31B:
2 lions -- II 3.306
    flank the bull's face
        betw the 2 lions
    2 dogs -- HMs 233 (KSPI R88)
    dots ab
PT 37A cl: 2 lions -- V 493
dots infr of & bel each lion
PT 39A:
lion L vs stag -- X 129
    inb
dog L vs agrimi/kid-man --
    XII 242
    2 (= Figure-8 Shield?)
        bel lion
    4 dots infr of sphinx
PT 47A: dog R vs bull -- XII
    265
bel bull
PT 48A: lion vs agrimi -- VII
180
    betw
Ch. 2C: Women
(1, stands frontal) --
    HM G 3103 (CMCG 366)

2 groups of 3 dots
    flank
(pair, salute)
    I Supp. 133 -- flank
    I Supp. 134 -- flank
    I Supp. 135 -- in the
        field
Ch. 2E: People at a Shrine --
    II 3.114
wavy line of dots
    (necklace?) ab bird
Ch. 3A: Man & Animals
(bull) -- IX 146
    2 dots/balls ab
(several) -- AM 1938.1091
    vertical line topped
        with a rayed dot
    2 dots separate the men
        from the genius
Ch. 3D: Men In Chariots --
    Louvre A02188
in the field
Ch. 4A: Women & Animals
(woman seated L at right)
    -- I 179
    dots (Stars?) fill the
        area ab the Heaven
        Line
(antithetic)
    XIII 135 -- inb
    AM 1938.1139 -- row of
        dots ab
Ch. 5B: Animal Faces (bulls)
V 347 -- 3 ab
V 623 -- 2 flank
AM 1938.952 (CS 104) --
    encircle
HMs 6b (KZ 83) -- wavy line
    with 3 dots ab
HMs 24a (KZ 81) -- bel
Ch. 5C: Animal Heads
(lions) -- II 2.48 encircle
(bulls) -- AM 1938.970
    (CS 206)
    2 ab & 1 bel

Ch. 5D: Protomes (caprid) --
    I 403
infr of each protome
Ch. 5E: Birds & Waterbirds
    (waterbirds, pair) --
V 422a
    in the field
Ch. 5F: Alerions (head L) --
    XII 254
2 flank the head
Ch. 5G: Insects (butterflies,
    1) -- VII 71
arch ab with a central dot
Ch. 5I: Dolphins (1) -- II
    3.34
2 ab & 1 bel
Ch. 6A: People-Animals:
Eagle-Woman (head R) -- II
    4.137
    2 large dots flank
Winged Agrimi-Woman -- XII
    276b
    bel head
Ch. 6D: Misc. Monsters -- HMs
    10b (KZ 48)
wavy line with dots
Ch. 7A: Branches (2 Branch 1)
V 156
X 209 -- central dot
Ch. 7B: Misc. Plants -- AM
    1938.1053 (CS 251)
dots encircle
Ch. 8E: Helmets (plumed, L)
X 243 -- row inb
HMs 494 (AT 6) -- row ab &
    at right
Ch. 8F: Figure-8 Shield -- II
    3.113
betw each shield
Ch. 9B: Concentric Circles (7)
    -- II 4.186
Ch. 9C: Arcs
I Supp. 139 -- at each focus
V 245 -- at each focus
VII 202 -- 2 between
Ch. 9F: Meanders -- V 332
in center

Ch. 9G: Rosettes -- XII 157
large dot with superimposed
    circle in center
Ch. 9Q: Misc. Lines
X 199 -- dots
X 202 -- encircling
    center dot
X 237 -- dots

17I
Arcs

PT 1A, L; Filler: agrimi
IV 225 -- 2 infr
X 113b -- ab
PT 5A, R; Filler: agrimi --
VIII 93
    bel
PT 6, L; Filler: Babylonian
Dragon -- HM G 3138 (CMCG
283)
    bef neck
PT 37C ccl: 4 caprids -- I 323
engraved over the center of
    the seal
Ch. 2C: Women (1, at Altar) --
I 410
    the woman seems to hold
        a stick crowned with
        2 arcs
    arcs (decoration?) bel
        the Altar/Table
Ch. 2E: People at a Shrine
(person at left) -- IX 163
    arc (= necklace?) bel
    Shrine
Ch. 3A: Man & Animals
(several) --
    AM 1938.1091
        dotted arcs ab the 2
        men

Ch. 3C: Man Hunts Animals
   (fisherman) -- HMs 164
         (KSPI K3)
   in the field
Ch. 5E: Birds & Waterbirds
   (birds, 1) -- X 117
      3 bel & 2 sets of 3
         flank bird
   (birds, misc.) -- VIII 135
   bel
Ch. 9E: Spirals -- X 235
   outlined by arcs
Ch. 9G: Rosettes -- V 370
   parallel arcs surround each
   "grain/leaf"
Ch. 9H: Cross -- V 190
   cross, the ends capped with
      arcs, & an arc betw each
      leg of the cross, all
      inside a square (random
      arcs in the other square)

17J
Arcade/Shell Pattern

PT 12, R: bull -- I 283
   reverse: arcades filled
      with blue glass
Ch. 2B: Men (1) -- Chania 1563
   as rock projections = coast-
   line
Ch. 2C: Women (1, misc.) --
   HMs 392 (KSPI Cc)
   shell pattern beh
Ch. 2E: People at a Shrine
   (tree-pulling, no Omphalos)
   -- Once in the Evans Coll.,
   The Ring of Minos
      Shrine on the top of a
         mountain, decorated
         with an arcade pattern

17K
Circles/Drill Marks/Rings

(see: Ch. 9B: Circles; & 9E:
Spirals -- HMs 147 [KZ 174])

PT 1A, L; Filler: Babylonian
   Dragon -- V 581
   5 drill marks & 1 circle ab
PT 2, L; Filler: bull -- IX 123
   circle ab rump & bel
PT 2, R; Filler: bull -- HM
   2301
   3 (5) rings ab
PT 8, L
   lion -- VIII 104
      circle encircles
   dog/calf/lion -- XII 135a
      Frond with circle ab
PT 10A, L: bull -- I 281
   circle infr
PT 11, L; Filler: agrimi -- I
   Supp. 92
   circle engraved (later?)
      over the center of the
      seal
PT 12, L: bull -- II 3.101
   circle bef the back & 2 bel
      (ab hindleg)
PT 12, R: bull -- X 187*
   2 centered circles ab
PT 13A, R: bull
   VIII 141 -- 1 small circle
      bef the shoulder & 2
      small circles bel
   IX 193 -- Dado 6d with 6
      circles ab
PT 14A, L: agrimi -- X 137
   2 circles bel
PT 18B, R: cow & calf
   I 67 -- 6 circles ab
   V 317 -- circle ab
PT 30A
   2 bulls -- XIII 11
      2 circles ab

2 goats -- I 48
  a circle on near goat's
    neck & hip
  a circle on far goat's
    neck
PT 30B: 2 bulls -- I 197
  3 circles ab
PT 36 ccl: 2 lions -- HM G
  3432 (CMCG 296)
    centered circle infr of
      each
PT 38, L: lion vs bull -- AM
  1938.1036 (CS 318)
    3 circles infr
PT 39A: lion R vs kid --
  Oxford, MS
    circle ab & 2 bel
Ch. 2C: Women
  (1, frontal) -- I 3.239
    in the field
  (stands R) -- II 4.55
    2 flank
Ch. 3A: Man & Animals
  (lion) -- II 3.52
    2 infr & 1 ab
  (several)/Ch. 5C: Animal
    Heads (groups) -- HMs
    656 (KSPI U115)
      ab at left
Ch. 3E: Animal-Sacrifice -- I
  203
    3 ab
Ch. 5B: Animal Faces (bulls)
  -- HMs 152 (KSPI S5)
    dotted ab
Ch. 5C: Animal Heads (groups)
  -- HMs 656 (KSPI U115)
  centered circle ab at left
Ch. 5E: Birds & Waterbirds
  (waterbirds, 1)/Ch. 5F:
    Alerions (head
    direction unknown) --
    XII 210
      centered circle ab &
        5 centered circles
        in the field
Ch. 5G: Insects (butterflies,

1) -- HM G 3185 (CMCG 329)
  2 ab
Ch. 5H: Fish (1, conventional)
  -- AM 1925.44 (CS 189)
    centered circle ab
Ch. 7A: Branches (2 Branch 2)
  I Supp. 10 -- 3 centered
    circles in the center
  II 3.383 -- 2 pairs flank
    Branch 1
  AM 1941.107 (CS 194) -- a
    centered circle in each
      quadrant
Ch. 9D: Dots
  II 3.85 -- a: 2 (-4?)
    centered circles & b: 3
    centered circles
    preserved
  X 197 -- circumscribed by 2
    hand-engraved circles
Ch. 9G: Rosettes
  V 180a -- circle in center
  V 408 -- centered circle in
    center
  X 105 -- large centered
    circle in center
Ch. 9H: Cross
  II 3.150
  V 190 -- a circle in the
    center (random circles in
    the other square)
  V 494
  VII 244
  VII 245
Ch. 9M: Reticulation
  I Supp. 60 -- long sides: 2
    concentric circles
  V 420 -- sides: 3 centered
    circles
Ch. 9P: Misc. Lines -- I Supp.
  12
Ch. 9Q: Misc. Lines
  II 4.189 -- a circle top &
    bottom
  V 448 -- sides: 2 centered
    circles

17L
Miscellaneous Patterns

Cross
PT 37C ccl:
    4 bulls -- XIII 12
        quarters the field
    4 caprids -- I 323
        quarters the field
Ch. 9B: Centered Circles (4)
    I 34 & II 4.14
Ch. 9E: Spirals -- HMs 11
    (KZ 134)
    cross made by interlocking
        C-spirals
Ch. 9L: Hatching -- V 375
Ch. 9P: Flaked Obsidian Disks
    -- VII 38b

Spirals
Ch. 6B: Genii -- XII 212
    2 rows of spirals flank
Ch. 7B: Misc. Plants (Papyrus)
    -- HMs 172a (KZ 172)
        volute spiral
Ch. 9B: Centered Circles
    (2) -- II 3.127
        S-shaped spiral betw
    (misc.) -- XII 179
        a groove spirals around
            the face

Stars (see: Ch. 12I: Suns)
PT 1A, L; Filler: quadruped --
    II 4.43
PT 1A, R; Filler: bull -- X
    186
        ab
PT 5A, R; Filler: agrimi -- I
    Supp. 164b
        the hole bel was made
            into a star
Ch. 2C: Women (1, at Altar) --
    I 410
    the woman seems to hold a
        stick crowned with 2

arcs ending in a star-
    like object

Triangles
PT 1A, R; Filler: agrimi -- V
    339
    2 ab & 3 bel
PT 13A, R: bull -- V 280
    bel

Diamonds
Ch. 9E: Spirals -- HMs 11 (KZ
    134/CS S10b)
        in the center

Hearts (or murex shells/
    peppers)
Ch. 5K: Shellfish
    VII 188 -- 2
    AM 1938.975 (CS 379) -- 5

V's
PT 40: lion R vs bull -- X 241
    inverted infr
PT 46; Attacker Right: griffin
    vs stag -- V (= seagull-
        type bird?) ab
Ch. 9J: Quadripartite -- I
    Supp. 47

X's
PT 11, L; Filler: lion -- IV
    282
    engraved later over lion
PT 39A: dog L vs agrimi/kid-man
    -- XII 242
    inb of sphinx & X (or
        crossed tail inb of fawn)
PT 25B, R: lion & agrimi -- I
    115
    infr
Ch. 3A: Man & Animals (bulls)
    -- VII 100
    bel
Ch. 4A: Women & Animals (woman
    inb) -- BSA cast 188
        2 X's betw

Ch. 5B: Animal Faces (bulls) --
   HMs 152 (KSPI S5)
      betw horns
Ch. 9B: Circles (2)/Ch. 9M:
   Reticulation -- I Supp. 11
      ends

Flaked
Ch. 5I: Dolphins (1)
   I Supp. 120 -- bel
   IV 166b -- bel
Ch. 9B: Centered Circles (4)
   -- VIII 143b

Miscellaneous
PT 1A, R; Filler: goat -- HMs
   335 (KSPI L26)
      swastika ab
PT 18B, R: cow & calf -- V 404
   reverse: 6 drilled holes
Ch. 9E: Spirals (C-spiral) --
   HMs 116 (KSPI O11)
      wedge betw
Ch. 9G: Rosettes -- V 165
   line/wedges encircle

PART III

INDEX OF RARE ANIMALS

Apes/Monkeys
PT 31B: 2 monkeys -- HM G 3311
   (CMCG 355)
Ch. 3A: Man & Animals
   (misc.) -- I 377
      an ape infr to L with
         arms up-raised
   (several) -- HMs 160 (KSPI
      Q19)
      at right: ape seated L
         on a campstool
Ch. 5A: Misc. Quadrupeds
   (monkeys) -- V 233

Cat
PT 1A, R; Filler: cat? -- IV
   311

Donkey
PT 1B, R; donkey? -- HM G
   3102

Horse (see: PT 1A, R; Filler:
   HM G 3211 [CMCG 338])

PT 1A, R; Filler: horse? --
   Melos 574
PT 1B, L: horse -- V 365
PT 5A, L; Filler: horse -- HMp
   4793-5
PT 20, L: 2 horses? -- I 390

PART IV

ICONOGRAPHIC BIBLIOGRAPHY

with

Commentary

Composition Principles
Biesantz 1958
Jung 1986
Pini 1986
Sourvinou-Inwood 1986
van Effenterre 1980

Animal Pose Types
General
    Younger 1973: 255-358

Specific
    PT 13 -- Sakellariou 1966:
      50-52
    PT's 16 & 17 -- Younger
      1974
    PT's 28 & 29 -- Deonna
      1968
    PT's 38-54 -- Pini 1985
    PT's 38 & 39 -- Sakellariou
      1966: 54-56, types II &
      IV
    PT's 42 & 43 -- Sakellariou
      1966: 54-57, types III,
      VI, & VII
    PT 44 -- Sakellariou 1966:
      54
    PT's 46 & 47 -- Sakellariou
      1966: 54-55, type III
    PT's 48-50 -- Sakellariou
      1966: 56-57, types V &
      VIII
    PT 54 -- Sakellariou 1966:
      57, type X

People
General
    Deonna 1926

Merrillees 1980
Tamvaki 1977 & 1986

Faces/Heads
    Betts 1981
    Biesantz 1954b
    Blegen 1962
    Marinatos 1962
    Sakellariou 1966: 25-6

Figures
Men
    Single Robed figure --
      PM IV 404 f. &
        412-414
    Master of Animals
      Betts 1965
      Sakellariou 1958:
        82-85
        1966: 70-72
      Younger 1973: 241-247
Women
    With upraised arms
      Alexiou 1958
      Hoglund 1981
      Karageorghis
        1977-1978
    Seated
      Sakellariou 1966: 67
    With Animals
      Potnia Theron
        Christou 1968
        Demargne 1939
        Gill 1969
          (Snake Frame)
        Sakellariou 1966:
          70-72
        van Leuven 1979
        Younger 1973:
          238-241
      "Crossed" by a caprid --
      Sakellarakis 1972b

Costumes
General
    Bielefeld 1968
    Marinatos 1967

Sapouna-Sakellaraki 1971

Jewelry
    Necklaces resemble boat-
        cabin decorations &
        ship rigging on the
        Thera Ship fresco
        (Marinatos 1974: color
        pls. 4 & 9; Laffineur
        1984; Morgan 1984) &
        perhaps as decorations in
        windows (as depicted in
        frescoes: Rodenwaldt
        1911: pl.IX.2) & in
        Shrines (cf. I 126).
        Ladies also swing or hold
        them on frescoes from
        Thera, Knossos, &
        Mycenae.
    Earrings -- see: Schliemann
        1880: fig. no. 293 &
        Marinatos 1974: color
        pl. 5 right

Coiffure
    Marinatos 1967
    Sapouna-Sakellaraki 1968

Activities
Fishing
    Guest-Papamanoli 1983
    Sakellarakis 1974

Hunting
    Sakellariou 1966: 60-62
    Younger 1973: 247-8

Bull-Games
    Berger 1986
    Evans 1921
    Lendle 1965
    Pinsent 1983
    Reichel 1909
    Sakellariou 1958 (CMCG):
        85-9 & 1966: 57-60
    Ward 1968
    Younger 1976 & 1984

Bull-Sacrifice
    Sakellarakis 1970

Conveyances
Ships/Boats
    General
        Alexiou 1971
        Betts 1973
        Casson 1975
        Doumas 1970
        Gray 1974
        Johnston 1982
        Raban 1894
        van Effenterre 1978

    Animal-Head Bow/Prow
        Aegis's appear, always
        facing forward, on both
        the bow & stern of the
        ceremonial barge of the
        god Amun (Egypt: XVIIIth
        Dynasty; Millet &
        Champion 1983: fig. 8;
        cf. fig. 11, a warship
        of Ramses III with a
        lioness-head prow); a
        monster-head terminal
        decorates the royal Thai
        barge (Everingam 1982:
        ill. on p. 489, lower
        right); several ships on
        the Thera Ship fresco
        have butterflies-in-
        profile, flying birds,
        or rosettes like
        dandelion puffs for prow
        terminals & crouching
        lions or falcon-heads
        with elongated necks for
        the stern terminals that
        face backwards (Marina-
        tos in Gray 1974: G
        145).

    Chariots -- Vermeule &
        Karageorghis 1982:
        181-187 for bibliography

Drawn by griffins -- AJA 76
(1972) 327 & 437

Vessels
General -- Davis 1977

Goblet (KSPI Q22) --
Evans TDA pp. 26-30
Jugs
Chapouthier 1946
Sakellariou 1966: 40-41

Military
General
Buchholz & Wiesner
1977, & Buchholz 1980
Guida 1973
Sakellariou 1966:
43-44 & 63-4; 1971; 1974;
& 1975

Helmets
Alexiou 1954
Borchhardt 1972
Deonna 1954
Holland 1929
Kalligas 1981
Sakellariou 1953 & 1973
Vavaregou 1981

Points -- Arrows & Spears
(for lances, see Hood &
de Jong 1952: no. A1;
Hesperia 35, 1966, 74-5;
& Sakellarakis 1981b:
206)
Avila 1983
Buchholz 1976 & 1980
Hockman 1980
Kaiser 1974: 50-52

Shields
Deroy 1979
Buchholz & Wiesner 1977

Swords
Hood 1980

Sandars 1961 & 1963

Architecture (see: Shrines,
below)
General
Graham 1969
Hallegar 1985
Sakellariou 1966: 35-36
Shaw 1971

Columns
Brommer 1981

Religious Activity
General
Gesell 1985
Herkenrath 1937
Long 1974
Mylonas 1977
Niemeier 1986
Rutkowski 1981
Sourvinou-Inwood 1971 &
1986

Tree-Worship
Marinatos, N. 1986
Taylor 1979

Bull-Sacrifice --
Sakellarakis 1970

Religious Buildings -- Shrines
Shaw's Tripartite Shrine
(Shaw 1978), though
undoubtedly a reality, does
not, however, seem to be
depicted on sealstones &
rings. The glyptic Shrine
is a simple cella,
sometimes fronted by a
porch, often raised on a
masonry base. A tree grows
either from the top or,
more likely, from the
interior of the Shrine &
through the top. The sima
of the Shrine is often

decorated with <u>Horns of Consecration</u> antefixes.

Gesell 1978 & 1985 describes similarly simple structures (cf.the one-room shrine at Gournia: Russel 1979).

General
   Gesell 1983

Sanctuaries -- Hagg & Marinatos 1981

Religious -- Epiphanies
   (for the <u>Potnia Theron</u> & Master of Animals, see People, above).

   Th. Corsten, "Zu den Sogenannten Schwebendem Gottheiten," Das Ende der mykenischen Welt, Koln Kolloquium (7-8 July 1984) suggests that some of these small figures are to be interpreted as figures at a distance; such a suggestion might explain the small figure on the Isopata Ring but few others.

Goddess with the Upraised Arms
   Alexiou 1958

Shield-god/goddess (cf. the trophy VII 158 & the small figure carrying a shield on I 17)
   Barrelet 1955
   Buchholz 1962
   Rehak 1982
   Small 1966
   Vermeule 1958

Religious Objects
Cypress Branch
   The <u>Cypress Branch</u> appears often in the upper field of religious scenes, once above the <u>Heaven Line</u> (I 179) along with the <u>Sun</u> & <u>Moon</u>; is it there another heavenly body, perhaps a shooting star or a comet? (e.g., Halley's comet might have been visible about the year 1510 B.C., a not impossible date for the Tiryns ring)

Double Ax
   Hodge 1985
   Mavriyannaki 1983
   Sakellariou 1966: 43-44

Horns of Consecration
   Loulloupis 1973
   Powell 1977
   Willetts 1978

Omphaloi
   Gill 1964: 8
   Renfrew 1985

Omphaloi/<u>Squills</u> -- Warren 1984
   While the sea squill, especially when doubled, looks very much like the smaller versions of the <u>Omphalos</u>/<u>Squill</u>, the larger ones at which people kneel must be thought of as something slightly different -- perhaps a baetyl with a squill placed on it.

Pithoi/<u>Shields-in-Profile</u>

   Rutkowski 1981: 30
      The object or objects

which occasionally frame
a cult scene are here
called Pithoi/Shields-in-
Profile; Sourvinou-Inwood
identifies these objects
as pithoi (1971 & 1986).
Two seals clearly depict a
Figure-8 Shield in profile:
I 219 (Ch. 2B: Men
[single]; & HMs 195 [KZ
195]; Ch. 2D: Men & Women
[pair]). A third, the ring
from Varkiza T. 1 (Ch. 3A:
Men & Animals [bull]) may
also carry a Figure-8
Shield in profile. One seal
may carry a tower shield in
profile: HMm 1034 (Ch. 2B:
Men [single]). The remaining
seal, AM 1938.1129 (CS 250;
Ch. 2D: Men & Women [with a
boat]), has been published
only in a drawing. The
object at the left seems
there to be a pithos; until
better photographs are made
available the object is here
identified according to its
iconographic parallels.

Sacred Heart
    It is difficult to
identify this object. It
may be shaped like the
pomegranite buds that
dangle from such necklaces
as Karo 78 from Mycenae
Shaft Grave III, or, if
understood as cordiform
in shape, we can then
see this object imitated
in other media: as a shape
for sealstones carrying an
alerion: the amethyst AM
1938.977 (CS 187) from
Knossos; & one of
cornelian in the HM, no.

unknown, from Kamilari (MM
III-LM I context; Annuario
39-40, 1961-2, 7-148 no. 17
figs. 125 & 143); as a
shape for pendants, all in
the HM: HM 2350 of agate (SH
across the top; EtCret VII
pl. 22); one of cornelian
from Knossos (JHS 14 p.281;
Cretan Pictographs p.12 fig.
8); one of rock crystal from
Gournia (Gournia 55 fig.
35.3a & b, & n. 21), &
another? from Iouktas; one
of magnetite from Avgo
(Hastings 1905: 284 pl.
10.23); & one of gold, from
Knossos (PM III 411 fig.
273); as a shape for
miniature stone palettes,
cosmetic dishes, or ladles
(HM 3553, 3645, 3794, & 2
others in HM case 21a; see
Warren 1969: 48-49, Shape
23).

Sacred Knot/Robe (PM I 429-
    435)
    Alexiou: 1967
    Demargne: 1948
    Korres 1980

Snake Frame
    Gill 1969
    Hagg & Lindau 1984

Tables/Sacrificial Tables
    Sakellarakis 1970

Trees
    Marinatos, N.: 1986
    Moebius 1933: 35

Waisted Altar
    There is one? in niello
on the gold cup Karo 390
from Mycenae Shaft Grave IV

with 5 <u>Branch 1</u>'s.

Signs
   General
      Gill 1966: 11-16
      Kenna 1962-1964

   Tailed Linear B -a-
      Vermeule 1961: 145, n.5
   <u>Impaled Triangle</u>
      Gill 1966: 15 nos. 1-24
      Kenna 1966: 55-57
      Palmer: Nestor p. 1830

Animals (for perspectives &
   movement, see Amiran 1956
   & Slusser 1945-1947)

Lions
   Deonna 1948
   Persson 1942: 125
      (emblems of Mycenae)
   Richardson 1978
   Sakellariou 1966: 4-7

Boars
   Sakellariou 1966: 10
   Younger 1973: 319-321

Bulls
   Persson 1931: 125-126
      (as emblems of the
      House of Minos)

Cows & Calves (PT 16 & 17)
   Buchanan 1954
   Kenna 1968c: 1219-1220

Deer -- Sakellariou 1966:
   7-10

Dogs
   Sakellariou 1966: 11 & 52
   Younger 1973: 321-322

Birds
   Kenna 1968b

PM III 115-118
Sakellariou 1966: 12-14
Insects
   Butterflies/Dragonflies
      PM II 787-790
      Sakellariou 1966: 15

Marine Animals
   Fish
      PM I 678 etc.
      Sakellariou 1966: 14

   Shellfish
      Conch -- cf. Furumark
      1972, Analysis FM
      23a. They are blown
      during the Goat Dance
      in Skyros (The
      Athenian, March 1978,
      p. 43) & in Cretan
      villages to announce
      the arrival of the
      mail (Alexiou, Cretan
      Civilization, p. 108;
      cf. The Athenian,
      April 1978, pp.
      46-8); & were used in
      Classical times as
      trumpets (CVA
      Ashbury/Northampton
      57 pls. 33 & 62 =
      ARV2 124, no. 7, a
      cup by the
      Nikosthenes Ptr.).
      Many have been found
      with their ends sawn
      as if to function as
      trumpets. There are
      imitations in
      terracotta, stone, &
      faience (Warren 1969:
      90, class 35, to which
      add: Baurain & Darcque
      1983; Foster 1979:
      passim).

Monsters

Comments: some of these people-monsters do not necessarily have to be "real" monsters, but rather people dressed or masked as lions, bulls, goats, agrimia, etc. The sealing KZ 135 shows six lion heads with the faces omitted, as if cut out in order to function as masks; cf. the "unusually large bull's skull ... (from Toumba tou Skourou, that) had been trimmed of its back & lower jaw so a priest could slip it over his head as a ceremonial mask" (Vermeule 1974: 10 & 24, the caption to fig. 29). A pictorial vase & a larnax now in Germany (Vermeule & Karageorghis 1982: 54 no. V 103) & the seal VIII 110a depict a bucranium hanging from a chain; these may be masks.

Bibliography for Monsters
General
    Davaras 1980
    N. Schlager, Damonen-darstellungen in der minoischen und mykenischen Glyptik. Eine Typologie (Archaeological Institute of Vienna, PhD dissertation announced in Nestor p. 1271); Weingarten 1983

Babylonian Dragon
    Gill 1963
    Poursat 1976

Fish-Monster = shark?
    Cf. Admiralty General Section: A Handbook of Serbia; on pictorial vases -- Vermeule & Karageorghis 1982: 40 no. V.18, & n. 15

Genius
    Gill 1964 & 1970
    Sakellariou 1966: 22-24
    Von Straten 1966

    To Gill's & Van Straten's lists of depictions of genii, add those listed in Ch. 6B & the one painted on the shoulder or haunch of a bull rhyton from Tiryns (AJA 82, 1978, 339-340 fig. 4)

Goat-Man
    Sakellariou 1966: 16

Griffin
    Benson 1969
    Desenne 1957
    Frankfort 1936-7
    Sakellariou 1966: 20-22

Sphinx
    Demisch 1977
    Mylonas 1980
    Sakellariou 1966: 8-19

Lion-Man -- Sakellariou 1966: 16

Minotaur -- Schlager 1986

Miscellaneous -- Betts 1965

Protomes & Body Parts
   Sakellariou 1966: 15-16
   Younger 1973: 382-383

Plants (Mobius 1933)
Cypress -- see Religious
   Objects, above
Fronds -- Betts 1968
Lilies -- Petrakis 1980
Papyrus
   Betts 1978
   Warren 1977
Palm-- N. Marinatos 1984

Setting
Dadoes -- PM I 685-689

Geometric
      A Mount-Guide is a short
   line on the sealface,
   perpendicular to the SH &
   near its mouth, usually one
   at each SH mouth; on Cyl's,
   a line circumscribes top &
   bottom. Because of their
   position, these lines
   resemble (in impression & in
   relief) the intaglio marks
   left (in impression) by
   gold mounts & caps.

Flaking
   Schiering 1968
   Renfrew 1985: ch. 7, 296-7

PART V

CONCORDANCE

A

CMS Volumes

CMS I

5 -- Ch. 2A: Body Parts (man's head)
8 -- PT 5B, L; Plain: bull
9 -- Ch. 3C: Man Hunts Animals (lions)
10 -- PT 6, L; Filler: lion
11 -- Ch. 2B: Men (duels)
12 -- Ch. 2B: Men (duels)
13 -- PT 17A, L: doe & fawn
14 -- Ch. 9B: Centered Circles (misc.)
15 -- Ch. 3D: Men In Chariots
16 -- Ch. 2B: Men (battles)
17 -- Ch. 2C: Women (4 or more)
18 -- Ch. 5B: Animal Faces (misc. faces)
19 -- PT 28A: 2 bulls
20 -- PT 28A: 2 pairs of cow & calf
21 -- Ch. 5C: Animal Heads (caprids)
23 -- PT 5A, R; Filler: bull
24 -- PT 6, R; Filler: goat
25 -- PT 1C, R; bull
26 -- PT 5C, R: calf?/kid?
28 -- Ch. 9H: Cross
29 -- PT 6, R; Filler: quadruped
30 -- PT 25C, R: 2 goats
31 -- PT 6, R; Filler: quadruped
32 -- PT 1A, R; Filler: quadruped
34 -- Ch. 9B: Centered Circles (4)
35 -- PT 10B, L: bull
36 -- PT 44A: lion R vs bull

37 -- PT 6, L; Plain: agrimi
38 -- PT 1A, L; Filler: quadruped
39 -- PT 1A, R; Filler: quadruped
40 -- PT 29A: 2 goat forequarters
41 -- PT 13C, R: stag
42 -- Ch. 2B: Men (religious)
43 -- PT 13A, L: lion
44 -- PT 13A, R: lion
45 -- PT 19A, R: 2 agrimia
46 -- PT 31A: 2 lions conjoined
47 -- PT 37B ccl: 3 quadrupeds (bulls?)
48 -- PT 30A: 2 goats
49 -- PT 13C, R: bull
50 -- PT 21, R: 2 bulls
51 -- PT 14A, R: lion
53 -- PT 36 cl: 2 bulls
54 -- PT 5A, R; Filler: lion
55 -- PT 10B, L: bull
56 -- PT 11, R; Filler: lion
58 -- PT 28B: 2 calves
59 -- PT 2, L; Filler: bull
60 -- PT 34B: 2 lions
62 -- PT 17B, R: lion & cub
64 -- PT 13A, R: bull
65 -- PT 11, R; Filler: bull
66 -- PT 12, L: bull
67 -- PT 18B, R: cow & calf
68 -- Ch. 2B: Men (1)
69 -- PT 21, L: 2 bulls
70 -- PT 39A, R: lion vs bull
71 -- PT 21, R: 2 lions
72 -- PT 21, R: 2 calves
73 -- PT 31A: 2 griffins
74 -- PT 19B, L: 2 goats
76 -- PT 2, R; Filler: bull
77 -- PT 44B: lion-man L vs kid?
78 -- PT 18C, R: lioness & cub
79 -- Ch. 3E: Animal Games (bull-leaping, Floating)
80 -- Ch. 4D: Women & Animals (misc.)

81 -- PT 52B: 2 dogs vs stag L
82 -- Ch. 3E: Bull-Leaping
(Uncertain Poses)
83 -- PT 6, R; Filler: calf
84 -- PT 13A, R: lion
85 -- PT 8, R; griffin
86 -- Ch. 2E: People at a
Shrine (person at left)
87 -- PT 28A: 2 sphinxes
88 -- PT 1B, R: bull
89 -- Ch. 3B: Master of
Animals (lions)
90 -- PT 31: 2 agrimia
91 -- PT 3B/24, R: 2 bulls
92 -- PT 34B: 2 bulls
93 -- PT 19A, R: 2 goats
95 -- Ch. 3E: Animal Games
(bull-wrestling)
97 -- PT 30A: 2 goats
98 -- PT 31B: 2 griffins
99 -- PT 31B: 2 agrimia
100 -- PT 39A: lion L vs bull
101 -- Ch. 2D: Men & Women (2)
102 -- PT 29B: 2 griffins
103 -- PT 35/36 cl: 2 pairs of
a lion vs a sheep
104 -- PT 18B, L: cow & calf
105 -- PT 27A, R: 3 goats
106 -- PT 18A, R: lioness &
cub
107 -- Ch. 2B: Men (1)
108 -- Ch. 2E: People at a
Shrine (person at left)
109 -- PT 24, R: 2 bulls
110 -- Ch. 5B: Animal Faces
(lion)
112 -- Ch. 3C: Man Hunts
Animals (lions)
113 -- PT 27B, R: 3 sheep
114 -- Ch. 8D: Vessels
115 -- PT 25B, R: lion &
agrimi
116 -- PT 44A: lion L vs bull
117 -- PT 33A: 2 lions
119 -- Ch. 2E: People at a
Shrine (tree-pulling)
120 -- PT 6, R; Plain:

quadruped
121 -- PT 6, L; Plain: bull
122 -- PT 5A, R; Filler: calf
123 -- PT 32B: 2 agrimia
124 -- PT 30A: 2 stags
125 -- PT 18B, R: cow & calf
126 -- Ch. 2E: People at a
Shrine (tree-pulling)
127 -- Ch. 2E: People at a
Shrine (2 women flank)
128 -- Ch. 4A: Women & Animals
(woman at right)
129 -- PT 10A, R: sphinx
130 -- PT 19B, L: 2 bovines
131 -- Ch. 2B: Men (2)
132 -- Ch. 2C: Women (3)
133 -- PT 7, R; lion/Ch. 3A:
Men & Animals (lion)
134 -- Ch. 2C: Women (2)
135 -- PT 1A, R; Filler: boar
137 -- Ch. 3E: Animal Games
(bull-wrestling)
138 -- PT 1/2, R; bull
139 -- PT 5B, L; Plain: bull
140 -- PT 18B, L: cow & calf
141 -- PT 6, L; Plain: lion
142 -- PT 24, L: 2 bulls
143 -- PT 10A, R: agrimi
144 -- Ch. 4B: Potnia Theron
(lions)
145 -- Ch. 4B: Potnia Theron
(lions)
147 -- PT 1C, R; bull
148 -- PT 5A, R; Filler:
caprid
149 -- PT 8, L; lion
150 -- Ch. 5E: Birds &
Waterbirds (birds, 1)
151 -- Ch. 5E: Birds &
Waterbirds (waterbirds,
pair)
152 -- Ch. 3E: Animal Games
(bull-leaping, Diving)
153 -- Ch. 8E: Helmets
154 -- PT 1A, L; Plain: bull
155 -- PT 28A: 2 agrimia
156 -- Ch. 8A: Writing

157 -- PT 34B: 2 quadrupeds
158 -- PT 10A, R: agrimi
159 -- Ch. 2C: Women (3)
160 -- PT 13C, R: bull
161 -- PT 32B: 2 dogs
162 -- Ch. 2C: Women (3)
163 -- Ch. 3B: Master of
Animals (agrimia)
164 -- PT 6, R; Plain: dog
165 -- Ch. 3C: Man Hunts
Animals (lions)
166 -- Ch. 5C: Animal Heads
(caprids)
167 -- Ch. 4A: Women with
Animals (woman rides)
168 -- PT 16B, R: nanny & kid
169 -- PT 1D, R; bull
170 -- Ch. 2B: Men (3)
171 -- PT 28B: 2 griffins/ Ch.
6C: Griffins
172 -- PT 28B: 2 lions
173 -- Ch. 9B: Centered
Circles (2)
175 -- PT 25B, L: 2 bulls
176 -- PT 27B, R: 3 sheep
177 -- Ch. 9B: Centered
Circles (4)
178 -- PT 1A, L; Plain: agrimi
179 -- Ch. 4A: Women & Animals
(woman at right)
180 -- Ch. 2D: Men & Women
(with a boat)
182 -- PT 49B, L: lion vs kid
183 -- PT 25B, L: bull & lion
184 -- PT 36 cl: 2 boars
185 -- PT 39A, R: lion vs bull
186 -- PT 51E: 2 lions vs bull
R
187 -- PT 30A: 2 sheep
188 -- PT 1A, R; Filler: goat
189 -- PT 28A: 2 sheep/Ch. 5D:
Protomes
190 -- PT 42C, L: lion vs bull
191 -- Ch. 2E: People at a
<u>Shrine</u> (person at left)
192 -- PT 1A, L; Plain: boar
193a -- PT 23A, R: 2 agrimia

193b -- PT 40: lion R vs agrimi
194 -- PT 37B ccl: 3 lions
195 -- Ch. 2B: Men (1)
196 -- PT 31B: 2 griffins
197 -- PT 30B: 2 bulls
198 -- PT 32B: 2 bulls
conjoined
199 -- Ch. 3A: Man & Animals
(caprid)
200 -- Ch. 3E: Animal Games
(bull-leaping, Diving)
201 -- PT 3, L: bull
(-leaping?)
202 -- PT 13A, R: kid
203 -- Ch. 3F: Animal-
Sacrifice
204 -- PT 39C, L: lion vs bull
205 -- Ch. 8G: <u>Sacred Knot/</u>
<u>Robe</u>
206 -- PT 7, R; griffins &
lions
209 -- PT 10A, L: bull
210 -- PT 1A, R; Filler: agrimi
211 -- Ch. 5F: Alerions (misc.)
212 -- PT 5A, L; Filler: agrimi
213 -- PT 31B: 2 waterbirds
214 -- PT 40, L: lion vs bull
215 -- PT 26, L: 3 calves
216 -- PT 13A, L: calf-man
217 -- PT 13A, R: lion
219 -- Ch. 2D: Men & Women
(2)
220 -- Ch. 4C: Women "Crossed"
by a Caprid
221 -- Ch. 4C: Women "Crossed"
by a Caprid
222 -- Ch. 4C: Women "Crossed"
by a Caprid
223 -- Ch. 3A: Man & Animals
(griffins)
224 -- Ch. 3C: Man Hunts
Animals (lions)
225 -- Ch. 2B: Men (1)
226 -- Ch. 2C: Women (1)
227 -- Ch. 3C: Man Hunts
Animals (boars)
228 -- Ch. 3C: Man Hunts

Animals (lions)
229 -- Ch. 3D: Men In Chariots
230 -- Ch. 3D: Men In Chariots
231 -- Ch. 6B: Genii
232 -- Ch. 6B: Genii
233a -- Ch. 4B: <u>Potnia Theron</u>
 (waterbirds)
233b -- PT 5C, L; Plain: bull
234 -- PT 5B, L; Plain: bull
235 -- PT 13B, L: bull
236 -- PT 10A, R: bull
237 -- PT 12, L: bull
238 -- PT 26, R: 3 calves
239 -- PT 35 ccl: 2 bulls
240 -- PT 24, L: 2 bulls
241 -- PT 24, L: 2 bulls
242 -- PT 5B, R; Filler:
 agrimi
243 -- PT 8, R: lion
244 -- PT 11, L; Filler: lion
245 -- PT 5A, R; Plain: lion
246 -- PT 1B, R; lioness
247 -- PT 13A, R: lion
248 -- PT 12, R: lion
249 -- PT 36 ccl: 2 lions
250 -- PT 37A cl: 2 lions
251 -- PT 44B: lion R vs bull
252 -- PT 39C, R: lion vs bull
253 -- PT 46: lion R vs bull
254 -- PT 50B cl: lion vs
 bull?
255 -- PT 8, R: dog scratching
256 -- PT 8, L: dog scratching
257 -- Ch. 5C: Animal Heads
 (sheep)
258 -- PT 19A, R: waterbirds
259 -- Ch. 5 : Dolphins (2)
260 -- Ch. 8E: Helmets
262 -- PT 19A, L: 2 goats
263 -- Ch. 2B: Men (battles)
264 -- PT 1B, R; bull
265 -- PT 12, R: bull
266 -- PT 31: 2 agrimia
267 -- PT 49B, L: bull vs bull
268 -- PT 13A, L: bull
269 -- PT 1A, L; Plain:
 griffiness

270 -- Ch. 5G: Insects (misc.)
272a -- PT 11, L; Filler: lion
272b -- PT 11, L; Filler: stag
273a+b -- Ch. 5E: Birds &
 Waterbirds (waterbirds,
 pair)
274 -- Ch. 3E: Animal Games
 (bull-catching)
275 -- PT 24, R: 2 bulls
276 -- PT 23A, L: 2 boars
277 -- PT 13C, R: lion
278 -- PT 44A: lion R vs bull
279 -- Ch. 2E: People at a
 <u>Shrine</u> (person at right)
280 -- PT 25C, L: 2 lions
281 -- PT 10A, L: bull
282 -- PT 23A, R: 2 griffins
283 -- PT 12, R: bull
285 -- Ch. 3A: Man & Animals
 (griffin)
286 -- PT 49A, R: lion vs bull
287a -- PT 12, L: lion
287b -- PT 6, R; Filler: calf
290 -- Ch. 3C: Man Hunts
 Animals (lions)
291 -- PT 17A, L: cow & calf
292 -- Ch. 2E: People at a
 <u>Shrine</u> (person at left)
293 -- PT 11, R; Filler:
 griffin
294 -- Ch. 3C: Man Hunts
 Animals (boars)
297 -- PT 28A: 2 agrimi
298 -- PT 13A, R: kid
300 -- PT 1/2, R; bull
301 -- Ch. 9K: Lines/Strokes/
 Gouges
302 -- Ch. 3C: Man Hunts
 Animals (lions)
303 -- PT 50A ccl: lion vs
 goat
304 -- PT 28B: 2 pairs of a
 griffiness & fledgling
305 -- Ch. 3E: Animal Games
 (man infr)
306 -- Ch. 2B: Men (battles)
307 -- Ch. 3C: Man Hunts

Animals (lions)

308 -- PT 49A, R: dog vs agrimi

309 -- Ch. 3A: Man & Animals (griffins)

310 -- PT 40, R: lion vs bull

312 -- Ch. 5I: Dolphins (4 or more)/Ch. 5J: Octopus

313 -- Ch. 2C: Women (4 or more)

314 -- Ch. 3E: Animal Games (bull-leaping; Diving)

315 -- PT 6, R; Filler: bull

316 -- PT 10A, R: griffin

317 -- PT 36 cl: 2 bulls

318 -- PT 24, L: 2 bulls

319 -- PT 31A: 2 lions

321 -- Ch. 2C: Women (3)

322 -- PT 5B, L; Filler: caprid

323 -- PT 37C ccl: 4 caprids

324 -- PT 39A: 2 pairs of griffins vs stags/Ch. 3B: Master of Animals (griffins)

325 -- Ch. 6A: People-Animals (caprid-people)

326 -- Ch. 6A: People-Animals (caprid-people)

328 -- PT 6, R; Filler: quadruped

329 -- PT 10A, L: lions & griffins

330 -- PT 49A, L: lion vs bull

331 -- Ch. 3C: Man Hunts Animals (lions)

332 -- PT 1A, R; Plain: lion

333 -- PT 41: lion L vs quadruped

334 -- PT 6, L; Plain: bull

335 -- PT 49B, R: quadruped vs quadruped

336 -- PT 2, R; Plain; caprid

337 -- PT 6, R; Plain: quadruped

338 -- PT 5/6, L: quadruped

339 -- PT 5A, L; Plain: quadruped

340 -- Ch. 2B: Men (battles)

341 -- Ch. 6C: griffins

342 -- Ch. 3E: Animal Games (bull-wrestling)

343 -- PT 1B, L; boar

344 -- Ch. 4B: <u>Potnia Theron</u> (dolphins)

345 -- PT 1A, R; Plain: calf?

346 -- PT 10A, R: bull

347 -- PT 28A: 2 quadrupeds

348 -- PT 25B, L: 2 calves

349 -- PT 19B, R: 2 quadrupeds

350 -- PT 1B, R: quadruped

352 -- PT 30A: 2 quadrupeds

353 -- PT 1A, L; Plain: quadruped

354 -- Ch. 9D: Dots

355 -- PT 6, R; Filler: agrimi

356 -- Ch. 3B: Master of Animals (misc.)

357 -- PT 6, L; Plain: quadruped

358 -- PT 14A, R: lion

359 -- Ch. 3A: Man & Animals (lions)

360 -- PT 36 ccl: 2 quadrupeds

361 -- Ch. 2C: Women (4 or more)

362 -- PT 30A: 2 quadrupeds

363 -- PT 49A, L: dog vs stag

364 -- PT 17A, R: cow & calf

365 -- PT 2, R; Plain: quadruped

366 -- PT 6, R; Filler: quadruped

367 -- PT 5C, L; Filler: bull

368 -- PT 54: 2 lions vs bull L

369 -- Ch. 2B: Men (religious)

370 -- Ch. 3E: Animal Games (bull-leaping; Diving)

371 -- PT 36 ccl: 2 quadrupeds

372 -- PT 30A: 2 bulls

373 -- PT 1A, R; Filler: bull

374 -- Ch. 3A: Man & Animals (lions)

375 -- PT 29A: 2 calves
376 -- PT 18B, R: cow & calf
377 -- Ch. 3A: Man & Animals
(misc.)
378 -- Ch. 3E: Animal Games
(bull-leaping; Floating)
379 -- Ch. 4B: Potnia Theron
(misc.)
380 -- PT 14B, R: bull
381 -- PT 30A: lion & goat/
Ch. 5D: Protomes
383 -- PT 10A, R: griffin
384 -- PT 44A: lion R vs bull
385 -- PT 33A: 2 lions
386 -- PT 21, R: 2 goats
387 -- PT 10A, L: lion
388 -- PT 46: lion R vs bull
389 -- PT 11, R; Filler:
griffin
390 -- PT 20, L: 2 horses?
391 -- PT 6, R; Filler:
quadruped
393 -- PT 15, R: agrimi
394 -- PT 3, R: quadruped
395 -- PT 39A, L: quadruped vs
quadruped
396 -- PT 35 ccl: 2 agrimia
protomes conjoined/Ch. 5D:
Protomes
397 -- Ch. 9B: Centered
Circles (4)
398 -- PT 28B: 2 quadrupeds
399 -- PT 1A, R; Filler:
agrimi
400 -- PT 1A, R; Plain:
quadruped
401 -- Ch. 9B: Centered
Circles (misc.)
402 -- Ch. 9B: Centered
Circles (4)
403 -- Ch. 5D: Protomes
404 -- PT 10A, R: agrimia
405 -- PT 10A, L: lion
406 -- Ch. 5F: Alerions
(misc.)
407 -- PT 39A, R: quadruped
vs quadruped

408 -- Ch. 3E: Animal Games
(bull-leaping; Floating)
409 -- Ch. 5I: Dolphins (2)
410 -- Ch. 2C: Women (1,
religious)
411 -- PT 25B, L: 2 calves?
412 -- PT 51C: 2 dogs vs stag?
R
467 -- Ch. 5B: Animal Faces
(bulls)
468 -- Ch. 6A: People-Animals
(caprid-people)
469 -- Ch. 5F: Alerions (head
R)
471 -- PT 19A, R: waterbirds
472 -- PT 1A, R; Filler:
griffin
473 -- PT 1A, R; Plain: griffin
474 -- PT 10B, L: griffin
475 -- PT 2, L; Plain: griffin
476 -- Ch. 6A: People-Animals
(caprid-people)
477 -- Ch. 6A: People-Animals
(caprid-people)
479 -- PT 1C, L: bull
481 -- PT 5A, L; Filler: agrimi
482 -- PT 5A, L; Filler: agrimi
483 -- PT 5B, L; Plain: bull
484 -- PT 6, L; Filler: kid
486 -- PT 10A, L: agrimi
487 -- PT 1A, R; Filler: kid
488 -- PT 25A, R: 2 agrimia
489 -- PT 5A, L; Plain: agrimi
490 -- PT 5A, R; Filler: agrimi
492 -- PT 5A, L; Filler: bull
493 -- PT 13A, R: bull
494 -- PT 5A, L; Filler: bull
495 -- PT 1C, L: kid
496 -- PT 14A, R: bull
497 -- PT 5B, L; Plain: stag
498 -- PT 5B, L; Plain: stag
499 -- PT 5A, L; Plain: stag
500 -- PT 5A, L; Plain: stag
501 -- PT 5A, L; Filler: stag
504 -- PT 5A, L; Filler: lion
505 -- PT 5A, L; Filler: lion
506 -- PT 11, L; Filler: lion

508 -- PT 13A, R: lion
509 -- PT 18B, R: cow & calf
510 -- PT 50B cl: quadruped vs
  quadruped
511 -- PT 39A, R: dog vs agrimi
512 -- Ch. 3A: Men & Animals
  (lions)
513 -- Ch. 2C: Women (1)
515/KN HMs 109 (KSPI J2) -- PT
  19B, L: 2 bulls
516 -- PT 2/8, R; Filler:
  quadruped
517 -- Ch. 3D: Animal Games
  (bull-leaping; Evans)

CMS II1

1.419 -- PT 44A: lion R vs
  bull

CMS II2

2.36 -- Ch. 5C: Animal Heads
  (lions)
2.43 -- Ch. 5E: Birds (1,
  flies L)
2.48 -- Ch. 5C: Animal Heads
  (lion)
2.57a -- Ch. 9E: Spirals
  (plain)
2.57b -- Ch. 5C: Animal Heads
  (bulls)
2.60 -- PT 5B, R; Filler:
  bull
2.68 -- Ch. 7: Hatching
2.211 -- Ch. 5C: Animal Heads
  (bulls)
2.213a -- Ch. 5C: Animal Heads
  (boar)
2.213b -- Ch. 8A: Writing

CMS II3

3.3 -- Ch. 2C: Women (1,
  stands L)
3.4 -- Ch. 6A: People-Animals
  (eagle-woman, head R)
3.5 -- PT 32B: 2 caprids
3.7 -- Ch. 2B: Men (religious,
  at Altar)
3.8 -- Ch. 2C: Women (1,
  carries object)
3.9 -- Ch. 3A: Men & Animals
  (lions)
3.10 -- PT 37 ccl: lion-man &
  stag-man
3.11 -- Ch. 5B: Animal Faces
  (bulls)
3.13a -- Ch. 2A: Human Body
  Parts (man's head, bearded)
3.13b -- Ch. 5C: Animal Heads
  (lions)
3.14 -- Ch. 3C: Man Hunts
  Animals (lions)
3.15 -- Ch. 2E: People at a
  Shrine (woman at left)
3.16 -- Ch. 2C: Women (1,
  carries object)
3.17 -- Ch. 2C: Women (pair,
  salute)
3.18 -- PT 2, R; Plain: lion
3.19 -- PT 6, L; Plain: lion
3.20 -- PT 5A, R; Plain: bull
3.21 -- PT 24, R: 2 boars
3.22 -- Ch. 5G: Insects
  (butterfly, trio)
3.23 -- Ch. 8A: Writing
3.24 -- Ch. 3A: Men & Animals
  (lions)
3.25a -- PT 50B, Attacker R:
  griffin vs stag
3.25b -- PT 45, Victim L:
  griffin vs boar/Ch. 6C:
  Griffins (with other
  animals)
3.27 -- Ch. 3A: Men & Animals
  (lions)
3.32 -- Ch. 2B: Men (2)

3.33 -- Ch. 3A: Men & Animals (agrimia)

3.34 -- Ch. 5I: Dolphins (1)

3.38 -- Ch. 8A: Writing

3.39 -- PT 10A, R: sphinx

3.40 -- PT 1A, R; Filler: caprid

3.41 -- PT 13B, R: lion

3.44 -- PT 49A, R: lion vs bull

3.46 -- Ch. 5G: Insects (butterfly, 1)

3.49 -- Ch. 5H: Fish (1, flying fish)

3.50 -- PT 10A, L: agrimi

3.51 -- Ch. 2C: Women (4, misc.)

3.52 -- Ch. 3A: Men & Animals (lions)

3.54 -- PT 17C, R: nanny & 2 kids

3.55 -- PT 25C, R: 2 agrimia

3.56 -- Ch. 2E: People at a Shrine (2 women antithetic)

3.57 -- Ch. 9B: Centered Circles (6)

3.60 -- PT 44A, Attacker L: lion vs bull

3.61 -- PT 11, L; Plain: lion

3.62 -- PT 24, L: 2 bulls

3.63 -- Ch. 4B: Potnia Theron (griffins)

3.64a -- PT 10A, L: bull

3.64b -- PT8, R: lion

3.65 -- PT 5/6, R: agrimi

3.66 -- Ch. 3A: Men & Animals (stags)

3.67 -- PT 14C, L: Minotaur

3.68 -- PT 1A, R; Filler: bull

3.69 -- PT 1A, R; Plain: bull

3.70 -- Ch. 9B: Centered Circles (misc., countable)

3.71 -- Ch. 5I: Dolphins (2)

3.72 -- Ch. 2C: Women (1, stands L)

3.73 -- PT 1A, R; Filler: waterbird

3.74 -- PT 5A, R; Filler: quadruped

3.75 -- Ch. 5I: Dolphins (4)

3.77 -- Ch. 6A: People-Animals (eagle-woman, head R)

3.78 -- Ch. 5E: Birds & Waterbirds (waterbirds, pair)

3.79 -- PT 11, L; Plain: lion

3.84 -- Ch. 9B: Centered Circles (3)

3.85 -- Ch. 9D: Dots

3.86 -- Ch. 4C: Woman "Crossed" by a Caprid

3.87 -- Ch. 5C: Animal Heads (lions)

3.88 -- Ch. 2A: Parts of the Human Body (man's face, beardless)/Ch. 5E: Birds & Waterbirds (waterbirds, pair)

3.89 -- PT 5B, L; Plain: bull

3.90 -- PT 5B, R; Filler: bull

3.91 -- Ch. 5K: Shellfish (argonaut)

3.92 -- Ch. 5J: Octopus (conventionalized)

3.93 -- Ch. 5G: Insects (spider)

3.94 -- Ch. 5F: Alerions (head R)

3.95 -- Ch. 5F: Alerions (head R)

3.96a -- Ch. 5F: Alerions (head R)

3.96b -- Ch. 5E: Birds & Waterbirds (waterbirds, 1)

3.96c -- Ch. 5B: Animal Faces (bulls)

3.99 -- PT 51A, R: lioness & cub vs agrimi

3.100 -- PT 40, Attacker R: lion vs caprid

3.101 -- PT 12, L: bull

3.102 -- PT 35 cl: 2 bulls

3.103 -- Ch. 4A: Women &

Animals (friezes)
3.104 -- PT 1A, L; Filler: agrimi
3.105a -- Ch. 6B: Genii
3.105b -- Ch. 3E: Animal Games (bull-wrestling)
3.106 -- PT 19D, L: 2 bulls
3.107 -- PT 32B: 2 agrimia
3.108 -- PT 34A: 2 goats
3.109 -- PT 35 cl: 2 calves?
3.110 -- PT 35 cl: 2 goats
3.111 -- PT 1A, R; Filler: goat
3.112a -- PT 13A, L: lion
3.113 -- Ch. 8F: Figure-8 Shield
3.114 -- Ch. 2E: People at a Shrine (tree-pulling)
3.115 -- PT 35 cl: 2 goats
3.117 -- Ch. 4C: Woman "Crossed" by a Caprid
3.118 -- PT 5A, L; Filler: lion
3.119 -- PT 24, F: 2 bulls
3.120 -- PT 5A, R; Plain: agrimi
3.122 -- PT 2, R; Filler: lioness
3.123 -- PT 25B, R: 2 agrimia
3.124 -- Ch. 2C: Women (1, stands R)
3.125 -- PT 6, L; Filler: calf
3.126 -- PT 5A, L; Filler: agrimi
3.127 -- Ch. 9B: Centered Circles (2)
3.129 -- PT 40, Attacker R: lion vs bull
3.131 -- PT 6, R; Plain: goat
3.132 -- Ch. 5F: Alerions (head L)
3.133 -- PT 32B: 2 agrimia
3.134 -- PT 6, L; Filler: calf
3.135 -- PT 6, R; Plain: calf
3.140 -- Ch. 9I: Stars
3.141 -- PT 5A, R; Filler: bull
3.142 -- Ch. 5E: Birds &

Waterbirds (waterbirds, pair)
3.145 -- Ch. 2D: Men & Women (2)
3.146 -- Ch. 2C: Women (2)
3.147 -- Ch. 2B: men (1)
3.148 -- Ch. 5F: Alerions (head R)
3.149 -- Ch. 5B: Animal Faces (bulls)
3.150 -- Ch. 9H: Cross
3.152 -- PT 2, L; Filler: lion
3.153 -- PT 1A, L; Filler: lion
3.160 -- PT 1C, R: quadruped
3.166 -- PT 5A, L; Plain: agrimi
3.167 -- Ch. 3B: Master of Animals (griffins)
3.168 -- Ch. 4A: Women & Animals (antithetic)
3.169 -- Ch. 2C: Women (pair, salute)
3.170 -- Ch. 2C: Women (1)
3.171 -- Ch. 2C: Women (1)
3.172 -- Ch. 5A: Misc. Quadrupeds
3.173 -- PT 39A, R: lion vs bull
3.174 -- PT 5A, L; Filler: bull
3.175 -- PT 5B, L; Plain: bull
3.176 -- PT 5A, L; Filler: agrimi
3.179 -- Ch. 5E: Birds & Waterbirds (waterbirds, pair)
3.186 -- Ch. 9H: Cross (hatched)
3.187 -- Ch. 9H: Cross (hatched)
3.188 -- Ch. 9H: Cross (hatched)
3.191 -- PT 23C, L: 2 goats
3.192 -- PT 10A, R: lion
3.193 -- Ch. 3B: Master of Animals (misc.)

3.194 -- Ch. 5F: Alerions (head L)

3.196 -- Ch. 2A: Body Parts (man's face)

3.197 -- PT 6, R; Filler: bull

3.198 -- Ch. 2B: Men (1)

3.199 -- Ch. 3D: Men In Chariots

3.200 -- PT 5A, L; Filler: agrimi

3.202 -- PT 6, R; Filler: bull

3.209 -- Ch. 5H: Fish (1)

3.210 -- -- PT 39A, R: lion vs stag

3.212 -- PT 2, R; Filler: bull

3.213 -- Ch. 4C: Woman "Crossed" by a Caprid

3.216 -- PT 13C, R: bull

3.217 -- PT 1C, L: bull/calf

3.218 -- Ch. 2C: women (3)

3.219 -- PT 10B, R: griffin

3.221 -- Ch. 3A: Men & Animals (lions)

3.222 -- PT 5A, R; Filler: agrimi

3.224 -- PT 13A, L: bull

3.225 -- PT 6, L; Plain: bull

3.226 -- PT 5A, R; Filler: bull

3.227 -- PT 12, L: lion

3.236 -- Ch. 2C: Women (pair, salute)

3.237 -- Ch. 5G: Insects (butterflies)

3.238 -- PT 5A, L; Filler: bull

3.239 -- Ch. 2C: Women (1)

3.245a & b -- Ch. 5H: Fish (1)

3.250 -- Ch. 5E: Birds & Waterbirds (waterbirds, pair)

3.251 -- Ch. 5J: Octopus

3.252 -- Ch. 2E: People at <u>Shrine</u> (person at left)

3.254a -- Ch. 5F: Alerions (head R)

3.257 -- PT 10A, L: lion

3.258 -- PT 5A, L; Filler: agrimi

3.259 -- PT 1A, L; Filler: agrimi

3.269 -- Ch. 5E: Birds & Waterbirds (birds, 1)

3.271 -- Ch. 3E: Animal Games (bull-leaping, Floating)

3.276 -- Ch. 4B: <u>Potnia Theron</u> (griffins)

3.277 -- PT 11, L; Filler: lion

3.278 -- PT 1A, L; Filler: agrimi

3.279 -- Ch. 5E: Birds & Waterbirds (waterbirds, pair)/Ch. 5I: Dolphins (2)

3.282 -- Ch. 4A: Women & Animals (friezes)

3.283 -- PT 44A, Attacker R: lion vs bull

3.287 -- Ch. 4C: Woman "Crossed" by a Caprid

3.288 -- PT 18B, R: cow & calf

3.290 -- PT 5A, L; Filler: lion

3.292 -- PT 11, R; Filler: lion

3.293 -- PT 10A, L: bull

3.302 -- PT 2, R; Filler: lion

3.303 -- PT 14A, R: agrimi

3.304 -- Ch. 2C: Women (1, frontal)

3.305 -- Ch. 2D: Men & Women (woman at left, man at right)

3.306 -- PT 31B: 2 lions

3.307 -- Ch. 5E: Birds & Waterbirds (waterbirds, pair)

3.309 -- Ch. 4A: Women & Animals (animal inb)

3.310 -- PT 36 ccl: 2 bulls

3.316 -- Ch. 5H: Fish (2)

3.317 -- Ch. 5H: Fish (2)

3.322 -- Ch. 9G: Rosette (early)

3.323 -- Ch. 9B: Centered
    Circles (8)
3.327 -- Ch. 4B: <u>Potnia Theron</u>
    (dolphins)
3.328 -- Ch. 3A: Men & Animals
    (griffins)
3.329 -- Ch. 3A: Men & Animals
    (lions)
3.330a -- PT 5A, R: lion
3.330b -- Ch. 2B: Men (1,
    religious)
3.331 -- PT 14D, R:
    agrimi-man
3.332 -- Ch. 6A: People-Animals
    (caprid-people)
3.333 -- PT 40, R: lion vs
    caprid
3.334 -- PT 41, Attacker L:
    griffin vs bull
3.335 -- PT 13A, R: bull
3.336 -- PT 2, R; Filler: calf
3.337 -- PT 6, L; Filler: bull
3.338 -- Ch. 3E: Animal
    Sacrifice (bull-sacrifice)
3.339 -- PT 11, R; Filler:
    agrimi
3.340 -- PT 10A, R: agrimi
3.341 -- PT 1A, L; Filler: lion
3.342 -- PT 5A, L; Filler:
    agrimi
3.343 -- PT 5A, L; Plain:
    agrimi
3.344 -- PT 18B, R: lioness &
    cub
3.345 -- PT 8, L: lion
3.346 -- PT 10A, L: lion
3.348 -- PT 37 ccl: 2 lions
3.349 -- PT 10A, L: griffin
3.350 -- Ch. 5E: Birds & Water-
    birds (waterbirds, 1)
3.351 -- Ch. 5E: Birds &
    Waterbirds (waterbirds,
    pair)
3.352 -- PT 19A, R: waterbirds/
    Ch. 5E: Birds & Waterbirds
    (waterbirds, pair)
3.353 -- Ch. 5E: Birds &

Waterbirds (waterbirds,
    pair)
3.354 -- Ch. 5F: Alerions
    (head R)
3.355 -- Ch. 5F: Alerions
    (head R)
3.356 -- Ch. 5F: Alerions
    (head L)
3.375 -- Ch. 5I: Dolphins
    (1)
3.378 -- Ch. 9H: Cross
    (hatched)
3.379 -- Ch. 9H: Cross
    (hatched)
3.380 -- Ch. 9H: Cross
    (hatched)
3.381 -- Ch. 9H: Cross
    (hatched)
3.382 -- Ch. 9H: Cross
    (hatched)
3.384 -- Ch. 9B: Centered
    Circles (7)
3.387 -- Ch. 5E: Birds &
    Waterbirds (birds, 1)
3.396c -- Ch. 5B: Animal Faces
    (bull-face)

<u>CMS</u> II4

4.1 -- PT 2, L; Filler: lion
4.3 -- Ch. 9B: Centered
    Circles (16)
4.4 -- PT 2, R; Filler: bull
4.5 -- PT 25B, R: 2 bulls run
4.6 -- PT 5A, L; Plain:
    quadruped
4.7 -- PT 2, R; Plain:
    lion/bull
4.8 -- PT 2, R; Plain: bull?
4.9 -- PT 10A, L: stag?
4.11 -- PT 5B, R; Plain:
    stag
4.12 -- PT 1A, L; Filler:
    agrimi
4.13 -- Ch. 5E: Birds &
    Waterbirds (birds, 1)/

Ch. 5I: Dolphins (1)
4.14 -- Ch. 9H: Cross
4.16 -- PT 36 cl: 2 quadrupeds
4.17 -- PT 1A, R; Filler:
    lioness
4.18 -- PT 1A, R; Filler: lion
4.19 -- PT 10A, L: lion
4.21 -- PT 1A, L; Filler:
    agrimi
4.22 -- Ch. 2C: Women (pair,
    salute)
4.24 -- PT 2, R; Plain: lion
4.25 -- PT 50B cl: lion vs
    bull?
4.26 -- Ch. 9L: Hatching
4.27 -- Ch. 9L: Hatching
4.28 -- Ch. 2C: Women (1,
    stands frontal)
4.29 -- Ch. 9Q: Misc. Lines
4.30 -- PT 54: 2 lions vs
    caprid
4.31 -- PT 5A, L; Plain: agrimi
4.32 -- Ch. 5F: Alerions (head
    L)
4.35 -- Ch. 4C: Women "Crossed"
    by a Caprid (head unclear)
4.36 -- PT 36 ccl: 2 bulls
4.37 -- PT 5A, L; Plain: bull
4.38 -- PT 6, L; Filler: lion
4.39 -- PT 6, R; Filler: lion?
4.40 -- PT 1B, R: boar
4.42 -- Ch. 9B: Centered
    Circles (2)
4.43 -- PT 1A, L; Filler:
    quadruped
4.44 -- PT 6, R; Filler: agrimi
4.45 -- PT 1A, R; Filler: lion
4.46 -- PT 1A, L; Filler: lion
4.47 -- PT 6, R; Plain: griffin
4.48 -- PT 13A, R: lion
4.49 -- PT 6, L; Plain: lion
4.50 -- PT 5A, L; Filler: stag?
4.51 -- PT 6, L; Filler: lion
4.52 -- PT 5A, L; Filler:
    agrimi
4.54 -- Ch. 9Q: Misc. Lines
4.55 -- Ch. 2C: Women (1,

    stands R)
4.56 -- PT 5A, L; Plain: bull
4.57 -- PT 19B, L: 2 goats
4.58 -- PT 49B, R: lion vs bull
4.59 -- Ch. 9H: Cross
4.60 -- PT 7, L: lion
4.61 -- PT 5B, L; Plain:
    griffin
4.62 -- PT 5A, R; Filler:
    quadruped
4.63 -- Ch. 5J. Octopus
4.64 -- Ch. 6B: Genii
4.65 -- PT 29A: bull protome &
    lion? protome/Ch. 5D:
    Protomes
4.66 -- PT 37A ccl: 2 lions
4.67 -- PT 1A, R; Filler:
    caprid?
4.68 -- Ch. 9B: Centered
    Circles (3 & 6)
4.70 -- Ch. 2C: Women (pair,
    salute)
4.71 -- PT 10A, L: griffin
4.72 -- PT 10A, L: griffin
4.73 -- PT 45: griffin vs lion
    L
4.74 -- PT 1A, R; Filler: lion
4.75 -- PT 1A, L; Filler: lion
4.76 -- PT 6, L; Filler: lion
4.77 -- PT 5A, L; Plain: lion
4.78 -- PT 7, L: lion
4.79 -- PT 25A, L: lion &
    agrimi protome
4.80 -- PT 40, L: lion vs bull
4.81 -- Ch. 3E: Animal Games
    (bull-leaping, Floating)
4.82 -- PT 5A, L; Plain: bull
4.83 -- PT 1B, R; Filler: bull
4.84 -- PT 13A, R: bull
4.85 -- PT 1A, L; Filler:
    agrimi
4.86 -- PT 5A, L; Plain:
goat
4.87 -- PT 6, R; Filler:
    agrimi?
4.88 -- PT 1A, R; Plain:
    agrimi

4.89 -- PT 25B, R: 2 agrimia?
4.90 -- PT 25C, R: 2 goats
4.91 -- PT 25B, R: bull &
sheep protome
4.93 -- PT 5A, L; Filler:
quadruped
4.97 -- Ch. 9H: Cross
4.99 -- Ch. 9B: Centered
Circles (20?)
4.104 -- Ch. 6A: People-
Animals (eagle-woman, head
L)
4.105 -- PT 5B, L; Plain:
bull
4.106 -- PT 5A, L; Plain:
agrimi
4.109 -- Ch. 9B: Centered
Circles (misc.)
4.111 -- Ch. 4C: Women
"Crossed" by a Caprid
4.112 -- Ch 2C: Women (1)
4.113 -- PT 5A, L; Filler:
agrimi
4.115 -- Ch. 9B: Centered
Circles (4 & 8)
4.116 -- PT 6, R; Plain:
griffin
4.117 -- PT 6, L; Filler: lion
4.119 -- Ch. 9H: Cross
4.120 -- Ch. 9H: Cross
4.121 -- Ch. 2C: Women (2)
4.122 -- PT 6, R; Filler:
goat
4.123 -- PT 1A, R; Filler:
agrimi
4.125 -- Ch. 4A: Women &
Animals (antithetic)
4.126 -- PT 1B, L: bull
4.127 -- PT 5A, L; Filler:
agrimi
4.130 -- PT 5B, L; Plain:
bull
4.131 -- PT 6, R; Plain:
agrimi?
4.132 -- PT 5B, L; Plain:
bull
4.133 -- Ch. 9G: Rosettes

4.134 -- Ch. 9B: Centered
Circles (10)
4.135 -- Ch. 9B: Centered
Circles (4)
4.136 -- Ch. 6a: People-Animals
(caprid-person)
4.137 -- Ch. 6A: People-Animals
(eagle-woman, head R)
4.138 -- PT 6, L; Filler: lion
4.139 -- PT 10A, L: lion
4.140 -- PT 5A, L; Filler: stag
4.141 -- PT 2, R; Filler: bull
4.142 -- PT 18B, L: cow & calf?
4.143 -- PT 37A cl: 2 calves
4.144 -- PT 6, R; Filler: goat
4.145 -- Ch. 5E: Birds & Waterbirds (waterbirds, 1)
4.146 -- Ch. 5E: Birds & Waterbirds (waterbirds, 1)
4.147 -- Ch. 9B: Centered
Circles (4)
4.148 -- Ch. 9B: Centered
Circles (50)
4.150 -- PT 1B, L: bull
4.151 -- PT 25B, R: 2 bulls
run
4.152 -- PT 5A, L; Plain:
agrimi kid
4.153 -- PT 5B, R; Plain: calf
4.154 -- PT 6, R; Plain: bull
4.155 -- Ch. 5I: Dolphins
(1)
4.156 -- PT 12, R: lion
4.157 -- Ch. 3E: Animal Games
(bull-leaping, Floating)
4.158 -- PT 34B: 2 bulls
4.159 -- PT 18B, R: cow & calf
4.160 -- PT 18B, R: cow & calf
4.161 -- PT 14B, R: bull
4.162 -- Ch. 3E: Animal Games
(bull-leaping, Diving)
4.163 -- PT 2, L; Filler: lion
4.164 -- PT 25C, R: 2 goats
4.165 -- Ch. 2C: Women (1)
4.166 -- PT 11, L; Plain:
griffin
4.167 -- PT 49B: lion vs

bull
4.168 -- Ch. 5F: Alerions
   (head L)
4.169 -- Ch. 9B: Centered
   Circles (4)
4.171 -- PT 6, R; Filler:
   griffin
4.172 -- PT 13A, R: bull
4.174 -- PT 5A, L; Plain: stag
4.175 -- PT 6, R; Filler: lion
4.176 -- Ch. 5F: Alerions
   (head L)
4.177 -- Ch. 9R: Misc.
   Patterns
4.178 -- PT 25A, L: lion &
   agrimi protome
4.179 -- PT 6, R; Filler: bull
4.180 -- PT 5A, L; Filler:
   bull
4.181 -- PT 5A, L; Plain:
   agrimi
4.182 -- PT 49B, L: dog? vs
   stag
4.183 -- PT 10A, L: agrimi
4.184 -- PT 1B, R: boar
4.185 -- Ch. 9B: Centered
   Circles (7)
4.186 -- Ch. 9B: Centered
   Circles (7)/Ch. 9G: Rosettes
   (misc.)
4.187 -- Ch. 9B: Centered
   Circles (15)
4.188 -- PT 6, L; Plain: lion
4.190 -- PT 6, R; Plain: lion
4.191 -- Ch. 5E: Birds &
   Waterbirds (waterbirds,
   pair)
4.193 -- Ch. 9M: Reticulation
4.194 -- Ch. 5E: Birds &
   Waterbirds (birds, pair)
4.195 -- PT 1A, R; Filler:
   bull
4.196 -- Ch. 4C: Woman
   "Crossed" by a Caprid (head
   unclear)
4.197 -- PT 19A, R: 2 goats
4.198 -- PT 13A, L: lion

4.199 -- PT 5A, R; Plain: bull
4.200 -- PT 2, R; Filler: lion
4.201 -- PT 5A, L; Plain:
   agrimi
4.202 -- PT 51A, L: 2 lions vs
   bull
4.203 -- PT 28B: 2 bulls
4.204 -- Ch. 4C: Women
   "Crossed" by a Caprid
4.206 -- PT 2, R; Filler: lion
4.207 -- PT 1A, L; Filler: lion
4.208 -- Ch. 9B: Centered
   Circles (6)
4.210 -- Ch. 9R: Misc. Patterns
4.211 -- Ch. 9H: Cross
4.214 -- PT 1A, L; Filler: bull
4.215 -- Ch. 9H: Cross
4.216 -- PT 1A, R; Filler: lion
4.217 -- PT 13A, R: agrimi?
4.218 -- PT 29A: 2 lion
   protomes/Ch. 5D: Protomes
   (lions)
4.219 -- PT 40, R: lion vs
   agrimi kid
4.220 -- PT 2, L; Plain: bull
4.221 -- PT 1B, L: bull
4.222 -- PT 5A, R; Plain: bull
4.223 -- PT 5A, L; Plain: bull
4.224 -- PT 5A, L; Filler:
   agrimi
4.225 -- PT 5C, L; Plain: bull
4.226 -- PT 5B, L; Filler:
   stag
4.227 -- PT 6, L; Plain: lion
4.228 -- PT 1B, R: goat?
4.230 -- PT 49B, L: small lion
   vs bull
4.235 -- Ch. 9B: Centered
   Circles (4)
4.236 -- Ch. 9B: Centered
   Circles (9)
4.237 -- Ch. 9B: Centered
   Circles (10)
4.238 -- Ch. 9Q: Misc. Lines

CMS IV

166 -- Ch. 7: Flaked Obsidian
    Disks/a: PT 5A, R; Filler:
    agrimi; b: Ch. 5I: Dolphins
    (1)
168 -- Ch. 5C: Animal Heads
    (bulls)
185 -- PT 8, R: dog
    scratching
221 -- Ch. 9L: Hatching
222 -- Ch. 9H: Cross
225 -- PT 1A, L; Filler:
    agrimi
228 -- PT 10A, L: lion
229 -- PT 10A, R: lion
233 -- Ch. 3C: Man Hunts
    Animals (lions)
240 -- PT 30A: 2 boars
245 -- PT 1A, L; Filler:
    agrimi
246 -- PT 19A, R: waterbirds
248 -- PT 10A, R: griffin
256 -- PT 19C, R: 2 bulls
257 -- Ch. 5E: Birds &
    Waterbirds (waterbirds,
    1)
258 -- PT 11, R; Filler:
    lion
259 -- PT 40: lion R vs bull
260 -- Ch. 5F: Alerions (head
    R)
261 -- PT 5A, L; Plain: agrimi
262 -- PT 39A: lion L vs
    agrimi
263 -- PT 10A, R: agrimi
264 -- PT 5A, L; Filler: goat
265 -- PT 19A, R: waterbirds
266 -- PT 6, L; Filler:
    griffin
267 -- PT 13A, R: bull
268 -- PT 11, R; Filler: bull
269 -- PT 2, R; Plain: stag
270 -- PT 5A, L; Plain: agrimi
271 -- Ch. 9B: Centered Circles
    (misc.)
272 -- PT 18B, R: cow & calf

273 -- PT 5A, R; Plain: agrimi
274 -- PT 11, L; Plain: lion
275 -- PT 6, R; Filler: bull
276 -- PT 25C, L: lion & agrimi
277 -- PT 6, L; Plain: lion
278 -- PT 5B, L; Filler:bull
279 -- PT 1A, R; Plain: lion
280 -- PT 5D, R: bull
281 -- PT 5B, L; Plain: bull
282 -- PT 11, L; Filler: lion
283a -- PT 8, R: griffin
283b -- Ch. 2C: Women (1,
    (stands frontal)
284 -- PT 2, L; Filler: bull
285 -- PT 49B, R: lion vs
    agrimi kid
286 -- PT 6, R; Plain:
    calf/dog
287 -- PT 5A, L; Filler:
    griffin
288 -- PT 5A, L; Filler:
    agrimi
289 -- Ch. 3E: Animal Games
    (bull-leaping, Floating)
290 -- Ch. 6A: People-Animals
    (agrimi-woman, head L)
291 -- PT 36 ccl: 2 bulls
292 -- PT 5A, L; Plain: agrimi
293 -- PT 54: 2 lions vs man
    (Master of lions?)
294 -- PT 30A: 2 lions
295 -- Ch. 4B: Potnia Theron
    (lions)
296 -- PT 5A, L; Filler: agrimi
297 -- PT 5A, L; Plain: agrimi
298 -- Ch. 5F: Alerions (head
    R)
299 -- PT 6, L; Plain: bull
300 -- PT 5A, L; Filler:
    bull
301 -- Ch. 5B: Animal Faces
    (bulls)
302 -- PT 50B: lion R vs
    quadruped
303 -- PT 5A, L; Plain:
    agrimi
304 -- PT 31A: 2 lions

305 -- PT 10B, L: bull
306 -- PT 10A, R: bull?
307 -- Ch. 4A: Women & Animals
   (woman inb)
308 -- PT 5A, L; Plain: goat
309 -- PT 1A, L; Plain:
   agrimi
310 -- PT 11, L; Filler:
   lion
311 -- PT 1A, R; Filler:
   cat?
313 -- PT 5A, L; Filler:
   griffin
314 -- Ch. 6D: Misc. Monsters
317 -- PT 1C, R: bull
318 -- PT 6, L; Plain:
   griffin
319 -- PT 6, R; Filler: lion
320 -- Ch. 6D: Misc. Monsters
321 -- PT 5A, R; Filler:
   agrimi
322 -- PT 5A, R; Plain:
   bull

33D -- Ch. 5G: Insects
   (misc.)
35D -- Ch. 6A: People-Animals
   (agrimi-woman, head R)
37D -- Ch. 3D: Men In Chariots
38D -- Ch. 3B: Master of
   Animals (agrimia)
39D -- PT 10A, L: griffin
40D -- PT 31A: 2 lions
41D -- PT 1A, L   Filler:
   agrimi
42D -- PT 3, R: <u>Babylonian
   Dragon</u>
53D -- PT 6, L; Filler:
   agrimi
54D -- PT 1A, R; Filler:
   agrimi
55D -- Ch. 2C: Women (1,
   stands frontal)
58D -- PT 1A, R; Filler:
   griffin

<u>CMS</u> V

2 -- PT 13A, L: lion
3 -- PT 1A, R; Filler: bull
4 -- PT 2, R; Filler: quadruped
5 -- PT 28B: 2 quadrupeds
7 -- PT 13A, L: bull
8 -- PT 2, R; Filler: bull
9 -- PT 2, R; Filler: agrimi
11 -- Ch. 2B: Men (1,
   religious)
13 -- Ch. 9B: Centered Circles
   (2)
23 -- PT 14A, R: bull
29 -- PT 1A, R; Filler: agrimi
30 -- PT 1A, R; Filler:
   quadruped
31 -- Ch. 5B: Animal Faces
   (bulls)
32 -- PT 13A, R: bull
33 -- PT 5A, R; Filler:
   quadruped
34 -- Ch. 9R: Misc. Patterns
42 -- PT 2, R; Filler:
   quadruped
150 -- PT 5A, R; Filler: bull
151 -- PT 29B: 2 bulls
152 -- Ch. 9B: Centered Circles
   (4)
153 -- PT 13A, R: bull
154 -- Ch. 9B: Centered Circles
   (3)
156 -- Ch. 7A: Branches (<u>Branch
   1</u>)
157 -- PT 1B, L: bull
158 -- PT 1A, R; Filler: agrimi
159 -- PT 1A, R; Filler: bull
160 -- PT 1B, R: agrimi
161 -- PT 2, R; Filler:
   quadruped
162 -- PT 6, L; Filler:
   quadruped
163 -- Ch. 7A: Branches (Branch
   3)
164 -- Ch. 9Q: Misc. Lines
165 -- Ch. 9G: Rosettes
166 -- Ch. 9G: Rosettes

167 -- Ch. 9G: Rosettes
169 -- PT 1A, R; Filler: agrimi
170 -- PT 1A, R; Filler: agrimi
171 -- Ch. 9Q: Misc. Lines
172 -- PT 2, R; Filler: bull
173 -- Ch. 2D: Men & Women (man & women)
174 -- Ch. 5F: Alerions (head R)
175 -- Ch. 9B: Centered Circles (4)
176 -- Ch. 5I: Dolphins (3)
180a -- Ch. 9G: Rosettes
180b -- Ch. 2B: Men (duels)
181 -- Ch. 3C: Man Hunts Animals (fishermen)
182 -- PT 10A, R: lion
184a -- PT 39A: dog L vs stag
184b -- Ch. 2B: Men (2)
186 -- PT 1A, L: Filler: agrimi
187 -- PT 2, R; Filler: quadruped
189 -- Ch. 2B: Men (1, religious)
190 -- Ch. 9H: Cross
191a -- PT 11, L; Filler: lion
191b -- PT 10B, L: bull
191c -- PT 10B, L: agrimi
192 -- PT 7, L: lion
193 -- PT 25B, L: 2 lions
194 -- PT 44A: lion L vs bull
195 -- PT 24, L: 2 bulls
196 -- PT 25B, L: 2 bulls
198 -- PT 10A, R: bull
199 -- Ch. 2E: People at a Shrine (woman sits on Shrine)
200 -- PT 13C, R: bull
201 -- Ch. 3B: Master of Animals (monsters)
208 -- PT 10B, L: griffin
209 -- Ch. 6B: Genii
215 -- PT 8, L: griffin
216 -- PT 52A: 2 griffins vs

bull R
217 -- Ch. 7A: Branches (Branch 1)
219 -- PT 2, R; Filler: bull
220 -- PT 39A: lion R vs bull
221 -- PT 19B, R: 2 agrimia
222 -- PT 25C, L: lion & stag
224 -- Ch. 9K: Lines/Gouges/ Strokes
225 -- Ch. 9B: Centered Circles (1)
226 -- Ch. 9B: Centered Circles (4)
227 -- PT 1A, R; Filler: bull
228 -- PT 5A, L; Filler: quadruped
229 -- Ch. 7A: Branches (Branch 1)
233 -- Ch. 5A: Misc. Animals (quadrupeds)
234 -- Ch. 5E: Birds & Waterbirds (waterbirds, 1)
235 -- PT 39A: lion R vs bull
236 -- PT 25B, L: 2 lions
239 -- Ch. 2B: Men (1)
241 -- PT 10A, L: lion
242 -- PT 6, L; Filler: lion
243 -- PT 6, R; Plain: bull
244 -- Ch. 2B: Men (1, religious)
245 -- Ch. 9C: Arcs
246 -- PT 14A, L: lion/ Ch. 3A: Men & Animals (caprids)
247 -- PT 2, R; Filler: bull
248 -- PT 1A, L; Filler: agrimi
249 -- PT 25C, L: 2 calves run
250 -- PT 1A, R; Filler: agrimi
252 -- PT 5C, R: bull
254 -- PT 1A, R; Filler: bull
255 -- PT 5A, R; Filler: agrimi
258 -- PT 1A, R; Filler: bull
259 -- Ch. 9B: Centered Circles (misc.)
261 -- PT 2, R; Plain: quadruped
264 -- PT 1A, L; Filler: lion

265 -- PT 41: lion R vs caprid

267 -- Ch. 3E: Animal Games
(bull-leaping, Diving)

270 -- Ch. 9B: Centered Circles
(8)

271 -- Ch. 9H: Cross (hatched)

272 -- PT 1A, R; Filler: agrimi
kid

274 -- Ch. 6A: People-Animals
(caprid-people)

275 -- PT 2, R; Filler: bull

277 -- Ch. 9H: Cross (hatched)

278 -- Ch. 9L: Hatching

279 -- PT 5C, L; Filler: bull

280 -- PT 13A, R: bull

281 -- PT 2, L; Filler: bull

282 -- PT 2, L; Filler: bull

283 -- PT 11, R; Filler:
agrimi?

297 -- PT 25A, L: 2 stags

298 -- PT 18B, R: cow & calf

304 -- PT 2, L; Filler:
lioness

309 -- PT 2, R; Plain: agrimi

310 -- PT 2, R; Filler:
quadruped

311 -- PT 25B, L: 2 quadrupeds

312a + b -- PT 13A, R: bull

313 -- PT 51F: 2 lionesses or
cubs vs bull L

314 -- PT 1B, L: boar

315 -- PT 2, R; Filler: bull

316 -- PT 6, R; Filler: calf

317 -- PT 18B, R: cow & calf

318 -- PT 37A ccl: 2 bulls

319 -- PT 14A, R: bull

320 -- PT 14A, L: bull

321 -- PT 2, R; Filler:
quadruped

322 -- PT 2, L; Filler: bull

323 -- PT 2, L; Filler:
quadruped

324 -- PT 1A, L; Filler:
quadruped

325 -- PT 1A, R; Plain:
quadruped

326 -- Ch. 5B: Animal Faces
(bulls)

327 -- Ch. 5B: Animal Faces
(bulls)

328 -- Ch. 5B: Animal Faces
(bulls)

329 -- Ch. 9A: Paisley

330 -- Ch. 9B: Centered
Circles (6)

331 -- Ch. 9K: Lines/Strokes/
Gouges

332 -- Ch. 9F: Meanders

336 -- PT 6, R; Plain: stag

337 -- PT 28A: 2 bulls

338 -- PT 1A, R; Filler: agrimi

339 -- PT 1A, R; Filler: agrimi

340 -- PT 1A, R; Filler: agrimi

341 -- PT 1A, R; Filler: agrimi

342 -- PT 1A, L; Filler: agrimi

343 -- PT 2, R; Filler: agrimi/
caprid

344 -- PT 1A, L; Filler: agrimi

345 -- PT 2, R; Filler:
quadruped

346 -- Ch. 5B: Animal Faces
(bulls)

347 -- Ch. 5B: Animal Faces
(bulls)

348/349/350/392 -- PT 25A, R: 2
goats

351/352 -- PT 36 cl: 2 calves

353/354 -- PT 31B: 2 calves

355 -- PT 33A: goats

356 -- PT 5C, L; Filler: calf

357 -- PT 1A, R; Filler: goat

358 -- PT 6, R; Plain: bull

359 -- PT 25B, L: 2 calves

360/383 -- PT 6, R; Filler:
calf

361 -- PT 39A: lion R vs bull

362 -- PT 5A, L; Filler: lion

363/364/385 -- PT 12, R: lion

365 -- PT 1B, L: horse?

367 -- Ch. 6B: Genii (flanking)

368 -- Ch. 9Q: Misc. Lines

369 -- Ch. 9G: Rosettes

370 -- Ch. 9G: Rosettes

371 -- Ch. 9A: Paisleys

372 -- Ch. 9Q: Misc. Lines
373 -- Ch. 7A: Branches (Branch 1)
374 -- Ch. 9L: Hatching
375 -- Ch. 9L: Hatching
376 -- Ch. 9B: Centered Circles (2)
377 -- PT 2, R; Filler: bull
378 -- PT 2, R; Filler: agrimi
379 -- PT 2, R; Filler: bull
381/382 -- PT 6, R; Plain: bull
383 -- PT 6, R; Filler: calf
385 -- PT 12, R: lion
386 -- Ch. 5J: Octopus
387 -- Ch. 9B: Centered Circles (6)
389 -- Ch. 9H: Cross
390 -- Ch. 7A: Branches (Branch 1)
391 -- Ch. 9M: Reticulation
392 -- PT 25A, R: 2 goats
393 -- PT 6, R; Filler: calf
394 -- PT 1A, L; Plain: agrimi
395 -- Ch. 9G: Rosettes
396 -- Ch. 9Q: Misc. Lines
397 -- Ch. 9Q: Misc. Lines
398 -- Ch. 5B: Animal Faces (bulls)
399 -- PT 5B, R; Plain: bull
400 -- PT 5A, L; Filler: winged agrimi
401 -- PT 1A, R; Filler: agrimi
402 -- PT 1D, R: agrimi
403 -- PT 6, R; Filler: quadruped
404 -- PT 18B, R: cow & calf
406 -- Ch. 9G: Rosettes
407 -- Ch. 9G: Rosettes
408 -- Ch. 9G: Rosettes
409 -- Ch. 9K: Lines/Strokes/ Gouges
410 -- Ch. 9K: Lines/Strokes/ Gouges
411 -- Ch. 9K: Lines/Strokes/ Gouges

412 -- Ch. 9H: Cross
413 -- Ch. 9B: Centered Circles (6)
414 -- Ch. 9B: Centered Circles (7)
415 -- Ch. 8A: Writing
417 -- PT 2, R; Filler: bull
418 -- PT 6, L; Plain: calf
419 -- Ch. 9B: Centered Circles (1)
420 --Ch. 9B: Centered Circles (3)/Ch. 9M: Reticulation
422a -- Ch. 5E: Birds & Waterbirds (waterbirds, pair)
422b -- Ch. 2E: People at a Shrine (person at right)
424 -- PT 40: lion L vs bull
425 -- PT 1A, R; Filler: quadruped
427 -- Ch. 9Q: Misc. Lines
428 -- PT 49B, L: lion vs kid
429 -- Ch. 9B: Centered Circles (2)
431 -- Ch. 2A: Body Parts (man's face)
432 -- PT 24, L: 2 bulls
433 -- PT 24, R: 2 bulls
434 -- PT 25B, L: 2 bulls
435 -- PT 40: lion L vs bull
436 -- PT 44A: lion L vs bull
437 -- PT 8, L; griffin
438 -- PT 11, L; Filler: griffin
439 -- Ch. 5E: Birds & Waterbirds (waterbirds, pair)
440 -- Ch. 6B: Genii
442 -- PT 2, R; Filler: bull
443 -- PT 2, R; Plain: quadruped
444 -- Ch. 7A: Branches (Branch 2)
446 -- Ch. 9Q: Misc. Lines
448 -- Ch. 9Q: Misc. Lines

448 -- Ch. 9B: Centered Circles (2)
493 -- PT 37A cl: 2 lions
494 -- Ch. 9H: Cross
495 -- Ch. 9B: Centered Circles (4)
496 -- Ch. 5J: Octopus
497 -- PT 1B, R: bull
498 -- PT 8, L: lion
499 -- PT 5B, L; Plain: kid
500 -- PT 13A, R: bull
510 -- PT 1A, R; Filler: quadruped
512 -- PT 2, R; Filler: bull
511 -- PT 25B, L: bull & lion
513 -- Ch. 5B: Animal Faces (bulls)
517 -- Ch. 3E: Animal Games (bull-Leaping, Floating)
528 -- PT 6, L; Filler: kid
572 -- Ch. 9R: Misc. Patterns
574 -- Ch. 8F: <u>Figure-8 Shields</u>
575 -- PT 6, R; Filler: bull
579 -- Ch. 5G: Insects (misc.)
580 -- PT 3, L: bull
581 -- PT 1A, L; Filler: <u>Babylonian Dragon</u>
582 -- Ch. 5E: Birds & Waterbirds (waterbirds, trio)
583 -- PT 2, R; Plain: griffin
584 -- Ch. 4A: Women & Animals (woman rides)
585 -- Ch. 3D: Men In Chariots
586 -- PT 10B, L: bull
587 -- PT 14A, R: agrimi
588 -- PT 14A, R: lion
589 -- PT 25B, R: 2 lions
590 -- PT 10B, L: griffin
592 -- Ch. 5B: Animal Faces (bulls)
593 -- Ch. 7A: <u>Branches</u> (<u>Branch 1</u>?)
594 -- Ch. 3B: Master of Animals (stags)
595 -- Ch. 4A: Women & Animals (antithetic)

596 -- PT 52B: 2 griffins vs quadruped (bull?) L
597 -- Ch. 3E: Animal Games (bull-leaping, Diving)
598 -- PT 1A, R; Filler: goat
599 -- PT 13/14: lion
600 -- PT 25B, R: 2 goats
602 -- PT 39A: lion R vs bull
604 -- PT 6, L; Filler: lion
605 -- Ch. 5E: Birds & Waterbirds (birds, 1)
606 -- PT 2, R; Filler: quadruped
607 -- PT 28A: 2 bulls conjoined
608 -- Ch. 2B: Men (1, religious)
610 -- PT 2, L; Filler: quadruped
612 -- Ch. 9B: Centered Circles (3)
613 -- Ch. 9Q: Misc. Lines
614 -- Ch. 7A: <u>Branches</u> (<u>Branch 1</u>?)
615 -- PT 1A, R; Filler: quadruped
617 -- Ch. 7A: <u>Branches</u> (branch)
620 -- Ch. 5I: Dolphins (3)
623 -- Ch. 5B: Animal Faces (bulls)
625 -- PT 1A, R; Filler: agrimi
626 -- PT 2, R; Filler: bull
627 -- Ch. 9A: Paisleys
628 -- Ch. 7: Lines/Strokes/ Gouges
630 -- PT 1A, R; Filler: bull
631 -- PT 2, R; Plain: quadruped
638 -- Ch. 3E: Animal Games (rides other animals)
641 -- PT 19A, R: 2 agrimia
642 -- PT 47B: griffin L vs stag
643 -- Ch. 2B: Men (duels)
644 -- PT 5B, R; Plain: stag
645 -- PT 5B, R; Filler: bull

646 -- PT 5B, R; Filler: bull
649 -- PT 49B, L: dog vs goat
650 -- Ch. 6C: Griffins
651 -- PT 1A, L; Plain: lion
652 -- PT 2, R; Plain: lion
653 -- Ch. 9H: Cross
654 -- Ch. 4B: <u>Potnia Theron</u>
   (griffins)
655 -- PT 11, R; Filler: lion
656 -- Ch. 3C: Man Hunts
   Animals (agrimia)
659 -- PT 6, L; Plain: kid
660 -- PT 40: lion R vs bull
661 -- Ch. 5B: Animal Faces
   (bulls)
663 -- PT 18B, L: cow & calf
664 -- PT 6, L; Filler: bull
665 -- PT 10A, R: stag
666 -- PT 23A, R: 2 boars
667 -- PT 6, R; Filler: caprid
669 -- Ch. 3B: Master of
   Animals (griffins)
670 -- PT 1A, L; Filler:
   quadruped
671 -- PT 2, L; Plain: lion
672 -- PT 11, R; Plain: griffin
673 -- PT 19B, R: 2 calves
674 -- Ch. 3E: Animal Games
   (bull-Leaping, Diving)
675 -- Ch. 3B: Master of
   Animals (lions)
676 -- PT 5A, R; Filler: calf?
677a -- PT 8, R: dog
   scratching
677b -- Ch. 5G: Insects
   (butterflies)
677c -- Ch. 5G: Insects
   (butterflies)
678 -- PT 39A: lion L vs bull
679 -- Ch. 9Q: Misc. Lines
680 -- PT 13A, L: lion
682 -- Ch. 5B: Animal Faces
   (bulls)
683 -- PT 1A, R; Filler: bull
684 -- PT 11, L; Filler:
   griffin
685 -- Ch. 9E: Spirals

686 -- PT 6, R; Plain: stag
687 -- PT 1B, R: agrimi
688 -- PT 39B, L: lion vs bull
689 -- PT 6, L; Filler: bull
690 -- PT 5A, L; Filler:
   griffiness
725 -- PT 25C, L: lion &
   agrimi
726 -- PT 43: dog L vs agrimi
728 -- Ch. 2E: People at a
   <u>Shrine</u> (person at left)
729 -- PT 2, R; Filler: bull
730 -- PT 10A, L; Filler:
   agrimi
731 -- Ch. 7A: <u>Branches</u>
   (<u>Branch 1</u>)
732 -- PT 5A, L; Filler: goat
733 -- PT 13/14: lion
734 -- PT 1A, R; Filler:
   quadruped
735 -- Ch. 9H: Cross
736 -- Ch. 9G: Rosettes
737 -- Ch. 9G: Rosettes
738 -- Ch. 9E: Spirals
739 -- Ch. 9H: Cross
740 -- PT 1A, R; Filler:
   quadruped
741 -- PT 5A, L; Plain: agrimi
742 -- Ch. 7A: <u>Branches</u>
   (<u>Branch 1</u>)
743 -- Ch. 7A: <u>Branches</u>
   (<u>Branch 1</u>)
744 -- Ch. 9R Misc. Patterns
745 -- PT 10A, L: lion
746 -- PT 1A, L; Filler: bull
747 -- PT 28A: 2 kids
748 -- Ch. 5B: Animal Faces
   (bulls)
749 -- Ch. 5J: Octopus
750 -- PT 25C, R: lion & agrimi
   protome
751 -- PT 1A, R; Filler: bull

CMS VII

37a & b -- Ch. 9P: Flaked
  Obsidian Disks
38 -- Ch. 9H: Cross/ Ch. 9P:
  Flaked Obsidian Disks
42 -- PT 5A, L; Filler: agrimi
44 -- Ch. 5E: Birds &
  Waterbirds (waterbirds, 1)
64 -- PT 1A, L; Plain
65 -- PT 1C, L: bull
66 -- PT 17C, L: bitch & 2
  puppies
67 -- PT 2, R; Plain: stag
68 -- PT 39B, R: 2 agrimia
  copulating
70 -- Ch. 5G: Insects (misc.)
71 -- Ch. 5G: Insects
  (butterflies)
87 -- Ch. 3E: Men In Chariots
88 -- Ch. 3C: Man Hunts Animals
  (fisherman)
89 -- PT 26, R: 4 agrimia
90 -- PT 37A, cl: 2 lions
93 -- PT 10A, L: griffin
94 -- PT 5A, L; Filler:
  lion
95 -- Ch. 3A: Man & Animals
  (monsters)
96 -- PT 49B, R: lion vs bull
97 -- PT 2, L; Plain: bull
98 -- PT 19B, R: 2 goats
99 -- PT 13B, R: bull
100 -- Ch. 3A: Man & Animals
  (bulls)
102 -- Ch. 3A: Man & Animals
  (bulls)
103 -- PT 19B, R: 2 calves
105 -- PT 10B, L: calf
106 -- PT 6, R; Plain: bull
108 -- Ch. 3E: Animal Games
  (bull-leaping, Diving)
109 -- Ch. 3E: Animal Games
  (bull-leaping, Floating)
110 -- PT 5B, R; Plain: bull
113 -- PT 2, R; Filler: bull
114 -- PT 13A, R: lion

115a -- PT 46: lion L vs bull
115b -- PT 25B, R: 2 calves
115c -- PT 14A, R: lion
116 -- PT 54: griffin & lion
  vs bull
117 -- PT 53: 2 dogs vs kid R
120 -- PT 11, R; Plain:
  griffin
121 -- PT 11, L; Filler: lion
124 -- PT 14A, L: agrimi
125 -- PT 49A, R: lion vs
  agrimi
126 -- PT 29B: 2 dog protomes
127 -- PT 24, L; Plain: 2
  bulls
129 -- Ch. 2B: Men (duels)
130 -- Ch. 2B: Men (battles)
131 -- Ch. 3C: Man Hunts
  Animals (agrimia)
134 -- Ch. 4B: Potnia Theron
  (waterbirds)
135 -- PT 8, L; griffin
136 -- PT 13A, R: calf
137 -- PT 12, R: lion
138 -- PT 14D, R: agrimi-man
139 -- PT 5A, R; Filler:
  agrimi
140 -- PT 10A, R: griffin
143 -- Ch. 6A: People-Animals
  (caprid-people)
145 -- PT 5A, L; Filler: bull
148 -- PT 14A, L: bull
151 -- PT 11, L; Filler: lion
152 -- PT 5A, L; Filler: stag
153 -- PT 5A, L; Filler:
  agrimi
155 -- PT 2, R; Filler:
  quadruped
156 -- PT 13A, R: bull
157 -- PT 13A, R: bull
158 -- Ch. 8J: Misc. Patterns
159 -- PT 21, variant: 2
  ibex/bulls
160 -- PT 41: dog R vs cow &
  calf
161 -- PT 2, R; Filler: bull
162 -- PT 2, R; Filler: bull

163 -- PT 1B, R; bull
164 -- Ch. 5E: Birds &
Waterbirds (birds, 1)
165 -- Ch. 5E: Birds &
waterbirds (birds, 1)
166 -- PT 5B, L; Plain: bull
167 -- PT 1A, L; Filler: goat
168 -- PT 8, R: lion
169 -- Ch. 3A: Man & Animals
(lions)
170 -- PT 1A, L; Filler: agrimi
171 -- PT 8, R: lion
175 -- PT 51C: bird & dog vs
agrimi
176 -- PT 52A: dog & cat vs
calf L
177 -- PT 1A, R; Filler: bull
178 -- PT 10A, L: lion
179 -- PT 19A, L: 2 kids
180 -- PT 48A: lion vs agrimi
181 -- PT 54: 2 lions vs bull
184 -- PT 6, L; Filler: agrimi
186 -- PT 19C, R: 2 caprids
187 -- PT 28A: 2 griffin
protomes
188 -- Ch. 5K: Shellfish
190 -- PT 2, R; Filler: bull
191 -- PT 1A, L; Filler: goat
192 -- PT 6, L; Filler:
calf/bull
193 -- PT 5B, L; Plain: bull
194 -- Ch. 7A: Branches (Branch
1)
195 -- Ch. 8E: Helmets
196 -- PT 6, L; Filler: agrimi
197 -- PT 25C, L: lion & agrimi
198 -- PT 25C, L: lion &
griffin
200 -- PT 1C, R: bull
201 -- PT 1A, L; Plain
202 -- Ch. 9C: Arcs
203 -- Ch. 8F: Figure-8 Shield
204 -- PT 2, R; Filler: bull
205 -- PT 2, R; Filler: bull
233 -- PT 17B, R: nanny & kid
235 -- PT 8, L; lion
236 -- PT 18B, R: cow & calf

237 -- PT 40: lion L vs bull
239 -- PT 1A, R; Filler: agrimi
240 -- PT 10B, L: griffin
241 -- Ch. 2C: Women (2, plain)
242 -- PT 5A, R; Plain: agrimi
243 -- PT 5B, R; Plain: bull
244 -- Ch. 9H: Cross
245 -- Ch. 9H: Cross
247 -- PT 1A, L; Filler:
agrimi
248 -- PT 13C, R: bull
249 -- PT 6, L; Filler:
dog/lion cub
250 -- PT 6, R; Filler: agrimi
251 -- PT 1B, L; Filler:
bull/calf
252 -- PT 5A, L; Filler:
kid/calf
256 -- Ch. 9L: Hatching
257 -- Ch. 3E: Animal Games
(bull-leaping, Floating)
258 -- PT 11, R; Filler:
griffin
260 -- PT 40: lion R vs bull
261 -- PT 6, R; Filler: bull
262 -- PT 6, L; Filler: stag
263 -- PT 1A, R; Filler:
agrimi
264 -- Ch. 5B: Animal Faces
(bulls)

CMS VIII

39a & b -- Ch. 9P: Flaked
Obsidian Disks
40a & b -- Ch. 9P: Flaked
Obsidian Disks
47a -- PT 3, R: goat
47b -- PT 5B, L; Filler: bull
52 -- PT 9, L: bull
53 -- PT 13B, L: boar
57 -- Ch. 5F: Alerions (head
R)
65 -- Ch. 6B: Genii
66 -- PT 6, R; Plain: calf
75 -- PT 5A, R; Filler: lion

76 -- PT 5A, L; Plain: agrimi
77 -- PT 5B, L; Plain: bull
78 -- PT 5A, R; Filler: lion
80 -- PT 25C, L: lion &
   agrimi? protome
81 -- PT 5A, L; Plain: agrimi
82 -- PT 5B, R; Plain: bull
83 -- Ch. 5F: Alerions (head
   R)
84 -- PT 29B: 2 kids? con-
   joined/Ch. 5D: Protomes
88 -- PT 10/11, L: griffin
89 -- PT 39C: lion L vs bull
90 -- PT 28B: 2 calves
91 -- PT 16/17, L: cow & calf
92 -- PT 10A, R: lion
93 -- PT 5A, R; Filler: agrimi
94 -- PT 5A, R; Plain: agrimi
95 -- Ch. 4A: Women & Animals
   (antithetic)
97 -- PT 39A: lion R vs bull
98 -- PT 2, R; Filler: goat
99 -- PT 2, R; Filler: bull
101 -- PT 5A, L; Filler:
   agrimi
104 -- PT 8, L: lion
107 -- PT 6, L; Filler: bull
108 -- PT 25B, R: bulls
110a -- Ch. 5B: Animal Faces
   (bulls)
110b -- Ch. 2A: Body Parts
   (man's head)
115 -- Ch. 5C: Animal Heads
   (lions)
116 -- Ch. 5B: Animal Faces
   (bulls)
119 -- PT 1B, R; boar
121 -- PT 39A: lion R vs bull
124 -- PT 1A, R; Filler: lion
125 -- PT 11, L; Plain: lion
126 -- PT 5A, L; Plain: bull
127 -- PT 6, R; Plain: agrimi
128 -- Ch. 2C: Women (1)
129 -- PT 1A, L; Filler:
   agrimi
130 -- PT 6, R; Plain: calf
135 -- Ch. 5E: Birds & Water-

birds (birds, misc.)
137 -- PT 11, R; Plain: lion
141 -- PT 13A, R: bull
143 -- Ch. 9B: Centered Circles
   (4)
144 -- Ch. 4C: Women "Crossed"
   by a Caprid
145 -- PT 1A, R; Filler: bull
146 -- Ch. 4A: Women & Animals
   (antithetic)
148 -- PT 12, R: bull
149 -- PT 39A: lion L vs bull
150 -- PT 50B: dog vs stag
152 -- Ch. 5G: Insects
   (butterflies)
154 -- PT 47B, L: lion vs
   agrimi kid
155 -- Ch. 5F: Alerions (head
   L)
156 -- PT 6, R; Filler: bull
158 -- Ch. 5F: Alerions (head
   R)

<u>CMS</u> IX

61 -- Ch. 5F: Alerions (head
   R)
62 -- Ch. 5F: Alerions (head
   L)
73 -- Ch. 5I: Dolphins (3)
74 -- Ch. 5H: Fish (3)
101 -- PT 1A, L; Filler:
   agrimi
102 -- PT 1A, L; Filler:
   agrimi
103 -- PT 1A, L; Filler:
   agrimi
104 -- PT 11, L; Plain:
   griffin
105 -- PT 11, R; Filler:
   griffin
107 -- PT 13C, R: lion
108 -- PT 1B, R: bull
109 -- PT 13B, L: bull
110a -- PT 5B, L; Filler: bull
111 -- PT 21, R: 2 calves

112 -- PT 30C: lions
113 -- PT 28B: 2 birds/storks
114 -- Ch. 3C: Man Hunts
    Animals (lions)
118 -- PT 14A, R: bull
119 -- PT 5B, R; Filler: bull
120 -- PT 6, R; Filler: bull
121 -- PT 5B, L; Plain: bull
122 -- PT 13C, R: stag
123 -- PT 2, L; Filler: bull
124 -- PT 6, L; Filler: bull
125 -- PT 14A, L: bull
126 -- PT 14C, R: bull
127 -- PT 14D, L: <u>Minotaur</u>
128 -- PT 14D, L: agrimi-man
129 -- Ch. 6B: Genii
131 -- PT 35 cl: 2 bulls
133 -- PT 33B: 2 bulls
135 -- PT 54: 2 lions vs
    salient calf L
136 -- PT 23C, L: 3 boars
137 -- PT 28A: 2 bulls & 2
    calves
138 -- PT 8, L; griffin
139 -- PT 5A, L; Filler: agrimi
140 -- PT 5A, L; Filler: agrimi
141 -- PT 5A, R; Filler: agrimi
142 -- PT 40: lion R vs bull
143 -- PT 37A cl: 2 lions
144 -- PT 14D, L: <u>Minotaur</u>
145 -- PT 53: 2 dogs vs kid L
146 -- Ch. 3A: Man & Animals
    (bulls)
147 -- PT 1B, L: bull
148 -- PT 46: lion L vs griffin
149 -- PT 1A, R; Filler: lion
150 -- PT 13A, R: lion
151 -- PT 2, R; Filler: lion
152 -- Ch. 3C: Man Hunts
    Animals (lions)
154 -- Ch. 4B: <u>Potnia Theron</u>
    (waterbirds)
155 -- PT 18B, R: cow & calf
156 -- PT 3, L: calf/PT 18B, R:
    cow & calf
157 -- PT 1B, R; bull
158 -- Ch. 2B: Men (battles)

161 -- PT 11, L; Filler: lion
162a -- Ch. 5G: Insects
    (butterflies)
162b -- Ch. 5E: Birds & Water-
    birds (waterbirds, trio)
162c -- PT 3, L: griffin
163 -- Ch. 2E: People at a
    <u>Shrine</u> (person at left)
164 -- Ch. 2C: Women (2,
    salute)
165 -- Ch. 6A: People-Animals
    (caprid-people)
166 -- Ch. 8E: Helmets
167 -- Ch. 8E: Helmets
168 -- PT 6, R; Plain: bull
169 -- PT 6, L; Filler: bull
170 -- PT 5B, L; Plain: stag
171 -- PT 5A, L; Plain: stag
172 -- PT 5B, R; Plain: kid
173 -- PT 5A, L; Plain: agrimi
174 -- PT 1A, L; Filler: bull
175 -- PT 1A, L; Plain: lion?
176 -- PT 1A, R; Filler: agrimi
177 -- PT 1B, R; boar
178 -- PT 1B, L: griffin
179 -- PT 10A, L: griffin
180 -- PT 25B, R: lion & agrimi
    protome
181 -- PT 12, R: lion
184 -- Ch. 5J: Octopus
189 -- PT 19D, L: 2 agrimia
190 -- PT 6, R; Plain: bull
191 -- PT 5C, R: bull
192 -- PT 6, L; Plain: calf
193 -- PT 13A, R: bull
194 -- PT 18B, R: cow & calf
195 -- PT 41: dog R vs agrimi
197 -- Ch. 9G: Rosettes
198 -- Ch. 5B: Animal Faces
    (bulls)
199 -- Ch. 5B: Animal Faces
    (bulls)
201 -- PT 1A, R; Filler: bull
202 -- PT 1A, R; Filler:
    agrimi
203 -- PT 2, R; Filler: bull
204 -- PT 2, R; Filler: bull

6Da -- Ch. 2A: Body Parts
   (man's head)
6Db -- Ch. 2A: Body Parts
   (man's head)
6Dc -- Ch. 2A: Body Parts
   (woman's face)
7D -- Ch. 3C: Man Hunts
   Animals (lions)
10D -- Ch. 5J: Octopus
11D -- PT 13A, R: bull
12D -- PT 21, R: 2 stags
13D -- PT 25B, L: 2 lions
14D -- PT 5B, R; Plain: bull
15D -- PT 8, L; lion
16D -- PT 25C, L: lion &
   agrimi protome
17D -- PT 1B, R: bull
18D -- PT 1A, R; Filler:
   griffin
19D -- PT 5A, L; Filler: bull
20D -- PT 46: griffin R vs
   stag
22D -- PT 10B, R: griffin
23D -- PT 13A, R: bovine
24D -- PT 18B, R: cow & calf

<u>CMS</u> X (* following a number
   marks it as a Gemma
   Dubitanda)

1 -- PT 11, L; Filler: lion
2 -- PT 25A, R: 2 goats
58 -- Ch. 9B: Centered Circles
   (misc.)
68 -- Ch. 5B: Animal Faces
   (bulls)
69* -- Ch. 8J: Misc.
95 -- Ch. 5G: Insects
   (butterflies)
102 -- Ch. 5G: Insects
   (butterflies)
105 -- Ch. 9G: Rosettes
113b -- PT 1A, L; Filler:
   agrimi
114 -- PT 1A, R; Filler: agrimi
115 -- PT 1A, L; Filler: agrimi

116 -- PT 1A, L; Filler:
   agrimi/Ch. 5H: Fish (2)
117 -- Ch. 5E: Birds &
   Waterbirds (birds, 1)
118 -- Ch. 9H: Cross (misc.)
120 -- Ch. 7B: Misc. Plants
121 -- PT 6, R; Plain: agrimi
122* -- PT 1A, R; Filler: sheep
123 -- PT 5A, R; Plain: agrimi
124 -- PT 1A, L; Filler: agrimi
125 -- PT 39A: griffin R vs kid
126 -- PT 39A: griffin R vs
   stag
127 -- PT 39A: lion R vs bull
128 -- PT 50B: lion L vs stag
129 -- PT 39A: lion L vs stag
130 -- PT 51C: 2 dogs vs kid R
131 -- PT 44A: lion R vs bull
132 -- PT 10A, R: lion
133* -- PT 8, L; lion
134 -- PT 6, R; Filler: griffin
135* -- Ch. 3A: Man & Animals
   (lions)
136 -- PT 6, L; Filler: kid
137 -- PT 14A, L: agrimi
138 -- PT 18B, R: cow & calf
139 -- PT 1B, R: bull
141 -- Ch. 3E: Animal Games
   (bull-leaping, Floating)
142* -- PT 2, R; Filler: bull
143* -- PT 12, L: bull
145 -- PT 14D, L: <u>Minotaur</u>
147* -- Ch. 5F: Alerions
   (head L)
149* -- Ch. 8E: Helmets
150 -- PT 10B, L: lion
151 -- PT 6, L; Filler: lion
152 -- PT 6, L; Filler: lion
153 -- PT 25C, L: lion &
   agrimi
154 -- PT 13A, R: lion
158 -- PT 40: dog L vs kid
160 -- Ch. 4A: Women with
   Animals (antithetic)
161* -- Ch. 3A: Man & Animals
   (lions)
162 -- PT 1A, L; Plain

164 -- PT 1A, R; Filler: lion
165 -- PT 1A, R; Filler:
  agrimi
166 -- Ch. 3E: Animal Games
  (rides other animals)
167 -- PT 2, L; Filler: bull
168 -- PT 5A, R; Plain: agrimi
169 -- PT 5B, L; Plain: bull
170 -- PT 10A, R: griffin
171* -- PT 6, R; Filler: bull
172 -- PT 2, R; Filler: lion?
173 -- PT 6, L; Filler: bull
174 -- PT 25C, R: 2 goats
175 -- PT 2, R; Filler: bull
176 -- PT 1A, L; FIller: bull?
178 -- PT 1C, L: agrimi
179 -- PT 2, L; Filler: agrimi
180 -- PT 2, R; Filler: bull
181 -- PT 2, R; Filler: goat
183 -- PT 6, R; Plain: agrimi
184 -- PT 39A: quadruped R vs
  quadruped
185 -- PT 5A, R; Filler:
  agrimi
186 -- PT 1A, R; Filler: bull
187* -- PT 12, R: bull
188 -- Ch. 9B: Centered
  Circles (misc.)
189 -- Ch. 9B: Centered
  Circles (8)
190 -- Ch. 9B: Centered
  Circles (3)
191 -- Ch. 9B: Centered
  Circles (misc.)
192a* -- Ch. 9B: Centered
  Circles (misc.)
192b* -- Ch. 5E: Birds &
  Waterbirds (birds, 1)
193 -- Ch. 9B: Centered Circles
  (4)
194 -- Ch. 9B: Centered
  Circles (misc.)
195 -- Ch. 9B: Centered Circles
  (3)
196 -- Ch. 9B: Centered Circles
  (2)
197 -- Ch. 9D: Dots

198 -- Ch. 5B: Animal Faces
  (bulls)
199 -- Ch. 9Q: Misc. Lines
200 -- Ch. 5B: Animal Faces
  (bulls)
201 -- Ch. 9G: Rosettes
202 -- Ch. 9Q: Misc. Lines
203 -- Ch. 9E: Spirals
204 -- Ch. 9K: Lines/Strokes/
  Gouges
205 -- Ch. 9O: Chevrons
206 -- Ch. 7A: <u>Branches</u>
  (<u>Branch 1</u>)
207 -- Ch. 9Q: Misc. Lines
208 -- Ch. 9H: Cross
209 -- Ch. 7A: <u>Branches</u>
  (<u>Branch 3</u>)
210 -- Ch. 7A: <u>Branches</u>
  (<u>Branch 4</u>)
215 -- PT 5A, R; Filler:
  agrimi
216 -- PT 18B, R: cow & calf
217 -- PT 18B, R: cow & calf
218 -- PT 39A: lion R vs bull
220* -- PT 5B, L; Filler:
  griffiness
221 -- PT 5A, R; Filler: agrimi
222 -- PT 1B, R; Filler: bull
224* -- PT 19A, L: waterbirds
233 -- PT 5A, L; Filler: winged
  agrimi
234 -- PT 1A, L; Filler: agrimi
235 -- Ch. 9E: Spirals
236 -- Ch. 5B: Animal Faces
  (bulls)
237 -- Ch. 9Q: Misc. Lines
238 -- Ch. 7A: <u>Branches</u>
  (<u>Branch 4</u>)
241 -- PT 40: lion R vs bull
242 -- Ch. 4B: <u>Potnia Theron</u>
  (lions)
243 -- Ch. 8E: Helmets
244 -- PT 2, R; Filler: bull
248 -- Ch. 5F: Alerions (head
  L)
249 -- PT 25B, R: 2 dogs
250 -- PT 37B cl: 3 lions

251 -- PT 5A, L; Filler: agrimi
252 -- PT 26, L: 3 agrimia
254 -- PT 24, R; Plain: 2 bulls
255 -- PT 18B, R: cow & calf
256 -- PT 34A: 2 bulls
257 -- PT 39A: lion R vs bull
258 -- PT 6, R; Filler: bull
259 -- Ch. 3A: Man & Animals
   (bulls)
260 -- PT 25C, R: 2 agrimia
261* -- Ch. 2D: Men & Women
   (2)
262 -- Ch. 2C: Women (1)
263 -- PT 1A, R; Filler: bull
264 -- PT 25C, R: lion & agrimi
   protome
267 -- PT 11, R; Plain: griffin
269 -- PT 14B, L: bull
270 -- Ch. 2C: Women (1)/Ch.
   2E: People at a <u>Shrine</u>
   (woman in a <u>Shrine</u>)
271 -- PT 40: lion L vs calf
277a -- PT 10A, R: lion
277b -- Ch. 5F: Alerions (head
   R)
278* -- Ch. 2A: Body Parts
   (man's head)
279 -- PT 50B: lioness L vs 2
   deer
281 -- PT 10A, R: agrimi
288 -- Ch. 9B: Centered Circles
   (3)
289 -- Ch. 5E: Birds &
   Waterbirds (birds, 1)
296 -- PT 5B, R; Plain: bull
297 -- PT 5B, L; Filler: bull
298 -- PT 6, L; Filler: calf
299 -- PT 19B, L: 2 goats
300 -- PT 5A, R; Plain: stag
301* -- PT 39B, L: lion vs bull
302 -- PT 14A, L: lion
303 -- PT 2, R; Filler: lioness
304 -- PT 25B, L: 2 lions
305* -- Ch. 5E: Birds & Waterbirds (waterbirds, 1)
308 -- PT 25B, L: 2 quadrupeds
309 -- Ch. 5D: Protomes

310 -- PT 6, R; Filler:
   quadruped
311 -- PT 6, R; Filler: bull
314 -- PT 2, R; Filler: bull
316 -- PT 24, L; Plain: 2 bulls
318 -- Ch. 5F: Alerions (head
   R)
319 -- PT 5A, L; Plain: agrimi
321 -- PT 14B: agrimi

<u>CMS</u> XII

79 -- Ch. 9B: Centered Circles
   (misc.)
104 -- PT 5A, L; Plain: stag
135a -- PT 8, L: dog/calf/lion
135b -- PT 10A, L: agrimi
136 -- PT 1B, L: sheep
137 -- PT 10A, L: calf
138 -- Ch. 5H: Fish (2)
141 -- Ch. 5E: Birds &
   waterbirds (birds, 1)
142 -- Ch. 5G: Insects (misc.)
147 -- Ch. 9H: Cross
150a -- Ch. 5E: Birds & Waterbirds (waterbirds, 1)
151a -- PT 5A, R; Filler: bull
151b -- Ch. 7B: Misc. Plants
157 -- Ch. 9G: Rosettes
158 -- Ch. 5I: Dolphins (4)
162a -- Ch. 5B: Animal Faces
   (bulls)
162b -- Ch. 5F: Alerions (head
   L)
168 -- Ch. 2C: Women (pair,
   salute)
174a/AM AE 1802 (CS 11Sa; KZ
   21) -- Ch. 6A: People-
   Animals (caprid-people)
174b -- Ch. 5E: Birds & Waterbirds (birds, 1)
174c (KZ 61) -- Ch. 5B: Animal
   Faces (bulls)/Ch. 6A:
   People-Animals (lion-people)
195 -- PT 1A, L; Filler: agrimi
196 -- PT 1A, L; Plain: agrimi

382

203 -- PT 19A, L: waterbirds
205 -- Ch. 5J: Octopus
207 -- Ch. 3A: Man & Animals (lions)
208 -- PT 10A, R: lion
209 -- PT 5B, L; Plain: bull
210 -- Ch. 5E: Birds & Water-birds (waterbirds, 1)/Ch. 5F: Alerions (misc.)
211 -- PT 5B, L; Plain: bull
212 -- Ch. 6B: Genii
213 -- PT 44A: lion R vs kid/calf
214 -- Ch. 5E: Birds & Waterbirds (birds, 1)
215 -- PT 1A, R; Plain: agrimi
219 -- Ch. 5F: Alerions (head R)
223 -- PT 6, L; Plain: kid
225 -- PT 13A, R: bull
228 -- PT 45: griffin vs bull L
229 -- PT 11, L; Filler: lion
232 -- PT 1A, L; Filler: agrimi
233 -- PT 11, R; Filler: griffin
235 -- PT 11, R; Filler: bull
236 -- PT 6, L; Plain: stag
237 -- PT 5B, R; Filler: bull
238 -- PT 13A, R: hornless <u>Minotaur</u> (= calf-man?)
239 -- Ch. 4C: Women "Crossed" by a Caprid
240 -- PT 1B, R: boar/Ch. 3A: Men & Animals (boars)
241 -- PT 19B, R: 2 agrimia
242 -- PT 39A: dog L vs agrimi/kid-man
243 -- PT 49B, R: small lion vs bull
244 -- PT 12, L: lion
247 -- PT 11, R; Filler: griffin
248 -- PT 10A, R: bull
249 -- PT 10A, L: bull
250 -- PT 36 cl: bulls
251 -- PT 51D, R: 2 lions vs bull

252 -- PT 1A, L; Filler: agrimi
253 -- PT 11, L; Plain: griffin
254 -- Ch. 5F: Alerions (head L)
255 -- Ch. 5F: Alerions (head L)
261 -- PT 5A, L; Filler: agrimi
262a -- PT 6, R; Plain: agrimi
262b -- PT 6, L; Plain: bull
262c -- PT 1A, R; Plain; goat
263 -- PT 21, R: 2 calves
264 -- Ch. 2E: People at a <u>Shrine</u> (person at right)
265 -- PT 47A: dog R vs bull
266 -- PT 11, L; Plain: griffin
267 -- PT 5A, L; Filler: agrimi
268 -- PT 13A, R: bull
269 -- Ch. 9B: Centered Circles (misc.)
270 -- Ch. 9Q: Misc. Lines
271 -- PT 47A: lion L vs kid?
272 -- PT 10A, L: bull
273 -- PT 5A, R; Filler: lion
274 -- PT 5A, L; Filler: agrimi
275 -- PT 5A, L; Filler: agrimi
276a -- Ch. 4C: Women "Crossed" by a Caprid
276b -- Ch. 6A: People-Animals (caprid-people)
277 -- Ch. 6A: People-Animals (caprid-people)
278 -- PT 5B, L; Filler: bull
279 -- Ch. 5F: Alerions (misc.)
281 -- Ch. 5F: Alerions (misc.)
282 -- Ch. 5F: Alerions (misc.)
283 -- Ch. 5F: Alerions (misc.)
284 -- Ch. 3E: Animal Games (bull-leaping, Floating)
285 -- PT 40: lion L vs agrimi
286 -- PT 17A, L: lioness & cub
287 -- PT 21, R: 2 bulls
289 -- PT 10A, L: bull
291 -- PT 47B: griffin L vs <u>Babylonian Dragon</u>
292 -- Ch. 2B: Men (duels)
293 -- PT 6, L; Plain: <u>Babylonian Dragon</u>

294 -- Ch. 5B: Animal Faces
   (bulls)
296 -- PT 5A, L; Filler:
   agrimi
297 -- PT 13A, R: bull
298 -- PT 5B, L: bull
300 -- PT 1A, R; Filler:
   griffin
301 -- PT 1A, R; Filler:
   griffin
302 -- Ch. 6B: Genii
303 -- PT 1B, R; bull
304 -- PT 5A, L; Filler: bull
305 -- PT 1A, R; Filler: bull
306 -- PT 17B, L: cow & calf
307 -- PT 5A, R; Plain: bull
308 -- PT 1A, L; Filler:
   agrimi
310 -- Ch. 5B: Animal Faces
   (bulls)
12D -- Ch. 2C: Women (1)
13D -- Ch. 2B: Men (duels)
14D -- PT 18B, R: cow & calf
15D -- PT 43: dog L vs agrimi

<u>CMS</u> XIII

3 -- Ch. 6A: People-Animals
   (caprid-people)
4 -- Ch. 5F: Alerions (head R)
5 -- Ch. 5H: Fish (3)
6 -- PT 1A, L; Filler: goat
7 -- PT 19B, R: 2 goats
8 -- PT 24, R; Filler: 2 bulls
9 -- PT 11, R; Filler: lion
10 -- PT 2, R; Plain: bull
11 -- PT 30A: 2 bulls
12 -- PT 37C ccl: 4 bulls
13 -- PT 7, L; lion
19 -- PT 10A, L: agrimi
20 -- PT 54: 2 lions vs stag R
21 -- PT 14C, R: lion
22 -- PT 11, R; Filler: lion
23 -- PT 11, R; Filler: lion
24 -- PT 23C, R: 2 lions
26 -- PT 49A, R: lioness vs

bull
27 -- PT 28B: 2 calves
28 -- PT 18B, L: cow & calf
29 -- PT 18B, L: cow & calf
30 -- PT 17A, L: cow & calf
31 -- PT 13B, L: bull
32 -- PT 2, L; Filler: bull
33 -- PT 14B, R: bull
34 -- PT 13A, L: <u>Minotaur</u>
35 -- Ch. 3A: Man & Animals
   (bull)
35 -- PT 4, R: bull
40 -- PT 25A, L: 2 lions
43 -- PT 14A, R: bull
44 -- PT 1A, L; Filler: agrimi
54 -- PT 10B, L: griffin
55 -- PT 10A, L; Plain: griffin
56 -- PT 6, R; Filler: griffin
57 -- PT 2, L; Filler: lion
58 -- PT 44A: lion R vs bull
59 -- PT 25C, R: 2 bulls
60 -- Ch. 6A: People-Animals
   (winged-man)
61 -- PT 14D, L: <u>Minotaur</u>
67 -- Ch. 5J: Octopus
68 -- PT 19D, R: 2 bulls
71 -- PT 49A, R: dog vs kid
76 -- PT 5A, L; Filler: agrimi
77 -- Ch. 5I: Dolphins (4 or
   more)
78 -- PT 24, L; Plain: 2 bulls
82 -- PT 1B, R: lion
83 -- PT 13B, R: bull
84 -- Ch. 6A: People-Animals
   (bull-people)
118 -- Ch. 5F: Alerions (head
   R)
124 -- PT 25A, L: 2 lions
126 -- PT 25B, L: 2 kids
127 -- PT 5A, L; Plain: agrimi
128 -- PT 5A, L; Plain: agrimi
129 -- PT 5B, L; Plain: bull
130 -- PT 5B, L; Plain: bull
131 -- PT 2, L; Filler: bull
133 -- PT 17B, L: cow & calf
134 -- PT 1B, R: goat?
135 -- Ch. 4A: Women &

Animals (antithetic)
136 -- Ch. 2B: Men (warriors)
137 -- Ch. 2B: Men (warriors)
138 -- PT 10A, R: zig-zag/lion
144 -- PT 1A, L; Filler: agrimi

3D -- PT 21, R: 2 calves
4D -- PT 49A, R: lion vs bull
5D -- Ch. 4C: Women "Crossed"
   by a Caprid
13D -- PT 11, R; Filler: kid?
16Da -- Ch. 6A: People-Animals
   (caprid-people)
16Db -- Ch. 2B: Men (1)
19D -- PT 12, L: lion
20D -- PT 11, R; Filler: lion
21D -- PT 40: lion R vs bull
22D -- Ch. 2A: Body Parts
   (man's head)/Ch. 5B: Animal
   Faces (lions; bulls)

B
Museums

(alphabetical by city)

Athens
British School of Archaeology,
Cast Coll.

135 -- Ch. 4B: Potnia Theron
   (lions)
168 -- PT 10A, R: agrimi
170 -- PT 51C: 2 dogs vs kid L
172 -- PT 17A, L: cow & calf
182 -- PT 6, R; Filler: bull
183 -- PT 8, R: lion
184 -- PT 36 cl: 2 lions
186 -- Ch. 6A: People-Animals
   (bull-people)
188 -- Ch. 4A: Woman & Animals
   (woman inb)

National Museum
from Asine ChT 1 -- PT 44A:
   lion R vs calf
from Athens, Acropolis -- PT
   2, R; Filler: quadruped
from Prosymna T. 8 -- PT 1B,
   R; bull
from Tiryns -- PT 41: lion R
   vs bull

Ayios Nikolaos
4653 -- Ch. 2C: Women (1)
11384 -- Ch. 2C: Women (3)

Berlin
FG 2 (AGDS II 20) -- Ch. 2C:
   Women (1)
FG 3 (AGDS II 21) -- Ch. 4A:
   Women & Animals (woman
   inb)
FG 6 (AGDS II 25) -- Ch. 2B:
   Men (duels)
FG 7 (AGDS II 24) -- Ch. 3C:
   Man Hunts Animals (lions)
FG 8 (AGDS II 22) -- PT 13A, L:
   bull/Ch. 3A: Men & Animals
   (bull)
FG 10 (AGDS II 27) -- Ch. 3B:
   Master of Animals (genii)
FG 11 (AGDS II 28) -- Ch. 6B:
   Genii
FG 12 (AGDS II 29) -- Ch. 6B:
   Genii
FG 13 (AGDS II 30) -- Ch. 6B:
   Genii
FG 14 (AGDS II 31) -- PT 8, L:
   griffin
FG 15 (AGDS II 34) -- PT 41:
   lion R vs stag
FG 16 (AGDS II 40) -- PT 12,
   L: lion
FG 17 (AGDS II 35) -- PT 48B:
   lion vs bull
FG 18 (AGDS II 39) -- PT 39A,
   L: quadruped (dog?) L vs
   bull?

FG 19 (AGDS II 41) -- PT 1B,
R; lion

FG 20 (AGDS II 46) -- PT 5B,
L; Filler: bull

FG 21 (AGDS II 56) -- PT 5A,
L; Filler: agrimi

FG 22 (AGDS II 44) -- PT 10A,
R: bull/Ch. 3F: Animal-
Sacrifice

FG 24 (AGDS II 47) -- PT 18B,
R: cow & calf

FG 26 (AGDS II 48) -- PT 25B,
L: 2 bulls

FG 30 (AGDS II 42) -- PT 25C,
L: lion & agrimi

FG 31 (AGDS II 57) -- PT 39A,
L: fish monster/quadruped
vs agrimi

FG 32 (AGDS II 52) -- PT 2, R;
Filler: lion

FG 33 (AGDS II 43) -- PT 2, L;
Filler: bull

FG 34 (AGDS II 39) -- PT 31B:
2 lions

FG 36 (AGDS II 58) -- Ch. 5F:
Alerions (head L)

FG 39 (AGDS II 14) -- Ch. 9N:
Architectonic

FG 40 (AGDS II 23) -- Ch. 3C:
Man Hunts Animals (boars)

FG 41 (AGDS II 26) -- Ch. 6B:
Genii

FG 42 (AGDS II 37) -- PT 39A,
L: lion vs bull

FG 43 (AGDS II 36) -- PT 45:
griffin vs lion R

FG 44 (AGDS II 49) -- PT 21,
R: 2 calves

FG 49a (AGDS II 45a) -- PT 24,
R; Filler: 2 bulls

FG 49b (AGDS II 45b) -- PT
23A, R: 2 boars

FG 50a (AGDS II 12a) -- Ch. 2C:
Women (1)

FG 50c (AGDS II 12c) -- Ch. 5H:
Fish (1)

FG 51 (AGDS II 33) -- PT 41:

griffin R vs kid

FG 61 (AGDS II 60) -- PT 1C, R:
agrimi

FG 122 (AGDS II 13) -- Ch. 2A:
Body Parts (man's head)

Staatliche Museen
Preussischer Kulturbesitz,
Antikenabteilung

no. unknown -- Ch. 2E: People
at a Shrine (woman sits on
Shrine)

Bodrum
no. unknown from the Kas wreck
-- Ch. 5B: Bucranium (pair,
addorsed)

Brussels, Musee Cinquantenaire
no. unknown from Argos -- PT
21, R: 2 calves

Chania
1002 -- PT 5B, L; Filler: calf
1005 -- Ch. 5G: Insects
(butterflies)
1014/1016 -- PT 37A ccl:
waterbird & argonaut
1017 -- PT 13B, L: bull
1018 -- PT 16A, R: nanny & kid
1021 -- PT 13A, L: lion
1024 -- Ch. 2D: Men & Women
(2)
1503/1513 -- Ch. 4A: Women &
Animals (woman at right)
1527 -- PT 10A, L: bull
1528 a & b -- Ch. 2C: Women
(3)
1529/1530 -- Ch. 3A: Men &
Animals (bull)
1536 -- Ch. 3C: Man Hunts
Animals (misc.)
1542/1544 -- PT 5C, R: calf
1547-1556 -- Ch. 3E: Animal
Games (man inb)

1557 -- PT 11, L; Filler: bull
2018 -- Ch. 5G: Insects
   (butterflies)
2045 -- Ch. 5E: Birds &
   Waterbirds (birds, 1)
2052 -- PT 18B, L: nanny & kid
2053 -- PT 2, R; Filler: dog
2055 -- Ch. 2E: People at a
   Shrine (person at left)
2058 -- PT 18B, R: nanny & kid
2065 -- PT 1A, R; Filler:
   quadruped
2066 -- Ch. 5C: Animal Heads:
   bulls
2067/2068 -- PT 10A, L:
   griffin
2071/2112 -- Ch. 2E: People at
   a Shrine (2 women
   antithetic)
2094 -- PT 11, L; Filler: lion
2097 -- Ch. 2E: People at a
   Shrine (woman sits on
   Shrine)
2100 -- PT 19A, R: waterbirds
Sigma 58 -- Ch. 7A: Branches
   (Branch 1)
Sigma 92 -- PT 12, R: lion

no. unknown (Papapostolou
   1977: no.18) -- PT 2, R;
   Filler: waterbird
no. unknown -- PT 12, R: lion

Chora
no. unknown -- PT 11, L;
   Plain: griffin

**Columbia, Missouri University
   Museum**
57.8 -- Ch. 3E: Animal Games
   (bull-leaping, Floating)

Copenhagen
1364 -- PT 2, L; Filler:
   lioness

Epidauros
no. unknown from Apollo
   Maleatas -- Ch. 4C:
   Women "Crossed" by a
   Caprid

Eretria
no. unknown from Lefkandi T.
   12B.3 (Popham & Sackett
   1980: 225) -- PT 1B, R:
   quadruped
no. unknown from Lefkandi T.
   12B.4? (Popham & Sackett
   1980: 225) -- PT 12, R:
   lion

Florence Archaeological Museum
82430 -- Ch. 7B: Misc. Plants
82528 -- PT 8, L; lion
82690 -- PT 5A, L; Filler:
   lion
82820 -- PT 6, R; Filler:
   calf
82822 -- Ch. 6A: People-Animals
   (caprid-people)
84708 -- Ch. 2C: Women (2)
85490 -- PT 1A, L; Filler:
   agrimi

Hamburg
1964.286 (AGDS IV 6) -- Ch. 5E:
   Birds & Waterbirds (birds,
   1)
1964.287 (AGDS IV 5) -- PT 1A,
   R; Filler: agrimi
1964.288 (AGDS IV 7) -- PT 8,
   L; lion
1964.289 (AGDS IV 8) -- PT 37,
   cl: 2 lions

Hannover
1935.119 (AGDS IV 6) -- PT 1A,
   R; Filler: goat
1967.30 (AGDS IV 9) -- Ch. 9G:
   Rosettes
1972.33 (AGDS IV 8) -- PT 11,
   L; Filler: lion

1973.2 (AGDS IV 7) -- PT 51C: 2
dogs vs agrimi L

**Herakleion Museum, Sealstones
(HM)**
610 -- Ch. 2C: Women (1)
888 -- PT 37A ccl: 2 lions
907 -- PT 1A, R; Filler: lion
922 -- Ch. 9B: Centered Circles
(3)
1559 -- Ch. 2C: Women (4 or
more)
1654 -- Ch. 4B: <u>Potnia Theron</u>
(griffins)
1961 -- Ch. 2C: Women (pair,
salute)
2067 -- Ch. 9H: Cross
2092 -- Ch. 6C: Griffins
2093 -- PT 5B, L; Plain:
bull
2094 -- Ch. 2C: Women (1)
2096 -- PT 10A, L: boar
2114 -- Ch. 3A: Men & Animals
(caprid)
2116 -- PT 10B, R: bull
2123 -- PT 10A, R: lion
2124 -- Ch. 5E: Birds &
Waterbirds (waterbirds,
pair)
2128 -- PT 39B, L: lion vs
bull
2163 -- PT 1A, R; Filler:
agrimi
HM 216-) -- Ch. 5F: Alerions
(head L)
2170 -- PT 6, L; Filler:
griffin
2236 -- PT 1A, R; Plain: bull
2243 -- PT 40: lion R vs bull
2250 -- PT 18B, R: cow & calf
2271 -- PT 30C: agrimia
2301 -- PT 2, R; Filler: bull
2343a -- Ch. 8D: Vessels
2343b -- Ch. 8G: <u>Sacred
Knots/Robes</u>
2343c -- Ch. 9C: Arcs
2344b -- Ch. 8D: Vessels

2344c -- Ch. 5G: Insects
(misc.)
2346 -- Ch. 5H: Fish   (1)
2347 -- Ch. 9Q: Misc. Lines
2348 -- Ch. 9H: Cross
2383 -- Ch. 5D: Protomes
2384 -- PT 14B, L: bull
2393 -- PT 24, R; Filler: 2
bulls
2505 (Knossos, MUM no. M35) --
PT 11, R; Filler: lion
2506 (Knossos, MUM no. P136)
-- PT 10A, L: lion
2507 (Knossos, MUM no. J/K3)
-- PT 10A, L: agrimi
2617? -- PT 1A, L; Filler
2624 -- Ch. 6A: People-Animals
(caprid-people)
2770 (Knossos, MUM Misc. 9) --
PT 25B, R: 2 goats
2772 (Knossos, MUM NP18) -- PT
10A, R: lion
2780 -- PT 5A, R; Filler:
quadruped
2781 -- PT 6, L; Plain: bull
2784 -- PT 1A, R; Filler: bull
2785 -- Ch. 6D: Misc. Monsters
2807a -- Ch. 2A: Body Parts
(man's head)
2807b -- Ch. 2C: Women (1)

no. unknown from Archanes,
Anemospilia Temple -- Ch.
2B: Men (1)
no. unknown from Kalyvia T. 9
-- PT 10A, R: griffin
-- PT 3, R: bull
no. unknown from Kalyvron Mylo-
potamou -- Ch. 2C: Women
(1)
no. unknown from Kamilari
-- PT 1B, R; bull
no. unknown from Kato Souli --
Ch. 5H: Fish (2)

nos. unknown from Knossos, MUM
(Popham et al. 1984:

NC 20) -- Ch. 5C: Animal
  Heads (bulls)
Misc. no. 1) -- Ch. 5G:
  Insects (misc.)
Misc. no. 2) -- PT 50B,
  Attacker L
Misc. no. 5) -- Ch. 9I:
  Stars
Misc. no. 6) -- Ch. 9H:
  Cross
Misc. no. 7) -- Ch. 5B:
  Animal Faces (bulls)
Misc. no. 8) -- PT 5A;
  Filler: bull
Misc. no. 11) -- PT 1A, L;
  Filler: quadruped
Misc. no. 12) -- PT 25B, L:
  2 calves
Misc. no. 13) -- PT 1A, L;
  Plain
Misc. no. 14) -- Ch. 9K:
  Lines/Strokes/Gouges
nos. unknown from Kommos (Shaw:
  1982: 166 pl. 40b) -- Ch.
  9H: Cross
  1979: pl. 53d) -- Ch. 9M:
  Reticulation
no. unknown from Mallia -- PT
  1B, L: quadruped
no. unknown from Mochlos --
  Ch. 5E: Birds & Waterbirds
  (birds, 1)
no. unknown from Zafer Papoura
  T. 99 -- PT 2, L; Plain:
  lion
nos. unknown from Crete
  (Xanthoudides 1907: pl.8.
    104) -- Ch. 5E: Birds &
    Waterbirds (water-
    birds, 1)
    148) -- PT 5A, L;
    Filler: bull
  (Younger & Betts 1979:
    no. 1) -- PT 35 cl: 2
    lion forequarters
    no. 2) -- PT 1B, R;
    lion

no. 3) -- PT 1A, L;
  Filler: agrimi
no. 4) -- PT 1/5A, L;
  agrimi
no. 5) -- Ch. 9B:
  Centered Circles 4)
no. 6) -- Ch. 9B:
  Centered Circles
  (misc.)
no. 7) -- Ch. 9K:
  Lines/Strokes/Gouges

Herakleion Museum, Rings (HMm)
989 -- Ch. 2E: People at a
  Shrine (tree-pulling)
990 -- Ch. 8H: Friezes:
  Shields & Sacred Knots/
  Robes
1002-4 -- Ch. 8F: Figure-8
  Shields
1017 -- Ch. 4A: Women &
  Animals (woman inb)
1034 -- Ch. 2B: Men (1,
  religious)
1035 -- PT 11, L; Filler:
  griffin

**Herakleion Museum, Pottery/
  Terracotta (HMp)**
4793-5 -- PT 5A, L; Filler:
  horse
4798-4802 -- PT 44A: lion L vs
  bull
4813 -- PT 1A, R; Filler: goat
4819 -- PT 36 cl: 2 goats?

nos. unknown from Knossos,
  Magazine of the Medallion
  Pithoi -- Ch. 9N:
  Reticulation?
  -- PT 1A, R; Filler: lion

Herakleion Museum, Sealings (HMs)

Ayia Triada Sealings

26 (AT 87) -- PT 39A:
quadruped R vs quadruped

47 (AT 47) -- PT 8, R: dog
scratching

63 (AT 31) -- Ch. 9R: Misc.
Patterns

69 (AT 112) -- Ch. 2B: Men
(1)

71 (AT 71) -- PT 5A, L;
Plain: agrimi

73 (AT 132) -- Ch. 4A:
Women & Animals (woman
rides)

77 (AT 77) -- PT 2, L; Filler:
bull

101, 497 (AT 54) -- Ch. 3A:
Men & Animals (bull)

102 (AT 145, Sk 3) -- Ch.
3D: Animal Games
(bull-leaping, Evans)

108 (AT 91) -- Ch. 5E:
Birds & Waterbirds (birds,
1)

159 (AT 84) -- Ch. 2C:
Women (1)

434 (AT 118) -- Ch. 2C:
Women (1)

435 (AT 13) -- Ch. 5E:
Birds & Waterbirds (birds,
1)

441 (AT 125) -- Ch. 2B: Men
(religious)

452 (AT 95) -- PT 37A ccl:
griffin & griffiness

456 (AT 79) -- PT 20, R: 2
agrimia?

459 (AT 116) -- Ch. 2B: Men
(warriors)

467 (AT 105) -- Ch. 2C:
Women (1)

470 (AT 45) -- PT 2, L;
Plain: lion

472 (AT 44) -- PT 6, L;
Plain: lion

474 (AT 9) -- Ch. 5H: Fish
(2)

476 (AT 32) -- Ch. 5H: Fish
(1)

477 (AT 38) -- PT 2, L;
Plain: lioness

480 (AT 33) -- Ch. 5H: Fish
(2)

482 (AT 78) -- PT 9, R: bull

483 (AT 113) -- Ch. 2B: Men
(battles)

484 (AT 12) -- Ch. 9G:
Rosettes

485 (AT 135) -- Ch. 2B: Men
(religious)

486 (AT 122) -- Ch. 2C: Women
(pair, salute)

487 (AT 136) -- Ch. 2E:
People at a Shrine
(person at left)

492 (AT 16) -- Ch. 5F:
Alerions (head L)

493 (AT 14) -- Ch. 5E: Birds
& Waterbirds (birds, 1)

493 (AT 17) -- Ch. 5F:
Alerions

494 (AT 6) -- Ch. 8E: Helmets

495 (AT 27) -- PT 31B: 2
waterbirds

497 (AT 54) -- Ch. 3E: Animal
Games (man inb)

500 (AT 56) -- Ch. 3E:
Animal Games (bull-riding)

501 (AT 59) -- PT 24, R;
Plain: 2 bulls

502 (AT 51) -- Ch. 3E:
Animal Games (bull-
leaping, Diving)

503 (AT 57) -- PT 2, R;
Filler: bull

504 (AT 55) -- PT 9, L: bull

508 (AT 134) -- Ch. 3A: Men &
Animals (lion)

509 (AT 73) -- PT 1A, L;
Filler: agrimi

512 (AT 86) -- PT 35 ccl: lion

& lioness
513 (AT 18) -- Ch. 5F:
Alerions (head L)
515 (AT 63) -- PT 1B, L:
bull
516 (AT 110) -- Ch. 3E:
Animal Games (bull-
leaping, Diving)
516 (AT 117) -- Ch. 3D: Men
In Chariots
517 (AT 81) -- PT 13A, R:
dog
520 (AT 43) -- PT 6, R;
Plain: lion
521 (AT 97) -- PT 39A, R:
griffin vs lion
522 (AT 139) -- Ch. 2C: Women
(pair, salute)
523 (AT 138) -- Ch. 2C: Women
(1)
525 (AT 74) -- PT 19A, L: 2
agrimia
527 (AT 8) -- Ch. 5B: Animal
Faces (misc. faces)/Ch. 5C:
Animal Heads (misc.)
530 (AT 35) -- Ch. 5G: Insects
(butterflies)/Ch. 5K:
Shellfish
531 (AT 36) -- PT 2, L;
Filler: lion
534 (AT 130) -- Ch. 2C: Women
(1)
535 (AT 123) -- Ch. 2C: Women
(1)
539 (AT 104) -- Ch. 6A:
People-Animals (caprid-
people)
540 (AT 68) -- PT 6, L; Plain:
stag
541 (AT 66) -- PT 2, L; Plain:
bull
544 (AT 109) -- Ch. 3E: Animal
Games (bull-riding)
545 (AT 80) -- PT 23A, R: 2
boars
546 (AT 72) -- PT 5A, L;
Plain: bull

547 (AT 21) -- Ch. 5E: Birds &
Waterbirds (waterbirds,
1)
548 (AT 58) -- PT 25B, R: 2
bulls
552 (AT 30) -- Ch. 5G: Insects
(butterflies)
555 (AT 10) -- Ch. 7A: Branches
(Branch 1)
559 (AT 65) -- PT 5A, L;
Plain: agrimi
561 (AT 24) -- Ch. 5E: Birds &
Waterbirds (waterbirds,
trio)
561 (AT 40) -- PT 1B, L: lion
563 (AT 69) -- PT 2, R;
Plain: bull
564 (AT 99) -- PT 6, L;
Filler: griffin
569/570 (AT 93) -- Ch. 3A: Men
& Animals (misc.)/Ch. 5E:
Birds & Waterbirds
(waterbirds, pair)
571 (AT 82) -- PT 8, R: dog
scratching
572 (AT 25) -- Ch. 5E: Birds &
Waterbirds (waterbirds,
trio)
574 (AT 53) -- PT 5B, L;
Filler: bull
575 (AT 37) -- PT 1A, R; Plain:
dog
576 (AT 137) -- Ch. 2C: Women
(pair, salute)
577 (AT 49) -- PT 31A: 2 lions
578 (AT 121) -- Ch. 2C: Women
(1)
579 (AT 19) -- Ch. 5E: Birds &
Waterbirds (waterbirds,
1)
580a (AT 42) -- PT 11, L;
Filler: lion
580rho (AT 7) -- Ch. 5B:
Animal Faces (bulls)
581 (AT 61) -- PT 9, L: bull
583 (AT 62) -- PT 6, R; Plain:
bull

583a (AT 126) -- Ch. 3A: Men &
   Animals (caprid)
584 (AT 128) -- Ch. 4A: Women
   & Animals (woman seated at
   right)
585 (AT 127) -- Ch. 3A: Men &
   Animals (bull)
586a (AT 28) -- Ch. 5E: Birds &
   Waterbirds (birds, 1)
587 (AT 41) -- PT 12, R: lion
588 (AT 88) -- PT 12, R: bull
590 (AT 23) -- Ch. 5E: Birds &
   Waterbirds (waterbirds,
   trio)
592 (AT 124) -- Ch. 2D: Men &
   Women (2)
597 (AT 101) -- Ch. 6D: Misc.
   Monsters
598 (AT 100) -- Ch. 6D: Misc.
   Monsters
660 (AT 70) -- PT 1A, L;
   Filler: agrimi
791 (AT 103) -- Ch. 6A:
   People-Animals (caprid-
   people)
1347 (AT 107) -- Ch. 6B: Genii
1348 (AT 15) -- Ch. 5F:
   Alerions (head L)

KE (AT 151/153) -- PT 6, R;
   Filler: bull

nos. unknown
   (AT 1) -- Ch. 9R: Misc.
      Patterns
   (AT 11) -- Ch. 5H: Fish
      (1)
   (AT 22a) -- Ch. 5E: Birds &
      Waterbirds (waterbirds,
      pair)
   (AT 26) -- Ch. 5E: Birds &
      Waterbirds (waterbirds,
      trio)
   (AT 29) -- Ch. 5G: Insects
      (butterflies)
   (AT 39) -- PT 1B, R; lion/
      dog

(AT 46) -- PT 4, L: stag
(AT 48) -- PT 12, R: lion
(AT 50) -- PT 10A, L: bull
(AT 60) -- PT 1B, R; bull
(AT 64) -- PT 5A, L; Plain:
   bull
(AT 67) -- PT 5C, L; Plain:
   bull
(AT 75) -- PT 11, L; Plain:
   bull?
(AT 83) -- PT 2, R; Filler:
   lion
(AT 85) -- PT 43: dog/
   lioness R vs dog/lioness
(AT 89) -- PT 49A, R: lion
   vs caprid
(AT 90) -- PT 49A, R: lion?
   vs bull?
(AT 94) -- PT 11, R; Plain:
   griffin
(AT 96) -- PT 31A: 2
   agrimia
(AT 98) -- PT 47B: lion? L
   agrimi
(AT 102) -- Ch. 6A: People-
   Animals (caprid-people)
(AT 108) -- Ch. 3E: Animal
   Games (bull-riding)
(AT 111) -- Ch. 4D: Women &
   Animals (misc.)
(AT 115) -- Ch. 2B: Men
   (duels)
(AT 119) -- Ch. 2C: Women
   (1)
(AT 129) -- Ch. 4A: Women &
   Animals (animal inb)
(AT 130) -- Ch. 4A: Women &
   Animals (woman seated at
   right)
(AT 133) -- PT 25B, R: 2
   Babylonian Dragons
(AT 140) -- Ch. 2E: People
   at a Shrine (at the
   Shrine)
(AT 141) -- Ch. 2D: Men &
   Women (2)

(AT 142) -- Ch. 2D: Men &
   Women (2)
(AT 143) -- Ch. 2C: Women
   (1, religious)
(AT 151/153) -- PT 6, R;
   Filler: bull
(AT 152) -- PT 1A, L; Plain
(AT 154) -- PT 12, R: bull
(AT 155) -- PT 5B, L;
   Filler: calf
(AT 160) -- Ch. 2C: Women
   (1)

Gournia Sealings

101/497/etc. -- Ch. 3E:
Animal Games (man inb)

Kato Zakro (see: XII 174; AM
AE 1802 [CS 11S])

1 (KZ 134/CS S10b) -- Ch. 9E:
   Spirals
1a (KZ 80/AM AE 1801 [CS
   10Sa]) -- Ch. 6D: Misc.
   Monsters
2a (KZ 127) -- PT 2, R; Plain:
   quadruped = monster?
2b (KZ 17) -- Ch. 6A:
   People-Animals (bull-people)
3a (KZ 36) -- Ch. 6A:
   People-Animals (winged-man)
3b (KZ 64) -- Ch. 5B: Animal
   Faces (boars)
4b (KZ 52) -- PT 31B: 2 geese?
   protomes?
5a (KZ 43) -- Ch. 6A:
   People-Animals (caprid-
      people)
5b (KZ 39) -- Ch. 6A:
   People-Animals (caprid-
   people)
6a (KZ 18) -- Ch. 6A:
   People-Animals (bull-
   people)
6b (KZ 83) -- Ch. 5B: Animal
   Faces (bull)

7a (KZ 175) -- Ch. 6A
   People-Animals (lion-
   people)
7b (KZ 75) -- Ch. 6A:
   People-Animals (sphinxes)
8 (KZ 184) -- Ch. 6D:
   Misc.Monsters
8a (KZ 13) -- Ch. 2B: Men
   (battles)
10a (KZ 78) -- Ch. 2A: Body
   Parts (man's face)/Ch. 6A:
   People-Animals
   (sphinxes)
10b (KZ 48) -- Ch. 6A:
   People-Animals (misc.)
10 gamma (KZ 44) -- Ch. 6A:
   People-Animals
   (caprid-people)
11 (KZ 129) -- Ch. 5E: Birds
   & Waterbirds (waterbirds,
   1)
11 (KZ 134) -- Ch. 9E: Spirals
11 (KZ 198) -- PT 1A, L;
   Filler: bull
11a (KZ 92a) -- Ch. 6A:
   People-Animals (bull-
   people)
12 (KZ 96) -- Ch. 3E: Animal
   Games (bull-Leaping,
   Diving)
15 (KZ 132) -- Ch. 7B: Misc.
   Plants/Ch. 9R: Misc.
   Patterns
15a (KZ 88) -- Ch. 5B: Animal
   Faces (bulls)
16 (KZ 33) -- Ch. 5F:
   Alerions (misc.)
17a (KZ 97) -- Ch. 3E: Animal
   Games (bull-Leaping, Evans)
18a (KZ 186) -- Ch. 2B: Men
   (2)
18b (KZ 188) -- Ch. 2B: Men
   (1, religious)
19 (KZ 120) -- PT 2, R;
   Filler: bull
21b (KZ 71) -- Ch. 5B: Animal
   Faces (boars)

22 (KZ 121) -- PT 2, R;
Filler: agrimi/caprid

23a (KZ 74) -- Ch. 6A:
People-Animals (sphinxes)

23b (KZ 58) -- PT 28A: 2
waterbirds

23 gamma (KZ 84) -- Ch. 5B:
Animal Faces (bulls)

24 (KZ 108) -- PT 2, R;
Filler: stag

24a (KZ 81) -- Ch. 5B: Animal
Faces (bulls)

24 gamma (KZ 82) -- Ch. 5B:
Animal Faces (bulls)

25 (KZ 130) -- Ch. 8E: Helmets

25a (KZ 49) -- Ch. 8B:
Buildings

26b (KZ 70) -- Ch. 7B: Misc.
Plants

27a (KZ 53) -- Ch. 6D: Misc.
Monsters

27b (KZ 45) -- Ch. 6A:
People-Animals (misc.)

28 (KZ 31) -- Ch. 8E: Helmets

29a (KZ 69) -- Ch. 5B: Animal
Faces (boars)

30 (KZ 133) -- Ch. 9F: Meanders

31 (KZ 34) -- Ch. 6A: People-
Animals (caprid-people)

31b (KZ 65) -- Ch. 5B: Animal
Faces (boars)

36 (KZ 125) -- PT 1A, R;
Filler: agrimi

37 (KZ 86) -- Ch. 8E: Helmets

37 (KZ 98) --PT 3, R: (bull-
leaping?)/Ch. 3E: Animal-
Games (uncertain poses)

38 gamma (KZ 60) -- Ch. 5B:
Animal Faces (lions)

39 (KZ 167) -- Ch. 5B: Animal
Faces (lions)

39a (KZ 38) -- Ch. 6A:
People-Animals (caprid-
people)

40/321, Pigorini no. unknown
(KN KSPI R37, AT 146, KZ
105) -- PT 20, R: 2 lions

41 (KZ 99) --PT 1B, R; bull

42 (KZ 128) -- PT 28B: 2 lions

43 (KZ 14) -- Ch. 2B: Men
(duels)

45 (KZ 131) -- Ch. 8B:
Buildings

45b (KZ 19) -- Ch. 6A: People-
Animals (caprid-people)

46 (KZ 85) -- Ch. 5B: Animal
Faces (bulls)

49 (KZ 103) -- PT 2, R;
Filler: bull

50a (KZ 76) -- Ch. 2A: Body
Parts (man's face)/Ch. 6A:
People-Animals (lion-
people)

51 (KZ 182) -- PT 47B: griffin
in PT 3 vs agrimi

51 (KZ 41) -- PT 11, L; Plain:
griffin

53 (KZ 62) -- Ch. 5B: Animal
Faces (boars)

54 (KZ 47) -- Ch. 2A: Body
Parts (body parts)

55a (KZ 46) -- Ch. 6A: People-
Animals (bull-people)

57 (KZ 94) -- Ch. 9G: Rosettes

58 (KZ 91) -- Ch. 5E: Birds &
Waterbirds (birds, 1)

60 gamma (KZ 79) -- PT 2, L;
Plain: griffin

60a (KZ 111) -- PT 29A: 2 lion
protomes/Ch. 5D: Protomes

60b (KZ 93) -- Ch. 5B: Animal
Faces (lions)

61 (KZ 113) -- Ch. 5C: Animal
Heads (lions)

65a (KZ 193) -- Ch. 3C: Man
Hunts Animals (lions)

66a (KZ 40) -- PT 5A, L;
Plain: griffin

68 (KZ 177) -- PT 32A: griffin
& agrimi

68 (KZ 181) -- PT 32C: lion &
griffin

69a (KZ 87) -- Ch. 5B: Animal
Faces (bulls)

72 (KZ 124) -- PT 2, L;
Filler: caprid
73 (KZ 100) -- PT 1B, R; bull
74 (KZ 156) -- PT 6, L; Plain:
bull
77 (KZ 126) -- PT 17A, L: cow
& calf
78 (KZ 101) -- PT 13A, R: bull
79 (KZ 109) -- PT 11, L;
Filler: lion
80a (KZ 66) -- Ch. 5B: Animal
Faces (boars)
81a (KZ 63) -- Ch. 5B: Animal
Faces (boars)
81b (KZ 56) -- Ch. 5B: Animal
Faces (lions)
85 (KZ 102) -- Ch. 3A: Men &
Animals (bull)
87 (KZ 143) -- PT 10A, R: lion
88 (KZ 42) -- PT 1A, R; Filler:
griffin
89 (KZ 32) -- Ch. 6A: People-
Animals (eagle-woman, head
misc.)
90 (KZ 164) -- PT 46A: genius L
vs bird
90 (KZ 170) -- Ch. 5D: Protomes
91 (KZ 196) -- Ch. 2B: Men
(1)
91b (KZ 72) -- Ch. 5G: Insects
(butterflies)
92a (KZ 37) -- Ch. 6A: People-
Animals (caprid-people)
92b (KZ 54) -- Ch. 5E: Birds &
Waterbirds (birds, misc.)
93 (KZ 135) -- Ch. 5B: Animal
Faces (lions)
93 (KZ 15) -- Ch. 3A: Men &
Animals (caprid)
97 (KZ 178) -- PT 1A, R;
Filler: griffin
106 (KZ 106) -- PT 8, R: dog
scratching
141 (KZ 141) -- Ch. 5B: Animal
Faces (lions)
146 (KZ 146) -- Ch. 9M:
Reticulation

147 (KZ 174) -- Ch. 9E: Spirals
149 (KZ 149) -- Ch. 5G: Insects
(misc.)
153 (KZ 153) -- PT 3, L: agrimi
154 (KZ 154) -- PT 1A, R;
Filler: lion?
155 (KZ 155) -- PT 11, L;
Plain: lion
157 (KZ 157) --PT 5A, R; Plain:
bull
159 (KZ 159) -- PT 5B, L;
Filler: bull
160 (KZ 160) -- PT 5/6, R: bull
162 (KZ 162) -- PT 2, L; Plain:
bitch
163 (KZ 163) -- PT 17A, L:
nanny & kid
165 (KZ 165) -- Ch. 5B: Animal
Faces (bulls)
168 (KZ 168) -- Ch. 8G: Sacred
Knots/Robes
169 (KZ 169) -- Ch. 5B: Animal
Faces (boars)
171 (KZ 171) -- Ch. 2B: Men
(1)
172a (KZ 172) -- Ch. 7B: Misc.
Plants/Ch. 9E: Spirals
173 (KZ 173) -- Ch. 6A:
People-Animals (caprid-
people)
176a (KZ 176) -- Ch. 2C: Women
(1)
179 (KZ 179) -- PT 3, L:
griffin
180 (KZ 180) -- PT 36 cl:
griffin & quadruped
182 (KZ 182) -- PT 2/6, L;
bull
185 (KZ 185) -- PT 1A, L;
Plain: griffin
189 (KZ 189) -- Ch. 3E: Animal
Games (bull-Leaping, Evans)
190 (KZ 190) -- Ch. 2B: Men
(duels)
191 (KZ 191) -- Ch. 4A: Women
& Animals (animal inb)

192 (KZ 192) -- Ch. 4A: Women & Animals (antithetic)

194 (KZ 194) -- Ch. 3A: Men & Animals (lion)

195 (KZ 195) -- Ch. 2D: Men & Women (2)

199 (KZ 199) -- Ch. 2C: Women (1)

200 (KZ 200) -- Ch. 2C: Women (pair, salute)

321/40, Pigorini no. unknown (KN KSPI R37, AT 146, KZ 105) -- PT 20, R: 2 lions

345 (KZ 55) -- Ch. 6A: People-Animals (caprid-people)

nos. unknown

(KZ 1) -- Ch. 2E: People at a _Shrine_ (person at right)

(KZ 2) -- Ch. 2B: Men (religious)

(KZ 4) -- Ch. 4C: Women "Crossed" by a Caprid

(KZ 5) -- Ch. 2C: Women (pair, salute)

(KZ 6) -- Ch. 2B: Men (religious)

(KZ 7) -- Ch. 2B: Men (religious)

(KZ 8) -- Ch. 2B: Men (2)

(KZ 9) -- Ch. 2C: Women (pair, salute)

(KZ 10) -- Ch. 2D: Men & Women (2)

(KZ 20) -- Ch. 6A: People-Animals (caprid-people)

(KZ 22) -- Ch. 6A: People-Animals (caprid-people)

(KZ 24) -- Ch. 6A: People-Animals (caprid-people)

(KZ 25) -- Ch. 6A: People-Animals (caprid-people)

(KZ 26) -- Ch. 6A: People-Animals (caprid-people)

(KZ 27) -- Ch. 6A: People-

Animals (caprid-people)

(KZ 28) -- Ch. 6A: People-Animals (caprid-people)

(KZ 123) -- Ch. 3E: Animal Games (bull-leaping, Evans)

(KZ 138) -- Ch. 6A: People-Animals (caprid-people)

(KX 139) -- Ch. 6A: People-Animals (caprid-people)

(KZ 145) -- Ch. 3A: Men & Animals (misc.)

(KZ 185) -- PT 1A, L; Plain: griffin

(KZ 187) -- Ch. 2B: Men (1)

(Platon 1971: 147) -- Ch. 6D: Misc. Monsters

(Platon 1971: 159) -- Ch. 2C: Women (1, religious)

Knossos Sealings

106 (KSPI O3) -- PT 41: lion R vs bull

108 (KSPI O4) -- Ch. 3E: Animal Games (bull-leaping, Diving)

110 (KSPI N2) -- PT 26, R: 3 calves

111 (KSPI N6) -- PT 13A, R: bull

112 (KSPI N11) -- Ch. 9E: Spirals

113 (KSPI G11) -- PT 51E: 2 lions vs bull R

114 (KSPI K2/11) -- Ch. 2D: Men & Women (2)

116 (KSPI O11) -- Ch. 9E: Spirals

118 (KSPI O5) -- PT 32B: 2 bulls

119 (KSPI Vc) -- PT 13A, R: lion

121 (KSPI N10) -- PT 14B, R: bull

122 (KSPI N7) -- PT 16A, R: nanny & kid

126 (KSPI Pa) -- PT 11, L; Filler: deer

128 (KSPI Pb) -- Ch. 5H: Fish (1)

129 (KSPI J1; CS 45S) -- PT 1A, R; Filler: bull

131 (KSPI Pe) -- Ch. 3A: Men & Animals (caprid)

132 (KSPI P73) -- PT 49A, R: dog vs deer

133 (KSPI O2) -- Ch. 2B: Men (1)

134 (KSPI Q14) -- Ch. 3A: Men & Animals (misc.)/Ch. 5E: Birds & Waterbirds (birds, pair)

136 (KSPI G8) -- PT 37B cl: 3? quadrupeds

139 (KSPI C51) -- PT 28B: 2 pairs of bulls

141 (KSPI M1-4) -- Ch. 2E: People at a Shrine (person at right)

142 (Sakellarakis 1970: 217 no. B3) -- Ch. 3F: Animal-Sacrifice (bulls)

143 (KSPI Q20) -- Ch. 3A: Men & Animals (bull)

144 (KSPI Pd) -- PT 10A, L: agrimi

146 (KSPI J3) -- Ch. 8C: Ships

147/313 (Gill 1966: no. 7) -- PT 13A, R: bull

148 (KSPI R2) -- PT 5A, R; Filler: stag

149 (KSPI S4) -- Ch. 2D: Men & Women (man, women)

150 (KSPI S6) -- Ch. 8G: Sacred Knots/Robes

152 (KSPI S5) -- Ch. 5B: Animal Faces (bulls)

153 (KSPI R102) -- Ch. 2A: Body Parts (body parts)

156 (KSPI O7) -- PT 28B: 2 bulls

157 (KSPI R91) -- Ch. 4A: Women & Animals (woman at right)

158/662 (KSPI R32) -- Ch. 4B: Potnia Theron (lions)

160 (KSPI Q19) -- Ch. 3A: Men & Animals (misc.)

163 (KSPI R92) -- PT 31B: 2 griffins

164 (KSPI K3) -- Ch. 3C: Man Hunts Animals (fisherman)

165 (KSPI G12) -- PT 14A, R: agrimi

167 (KSPI K8) -- Ch. 3A: Men & Animals (misc.)

179a (KSPI P71) -- Ch. 2A: Body Parts (man's head)

180a (KSPI Pf) -- Ch. 2A: Body Parts (man's head)

190 (KSPI P72) -- Ch. 5B: Animal Faces (bulls)

201 -- Ch. 5E: Birds & Waterbirds (waterbirds, pair)

202 (KSPI H?) -- Ch. 6B: Genii

205 (KSPI O1) -- PT 41, Attacker L: lion L vs calf

208 (KSPI R7) -- PT 1A, R; Filler: sheep

209 (KSPI G10) -- PT 39A: lion L vs bull

210 (KSPI R29) -- PT 26, L & R: 2 sheep

211 (KSPI R13) -- Ch. 3F: Animal-Sacrifice (bulls)

212/1000/1005 (KSPI R6) -- PT 10A, L: bull

214/287 (KSPI F2/K4/K7/K12/Q21/ R53/CS 40S) -- PT 2, R; Filler: bitch

216 (KSPI R86) -- PT 19A, R: 2 bulls

218 (KSPI R44) -- Ch. 3B: Master of Animals (lions)

219 (KSPI R43) -- Ch. 3B: Master of Animals (lions)

221 (KSPI R10) -- PT 18B, R: cow & calf

222 (KSPI R15) -- PT 10B, L:
griffin
225 (KSPI O6) -- PT 13A, L:
lion
226 (KSPI R103) -- Ch. 6A:
People-Animals (caprid-
people)
229 (KSPI R36) -- Ch. 7A:
Branches (Branch 1)
232 (KSPI R17) -- PT 21, L: 2
calves
233 (KSPI R88) -- PT 31B: 2
dogs
239 (KSPI G5+6/CS 52S) -- Ch.
3E: Animal Games (bull-
wrestling)
240+1023 (KSPI G3/Betts 17) --
PT 35 cl: 2 bulls
242 (KSPI R50) -- Ch. 2B: Men
(3 or more)
250 (KSPI R8) -- Ch. 3E:
Animal Games (bull-leaping,
Diving)
251 (KSPI R9) -- Ch. 3A: Men &
Animals (bull)/Ch. 3E:
Animal Games (uncertain
poses)
253 (KSPI N1) -- PT 14A, R:
lion
255 +? (Pini 1973: 221-230) --
PT 51F: 2 griffins vs stag
R
256a (KSPI R88?) -- PT 28B: 2
lions
257 (KSPI R81) -- Ch. 6B:
Genii
259 (KSPI C15) -- PT 29B: 2
griffins
260 (KSPI R60 + 63) -- Ch. 2B:
Men (3 or more)
264 (KSPI R100) -- Ch. 8I:
Double Axes
265 (KSPI R18) -- PT 14A, R:
lion
266 (KSPI R22) -- Ch. 8F:
Figure-8 Shields
267 (KSPI R61) -- Ch. 3A: Men

& Animals (bull)
270 (KSPI R34) -- PT 13C, R:
bull
272 (KSPI R66) -- Ch. 4A:
Women & Animals (friezes)
277-283 (KZ 3; KSPI Q22/R1/
R51/R54) -- Ch. 2E: People
at a Shrine (woman sits on
Shrine)
284 (KSPI G13) -- PT 19, L: 2
bulls
285 (KSPI G14) -- PT 31A: 2
dogs/lions
286 (Gill 1966: 16 no. 20) --
PT 13, R: bull
287 (KSPI R69) -- PT 25A, L: 2
goats
288 (KSPI R85) -- PT 31: 2
agrimia
289 (KSPI R3) -- PT 37A ccl: 2
calves
291 (KSPI R35) -- Ch. 3A: Men &
Animals (monster)
292/Zeta (KSPI R19/30) -- PT
34A: 2 bulls
293 (KSPI R4) -- PT 40: lion L
vs bull
295/329/LambdaBeta (KSPI
K6/R46) -- PT 17B, L: cow &
calf
296 (KSPI K10) -- PT 1A, R;
Filler: goat
298 (KSPI K9) -- PT 1A, R;
Filler: quadruped
300/NH (KSPI R12/14/27)
-- PT 53, Victim R: 2 dogs
vs caprid
302 (KSPI R33) -- PT 13A, L:
lion
308I/RhoZeta (KSPI R74/97?) --
PT 2, R; Filler: bull
309I (KSPI R83) -- Ch. 9B:
Centered Circles (7)
309a (KSPI R82) -- Ch. 9B:
Centered Circles (7)
310 (KSPI R42) -- PT 40: lion R
vs bull

311/KZ (KSPI R84) -- PT 1B, R;
 bull

312 (Gill 1966: 15 no. 8) --
 Ch. 5B: Animal Faces (bulls)

315 (KSPI R41) -- PT 1A, R;
 Filler: lion

316/317 (KSPI R49) -- PT 11, R;
 Plain: griffin

319 (KSPI R77) -- PT 13A, R:
 lioness

320 (KSPI R79) -- PT 1A, L;
 Filler: lion

321 (KSPI R37) -- PT 3, R: lion

328/1008 (Betts 66) -- PT 49A,
 R: lion vs quadruped

330 (KSPI R48) -- PT 1A, R;
 Filler: bull

330a/KsiH (KSPI R52) -- PT
 1B, R: bull

331/332 (KSPI R76) -- PT 36
 cl: 2 goat protomes

335 (KSPI L26) -- PT 1A, R;
 Filler: goat

336 (KSPI L50) -- Ch. 2B: Men
 (2)

337 (KSPI L49) -- Ch. 2B: Men
 (1)

340 (KSPI L43) -- Ch. 5K:
 Shellfish

343 (KSPI L47) -- Ch. 2B: Men
 (1)

344 (KSPI La) -- PT 11, L;
 Filler: deer/cow

345B/399 (KSPI L27) -- PT 10A,
 R: bull

347 (KSPI L?/Na?) -- Ch. 3D:
 Men In Chariots

348 (KSPI L42) -- Ch. 5H: Fish
 (3)

358 (KSPI L?) -- Ch. 5E: Birds
 & Waterbirds (waterbirds,
 1)

360 (KSPI Q16) -- Ch. 6B:
 Genii

362 (KSPI K16) -- Ch. 2B: Men
 (3 or more)

364 (KSPI R16) -- PT 19A, L: 2
 griffins?

367 (KSPI R38) -- PT 34A: 2
 lions/Ch. 5B: Animal Faces
 (bulls)

369/526/no No. 116 (KSPI Ec
 [Betts 12] & AT 114/144) --
 Ch. 2B: Men (battles)

377/OTheta (KSPI Va/CS 51S)
 -- Ch. 5E: Birds &
 Waterbirds (waterbirds,
 pair)

382 (KSPI Ca) -- Ch. 3B:
 Master of Animals (lions)

383I (KSPI L46) -- Ch. 3A:
 Men & Animals (lion)

384 (KSPI L15/22) -- Ch. 8C:
 Ships

386 (KSPI L24) -- Ch. 5C:
 Animal Heads (sheep)

387i/CS 7Sa (KSPI L13) -- Ch.
 5K: Shellfish

387ii (KSPI L25; CS 7Sa) -- PT
 1A, R; Filler: goat

388b (KSPI L40) -- Ch. 5K:
 Shellfish

391 (KSPI L38) -- PT 28A: 2
 pairs of owls/Ch. 5E: Birds
 & Waterbirds (birds, misc.)

392 (KSPI Cc) -- Ch. 2C: Women
 (1)

393 (KSPI L39) -- Ch. 5G:
 Insects (misc.)

396 (KSPI L48) -- Ch. 3E:
 Animal Games (bull-leaping,
 Evans)

404a (KSPI L41) -- Ch. 5I:
 Dolphins (1)

418 (KSPI E1) -- Ch. 2E: People
 at a Shrine (person at left)

421 (KSPI U2) -- Ch. 2D: Men &
 Women (2)

423 (KSPI U12) -- Ch. 5C:
 Animal Heads (caprids)

650 (KSPI U?) -- Ch. 3A: Men &
 Animals (misc.)

653 (KSPI U?) -- Ch. 2A: Body
    Parts (man's face)
654 (KSPI U106) -- Ch. 2A: Body
    Parts (man's face)
655 (KSPI U?) -- Ch. 2D: Men &
    Women (pair, alone)
656 (KSPI U115) -- Ch. 3A: Men
    & Animals (misc.)/Ch. 5C:
    Animal Heads (misc.)
659 (KSPI U117) -- Ch. 5E:
    Birds & Waterbirds
    (waterbirds, pair)
661 (KSPI Cb) -- Ch. 2C: Women
    (1)
664 (KSPI C11) -- Ch. 8H:
    Friezes: Shields & Sacred
    Knots/Robes
665 (KSPI R101) -- Ch. 5B:
    Animal Faces (bulls)
666 (KSPI Ve) -- Ch. 9N:
    Architectonic
668 (KSPI C10) -- Ch. 2C: Women
    (4 or more)
669 (KSPI C9) -- Ch. 2C: Women
    (1)
670 (KSPI C43) -- Ch. 3E:
    Animal Games (bull-
    wrestling)
671 (KSPI Ce) -- Ch. 9N:
    Architectonic
1001 -- Ch. 3E: Animal Games
    (bull-leaping, Floating)
1007 (Betts 47) -- Ch. 6A:
    People-Animals (caprid-
    people)

1010 (Betts 54) -- Ch. 3A: Men
    & Animals (bulls)
1014 (Betts 46) -- PT 2, R;
    Filler: bull
1017 (Betts 53) -- Ch. 2B: Men
    (1)
1033 (Betts 10) -- Ch. 3E:
    Animal Games (man inb)
1039 (Betts 6) -- Ch. 3A: Men
    & Animals (misc.)
1042 (Betts 4) -- Ch. 6B:

Genii

KE -- PT 6, R; Filler: bull
LamdaDelta -- PT 37A ccl:
    goats
LamdaGamma -- Ch. 3E: Animal
    Games (bull-leaping,
    Diving)
PA (KSPI L14) -- Ch. 8E:
    Helmets
XZ (KSPI R70) -- Ch. 2B: Men
    (1, religious)

nos. unknown
    (KSPI C42) -- Ch. 3E: Animal
        Games (bull-riding)
    (KSPI R105) -- Ch. 5I:
        Dolphins (3)
    (KSPI U5) -- Ch. 3E: Animal
        Games (bull-leaping,
        Floating)

Knossos Area Sealings

415 from Isopata, the Royal
    Tomb -- PT 11, R Filler:
    bull

no. unknown from Knossos, MUM
    (Popham et al. 1984: Misc.
    16) -- PT 6, R; Plain:
    bull

Mallia Sealings
1049 -- (Sakellarakis 1970:
    169 fig. 8.5) -- Ch. 3F:
    Animal-Sacrifice (bulls)
1095 -- PT 2/6: agrimi

Myrtos Pyrgos Sealings

1096 from Myrtos Pyrgos -- Ch.
    5E: Birds & Waterbirds
    (waterbirds, pair)
1097 from Myrtos Pyrgos -- PT
    51D, R: 2 lions vs bull

1098 from Myrtos Pyrgos -- PT
19A, R: 2 boars

Sklavokambos Sealings

611 (Sk 1) -- Ch. 2B: Men (2)
613-24/626/627/649 (Sk 4) --
Ch. 3E: Animal Games (bull-
leaping, Diving)
625 (Sk 5) -- Ch. 3E: Animal
Games (bull-leaping, Diving)
628/629 (Sk 2) -- Ch. 3E:
Animal Games (man inb)
630 (Sk 6) -- Ch. 3E: Animal
Games (bull-leaping, Evans)
631 (Sk 7) -- PT 10A, R: bull
632-636 (Sk 8) -- Ch. 3E: Men
In Chariots
636/647 (Sk 10) -- PT 50B: lion
L vs quadruped (bull?)
637 (Sk 11) -- PT 5A, L;
Filler: Babylonian Dragon
638-648 (Sk 12) -- PT 3, R:
griffin
642
(SK 13) -- Ch. 2C: Women
(1)
(Sk 14) -- Ch. 2C: Women
(1)
(Sk 15) -- Ch. 2C: Women
(2)
(Sk 16) -- Ch. 5B: Animal
Faces (bulls)
643/644 (Sk 17) -- Ch. 5B:
Animal Faces (caprids)
648 (Sk 19) -- PT 5A, R; Plain:
bull

**Herakleion Museum, Giamalakis
Collection**
3006 (CMCG 294) -- PT 25C, R: 2
quadrupeds
3007 (CMCG 230) -- PT 5B, L;
Plain: bull
3011 (CMCG 276) -- PT 16B, L:
lion & cub?/quadruped
3015 (CMCG 335) -- PT 11, R;

Filler: griffin
3022 (CMCG 374) -- Ch. 6A:
People-Animals (caprid-
people)
3025 (CMCG 177) -- PT 19B, R:
2 waterbirds
3027 (CMCG 304) -- PT 17A, L:
cow & calf
3031 (CMCG 373) -- Ch. 6A:
People-Animals (caprid-
people)
3032 (CMCG 236) -- PT 5B, L;
Plain: goat
3033 (CMCG 311) -- PT 39A, L:
lion L vs bull
3034 (CMCG 362) -- Ch. 4C:
Women "Crossed" by a Caprid
3045 (CMCG 171) -- PT 1A, L;
Filler: agrimi
3046 (CMCG 320) -- Ch. 5I:
Dolphins (2)
3054 (CMCG 359) -- Ch. 4A:
Women & Animals
(antithetic)
3064 (CMCG 308) -- PT 25C, R:
lion & bull
3065 (CMCG 287) -- PT 25B, L:
2 lions
3066 (CMCG 277) -- PT 37A ccl:
2 lions
3067 (CMCG 319) -- Ch. 5I:
Dolphins (3)
3075a (CMCG 122a) -- PT 1A, L;
Filler: sheep
3078 (CMCG 378) -- PT 31A: 2
genii
3080 (CMCG 301) -- PT 37A ccl:
2 lions
3081 (CMCG 269) -- PT 11, L;
Plain: lion
3083 (CMCG 264) -- PT 11, L;
Plain: lion
3085 (CMCG 271) -- PT 6, L;
Plain: lion
3086 (CMCG 242) -- PT 5A, L;
Plain: agrimi

3088 (CMCG 376) -- Ch. 6A:
People-Animals (caprid-
people)

3089 (CMCG 262) -- PT 10A, R:
lion

3091 (CMCG 227) -- PT 14A, R:
bull

3100 (CMCG 291) -- PT 50B, R:
small lion R vs bull

3101 (CMCG 232) -- PT 5B, L;
Plain: bull

3102 (CMCG 279) -- PT 1B, R:
donkey?

3103 (CMCG 366) -- Ch. 2C:
Women (1)

3104 (CMCG 275) -- PT 10A, R:
lion

3112 (CMCG 309) -- PT 49B, L:
lion vs caprid

3113 (CMCG 422) -- Ch. 6A:
People-Animals (eagle-woman,
head R)

3115 (CMCG 365) -- Ch. 6A:
People-Animals (eagle-woman,
head R)

3117 (CMCG 358) -- Ch. 3B:
Master of Animals (lions)

3123 (CMCG 226) -- PT 5A, L;
Filler: bull

3130 (CMCG 289) -- PT 25C, L:
lion & agrimi

3132 (CMCG 229) -- PT 5A, R;
Plain: bull

3133 (CMCG 300) -- PT 37A cl: 2
lions

3134 (CMCG 246) -- PT 5B, L;
Plain: bull

3135 (CMCG 313) -- Ch. 5E:
Birds & Waterbirds
(waterbirds, 1)

3136 (CMCG 172) -- PT 11, L;
Filler: agrimi

3138 (CMCG 283) -- PT 6, L;
Filler: <u>Babylonian Dragon</u>

3139 (CMCG 295) -- PT 25C, R: 2
quadrupeds

3142 (CMCG 273) -- PT 8, L:
lion

3143 (CMCG 261) -- PT 10A, L:
lion

3145 (CMCG 367) -- Ch. 2C:
Women (1)

3146 (CMCG 253) -- PT 5A, L;
Filler: agrimi

3157 (CMCG 375) -- Ch. 6A:
People-Animals (caprid-
people)

3158 (CMCG 363) -- Ch. 2C:
Women (1)

3177 (CMCG 270) -- PT 11, L;
Filler: lion

3181 (CMCG 268) -- PT 12, L:
lion

3185 (CMCG 329) -- Ch. 5G:
Insects (butterflies)

3192 (CMCG 302) -- PT 23A, L:
2 boars

3198 (CMCG 418) -- Ch. 5F:
Alerions (head L)

3205 (CMCG 425) -- Ch. 5E:
Birds & Waterbirds
(waterbirds, 1)

3208 (CMCG 224) -- PT 13B, R:
bull

3209 (CMCG 357) -- Ch. 3E:
Animal Games (bull-leaping,
Diving)

3210 (CMCG 312) -- Ch. 5E:
Birds & Waterbirds
(waterbirds, pair)

3211 (CMCG 338) -- PT 1A, R;
Filler: lion/Ch. 2A: Body
Parts (man's head)

3212 (CMCG 241) -- PT 2, R;
Filler: bull

3214 (CMCG 234) -- PT 5B, L;
Plain: bull

3216 (CMCG 231) -- PT 5B, L;
Plain: bull

3217 (CMCG 243) -- PT 5B, R;
Plain: agrimi

3218 (CMCG 292) -- PT 24, L;
Plain: 2 bulls

3219 (CMCG 245) -- PT 5B, L;
   Plain: bull
3220 (CMCG 233) -- PT 5B, L;
   Plain: bull
3221 (CMCG 265) -- PT 13B, L:
   lion
3222 (CMCG 240) -- PT 6, R;
   Plain: agrimi
3223 (CMCG 337) -- PT 10A, L:
   griffin
3224 (CMCG 247) -- PT 5A, L;
   Filler: deer
3227 (CMCG 272) -- PT 6, L;
   Filler: lion
3258 (CMCG 252) -- PT 1A, L;
   Plain
3259 (CMCG 290) -- PT 50B cl:
   lion L vs quadruped
3260 (CMCG 307) -- PT 39A, R:
   lion R vs bull
3264 (CMCG 362) -- Ch. 4C:
   Women "Crossed" by a Caprid
3278 (CMCG 380) -- PT 47B, R:
   genius & stag
3285 (CMCG 260) -- PT 2, L;
   Filler: lion
3288 (CMCG 419) -- Ch. 5F:
   Alerions (head R)
3293 (CMCG 288) -- PT 25C, L:
   lion & agrimi
3296 (CMCG 170) -- PT 1A, R;
   Filler: goat
3298 (CMCG 426) -- Ch. 2A: Body
   Parts (face parts)
3299 (CMCG 228) -- PT 6, R;
   Filler: bull
3303b (CMCG 186b) -- PT 5B, L;
   Filler: agrimi
3305 (CMCG 254) -- PT 5A, R;
   Plain: caprid
3306a (CMCG 186a) -- PT 1A, R;
   Plain: agrimi
3307 (CMCG 353) -- Ch. 5B:
   Animal Faces (bulls)
3309 (CMCG 303) -- PT 18B, R:
   cow & calf
3311 (CMCG 355) -- PT 31B:
   monkeys
3313 (CMCG 274) -- PT 2, L;
   Plain: lion
3316 (CMCG 379) -- PT 6, L;
   Filler: Minotaur
3324a (CMCG 185a) -- PT 10A, L:
   griffin
3324b (CMCG 185b) -- PT 5A, L;
   Plain: agrimi
3324c (CMCG 185c) -- PT 10A, L:
   lion
3325 (CMCG 281) -- PT 10A, L:
   dog?
3331 (CMCG 121) -- PT 1B, R;
   lion
3333 (CMCG 282) -- PT 1A, R;
   Filler: quadruped
3349 (CMCG 368) -- Ch. 2C:
   Women (1)
3350 (CMCG 423) -- Ch. 5F:
   Alerions (head L)
3351 (CMCG 267) -- PT 10A, R:
   lion
3356 (CMCG 293) -- PT 25C, R: 2
   goats
3365 (CMCG 421) -- Ch. 5F:
   Alerions (head R)
3369 (CMCG 280) -- PT 1B, L:
   dog
3372a (CMCG 190a) -- PT 33A: 2
   caprids
3372b (CMCG 190b) -- PT 35
   ccl: 2 bull protomes/Ch.
   3A: Men & Animals (misc.)
3372c (CMCG 190c) -- PT 14B,
   R: bull
3415 (CMCG 169) -- PT 10A, L:
   sheep
3422 (CMCG 249) -- PT 6, L;
   Plain: bull
3432 (CMCG 296) -- PT 36 ccl:
   2 lions
3434 (CMCG 263) -- PT 11, L;
   Filler: lion
3437 (CMCG 377) -- Ch. 6A:
   People-Animals (caprid-
   people)

3446 (CMCG 361) -- Ch. 2C:
Women (1)

3450 (CMCG 244) -- PT 5A, L;
Plain: agrimi

3452 (CMCG 259) -- PT 1A, R;
Filler: agrimi kid

3495 (CMCG 336) -- PT 10A, R:
griffin

3496 (CMCG 238) -- PT 6, R;
Plain: bull

3497 (CMCG 237) -- PT 6, R;
Filler: bull

3500 (CMCG 239) -- PT 5A, L;
Plain: goat

3502 (CMCG 257) -- PT 5A, L;
Filler: agrimi

3503 (CMCG 297) -- PT 37A cl:
2 lions

3505 (CMCG 298) -- PT 37A cl:
2 lions

3507 (CMCG 420) -- Ch. 5F:
Alerions (head L)

3511 (CMCG 328) -- PT 19D, L:
2 waterbirds/Ch. 5E: Birds &
Waterbirds (waterbirds,
pair)

3514 (CMCG 299) -- PT 37A cl:
2 lions

3517 (CMCG 235) -- PT 6, R;
Plain: bull

3518 (CMCG 248) -- PT 1A, L;
Filler: bull

3519 (CMCG 321) -- Ch. 5I:
Dolphins (2)

3520 (CMCG 352) -- Ch. 5B:
Animal Faces (bulls)

3521 (CMCG 225) -- PT 15, L:
bull

3525 (CMCG 305) -- PT 36 cl: 2
bulls

3526 (CMCG 266) -- PT 1A, R;
Filler: lion

3527 (CMCG 310) -- PT 49B, L:
quadruped vs quadruped

3528 (CMCG 278) -- PT 1B, L:
boar

3556 (CMCG 424) -- Ch. 6A:
People-Animals (caprid-
people)

3557 (CMCG 256) -- PT 5A, L;
Plain: deer

3561 (CMCG 306) -- PT 39A, L:
dog vs stag

**Herakleion Museum, Metaxas
Collection** (see: CMS IV)
1385 -- Ch. 3E: Animal Games
(bull-leaping, Floating)

Jerusalem, Rockerfeller Museum
no. unknown from Tell Abu Hawam
-- PT 21, R: 2 calves

Kassel
no. unknown from Menidi (AGDS
III 6) -- Ch. 4B: Potnia
Theron (lions)

Knossos, Stratigraphical Museum
no. unknown from the Strat.
Mus. Ext. (Warren 1980) --
side b: Ch. 2A: Body Parts
(man's face); side a: ?Ch.
2C: Women (1, religious)
no. unknown from Knossos
(Younger & Betts 1979: no.
9) -- PT 37A, ccl: lions

Lamia
BE 956 -- PT 31B: 2 lions
no. unknown from Kalapodi --
PT 31B: 2 lions

London

<u>British Museum</u> (see: CMS
    VIII)
97.4.64 -- Ch. 3A: Men &
    Animals (bull)
no. unknown -- Ch. 2C: Women
    (3)

<u>Victoria & Albert Museum</u>
8793-1863 -- PT 37A ccl: 2
    lions

**Los Angeles, J. Paul Getty
Museum**
no. unknown (Boardman 1975: no.
    4) -- PT 13A, L: dog

no. unknown (Boardman 1975: no.
    5) -- PT 19B, L: 2 goats

Mallia, Excavation Storeroom
no. unknown -- PT 2,R; Filler:
    calf

Melos
568 -- PT 5A, L; Filler: agrimi
569 -- PT 1A, R; Filler: bull
570 -- PT 1A, R; Filler: agrimi
571 -- PT 13A, R: calf
572 -- PT 5A, L; Filler: goat
573 -- PT 1A, R; Filler: bull
574 -- PT 1A, R; Filler: horse?
575 -- PT 2, R; Plain:
    quadruped
576 -- PT 6, L; Plain:
    bull/stag
578a -- PT 1A, R; Plain: agrimi
578b -- Ch. 5F: Alerions (head
    L)

Munich
A.1163a (AGDS I 84a) -- PT 5A,
    R; Filler: agrimi

A.1164 (AGDS I 55) -- PT 7, L;
    griffin
A.1165 (AGDS I 85) -- PT 5A, R;
    Plain: agrimi
A.1169 (AGDS I 53) -- PT 2, L;
    Plain: bull
A.1170 (AGDS I 86) -- PT 5A, R;
    Plain: stag
A.1171 (AGDS I 87) -- Ch. 3A:
    Men & Animals (lion)
A.1172 (AGDS I 54) -- PT 25C,
    L: 2 lions
A.1180 (AGDS I 45) -- Ch. 3E:
    Animal Games (bull-leaping,
    Floating)
A.1181 (AGDS I 46) -- PT 48A:
    lion vs stag
A.1186 (AGDS I 40) -- PT 44A:
    lion R vs bull
A.1187 (AGDS I 82) -- PT 21, L:
    2 bulls
A.1188 (AGDS I 61) -- PT 13A,
    R: bull
A.1189 (AGDS I 62) -- PT 14B:
    bull
A.1192 (AGDS I 37) -- PT 40, L:
    dog vs agrimi
A.1193 (AGDS I 38) -- PT 24, L;
    Filler: 2 bulls
A.1194 (AGDS I 63) -- PT 10A,
    L: agrimi
A.1195 (AGDS I 64) -- PT 8, R:
    lion
A.1196 (AGDS I 47) -- PT 10B,
    L: griffin
A.1197 (AGDS I 48) -- PT 10B,
    R: bull
A.1198 (AGDS I 65) -- PT 1A, L;
    Filler: agrimi
A.1199 (AGDS I 66) -- PT 2, L;
    Filler: lion
A.1200 (AGDS I 35) -- PT 3, L:
    agrimi
A.1201 (AGDS I 49) -- Ch. 5F:
    Alerions (head L)
A.1216b (AGDS I 70b) -- PT 1A,
    L; Filler: griffin

A.1307 (AGDS I 88) -- PT 13A,
  R: bull
A.1308 (AGDS I 89) -- PT 2, R;
  Filler: bull
A.1321 (AGDS I 50) -- Ch. 5H:
  Fish (2)
A.3161 (AGDS I 51) -- Ch. 5B:
  Animal Faces (lions)

acc. 18211 (AGDS I 23) -- PT 4,
  R: lion/dog
acc. 21765 (AGDS I 24) -- Ch.
  5B: Animal Faces (bulls)
acc. 21767 (AGDS I 93) -- PT
  5A, L; Plain: agrimi
acc. 21768 (AGDS I 44) -- PT
  40: lion R vs caprid
acc. 22846 (AGDS I 76) -- PT
  1A, L; Filler: bull

no. unknown (AGDS I
  52) -- PT 5A, L; Plain: goat
  74) -- PT 18B, L: cow & calf
  77) -- PT 2, R; Filler:
    quadruped
  78) -- PT 1A, R; Filler:
    agrimi
  94) -- Ch. 6A: People-
    Animals (caprid-people)

Antike Sammlung
SL681 -- Ch. 3C: Man Hunts
  Animals (lions)

Nafplion
no. unknown from
  Aidonia T. 7 -- PT 8, R:
    lion
  Apollo Maleatas -- PT 1A,
    L; Plain: agrimi
  Apollo Maleatas -- Ch. 5F:
    Alerions (head L)
  Tiryns -- PT 2/6, R; bull
  Tiryns -- Ch. 2A: Body Parts
    (man's face)
  Tiryns -- Ch. 5B: Animal

Faces (bulls)
  Tiryns -- Ch. 9A: Paisleys
  Tiryns -- Ch. 9E: Spirals
  Tiryns -- Ch. 9G: Rosettes

Naples
1404 -- PT 6, L; Filler: caprid

New York
Metropolitan Museum (see: CMS
  XII)

26.31.218 -- Ch. 2A: Body Parts
  (man's head)

L. Morgan Library
1077 (Pini 1980: no. A5) -- PT
  39A: griffin L vs bull

Nicosia, Cyprus Museum
1953/IX-3/6 from Analiondas
  (Pini 1980: no. B2) -- PT
  39A, R: lion vs bull/Ch. 3E:
  Men In Chariots
no. unknown, ring from Enkomi
  T. 18 -- PT 2, L; Plain:
  lion

Oxford, Ashmolean Museum
1873.129 (CS 330) -- PT 2, L;
  Filler: lioness
1889.289 (CS 375) -- Ch. 2C:
  Women (pair, salute)
1889.999 (CS 397) -- Ch. 7A:
  Branches (Branch 2)
1893.234 (CS 18P) -- PT 2, R;
  Filler: bull
1893.235 (CS 26P) -- PT 5A, R;
  Plain: stag
1893.238 (CS 327) -- PT 10A, R:
  griffin
1895.3 (CS 40P) -- Ch. 2B: Men
  (1, religious)

1919.56 -- Ch. 2C: Women (1, religious)

1920.116 (CS 8P) -- PT 6, R; Filler: agrimi

1925.128 (CS 6P) -- PT 51B, L: lion & dog vs agrimi

1925.44 (CS 189) -- Ch. 5H: Fish (1)

1925.45 (CS 348) -- PT 14B, R: agrimi

1925.47 (CS 25P) -- PT 5B, L; Plain: stag

1925.49 (CS 385) -- PT 5B, L; Plain: bull

1925.50 (CS 388) -- PT 6, R; Plain: bull

1925.52 (CS 387) -- PT 6, L; Plain: bull

1925.53 (CS 389) -- PT 6, R; Filler: bull

1925.54 (CS 27P) -- PT 5A, L; Plain: stag

1938.861 (KSPI G15; CS 50S) -- PT 51A, R: 2 lions vs bull

1938.941 (CS 1S/KSPI L1-6?) -- Ch. 9Q: Misc. Patterns

1938.946 (CS 201) -- PT 6, L; Filler: agrimi

1938.947a, b (CS 47S & 48S/KSPI R94) -- Ch. 9G: Rosettes

1938.948 (CS 2S) -- Ch. 7B: Misc. Plants

1938.948 (CS 2Sb; KZ 29) -- Ch. 5E: Birds & Waterbirds (birds, misc.)

1938.951 (CS 105) -- Ch. 5B: Animal Faces (bulls)

1938.952 (CS 104) -- Ch. 5B: Animal Faces (bulls)

1938.953 (CS 200) -- PT 1A, R; Plain: sheep

1938.954 (CS 227) -- PT 1B, R; Filler: agrimi

1938.956 (CS 205) -- Ch. 3C: Man Hunts Animals (fisherman)

1938.957 (CS 228) -- Ch. 8C: Ships

1938.962 (CS 226) -- Ch. 3C: Man Hunts Animals (agrimia)

1938.963 (CS 203) -- Ch. 5I: Dolphins (2)

1938.964 (CS 202) -- Ch. 3E: Animal Games (bull-leaping, Diving)

1938.967 (CS 195) -- Ch. 5J: Octopus

1938.968 (CS 233) -- Ch. 5G: Insects (butterflies)

1938.969 (CS 301) -- PT 1C, R: calf/bull

1938.970 (CS 206) -- Ch. 5C: Animal Heads (bulls)

1938.971 (CS 297) -- Ch. 5E: Birds & Waterbirds (waterbirds, trio)

1938.972 (CS 232) -- Ch. 5H: Fish (1)

1938.973b (CS 220) -- Ch. 5E: Birds & Waterbirds (birds, misc.)

1938.975 (CS 379) -- Ch. 5K: Shellfish (shells)

1938.976 (CS 291) -- Ch. 5B: Animal Faces (bulls)

1938.977 (CS 187) -- Ch. 5F: Alerions (head R)

1938.978 (CS 223) -- Ch. 5E: Birds & Waterbirds (waterbirds, 1)

1938.979 (CS 181) -- Ch. 5E: Birds & Waterbirds (waterbirds, 1)

1938.981 (KSPI K1) -- PT 20, R: lion & lioness

1941.982 (CS 5S) -- PT 11, L; Filler: deer

1938.1007 (CS 355) -- Ch. 5I: Dolphins (4 or more)

1938.1009 (CS 284) -- Ch. 2D: Men & Women (2)

1938.1013 (CS 295) -- Ch. 2C: Women (3)

1938.1017 (CS 237) -- PT 10A,
R: dog
1938.1018 (CS 236) -- PT 9, L:
bull
1938.1019 (CS 316) -- PT 16A,
R: nanny & kid/PT 33A: lion
& nanny & kid (PT 16A, R)
1938.1020 (CS 302) -- Ch. 5E:
Birds & Waterbirds
(waterbirds, pair)/Ch. 5G:
Insects (butterflies)/Ch.
5K: Shellfish
1938.1021 (CS 242) -- PT 17A,
L: nanny & kid/Ch. 3A: Men &
Animals (bull)
1938.1022 (CS 320) -- Ch. 3C:
Man Hunts Animals (agrimia)
1938.1023 (CS 285) -- Ch. 3C:
Man Hunts Animals (agrimia)
1938.1024 (CS 309) -- Ch. 3A:
Men & Animals (caprid)
1938.1026 (CS 300) -- Ch. 3A:
Men & Animals (bull)
1938.1029 (CS 311) -- PT 24, L;
Plain: 2 bulls
1938.1030 (CS 312) -- PT 24, L;
Filler: 2 bulls
1938.1031 (CS 317) -- PT 5C, R:
bull
1938.1032a (CS 243a) -- Ch. 5B:
Animal Faces (boars)
1938.1032b (CS 243b) -- PT 18B,
R: cow & calf
1938.1035 (CS 331) -- PT 39A:
lion R vs bull
1938.1036 (CS 318) -- PT 38, L:
lion vs bull
1938.1037 (CS 314) -- PT 13A,
R: lioness
1938.1039 (CS 292) -- Ch. 5B:
Animal Faces (bulls)
1938.1040 (CS 307) -- PT 1A, R;
Filler: bull
1938.1041 (CS 306) -- PT 1A, R;
Filler: bull
1938.1042 (CS 305) -- Ch. 6B:
Genii

1938.1043 (CS 304) -- Ch. 6B:
Genii
1938.1044 (CS 338) -- Ch. 6B:
Genii
1938.1045 (CS 303) -- Ch. 6B:
Genii
1938.1947 (CS 49S) -- PT 37A
ccl: goats
1938.1048 (CS 10P) -- PT 11, R;
Filler: lion
1938.1049 (CS 294) -- Ch. 2B:
Men (1)
1938.1050 (CS 293) -- Ch. 3A:
Men & Animals (misc.)
1938.1051 (CS 308) -- Ch. 3D:
Men In Chariots
1938.1052 (CS 224) -- PT 6, R;
Filler: bull/Ch. 5H: Fish
(1)
1938.1053 (CS 251) -- Ch. 7B:
Misc. Plants
1938.1054 (CS 9P) -- Ch. 3B:
Master of Animals (lions)
1938.1058 (CS 315) -- PT 14A,
R: lion
1938.1059 (CS 319) -- PT 43:
lion L vs agrimi
1938.1060 (CS 298) -- PT 18B,
R: lioness & cub
1938.1061 (CS 240) -- PT 2, R;
Filler: bitch
1938.1062 (CS 238) -- Ch. 3A:
Men & Animals (misc.)
1938.1063 (CS 349) -- PT 51C: 2
dogs vs kid L
1938.1064 (CS 5P) -- PT 39A:
lion L vs bull
1938.1065 (CS 350) -- PT 53,
Victim R: 2 dogs vs kid
1938.1066 (CS 343) -- PT 26, R:
3 waterbirds
1938.1068 (CS 51S) -- Ch. 5E:
Birds & Waterbirds
(waterbirds, pair)
1938.1069 (CS 321) -- PT 37A
cl: Lion-man & Minotaur

1938.1070 (CS 325) -- PT 14D,
   L: <u>Minotaur</u>
1938.1071 (CS 322) -- PT 13A,
   L: <u>Minotaur</u>
1938.1072 (CS 323) -- Ch. 6A:
   Animal-People (bull-people)
1938.1074 (CS 209) -- Ch. 3E:
   Animal Games (bull-leaping,
   Diving)
1938.1075 (CS 342) -- PT 52A: 2
   griffins vs bull R
1938.1076 (CS 247) -- Ch. 3A:
   Men & Animals (bulls)
1938.1077 (CS 246) -- Ch. 3E:
   Animal Games (bull-leaping,
   Diving)
1938.1078 (CS 248) -- Ch. 3E:
   Animal Games (bull-leaping,
   Floating)
1938.1079 (CS 249) -- Ch. 3E:
   Animal Games (bull-leaping,
   Floating)
1938.1080 (KSPI G5 + 6/CS 246)
   -- Ch. 3E: Animal Games
   (bull-wrestling)
1938.1082 (CS 44S) -- PT 11, R;
   Filler: bull
1938.1083 (CS 328) -- PT 47B:
   lion L vs bird
1938.1084 (CS 344) -- PT 39A,
   R: cat vs waterbird
1938.1085 (CS 345) -- PT 14B,
   L: bull
1938.1086 (CS 332) -- PT 1B, L:
   boar
1938.1087 (Matrix) -- PT 18A,
   R: cow & calf
1938.1091 -- Ch. 3A: Men &
   Animals (misc.)
1938.1093 (CS 282) -- Ch. 4D:
   Women & Animals (misc.)
1938.1094 (CS 336) -- Ch. 5D:
   Protomes
1938.1095 (CS 239) -- PT 6, L;
   Plain: bitch
1938.1096 (CS 19P) -- PT 1A, R;
   Filler: agrimi

1938.1097 (CS 21P) -- Ch. 4A:
   Women & Animals (antithetic)
1938.1099 (GGFR pl. 197) -- Ch.
   9A: Paisleys
1938.1100 (CS 367) -- PT 13A,
   R: griffin
1938.1108 (CS 34) -- Ch. 3E:
   Animal Games (bull-leaping,
   Floating)
1938.1126 (CS 340) -- PT 29B: 2
   lions
1938.1127 (CS 250) -- Ch. 2E:
   People at a <u>Shrine</u> (person
   at left)
1938.1129 -- Ch. 2D: Men &
   Women (& a boat)
1938.1130, The Ring of Nestor
   -- Ch. 2D: Men & Women
   (misc.)
1938.1136a (CS 398a) -- PT
   1/2, R; bull?
1938.1146 (CS 253) -- Ch. 2C:
   Women (pair, salute)
1938.1147 (CS 252) -- Ch. 2C:
   Women (pair, salute)
1938.1150 (CS 22P) -- PT 5A, R;
   Filler: <u>Babylonian Dragon</u>
1938.1153h:A (Pini 1982: 1-4)
   -- PT 46: lion L vs 2 bulls
1938.1439a (CS 7S) -- Ch. 5K:
   Shellfish
1938.1440a (CS 9S) -- Ch. 5K:
   Shellfish
1938.1441 (CS 43S)-- PT 1/2, R;
   lion
1941.89 (CS 4P) -- PT 40: lion
   R vs stag
1941.91 (CS 191) -- Ch. 5I:
   Dolphins (2)
1941.92 (CS 383) -- PT 25B, R:
   2 calves
1941.94 (CS 245) -- PT 37A cl:
   2 lions
1941.95 (CS 244) -- PT 37A cl:
   2 lions
1941.98 (CS 373) -- PT 11, L;
   Filler: lion

1941.99 (CS 386) -- PT 5A, L;
Plain: agrimi

1941.101 (CS 290) -- PT 19A, R:
waterbirds

1941.107 (CS 194) -- Ch. 7A:
<u>Branches</u> (<u>Branch 2</u>)

1941.119 (CS 3P) -- PT 39A: dog
L vs kid

1941.120 (CS 283) -- Ch. 4C:
Women "Crossed" by a Caprid

1941.121 (CS 286) -- PT 27B, R:
3 goats

1941.123 (CS 326) -- PT 14D, L:
agrimi-man

1941.124 (CS 263) -- PT 1A, L;
Filler: agrimi

1941.125 (CS 299) -- PT 10A, L:
bull

1941.126 (CS 41P) -- Ch. 2C:
Women (1)

1941.128 (CS 23P) -- PT 1A, R;
Filler: griffin

1941.129 (CS 347) -- PT 47A;
Attacker R: griffin vs lion

1941.124 (CS 263) -- PT 1A, L;
Filler: agrimi

1941.130 (CS 366) -- PT 45:
griffin vs bull L

1941.134 (CS 20P) -- PT 1A, R;
Filler: agrimi

1941.136 (CS 190) -- PT 10A, L:
agrimi

1941.137 (CS 11P) -- PT 5B, L;
Filler: bull

1941.138 (CS 12P) -- PT 25B, L:
bull & goat protome

1941.142 (CS 368) -- PT 7, L;
griffin

1941.144 (CS 363) -- PT 25B, R:
2 sheep

1941.146 (CS 369) -- PT 6, L;
Filler: lion

1941.147 (CS 28P) -- PT 6, L;
Filler: lion

1941.148 (CS 370) -- PT 49B, R:
lion vs bull

1941.155ba (CS 30Pa) -- PT 2,

L; Filler: lion

1941.155bb (CS 30Pb) -- PT 8,
L; lion

1941.246 (CS 7P) = CMS II 3.40
-- PT 1A, R; Filler: goat

1941.1228 (CS 24P) -- PT 6, L;
Plain: stag

1941.1229 (CS 234) -- Ch. 5G:
Insects (butterflies)

1941.1231 (CS 289) -- Ch. 5E:
Birds & Waterbirds
(waterbirds, pair)

1941.1233 (CS 287) -- PT 6, R;
Plain: goat

1941.1238 (CS 235) -- Ch. 5F:
Alerions (head L)

1941.1241 (CS 346) -- PT 12, L:
lion

1941.1242 (CS 335) -- PT 1,
L; quadruped

1953.116 (CS 31P) -- Ch. 9N:
Architectonic

1953.117 (CS 32P) -- PT 5A, R;
Plain: griffin

1953.119 (CS 34P) -- PT 10A, L:
griffin

1953.120 (CS 35P) -- PT 11, L;
Plain: griffin

1953.121 (CS 36P) -- PT 1A, R;
Plain: lion

1953.122 (CS 37P) -- Ch. 2B:
Men (2)

1971.1136 (Boardman 1973: no.
7) -- PT 49B, L: lion vs kid

1971.1137 (Boardman 1973, no.
8) -- PT 45: griffin vs lion
L

1971.1138 (Boardman 1973: no.
17) -- Ch. 9G: Rosettes

1971.1139 (Boardman 1973, no.
6) -- Ch. 4A: Women &
Animals (antithetic)

1971.1140 (Boardman 1973, no.
11) -- PT 5B, L; Filler:
bull

1971.1141 (Boardman 1973, no.
    3) -- PT 6, R; Filler: bull
1971.1142 (Boardman 1973, no.
    4) -- Ch. 8E: Helmets
1971.1143 (Boardman 1973, no.
    12) -- PT 5B, L; Plain: bull
1971.1144 -- PT 2, L; Plain:
    lion
1971.1145 (Boardman, 1973, no.
    5) -- Ch. 4B: Potnia Theron
    (dolphins)
1971.1147 (Boardman 1973, no.
    18) -- Ch. 9K:
    Lines/Strokes/Gouges
1971.1148 (Boardman 1973 no. 2)
    -- Ch. 2A: Body Parts (man's
    head)
1971.1149 -- PT 5A, L; Plain:
    agrimi
1971.1150 (Boardman 1973, no.
    3) -- PT 8, R: dog
    scratching
1971.1151 (Boardman 1973, no.
    10) -- PT 10A, L: lion

AE 689 (CS 351) -- Ch. 4B:
    Potnia Theron (griffins)
AE 690b (CS 334b) -- PT 12, L:
    bull
AE 693 (CS 16P) -- PT 10A, R:
    griffin
AE 695 (CS GD pl. 20) -- PT
    39A/40: lion R vs bull
AE 696 (CS 324) -- PT 44A:
    Minotaur L vs caprid?
AE 697 (CS 17P) -- PT 2, L;
    Plain: bull
AE 700 (CS 364) -- PT 5A, L;
    Filler: agrimi
AE 1200b (CS 15P) -- PT 7, L;
    griffin
AE 1227 (CS 384) -- PT 5A, R;
    Plain: caprid
AE 1230 (CS 14P) -- PT 44A:
    lion L vs bull
AE 1786 (CS 371) -- PT 5A, L;
    Filler: agrimi

AE 1787 (CS 372) -- PT 39C:
    (lion R vs ?) goat
AE 1790 (CS 392) -- Ch. 9B:
    Centered Circles (misc.)
AE 1793 (CS 13P) -- PT 5A, L;
    Filler: agrimi
AE 1795 (CS 29P) -- PT 2, L;
    Filler: quadruped
AE 1796 (CS 42P) -- PT 1A, L;
    Filler: quadruped
AE 1798 (CS 48P) -- Ch. 9K:
    Lines/Strokes/Gouges
AE 1801a (CS 10Sa) -- Ch. 6D:
    Misc. Monsters
AE 1801b (CS 10Sb) -- Ch. 9E:
    Spirals
AE 1802a/XII 174a (CS 11Sa; KZ
    21) -- Ch. 6A: Animal-People
    (caprid-people)
AE 1802b (CS 11Sb) -- Ch. 5E:
    Birds & Waterbirds (birds,
AE 1802c (CS 11Sc; KZ 61) --
    Ch. 5B: Animal Faces (bulls)
AE 2237, The Archanes Ring --
    Ch. 3E: Animal Games
    (bull-leaping, Diving)

no No. 8 (KSPI Ce) -- Ch. 9N:
    Architectonic

Oxford, Mississippi University Museums

J21 -- PT 1B, R: sheep
J22 -- PT 1B, R: bull
J25 -- PT 12, L: lion

no. unknown -- PT 39A, R: lion
    vs kid

Paris
Cabinet des Medailles (see: CMS
    IX)

Coll. Schlumberger 43 (Pini
    1980: no. A6) -- PT 39A:
    griffin L

Louvre Museum
    AO 2188 -- Ch. 3D: Men In
        Chariots

Patras
2440/2442 -- PT 13A, L: bull
2443 (Pini 1981: no. 88) -- PT
    30A: 2 goats

Piraieus
no. unknown, ring from Varkiza
    (AAA 7, 1974, 423-433) --
    Ch. 3A: Men & Animals
    (bulls)

Peronne
no. unknown from Thessalonike,
    the Danicourt Ring -- Ch.
    3C: Man Hunts Animals
    (lions)

Pylos
no. unknown from Koukounara,
    Phyties -- PT 42A, R: dog vs
    agrimi

Rome
Pigorini Museum
    71974 (AT 145, Sk 3) -- Ch.
    3E: Animal Games
    (bull-leaping, Evans)

Villa Giulia
    no. unknown -- Ch. 3B:

Master of Animals (monsters)

Sofia, Rumania Academy
433 -- PT 13A, L: bovine
434 -- PT 6, R; Filler: goat

Sparta
no. unknown from
    Ayios Stephanos -- PT 2, R;
        Filler: quadruped
    the Menelaion
        -- PT 19A, L: 2 goats
        -- PT 34B: 2 bulls
            conjoined

Thera
    no. unknown from Acrotiri --
    Ch. 9K: Lines/Strokes/Gouges

Vienna
1357 -- Ch. 3B: Master of
    Animals (lions)

VC
Collections

(alphabetical by collector)

Brummer Collection, NY
-- PT 1B, L: sow
-- PT 25C, L: lion & bull
    protome

Eccles Collection
(Betts 1979: 277-8) -- PT 47B:
    lion R vs kid

Dr Hamerton Collection
(Boardman 1973: no. 1) -- PT
    14A, R: goat

Younger Collection
PT 5B, L; Plain: bull

                    VD

        Whereabouts Unknown

Holland
(Crouwel 1975) -- Ch. 6A:
    People-Animals (bull-people)

Turkey
Lentoid from Besiktepe -- Ch.
    5B: Animal Faces (bulls)

Once Arndt Coll.
(GGFR pl. 186) -- Ch. 3D: Men
    In Chariots

Once Evans
(GGFR
    pl. 115) -- PT 1A, R;
        Filler: dog
    pl. 135) -- PT 5A, R;
        Filler: bull
the Ring of Minos -- Ch. 2E:
    People at a <u>Shrine</u>
    (tree-pulling)

Once Schliemann
from the Argive Heraeum -- Ch.
    5B: Animal Faces (bulls)

Lentoid
Furtwangler, Antike Gemmen pl.
    VI.6) -- Ch. 6A: People-
    Animals (caprid-people)

PART VI

BIBLIOGRAPHY
(see Abbreviations)

Alexiou, S.
1954   "The Boar's Tusk Helmet," Antiquity 28 (1954)
                   211-213

1958a   He Minoike Thea meth' Hypsomenon Cheiron
                   (Herakleion, Crete, 1958; also published in
                   KretKhron 12, 1958, 179-301)

1958b   "Ho Daktylios tes Oxfordes," Minoica: Festschrift
                   Geburtstag J. Sundwall (Berlin 1958)

1967   "Sacred Knot," Europa, Festschrift E. Grumach
                   (de Gruyter, Berlin 1967) 1-6

1971   "Nea Paratasis Ploiou epi Minoikes Larnakes,"
                   CretCong III (1971) 3-12

Amiran, R.
1956   "A Seal from Brak: Expressions of Consecutive
                   Movements in Late Minoan Glyptic," Iraq 18
                   (1956) 57-59

Atkinson, T.D., et al.
1904   Excavations at Phylakopi in Melos (JHS
                   Supplementary Paper 4; London, 1904)

Avila, R.J.
1983   Bronzene Lanzen- und Pfeilspitzen der
                   griechischen Spatbronzezeit Prahistorische
                   Bronzefund 5, 1 (Munich 1983)

Barrelet, M.-T.
1955   "Les Deesses armees et ailees," Syria 32 (1955)

Battaglia, G.B.
1980   Gioielli antichi dal'eta micenea all'ellenismo
                   (Edizioni Quasar; Rome 1980)

Baurain, C. & Darcque, J.
1983   "Un Triton en pierre a Mallia," BCH 107 (1983)
                   3-73

Benson, J.L.
1969   "The Three Maidens Group," AJA 73 (1969) 109-122

Betts, J.H.
1965   "Notes on a Possible Minoan Forgery," BSA 60
                        (1965) 203-206

1967a   "New Light on Minoan Bureaucracy," Kadmos 6
                        (1967) 15-40

1967b   "Some Unpublished Knossos Sealings and
                        Sealstones," BSA 62 (1967) 27-45

1968   "Trees in the Wind on Cretan Sealings," AJA 72
                        (1968) 149-150

1973   "Ships on Minoan Seals," Marine Archaeology
                        (Colston Papers 23, 1973) 325-338

1974   Review of Kenna 1969, in BibO 31.3/6   (May-
                        November 1974) 309-31 4

1978   "More Aegean Papyrus: Some Glyptic Evidence,"
                        AAA 11 (1978) 61-74

1981a   "The 'Jasper Lion Master': Some Principles of
                        Establishing LM/LH Workshops and Artists,"
                        CMS Beiheft I (1981) 1-15

1981b   "The Seal from Shaft Grave Gamma: A 'Mycenaean'
                        TUAS 6 (1981) 2-8

Bielefeld, E.
1968   Schmuck (ArchHom C, 1968)

Biesantz, H.
1954a   Kretisch-mykenisch Siegelbilder.
                        Stilgeschichtliche und chronologische
                        Untersuchungen (Marburg, 1954)

1958   "Die minoischen Bildnissgemmen," Marburger
                        Winckellmann-Programm 1958, 9-23

Blegen, C.W.
1937   Prosymna (Cambridge UP, 1937)

1962   "Early Greek Portraits," AJA 66 (1962) 245-247

Boardman, J.
1970a   Greek Gems and Finger Rings (Thames & Hudson,
                 London 1970)

1970b   "The Danicourt Ring," RA 1970, 3-8

1973   "The de Jong Gems," Antichita Cretese. Studi in
                 Levi I (Cronache di Archeologia
                 12, 1973) 116-121

Borchhardt, J.
1972   Homerische Helme (Philipp van Zabern, Mainz am
                 Rhein, (1972)

Bordan, M.
1946   Arte Cretese-Micenea nel Museo Pigorini di Roma
                 Istituto di Archeologia e Storia dell'Arte;
                 Rome 1946)

Bowman, J.
1978   Crete (New York, 1st ed. 1962; 2nd ed. 1978)

Brice, Wm
1961   Inscriptions in the Minoan Linear Script of
                 Class A (Oxford 1961)

Brommer, F.
1981   "Zur Minoischen Saule," AA 1981, 20

Broneer, O.
1939   "A Mycenaean Fountain on the Athenian
                 Acropolis," Hesperia 8 (1939) 317-433

Buchanan, W.B.
1954   "The Cow and Calf," AJA 58 (1954) 144

Buchholz, H.-G.
1962   "Eine Kultaxt aus der Messara," Kadmos 1 (1962)

1976   "Pfeilspitzen. Weitere Beobachtungen," AA 1976,

1980   Kriegswesen, Teil 2: Angriffswafen (ArchHom E,
                 Teil 2; 1980)

Buchholz, H.-G. & Wiesner, J.
1977   Kriegswesen, Teil 1: Schutzwaffen und Wehrbauten
                 E, Teil 1; 1977)

Casson, L.
1975   "Bronze Age Ships. Evidence of the Thera Wall
                        Paintings," IJNA 4 (1975) 3-10

Catling, H.
1964   Cypriot Bronzework in the Mycenaean World
                        (Oxford UP, 1964)

Catling. H., Catling, E., & Smyth, D.
1979   "Knossos 1975: Middle Minoan III and Late Minoan
                        by the Acropolis," BSA 74 (1979) 1-80

Chapouthier, F.
1932   "A travers trois gemmes prismatiques," Melanges
                        Glotz I (Paris 1932) 183-201

1946   "Glyptique cretoise et continuite de la
                        civilization minoenne," BCH (1946) 78-90

Chittenden, J.
1947   "The Master of Animals," Hesperia 16 (1947) 89-
                        114

Christopoulos, G.A. & Bastias, J.C.
1970   Prehistory and Protohistory (Ekdotike Athenon;
                        Athens, 1970)

Christou, Chr.
1968   Potnia Theron. Eine Untersuchung uber Ursprung,
                        Erscheinungsformen und Wandlungen der Gestalt
                        einer Gottheit (1968)

Davis, E.N.
1977   The Vapheio Cups and Aegean Gold and Silver Ware
                        Publishing Inc., New York & London 1977)

Dawkins, R.M.
1909-10   "Laconia. Excavations at Sparta, 1910; 2. The
                        Mycenaean City near the Menelaion," BSA 16
                        (1909-1910) 4-11

Demargne, P.
1939   "Le Maitre des animaux sur une gemme cretoise du
                        MM I," Melanges Syriens offerts Monsieur Rene
                        (Paris 1939) I 121-127

1948   "La Robe de la Deesse minoenne sur une cachet de
                                 a Mallia," Melanges Picard (RA 29-30, 1948) I
                                 280-288

Demisch, H.
1977   Die Sphinx (Stuttgart 1977)

Deonna, W.
1926   "Les Origines de la representation humaine dans
                                 l'art grec," BCH 50 (1926) 319-382

1948   "Les Lions attaches a la colonne," Melanges
                                 Picard (RA 29-30, 1948) I 289-308

1954   "Casque grave sur une hache minoenne," BCH 78
                                 (1954) 253-257

Deroy, L.
1979   "Boucliers, formules et vieilles meprises, a
                                 propos de quelques termes homeriques," EtCl
                                 47 (1979) 235-243

Dessenne, A.
1957   "Le Griffon creto-mycenien. Inventaire et
                                 remarques," BCH (1957) 203-215

Devaras, K.
1980   "Composite Sacred Monsters from the Peak
                                 Sanctuary of Petsopha," CretCongIV (1980),
                                 88-93

Doumas, Chr.
1970   "Remarques sur la forme du bateau egeen a l'age
                                 du bronze ancien," Valamonica Symposium
                                 (1970) 227-233

Eccles, E.
1939-40   "Unpublished Objects from Palaikastro and
                                 Praisos II. The Seals and Sealings," BSA 40
                                 (1939-1940) 43-49

Evans, A.J.
1905   "The Prehistoric Tombs of Knossos," Archaeologia
                                 59 part 2 (1905) 391-562 (also published
                                 separately, London 1906)

1913   "The Tomb of the Double Axes and Associated
                              Group at Knossos," Archaeologia 65 (1913) 1-
                              94

1921   "On a Minoan Bronze Group of a Galloping Bull
                              and Acrobatic Figure from Crete," JHS 41
                              (1921) 247-259

Everingham, J.
1982   "Thailand's Working Royalty," NatGeogMagazine
                              162.4 (October 1982) 486-499

Forsdyke, E.J.
1926-7   "The Mavro Spelio Cemetery at Knossos," BSA 28
                              (1926-7) 243-296

1952   "Minos of Crete," JWarb 15 (1952) 13-19

Foster, K.P.
1979   Aegean Faience of the Bronze Age (Yale UP 1979)

Frankfort, H.
1936-7   "Notes on the Cretan Griffin," BSA (1936-7) 106-

Frodin, O. & Persson, A.
1938   Asine. Results of the Swedish Excavations 1922-
                              1930 (Stockholm 1938)

Furumark, A.
1972a   Mycenaean Pottery I. Analysis (Stockholm, 1972)

1972b   Mycenaean Pottery II. Chronology (Stockholm,
                              1972)

Gesell, G.
1979   "The Minoan Town Sanctuary," AJA 83 (1979) 229

1983   "The Place of the Goddess in Minoan Society,"
                              Minoan Society. Proceedings of the Cambridge
                              Colloquium, 1981 (BCP 1983) 93-99

1985   Town, Palace, and House Cult in Minoan Crete
                              (SIMA 67, 1985)

Gibson, McG. & Biggs, R.D., eds.
1977   Seals and Sealing in the Ancient Near East
                              (Bibiotheca Mesopotamica 6, 1977)

Gill, M.A.V.
1961   "Note on the Hagia Pelagia Cylinder," BICS 8
                   (1961) 7-13

1963   "The Minoan Dragon," BICS 10 (1963) 1-12

1964   "The Minoan Genius," AthMit 79 (1964) 1-21

1965   "The Knossos Sealings: Provenience and
                   Identification," BSA 60 (1965) 58-98

1966   "Seals and Sealings: Some Comments," Kadmos 5
                   (1966) 1-16

1969   "The Minoan 'Frame' on an Egyptian Relief,"
                   Kadmos 8 (1969) 85-102

1974   "The Knossos Sealings. Some Reflections," CMS
                   Beiheft 0 (1974) 30-36

1981   "The Human Element in Minoan and Mycenaean
                   Glyptic Art," CMS Beiheft I (1981) 83-90

Graham, J.W.
1969   The Palaces of Crete (Princeton UP 1969)

Gramatapoulos, M.
1974   "Les Pierres gravees du Cabinet Numismatique de
                   l'Academie Roumaine," CollLatomus 138 (1974)
Gray, D.
1974   Seewesen (ArchHom G; 1974)

Guest-Papamanoli, A.
1983   "Peche et pecheurs minoens: proposition pour une
                   recherche," Minoan Society. Proceedings of
                   the Cambridge Colloquium 1981 (BCP 1983) 101-
                   110

Guida, P.C.
1973   Le Armi difensive dei Micenei nell figurazioni
                   (1973)

Hagg, R. & Lindau, Y.
1984   "The Minoan 'Snake Frame' Reconsidered," OpusAth
                   67-77

Hagg, R. & Marinatos, N., eds.
1981   Sanctuaries and Cults in the Aegean Bronze Age
              (Skrifter Utgivna av Svenska Institutet i
              Athen, 4o, XXVIII, 1981)

Hall, E.
1912   "Excavations in Eastern Crete, Sphoungaras,"
              Museum Anthropological of the University of
              Pennsylvania 3.2 (1912) 43-72

Hallager, E.
1985   The Master Impression (SIMA 69; Goteborg 1985)

Hastings, H.R.
1905   "A Bronze Age 'Pocket' from Avgo (Crete)," AJA 9
              (1905) 279-287

Hatzidakis, I.
1912   "Tylissos Minoike," ArchEph 1912, 197-233

Hawes, H.B.
1908   Gournia (Philadelphia 1980)

Herkenrath, E.
1937   "Mykenische Kultszenen," AJA 41 (1937) 411-423

Hockman, O.
1980   "Lanze und Speer in spatminoischen und
              mykenischen Griechenland," JRGZM 27 (1980)
              41-47

Hodge, A.T.
1985   "The Labrys: Why was the Double Axe Double?" AJA
              89 (1985) 307-308

Hoglund, K.S.
1981   "The Up-Raised Arm Motif in Predynastic Art," MA
              Thesis, Northern Illinois University (1981)

Hood, S.
1956   "Another Warrior-Grave at Ayios Ioannes near
              Knossos," BSA 51 (1956) 81-99

1980   "Shaft Grave Swords: Mycenaean or Minoan?"
              CretCong IV (1980), 233-242

Hood, S. & de Jong, P.
1952   "Late Minoan Warrior-Graves from Ayios Ioannes
                        and the New Hospital Site at Knossos," BSA 47
                        (1952) 243-279

Hood, S., et al.
1958-9   "A Minoan Cemetery on Upper Gypsades," BSA 53-4
                        (1958-9) 194-262

Hoopes, T.
1947   "A Cretan Gold Ring," Bulletin of the City Art
                        Museum of St. Louis, 32 (1947) 99-103

Johnston, P.F.
1982   "Bronze Age Cycladic Ships: an Overview," TUAS 7

Jung, H.
1986   "Methodisches zur Hermeneuttik der minoischen
                        und mykenischen Bilddenkmaler," CMS Beiheft 3
                        (forthcoming)
Kaiser, B.
1974   "Zur Datierung von Kammergrab 26 in Mykene," CMS
                        Beiheft (1974) 37-57

Kallegas, P.G.
1981   "Mycenaean Helmets from Kephallenia,"
                        Archaeologia 1 (1981) 77-83

Kapake, K.
1984   "Une Bague minoenne de Mallia," BCH 108 (1984)
                        3-12
Karageorghis, V.
1977-8   The Goddess with Uplifted Arms (Humanistiska
                        Vetenskapssamfundet i Lund. Scripta Minora
                        1977-1978.2)

Kenna, V.E.G.
1960   Cretan Seals (Oxford UP 1960)

1962   "Seals and Script with Special Reference to
                        Ancient Crete," Kadmos 1 (1962) 1-15

1963   "Seals and Script II," Kadmos 2 (1963) 1-6

1964   "Seals and Script III.   Cretan Seal Use and the
                 Dating of Linear Script B," Kadmos 3 (1964)
                 29-57

1968a   "Design for a Water Garden," Marburger
                 Winckelmann-Programm 1968, 1-4

1968b   "Studies of Birds on Seals of the Aegean and
                 Eastern Mediterranean in the Bronze Age,"
                 OpusAth 8 (1968) 23-38

1968c   "Should Differences between Cretan and Helladic
                 Seal Use Imply Differences in their
                 Respective Use of Linear B?" Congresso
                 Internazionale di Micenologia III (Rome 1968)

1969   The Cretan Talismanic Stone in the Late Minoan
                 Age (SIMA 24; Lund 1969)

Korres, G.
1980   "Representations of Offerings of Sacred Dress
                 and Sacred Peplos and the Problems about them
                 and Related Works," CretCongIV 659-688

Laffineur, R.
1984   "Mycenaeans at Thera: Further Evidence?" The
                 Minoan Thalassocracy. Myth and Reality
                 (Skrifter Utgivna av Svenska Institutet i
                 Athen, 4o, XXXII; Stockholm 1984)

Laviosa, C.
1969   "La Collezione di Sigilli e Cretule
                 Minoico-Micenei del Museo Archeologico di
                 Firenze," SMEA 40 (1969) 7-18

Lembessi, A.
1967   "Anaskaphai Porou," Praktika 1967, 197-209

Lendle, O.
1965   "Das Kretische Stiersprungspiel," Marburger
                 Winckelmann-Programm 1965, 30-37

Levi, D.
1925-6a   "Le cretule di Hagia Triada," ASAtene 8-9 (1925-
                 6) 71-156

1925-6b   "Le cretule di Zakro," ASAtene 8-9 (1925-6) 157-
                 201

1961-2   "La Tomba a tholos di Kamilari presso a Festos,"
                    ASAtene 39-40 (1961-2) 7-148

Long, C.R.
1974   The Ayia Triadha Sarcophagus: A Study of Late
                    Minoan and Mycenaean Funerary Practices and
                    Beliefs (SIMA 41, 1974)

Loulloupis, M.
1973   "Mycenaean 'Horns of Consecration' in Cyprus,"
                    Acts of the International Archaeological
                    Symposium "The Mycenaeans in the Eastern
                    Mediterranean" (Nicosia 1973) 225-244

Marinatos, N.
1984   "The Date Palm in Minoan Iconography and
                    Religion," OpusAth 15 (1984) 115-122

1985   "The Tree as a Focal Point of Ritual Action,"
                    CMS Beiheft 3 (forthcoming)

Marinatos, S.
1941   "To Minoikon Megaron Sklavokampou," ArchEph
                    1939-1941, 69-96

1962   "Minoische Portrats," Festschrift Max Wegner
                    (Munster 1962) 9-12

1967   Kleidung, Haar- und Barttracht (ArchHom A & B,
                    1967)

1974   Thera VI (Bibliotheke tes en Athenais
                    Archaiologikes Hetaireias no. 64; Athens,
                    1974)

Marinatos, S. & Hirmer, M.
1960   Crete and Mycenae (Thames & Hudson, London 1960)

Mavriyannaki, C.
1981   "La Double hache dans le monde hellenique a
                    l'age du Bronze," RA 1983, 195-228

Merrillees, R.S.
1980   "The Representation of the Human Form in
                    Prehistoric Cyprus," OpAth 13 (1983) 171-184

Millet, N. & Champion, D.
1983   Ancient Egyptian Ships (Toronto, Royal Ontario
                        Museum, 1983)

Mylonas, G.
1977   Mykenaike Threskeia. Naoi, Bomoi kai Temene
                        (Pragmateiai Akademias Athenon 39, 1977)

1980   "Creto-Mycenaean Sphinx," CretCongIV (1980) 352-

Niemeier, W.-D.
1986   "Zur Ikonographie der 'Kultszenen' auf
                        minoischen und mykenischen Sieglen," CMS
                        Beiheft 3 (1986), forthcoming

Papapostolou, I.
1977   Ta Sphragismata ton Khanion (Bibliotheke tes en
                        Athenais Archaiologikes Hetaireias no. 7;
                        Athens, 1977)

Persson, A.
1931   The Royal Tombs at Dendra near Midea (Lund 1931)
                        (Lund 1942)

Petrakis, S.
1980   "Madonna Lilies in Aegean Wall Paintings," TUAS
                        5 (1980) 15-21

Pini, I.
1973   "Ein Siegelabdruck im Archaologischen Museum
                        Iraklion," a CretCongress III (1973) 221-230

1979   "Cypro-Aegean Cylinder Seals. On the Definition
                        and Origin of the Class," Acts of the
                        International Archaeological Symposium "The
                        Relations between Cyprus and Crete, ca.
                        2000-500 B.C." (Nicosia 1979) 121-127

1980   "Kypro-Agaische Rollsiegel. Ein Beitrag zur
                        Definition und zum Ursprung der Gruppe," JDI
                        95, 1980, 77-108

1981   "Spaetbronzezeitliche agaische Glassiegel,"
                        JRGZM 28 (1981) 48-81

1982   "Eine Tonplombe aus Knossos im Ashmolea n
                        Museum," Kadmos 21 (1982) 1-4

1983a   "Mitanni-Rollsiegel des 'Common Style' aus
               Griechenland," PZ 58 (1983) 114-126

1983b   "Neue Beobachtungen zu den tonernen
               Siegelabdrucken von Zakros," AA 1983, 559-
               572

1984   "Minoische und Helladische Tonsiegel," Aux
               Origines de l'Hellenisme: La Crete et la
               Grece. Hommages a Henri Van Effenterre
               (Publications de la Sorbonne. Histoire
               Ancienne et Medievale no. 15; Paris 1984)
               73-81

1985   "Das Motiv des Lowenuberfalls in der
               spaetminoischen und mykenischen Glyptik,"
               L'Iconographie minoenne (BCH Supplement 11,
               1985, 153-166)

1986   "Zur 'richtigen' Ansicht minoischer und
               mykenischer Siegel- und Ringdarstellungen,"
               CMS Beiheft 3 (1986), forthcoming

Pinsent, J.
1983   "Bull-Leaping," Minoan Society. Proceedings of
               the Cambridge Colloquium, 1981 (BCP 1983)
               259-271

Platon, N.
1967a   "Anaskaphai Zakrou," Praktika 1967, 187-224

1967b   Crete (London, 1966)

Popham, M.
1974   "Sellopoulo Tombs 3 and 4. Two Late Minoan
               Graves near Knossos," BSA 69 (1974) 195-257

Popham, M. & Sackett, H.
1980   Lefkandi I. The Iron Age (British School of
               Archaeology at Athens, 1980)

Popham, M. et al.
1984   The Minoan Unexplored Mansion at Knossos
               (British School of Archaeology at Athens:
               Thames and Hudson, London 1984)

Poursat, J.-C.
1976   "Notes d'iconographie prehellenique. Dragons et
                    crocodiles," BCH 100 (1976) 461-474

1977a   Les Ivoires myceniens (Bibliotheque des Ecoles
                    francaises d'Athenes et de Rome, fasc. 230a;
                    Paris 1977)

1977b   Catalogue des ivoires myceniens du Musee National
                    d'Athenes (Bibliotheque des Ecoles franciases
                    d'Athenes et de Rome, fasc. 230b; Paris 1977)

Powell, B.B.
1977   "The Significance of the so-called 'Horns of
                    Consecration'," Kadmos 16 (1977) 70-82.

Raban, A.
1984   "The Thera Ships: Another Interpretation," AJA 88
                    (1984) 11-19

Rehak, P.
1982   "New Observations on the Mycenaean 'Armed
                    Goddess'," AJA 86 (1982) 282

Renfrew, A.C., et al.
1985   Phylakopi (British School of Archaeology at
                    Athens: Cambridge UP 1985)

Richardson, E.C.
1978   Lions in Bronze Age Aegean Art (Cincinnati MA
                    thesis, 1978)

Reichel, A.
1909   Stierspiele in der kretisch-mykenische Kultur,"
                    AM 34 (1904) 85-99

Robinson, D.
1949   "The Robinson Collection of Greek Gems, Seals,
                    Rings, and Earrings," Hesperia Supplement 8
                    305-323

Rodenwaldt, G.
1911   "Fragmente mykenischer Wandgemalde," AthMit 36
                    (1911) 221-250

Russel, P.
1979   "The Date of the Gournia Shrine," TUAS 4 (1979)
                    27-33

Rutkowski, B.

1972   Cult Places in the Aegean World (Warsaw 1972)

1981   Fruehgriechische Kultdarstellungen (MdI AthAbt
              Beiheft 8, 1981)

Sakellarakis, J.

1966   "The First Untouched Royal Burial Found in
              Crete," ILN 26 (March 1966) 32-3

1967a   "Minoan Cemeteries at Arkhanes," Archaeology 20
              276-281

1967b   "Anaskaphai Archanon," Praktika 1967

1970   "Das Kuppelgrab A von Archanes und das kretisch-
              Tieropferritual, PZ 45 (1970)" 135-219

1972a   "To Proschedion tes Sphragidos CMS I 220 ek
              Vapheiou," ArchEph 1972, 234-244

1972b   "To Thema tes pherouses Zoon Gynaikos eis ten
              kretomykenaiken Sphragidoglyphian," ArchEph
              245-258

1974   "Le Theme du pechueur dans l'art prehistorique,"
              370-390

1981a   "Matrizen zur Herstellung von Siegelringe," CMS
              Beiheft 1 (1981) 167-179

1981b   "Drama of Death in a Minoan Temple," NatGeogMag
              159.2 (Feb. 1981) 204-222

Sakellariou, A.

1953   "La Representation du casque en dents de sanglier
              (epoque minoenne), BCH 77 (1953) 46-58

1958   Les Cachets minoens de la Collection Giamalakis
              Paris 1958)

1962   "Hena Sphragisma apo ten Pylo," Festschrift fur
              Friedrich Matz (Philipp von Zabern, Mainz am
              19-21

1966   Mykenaike Sphragidoglyphia (Athens 1966)

1971   "Scene de bataille sur un vase mycenien en
                       pierre?" RA 1 (1971) 3-14

1973   "A Propos des cimiers du casque en dent de
                       sanglier," Antichita Cretesi. Stud in onore
                       (Chronache di Archaeologia 12, 1973) I 122-126

1974   "Un Cratere d'argent avec scene de bataille
                       provenant de la IVe tombe de Mycenes,"
                       Antike Kunst 17 (1974) 3-20

1975   "La Scene du 'Siege' sur le rhyton d'argent de
                       Mycenes d'apres un nouvelle reconstruction,"
                       195-208

Sandars, N.K.
1961   "The First Aegean Swords and their Ancestry," AJA
                       65 (1961) 13-29

1963   "Later Aegean Bronze Swords," AJA 67 (1963) 117-
                       153

Sapouna-Sakellaraki, E.
1968   "Hair Styles in the Minoan Age," Lefkoma
                       Diethnous Ektheseos Thessalonikes 1968, 247-
                       277

1971   Minoikon Zoma (Bibliotheke tes en Athenais
                       Archaiologies Hetaireias no. 71;
                       Athens, 1971)

Savignoni, L.
1904   "Scavi e scoperte nella necropoli di Phaestos,"
                       14 (1904) 501-675

Schiering, W.
1968   "Eine Bemerkung zur minoischen Siegelkunst,"
                       Wissenschaftliche Zeitschrift der
                       Universitat Rostock 17 (1968) 775-776

1984   "Bemerkungen zu den sogenannte architektonischen
                       Motiven der minoischen Siegelkunst," Aux
                       Origines de l'Hellenisme: La Crete et la
                       Grece. Hommages a Henri Van Effenterre
                       (Publications de la Sorbonne. Histoire

Ancienne et Medievale no. 15; Paris 1984) 65-71

Schliemann, H.
1880   Mycenae (London & New York 1880; reprinted by B. York 1967)

Schlager, N.
1986   "Minotauren in der aegaischen Glyptik?" Beiheft 3 (1986), forthcoming

Seager, R.
1912   Explorations in the Island of Mochlos (Boston and New York, 1912)

Shaw, J.
1971   "Minoan Architecture. Materials and Techniques," ASAtene 49 (1971) 1-256

1978   "Evidence for the Minoan Tripartite Shrine," AJA 429-448

1981   "Excavations at Kommos (Crete) During 1980," Hesperia 50 (1981) 211-251

1982   "Excavations at Kommos (Crete) During 1981," Hesperia 51 (1982) 164-195

Slusser, M.S.
1945-1947   "The Animal Seen from Above in Migration Art: Its Form and Magical Meaning," Marsyas 4 (1945-1947) 47-67

Small, T.
1966   "A Possible Shield-Goddess from Crete," Kadmos 5 (1966) 103-107

Sourvinou-Inwood, Ch.
1971   "On the Authenticity of the Ashmolean Ring 1919.56," Kadmos 10 (1971) 60-69

1973   "On the Lost 'Boat' Ring from Mochlos," Kadmos 12 (1973) 149-158

1986   "Space in Late Minoan Religious Scenes: Some Remarks," CMS Beiheft 3 (forthcoming)

Tamvaki, A.
1973   "A Late Minoan Seal in the N. Metaxas Collection,"
                        AAA 6 (1973) 308-315

1977   "Katagoge, Exelixe kai Hermeneia ton
                        Anthropomorphon Eidolion tes Proistorikes
                        Epoches sto Aigaio," Anthropos 4.1/2 (1977)
                        264-337

1986   "The Human Element in the Glyptic of the Aegean
                        Late Bronze Age: Some Thoughts," CMS Beiheft
                        3 (1986), forthcoming

Taylor, R.W.
1979   "Tree Worship," The Mankind Quarterly 20 (1979)
                        79-141

Van Effenterre, H. & M.
1955   "Terre, ciel et mer dans l'iconographie de la
                        glyptique creto mycenienne," BCH Supp. XI:
                        L'Iconographie Minoenne (Paris 1985) 83-93

Van Effenterre, M.
1978   "Cretan Ships on Sealstones: Some Observations,"
                        Thera and the Aegean World I (London 1978)
                        593-597

1980   "Description normalisee des sceaux creto-
                        myceniens," Symposium in Paris 1980, held
                        under the auspices of CNRS, Universite de
                        Paris I

Van Leuven, J.C.
1979   "Mycenaean Goddesses Called Potnia," Kadmos 18
                        (1979) 112-129

Van Straten, F.
1969   "The Minoan 'Genius' in Mycenaean Greece,"
                        BABesch 44 (1969) 110-121

Varvaregou, A.P.
1981   The Mycenaean Boar's Tusk Helmet. The Technique
                        of Construction (Athens 1981)

Vermeule, E.
1958   "Mythology in Mycenaean Art," CJ 54 (1958) 99-108

1966   "A Mycenaean Dipinto and Grafitto," Kadmos 5 (1966)
                142-146

1974   Toumba tou Skourou (Harvard University-Museum of
                Fine Arts, Boston, Cyprus Expedition 1974)

Vermeule, E. & Karageorghis, V.
1982   Mycenaean Pictorial Vase Painting (Harvard UP
                1982)

Walters, H.G.
1912   Catalogue of the Greek and Etruscan Vases in the
                British Museum I.2 (London 1912)

Warren, P.
1969   Minoan Stone Vases (Cambridge UP 1969)

1976   "Did Papyrus Grow in the Aegean?" AAA 9 (1976)
                89-95

1980   "Surprising Discoveries in Crete," University of
                Bristol Newsletter 10.8 (10 January 1980) 1
                & 3

1984   "Of Squills," Aux Origines de l'Hellenisme. La
                Crete et la Grece (Hommage a Henri Van
                Effenterre (Publications de la Sorbonne,
                Histoire ancienne et medievale, 15; Paris
                [1984]) 17-24

Warren, P. & Hughes, H.
1963   "Two Sealstones from Mochlos," KretKhron 17,
                (1963) 354-356

Weingarten, J.
1983   "The Zakro Master and his Place in Prehistory,"
                SIMA Pocketbook 2 (Astroms Forlag, Goteborg
                1983)

1986   "Formulaic Implications of Some Late Bronze Age
                Three-Sided Prisms," CMS Beiheft 3
                (forthcoming)

Willetts, R.F.
1978   "More on the 'Horns of Consecration'," Kadmos 17
                        (1978) 172-173

Xanthoudides, St.
1907   "Ek Kretes," ArchEph 1907, 141 ff.

Younger, J.G.
1973   Towards the Chronology of Aegean Glyptic in the
                        Late Bronze Age (Cincinnati, PhD
                        dissertation, 1973; University Microfilms
                        73-24, 867)

1974   "A Glyptic Sketch from Isopata, HM 908," Kadmos
                        13 (1974) 1-5

1976   "Bronze Age Representations of Aegean Bull-
                        Leaping," AJA 80 (1976) 125-137

1977   "Non-Sphragistic Uses of Minoan-Mycenaean
                        Sealstones and Rings," Kadmos 16 (1977) 141-
                        159

1984   "A New Look at Aegean Bull-Leaping," Muse 17
                        (1983) 72-79

Younger, J.G. & Betts, J.H.
1979   "Eight Sealstones and a Sealing from the
                        Statigraphical Museum at Knossos," BSA 74
                        (1979) 270-278

Yule, P.
1981   Early Cretan Seals. A Study of Chronology
                        (Philipp von Zabern; Main am Rhein 1981)